Ulrich Pfammatter

BUILDING THE
FUTURE

Building Technology
and Cultural History from the
Industrial Revolution until Today

PRESTEL
MUNICH · BERLIN · LONDON · NEW YORK

Table of Contents

Introduction

1, 2: Iron Bridge Coalbrookdale, England, 1775–79; architect and engineer: Thomas Farnolls Prichard; iron foundry: John Wilkinson and Abraham Darby III. Translation of a Roman stone-arch bridge into cast- and wrought-iron techniques; section of the bridge, detail of a junction

3: 'La Bolla' event space in the port of Genoa, 2000/2001; architects: Renzo Piano Building Workshops, engineers: Ove Arup & Partners

4: Concrete shell technology by Heinz Isler: indoor tennis halls, Marin-La Thène, near Neuenburg, Switzerland, 1983; architect: J. Copeland

In the 200 years since the Industrial Revolution, or more precisely since the erection in 1775 of the Iron Bridge in Coalbrookdale in the English Midlands (which was its first built manifestation), architecture, civil engineering and their worlds of images have changed radically (ills. 1, 2).

Since the building of the Pantheon in Rome, in which the load-bearing structure marked the limits of concrete technology at that time, architecture has shown a tendency to dissolve mass: space has moved towards 'liberated space', towards 'transparency';[1] load-bearing walls tend to be metamorphosed into partitions or a skin; increasingly and with ever-growing speed new materials and technologies are borrowed from areas such as motor car, ship and airplane building and space travel technology and 'translated' into building techniques. At the same time there is a growing attempt to visualise and understand – intellectually, emotionally or with senses not usually employed – material technologies that cannot be directly understood, such as prestressed concrete, or glass structures, composite materials with concealed qualities and functions, transformed traditional building materials or 'bionically' oriented composites.[2]

The history of important, model buildings since the Hanging Gardens of Semiramis in Babylon can also be read as a history of 'brands'. The protagonists in building have always attempted to leave behind traces. Only anonymous building, what is known as 'vernacular architecture', refuses to include a conscious language of images in its view of itself, although it has exerted and continues to exert a strong influence on *architettura maggiore*. This is shown by the 'primitive huts' that regularly occur in the relevant literature or by Gottfried Semper's meaningful reference to the Caribbean Hut, which he discovered on the occasion of the first *World's Fair*, in the Crystal Palace in London in 1851, and used to illustrate his theory in his magnum opus, *Der Stil* (1863). Here Semper pointed out the tendency towards the *stoffliche* (textile), towards dematerialisation and lightness in the culture of building. Two thousand years after the Pantheon, Richard Buckminster Fuller made the dream of lightweight building reality with his 'geodesic dome', 1,000 times lighter but with the same span as the domed Roman building. Since Fuller's time this development has continued unabated (ill. 3). The tendency towards the dissolution of mass even reached concrete technology, which in projects by Heinz Ilser, Eladio Dieste, Eduardo Torroja, among others, approached borderline areas in which this material becomes a 'membrane' (ill. 4).[3]

Pioneering changes in building occurred in glass technology: in their palm house in Bicton Gardens in Devonshire, the Bailey Brothers combined an essentially unstable web of iron bars with small glass panes to create a structurally stable 'blob', thus using glass to help transfer the loads. Schwedler's invention in 1865 of the structural joint in ironwork revolutionised architecture in iron and steel construction, while in the field of concrete the design possibilities for architects and engineers were expanded in a previously unimaginable way when, in 1892, with his forward-looking patent, François Hennebique introduced reinforced concrete as a sculptural-spatial and constructive-structural method of building.

The skeleton or frame building which developed from the constraints, necessities and simplifications required by industrial production first established itself in the textile industry in the English Midlands, and led step by step to a way of seeing things that made the traditional brick-built massive façade superfluous, and allowed it to be 'liberated' from its load-bearing role. This set in motion the development of the front-hung building envelope that today still offers architects and engineers unrestricted design opportunities.

The growing possibilities offered by industrial production form a permanent motor of development that repeatedly influences the world of building. The replacement of handmade production methods by industrial techniques led, early on, from production based on immediate need to market-oriented and mass production, while the transfer of computer-operated component or system production from mechanical engineering technology to the planning, production and assembly processes in building simplified, in a later phase, the transition from mass to made-to-measure production by means of computer programmes. However, the purely technical, machine-made or mechanical processing of 'bespoke' building elements removes the possibility of any emotional approach to the perception and understanding of their function or meaning. To recreate a sensitivity to materials, attempts are being made to employ hybrid techniques which, in the case of English engineer Peter Rice, was a key aspect in building the Centre Georges Pompidou in Paris: the explanation of large building elements that are difficult to understand in the overall context of the building is achieved by the use of classic cast elements and hand-finishing (ill. 6).

The culture of work, the instruments and tools, and office structures, have also changed. Since the Industrial Revolution, a tendency has developed to separate the professional disciplines of architect and engineer, even though a school of thought inspired by Saint-Simon in the framework of a new kind of multidisciplinary educational institution, the École Centrale des Arts et Manufactures (founded in Paris in 1829/30), was able to delay this split until the mid-19th century, that is, until the age of iron and glass, and indeed produced an entire series of prominent 'engineer-architects'. This educational system, which has entered history under the name 'method school', contrasted with the 'style school' of the École des Beaux-Arts, which was more anchored in tradition (ill. 7).[4]

Whereas until well into the 20th century numerous architects practices were run as 'Beaux-Arts studios', under the influence of the *ingénieurs centraliens*, as well as of industrialisation, a new type of office organisation grew up that was first introduced in a comprehensive form as the 'industrial office' by Albert Kahn in the motor car town Detroit. This new multidisciplinary work structure, initially based on production methods and work models taken from Henry Ford and Frederick W. Taylor, was later replaced by more democratic forms, as in the practice of Skidmore, Owings & Merrill, and subsequently transformed by changes resulting from environmental and energy questions into modern interdisciplinary workshops, of the kind introduced by Renzo Piano, Günter Behnisch or Ove Arup – the work worlds of the future. Ove Arup indeed founded a modern ethics of building in a speech that is printed in the appendix to this book.

5: Warehouse of the Franz Carl Weber games factory in Zurich by Heinz Ronner (at Rudolf Kuhn), façade cladding of front-hung Durisol elements that project out further from storey to storey, 1955/56

6: 'Gerberette' as a prominent cast element in the structural context of the Centre Georges Pompidou; it was finished by hand at Krupp; architects: Renzo Piano, Richard Rogers; engineers: Peter Rice, Ove Arup & Partners

7: The École Centrale des Arts et Manufactures (founded 1829/30 in Paris) was a building college where 'the art of building' rather than 'building as art' was taught and learnt. The *ingénieurs centraliens* included both prominent engineers and architects, such as Gustave Eiffel and William Le Baron Jenney

Inventions in building materials and techniques, and new forms of work along with other epochal shear forces formed the background to the uninterrupted development of this view of building. In the process a question arose that, most probably, can never be fully answered: Why always something new? (ill. 8).

The ceaseless striving for perfection, and the constant search for "a better world" (Ove Arup & Partners) lie in a field of tension between unrestricted and controlled growth. *The Unbound Prometheus* (David S. Landes)[5] emerges regularly as an antagonist to the tendency – also constantly pursued, and not only since Rio – towards 'sustainable development'. Whereas in the 'old' or 'first' world sustainable know-how is built up in a scientific and technical way and formulated by politicians and lawmakers, in other, still intact cultures, techniques and behaviour patterns have survived from which much can still be learned as regards the constant regeneration of the living space of generations to come. The empirical and scientific approach to naturally oriented structures, forms and cultural techniques is an intercultural research area of the future (ill. 9).

On the layout of this book   Each of the six chapters of this book is divided into sections accompanied by case studies. Both the themes of the chapters, as well as the projects, tendencies and buildings selected naturally follow a 'construct' of the author's that is aimed at choosing the most important inventions and developments that produced new aspects in every epoch, pointed the way to the future or indicated a tendency, at putting these in their historical context and at underlining their significance by documenting and visualising their special and emotional appeal. The original manuscript was three times as long as the present book but the wise advice offered by the publishers and the editors on shaping it into its present form have meant that the present book is more concentrated and can be used both as a manual and a textbook.

Thanks   My greatest thanks are due to my wife, Johanna, who constantly accompanied both the progress of this book project and the lectures at the ETH Zurich that formed the basis for it and who kept alive the continuous discussion on its *perfectionnement*. I owe a debt of gratitude to my parents, who attracted me to the path of building and different schools of thought. My teachers in the architecture department of the ETH Zurich – Bernhard Hoeli, Heinz Ronner, Herbert E. Kramel, Hans Ess, Adolf Max Vogt, Paul Hofer and others – honed the critical view of an entire 'post-war generation', conveyed an awareness of the problems and processes, and balanced the older style school with a method-oriented model of the future. Heinz Rohmer, in particular, should be thanked for imparting his critical view of ways of presenting the history of building and building technology that are often confined to the viewpoint of art history alone.

I am grateful to many colleagues for valuable discussions, suggestions and for pointing out mistakes, gaps or inadequacies. As an architect and building historian, I am indebted to the engineers Jörg Schlaich, Heinz Isler, Christian Menn, Peter Marti, Jürg Conzett, Joseph Schwartz, Aurelio Muttoni, Daniel Meyer, Chris Luebkeman, Florian Niggli and others for reflections on questions of interdisciplinary design and construction that have both deepened and advanced my knowledge.[6] Architects whom I met during excursions, seminar weeks with students, study trips and explorations, as well as my colleagues in the teaching projects Karin Bucher, Christian Fierz, Armando Meletta and Mathias Fey stimulated interesting discussions about basic questions of architecture, construction and

8

8: Steiff-Werke, Giengen a.d. Brenz, 1903: modern daylight factory with very early use of logical construction and material technology, not conceived by a prominent industrial architect but by the inventor of the teddy bear, Richard Steiff!

9: Jean-Marie Tijbaou Cultural Centre, Nouméa, New Caledonia, 1991–98; architects: Renzo Piano Building Workshop; engineers Arup; sustainable as an intercultural field of learning

9

technology and about the approaches and positions in current debates. Many of the examples here are a tribute to their work.

Joint teaching projects with Richard Horden (TU Munich)[7] broadened the approach to new areas of research and new research partners, to new areas on the boundaries of design construction and material technology, to a new school of thought and culture of cooperation, also in conjunction with his team, which includes Lydia Haack, Walter Klasz, Burkhard Franke, Hendrik Müller, Wieland Schmidt, Nadine Zinser, Birgitta Kunsch, Tim Wessbecher and others (ill. 10).

Years of collaboration in building up a new teaching model, new research projects and experimental and new projects such as Newspirit or Peak_Lab, City Mall and Event Center[8] link me to architect Christian Fierz. A project that represents a particular challenge is the "architecture gallery of good concrete buildings" that are accessible in virtual space, which was developed (and is regularly expanded) on the Internet by the author together with the architects Thomas Suter and Marco Homberger; it forms a framework for meetings and excursions with architecture schools.[9]

I should like to thank the sponsors of this book for their generous support, especially the G. und N. Schnitter Fonds zur Förderung der Technikgeschichte an der ETH Zürich, which supported the research section, the Gesellschaft für Ingenieurbaukunst (Prof. Dr. Peter Marti, ETH Zürich), which introduced the book to a wide circle of civil engineers, and in particular also the sponsors of this English edition, the engineering consulting firm Ove Arup London, as well as the following firms from the Swiss building industry: USM Münsingen (Canton Berne), SIKA (Schweiz) Zürich, Glas-Trösch Bützberg (Canton Berne), Tuchschmid Frauenfeld (Canton Thurgau), Gasser-Membranbau Lungern (Canton Obwalden) und Ruch-Griesemer Altdorf (Canton Uri). Fritz Haller (bauen und forschen GmbH Solothurn), Jörg Schlaich (Schlaich Bergermann und Partner Stuttgart) and Hanspeter Setz (Oskar Setz AG, Dintikon, Canton Aargau) also provided valuable support.

My thanks also to the publisher, Jürgen Krieger, editor-in-chief Katharina Haderer, the translators Jeremy Gaines and James Roderick O'Donovan, as well as all the people in the background at Prestel Verlag in Munich who, with painstaking care and great commitment, expertly monitored and supervised the planning, production and new English edition of the book.

On the sources   Most of the images are from the architects and engineers themselves, their offices or from photographers whom they commissioned, as well as from the author (own photos, archive images or archive from the estate of Professor Heinz Ronner). These sources have been listed with the respective names; cooperation at the personal level was extremely friendly and the author wishes at this point to thank all involved: Richard Horden, Jörg Schlaich, Fritz Haller and Therese Beyeler, Heinz Isler, Cuno Brullmann, Chris Williams, Renzo Piano Building Workshop and Bernhard Plattner, Shigeru Ban Architects, Norman Foster Associates, Schneider + Schumacher (Michael Schumacher), Bothe Richter Teherani, Christian Fierz, Karin Bucher, Christian Sumi, Rodolphe and André Luscher, Hans-Peter Bärtschi prospective concepts ag. All other illustrations are acknowledged by references to the relevant sources, archives or literature. In comparison with the German edition of this book, a number of aspects have been made more precise, including the complex area of the sources for Jean Prouvé's work; here the author is especially indebted to Peter Sulzer.

10: Richard Horden with the author at one of the numerous workshops at the TU Munich

10

1 From Greenhouse to 'High-tech Hothouse' –
Virtual Event Space of Industrial
and Communicative Societies

When in 1817 the landscape gardener John Claudius Loudon built an experimental glasshouse in Bayswater in London he could not possibly have known that he was setting in motion the development of glasshouse architecture that has continued down to the present day. A look backwards shows that both his venture into the realm of architecture and the application of glass and iron technology to a new problem were a first milestone in the history of architecture in glass and glasshouse technology, as well as providing the initial spark for the development of glass-building schools in the old world (ill. 1.1).

Glasshouse pioneers   Whereas the English pioneers did not enjoy any formal training in architecture or engineering and arrived in new territory through experimentation, the French masters of building had the advantage of a wide-ranging school culture. This allowed them to adopt a scientific approach to the composition of space and construction, materials and technology.

In England the apprenticeship system was dominant, the combination of handcraft skills, a trade or other practical activity with individually acquired knowledge – an educational ideal that had been postulated as early as 1693 by the pre-Enlightenment English philosopher John Locke.[1] Over a period of 150 years this approach shaped entire generations – also in the field of building – and was regarded as appropriate both for the sons of noble families and for those of working-class origins. Locke's educational ideal was for a long period the motor of inventions that were made at an astonishingly early date, brought about considerable industrial changes and gave England the leading position worldwide in the area of building technology.[2]

The exceptional achievements of English and French pioneers consisted to a certain extent in translating the new glasshouse into an acceptable kind of architecture and in their success in positioning 'engineering architecture' as a modern style alongside classicism and historicism. In England it was unavoidable that Victorian taste should be challenged in the process. And that in France the first modern glasshouse could be built only after the July revolution of 1830 (Charles Rohault de Fleury, 1833) is equally obvious. In France the restoration regime suppressed industrial innovation and it was only with the 'Citizen King' Louis-Philippe Duc d'Orleans that the modern bourgeoisie was able to assert itself – not least of all due to the merciless impact of railway construction.

Between the first true palm house in Bicton Gardens in south-west England (around 1825) and the still attractive Great Palm House by Richard Turner in Kew Gardens near London (1846–48) there were just two decades of architec-

1.0: Orang-utan House, Hagenbeck's
Zoological Garden, Hamburg, 2004

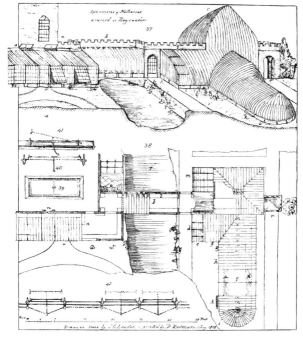

1.1

1.1: John Claudius Loudon's experimental glasshouse complex in Bayswater, 1817 – the search for architectural competence in creating spatial form and constructive-technical structure

1.2: Jardin d'Hiver in Paris, 1846/47: the change in the function of the glasshouse from botanical greenhouse to urban meeting place for the virtual experience of an assembled world

1.2

1.3

1.4

tural and technical development – the pioneering phase of glasshouse construction. Also built during this period were the experimental greenhouses by Joseph Paxton in the park of Chatsworth House (1833–49) and the glass pavilion by Charles Rohault de Fleury in the Jardin des Plantes in Paris (1833). The end of the pioneering period in France is marked by the Jardin d'Hiver on the Champs Élysées from 1846/47 which – together with Kew Gardens – marked a turning point: away from the purely botanical greenhouse to the 'event space' of the colonial capitals where the significance of global alliances and domination was animated and presented using all the arts and moods and activating all the senses (ill. 1.2).

The glasshouse in the architectural repertoire of the 19th century The transition from the pioneering phase to standardised building type took place with the Crystal Palace in London (1850/51) and the Glaspalast in Munich (1853/54). From this point, glasshouses formed part of the cultural substance and of the repertoire available to architect, engineer, draughtsman and entrepreneur.[3] The first functional change was made in the Jardin d'Hiver, the technical possibilities were explored to the limits in the palm house in Kew and industrialisation was introduced by the glass palaces in London and Munich. Although glasshouse architecture experienced a boom in the second half of the 19th century, after the mid-century technical or architectural and spatial innovations were revealed only by a few exhibition buildings,[4] in particular the Crystal Dome erected by William Le Baron Jenney in Chicago in 1893 for the *World's Columbian Fair* (hardly mentioned in the specialist literature), which marked the end of the 'Age of Iron' and which lies typologically between the Paris grain hall and the 'domes' by Richard Buckminster Fuller.

In German-speaking Europe the green and glasshouses illustrate a field of tension that stretches between a formal idiom still based on the classic style-oriented schools and the engineering art of the future. The Großes Palmenhaus in the park of Schönbrunn Palace in Vienna (1880–82) is an example of a complete iron-and-glass construction suited to the nature of the materials used which aims at establishing a new style in the 'Age of Iron' (ill. 1.3).

Between style and method – modernism and post-war modernism A number of glass pavilions at various World Fairs after 1893 show how equally fascinating spaces could be made with the new material reinforced concrete as with the iron and metal: for example the glasshouse by Bruno Taut (1914) or the Saint-Gobain exhibition pavilion at the Paris *Expo* in 1937. But these are individual cases; modernism in the period between the wars had a differently focused building programme. Frank Lloyd Wright's 'work worlds' under glass are here an exception.

In the era of post-war modernism after 1945 it was above all Richard Buckminster Fuller who investigated the 'new type' of glasshouse – the 'geodesic dome'. He experimented in building the globe shape using lightweight construction methods, and succeeded in a number of projects, also using glass and plastics (ill. 1.4). The US pavilion at the 1967 *Expo* in Montreal formed a highpoint. In 1971 it was followed by the Climatroffice, which he designed together with Norman Foster: a vision of a work landscape enclosed in a translucent membrane and a net structure of aluminium, with platforms positioned freely in space. Other visions, such as Frei Otto's Arctic City or the American *Expo* pavilion in Osaka in 1970 with its artificially conditioned indoor climate, announced the end

From Greenhouse to 'High-tech Hothouse'

of the "architecture of the well-tempered environment". In October 1973 the oil crisis that had been caused by the war in the Middle East introduced a further turning point in the world of building.

After 1973   The new glasshouse that followed as a consequence of the energy crisis that began in October 1973 is the expression of a struggle, conducted largely by English building teams, against the reestablishment of solid building methods and 'hole-in-the-wall' windows as well as against the closed nature of postmodernism. Even the first architectural reactions after 1973 announced the 'triumph of glass', for example, the projects in Ipswich and Norwich by Norman Foster with their all-glass façades and glass strips as wind-bracing, or the glass pavilions of the Museum of Science and Industry in La Villette in Paris by Peter Rice. In the case of the latter, Rice, an engineer with Arup, took up a theme that had appeared in the palm house in Bicton Gardens: the connection of two unstable part systems – cable tensioning and large, silicone-fixed glass sheets for La Villette, as well as slender and structurally reduced iron bars and small glass panes in Bieton Gardens – to form a structure. Rice's invention of 'structural glazing' in La Villette[5] meant a second revolution in glasshouse technology, which this time was a scientific and methodical one. This achievement was rapidly perfected, also by Peter Rice himself, and up until the present day forms an accepted standard that is a fixed element in our culture of building, once again initiated by an English school of thought (ill. 1.5).

On the threshold of the future   For a number of years now, with the help of CAAD tools it has been possible to develop new, free plane load-bearing structures curved in a number of directions whose structure and form are made of computer-generated bespoke components. It is no longer standard and mass, modules and series of elements but made-to-measure production that creates an entirely new and expanded design field for architects and engineers that more strongly calls for interdisciplinary work. Additionally, glass is no longer the only material: ETFE foils, for example, point to a future of new worlds of images in which materials and technology are moved more clearly to the foreground and in which the 'learning area' of bionics will also be incorporated (ill. 1.6).

Spheres and blobs   Since classical antiquity, four areas of reference have been available to form-givers, and today all of them are still being employed: spheres and regular bodies as complete figures, bespoke forms, structures derived from biological phenomena and the free design area. Since mankind's first cultural expressions the processes of discovering form and structure have been the motor of the development of building techniques in the search for new possibilities of design and a new kind of space. The Pantheon in Rome, the Fuller 'domes', the Sydney Opera House and the Eden Project in Cornwall in England are based on spherical structures. Egyptian sarcophagi, the Guggenheim Museum in Bilbao by Frank O. Gehry and Peter Cook's Kunsthaus in Graz are 'bespoke tailoring'. African primitive huts, the culture centre in Nouméa by Renzo Piano, Heinz Isler's shell constructions made of reinforced concrete and the branching bars of the palm house in Bicton Gardens are 'translations' of natural structures. The Bedouin tent, the Millenium Bridge in London and Foster's Greater London Authority use the free form as their theme. The issue is always the generation of operable forms and structures for material, technology and production processes, this is also the case for new developmental methods such as design by algorithm, digital tectonics, etc. The qualities of materials are repeatedly newly

1.5

1.6

1.3: Großes Palmenhaus in the park of Schönbrunn Palace in Vienna, 1880–82

1.4: Richard Buckminster Fuller: Dome over Manhattan, project, 1960

1.5: Peter Rice/RFR (engineers): glass pavilion in Parc André Citroën, Paris, 1992; architect: Patrick Berger

1.6: Shigeru Ban: Centre Pompidou-Metz, competition design, 2004; reworked with Cecil Balmond, Arup

1.1 Glasshouse Pioneers

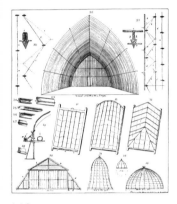

The beginnings:
the struggle for architectural acceptance

The modern glasshouse that was more than merely a purely functional hothouse can be regarded as the invention of the English landscape gardener John Claudius Loudon (1783–1843). With his new structures and forms Loudon aspired to attain architectural qualities. His invention of ambitious volumetric, curvilinear and spatial shells constructed around plants and nursery gardens by 1816 represented a first turning point in building in glass, and showed the direction for the development of glasshouse architecture that has continued down to the present day (ill. 1.1.1).

Loudon pursued the goal of using slender iron-bar sections to allow maximum utilisation of sunlight and zenithal light. Constructing the roofs with ridge and furrow forms optimised the angle of incidence of sunlight. But continuous curvilinear volumes brought even better results (ill. 1.1.2). He used the Bayswater experimental house (1817/18), with its different forms and structures, to carry out tests (see ill. 1.1).

In the field of theory, Loudon also made contributions to various books and specialist journals.[6] Two journeys to the European mainland (1813, 1819) expanded his knowledge of the state of glasshouse technology. His buildings and publications influenced all the pioneers of glasshouse architecture in England, France, and German-speaking Europe who followed him. After Loudon and down to the present day not only have new building types in glass (Expo pavilions, atriums, city malls) been developed, but also previously unknown worlds of spatial images have been created – and the future remains open.

While Loudon built prototypes, the brothers D. and E. Bailey (occasionally in collaboration with Loudon) attempted to use his discoveries, along with their own developments, in botanical gardens and parks. The first high point of a curvilinear vaulted tripartite space for a glasshouse of larger dimensions with a minimum quantity of iron bars was the → palm house in Bicton Gardens, built by the Bailey brothers around 1825.

The steps towards industrialisation

The desire of numerous botanical societies, educational associations and owners of large estates to have large glass- and hothouses encouraged the standardisation of construction and the development of glasshouse technology. It is certainly no accident that the rationalisation of glass building technology began in France and spread from there. This iron and glass 'school of building' was not based as much on experiment and empirical methods as the English school but more on mathematical science. Charles Rohault de Fleury, a student of Jean-Nicolas-Louis Durand at the École Polytechnique in Paris, was the first who attempted to 'translate' his teacher's design method – which was conceived for building in stone – into buildings made of iron and glass.[7] Fleury's → glass pavilions of 1833 in the Jardin des Plantes in Paris marked the beginning of the French 'serre chaude' (greenhouse).

In 1833, the year in which his glass pavilion was erected, Fleury made an educational trip to England, where he visited Loudon's and Bailey's glass- and hothouses and wrote about them in two issues of the Vienna *Allgemeine Bauzeitung*.[8] A year later the English gardener Joseph Paxton travelled to Paris, where he visited Fleury's glasshouses in the Jardin des Plantes.[9] Subsequently, Paxton built a number of pioneering hothouses in the park of Chatsworth House (ill. 1.1.3), including the Great Stove (1836–40), which combines the 'ridge and furrow' system with a curvilinear primary construction.

Transition: from hothouse to 'event space'

In 1846/47 French architects[10] designed the largest glass pavilion of its time, the Jardin d'Hiver on the Champs Élysées in Paris. Its filigree construction anticipated the principle of the lattice or net structure, which has only recently been revived, while the mechanical services in the building were a source of amazement for contemporaries (ill. 1.1.4).[11]

After a construction period of only eight months this multi-functional glass palace,which could accommodate 8,000 persons, was opened on 20 December 1847. This marks the first shift of function, as the pavilion was both hothouse with exotic plants as well as an event space, concert hall and ballroom and, in addition a 'shopping mall'[12] and thus did not solely serve the purpose of education in the natural sciences but was also used for com-

1.1.1: John Claudius Loudon, portrait

1.1.2: Forms and metal sections (plate) – attempt at combining constructive-technical innovations with architectural quality

1.1.3: First glass pavilions in a long series of experiments made by Joseph Paxton in the park of Chatsworth House up until the time of the Crystal Palace

From Greenhouse to 'High-tech Hothouse'

munication and pleasure – with horticulture as a pretext. Gottfried Semper, who visited the glass palace on his journey from Dresden to exile in London, was delighted (not only) by the atmosphere, which he described as follows: "One believes one has been transported into a world of dreams and is surrounded by the whispers of elves and elementary spirits." He was also convinced that this building, made entirely of steel and glass, would serve as a "model and criterion for all similar buildings" for winter gardens, railway station concourses and Expo pavilions.[13] As the Jardin d'Hiver was demolished only in 1852, both Henry Cole, the organiser of the 1851 *London Exhibition*, whom Prince Albert had sent on an exploratory mission to Paris in 1849, and Paxton during one of his visits to the continent were able to draw inspiration from this spectacular building.[14]

Twenty years after the Baileys' hothouses in Bicton Gardens and at the same time as the Jardin d'Hiver, Richard Turner, an engineer and founder of the Hammersmith Ironworks in Dublin, built the Great Palm House in Kew Gardens to the west of London (1846–48), in the process demonstrating a virtuoso, technically perfect and

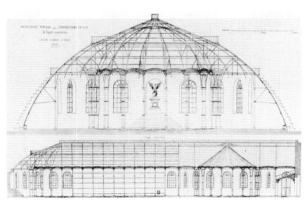

1.1.4

already industrial implementation of Loudon's original ideas in the context of the transition from botanical hothouse to a social and cultural event space.[15] Joseph Paxton, too, anticipated this transformation from glasshouse into an 'events space' – which is topical once again today – with his spectacular project for the Great Victorian Way in 1855 (see section 6.3).

Standardisation and the primacy of style

Between 1850 and 1900 the development of the glasshouse is marked by both standardisation and the formation of a style. In the German-speaking world the 'primacy of style' was characteristic of glasshouse architecture from the very start. The Glaspalast in Munich was preceded by a long series of ambitious and prominent hothouses and glasshouses. This tradition and the experience acquired extend over a period about the same length as in England. The builders in Munich (von Sckell, von Voit), Berlin (Schadow, Schinkel, Persius), Stuttgart (Zanth, Leins) or Vienna (von Sengenschmid, von Remy, Ohmann) all had in common a striving to combine a view of architecture that was shaped by the concept of style with the modern industrial opportunities offered by iron- and glass-building technology (ill. 1.1.5).

Between 1807 and 1820 Friedrich Ludwig von Sckell built three greenhouses in Munich in the Königlicher Hofgarten in Nymphenburg. The modular, structural composition of his glass pavilions allowed an easy transfer to the approaching age of industry, represented a kind of catalogue of types and contained a forward-looking programme for further developments. As a source of impulses Munich played a similarly important role like London or Paris, and it was no coincidence that the Munich Glaspalast was built immediately after the Crystal Palace in London and thus marked a further step in this development (see chapter 2, case studies 20 and 21).

Illustrative attempts at using modern, industrially influenced construction and material technology to popularise the aim of creating a style include, for example, the → Großes Palmenhaus as well as the Sonnenuhrhaus in the park of Schönbrunn Palace in Vienna.

1.1.4: Jardin d'Hiver, Paris, sections with views of interior: the pavilion measured 100 x 65 m, the glass barrel-vaulted roof spanned a width of 40 m with a maximum height of 18.5 m (the columns at the side were 9 m tall!), which led to a truly light-flooded space (after Victor Hugo, *Une fête de lumières*).

1.1.5: Friedrich Ludwig von Sckell: hothouse in the Königlicher Hofgarten in Nymphenburg, Munich

Palm House

Bicton Gardens,
Budleigh Salterton, Devon
England, around 1825
Built by D. and E. Bailey

1.1.6

The palm house in Bicton Gardens in Budleigh Salterton, which lies off the beaten tourist track (on a site above the sea, to the south-east of Exeter) was a gift by John Rolle, Lord of the Manor of Bicton, to his wife, Lady Louisa, and stands at the edge of an Italianate garden.[16] Given the high taxes levied on glass (window tax and glass tax) at the time, this glass construction was an extremely expensive undertaking.[17] Alongside the palm house in Kew Gardens near London the hothouse in Bicton Gardens is the largest surviving glass building in England from the pioneering period. It was renovated in 1985 and new planting was undertaken in 2000, as the palm trees had grown too large.

Geometry and spatial form The tripartite, axially symmetrical palm house, which is built against a rear wall, is made up of interlocking volumes that reveal a new kind of spatial interpenetration related to modern spherical worlds of images, such as those of Buckminster Fuller or the currently fashionable 'bubbles' (ills. 1.1.6 and 1.1.7). The central vault is 8.3 metres high and looks like a quarter sphere but is, in fact, a parabolic 'onion form' with a radius of 4.5 metres, which, however, is continued at the rear as a barrel vault over a rectangle with sides measuring 4.5 x 9 metres. As a result, a spherical, multiply-curved surface is created at the transitional areas that anticipates contemporary spatial figures such as those by Jörg Schlaich or Shigeru Ban (ill 1.1.8).

Statics, structure and construction The line of intersection in the valley of the roof is structurally strengthened internally by a flat iron section set on edge and by a cast-iron column 4.5 metres high and 5 cm in diameter (ills. 1.1.7 and 1.1.9). From the head of the column a further flat iron runs into the side wings as a ring-shaped, meridial tension element and is supported at the middle of the arc by a further column (ill. 1.1.10). The columns, four in all, are empirically positioned, which is astonishing, given the complex interpenetration and formal composition of the surfaces of the multiply-curved roof skin!

Load-bearing glass skin Loudon realised that the curved volume of the glass skin was advantageous, because curvilinear iron beams, despite using less material, achieve greater stability, aided by the fact that in cross-section the beam is deeper than it is wide, which increases the area of glass and, as a result of the continu-ous development of the glass envelope, leads to the more efficient exploitation of the light available. In using iron sections of this kind the Bailey brothers introduced a theme that, more than 100 years later, was to be investigated by Jean Prouvé and modernism (see chapter 6, case study 89).

Together with 18,000 small, slightly convex glass panes the slender, wrought-iron, 'curvilinear' iron bars form a glass skin that is a single constructive layer. The glass contributes structurally to the overall system by taking up meridial compression and shear forces. The slightly thicker edges of the glass panes were a result of the technique of glass-blowing at the time. In the fall line the glass panes do not only overlap like scales but are also cut in a slight curve to help water run off (ill. 1.1.11).[18] The iron bars rest on a vertical 'base element' that is covered by the same type of glass skin but that has, additionally, posts that form a ring-shaped bearing (ill. 1.1.12).

According to local information, the company of D. and E. Bailey built the palm house in accordance with a patent transferred to them by Loudon.[19]

The palm house in Bicton Gardens illustrates the tendency of early greenhouses to develop an architectural style and spatial transparency (see also ill. 1.2.10).[20] Writing about these glass construction techniques, engineer Peter Rice, the inventor of 'structural glazing' 170 years later, stated that this is where thinking in terms of structural glazing first appears: "The transparent surface of glass and struts forms a very fine skin: the load-bearing frame is reduced to an absolute minimum. Extremely small panes of glass rest on the supporting iron sections, producing a smooth, rounded form. The glass provides the bracing of the sections at the sides and thus plays a structural role. The glass and iron sections together form a transparent shell that recalls the spine of an animal and provides its own structural stability. The reduction of the load-bearing elements lessens their visual presence and maximises the transparency from either side."[21] (ill. 1.1.13; see also ill. 1.1.10).

Thus the Bailey brothers not only anticipate Turner's Palm House in Kew Gardens, but also point towards the future with these first indications of structural thinking in the form of nets or meshes (ill. 1.1.14).

1.1.7

1.1.8

1.1.9

1.1.10

1.1.11

1.1.12

1.1.13

1.1.14

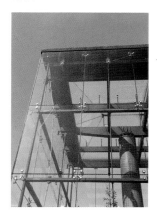

1.1.6: View from the side

1.1.7: Spatial transparency from the perspective of the interior

1.1.8: Spherical planar structure in the transition from paraboloid to barrel vault: load-bearing function of the glass and reduction of the bars – a kind of 'dematerialisation' appropriate to the nature of the materials used

1.1.9: Foot of column; diameter 5 cm

1.1.10: Head of column at the meridial ring

1.1.11: Glass panes, originally slightly convex and slightly scalloped to improve ventilation and help water run off. They are 12.5 cm long, in a test area of 7 bays (in the base element) measured by the author the width varies from 17.0 to 18.8 cm. The axial distance between two posts theoretically produces a division of 7 x 18 cm (in total 126 cm). Thinking in terms of construction axes naturally produces a narrower edge bay (13.2 cm) – a reoccurring problem in architecture with which Mies van der Rohe, for example, was confronted in his Lake Shore Drive Apartments. The slender, cross-shaped bars are 15 mm long externally, 16 mm internally and 15 mm wide, the bars are only 5 mm thick, and the glass rebates at the sides are also 5 mm. The glass is fitted from outside with the use of putty.

1.1.12: Bearing of the curvilinear roof bars on the base element

1.1.13: Tailor-made solution of the spherical structural system. As the bars are in the fall line the distance between them reduces as they curve upwards so that they form a pattern like the mesh of a piece of fabric and appear like a decorative 'rosette' (see also ill. 1.1.10).

1.1.14: Peter Rice/RFR: 'structural glazing' of the glass pavilions in Parc André Citroën,

Greenhouse and Glass Pavilions

Jardin des Plantes, Paris
France, 1833
Architect:
Charles Rohault de Fleury

1.1.15

Charles Rohault de Fleury (1801–75), who attended the design courses of Jean-Nicolas-Louis Durand at the École Polytechnique (1820–22), made his debut in the architecture of the restoration period in Paris.[22] Against this political background it seems astonishing that Fleury designed the first pure glass-and-iron pavilions before Paxton and Turner and as a student of Durand, whose design theory was still oriented on techniques of building in stone. But Durand initiated a method that pointed towards the future.

Durand: 'a Copernican turning point' in design methods
As the first teacher of architecture at the École Polytechnique (founded in 1794) Durand recognised the need to give composition and construction equal importance. By replacing the system of the classical orders, which was based on bodily dimensions, with the construction (unvisual!) grid, Durand introduced an entirely new way of thinking that was intended to open up to his students the future world of a culture of building shaped by industry.[23] Fleury's glass pavilions were the first products of this forward-looking school of thought (ills. 1.1.15 and 1.1.16).

Fleury's glass pavilions: applications of Durand's teaching
Fleury's 'serres chaudes' in the botanical gardens in Paris in 1833 meant (not in glass, but in iron technology and in the principles of construction) a 'parallel revolution' to the inventions of Loudon and the Bailey brothers.[24] They demonstrate a certain systematic grammar of constructive design based on the mathematical way of thinking that prevailed in the École at the time, as well as on Gaspard Monge's 'stéréometrie'.[25]

Fleury took over the didactic design model of the 4 x 4-m grid from Durand[26] and transferred it at a scale of 1:1 to his own design task: the lightweight, light-flooded and modern glasshouse could not be built using massive construction methods but had to use the new iron-and-glass technologies. In plan the central pavilions were made up of 3 x 5 bays of 4 metres, that is, they measured 12 x 20 metres, in elevation they consisted of 2 bays, that is to say, 8 metres. This three-dimensional, 4-metre grid produced not only a new kind of building and a new spatial typology but also a systematic overall composition – 'constructive economy', Fleury's translation of Durand's teaching (ills. 1.1.17 and 1.1.18).

Innovation and 'creative misunderstanding'
Although Fleury designed an iron truss with compression and tension members that spanned 12 metres he placed cast-iron posts at the junctions in the grid. Was he still thinking cautiously in Durand's stone dimensions? If he had recognised the new qualities of this structural system he would have dispensed with these columns (ill.1.1.19).[27] New types of structures spanning similar and, indeed, wider spaces without the use of columns followed only a short time later: in 1837, with Camille Polonceau's invention of the trussed beam[28] and in 1838 with the truss construction of Euston Station in London (that also spanned 12 metres) by Charles Fox, Robert Stephenson's assistant (see chapter 2, case study 16).

Constructive innovations
With standardised, self-supporting glass façades made of a frame of 8-metre-tall. cast-iron uprights Fleury achieved the highest level of development in glass-building technology at the time. The tall, slender columns consisted of two parts with intermediate pieces that used the side connections for the gallery running around the building to strengthen the critical buckling point. The internal columns were cruciform in plan: a precise, function-related reaction to the longitudinal and transverse beams, screwed to the column heads by means of positive locking.[29]

Travel and the international transfer of knowledge
In 1833, shortly before the erection of the glass pavilion, the French state authorities sent Fleury on a study trip to England. In the two illustrated articles referred to above, which were published in Förster's *Allgemeine Bauzeitung*,[30] he emphasised, above all, the remarkable spatial quality, the structurally advantageous curved structure and the even light of the glass pavilions by Loudon and the Bailey brothers (ill. 1.1.20). As, on the other hand, Paxton travelled to Paris (for example, in 1834) and visited Fleury's glass pavilions we have documentation of a cross-border exchange of information, which was supported by the international nature of the journal and newspaper business.

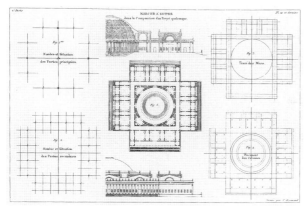

1.1.16

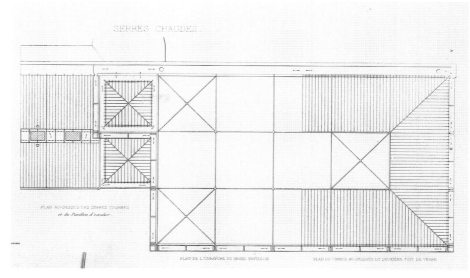

1.1.17

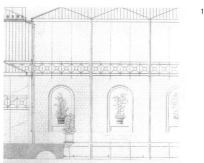

1.1.18

1.1.19

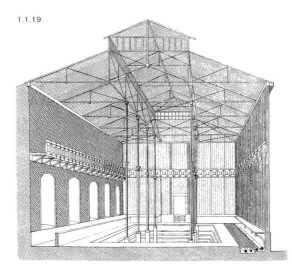

1.1.20

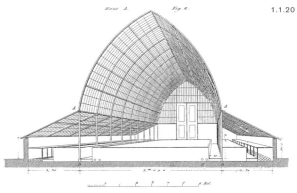

1.1.15: 'Serres chaudes' by Fleury in the Jardin des Plantes in Paris, 1833

1.1.16: 'Marche à suivre': the virtual construction grid as a basis of building composition in Durand's textbook *Precis des leçons d'architecture* (1802–05)

1.1.17: Plan of the structure with the 4 x 4-m grid

1.1.18: Section through the modulated space, height 2 x 4 m

1.1.19: Construction of the interior space

1.1.20: Illustration by Fleury made during his trip to England: combination of spatial quality, construction typology and incidence of light

Case Study 3
Greenhouses

Park of Chatsworth House
Derbyshire, England 1834–50
Built by: Joseph Paxton

Joseph Paxton (1803–65) was the son of a farmer. He trained as a gardener and as a 19-year-old worked for the Duke of Somerset in Wimbledon and then for the Horticultural Society in the gardens of Chiswick House, which belonged to the sixth Duke of Devonshire, who in 1826 appointed Paxton head gardener in his county seat, Chatsworth. Afterwards Paxton educated himself empirically in the fields of landscape design, greenhouse construction and building. He designed the park in Chatsworth, erected cottages and villages in Derbyshire and, finally, worked as the duke's general manager.[31]

First hothouses In 1833/34 Paxton travelled to Paris (his travel expenses were met by the Duke of Devonshire), where among the sights he visited were Fleury's glasshouses in the Jardin des Plantes. By initially building traditional orangeries (ills. 1.1.21 and 1.1.3) he gradually acquired knowledge of construction and materials, and then built his first real hothouse, a ridge and furrow construction with wooden glazing bars, cast-iron columns and small glass panes, which he published in 1834 in his own journal, *Paxton's Magazine of Botany* (ill. 1.1.22).

Great Stove Between 1836 and 1840 Paxton (with the support of the young architect Decimus Burton) carried out a large, new kind of hothouse: he overlaid the curvilinear, load-bearing structure with a ridge and furrow roof – essentially a combination of two of Loudon's principles. Water running off the upper part of the roof was drained internally at gallery level to provide moisture for the earth in which the plants grew.[32] As Paxton wanted to use large glass panes he consulted the glassmaker Lucas Chance (who since 1832 had worked with the cylindrical expansion process that he had learned about in France in 1830), and asked him to increase the length of the glass panes from three to four feet. Although initially unwilling Chance finally successfully complied with Paxton's wishes and, as a consequence, in 1850 received the contract to provide 300,000 panes of glass to cover the Crystal Palace. (ill. 1.1.23).[33]

Victoria Regia House Paxton's last glasshouse in Chatsworth was once more a folded roof construction but with a greater span and, most importantly, with effective natural air-conditioning, which meant that Paxton succeeded in getting the water lily *Victoria regia* to blossom in England for the first time (ill. 1.1.24).

The 'Paxton gutter' One of Paxton's most ingenious ideas came as a result of the awareness he had developed through his experience and practice that the best possible lighting of a wide space could be achieved only when the load-bearing building elements fulfilled several different functions. Paxton developed a timber load-bearing valley beam for use with any kind of folded roof which was modelled in a number of work processes so that it had a groove on either side to take the glass panes and, on the inside, two further notches that helped to drain off the condensation that formed below the panes. This 'Paxton gutter' was slightly cambered and pre-tensioned in the long direction by the use of tension rods and compression struts as spacers, so that the water was led off at the sides and the beam's structural properties strengthened. The patent for this gutter was granted in 1850, the same year in which the construction of the Crystal Palace began, where Paxton's invention was used over a total length of 40 km! (ill. 1.1.25)

Thanks to his success in Chatsworth, Paxton was able to enter the railway construction business at an early stage. In 1835 he became financially involved in the railway business and was the organiser and manager of several railway lines. The personal contacts he made as a result were of great use to him in realising his design for the Crystal Palace in 1850/51, as indeed was his experience as a glass-building engineer and a pioneer in the field of hothouses.

1.1.24

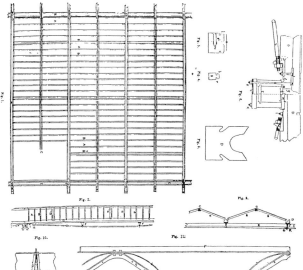

1.1.21: Orangery against the wall enclosing the park

1.1.22: Paxton's first folded roof construction

1.1.23: The Great Stove; test of the new glass construction

1.1.24: Construction of Victoria Regia House

1.1.25: Patent application plan of the 'Paxton gutter'

1.1.25

Case Study 4
Great Palm House

Kew Gardens, London
England, 1846–48
Built by: Richard Turner

Little is known of the background and biography of Richard Turner (1783–1843). An engineer and businessman, he ran the Hammersmith Ironworks in Dublin, which he had founded with his brother as business partner in 1818. His company acquired its reputation through innovative iron-and-glass constructions and catalogues offering different types of constructions and standard elements that it produced itself, but also through visionary projects. With the Great Palm House in Kew Gardens, Lime Street Station in Liverpool, 1847–49 (see chapter 2, case study 17) and his competition entry for the *Great Exhibition* (1850) Turner pointed the way to the future.[34]

First projects   With the construction of his first palm house in 1839 in the Botanical Garden in Belfast (design by architect Charles Lanyon), the winter garden in

1.1.26

Regent's Park (1842–46) and the greenhouse in the National Botanic Gardens in Glasnevin, Dublin (1842–50), Turner showed himself to be a great industrialist implementer and developer of the ideas of the pioneers Loudon and Bailey.

Glasshouse as 'event space'   The palm house in Kew was, after the Jardin d'Hiver in Paris, the second glasshouse to be conceived as an 'event space'. The size of the building and the spans were new, as was the perfection of the possibilities of achieving transparency on an industrial basis, in terms of both construction techniques and material technology (ill. 1.1.26). The volumetric concept of spatial interpenetration in three dimensions, as illustrated in an engraving published by Henry-Russell Hitchcock (ill. 1.1.27), pointed far into the future. This building

refers to modern worlds of images in that it creates an ambiguity of spatial references through the longitudinal and transverse directions, as well as through the fact that the height is stepped twice, which allows a simultaneous perception of space and time (four dimensions) and can therefore be viewed as an early form of modern 'transparency'.[35]

Decimus Burton's first design seems to have proposed the principle of the folded roof; but according to Hix, the execution of what still remains the most spectacular glasshouse is essentially Turner's work, on the basis of a ground figure by Burton.[36] The curvilinear formation of the figure and the use of larger and, at places, curved glass panes[37] add to the volumetric clarity, and were contributed by Turner.

The large dimensions required not only a strong primary structure with curved beams but also purlins made of slender tubes that take compression forces and that contain invisible continuous tension elements which run around the entire building (ill. 1.1.28). The building envelope is a secondary construction based on Loudon's curvilinear principle. All the building parts depict their function, in much the same way as current examples of the 'new constructivism', for example, Waterloo International Terminal by Nicholas Grimshaw and Anthony Hunt (see chapter 2, case study 28).

Like in the palm house in Bicton Gardens, the panes of glass are fixed like scales between curved cruciform profiles. A small gap allows the entry of fresh air and also allows the condensation that collects below the glass to be drained off outside (ill. 1.1.29).

The volumetric and technical perfection of industrially produced components in a framework of a rational order and geometrical precision is legible in the normally problematic areas of the valleys and ridges, which mark the intersections of the interpenetrating spaces (ill. 1.1.30).

The Great Palm House in Kew Gardens signals the end of the pioneering phase in England and the introduction of an industrial basis for glasshouse construction in the future. Despite his remarkable achievements Turner still has yet to achieve sufficient recognition in the world of building and technology research.

1.1.28

1.1.30

1.1.26: View of the glasshouse in its present state

1.1.27: Interpenetrating spaces: early view of 'transparency' as simultaneous perception of space and time (4D)

1.1.28: Build-up of the structure and the envelope; where they meet the beams, the compression rods form small rosettes: a depiction of the 'compressing' function; on the other hand, they conceal the tension bars; a paradoxical structural functionality (similar construction in glass 150 years later: see ills. 6.2.28–30)

1.1.29: Skin made of glass 'scales' for natural ventilation and to lead off condensation

1.1.30: Technically perfected solution of interpenetrating spaces and volumes

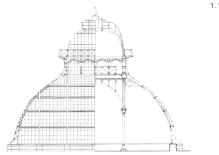

Case Study 5

Großes Palmenhaus

Schlosspark Schönbrunn
Vienna, Austria, 1880–82
Architect: Franz von Sengenschmid
Construction: Sigmund Wagner
Building: Ignaz Gridl

Sonnenuhrhaus

Schlosspark Schönbrunn
Vienna, 1885

1.1.31

In the history of the development of glasshouses since Loudon, the Bailey brothers and also von Sckell, the Großes Palmenhaus in Vienna comes at a very late stage. The court architect Franz von Sengenschmid, who had been sent on a study tour by Archduke Ferdinand Maximilian to inform himself about developments in glasshouse construction, utilised this advantage. The intention was that iron-and-glass building technology should here be brought to a new high point and integrated in an overall architectural composition to form a style. The Großes Palmenhaus in the park of Schönbrunn Palace was seen as a 'flower temple' and 'enchanted palace'.[38]

While the plan of the palm house is axially symmetrical, consisting of a central pavilion and pronounced end elements, in section the building describes a curvilinear figure (see ill. 1.3). This compositional design illustrates an attempt to apply the new technology of iron building and its possibilities, which had been explored mostly in railway and market halls, industrial complexes and bridge building, to a representative building at a prominent location (ills. 1.1.31 and 1.1.32).

Apart from a few cast-iron columns in the interior that support the vaulted pavilions, the entire iron structure is outside the glass skin and not in the same construction layer, unlike, for example, the palm house in Bicton Gardens. As a result, the new material, together with the constructional system, shapes the first impression made by this building, clearly showing what is new here when compared with the conventional stone buildings in classical and historicist Vienna and presenting self-confident architectural forms of a kind only possible with the use of iron (ill. 1.1.33).

The curvilinear, wrought-iron lattice beams made up of parts riveted together follow a rigid geometrical basic grid that allows the consistent formation of valleys and ridges (ill. 1.1.34) and thus translates basic laws of classical building into the medium of iron and glass – a precision of design and use of materials similar to Turner's palm house in Kew Gardens.

In accordance with the recommendations of the building commission for the Glaspalast in Munich in 1853/54 that, on account of the climate, glasshouses north of the Alps should be built in a more robust way, the Schönbrunn palm house is double-glazed. Despite the progress that had been made in glass technology the glass panes are rather small and in form are similar to the standard developed in the pioneering glasshouses, that is, slightly convex in cross-section and with a scalloped lower edge that naturally aids cross-ventilation and helps to lead condensation from inside to outside. Ventilation occurs primarily by means of opening flaps in the glass vault and through the pavilions.

Sonnenuhrhaus Whereas in the palm house the iron structure winds continuously like a creeper around all the curves and corners, conveying an image of an architecture related to the world of plants, the Sonnenuhrhaus, which is only a few steps away, seems like a rational, modern building. On the north side the slightly flattened, barrel-shaped roof rests on a wall, as was often the case with the earliest hothouses, for example, in Bicton Gardens; on the other three sides the iron beams of the vault connect to the lattice columns of the façade; each of the short ends of the building was made as a half cross-vault. The interior, which has no internal columns, is 14.5 metres wide. The structure is on the inside, the glass skin on the outside (ill. 1.1.35), only the corner column was placed outside (ill. 1.1.36). The image created is that of a plain, homogeneous and modern building, similar to a small railway station. Today, the Sonnenuhrhaus is used as an 'event space' with artificial deserts.

1.1.35

1.1.31: Großes Palmenhaus, Schlosspark Schönbrunn: construction as an eye-catcher

1.1.32: Palmenhaus: cross-section through the centre pavilion

1.1.33: Palmenhaus: precise geometry of the structure as a style-forming dimension in the architectural composition

1.1.34: Palmenhaus: detail solution of ridge and furrow

1.1.35: Sonnenuhrhaus: glass skin flush with the construction

1.1.36: Elegant solution of the corner column problem

1.1.36

1.2 Between Style and Method: Modernism and Post-war Modernism

Transitions: after the 'age of iron'

William Le Baron Jenney's → Crystal Dome was the surprising event space of the Horticultural Building at the *World's Columbian Fair* in Chicago in 1893, which was otherwise mostly a tasteless blend of styles at the end of

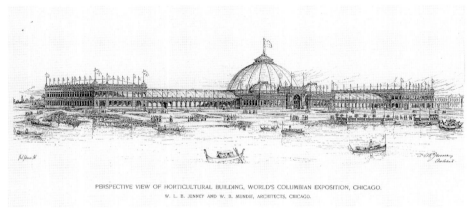

PERSPECTIVE VIEW OF HORTICULTURAL BUILDING, WORLD'S COLUMBIAN EXPOSITION, CHICAGO.
W. L. B. JENNEY AND W. B. MUNDIE, ARCHITECTS, CHICAGO.

1.2.1

1.2.2

a creative era. The dominance of the 'East Coast architects', the late-historicist Beaux Arts school of New York, seemed to announce the fatal end of the great era of iron construction, But the pioneering period of the lightweight, transparent and spherical glasshouses blossomed a final time – in the form of the Crystal Dome, which in the development of the glasshouse marks both the end of an era and the transition to modernism. Jenney, who was educated during the heyday of French iron-and-glass technology at the scientific and technical École Centrale des Arts et Manufactures (ECAM) in Paris (at the time the most modern school of its kind), 'rescued', so to speak, both this building type and, at the same time, the problem-solving, method-based school of thought which was then to form the basis of a regenerative modernism (ill. 1.2.1).

Following François Hennebique's pioneering patent in 1892, which decisively expanded the structural and design possibilities of concrete construction for architects and engineers, construction in iron and steel was shifted to the sidelines, as it were. Reinforced concrete, the new material, conquered the 20th century (see section 3.1).

The 1900 *World Exhibition* in Paris punctually announced this new world. Subsequently, lightweight pavilions crop up only as isolated cases, for example, in the 1925 *Exposition des Arts Decoratifs* in Paris, where in their theatre building the Perret brothers were able to achieve almost ideal entry of daylight by using a glazed, cross-ribbed concrete ceiling (ill.1.2.2).[39]

A specific discovery of modernism was the glass block, which combined in an ideal way a load-bearing concrete ribbed structure with a double-layered glass module that also helped carry loads. Innumerable forms and systems were and still are available, but only few glass pavilions were built using this material. An exception and an impressive exploration of this theme was the exhibition pavilion of the Saint-Gobain Company at the 1937 *World Exhibition* in Paris (ill.1.2.3).[40] It measured 24 x 15 metres and was 20 metres high. The glass blocks (30 x 30 cm, 10 cm thick)[41] were smooth on the outside face and ribbed on the inner side, and were used as modules of 15 x 15 elements with a composite metal (including aluminium) that formed integrally stable slabs which were fixed to the reinforced concrete frame. The distance between axes was around 5 metres and the reinforced ribs were 15 mm thin! Whereas the roof construction consisted of glass block panels measuring around 4.5 x 4.5 metres, the façade modules rose uninterrupted the entire height of the space (9 m). The designers used a concave, glazed entrance element to give the panels stability.[42]

The Glashaus, or pavilion, that Bruno Taut designed for the Luxfer-Prismen-Syndikat at the exhibition of the Deutscher Werkbund in Cologne in 1914 represents a historically important precursor. Taut cast Loudon's curvilinear structure in concrete (ill. 1.2.4).[43]

Spatial continuum and dream worlds under glass

Architect Frank Lloyd Wright investigated glass as a building material at an early stage. As industrial designer for the Luxfer Prism Company (1894–98) with his concept of glass modules consisting of prismatic rods that directed and increased light he opened up for architects a new approach to designing naturally-lit deep spaces, from which the Chicago School in particular benefited (see chapter 4, case study 55, as well as chapter 5, case study 69). In Wright's work horizontal glass ceilings also

From Greenhouse to 'High-tech Hothouse'

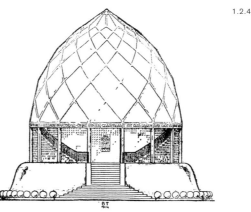

1.2.4

1.2.3

1.2.5

1.2.1: William Le Baron Jenney: Horticultural Building, *World's Columbian Fair*, Chicago, 1893

1.2.2: Auguste and Gustave Perret: theatre auditorium, *Exposition des Arts Décoratifs*, Paris, 1925

1.2.3: Glass pavilion of the Saint-Gobain company, *World Exhibition*, Paris, 1937.

1.2.4: Bruno Taut: Glass Pavilion, 1914

1.2.5: Frank Lloyd Wright: S. C. Johnson & Son Company, Racine, Wisconsin. Light-flooded interior with mush-room-head columns

1.2.6: Lattice of iron rods for the concrete dome of the Zeiss planetarium in Jena

play an important role, for example, in the "buildings for people working together" such as the Larkin Building in Buffalo, New York (1902–06), the administration building for S. C. Johnson & Son in Racine, Wisconsin (1936–39; ill. 1.2.5, see also chapter 3, case study 40) or the project for the Lenkurt Electric Company in San Carlos, California (1955–58). Wright's few 'pure' glass structures – the glass dome of the sport hotel for Huntington Hartford in Hollywood, California (1946–48) or the glass rotunda for Point Park Civic Center in Pittsburgh, Pennsylvania (first project 1947) – remained drawing board projects but show him to be a visionary designer, even in his late work.[44] Both projects were made at the same time as Buckminster Fuller began to experiment with 'geodesic domes'.

'Geodesic worlds'

Before the concrete was poured the net used as reinforcement for the thin concrete dome of the Zeiss Planetarium in Jena (1924/25)[45] – an icosahedric structure – formed the first geodesic figure (ill. 1.2.6).

A striving to achieve completely spherical buildings and, at the same time, a tendency to breakup building mass and weight is as old as architecture itself. Buckmin-

ster Fuller followed this trail with his concept of → 'geodesic domes' and was proud of the fact that his first weather-proof 'dome' – 50 metres wide without internal supports – weighed only 15 tons and was thus 1,000 times lighter than the Pantheon and the dome of St. Peter's in Rome, which are also 50 metres wide. "An earthquake would tumble both the Roman domes, but it would leave the geodesic unharmed."[46] Fuller's largest built 'dome', with a span of 76 metres, was the US pavilion at the *Expo '67* in Montreal.

Exploring new boundaries: visions before 1973

At the same time as Fuller, other teams, in particular Frei Otto and Ove Arup, began to define new boundaries for lightweight structures. Their vision of an → Arctic City for 15,000 to 45,000 inhabitants (1971) spanned a space measuring 2 km[2].[47] The US pavilion at the *Expo '70* in Osaka[48] was a visionary project that was actually carried out. Here and in other 'air-inflated domes' a synthetic shell was used that consisted of several membranes and was stabilised by the internal air pressure[49] (see chapter 2, case study 26). Nicholas Grimshaw's Eden Project is related to constructions of this type.

1.2.6

Horticultural Building and Crystal Dome

World's Columbian Fair
Chicago, USA, 1893
Architects:
William Le Baron Jenney,
William B. Mundie

1.2.7

Even though 'The Fair' in Chicago in 1893 gave the overall impression of a classical revival and suggested a "triumph of the École des Beaux Arts"[50] – with Baroque palaces, a copy of Florence Cathedral and Venetian bridges and gondolas – under the supervision of Chicago architect Daniel Burnham a number of pavilions in glass and steel were also built that reflected the state of European building technology in the 1860s, but all of which were clad in a historicist manner: the Manufacturer's Building (George B. Post), the Electricity Building (Henry van Brunt), the Agricultural Hall (Charles F. McKim) and others.[51] The Crystal Dome reveals the different background of William Le Baron Jenney, who was a graduate of the École Centrale des Arts et Manufactures in Paris (ECAM).

Jenney's Horticultural Building was the only truly original building. He erected it together with William B. Mundie, his colleague since 1884, and business partner since 1891. The building housed a world of tropical vegetation as well as numerous national presentations. It consisted of a long pavilion and the central Crystal Dome, at the time one of the world's largest domes with a diameter of more than 60 metres. In the context of this exhibition the dome represented a supremely ingenious architectural and constructional achievement.[52] The overall dimensions of the Horticultural Building were 333 x 95.5 metres; it was the largest glasshouse of its time (ill. 1.2.1).[53] The central domed space, the Crystal Dome, was 43.5 metres high and soared above the extensive pavilion complex (ill. 1.2.7).[54]

The construction of the dome consisted of 20 primary ribs (curved lattice beams) directly anchored in the foundations, with a secondary system of slender longitudinal beams (also lattice beams) between them and transverse purlins, a system of diagonal braces mounted across the entire internal surface of the dome as well as a curvilinear external glass skin with glazing bars (ills. 1.2.8 and 1.2.9). With a diameter of 60.5 metres this was the broadest construction of its kind at the time, it weighed 366 t and was erected in a period of only 39 days. The dome and the glass façades of the side pavilions were heated by means of a warm-air blower, the most modern of its time.[55]

The greenhouse erected in 1840 by the Bailey brothers in Chiswick near London employed a similar construction but was barrel-vaulted in shape: curved lattice beams, connected by transverse purlins, formed the primary load-bearing structure over which a shell made of a curvilinear lattice of bars carried the glazing which, analogous to the palm house in Bicton Gardens, lies in the same plane (ill. 1.2.10).[56]

One source of inspiration for this lattice beam and net structure, and for the impression it gave of the transparent spatial quality of architecture of the future, was the Halle au Blé, which Jenney knew from his time as a student at the École Centrale des Arts et Manufactures in Paris. This building was erected from 1809 to 1813 by the engineer François Brunet on the basis of an architectural form by François Joseph Bélanger, replaced the wood construction that burned in 1802, and was the first pure lattice dome to be built of iron.[57] Jenney's teacher of architecture and construction at the ECAM, Charles-Louis Mary, published the plate illustrating the construction of the Halle au Blé in 1852/53, the first year of Jenney's studies (ill. 1.2.11).

The Horticultural Building built by Jenney and Mundie in 1893 represents a transition – the end of the epoch of glass- and greenhouses made of iron and glass, and at the same time the proclamation of new, creative spatial and constructional inventions pointing in the direction of geodesic domes – the move forward to modernism.

1.2.8

1.2.7 Crystal Dome by William
Le Baron Jenney, Chicago,
1893

1.2.8. Construction of the dome
before cladding

1.2.9: Detail of part of the net
structure

1.2.10: D. and E. Bailey: glasshouse, Chiswick, 1840, interior

1.2.11: Plate showing the construction of the Halle au Blé
from the texbook of Charles-
Louis Mary (École Centrale des
Arts et Manufactures, 1852/53)

1.2.10

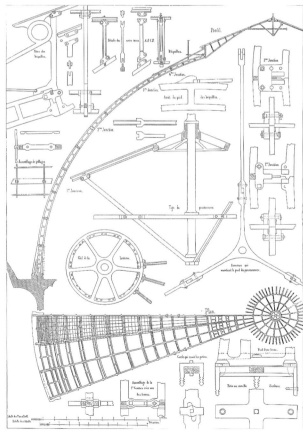

1.2.11

Case Study 7
Geodesic Domes

1949–83
Architect:
Richard Buckminster Fuller

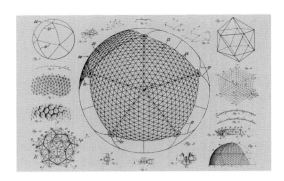

1.2.12: From one of Fuller's patent applications

1.2.13: Buckminster Fuller in his experiment workshop in Black Mountain College

1.2.14, 1.2.15: Industry hall of the Union Tank Car Company in Baton Rouge, Louisiana, 1958, with a span of 116 m: a combination of two unstable systems: honeycomb structure and folded plate as the envelope

1.2.16: First prototype with polyester and fibreglass with a span of 16.5 m, built on Long Island

1.2.17: Assembly by helicopter of a mobile theatre space for Ford, aluminium construction with a span of 30 m

1.2.18: US pavilion at the *Expo '67* in Montreal, with a span of 76 m. Not tied to a particular place, climate or culture: the use of Fuller's 'domes' around the entire world – even on aircraft carriers – illustrate the universality of this model.

1.2.19: Norman Foster: Greater London Authority building, London, 2002

1.2.20: Norman Foster, Anthony Hunt (engineer): greenhouse, Carmarthenshire, Wales, 2000

Richard Buckminster Fuller (1895–1983) never mentioned Jenney and Mundie's Crystal Dome at the 1893 *World's Columbian Fair* in Chicago. But this building – between the Pantheon in Rome and Fuller's architecture – stands on the threshold of a new development: with its span of 60.5 m, its weight of only 366 t and a construction period of only 39 days, the Crystal Dome broke all records and surpassed all earlier domes with its span and elegance. Although it seems that Fuller did not know the Crystal Dome, it was in a sense the point from which he started.

Among the most important areas of Fuller's research work, experiments and activity were his examinations of how to deal with the sphere in terms of operation, construction and the technology of materials in order to create a space-shaping, functional figure in architecture's repertoire of forms (ill. 1.2.12).

Fuller's studies on geodesic domes are closely linked to Black Mountain College, near Ashville North Carolina. It was founded in 1933 – at some distance from the machinery of the academic university world – and soon became a first refuge for exiled teachers and students from the Bauhaus in Dessau.[58] Fuller set up an experiment workshop there in 1948/49 (ill. 1.2.13).

The source of inspiration was the pioneering spherical construction of the Zeiss Planetarium in Jena (1924/25; see ill. 1.2.6; see also ills. 3.4.17 and 3.4.18). The hemispherical dome (radius 28.28 m), made of a net of flat steel rods, was covered with a 3-cm-thick layer of sprayed concrete. Before this layer was applied the net represented a completely new intellectual model: the net of rods was the materialised projection of a 20-face regular body, or icosahedron, on a virtual sphere. The refinement through the use of pentagons and hexagons (similar to the structure of a leather football) produced the typical regularity of a net structure, with which Fuller also worked.[59]

The tradition of the lightweight glasshouse was brought to life again by Fuller's geodesic domes and experienced an entirely new innovation phase, more than half a century after Jenney had built his Crystal Dome at the 1893 *Chicago Fair*. Fuller succeeded in going beyond the boundaries established by steel-and-glass constructions and ventured into new territory (ills. 1.2.14, 1.2.15).

His approach, which was not dependent on specific materials, encouraged thinking in different kinds of structures and techniques, forms and combinations and allowed an approach to materials still unfamiliar in the building world, such as aluminium structures or plastics, as well as the use of new transport and assembly methods (ills. 1.2.16 and 1.2.17). Fuller's thinking was characterised by experiment, trial and error, a methodical approach that seemed largely to have been lost since Loudon's Bayswater experimental building and Paxton's attempts in Chatsworth but that reached a highpoint with the US pavilion at the *Expo '67* in Montreal and that today is being discovered once again (ills. 1.2.18 and 1.2.19).[60]

With his geodetic problem type Fuller set a worldwide movement in motion, leading to a number of very different inventions, such as the 'Mero-System' by the German engineer Max von Mengeringhausen.[61]

It was not only load-bearing shells that interested Fuller but also the controlled internal climate. His own house, a cotton factory, and the visionary office landscape of the Climatroffice, developed together with Norman Foster, are a few of the case studies that illustrate a direction that focused on architecture and technical aspects of buildings and covered an important area of experiment. Thanks to this way of thinking, on the threshold of the events of October 1973 (the oil crisis), Fuller had already acquired a certain degree of far-sighted knowledge that has influenced project ideas and developments by other teams, such as Frei Otto, Jörg Schlaich, Norman Foster, Nicholas Grimshaw, to name but a few (ill. 1.2.20), from the decades after 1973 to the present time.

As early as 1944–48, Fuller made a thorough investigation of climate conditions and their incorporation in spatial structures, in particular with a system of natural room ventilation that utilises wind energy and which, with an airtight shell, in winter produces a climate that keeps the warmth inside and in summer creates a cool indoor climate. Here he used the concepts of Dymaxion House and Wichita House – early examples of a 'passive house model'![62] Fuller's motto was: "Don't fight the forces, use them!"

From Greenhouse to 'High-tech Hothouse'

1.2.13

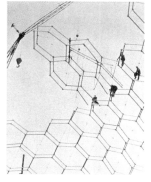

1.2.14

1.2.15

1.2.16

1.2.17

1.2.18

1.2.19

1.2.20

Arctic City

Project, 1971
Architects: Frei Otto with
Warmbronn Studio, Stuttgart
Urbanism: Kenzo Tange
with Urtec, Tokyo
Engineers: 'Structure 3' at Ove Arup
& Partners, London

A megastructure made of a transparent membrane filled with pressurised air was planned to create a town and living space for between 15,000 and 45,000 inhabitants on an area of 2 km² in the extreme Arctic climate.[63] Just after the *Expo '70* in Osaka, which was a field of experiment for new types of tent buildings (see chapter 2, case study 26), the design team of the US pavilion suggested expanding the type of the vinyl glass-roofed, pressurised air hall and using it to create the spatial and climatic envelope for an Arctic City. Both projects started from similar considerations. A parallel visionary project came from Buckminster Fuller: the Dome over Manhattan (1960, see ill. 1.4).

The Arctic City was not a piece of realistic urban planning but an intellectual model and prototype for the construction of urban landscapes under a weatherproof skin

intended to help the shell inflate into a regular form. Then the prefabricated membranes are spread out or their parts are sewn together (ill. 1.2.23). They are laid on top of and below a lattice structure of polyester cables with a diameter of 270 mm and connected with distance pieces made of rigid PVC that are laid around the cables and glued to them so that a continuous void with a minimum wide of 10 cm (even at the junctions) can be guaranteed (ill. 1.2.24).

During the 50-hour-long process of inflating the structure with pressurised air the structure increases in strength in the same way as the 'sieve' changes shape: what were originally squares become rhomboids with junctions of different angles (ill. 1.2.25).

A mesh structure that is similarly homogeneous but made with rigid steel rods and junctions was used to

1.2.21

that could regulate the climate. The question examined by the team was a multidisciplinary one, made more dramatic by the extreme climate. All the basic problems in the areas of architecture, planning, energy and technology were made more complex, which mercilessly influenced the thinking (ill 1.2.21).

The building procedure recalls the experiment with the 'flour sieve': it formed the practical basis for different approaches by Frei Otto and Jörg Schlaich, who referred to Frei Otto,[64] or by Richard Horden with Peter Heppel[65] (ill. 1.2.22).

Like a 'sieve', which needs a continuous circular frame to retain its shape, the Arctic City also needs a circular foundation. Balloons anchored in the interior are

cover the atrium of the British Museum in London (see case study 12).

The structural experiment of the Arctic City was pursued further and tried out in the exhibition pavilion at the Bundesgartenschau in Mannheim in 1971 (described under 'spheres and blobs' in section 1.4; see also ills. 5.4.6 and 6.2.9). During the development of new spatial landscapes over the past three decades, interest has been focused on the flattest possible geodetic envelopes and on perfecting them with the help of material technology. Loudon's dream of 'dematerialisation' has been realised and the borders of spatial and material transparency have been expanded

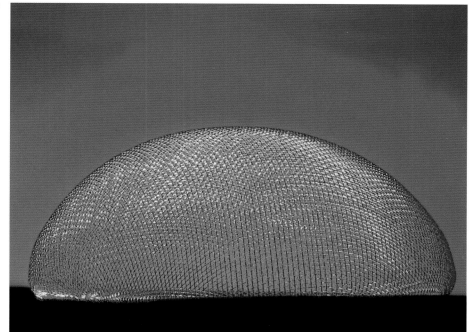

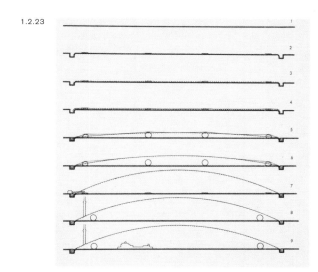

1.2.23

1.2.25

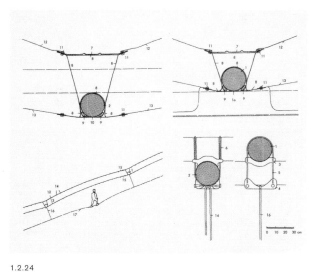

1.2.24

1.2.21: View of the model city

1.2.22: 'Flour sieve', illuminated from inside

1.2.23: The structure changes shape while it is inflated with pressurised air up to a height of 240 m.

1:2.24: Cross-sections through the structure of the membrane roof

1.2.25: View of interior of the Arctic City, photomontage

1.3 After 1973:
The New Type of Glasshouse

The architecture of the well-tempered environment – transitions

The reactions to the Middle East crisis in October 1973 were diverse. The tendency towards massive building methods and the use of increasingly thick layers of thermal insulation with the intention of saving energy encouraged post-modern approaches. It was hoped that neo-historical forms could save architecture, its permanence and representative quality, as well as the receptiveness to such qualities. At the same time, the concept of an artificial world with covered urban and work environments was still pursued by the same protagonists as before 1973: Richard Buckminster Fuller and Norman Foster, Frei Otto and Jörg Schlaich, among others. The lightness and flexibility of these structures suited the new

1.3.1

situation and they were used to react in a dynamic way to changing environmental conditions, without having to dispense with spatial and material transparency, on the contrary in fact. The project Autonomous Dwelling by Fuller and Foster (1982) depicts one such attempt (ill. 1.3.1).

Fritz Haller 'fled' into orbit to expose himself to the self-imposed constraints of autarchy: in 1987, in collaboration with Therese Beyeler, he designed a Space Colony, a settlement for 1,000 inhabitants in planetary space close to the earth (ill. 1.3.2).[66] New considerations were applied to the entire ecosystem of the human, plant and

1.3.1: Richard Buckminster Fuller, Norman Foster: Autonomous Dwelling, project, 1982

1.3.2: Fritz Haller, Therese Beyeler: Space Colony, project, 1987

1.3.3: Norman Foster: Microelectronic Centre, Duisburg: longitudinal section

1.3.4: Cuno Brullmann, Peter Rice: Piscine Cabrio, project

1.3.5: Soap film machine at the IL with soap film model in parallel light and camera

1.3.6: Olympic Stadium roof, Munich, part of model

animal worlds under extreme conditions, which could also influence 'earthly' concepts. This vision was further pursued in the International Space Station ISS.

Point of change in the way of thinking: the ecological crisis

The energy crisis unleashed highly innovative ideas in the development of glass architecture. The 'victory of glass' had already been announced in the City of London by the Lloyds Building, which is completely glazed and dispenses with conventional heating systems. The architect of this building, Richard Rogers, and his engineer Peter Rice from Ove Arup & Partners continued to follow this trail under the mottos 'sustainability building' and 'sustainable design'. Norman Foster, who had ventured into new territory with Fuller before 1973 (Climatroffice) and after 1973 (Autonomous Dwelling), was inspired by the energy crisis: an entire 'genealogy' of → Foster's projects can be drawn up that illustrates architectural themes ranging from platforms surrounded by space and the design connection of passive and active solar energy systems with a free-form building skin – Foster's trademarks. Early buildings, such as the office building in Ipswich, or later ones such as the law faculty of the University of Cambridge or the Microelectronic Centre in Duisburg (ill. 1.3.3) illustrate this. In Foster's series of sketches the projects are depicted as part of an environmental dynamic: a basis for reflections and questions that are dealt with in workshops with engineers, mostly from the Arup school of thought.

Foster's interest in the theme of the 'ecological glasshouse' remains unchanged. A direct typological and spatial reference to the origins of this theme can be seen in the Reichstag dome in Berlin. It was opened 105 years after Jenney's Crystal Dome in Chicago, is accessible and part of a sustainable, environment-related concept (see chapter 6, case study 98).

→ Peter Rice, whose 'apprentice piece' with Over Arup was the realisation of Jørn Utzon's design for the Sydney Opera House, later had the opportunity to work together with innovative architects such as Richard Rogers and Renzo Piano in the competition for the Centre Georges Pompidou in Paris.[67] After the completion of the Centre Pompidou he founded the consultancy office RFR,

From Greenhouse to 'High-tech Hothouse'

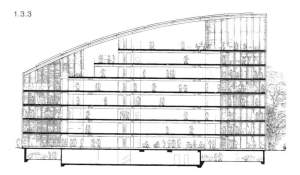

1.3.3

together with Martin Francis and Ian Ritchie. After the pavilions for IBM with Renzo Piano – the travelling pavilion as well as the mobile Lady Bird – he designed his first real 'serres chaudes' for the Museum in La Villette and the Parc André Citroën in Paris. The roofing of the Postautostation of Chur railway station in Switzerland and the Piscine Cabrio by Cuno Brullmann are also in the glasshouse tradition, but serve different functions (ill. 1.3.4; cf. also ills. 1.3.19 and 1.3.20).

The Stuttgart 'school of glass building'

Frei Otto (born in 1925) worked parallel to Fuller on lightweight structures. The Institut for leichte Flächentragwerke (IL) at Stuttgart University (on Pfaffenwaldring in Vaihingen) was set up in 1964 thanks to his initiative. He headed the IL until 1991. His successor is Werner Sobek (repositioned as The Institut für Leichtbau Entwerfen und Konstruieren, ILEK).[68] Frei Otto is an architect and engineer. From the very start he searched for form, diversity and processes of development and movement in 'natural constructions'. At the IL he had the opportunity and the means to develop a combination of experiment, scientific simulation and work with computer programs, which had not been available to Fuller when he designed his 'geodesic domes'. Through artificially initiated processes, by means of the 'method of the reverse direction' natural structures can become easier to understand: "Technical developments that are advanced in a highly qualified way allow a better understanding of the non-technical constructions of nature."[69] (ill. 1.3.5)

In addition to the tent structures it is, above all, net structures and pneumatic constructions used to produce free spatial forms curved in several directions that are of interest in our context. At the *Bundesgartenschau* in Mannheim in 1971 Frei Otto tested and constructed – in the framework of the IL – the large Multihalle as a first prototype for roofing spatial figures of any shape. → Jörg Schlaich, who as the project head for engineer Fritz Leonhardt, had worked with Frei Otto and Heinz Isler in developing the roof to the Olympic Stadium (ill. 1.3.6; see also case study 25) in Munich (the competition was held in 1972; architects: Behnisch & Partner, including Fritz Auer and Karl-Heinz Weber as project leaders, Stuttgart), at this time came into contact with the

IL school of thought[70] and subsequently pursued his own approaches in the areas of glass pavilions, roofs to atriums, etc. The indoor swimming pool in Neckarsulm and roof of the courtyard of the Museum für Hamburgische Geschichte illustrate the development from regular to free forms and the search for technical perfection in the production of new spatial qualities.

1.3.4

1.3.5

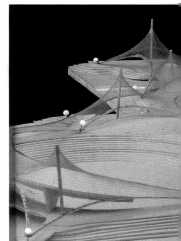

1.3.6

Case Study 9

Glasshouses in Transition after 1973

Architect:
Norman Foster

Norman Foster play a key role in positioning glasshouse architecture in the transitional period before and after the 'oil crisis' of 1973. His collaboration with Fuller between 1968 and 1982 meant that at the decisive moment when the signs of a change in architecture became apparent, Foster had at his disposal important knowledge, experience and visionary impulses with which he could more precisely define the glasshouse in terms of energy and could employ convincing arguments against the trend towards closed, solid building methods that had developed after 1973 and that, it was hoped, would help save energy. At the forefront, Norman Foster, Richard Rogers, Nicholas Grimshaw, engineers from Arup, also Renzo Piano, as well as Thomas Herzog, the German 'school of glass building' and others[71] attempted to combine the basic spatial principles of modernism with knowledge of construction and material technology, as well as energy-efficient strategies from current industrial research and in this way to venture into new territory. By now, the 'victory of glass' can no longer be ignored and along with it a 'new constructivism'.

After working on the visionary Climatroffice with Fuller (1971) Foster conducted further investigations in the field of internal climate, energy efficiency and building envelope technology – for example, in the office landscape for IBM 1971, the Modern Art Glass 1973 or the Fred Olsen Offices 1974 – which in the period up to the construction of the Willis-Faber office building in Ipswich (1975) achieved high standards of implementation and perfection. The sketches for the Fred Olsen project illustrate a methodically new way of thinking in relation to the environment and climate that today forms part of the repertoire of the architect and climate engineer: the depiction of the various architecturally relevant and technical ways in which buildings can react to the conditions of the environment (ill. 1.3.7).

In 1982 there followed the last joint project with Fuller, Autonomous Dwelling, the design of a residence for Fuller and his wife in Los Angeles (see ill. 1.3.1).

The spherical space is enclosed by an inner and outer membrane that can be moved independently of each other – an anticipation of the breathing building envelopes of the future. The model of two revolving shells to test reactions to different climatic conditions (summer/winter, day/night, transitions) was realised two decades later (2004) in the new Orang-utan House at Hagenbeck Zoo in Hamburg (ill. 1.3.8; see also ill. 1.0). A sliding hemisphere, the moving part structurally strengthened by arched three-dimensional trusses, allows the structure to be opened and closed. The construction consists of hemispherical lattice beams, cross purlins and three in-between layers of ETFE foils inflated with pressurised air, analogous to the membrane of the Eden Project in Cornwall or the Masoala Hall at the Zoological Gardens in Zurich (see ill. 6.2.4). Obviously, zoos are once again developing into areas of experiment in terms of space, structure and the technology of materials.

Foster's building for the Law Faculty of Cambridge University from 1996 represents a 'semi Climatroffice'. The multi-storey foyer, as well as the zones in front of the main spaces, are platforms placed in space and enclosed in a glazed shell (ill. 1.3.9). This transitional zone becomes an event and communications space in the area of tension between the interior life of the faculty and the external world of the university campus – within view of James Stirling's famous library for the History Faculty.[72] Here, for the first time, Foster used a lattice façade construction with triangular panes of glass (ill 1.3.10). An early competition project for the headquarters of Humana Inc., in Louisville, Kentucky, from 1982[73] already has diagonal trusses, as in the SwissRe high-rise building in London, but was never carried out.[74]

The visitors' centre in the dome of the Reichstag in Berlin is a special kind of glasshouse by Foster that fulfils the function of a pure 'event space'. It is part of a sustainable overall energy and climate concept (see chapter 6, case study 98).

1.3.7: Early sketches by Norman Foster: the building seen as part of the dynamic of the environment: offices for Fred Olsen Ltd. in Vestby, Norway (1974)

1.3.8: Hagenbeck's Zoological Garden, Hamburg, Orang-utan House, opened 2004

1.3.9: Law Faculty of Cambridge University, 1996, sketch of cross-section

1.3.10: Law Faculty of Cambridge University, interior at the interface

From Greenhouse to 'High-tech Hothouse'

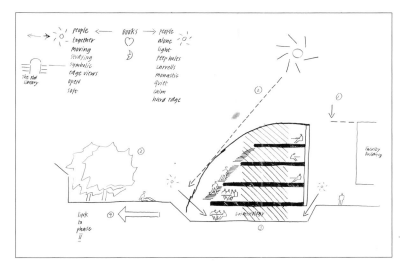

1.3.9

1.3.10

Peter Rice – Pioneer of 'Structural Glazing'

1.3.11

With the construction of the Centre Pompidou in Paris (1971–76) in the competition for which, on the initiative of the group 'Structure 3' at Ove Arup & Partners (Ted Happold, Peter Rice and others), the architects Richard Rogers and Renzo Piano had successfully taken part, the engineering practice of Ove Arup and also Peter Rice shaped a new school of thought in the field of glass-building technology. Rice's research work and practical implementations in conjunction with a number of innovative architects concentrated on new lightweight constructions combined with a new understanding of the technology of materials in relation to architecture, as well as, and especially, on the development of structural glazing.[75]

The IBM exhibition pavilion by Renzo Piano Building Workshop (1983–86) was the first glasshouse developed by Peter Rice:[76] a travelling pavilion that could be erected and taken down quickly (see chapter 6, case study 86). It was not the three-hinged arch that was new but the 'hybrid' combination of steel beams, polycarbonate glass pyramids, timber top and bottom chords and aluminium junctions, each of which contributes a structural function (ill. 1.3.11). Thus the transparent, 'dematerialised' edges of the pyramids, which are only glued, function as tension members in a 'virtual' space frame. This technical and constructional solution leads to a fractured interface between inside and outside (ill. 1.3.12).[77]

This experiment was followed by another that went even further: the mobile IBM travelling pavilion, Lady Bird (with Renzo Piano Building Workshop; ill. 1.3.13; see also chapter 6, case study 97). Here we can trace Buckminster Fuller's basic ideas on the 'geodesic dome' and they are also illustrated in Renzo Piano's work.[78] The structure stands like the jointed wings of a bat: they can be folded together and stored in a small space or transported. The envelope is a triple carbon-fibre-reinforced membrane, beneath which an intermediate layer of water-repellent and breathable Gore-Tex was used, probably for the first time. Unfortunately, unlike the IBM exhibition pavilion, it is not transparent; nevertheless, in terms of construction and material technology the combination is an intellectual model that is the precursor of Nicholas Grimshaw's Eden Project.

Rice's first glasshouse project after the IBM pavilion was the 'grandes serres' for the Museum for Science,

Technology and Industry in La Villette in Paris (1981–86). These glass structures are placed in front of the museum, a number of them are planted with trees, and they serve the entire complex as a 'power station' for exploiting passive solar energy (ill 1.3.14).

The architect Adrien Fainsilber, who dreamt of a similar glass construction to the Willis Faber office building in Ipswich, engaged Peter Rice as his engineer.[79] The glass buildings were intended to achieve maximum transparency and to pursue the visions of Loudon, the Bailey brothers and Paxton. The engineers, who around 1980 were beginning to develop highly modern glass technology, implemented the architectural and material-technology research goals in an industrial context, as a result setting in motion a multidisciplinary planning and thought process. The new questions concerned the behaviour of glass with point fixing, boring holes in glass itself, the boring method, the reduction of the structure that carried the glass to a minimum, the production of cast parts for fixing the glass and for the junctions or nodes of the structural system. Various companies, including Eiffel Constructions Métalliques and suppliers to the aircraft industry, had an important influence on the development of the constructional and technical system. A series of tests was used to examine behaviour in terms of construction and the technology of materials in order to assess the way in which the new system of 'structural glazing' would function (ill. 1.3.15).[80]

In the La Villette museum the modern glasshouse and its technology, 'structural glazing', were born, not as a prototype but as an industrial product for future development. In a book about La Villette, Peter Rice coined the term 'hierarchy', which is characteristic of the glasshouse: "The term hierarchy in a structure means that the elements forming it are placed in a naturally ordered relationship. In the case of the glass buildings in La Villette it means that each piece and each section is immediately identifiable as an integral part of the logic of the building as a whole. Natural structures also possess this quality."[81]

In other words, there is nothing superfluous, each component has a necessary function in the system. And: viewed alone, each part system or each element is unstable or senseless and achieves the full potential offered by its material performance only when it forms

1.3.12

1.3.13

1.3.14

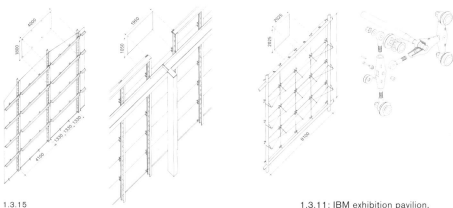

1.3.15

1.3.11: IBM exhibition pavilion, 1983–86; interplay of the components in the overall system

1.3.12: IBM exhibition pavilion, detail of materials and technology

1.3.13: IBM travelling pavilion, Lady Bird, 1986; skeleton frame

1.3.14: Museum for Science, Technology and Industry, Paris, La Villette, 1981–86; glass pavilion

1.3.15: Museum for Science, Technology and Industry: structural glazing and its development from the traditional post-and-beam glass façade for the Renault spare parts warehouse in Swindon (N. Foster) to La Villette

1.3.16

part of, and works together in the overall system – a new, forward-looking definition of the 'lightweight building method', and a new aesthetic of glass architecture (ill. 1.3.16).

The primary structure consists of 4 x 4 modules, each made up of 8 x 8-m glass sheets that contain 16 panes, each measuring 2 x 2 m; the secondary tension system connects with the nodes by means of horizontal compression struts, and the tertiary cable bracing of the glass skin is also connected to the primary structure. The glass modules are hung from the top and held horizontally by glass cables. Peter Rice writes: "We loaded this 10-mm-thick glass with up to 4.5 tonnes. However, glass is not capable of taking point or shock loads (. . .) We therefore used a compressed spring that functions as a shock absorber (. . .) Every individual element of this design is the result of the actual qualities of glass itself. This is, in my opinion, one of the ways in which you can achieve a direct relationship between the product and the design process."[82]

The greenhouses in the Parc André Citroën in Paris (1988–92; architect: Patrick Berger) represent a further development in structural glazing. In contrast to La Villette, the glass construction here is freed from the primary structure: the 15-m-high vertical tension cable is connected to the columns at only two points and the horizontal bracing envelops a central compression mem-

ber in the form of a tube (ill. 1.3.17). The four-point fixing of the glazing was also changed: as silicone fixing of the glass sheets tends to produce a rigid system and the experience gained in La Villette had shown that rhomboid deformation of the entire glass front is limited, the RFR team replaced the 'H' form with the aesthetically more perfect 'X' form of node (ill. 1.3.18).[83]

Peter Rice (RFR with Arup) developed a new kind of glass construction for the open roof of the Postautostation over the platforms of Chur railway station in Switzerland (1987–94).[84] Pairs of steel tube arches form a spherical figure that is spatially tensioned by a group of cables, anchored like a segment of spokes in wheel in a 'flying' junction (see chapter 2, case study 27).

The project Piscine Cabrio by Swiss architect Cuno Brullmann (1991), who works in Paris and Vienna, is a competition-winning design that was never built, based on a further invention by Peter Rice: a mobile glass construction for a swimming pool complex that can react to seasonal and climatic changes. Large, curved glass panels built up according to the principles of structural glazing are fixed to jointed, insect-like projecting arms. When the weather is fine sections can be opened and folded together to create an outdoor swimming pool; when the weather is inclement the reverse process provides a roofed, protected indoor pool (ills. 1.3.19 and 1.3.20; see also ill. 1.3.4).[85]

1.3.17

1.3.18

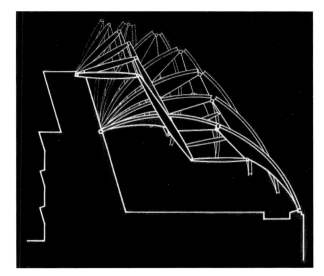

1.3.20

1.3.16: Museum for Science,
Technology and Industry: details
in the context of the overall
system

1.3.17: Greenhouses in Parc
André Citroën, Paris, 1987;
primary and secondary construction

1.3.18: Greenhouse in Parc
André Citroën: junction solution

1.3.19: Piscine Cabrio: vision

1.3.20: Piscine Cabrio: opening
roof

'Flying Glass Roofs'

Engineers: Jörg Schlaich,
Schlaich Bergermann
und Partner

Jörg Schlaich already had experience in designing, constructing and calculating lattice structures and net shells long before he and the engineering practice of Schlaich Bergermann und Partner (Stuttgart) became known for the roof over the atrium of the Museum für Hamburgische Geschichte in Hamburg. Schaich had been a leading member of the team of engineers responsible for the erection of the Olympic Stadium in Munich, together with his teacher Fritz Leonhardt, as well as his later office partner Rudolf Bergermann and the architects Behnisch & Partner (construction period: 1967–72; see case study 25).[86]

Influenced by the Multihalle of the Bundesgartenschau in Mannheim (1971), for the glass roof over the Aquatoll leisure swimming complex in Neckarsulm (architects: Bechler Krummlauf; 1990) Jörg Schlaich adopted the system of rods of equal length in a roof surface curved in two directions (ill. 1.3.21). The two systems of lines forming the lattice intersect at different angles in each case, at least in the squares above the circular floor plan (ill. 1.3.22). To illustrate this process of spherical deformation Schaich repeatedly uses the model of a flour or salad sieve that initially has a flat, orthogonal mesh that is then pressed into a hemispherical shape (see ill. 1.2.22). The lattice above the swimming pool in Neckarsulm was additionally strengthened with tension cables, thus creating a three-dimensional net structure.[87]

Using this approach, Schlaich Bergermann are also able to construct net shells above irregular plans and free spatial forms, as is illustrated by the roof to the atrium of the Museum für Hamburgische Geschichte. This museum was built in 1914–23 by Fritz Schumacher; in 1989/90 it was renovated by the architects von Gerkan, Marg und Partner (gmp).[88]

The principle of cable tensioning with 'flying' nodes, developed at the same time by Peter Rice for the roof above the Postautostation of the railway station in Chur (Switzerland; see chapter 2, case study 27), was used by RFR in the sculpture hall in the Louvre in Paris to achieve a glass roof with maximum transparency that admitted the maximum amount of daylight (see ill. 2.4.12).[89] In the Museum für Hamburgische Geschichte the construction of the glass roof above the courtyard by Jörg Schlaich involved a further material reduction of the structural system by dissolving it into a slender lattice of sections that frame the glass, and a tensioning system that intrudes into the space of the yard (ill. 1.3.23). In contrast to the Louvre, here the geometry of the bearing points on the parts of the building that define the courtyard was complex and irregular. Thanks to this glass roof with its suggestion of extreme lightness the existing clinker brick façade could be preserved and did not have to be expensively renovated and restored (ill. 1.3.24).

According to Jörg Schlaich, random double-curved structural forms are based on a simple basic pattern: "It consists of flat steel sections of equal length that are screwed together at the junctions in such a way that they can turn. It is only at the edges that, according to the geometry of the dome, rods of different lengths result. The angles of the mesh are determined by the form of structure required." To deal with snow and wind loads, "the quadrilateral elements of the mesh are diagonally braced with thin cables to provide the necessary triangulation."[90] Schlaich used a similar construction in the new Lehrter Central Railway Station in Berlin (see chapter 2, case study 29).

In contrast to Foster, who works mostly with triangular structures and strives to achieve a homogeneous shell (for example, in the roof to the atrium of the British Museum, London), with Schlaich the aspects of construction and structure are emphasised more – also spatially – through the expressive effect of the diagonal tensioning of the rhomboids – a depiction of the function and performance of the components in the overall structural figure. The structurally determined triangle remains a constant design element in both approaches (see ill. 2.4.27).

1.3.21

1.3.22

1.3.21. Aquatoll leisure pool,
Neckarsulm: interior

1.3.22: Aquatoll leisure pool,
Neckarsulm: detail of structure

1.3.23: Museum für Hamburgische Geschichte: interior of
atrium

1.3.24: Museum für Hamburgische Geschichte: axonometric
and plan of the structure and
construction of the glass roof

1.3.23

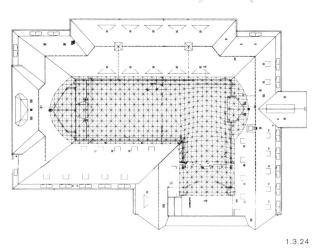

1.3.24

1.4 On the Threshold of the Future

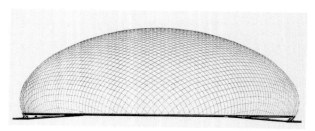

At present we can discern a number of different approaches or starting points that use computer-operated design, construction and production methods and exploit new possibilities in the technology of materials to present visionary and also virtual spatial figures as event worlds of the future.

Spatial figures and technology of materials

In terms of method the English architect Richard Horden develops Buckminster Fuller's way of thinking and working. From 1974 to 1985 Horden worked for Foster in London during a time when the latter was developing the project for the Autonomous Dwelling with Fuller (1982). As designer, initiator of international student workshops, inspirer and experimenter in his own office in London,[91] as well as at various schools, Horden developed innovative projects, particularly at Munich University of Technology, with his 'micro-architecture workshops'.[92] For the competition for the Scottish National Science Centre (SNSC) in Glasgow (1995), Horden, together with the engineer Peter Heppel, developed the concept of the 'droplet dome' (ill. 1.4.1): the drop-like shape of the exhibition hall is derived from three different radii and, compared to Fuller's 'geodesic domes', offers the same volume with a smaller total surface area, and, in addition, a lower and more easily utilisable internal height. The shell consists of an aluminium mesh that reduces the influence of wind forces and serves as a 'light spreader'.[93]

Richard Horden also used the 'droplet dome' model to secure the foot of the Wing Tower in Glasgow – a project he was working on simultaneously – against wind loads. The extremely light construction – weighing only 40 t – covers a span of 52 m. The platforms in the interior (ill. 1.4.2) suggest a similar image to Fuller and Foster's Climatroffice project.[94]

Norman Foster's → British Museum and also his building for the Greater London Authority point the way ahead to the world of free forms. The cable tensioning that Jörg Schlaich uses to create the structurally necessary triangles is omitted here, which means that the lattice structure made up of triangular units and the construction of the bearing area running around the edge must be made considerably stronger (ill. 1.4.3, see also frontispiece):

New green- and hothouses

Unlike the glass pavilions in La Villette, which serve as 'power stations' for the museum complex or the true greenhouses in Parc André Citroën, which form part of a public park (both constructed in Paris by RFR, see case study 10), → Nicholas Grimshaw's Eden Project near St. Austell in Cornwall (southwest England) represents a completely new and pioneering overall concept, which was developed out of the extreme topography of a disused clay pit, Cornwall's unique situation in terms of tourism and cultural history, and the area's uncertain weather conditions. Grimshaw and the Arup engineers constructed a new kind of space that, while it refers to the English tradition of glasshouse building, at the same time points to the future, and that is made even more fascinating by the use (for the first time at a larger scale) of a sculpturally-shaped foil membrane. The Masoala Hall at the Zoological Gardens in Zurich (ill. 1.4.4) and the new Orang-utan House at Hagenbeck Zoo in Hamburg (opened in 2004) are a continuation of the Eden project, also in terms of building technology.

New experiments: load-bearing glass

Since 1995 and a first appearance at the *glasstec '96* in Düsseldorf, various → schools of thought in the area of glass architecture together with the glass industry have played a leading role in the research and development of new architectural and spatially effective pure glass constructions. In addition to the Rheinland-Westfälische Technische Hochschule (RWTH) in Aachen, the Stuttgart 'school of glass building' in two faculties of the local university is carrying out pioneering work. As in glass buildings of the future, greater spans and more complex load-bearing systems can be expected, the specialist area of glass latice offers a promising research programme.[95] The visitors' centre at the glass works in Kingswinford (ill. 1.4.5) is one of the first pure glass buildings with a long-term function; although it does not have an experimental character it was constructed using the latest glass technology. The harmony achieved between the architectural aspirations and the structurally legible clarity make it a milestone for future developments.[96]

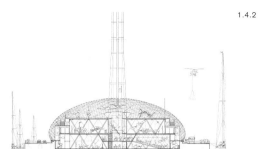
1.4.2

1.4.3

1.4.4

Spheres and blobs

The Multihalle at the *Bundesgartenschau* in Mannheim in 1971 can be regarded as an early 'blob' and a precursor of current designs (ill. 1.4.6; structural engineers: Ove Arup & Partners, including Ted Happold, later to work with Peter Rice on the Centre Pompidou). The theme of lattice and net structures was developed together with Frei Otto (Institut für leichte Flächentragwerke of the University of Stuttgart-Vaihingen, IL) and the architects Mutschler, Langner und Partner. The load-bearing system is a timber lattice. The roofing material was a transparent, PVC-coated mesh textile (which has since been renewed). The maximum span is 80 m, the total roofed area is 7,400 m². The entire mesh was first laid out on even ground and then lifted by scaffolding towers and brought into its final form, which is curved in several directions, while the junctions remained flexible. The final stability was achieved by the combined working of several elements: the fixing of the junctions, and additional tensioning with the help of a wire cable net with a wider mesh floor anchoring and the fixation of the membrane (see original). It was only the combination of all the components – each of them in itself unstable – that produced the overall system, stability and form of this new typology of lightweight building technology.[97]

Thirty years later, Japanese architect Shigeru Ban together with Frei Otto constructed an analogous free spatial form for the Japanese Pavilion at the *Expo 2000* in Hanover. Shigeru Ban's initial proposal was altered and the construction of the structure was strengthened on the basis of arguments concerning the northern climate of Central Europe and similar to those that had been put forward during the planning of the Glaspalast in Munich in 1853 (see chapter 2, case study 21). Since 'Hanover 2000' there has been a discernible → international movement that makes the design of free forms and (design) of new spacial figures a topic of discussion in the field of building typology and material technology and offers numerous examples that point in new directions. These include the successful competition entry by Shigeru Ban for the second Centre Pompidou, in Metz, in France (2004).

An operational question arises here concerning the technical realisation of arbitrary forms in material struc-

tures. There are numerous structures currently in development that can be compared to common geometrical shapes such as a sphere, a cylinder, a cone or hyperbolic paraboloid areas, etc. These structures fathom the possibility of irregular structural building and made-to-measure production of built components by means of computer generated forms and structural discovery processes.

View to the future

Defining the architectural and spatial outline conditions and the computer-supported processes that react to them

1.4.5

generates unsuspected structures and forms that are almost impossible to predetermine. The spectrum of proven operative models (such as Foster's or Schlaich's plane loadbearing structures curved in several directions) is thus expanded – the 'digital design space' of architects, engineers, mathematicians and design engineers opens up a new field of experiment for multi- and interdisciplinary work in the future.[98]

1.4.6

Great Court

British Museum, London
England, 1998–2001
Architects: Foster and Partners
Engineers: Buro Happold

The triangulated lattice structure of Norman Foster's law faculty building in Cambridge has established itself as a highly attractive spatial and technical strategy for new glass buildings and glass envelopes – one is reminded here of projects such as the roof over the courtyard of the British Museum in London (2001), the Greater London Authority building (2002), the SwissRe Tower (2004) and others. Whereas triangular glass sheets define Foster's typological 'brand' and convey the impression of homogenous plane loadbearing structures, the constructions by Jörg Schlaich use squares or rhombuses that are divided into structural triangles by diagonal bracing, thus giving the constructional and structural function a visual form. Nowadays, irregular structures are also possible.

The Great Court has been made into a modern atrium by the intervention of Foster and the team of specialists and engineers[99] involved. In a certain sense it is a reverse figure: what was once the external façade of a courtyard surrounded by a number of temple-like exhibition halls is today an internal façade. The central rotunda of the former British Library was expanded by adding the services nowadays usually found in a museum and was incorporated in the overall composition. Whereas previously the courtyard was not accessible, today it is a new, focal, light-flooded space that functions as visitors' centre, similar to the space that may have provoked fear among the visitors to the great machine hall of the 1889 Paris *World Exhibition* (see chapter 2, case study 22), because it lacked a "fullness of material".[100] (ill. 1.4.7)

The structural design of the shape of the glass roof starts from the curvilinear model of the English glasshouse, but exploits the current possibilities offered by the computer-generated forming of structure (ill. 1.4.8; see also ill. 5.4.15). Given the irregular nature and overall geometry of the existing complex, the greatest degree of precision was called for: the fixed bearing points of natural stone were overlaid with a steel lattice that follows the soft, multiply-curved form and in which the glass has a stiffening function (ill. 1.4.9).

The courtyard is symmetrical only in the long direction; the rotunda is 5 m closer to the north façade than to the south façade of the surrounding courtyard buildings. Similar to the Bailey brothers' palm house in Bicton Gardens, the roofing consists of series of differently sized glass panes, with the difference here being that the 3,312 glass triangles of different formats spanning between 5,162 steel rods, and the 1,826 junctions with different angles that make up the glass roof of the British Museum were calculated with the aid of computers (ill. 1.4.10).[101] The roof construction consists of three layers: a steel frame with nodes, on top of it an aluminium construction, with the silicone-fixed and framed glass panels as the outer climatic envelope (ill. 1.4.11). The entire roof construction weighs just 800 t: 478 t of steel and aluminium, 315 t of glass.

Steel rings with slide bearings on the stone cornices of the surrounding or enclosing buildings form the bearing points. This produces interstices between old and new which make the glass roof appear to hover, but which also are used for the natural ventilation and exhaust system.

The interaction of the stone pavilions and the light glass roof creates a dynamic play of shadows, similar to the effect created by the dome of the Reichstag in Berlin.

1.4.7: Atrium with play of shadows

1.4.8: Computer simulation of the canopy: lines running out radially from the rotunda are overlaid with structural lines that follow the rectangular edges of the courtyard.

1.4.9: Building site during the fixing of the roof

1.4.10: Glazing the structure of the envelope

1.4.11: Exploded axonometric of the construction of a node

1.4.7

1.4.9

1.4.10

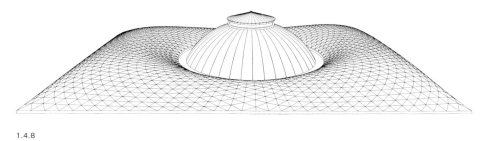

1.4.8

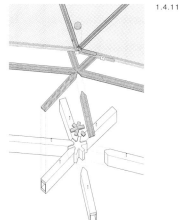

1.4.11

Eden Project

St. Austell, Cornwall, England
1995–2001
Architects:
Nicholas Grimshaw & Partners
Engineers:
Anthony Hunt Associates, Arup

The Eden Project by Nicholas Grimshaw near St. Austell, a small mining town in Cornwall in south-west England, points in the direction of the built implementation of visionary ideas as represented by the old greenhouse theme: a greenhouse complex made of a number of 'biomes' of different sizes in dimensions never achieved before. The complex lies in an abandoned porcelain clay pit in St. Austell Bay. The initiator of the Eden Project, Tim Smit, and his committed team pursued an idea of helping the relationship between mankind, plants and resources achieve a sustainable future. The 'new Garden of Eden' was not intended as a purely commercial leisure park but as a nature park that would demonstrate to visitors the relationships between man, culture and nature. The concept includes linking different climatic zones (specific plants) with the respective ethnic and cultural areas to create a learning space, augmented by art performances, exhibitions and workshops for school classes and groups of visitors – a revival of enlightenment themes in a modern, forward-looking educational and research project.[102]

As a platform for learning, communication and research in the context of sustainable design of the future, Eden also required the appropriate architecture. Nicholas Grimshaw and Anthony Hunt, designers of the Waterloo International Terminal in London (1993), and the engineers from Arup involved chose for this function a new kind of honeycomb structure in a spherical shell (biome) and joined four different 'domes', similar to Fuller's, that intersect to create an almost 500-metre-long coherent spatial continuum (spans 65–110 m, heights 35–55 m; ill. 1.4.12).

The innovation in comparison to Fuller's domes is the composition of the complex as a whole and the use of new material technology. "Whereas a standard Bucky dome is perhaps an over-familiar object, at Eden the intersection of domes of differing sizes gives the complex a unique architectural quality. As with so much of NGP's work there is an accretive sensibility to the arrangement of internal and external spaces."[103] The points at which the biomes intersect have not been solved in conformance with this system (ill. 1.4.13).

The curves of the intersections are supported by arched trusses. The honeycomb structure is fixed by steel tubes, the system of junctions (Mero) is additionally stabilised by internal compression struts (ill. 1.4.14).

The geometry of the load-bearing frame consists of hexagonal surfaces projected onto a system of four virtual spherical surfaces that intersect and have different radii (ill. 1.4.15).

Within the 11-m-wide hexagonal honeycomb structure made of aluminium sections the shell is formed by 'cushions' made of self-cleaning synthetic ETFE foils (ethylene tetrafluorethylene) in three layers that can be conditioned by pressurised air (to a thickness of 2 m). That is, they can react dynamically to different weather conditions (heat, cold, rain, snow) and the demands of the internal climate (internal temperature, humidity and air pressure of the tropical or Mediterranean zones). The cushions are not only light (less than 1 per cent of the weight of a glass pane the same size) and pulsating, but also insulate against heat and cold (U-value 1.4) and with a light transmission factor of 95 per cent are completely transparent – a new invention in the field of greenhouse technology with the maximum amount of daylight and the minimum loss of heat that realises the dream of Loudon, the Bailey brothers and Paxton (ills. 1.4.16 and 1.4.17).

The foils, which are welded at the edges, are held between two aluminium sections by the secondary construction and are fixed externally to the steel tubes; the aluminium substructure is a link between the cruder steel tube system and the soft synthetic cushions. This triple-layer envelope resembles the composition in the British Museum of the glass roof by Norman Foster (ill. 1.4.18).

The erection, which was carried out by 'skyworkers' trained in climbing techniques and was exposed to the elements, turned out to be extremely complex. To erect the structure and the honeycombs an enormous scaffolding with around 100,000 junctions was required, the largest ever. Each element in the system was numbered and coded – like the stone masonry work in a medieval cathedral (ill. 1.4.19). The lightweight structure consists of 700 t of steel as well as 831 hexagons, pentagons and triangles in the biome envelope (ill. 1.4.20). 14,000 elements had to be fixed by hand. At the junctions the biomes

1.4.12

1.4.12: Overview of the entrance area

1.4.13: Intersection of two biomes

1.4.14: Construction, honeycomb module and detail of the Mero junction

1.4.15. Wire model

1.4.16: Building site

1.4.14

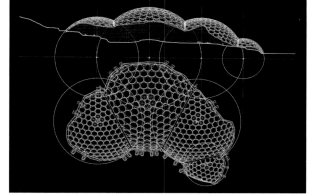

1.4.15

1.4.13

1.4.16

1.4.17

were subjected to a loading test by means of 'balloons' made of tear-proof material (each filled with 5 t of water). The largest biome withstood a load of 150 t and deformed only by between 9 and 13 mm!

Inside the spherical domes the climate is adapted to provide the tropical and Mediterranean environmental conditions by the use of spray systems, wind generators and heating systems, as well as natural ventilation (ill. 1.4.21). The crowing area of the 'geodesic domes' consists of 5 honeycombs with a core pentagon made of opening ventilation elements. A service stairway leads to this area of the biome (ill. 1.4.22).

The development of the climate conditioning and control represented the most important task for the Arup engineers. Their project (project leader Alistair Guthrie) pursued a strategy of environmentally-friendly, energy-efficient construction systems and material technology that used resources economically: "This was emphasised in the opening of the Environmental Statement – the project aimed 'to provide as far as possible, a sustainable environment maximising the use of renewable energy'."[104] This links this newly-built sustainability programme with the theoretical model of new spatial and climatic theme worlds.

A decisive economic and marketing problem was encountered in the area of time management. The delays to construction and fitting caused by the climate and weather that have already been referred to led a year before the planned completion to a question similar to that which had been put 150 years earlier to Joseph Paxton during the building of the Crystal Palace: "Can it be built in time?" (See chapter 2, case study 20) In January 2001, two months before the planned opening on 17 March, a despairing construction manager and a sceptical marketing manager asked at a crisis meeting: "Can it be finished?" Tim Smit answered: "It will be done by 17

March!" This was followed by the 24-hour non-stop deployment of all available staff plus additional resources, and Eden was opened on time on 17 March 2001.

It was also necessary to take into account the risks to the plants themselves, which came from overseas and from greenhouses in England (e.g. Kew Gardens) and the continent. Two transports were required: first of all, staggered deliveries were made to a temporary storage area (quarantine) – a specially equipped greenhouse where the plants could recover from the 'climate shock' and where their growth and any possible diseases could be monitored – and then within the shortest period possible to Eden. Over a period of three weeks around 72,000 plants, including 500 very large, full-grown trees weighing up to 4 t, were transported to St. Austell and planted in the Eden park.

The Eden Project revives old greenhouse ideas, in the same region of south-east England where the Bailey brothers' palm house in Bicton Gardens stands and can still be visited today, thus making a connection to the starting point of this chapter – two to three hours' travelling time today and 180 years of technological change lie between these two structures.

1.4.21

1.4.17: Mounting the ETFE file cushions (Foiltec company)

1.4.18: 3-layer engineering construction of the building's covering: primary system of steel tubes, secondary construction of aluminum terminal strips to attach the ETFE file cushions.

1.4.19: Erecting the structure by the 'skyworkers'

1.4.20: Standardised structural system of two overlaid hexagonal basic figures; the junctions are connected by triangular pyramids.

1.4.21: Ventilation flaps built into a bay of the structure

1.4.22: Air exhaust at the top of a biome, reached via stairs

1.4.22

Case Study 14
Schools of Thought in Glass-building Technology

The fact that, in addition to the Rheinland-Westfälische Technische Hochschule in Aachen and elsewhere,[105] a school of glass-building and a pioneering glass-building research programme developed in Stuttgart was no accident. Two factors in particular were involved here: the founding of the Institut für leichte Flächentragwerke (IL) of the University of Stuttgart-Vaihingen and the appointment in 1964 of Frei Otto to build up the IL on the initiative of Fritz Leonhardt, the best-known engineer of the time, in the period leading up to the Munich Olympic buildings (1967–72), as well as the influence of the Stuttgart architects practice Behnisch & Partner that prepared the way for a democratically oriented, transparent, open and light architecture in post-war Germany.

Werner Sobek, the successor to Frei Otto at the new ILEK (Institut für Leichtbau Entwerfen und Konstruieren since 1995), entered unknown territory with a 'glass arch', a shallow-curved structural system made of sheets of glass in which the glass takes compression forces and the tension forces are taken up by steel tension cables. A mature pilot construction was shown at the *glasstec '98* in Düsseldorf. It spanned 20 m, was 4 m wide, 5 m tall at the highest point and consisted of 14 sheets of glass (type TGV, 2 x 10 mm) that were strengthened at the edges of the arch construction by 160-mm-wide strips of 12-mm TVG. A breaking test made after the exhibition provided new knowledge in an area that was still new at the time (ill. 1.4.23).[106]

Pioneering attempts had been shown at the *glasstec '96*, such as, for example, a 'tensegrity' glass construction that referred to Fuller's 1959 'tensional integrity' project. Fuller constructed a 'geodesic dome' made of 'flying' compression struts that were held by tension cables (see ills. 2.3.11 and 2.3.12). At the University of Stuttgart students of the teaching and research department of Stefan Behling and Jörg Schlaich (visiting lecturer: Andrea Compagno) designed and constructed a glass structure in which the compression loads were taken by glass tubes. The sculptural effect was connected with a light game to produce a completely new and ambivalent spatial and transparent perception by means of the three-dimensional glass figure (ill. 1.4.24).[107]

Since that time certain aspects of pure glass technology, such as glass strips (first used in the Sainsbury Centre for Visual Arts in Norwich and in the Willis Faber office building in Ipswich, both by Norman Foster) and glass compression struts have formed part of the repertoire of contemporary architecture and are particularly popular in making atrium roofs and glass façades (see chapter 6, case study 91). However, glass research that goes further than this remains experimental.[108] Individual prototypes such as glass pavilions or abstract constructions that cannot yet be realised generate experience and ultimately also help the development of real 'structural design in glass' without the need to refer to other materials and technologies (wood, concrete). Permanently used spaces and structures of glass, such as the entrance and exhibition space already referred to in the glassworks in Kingswinford in the English Midlands (1994),[109] or footbridges, bridges and stairs, are proof of a knowledge that is already technically mature and is the product of concluded tests (ills. 1.4.25 and 1.4.26; see also ill. 1.4.5).

Generally, 'hybrid' constructions combining glass and steel (for reasons of safety) are developed in which the glass takes on a contributory structural function. While the Audi stand by Werner Sobek at the *Internationale Automobilausstellung* in Frankfurt (1999) represents an interior installation,[110] the construction of a public pedestrian bridge over Corporation Street in Manchester by Hodder Associates and Arup (2001; ill. 1.4.27; see also ill. 6.2.27) is a project designed for long-term use, exposed to the climate and with aspirations in terms of urban policy. Ten different triangular glass formats form the climatic skin; it is enclosed by a hyperboloid that consists of linear and circular steel tubes and is connected to the node points of the sheets of glass by means of tension cables.

1.4.24

1.4.25

1.4.27

1.4.23: Arch made entirely of glass; construction at ILEK: Werner Sobek, Matthias Kutterer

1.4.24: 'Tensegrity' sculpture by students of Stefan Behling and Jörg Schlaich

1.4.25: Visitors' centre at Kingswinford glassworks, 1994

1.4.26: Visitors' centre at Kingswinford glassworks: axonometric showing how the elements of the construction fit together

1.4.27: Glass footbridge in Manchester

1.4.26

Spheres and Blobs

The glass building of the future and the increasing complexity of building commissions will produce new interpretations that will also incorporate the new, expanded event space generated by new computer worlds: work worlds, educational landscapes, multi-functional centres for shopping, sport and entertainment, city malls, solar cities and Habitat models. Early visions have already been drawn and modelled: the Arctic City project or the Mannheim Multihalle, both designed 1970/71 under the leadership of Frei Otto and engineers from Arup. After three decades a revival is on the way.

Regular and irregular structures are not designed by different schools of thought; both involve the same protagonists, development offices and institutes. The leaders include Arup and the Stuttgart 'school of glass-building'. Whereas figures based on a sphere, cone, cylinder, hyperboloid, etc. aim at achieving large numbers of the same building parts (modules, series, standardised junctions), free forms demand the tailor-made and computer-generated production of constructional components. Today, the expense of design and of production is no greater for one approach than the other. Bespoke production has replaced mass production but the latter continues to exist (see section 5.4).

Innumerable forms of combinations are also imaginable. Original suggestions have come from the Japanese architect Itsuko Hasegawa for a Museum of Fruit in Yamanashi (1992–95; ill. 1.4.28; see also ill. 6.3.17). The tropical greenhouse developed with Arup that relates to both regular and irregular forms of fruit is generated from a shell of revolutions that turns along a free 'generatrix'. Unlike in translated net shells (e.g. the Hippopotamus House at the Berlin Zoo; engineer: Jörg Schlaich) that produce flat glass sheets, sheets curved in two directions were required here; for cost reasons, however, flat sheets were used that required an additional fixing construction between the steel structure and the glass building (ill.1.4.29).[111]

In 2004, architect Shigeru Ban, who trained at the New York Cooper Union and who carried out the Japanese Pavilion at *Expo 2000* in Hanover with Frei Otto (see chapter 6, case study 88),[112] won the international competition for the second Centre Pompidou, in Metz (the head of the architects on the jury was Richard Rogers).[113] A mega-structure developed together with Arup (London) spans all the functions of the museum and is a light membrane, visible from afar, which surrounds spaces that flow into each other (ill. 1.4.30, see also ill. 1.6). Like the Hanover pavilion it will be a mesh with traditional organic references: a wood lattice structure with strengthening steel elements carries a translucent, teflon-coated fibreglass skin and forms hexagonal modules that produce a free form that can react to the functional spatial qualities (ill. 1.4.31).

In addition to the concept of natural climate balance, Shigeru Ban also works with references to 'bionic' structure, organic building materials and revitalised cultural traditions. In the future the question of sustainability will challenge and shape spatial designs and the construction of structures even more strongly. 'Sustainable building design' will produce new materials, technologies and operative processes as well as unmistakeable worlds of images – 'sustainable branding' as the architecture project of the future (see section 6.4).

1.4.28

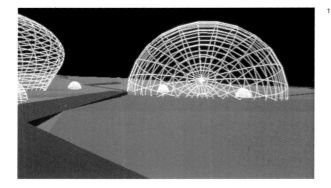

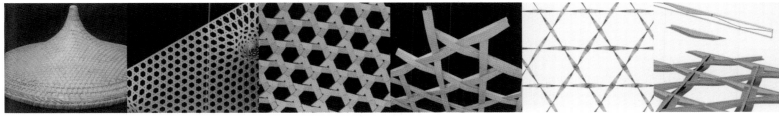

1.4.28 Itsuko Hasegawa:
Museum of Fruit; Yamanashi,
1992–95: computer-generated
form and structure of the greenhouse

1.4.29: Museum of Fruit, interior
of the cafeteria platform

1.4.30: Shigeru Ban: Centre
Pompidou-Metz, overall view,
competition entry, 2004; project
reworked with Cecil Balmond
(Arup)

1.4.31: Centre Pompidou-Metz,
constructional models of the
structure

On the Threshold of the Future

57

2 Building as an Art or the Art of Building?
Railway Sheds, Expo Pavilions, Terminals –
Spatial Landscapes of the Future

Whereas the glasshouses and greenhouses in the centres of colonial capital cities formed a fragile sheath around the virtual world of plants and exotic products collected in them, stations in the days of the pioneers marked the start of an adventurous journey in the opposite direction, out into the wide world. Into a world that still featured earthy boulevards for carriages and cumbersome goods transportation canals that wound their way across viaducts and through tunnels. The breathtaking speed of the first trains very quickly sounded the death knell of laborious, slow transport along waterways, while journeys by horse that had previously taken days, even weeks, were now replaced by swift, more direct and cheaper passenger traffic provided by competing railway companies (ill. 2.1).

The widespread introduction of the car after 1900 only halted the expansion strategy of the American railway companies, while in Europe, networking, improved safety and quality standards, and industrial design not only influenced the railway culture up until post-war Modernism but also produced trailblazing railway buildings. Ever since Nicholas Grimshaw and Anthony Hunt's Waterloo International Terminal in London (1993), above-ground station sheds in attractive urban surroundings and boasting spectacular construction techniques have been vying for middle-distance passengers; TGV, IC and EC stations bear witness to this future trend.

Space and time   The dynamic force of this new sensation of space and time was in stark contrast to the contemplative experience of glasshouses and the static presentation of different climatic zones and cultures. In 1843, Heinrich Heine expressed in highly descriptive terms his "real experience of the world" in Paris, the city in which he had chosen to live: "What changes there must now be in the way we view things, in our ideas! Even elementary terms such as time and space have become indeterminate. Railways are destroying space, and all we are left with is time. In four and a half hours you can now get to Orléans, and in the same amount of time to Rouen as well. What is going to happen when the lines have been extended to Belgium and Germany and linked up with the railways there! To me it is as if the mountains and forests were getting closer to Paris. I can already smell the scent of German linden trees; the North Sea is breaking in front of my door."[1] (ill. 2.2)

The heydays of greenhouse and glasshouse architecture described in chapter 1 occurred at the same time as the pioneering railway buildings; the two architectural experiences contrasted each other simultaneously. The master builders of low-tech greenhouses used and developed glass technology in order to maxi-

2.1

2.1: Painting from the pioneering days, USA

2.2: Railway network in France around 1855, twenty years after it was founded

2.2

2.0: Richard Turner: Lime Street Station,
Liverpool, 1847–49

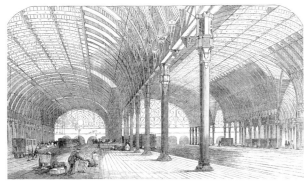

2.3

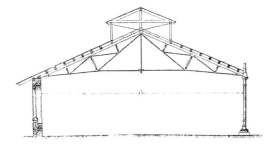

2.4

2.5

mise the use of daylight; those that designed railway sheds strived for ever wider spans, invented new forms of load-bearing structures, constructions and building structures made of iron, steel, and glass – in both cases with a 'dematerialisation' of the building sheath in order to create a spectacular urban space: the instrumentation of space and time through two design fields (ill. 2.3).

Railways conquer architecture   The first English constructors of railway sheds were the same who developed new-style iron bridges and influenced the school of thought with regard to constructing with iron: Robert Stephenson, Charles Fox, Joseph Paxton, Isambard Kingdom Brunel et al. It was the same group that to a large extent enabled the construction of the Crystal Palace at the 1851 *World Exhibition* in London. And so, as early as the middle of the century the first far-reaching step towards industrialisation – even of a major building site – had already been taken.

In France the school culture resulted in the invention of a totally new type of building and construction – the "Polonceau truss". Camille Polonceau drew this girder, which was based on compression and tension members, in 1837 at the École Centrale des Arts et Manufactures (ECAM) in Paris as part of his degree thesis on a locomotive depot (ill. 2.4).[2] The triangular structure the girder is based on provided the early basic principles of Karl Culmann's later *Graphic Statics*.[3] For some 40 years the Polonceau girder served as a standard construction, not just of French railway sheds. The first new, original interpretation of the Polonceau truss in an elegant sickle shape stems from Richard Turner: the 1848 wide-span roof over Lime Street Station in Liverpool, whose construction and experiment in load bearing Culmann was by chance able to follow on site, perplexed by the lack of theory.

Expo pavilions – a field of experimentation   To a certain extent exhibition architecture represents the experimental continuation of station sheds. The 115-metre-wide hall of the Palais des Machines at the 1889 *World Exhibition* in Paris, next to the Eiffel Tower, marked the highpoint of this trend, also with regard to the collaboration between architect and engineer (ill. 2.5). The new major building assignments for the railways as well as for exhibitions were a challenge for both disciplines: the initial coexistence of prestigious entrances and industrial sheds in the case of stations and monumental bases and filigree load-bearing structures in the case of exhibition pavilions increasingly gave way to synthetic projects that represented the contribution made by engineers in terms of construction and structure to the architectural concept. The 'collage' of two schools of thought and the interweaving of the construction disciplines resulted in several landmark buildings that are of particular interest here, as in the second half of the century the professions were taught in different institutions.[4]

In-between worlds: the avant-garde and fascination with construction   After 1900, major building structures generally reflected the new world of concrete construction (see chapter 3). Between the wars, railway sheds that followed industrial aesthetics were rare. Italian examples, such as the station in Florence and Pier Luigi Nervi's sheds, represented a continuation of the futurist avant-garde and, as such, links to today's stations. Sports, machine and Expo halls also used the type of wide-span constructions that emerged through the railways.

Disregarding the Modernist *zeitgeist,* Richard Buckminster Fuller is credited with having stubbornly and independently pursued a type of hall that was bound by neither era nor location: the geodesic dome. Somewhere in between the

Building as an Art or the Art of Building?

phenomena Pantheon and Planet Earth, he attempted to break down the dome into standardised construction components and perfect their material structure. In doing so he made a whole series of trailblazing discoveries, including the tensegrity structure. It was too early though. Nowadays the tensegrity form of construction is being rediscovered, advanced and used, for example, in sports arenas (ill. 2.6, see also ill. 2.2.16).

New types of terminals: station and airport buildings   The challenge of flying, even over middle distances, led to the rediscovery of exciting 19th-century stations, which had the advantage of being located centrally. However, the second advantage had to be invented: the station as an urban event space. And for this the backdrop of the city provides an outstanding pretext. Arriving slowly in the city, leaving behind the urban world and rapidly passing through fascinating landscapes are the new means of experiencing earthly occurances in terms of space and time through the combination of high speed and precision arrival.

On the one hand, stations are now turning into terminals with the range of services previously available only at airports, and on the other, airports necessarily link up with railways, which leads to an "amalgam", to a new type of terminal, to the "splendid station". Nowadays, the Expo halls that emerged from the construction technique used in railway sheds are discovering a new parallel field of experimentation in air terminal departure halls. It is not only the oversized, spatially fascinating and brightly lit setting of a virtual city and the vivid preparation for taking off by means of aircraft-like structures that characterise the world of airports. An airport also represents a new city with workspaces and lounges, congress centres, hotels, shopping malls, and even living space for stranded refugees and asylum seekers. Here, airports provide a concentrated city programme, a new ideal city, in a way that stations never can. All that these have is the city, as found, in which they are located, which they complement (ill. 2.7).

2.6

2.3: Paddington Station, London

2.4: 'Polonceau truss', drawing by Camille Polonceau, thesis at the École Centrale des Arts et Manufactures, 1837

2.5: Palais des Machines, *World Exhibition*, Paris, 1889, subtle overlaying of the engineering and artistic design in the front of the newstyle trussed arc designed to meet specific requirements and of the classic circular arc

2.6: Reinterpretation of the tensegrity structure: auditorium of the City of Utica (USA) by the engineer Lev Zetlin

2.7: Airside Center, Zurich Airport (architects: Nicholas Grimshaw, Itten+Brechbühl; engineers: Arup; steel/glass construction: Tuchschmid, Frauenfeld, Switzerland; 2002 – 03)

2.7

2.1 Railways Conquer Architecture

2.1.2

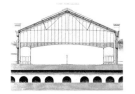

2.1.1

Railways and railway stations are visible signs and material symbols of the up-and-coming nation state. At the same time they represent the industrialisation process in the networking of domestic markets and the opening up of new territories. Ultimately, a public that since the Enlightenment and the French Revolution had been more self-confident became more mobile. In addition to political and economic impulses, tourism, adventure and the settlers' movement in the USA, as well as the shifting of military troops, were additional engine rooms in the development of the railways.

The English pioneers

The first railway shed to herald the forthcoming art of engineering during the pioneering phase of the railways was Charles Fox's → Euston Station in London (1835–38). It is a striking, extreme example of the presence of this new type of building in cities: the industrial engineering of the shed is concealed behind antiquating monumental buildings, hardly apt symbols of modern mobility, but referential figures of Victorian taste.

One new concept was the work of Richard Turner: the design for → Lime Street Station in Liverpool (1847–49), an interpretation of the trussed framework divided into triangles by compression members and tie rods that Camille Polonceau had first developed for his thesis at the École des Arts et Manufactures in Paris in 1837 (ill. 2.1.1).

The prominent British engineer Isambard Kingdom Brunel built Paddington Station in London between 1853 and 1857 (ill. 2.1.2; see also ill. 2.3). In terms of construction technique the iron-and-glass construction of what at the time was the largest station followed the model of Crystal Palace, which was built in 1851. In the middle the 213-metre-long three-bay shed is 31.2 metres wide and 10.3 metres high, at the side 20.7 metres wide and 21.3 metres high. Two 15.2-metre-wide transverse transept vaults that break up the entire length enable cross links, give the entire complex spatial depth and improve the lighting. The glass roof employs the ridge and furrow system in evidence in Crystal Palace – here, too, Fox & Henderson was the engineering company responsible for the construction work.[5] The Victorian architect Matthew Digby Wyatt helped Brunel in the 'stylistic' development of the station and façade cladding.[6]

The French school of railway construction

The world's first ever course in railway technology was taught at the École Centrale des Arts et Manufactures (ECAM; founded 1829–30) by Auguste Perdonnet. Its industrial, practical focus enabled numerous graduates to embark on a career in the up-and-coming railways (ill. 2.1.3).[7]

Polonceau's invention – stations for the next fifty years

Camille Polonceau, one of the first generation of ECAM graduates, came up with the most important invention in terms of construction and technology. His 1838 thesis, a design for a trussed framework-style iron girder for a locomotive depot for the Paris – Versailles – Rive gauche line, whose chief engineer was his teacher Perdonnet, went down in history as the 'Polonceau truss'. Spans of 15 to 40 metres were envisaged, yet engineers recognised and expanded the girder's capabilities, whose beauty and lightness enabled the construction of light-filled sheds and was even discovered by painters such as Claude Monet.

The Polonceau truss was used primarily in the construction of stations, exhibition pavilions and sports halls, with spans in the mid-1860s reaching in excess of 60 metres. This type of construction differentiates consistently between compression and tension elements. The compressed members are positioned vertically to the slanting rafter, form stable triangles on account of the truss and consisted initially of cross supports. These were positioned between two shaped pieces as 'joints' formed as parallel panels, which the hinged tie members also adjoined, a shaped fitting piece that followed function (ill. 2.1.4).

Its most consistent and, even today, imposing application is the → Gare d'Austerlitz in Paris with its 52.55-metre span.[8] Many of the other stations, for example, the Gare

2.1.1: Simplest use of the Polonceau trusss at the Gare de Lyon-Perrache, 1860; architect: Alexis Cendrier

2.1.2: Paddington station, London, construction of the spatial covering

2.1.3: Paris-Versailles building site, Auguste Perdonnet was the chief engineer, Camille Polonceau the site engineer and director

2.1.4: Construction tableau of the "Polonceau-Type"

2.1.5, 2.1.6: Multi-disciplinary collage of architectural and engineering expressive art: King's Cross railway station, London, 1850–52

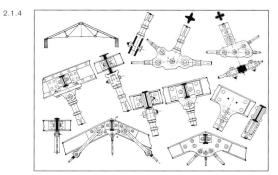

du Nord,[9] also used the Polonceau girder, but fronted it with prestigious premises, mostly with one or several large, round-arch windows in the front that in no way took into account the shape of the railway sheds behind but which reflected the taste of the time: reminiscences of thermal architecture that adulated Antiquity. In the case of the Gare de l'Est,[10] the architectural figure was identical to the engineer's concept, but rather than apply the Polonceau principle a round-arch girder was selected instead.

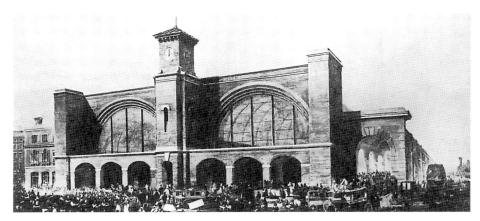

2.1.5

Railway architecture –
the 'primary school' of modern building

Two schools of culture struggled to lend stations their appearance: on the one hand, the style-oriented École des Beaux-Arts, and on the other, the technical, methodical schools of engineering that championed industrial matter-of-factness. Here, prestigious buildings featuring hotels and restaurants, and which reflected the representational needs of the Victorian, Napoleonic, Haussman and Wilhelmenian eras; there, light, bright, airy sheds that reflected the industrial shape of things to come, fascinating places in the era of emerging mobility and technical fascination with iron and glass that influenced a new perception of space and time. Although a division into two buildings – the head and the body – ensured the presence of both disciplines it did not solve the problem of the interfaces. The 'collage' of two schools of thought provided an approach that involved common processing, for example, in the provision of architecturally 'established' bearings as fitting pieces for the girders in St. Pancras Station in London,[11] the formal design of the compressed elements of the Polonceau girder in the buckling section in the Gare d'Austerlitz in Paris or the 'breakthrough' of the industrial railway shed on the front of King's Cross Railway Station in London (1850–52), designed by Lewis Cubitt (ills. 2.1.5 and 2.1.6).

The German school of railway building

→ Stations in the German cultural realm adhered to the French school of thought; after all, a visit to Paris and an inspection of the railway buildings was just as much a must for German master builders as a journey to Italy and Rome. The main station in Frankfurt/Main is a

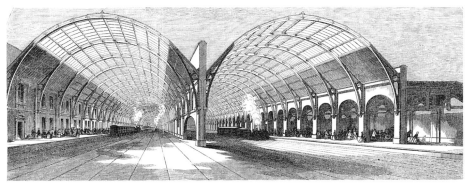

2.1.6

particular example of the 'amalgam' of architecture and engineering. The railwaystation 'Zoologischer Garten' in Berlin (1934–41) represents a late reconstruction of a pioneering type of iron construction. Other stations such as Dresden, Hamburg, Vienna, etc. followed the standard that emerged throughout Europe after the middle of the century, or were built later during the era of post-war Modernism.

Euston Station

London, England, 1835–38
Architect: Philip Hardwick
Engineer: Charles Fox

Euston Station was the point of departure for Birmingham, a line that was built by Robert Stephenson as the chief engineer. The spatial and structural concept was the work of Charles Fox, a young engineer who assisted Stephenson and was later to build Joseph Paxton's Crystal Palace (1850–51). Euston Station was Fox's first work and the first sign of forthcoming industrial engineering. The entire composition and architectural design of the urban front was in the hands of the Victorian architect Philip Hardwick.

Together with the rafters, a row of glass-covered lattice girders reduces the edifice to a structural minimum. Shortly ahead of Polonceau's invention, the mullions, divided into triangles and comprising hinged compression and tension members, represent a masterly English achievement. Each of the roofs, which span two tracks or 12 metres, rest on cast-iron supports, which lengthways are connected using arched girders (ill. 2.1.7). In addition, their static level is heightened through a series of wrought-iron rings, an invention of the builders of the Iron Bridge in Coalbrookdale in 1775, which later not only became a standard for many bridges, but also for roof constructions – an example of the influence of bridge-building techniques on architecture. In contrast to the monumental reception building, the railway shed conveys the impression of a 'dematerialised' architectural space (ill. 2.1.8).

For the main building's façade the architect Philip Hardwick drew the front of the station as an antiquating ensemble with a central arched entrance (the Arch of Euston) and on the sides two temple-like pavilions (ill. 2.1.9). In doing so he positioned representative examples of Victorian construction[12] as a counterpart to the light, filigree, glass-covered and thus transparent materials and shapes of forthcoming engineering methods.

If one looks at the footprint of the entire site (ill. 2.1.10) the ambiguity becomes apparent: the axially symmetric composition, with reception and entrance area, and infrastructure dominates and presents itself to the world, or the city, as a triumphal gate. The actual purpose building, the arrival and departure shed for the railway, lies alongside the significant axis, though likewise aligned in the side pavilions.

The construction of Euston Station triggered a trend towards new railway sheds influenced by engineers that no longer differed from factories, covered markets, and exhibition pavilions etc. A new field of design emerged featuring ever wider spans, more robust girder systems, and improved materials. The Palais des Machines at the 1889 *World Exhibition* in Paris (see case study 22) can be seen as an intermediate stage of this trend. In the meantime, hinges and heavy-duty joints have been perfected and – since Nicholas Grimshaw and Anthony Hunt's new Waterloo International Terminal (1993; ill. 2.1.11; see case study 28) – are once again a topic of debate.

Building as an Art or the Art of Building?

2.1.9

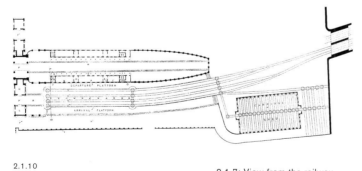

2.1.10

2.1.7: View from the railway shed

2.1.8: Light and airy construction is the dominant image of a new sense of time and space

2.1.9: The front of the first new station in London

2.1.10: Footprint of the station

2.1.11: Base hinge on Waterloo International Terminal, London, 1993

Case Study 17

Lime Street Station

Liverpool, England, 1847–49
Architect and engineer:
Richard Turner

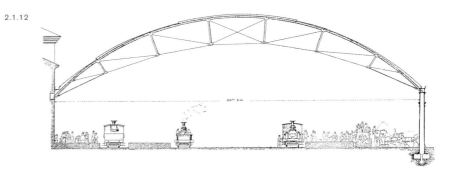

Lime Street Station was erected directly after the construction of Turner's large Palm House in Kew Gardens (see chapter 1, case study 4). Its span measures 153.5 feet, or around 50 metres. On one side the roof rested on the Classicist-style station building designed by the architect William Tite, and on the other on stand-alone cast-iron columns (ills. 2.1.12, 2.1.13). In contrast to Euston Station it is the engineering in the railway shed that dominates here, located as it is next to the entrance and not behind it. As the framework is self-supporting and does not produce any shearing loads it rests on the side on castors and hinges to balance out any fluctuations in the temperature. Because this construction principle was new it was subjected to tests with loads from all sides. Unfortunately, the framework was replaced between 1860 and 1870 and lost some of its elegance (ill. 2.1.14).

Whereas in France the Polonceau trusses and their use in railway sheds, covered markets and exhibition halls were preserved in their original form as saddle roofs, Turner masterfully applied the Polonceau principle to an arched girder. The compressed members were consistently positioned in a radial pattern and/or vertically to the arch, and the tension members diagonally; they intersect in the vertex; in addition, the bases of the compression members are pin-jointed with each other by means of tension members in the arch, as Polonceau envisaged. In the original version the vertex of the roof, approximately a third of the span, was glass.

The arched girder is thus braced by means of a framework system. In this way Turner created a type of synthesis of English arched girder typology and French bracing technology. In cutting edge halls in those days saddle roofs as well as vaults followed classic architectural typology. Not until the three-hinged joint on the Palais des Machines at the 1889 Paris *World Exhibition* was there a departure from familiar waters.

Around 1850, Turner's roof represented the very latest in technological thought, and not just in England. Karl Culmann, the inventor of 'graphic statics' and from 1855 the first professor of engineering sciences at the Swiss Federal Institute of Technology in Zurich, visited the Lime Street Station building site in Liverpool at the very moment the last two roof girders were being erected; he immediately recognized this as an interpretation of the Polonceau principle and quite simply referred to it as a "French construction":[13] "Mr. Turner himself just happened to be present when I visited the entrance hall and with the greatest courteousness showed and described his construction down to the very last detail, and he finally had the decency to invite me to a lecture he was giving at the Royal Mechanic Institution (a sort of engineer's association) about his roof. (...) He did not allow himself to be drawn on theoretical developments but was content to prove the load-bearing capacity of his roof by himself climbing upon his model without breaking it. In recognition of this, after the lecture he was made a member of the Institute. Incidentally, his roof is one of the most beautiful constructions of this type; it demonstrates the simplest, most purposeful application of the framework in roofs and is certain to be emulated."[14]
In terms of construction, Crystal Palace, which followed immediately afterwards, was not on the same level; it reveals other trailblazing features. In the 1850 "Great Exhibition" competition, however, Turner proposed applying the greatest dimensions to his model; the jury rejected the idea (see ill. 2.2.9).

As mentioned earlier the entire construction was replaced. Though structurally more robust it is, in fact, far more transparent, as more than half the roof consisted of glass (ill. 2.1.15). The original compression members and tension rods were joined in spindle-shaped combination by a central compression member and peripheral tension members and strengthened using rings in order to accommodate both types of thrust in a single element simultaneously (see ill. 2.0). The individual meridional sections are configured such that they overlap, the entire roof resembling a reptile's scale armour (ill. 2.1.16), an effect that the rear of Waterloo International Terminal references (see case study 28).

2.1.13

2.1.14

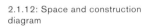

2.1.12: Space and construction diagram

2.1.13: Interior view of the present-day shed

2.1.14: Later load-bearing construction, around 1860–70

2.1.15: Advances on previous load bearing systems allows light to penetrate

2.1.16: Undulating roof

2.1.16

Case Study 18
Gare d'Austerlitz

Paris, France, 1865–69
Architect: Pierre-Louis Renaud
Engineer: Louis Sévène

The Gare d'Austerlitz is one of the most consistent interpretations of the Polonceau principle. The span of the large shed is 52.55 metres – at the time a record. At the same time a structural limit seemed to have been reached, also in terms of the numerous different individual pieces which had to be adapted and forged. The large number of parts now required in the construction of larger halls no longer justified their being made by hand – the transition to industrially manufactured load-bearing frameworks of riveted rolled sections was making its presence felt.

The Polonceau truss was used threefold: for the centre span of the passenger station and two side tracts of the freight station. The engineer achieved the span using just three compression members to the left and right of the centre span and exclusively isosceles triangles – pure,

side walls on the far outside, on the other hand, were designed by Pierre-Louis Renaud in Beaux Arts fashion. The shed and the connections to the side wings, as well as the large front, however, are the result of a multi-disciplinary design (ill. 2.1.20).

Schneider & Co. in Creusot, at the time one of the largest metal structure companies in France, produced and assembled this shed construction. Back then, Schneider was managed by R. P. Mathieu, an 'ingénieur centralien' who had been an awarded a diploma from the École Centrale in 1834. The company specialised in railway bridges (of which it completed a total of 450), stations, and exhibition pavilions.[15]

The contemporary Impressionist painter Claude Monet saw the tie rods of the Polonceau truss through the drifts of smoke from the steam trains with the eyes of

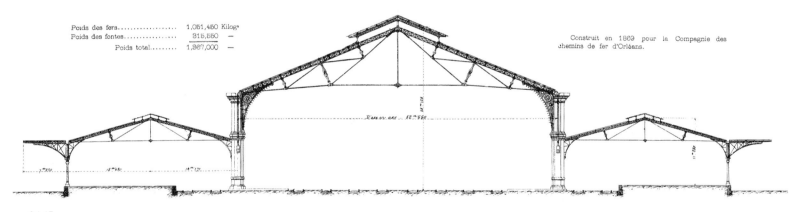

Poids des fers.................. 1,051,450 Kilog.
Poids des fontes.............. 315,550 —
Poids total........ 1,367,000 —

Construit en 1869 pour la Compagnie des chemins de fer d'Orléans.

2.1.17

unadulterated Polonceau teaching (ill. 2.1.17). In the middle, at the inflexion point, the compression members are structurally strengthened as cross supports, which also provide a sculptural, decorative look (ill. 2.1.18).

The rafters consist of lattice girders that are screwed at the vertex, thus forming a frame girder. At the side they rest on consoles that are part of a wall structured using pillars and bracing. The spatial, functional and visual permeability of these side walls represents an architectural reference to lightweight construction in steel and glass. The design of the front facing the city as a light and airy suspended glass façade illustrates that here, as opposed to other Parisian stations, the architect played second fiddle to the engineer (ill. 2.1.19). The

an artist, combining the wealth of light made possible by advanced building techniques with his impression of railway technology and the adventure of travel. His numerous pictures and studies of the Gare Saint-Lazare, in which he set up a temporary studio, were, however, staged: according to his fellow painter Renoir, Monet managed to convince the director of the Gare Saint-Lazare to stop trains, cordon off platforms and cram the locomotives with much coal "so that they spewed out just as much smoke as Monet wanted"[16] (ill. 2.1.21).

2.1.17: Cross-section of the entire shed

2.1.18: Compression member measure against buckling as a design feature

2.1.19: Interior of Gare d'Austerlitz

2.1.20: A hanging glass skin marks the end of the shed

2.1.21: Claude Monet, *Gare Saint-Lazare*, 1877

Stations Designed by German Master Builders

Main station
Frankfurt/Main, 1879–88
Architect: Georg P. Eggert

Zoologischer Garten Station
Berlin, 1934–41
Architect: Fritz Hane

Two German master builders, Jacob Ignaz Hittorff and Franz Christian Gau, with an architectural studio in Paris – Gottfried Semper served his apprenticeship there in 1826–27 and frequently visited the two men, for example, on his way into exile in London in 1847 – were successful station architects: the second building for the Gare du Nord in Paris (together with the engineer Edouard Gouche; 1861–65) is one example of their work. In addition to what since time immemorial had been standard trips to Italy and Rome, German master builders always paid at least one visit to Paris during the century of the railway. Friedrich Gilly, Friedrich von Gärtner, Friedrich Weinbrenner, Hittorff and Gau, Leo von Klenze, Peter Joseph Lenné et al., who since the founding of the École Polytechnique in Paris had been attending courses given by Jean-Nicolas-Louis Durand,[17] aroused interest in Paris and paved the way for future generations to familiarise themselves with the background and projects of the French school of thought with regard to iron constructions. The train stations of the 19th century located in German cultural areas are all based upon this example.

The stations in Germany in the Bismarck era (post-1870) served not only the free exchange of goods and passenger transport, but also the movement of troops. The neo-Classicist style most clearly expressed the new empire's need for self-portrayal, in particular in the design of stations as well.

In its structure the main station in Frankfurt/Main is based, despite the victory over Napoleon in 1871, on French counterparts, in particular Hittorff's Gare du Nord: it takes the form of a three-span iron-and-glass shed around 180 metres wide and 30 metres high covering the platforms, and with a prestigious front. It is however, precisely this interface that differs from the Gare du Nord: the industrial railway shed in Frankfurt is positioned over the solid structure and is visible from the perspective of the city (ill. 2.1.22). This 3D superimposition results in an original solution in terms of structure and construction as well as an exciting interplay between light and shadow on the inside (2.1.23). The main station in Frankfurt was not totally destroyed in World War II; the damaged parts were restored in 1958.[18]

In contrast to the Gare du Nord the architects of the station in Frankfurt embellished the iron construction with additional décor, which was very much in line with contemporary taste in the second half of the 19th century (ills. 2.1.24 and 2.1.25).

Though it was not built until 1934–41, in its poise the Zoologischer Garten station in Berlin references the stylistic repertoire of the second half of the 19th century. As a through station it had no front building or tract for purposes of prestige and ostentation, though it did boast a base that raised it from street level (ill. 2.1.26). Most of Berlin's downtown stations are raised – like the 'Loop' in Chicago – meaning that services, distribution and access are located below the glass hall. In the case of the Zoologischer Garten station it was precisely this base area, which is in the direct field of perception of visitors and passers-by, that was designed in the monumental style required during the Nazi regime. The functional modernistic steel construction on the upper level is, in contrast, remarkable (ill. 2.1.27).

2.1.22

Building as an Art or the Art of Building?

2.1.22: The main station in Frankfurt/Main: two overlapping figures seen from the perspective of the city; prestigious, historicising front and the 'footprint' of the industrial railway shed

2.1.23: Main station, Frankfurt/Main: transition point from the inside

2.1.24, 2.1.25: Iron construction in comparison main station, Frankfurt/Main, and Gare du Nord, Paris, 1861–65 (architect: Jacob Ignaz Hittorff, engineer Edouard Couche)

2.1.26, 2.1.27: Zoologischer Garten station, Berlin: overall view with railway shed on upper level

2.2 Field of Experimentation: Expo Pavilions

Sources of exhibition architecture

The most significant background in terms of structural engineering in the construction of large exhibition pavilions was Polonceau's invention in 1837. Though the Polonceau truss, or 'French construction' (Karl Culmann) was not used in the glass palaces in London (1850–51) or Munich (1853–54), it was employed for the inner rings in the spectacular exhibition premises in 1867 in Paris (ill. 2.2.1). In the vertex the roofs featured skylights (ill. 2.2.2).

The railways were the engine room of developments in construction in general, and specifically exhibition buildings, as here, too, it was a case of planning, producing, transporting and building swiftly. Even the building sites and organisation resembled each other – a sign of the beginning of time and money management. The tem-

2.2.1

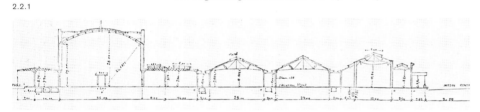

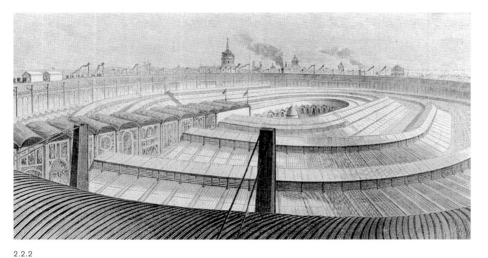

2.2.2

porary character of the exhibition structures led to new deliberations with regard to assembly and dismantling – this was the birth of lightweight construction and ephemeral decors.

The first glass palaces

It was not first and foremost greenhouse technology that turned the Crystal Palace into the "racehorse" of 19th-century structural engineering, but rather the background of British railways and the engineering company Fox & Henderson (ill. 2.2.3). The fact that two years after the Great Exhibition in London the Glass Palace in Munich set further construction records illustrates that the German construction and railway industries had quickly caught up lost ground and reached, indeed even overtaken, the state of the art of the era. Munich was the birthplace of trailblazing assembly techniques (ill. 2.2.4).

On the one hand, the → Crystal Palace in London (1850–51) enabled, for the first time in history, the presentation and confrontation of all countries – when not at war with each other – as competitors in terms of economy, industry, arts and crafts, culture and ethnology. On the other hand, England itself encountered highly developed US and French industry, which came as a shock to the organisers – after all, Great Britain had, until 1850, been the predominant industrial power: the outstanding achievements of France's scientific, technical university system in particular now confronted Britain's shop culture and exposed its shortcomings.[19]

With the → Glass Palace in Munich (1853–54) Maximilian II made a political statement for Bavaria's economic, industrial, scientific and cultural upswing. However, on account of the distance by which it was trailing foreign countries in terms of the economy and industry, and as a result of a lack of capital and raw materials, the desired success could not be achieved that quickly. However, the fact that voracious efforts were nonetheless put into creating new thrust is revealed by the company Cramer-Klett, which was involved with the construction of the Glass Palace. Theodor Cramer-Klett (1819–86) was one of the driving forces in the development of Bavarian industry and of finance and transport policies in the second half of the 19th century.[20] As after the *Great Exhibition* in London, here, too, the exhibition and its successes triggered the initiation of a university reform.

1889: Culmination of the World Exhibition mindset

The constructors of the Crystal Palace in London, the Glass Palace in Munich, and of the large Halles Centrales

2.2.1: Buildings at the *World Exhibition* in Paris, 1867, architect: Frédéric Le Play, engineers: Jean-Baptiste Krantz and Gustave Eiffel; cross-section of the load-bearing structures

2.2.2: Buildings at the *World Exhibition* in Paris, 1867: view of the roofs with the Polonceau structures

2.2.3: Joseph Paxton, Crystal Palace, London, 1850 – 51

2.2.4: August von Voit: Glass Palace, Munich, 1853 – 54

2.2.5: Pier Luigi Nervi, Guiseppe Vaccaro, Mario Campanella: main station, Naples, 1954

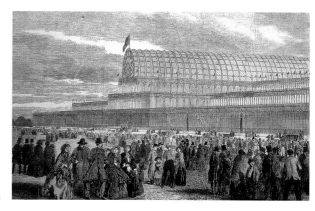

2.2.3

2.2.4

2.2.5

in Paris (1854 – 57) did not develop new types of load-bearing structures; their achievements lay rather in the pioneering application of industrial methods. The new major building assignments, the exhibitions themselves, the stations and covered markets, as well as arcades and atriums in department stores and hotels, modern factories and workshops, along with iron bridge projects, on the other hand, had an influence on industrial production and the development of new material technology.
The buildings at the *World Exhibition* in Paris in 1889 in particular bear witness to this; here, alongside the 'tour de 300 mètres' by the bridge designer Eiffel and his Swiss assistant Koechlin, a large-scale, three-hinged frame was used for the first time: the → Palais des Machines.

Upheaval around 1900

The pavilions for international exhibitions, in particular those in Paris in 1855, 1867, 1878, and 1889, as well as in Chicago in 1893, benefited on the one hand from the concepts of the railway sheds, while on the other hand they also represented unique contributions to the development of building technology and to a new interpretation of space. For the most part, the players – architects, engineers, builders, and entrepreneurs – came from the same schools of thought and 'schools of railway construction'. With the invention and patenting in 1892, by François Hennebique, of the reinforced concrete skeleton form of construction as an architectural means of design, this particular building material began leading the way. The *World Exhibition* in Paris in 1900 marked a demonstration of the transition: iron constructions were demoted to second place – the new era of concrete began punctually. Prototypes and uncompleted projects between the wars were ultimately followed in the 1950s and 1960s by broad-based influence and highpoints after World War II (ill. 2.2.5).

Crystal Palace

Glass Palace

Munich, 1853–54
Architect:
August von Volt
Engineer:
Ludwig Werder
(Cramer-Klett)

Crystal palace in London and the Glass Palace in Munich form part of a series of outstanding historical construction case studies of a new industrial mindset in building culture as well as of the innovative organisation of planning, building site and building process. The players were entering uncharted territories, had nothing comparable on which to work, indeed were thinking up the future. Crystal Palace demonstrated how constructing enormous volumes with the tightest of budgets and time restrictions and the greatest of precise detail could be achieved rationally and with an industrial mindset, and reveals an understanding of a building as a multi-layered overall system and the building process as a multi-disciplinary problem, which was new at the time and anticipated the future of modern construction (ill. 2.2.6). Through the use of iron tracks and cranes the Glass Palace in Munich advanced the rationalisation and industrialisation of major building sites as a task for future methods of construction (ill. 2.2.7).

Joseph Paxton and the railway system Paxton became involved with the British railway system in the pioneering era, 1835, before construction of the Great Stove in Chatsworth (see chapter 1, case study 3). As the 32-year-old head garden planner of the Duke of Devonshire he invested GBP 1,000 in the Furness Railway, the very first financially interesting railway line, of which he was later

to become director. In 1845 he assumed control of the Manchester Buxton Matlock and Midland Junction Railway, which crossed the land of his employer, the Duke of Devonshire; the railway pioneer George Stephenson was the chief engineer. Paxton's lobby was then established and expanded to include landowners, investors, shareholders and engineers. That same year, the Midland Railway – the result of the merger of three lines: Midland Counties, North Midland, Derby and Birmingham – appointed him director. Together with George Stephenson, Paxton made it into the most important traffic axis in England.[21]

The Munich master builders Since August von Voit, as opposed to Paxton, was a qualified architect[22] and did not gain experience in glass building architecture until after the construction of the Glass Palace, Voit and his engineer Ludwig Werder represented the two classic construction disciplines.[23] Voit's background found expression in the style to which modern iron and glass also paid deference. Ludwig Werder (1808–85), as of 1848 chief technical engineer at Cramer-Klett in Nuremberg was an industrial pioneer like Paxton and Fox and invented numerous new production and measuring facilities, assembly appliances, etc. A trained fitter, before joining Cramer-Klett he played a pivotal role in the construction and assembly of Leo von Klenze's Walhalla[24] in

2.2.6

2.2.7

Building as an Art or the Art of Building?

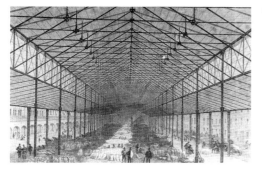

Regensburg, which marked a new form of iron truss construction in German building history, and also headed the royal carriage construction company in Nuremberg.

As an engineer and technical director at Cramer-Klett, Werder could avail himself of an experienced construction company as well as his experience with Voit in the construction of the winter garden for Maximillian II.[25] Cramer-Klett's most significant background with regard to iron-and-glass buildings immediately prior to the construction of the Glass Palace was Maximillian's grain store in Munich (ill. 2.2.8).

In 1857, as technical director at Cramer-Klett, Werder worked with Heinrich Gerber (the inventor of the Gerber girder) and Friedrich August von Pauli (the inventor of the Pauli girder) on the construction of the striking bridge over the River Isar near Grosshesselohe.[26] In the history of construction, Werder is a pioneer of engineering who is given far less attention than he deserves, like Charles Fox and Richard Turner, whose importance is also underestimated.

The story behind Crystal Palace   The Building Committee of the Royal Commissioners came into existence in January 1850 and comprised investors in railways, architects, and engineers.[27] Henry Cole was the inspirator behind the *Great Exhibition* and, prior to the royal decision to stage the first *World Exhibition* in London, had been dispatched by Prince Albert to Paris on a tour of investigation.

The size of building that was the subject of the competition announced by the Royal Commission in 1850 could scarcely have been built using conventional construction methods, on a low budget, and within the space of 11 months. As such it is astonishing that the only two entries, by Hector Horeau and Richard Turner, to feature contemporary load-bearing structures and metal constructions were not considered worthy of construction (ill. 2.2.9). Not one of the 245 projects satisfied the jury, which thus set about devising a concept from its own ranks.[28] This project was published in the *Illustrated London News* on 22 June 1850, which speeded up Paxton's intervention, who ten days previously had submitted his own proposal 'hors concours' to the Society of Arts – two weeks later he published his project in the same newspaper!

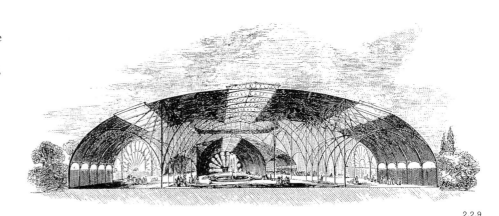

2.2.9

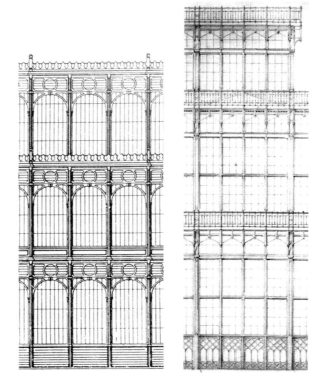

2.2.10

The parameters in Munich   The royal consent granted on 10 August 1853 served the construction of a major industrial exhibition pavilion based on Crystal Palace in London.[29] Within a week a discussion had begun that focused primarily on the materials iron and glass.[30] In the contract with Cramer-Klett dated 11 September

2.2.6, 2.2.7: Crystal Palace, London, and the Glass Palace, Munich: interiors

2.2.8: Schrannenhalle, Munich, 1851–53, architect: City Building Councillor C. Muffat. The grain storage hall was one of the first hall constructions based on the Polonceau system in Bavaria.

2.2.9: Richard Turner's competition entry, 1850

2.2.10: Crystal Palace, London, and the Glass Palace, Munich: cross-section of the wall structures in comparison

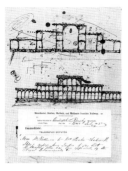

a date was set for the building to be handed over: 8 June 1854 – 9 months' construction time. A condition of the plans was that the exhibition building be suitable for subsequent conversion into a publicly accessible greenhouse – an early example of the reuse of a pavilion after an exhibition.

The site itself and construction of Crystal Palace were entrusted to Fox & Henderson with specific time and budget constraints, together with the approved project. In Munich, all construction details for the project were defined in the contract, and such that it was to outdo Crystal Palace in terms of the slenderness of the profiles, the lightness of the load-bearing structure, flexibility and conversion suitability: "The outer walls of the galleries are to be constructed in such a way that in the future, when the building is being used as a greenhouse, they can be easily removed and used on the inside at the end of the upper centre span"[31] – a premonition of the light construction method! (ill. 2.2.10).

Planning and construction – a chronology in comparison

The extraordinary story leading up to the building for the *Great Exhibition* and Paxton's daring intervention – and ultimate success – lend Prince Albert's decision-making process a masterful character. All the more so if one takes into account the 10 months and 20 days between Paxton's first sketch (ill. 2.2.11) and the opening of Crystal Palace!

In contrast, the planning and construction process in Munich seems to have been one of meticulous thoroughness: in two-day rhythm, experts worked out the fundamentals, decisions were prepared in the imperial building commission, applications considered and passed on to the imperial authorities, edicts drawn up by the latter, confirmed by the imperial Privy Counsellor, and approved for construction, etc. The time spent on planning and construction – from the date the decision was made to go ahead with construction (10 August 1853) to the opening (15 July 1854) – came to 11 months and 5 days.

In Munich, the time spent on preparation and planning from the first royal declaration of intent (2 August 1853) until the beginning of work on the building site (the first foundations were laid on 17 October) was 68 days, as opposed to 49 in London (Paxton's sketch: 11 June 1850; takeover of the site by Fox & Henderson:

30 July; ill. 2.2.12). The building was much smaller (a fifth of the size of Crystal Palace) and the journey there from Munich station along a specially laid streetcar track more comfortable (ill. 2.2.13).

Whereas in London construction of the carcass took 4 months (ill. 2.2.14), in Munich it needed 3 months and 10 days.[32] In contrast with Crystal Palace, in Munich the extremely short construction time (carcass and interior) of 100 days (from the first column to handing over of the fitted building) was achieved by means of measures that speeded up the process: through the direct railway link to the hall, the erection of various mobile scaffolding cranes that were adapted to the profile of the edifice and the various platforms, as well as the introduction of 'continuous' construction work.[33] This type of construction by processes represented an early form of industrial building site operations as was later to become necessary in the case of skyscrapers and car factories and even later in industrialised construction (ill. 2.2.15).

The time spent making diagrams is even more astonishing. Whereas there is hardly any difference in the pre-project phase (London four days, Munich six), August von Voit and Ludwig Werder together needed 63 days for the project development as opposed to the 30 days Joseph Paxton and Charles Fox needed for Crystal Palace, which was five times as big.[34] Their construction project took 18 days to produce and was approved in a fortnight.[35] According to sources available, between 22 June and 6 or 10 July 1850, Charles Fox produced the entire diagrams for the Crystal Palace project from Paxton's plans, also proving its technical and logistical feasibility (ill. 2.2.16). That comes to 18 working days at most for a surface area of one million square feet (over 85,000 square metres), five times the size of St. Peter's Basilica in Rome![36] Construction planning therefore required 42 days until load tests on the first cast parts on 6 September.

In Munich more than a third of the planning time was required for variations on the building site, debates about materials, applications, confirmations, expert opinions, approvals and decisions at various levels of the royal administrative authorities; the construction project was compiled at the same time as the building site and the first foundations were set up and required 75 days.

2.2.11: Joseph Paxton, 'blotting-paper sketch' of 11 June 1850

2.2.12: Industrially organised building site with machines, horses and manual labourers in Hyde Park, London

2.2.13: Industrialised building site with scaffolding crane

2.2.14: Assembling the transept arch of Crystal Palace by hand and rope winch

2.2.15: Combination of fixed and moving assembly equipment in Munich

2.2.16: As an example of the precise nature of information about the construction: façade slats with ventilation mechanism, Crystal Palace, London

2.2.17: Industrial and engine hall in Crystal Palace

2.2.14

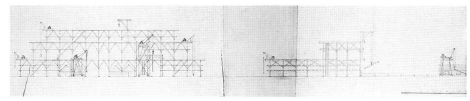

2.2.15

2.2.16

Finally, hurdles in production had to be overcome. For Crystal Palace alone the glass manufacturer Chance in Birmingham, who had already worked for Paxton in Chatsworth, had produced one third of his annual output within some 5½ months and in 6 weeks assembled 100,000 square metres of glass panels.

State of the art and what are new trends? Crystal Palace and the Glass Palace illustrate where the new trends are to be found: in the standardisation of building production and assembly thanks to a rational mindset and a grid with regard to space and construction – the key to high speed and low cost; in limiting the number of component parts to just a few, in prefabrication in workshops under controlled conditions (consistent quality), on-site dry assembly (apart from glass puttying) and a uniform design (dimensions, profiles, connections). Conditioned interior climates through natural ventilation and the efficient use of shade were also new, supplemented in Hyde Park by elms and fountains. The industrial mindset was at the same time a construction programme and ultimately determined spatial quality, method, shape, detailed figure creation and the perception of a new type of transparency. The exhibition pavilions did not, first and foremost, represent an architectural achievement but were rather the result of an organisational and construction process: nothing that had previously existed could

2.2.17

be imitated; even traditional building work and decision-making processes were doomed to failure; everything was new (ill. 2.2.17).

The players and advisors involved in building projects such as these were pioneers, inventors and innovative minds, influenced multi-disciplinary schools of thought, founded magazines and moved in the context of an epoch that promoted them. With the promoters they founded an early form of a 'lobby scientifique' as intellectual and commercial associations and clubs that functioned as places with a personal network in which to exchange ideas.

Case Study 22
Palais des Machines

World Exhibition, Paris,
France, 1889
Architect:
Charles-Louis-Ferdinand Dutert
Engineer and metal structure
entrepreneur: Victor Contamin

The machine hall for the *World Exhibition* in Paris in 1889, which was located directly adjacent to the Eiffel Tower, was the multi-disciplinary work of the engineer Contamin (1840–93) and the architect Dutert (1845–1906). Like Gustave Eiffel, Contamin was also a graduate of the École Centrale, taking his degree in 1860, five years after Eiffel, in other words well educated in the art of building under Mary, Perdonnet et al. Having graduated, Contamin started off as a draughtsman at the Compagnie du Chemin du Fer du Nord, where later on, as a 50-year-old, he served as a senior engineer. Dutert, on the other hand, studied at the École des Beaux Arts, winning, in 1869, the coveted Prix de Rome. The exhibition director and 'polytechnicien' Adolphe Alphand commissioned Charles Garnier, like Dutert a Beaux Arts pupil and winner of the Prix de Rome (1848), as architectural advisor, and Contamin as senior engineer and chief inspector of all metal constructions, including the 'tour de 300 mètres' – as such all the major construction schools were prominently represented on the Champs de Mars.[37]

Contamin's engineering achievement in the construction of the machine hall was in – for those days – the widest spanned application of the three-hinged arch. The width was 115 metres, the height of the vertex 43.5 metres (ill. 2.2.18). The bolts and supports of the hinges on the vertex and base displayed previously unknown dimensions (ill. 2.2.19).

In the upper section the arched girders became ever flatter and more slender; vertically downward, on the other hand, they became wider, before tapering towards the hinge. Twenty three-hinged arches produced what, at the time, was the enormous length of 420 metres. The middle span, not the side galleries, was made totally of glass. In *Bauen in Frankreich* (1928) Sigfried Giedion attempted to illustrate the contemporary perception around 1889 and the impression that the lightness of the girders and the lack of 'filling material' both in the girders themselves and in the roof must have left behind: "At the time, people were unsure and unnerved by what they saw, as the light cascading in from above swallowed up the thin glazing bars. Visually, the arches seemed to adopt an unusual hovering position."[38] (ill. 2.2.20)

In the measurement of the arched girders, which served as the framework, the engineers and designers at the time were able to avail themselves of Karl Culmann's now established 'graphic statics'. Recalculations using computer simulation (ill. 2.2.21) by the Arup engineer Angus Low, 100 years after Contamin, produced an almost identical form of framework and construction: "The conclusion from this exercise is that the designer's calculations gave a similar distribution of forces to those found with a modern computer analysis... They produced a well-conceived and elegant design."[39]

Low also referred to the outstanding material characteristics of the steel used, as well as to the fact that the rivets (32,000 per girder) were forged on the building site and, while not yet cool, forced together by two simultaneous blows with a hammer in such a way that they stuck together while cooling, thereby guaranteeing a lasting bond, a technique that was also used for the neighbouring Eiffel Tower.[40]

The contract to build and assemble the load-bearing structure was awarded to two of the largest metal construction companies in France: Fives-Lille & Cie., and Cail & Cie., both of which were run by graduates of the École Centrale. They each intended to progress from the side towards the middle. As they divided up the load-bearing system differently and consequently used different scaffolding, and furthermore had different numbers of workers present on the building site, the assembly developed into a competition. Despite the different approaches used, both companies completed their work at almost exactly the same time (ill. 2.2.22).[41]

2.2.18: A lightweight structure and plenty of natural light dominated what at the time was a large interior

2.2.19: Vertex hinge being assembled

2.2.20: Detail of the hall and size of the base hinge

2.2.21: Computer simulation of Contamin's arched girder by Angus Low/Arup

2.2.22: Two differing manufacturing and assembly methods by Cail & Cie. and Fives-Lille & Cie.

Building as an Art or the Art of Building?

2.2.18

2.2.19

2.2.20

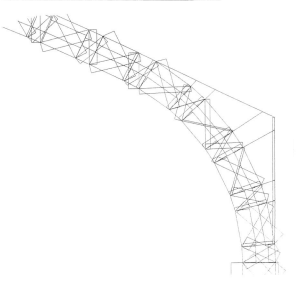

2.2.21

2.2.22

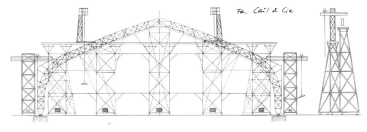

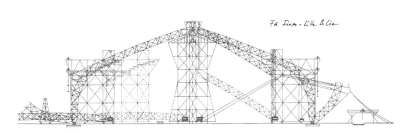

2.3 Interim Worlds: The Avant-garde and Fascination with Construction

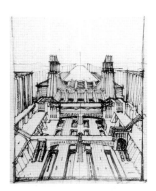

2.3.1

Whereas Pennsylvania Station in New York – which opened in 1910 and was designed by McKim, Mead and White, a steel construction consisting almost entirely of glass stretching into infinity and reminiscent of Piranesi's fantastic architecture – represented the end of the era of major iron constructions, Victor Laloux's Gare d'Orsay in Paris (1898–1900) heralded the beginnings of concrete. In terms of style both stations represent the Beaux-Arts school; using different materials both attempted to 'save' the predominance of the style over pure engineering beyond the turn of the century. As yet, Modernism had emerged only in isolated instances, such as the Hennebique pavilion for the Palais des Sciences et Arts at the 1900 *World Exhibition* in Paris (see ill. 3.2.3); there were, as yet, only indications of the avant-garde in Cubism and architecture.

Industrial aesthetics of the avant-garde and Modernism

Neither the promoters of the avant-garde architectural movements of de Stijl nor those of Russian Constructivism and Suprematism delivered any striking visions of stations. The needs of expression in architecture and buildings were different: in Holland the focus was on the pressing apartment question, in the Soviet Union on manifestations for the new state, its factories and claims to power; there were interesting visionary approaches in trade union and media buildings, for example.[42] This was not the case in Italian 'futurismo' prior to World War I: fascination and visionary ideas gripped all areas and their driving force was the industrial revolution – cities, traffic, power stations, factories – dynamic elements of the new sensation of space and time. Of the examples completed the FIAT Lingotto car factory in Turin, built between 1916 and 1920, stands out (see chapter 3, case study 36). The most important visionary draughtsman was Antonio Sant'Elia. What is interesting is the uninterrupted presence of the railroad as a motif and of stations, which, even earlier, were combined with airports.

As of 1914, Sant'Elia was the dominant figure of the futurist circle around Filippo Tommaso Marinetti, Umberto Boccioni, Carlo Carrà et al. His work consists primarily of a series of 16 drawings and several sketches,

2.3.2

which in March 1914 he published with a manifesto under the title *La Città Nuova*.[43] Sant'Elia's drawings depict possible cityscapes of the future. Among the total of 367 (!) unrealised projects there are numerous multi-functional traffic hubs with over-layered forms of traffic – a potent, dynamic weave in an urban concentration that links all futuristic themes with one another – a futuristic 'crystal way' (ill. 2.3.1).

Despite the immaterial manner of their portrayal Sant'Elia's metropolises of the future make use of new building materials and techniques: alongside specific steel constructions for wide-span passages, arcades and inclined transportation elevators (the precursor of escalators), the gigantic but slender structures and the dimensions of the towers could be overcome only by using reinforced concrete. The *Messagio* stated: "Calculations pertaining to the material's resistance and the use of reinforced concrete and iron rule out 'architecture' in the classical, traditional sense."[44]

Following Mussolini's seizure of power in 1922 all Italian architectural currents with an influence on style attempted to make themselves popular as the true artistic expression of the fascism that was establishing itself. This escaped neither Mussolini's dazzling, calculating cultural policy nor his guardians of art and culture. The multi-layered aspect geared to mobilising all tendencies corresponded to the fascist concept.[45] During the course of the power seizure process, the increasing monumentalism and militarism, Rome's cultural policy constantly and relentlessly brought into line all currents as

2.3.3

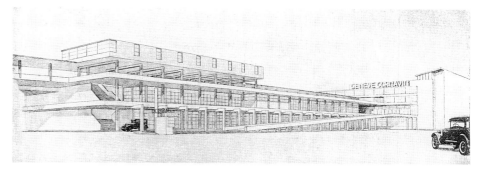
2.3.4

2.3.5

a demonstration of the regime's power. The avant-garde and Modernism also toed the line; scarcely any artists, architects or engineers went into exile, as had been the case in Germany. Nonetheless a few 'system eyesores' do stand out among the instrumentalised Italian architectural scene: for example, Casa Cattaneo in Cernobbio near Como (1938–39) and → Santa Maria Novella station in Florence. It is, and indeed was at the time, a protest against ideological domination. The project and its construction did not correspond to Rome's design guidelines: no axial symmetry (with regard to the object), no monumentality (with regard to the city), no militarism (with regard to the fascist idea of strength) – in other words, hardly any alignment with the forms of portrayal that the regime and party required.

Modernism

The protagonists of Modernism and their successors, such as Pier Luigi Nervi and the masters of concrete Eduardo Torroja and Eladio Dieste, attempted to arch large halls using light structures (see chapter 3, case studies 41, 44 and 45). In their designs they drew on the design opportunities presented by concrete and from the repertoire of pioneers such as Hennebique, Freyssinet, Dischinger, Finsterwalder et al developed new approaches of their own (ills. 2.3.2 and 2.3.3).

Representative of the rationalism of this 'Nordic-inspired' Modernism is, for example, the competition project submitted by Mart Stam (which was rejected by the jury) for Geneva-Cornavin station (1925), which by means of a simple concrete frame load-bearing structure if anything anticipates the spaciousness and lightness of post-War Modernism rather than imitating a Le Corbusier-style 'obsession with objects' (ill. 2.3.4). Stam emphasized the transmissibility between train and city and the openness of the building's structure.

Post-1945 lightweight construction

Alongside lighter forms of construction in steel and glass, of which the stations Amstel in Amsterdam and Rotterdam-CS represent 1950s' and 1960s' examples, with → Fuller's 'tensegrity' experiments a new mindset with regard to space, load-bearing structures and technology emerged in architects' and engineers' field of design.

The 'tensegrity' method of construction pointed in a new direction, was tested for the *Expo '67* in Montreal and *Expo '70* in Osaka, and with the engineer Lev Zetlin's roof structure over the auditorium in the city of Utica was reinterpreted in a way that around 1990 was used for large sports halls (ill. 2.3.5), and which is still in use today.[46] Even today, however, 'tensegrity' is still an experimental method of construction and provides grounds for further research. The new sports hall in Aigle in Switzerland represents one possible elegant interpretation (see ill. 2.3.14).

Post-1945 large halls increasingly became architectural and engineering assignments in the fields of sport, trade fair pavilions, 'middle-distance stations' and airport terminals. The → Olympic Stadium in Munich, which was a major test for the membrane building technique, as well as the project for the → US Pavilion at *Expo '70* in Osaka from Geiger Berger Associates, which was running at the same time, represented a new form of building and construction.

2.3.1: Antonio Sant'Elia: *Stazione per treni e aerei*, 1913–14: The 'horizontal' speeds are illustrated by railway tracks, partially underground routes, roads and runways, and vertical speeds by elevators, chimneys and towers.

2.3.2: Eduardo Torroja: design for a railroad station

2.3.3: Eladio Dieste: service sheds for the underground in Rio de Janeiro, Brazil

2.3.4: Mart Stam: competition project for Geneva-Cornavin station, 1925

2.3.5: Sports arena in St Petersburg, Florida, 1989; architects: Hellmuth, Obata & Kassabaum; engineers: Geiger Berger Associates; constructor: Birdair Inc.

Main Station
Santa Maria Novella

Florence, Italy, 1933–35
Architects: Gruppo Toscano
(Giovanni Michelucci and others)

Although not strictly assigned to the actual group of futurists, Gruppo Toscano,[47] which won the competition and was able to construct the new station in Florence in line with the project, referenced a central theme of 'futurismo', as did the engineer Giacomo Mattè Trucco with the FIAT Lingotto factory: the 'transposition' in terms of form and construction of momentum and speed – in some cases the railroad; in others, cars – in an architecturally functional building.

The competition for the new station in Florence in 1933 and the prizewinning project caused quite a stir. And an even bigger one when, on its completion in 1935, the building revealed a 'modernità' that was visible from afar. Roman academics accused the jury of having betrayed the noble aims of Italian culture, the real 'italianità'; in the Roman parliament the 'Florence case' was cited as a deterrent and a warning (ill. 2.3.6).[48]

This happened at a time when Mussolini was preparing for war with Abyssinia, surrounding himself primarily with monumental buildings made of 'national autarkic' materials that were intended to illustrate the power of the regime with the legend and splendour of the glory of Antiquity and victorious pose. At this time, with the militaristic, monumental Roman academicism headed by Marcello Piacentini, all architectural currents (neofuturism, architettura razionale, novecento) had already been forced into line.[49]

Seen in this light the station in Florence was the last sign the Modernists were able to make in the circle of architettura razionale, and one of the most consistent: The building does not possess an axial symmetry, but rather one that is functional, an architectural design and materials geared to cars (crosswise) and the railroad (lengthwise) – an example of the priority of function, structure, construction and shape over the regime's style requirements (ill. 2.3.7).

The materials were used for different purposes: steel, metal and glass for the entrance hall, with references to the direction of travel and materiality of the railroad, announced already by the slip-road (ill. 2.3.8); a concrete skeleton for the spatial frame, defining the spatial sequence level by level; cladding and the ground on the inside are a refined skin of modern elegance made of valuable natural stone (ill. 2.3.9), and the same applies to the outside, aimed at referencing the city centre close by but primarily the Santa Maria Novella Basilica.[50]

The metal-and-glass roof of the front hall is of extraordinary interest. It went against the trend for stone, columns and arched buttresses that the regime preferred at the time and as such triggered public attack,[51] and which was able to gain in influence in the competition for the Città Universiteria di Roma (1932–35) organised at the same time.[52]

The longitudinal girders take the form of a trussed framework. A secondary construction secured crosswise at the top flange serves for the glazing in the shed; between the two lower flanges, making these partially visible, is a second glass ceiling. This dual glass cover produces a climatic buffer zone.[53] The visible supporting ribs indicate the direction of travel of the trains, an effect that is increased by the supports taking the form of ever larger panels, linking the sequence of spatial layers as a 'filter': car approach – front zone – shed (ill. 2.3.10).

As such, through its spatial sequence and material structure, the entrance hall already announces the purpose of the site, while the platforms and roof are secondary. There has been a change in paradigm: it is no longer the shed, as an experience of space and construction that has priority, but rather the importance of the end of the building as the representative of railroad culture and its modern objectivity and as a part of the everyday cityscape of 'stone Florence' – the reverse of the Beaux-Arts type of station.

The Santa Maria Novella main station in Florence is one of the few examples of Modernism in stations between the two World Wars. It also had other focuses: large estates, factories, schools, swimming baths, sanatoriums, etc., whose structure and physiognomy also reflected a synthesis of steel, reinforced concrete, and glass.

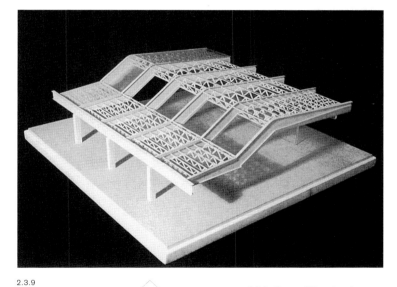

2.3.7

2.3.8

2.3.9

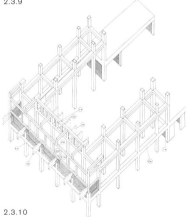

2.3.6: Competition drawing of the new station in the urban context of Santa Maria Novella Basilica

2.3.7: Side view

2.3.8: Entrance hall, interior

2.3.9: 'Cascata di vetro': model (1:50) of the entrance hall structure

2.3.10: Underside view of the shed's axonometry

2.3.10

'Tensegrity' Structures for Wide Halls – Richard Buckminster Fuller and the Consequences

2.3.11

2.3.12

Ever since the experimental phase at Black Mountain College in 1949 Richard Buckminster Fuller had been developing ever lighter and wider-span roofs with his 'tensegrity' structures. With the invention of 'tensegrity' he intended to develop spatial and engineering structures, which, thanks to the combination of linked tension elements under continual tension with discontinuous pressure from non-linked girders, created a new form of equilibrium: 'integral tensile stress' ('tensile + 'integrity' = 'tensegrity') was to be a new category of load-bearing structure. This 'hovering' structure has been fascinating architects and engineers alike ever since. In the past few years there have been reinterpretations and an attempt at a glass version aimed at increasing efficiency and reducing weight (see ill. 1.4.24).

Buckminster Fuller's dream   'Tensegrity' is not just an invention, it is also a discovery: the transfer of an already existing, perfected principle of the spoked wheel of a bicycle to building, spatial structures. The new way of thinking is based on reversal: a building's load-bearing components no longer weigh heavily on the ground, but are light and hover. The load-bearing system is broken down into 'flying' girders under pressure that are connected with each other by tension cables in such a way that the equilibrium is created without touching the compression members. Kenneth Snelson created an early 'tensegrity' structure that consisted of two 'hovering plywood crosses' connected by nylon chords (1948). Fuller referred to the sculpture as a "spiritual breakthrough" and "disruption of solid thought."[54] (ill. 2.3.11)

Subsequent experiments and students' theses served to implement the discovery that the static and dynamic forces in material characteristics, dimensions and technology could be used differently than before: "Don't fight the forces, use them." Initial experiments were geared to combining Fuller's previous discovery, the 'geodesic dome', with 'tensegrity' structures: 'tensegrity sphere' (ill. 2.3.12; see also ill. 6.1.3). Fuller saw that this paved the way for considerably wider spans.

As a vision Fuller came up with the Dome over Manhattan, a gigantic, drop-shaped 3.2-km spatial structure covering 50 blocks of Upper Manhattan, which he publicised by means of what became a famous photomontage (see ill. 1.4).

'Tensegrity' structures with glass   At *glasstec '96* in Düsseldorf a glass cube was introduced that had been developed by the University of Stuttgart and industry: a 'tensegrity' sculpture made of glass and steel. The compression members consisted of glass tubes that were, at the ends, covered with a steel plate and a mandrel to guarantee the transmission of force via the tensile cables (see chapter 1, case study 14). The steel and glass were stuck together with polyurethane. Assembly used the prestressing technique (ill. 2.3.13).[55]

More recent interpretations   For the roof of the new velodrome in Aigle in Switzerland a development that since Fuller had been advanced by several groups of engineers was referenced and an 'tensegrity' cell invented consisting of six compression members that hit against a central node, whose corners are connected in a bi-pyramid way with tensile cables; the sheaves of the compression members, on the other hand, have no connections. This type of construction increases performance and leads to a further reduction in weight of approx. 40–50 per cent (ills. 2.3.14 and 2.3.15).[56]

David Geiger's Cable Dome (1986), the sports arena in St Petersburg, Florida (1989, see ill. 2.3.5), M. Saithoh's Tension Strut Dome in Amagi, Japan (1991), M. Levy's Hyper Dome in Georgia (1992) and the engineer Lev Zetlin's spoked wheel roof over the auditorium in the city of Utica (ill. 2.3.16) are all precursors and 'interim examples' in the line of development. Two radial sheaves of parabolic tensile cables form a 'spatial cushion' of the Utica project; the vertical compressed members are placed in between and connected with each other diagonally using load cables. As opposed to the building in Aigle, the 'tensegrity' structure here is effective as a whole and not by means of integral components.[57]

2.3.13

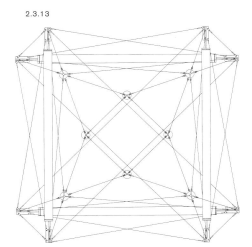

2.3.11: Buckminster Fuller with an experimental 'tensegrity' structure

2.3.12: 'Tensegrity sphere: experimental structure, developed at the University of Oregon; it was patented in 1956.

2.3.13: 'Tensegrity' glass sculpture at *glasstec '96*: construction drawing

2.3.14: Velodrome in Aigle, Switzerland; interior with strengthened 'tensegrity' structure

2.3.15: 'Anti-prism': advanced 'tensgrity' structural cells

2.3.16: Lev Zetlin: spoked wheel roof over the auditorium in Utica, USA (see ill. 2.6)

PERSPECTIVE-VIEW

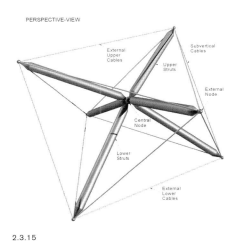

2.3.15

COMPRESSION RING   TENSION RING   UPPER CABLE

LOWER CABLE

SEPARATOR STRUT

240'

2.3.16

Case Study 25

Olympic Stadium

Munich, 1967–72
Architects: Behnisch & Partner
Engineers: Heinz Isler;
Leonhardt, Andrä und Partner
with Jörg Schlaich
Experiment models:
Frei Otto, IL Stuttgart

The 1972 roof over the Olympic Stadium in Munich represents another milestone in the development of a new, cosmopolitan and democratically inspired German post-war architecture that began with Egon Eiermann and Sepp Ruf's German pavilion at the *Expo '58* in Brussels. Günter Behnisch and his team in Stuttgart continued along these lines. As such, it was hardly by chance that under the aegis of the jury president, Egon Eiermann, the project submitted by Behnisch & Partner won the Olympic competition and that the engineers Leonhardt, Andrä und Partner, who had developed the concept for the German pavilion at *Expo '67* in Montreal, were taken on board for the construction of the Olympic stadium in Munich to complement the Swiss engineer Heinz Isler, whom Behnisch had hired for the competition.

The roof, which covers the central Olympic park like an enormous sail, was an integral part of the design of the park as a whole and a response to the hilly terrain that in parts still hid the rubble left over from the destruction of Munich in World War II (ill. 2.3.17).

In terms of structure and shape the complex roof with membranes could be determined only through experiments with models, methods which were investigated both in Heinz Isler's laboratory near Burgdorf in Switzerland as well as in Frei Otto's Institut für leichte Flächentragwerke in Stuttgart. An experiment with a 1:125 scale model was then conducted at the IL in Stuttgart. For several years engineers struggled to find ways to realise the original concept, until eventually a viable solution was found: a load-bearing structure consisting of strong pylons and 'flying' compression members that do not touch each other and that form a discontinuous system of stressed construction parts, and of a system of tensile cables that continually link all the fixed points on the roof, including the borders of the membranes, which have the effect of pure tie members (ill. 2.3.18).

The roof initially consisted of a square network of spring steel wire with movable nodes that was laid out flat. The entire system was hoisted into the correct position by means of the pylons, with the exact tension achieved through tensile elements bundled in a 'flying' node (ill. 2.3.19).

The different-sized, rhomboid-shaped acrylic glass panels, the calculations for which back then involved a laborious process, were then inserted and sealed. They have recently all been replaced. The deformation during the assembly process, as well as in the case of various loads (snow, wind), which were previously diagnosed by means of a photographic experiment (double exposure of the unstressed and stressed condition of the model) turned out, when the roof was given its final shape through pre-stressing, to be correct (ill. 2.3.20).

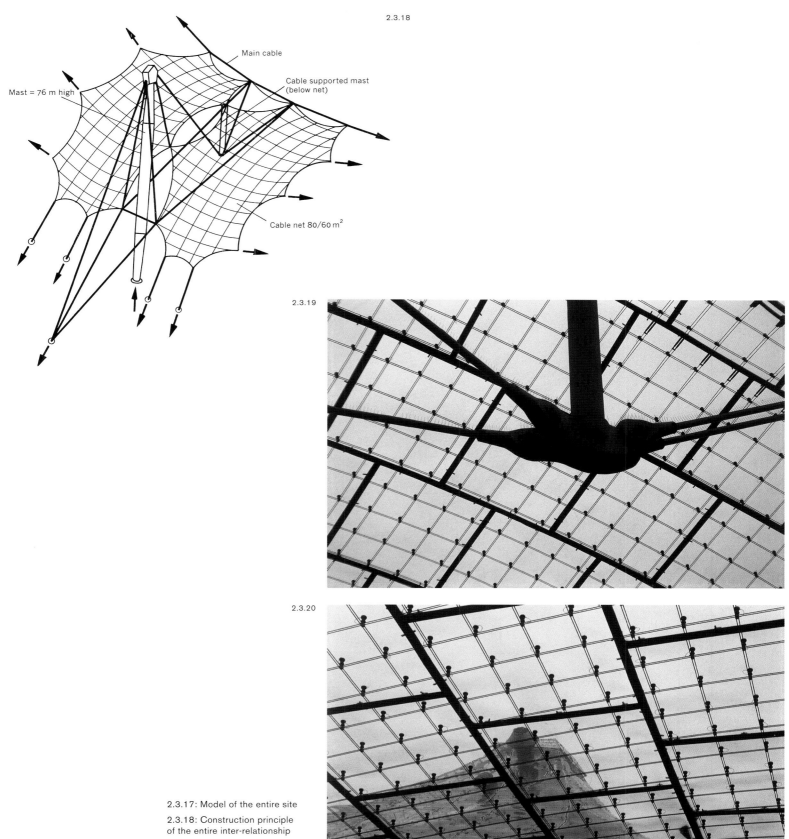

Main cable

Cable supported mast
(below net)

Mast = 76 m high

Cable net 80/60 m²

2.3.19

2.3.20

2.3.17: Model of the entire site

2.3.18: Construction principle
of the entire inter-relationship

2.3.19: 'Flying' node, the precursor of the 'spoked wheel system'

2.3.20: The roof's transparency
and lightness

US Pavilion

Expo, Osaka, Japan, 1970
Architects:
Davis, Brody, Chermayeff,
Geismar, de Harak
Engineers: Geiger Berger Associates
Constructor:
Taiyo Kogyo Corporation

For the light, textile surface structures that were partially reinforced with plastic and bent in several places and were developed by Frei Otto and other pioneers of the membrane, such as Walter Bird, Klaus-Michael Koch, Horst Berger and David Geiger, another area of application was found in pneumatic constructions, in other words, in air-inflated domes, dual or multi-shell membrane roofs pre-stressed by the inner air pressure, which were able to increase the span of large, support-free spaces quite considerably. The US pavilion at *Expo '70* in Osaka, Japan, designed by David Geiger for the architects Davis, Brody, Chermayeff, Geismar and de Harak, is regarded as the prototype.

One characteristic of these air-inflated membrane constructions is their flat camber even in the case of extreme spans, which offers less surface area for wind pressure. The US pavilion spanned a surface area of almost 10,000 square metres. The air-inflated membrane cushion was kept 'in shape' and stabilised by a cable mesh structure on the outside as well as a surrounding compression ring like a quilted cover (ill.2.3.21).

David Geiger developed this type of load-bearing structure during the time he headed the engineering consulting company Geiger Berger Associates together with Horst Berger. What was new about it was that it filled not the hall itself but the dual-shell membrane roof with pressurised air, thereby pre-stressing the foils. In order to control its shape and the volume of the pressurised air, additional steel cable bracing was necessary, which in this case consisted not of square-shaped steel cable sheaves but of a mesh of parallel running, high-quality steel cable sheaves that responded to the unequal lengths of the sides of the hall. (ill. 2.3.22)

The footprint, which was something in between a rectangle and an ellipse and measured 142 x 83 metres, was calculated covered with a cable mesh and in such a way that each of the nodes experienced the same tension while the outward shear forces could be regularly transferred to the outer ring. A computer program was used to scientifically calculate on a model all the structural forces and their impact, thereby overcoming all the initial calculations and experimental tests. A special feature of this structural invention is that roofs of this type that are up to 20 times as large always have the same weight of approx. 5 kg/m2.[58] Furthermore, the membranes are translucent, enabling a fascinatingly airy and light-filled spatial landscape to emerge (ill.2.3.23).

In the 1980s David Geiger and Horst Berger constructed several other halls of this type, such as, in 1983, the stadium on British Columbia Place in Vancouver, Canada (architects: PBK Architects; constructor: Birdair; ill. 2.3.24). This type of construction was subsequently used by other engineers and architects for warehouses, and tennis and sports halls. However, the running costs to permanently maintain the air pressure were so high that after just a few years they switched to self-supporting systems, in particular 'tensegrity domes'; in total, only eight extremely large halls that fully exploited this system were ever built.[59]

It is not surprising that following the prototype in Osaka this structural novelty and the rapidly developed new material technology of plastic sheaths (originally PTFE-coated fibre-glass fabric) led to visions such as the Arctic City and the Dome over Manhattan: Alongside David Geiger, Horst Berger and Walter Bird, Frei Otto and Richard Buckminster Fuller were also among the pioneers, setting in motion a light membrane construction movement and school of thought that are currently enjoying a revival (see chapter 6, case study 87).

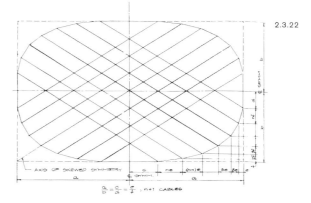

AXIS OF SKEWED SYMMETRY

$$\frac{a}{b} = \frac{c}{d} = \frac{e}{f} \; ; \; n+1 \; \text{CABLES}$$

2.3.23

2.3.21: The first pneumatic
load-bearing structure with air-
inflated membrane 'cushions'
for the US pavilion at *Expo '70*
in Osaka; engineer: David
Geiger

2.3.22: Diagram of the steel
cable bracing

2.3.23: Interior with translucent
roof under construction

2.3.24: Inflated air-membrane
hall of the BC Place Stadium
in Vancouver, Canada, 1983;
engineers: Geiger Berger
Associates

2.3.24

2.4 A New Type of Terminal: Station and Airport Buildings

2.4.1

2.4.2

2.4.1: Centre Georges Pompidou, Paris; competition model, 1971

2.4.2: 'Symbol zone' at the *Expo '70* in Osaka; architect: Kenzo Tange; engineer: Tsuboi

2.4.3: Norman Foster: project for St Pancras and King's Cross Station

2.4.4: Santiago Calatrava: train station for the 1998 *World Exhibition* in Lisbon

2.4.5: Renzo Piano: concept model for Kansai International Airport, Osaka, Japan

2.4.6: André Lurçat: Aéroport at the foot of the Eiffel Tower, 1932 (photomontage)

One effect of the 'oil shock' of October 1973 was that the world of construction changed, posing a challenge to innovative architects and engineers: the sparing use of materials and energy now called for promoted a trend towards lightweight construction as well as with regard to systems (improved performance, better efficacy with the use of less material), components (interchangeable parts) and the lifespan of buildings (life cycle strategies). Out of this a new architectural stance emerged, a 'new type of Constructivism'. It stood, and indeed still stands, in contrast to the trend towards solid-state construction and punctuated windows that referenced style reminiscences ("postmodernism"). Since the 1990s, stations, airport terminals, Expo pavilions, sports halls, event spaces, etc. have been characterised by construction systems featuring, in parts, colour coding for the various functions of material and technology that represent a new spatiality, sensitivity to materials, and a new world of images – the rediscovery and reinterpretation of the fascination of earlier ingenious architecture.

From functional building to event space: approaches to a 'new constructivism'

Ever since the challenge of the Centre Georges Pompidou in Paris (1971–78; see chapter 6, case study 83) the functional building mindset and post-modern Formalism have faced a new stance and a changed awareness. In view of the global networking of communicative societies, new urban locations become additionally necessary: an image of the virtual space in the event space of real time.

As a result of the inspiring influence of the wealth of ideas in the 1960s from Archigram and Buckminster Fuller's US pavilion at the 1967 *Expo* in Montreal, as well as being a European answer to 'le défi américain', in the eyes of the successful competition team Richard Rogers, Renzo Piano and Richard Rice, the planned cultural centre in Paris was to be a large, adaptable structure, dramatically revealing its entire infrastructure, and in which anything could take place – "an information machine",[60] a place for an open social environment (ill. 2.4.1).[61]

Designing a wide-span, steel space framework was a task for the engineers. At the time, Peter Rice visited the buildings at the 1970 *Expo* in Osaka and discovered the large space framework of the central 'symbol zone' with the cast-iron nodes (ill. 2.4.2).[62] For Rice, the fascinating 19th-century iron frameworks were also a source of inspiration: the Gare de Lyon, the Eiffel Tower and the Grand Palais in Paris, structures that render the hand-crafted, cast-iron parts visible and as such are comprehensible and reachable for the observer.

A sketch by Renzo Piano illustrates the intention behind the design: it reveals a complex edifice approx. 50 metres in depth, though as much urban space as possible was to be left undeveloped. Rice saw the solution in a sort of 'Gerber girder', which formed three parts of space connected by hinges: a support-free, 44.8-metre-wide interior and 6-metre-wide accessible outer zones. Serving as a basis, Gerber's bridge over the River Main near Hassfurt (1866–67) was now 'transposed' to the structure of the Centre Pompidou: the centre section was now the longest and the two side sections the shortest structural elements – the Gerber principle in reverse. This transformation by Peter Rice once again illustrates the creative power of the railroad technology and the inexhaustible source of ideas its pioneers had created: the problems the railroad posed broadened the design spectrum of architects and engineers.

For the architects Renzo Piano and Richard Rogers the Centre Pompidou was a joint experiment and piece of work; for Peter Rice it was the first major piece of work since the Sydney Opera House and reason enough to stay in Paris, where he set up the RFR studio.[63]

The Renault distribution centre in Swindon, England (Norman Foster, Ove Arup & Partners, 1983), Kansai International Airport near Osaka (Renzo Piano, Peter Rice, 1988–94), or the roof over the TGV airport station Roissy at Charles de Gaulle airport in Paris (architects: Paul Andreu, Jean-Marie Duthilleul; engineers: RFR; 1988–94) were direct consequences of the Centre Pompidou and the new Constructivism. At the same time Peter Rice, together with RFR, Arup, and the architects Richard Brosi and Robert Obrist, designed the spectacular, glass-roofed → post vehicle terminal at Chur station in Switzerland.

All the projects have a common guiding principle, which Peter Rice developed for the Centre Pompidou, namely the reintroduction of cast steel in the architecture

Building as an Art or the Art of Building?

2.4.3

2.4.4

2.4.5

of large buildings, and the contrast of a materiality that reflected craftsmanship with other parts of the construction, which were industrial and as such leave a perfect impression on the structural shape. This 'paradox liveliness' of large supporting frameworks made of steel and light glass sheaths is clearly visualised in these projects. As part of themes such as these Ove Arup founded an effective school of thought.[64]

→ Waterloo International Terminal in London, designed by Nicholas Grimshaw and Anthony Hunt (1993), was intended to represent a new era for the railroad in the 21st century, as well as its efficiency in space and time. Like an airport terminal it provides a wide range of services but has the advantage of being located in the heart of the city, carefully staged through views of Westminster and the Thames. British Rail wanted a new style of station, which in terms of originality and fascination was to carry on where Victorian stations such as St Pancras and Paddington had left off.

Waterloo International Terminal served as a thrust for future station architecture and the perception and prospects of new 'splendid stations' of the 21st-century. Without this impulse and the positive effect of the building, the new stations in Berlin, for example, the new → Lehrter main station, would have been unimaginable.

Norman Foster's project for an extension glass hall as joint 'event space' between St Pancras (actually the new Eurostar terminal from Paris to London) and King's Cross Station in London continues this new tradition (ill. 2.4.3), as do his designs for various underground stations that penetrate the city fabric.

'Splendid stations' of the 21st-century

Different tendencies characterise the forthcoming trend. The continuation of 'structural primacy' is foreseeable: beginning with concrete structures by the Swiss architect and engineer Santiago Calatrava (ill. 2.4.4) via TGV terminals and the planned stations for → Deutsche Bahn, for example, in Stuttgart (Ingenhoven, Overdiek und Partner; Frei Otto) and Dortmund (Bothe Richter Teherani) through to Dutch visions such as Arnhem Central station by UN Studio/Ben van Berkel and Arup engineers.

The ever more frequent building assignment of linking station and airport terminals is leading to a new type of building. Renzo Piano and Peter Rice's still classic Kansai International Airport can be regarded as a transition: a combination of a dinosaur-like, load-bearing framework and a Zeppelin sheath, which as a metaphor for the airship conveys the feeling of already being in a flying object (ill. 2.4.5). The ICE/airport terminal in Frankfurt/Main by Bothe Richter Teherani has already been completed.

The growing similarity between airports and stations as buildings and how they are experienced can be seen as a new trend.[65] What it involves is the renewed conquest of urban space, the advantages of inner-city stations. Yet air terminals far away on the outskirts can be nothing more than an artificial, virtual city, as current examples illustrate.[66] Earlier, the orchestration of an urban space for the sensation of taking off and landing was genuine, for example, in the 1925 Paris visions of the Plan Voisin by Le Corbusier or by André Lurçat in 1932 (ill. 2.4.6).

2.4.6

Case Study 27

Roofing Over the Postal Vehicle Shed

Chur, Switzerland, 1987–94
Architects: Richard Brosi,
Robert Obrist
Steelwork: Peter Rice, Paris;
Arup, London
Light planning:
Bartenbach, Innsbruck

2.4.7

2.4.8

The 1987 competition entry submitted by Brosi and Obrist for a roof over the station in Chur, Switzerland, the capital of the Swiss canton Graubünden, envisaged a light, hovering roof over the entire tracks. However, all that was actually completed was the cover over the section of track in the west for post buses. Though Chur might not now boast Switzerland's most fascinating station it does have the most lucid post vehicle shed.

Peter Rice, a former engineer at Arup and the main structural designer of the Centre Georges Pompidou, together with his RFR studio, was hired to devise a concept for the structural system and framework. The seemingly hovering glass roof was suspended on pylons in just a few places in order to make it appear even lighter (ill. 2.4.7).

The supporting structure consists of 12 curved, fish-bellied girders made of welded steel tubes; two of them are suspended from side pylons, which tower up 16 metres above the lower track level, such that with a span of 52 metres the entire area of some 5,000 square metres has no supports (ill. 2.4.8). The longitudinal bracing is conducted by 29 rails between the cross girders. To stay the transverse arched girders Rice used a sort of spoked wheel principle featuring a series of cable stays, which are attached at eight points on the pair of arched steel tubes or every fourth transverse purlin and are anchored in a 'flying' node; the lowest, horizontal ones in dual formation. The node is not only the result of structural load-bearing considerations but, similar to the 1837 Polonceau node (see ill. 2.1.4), illustrates the various functions of the inserted tension cables as visual design – force and coherence of shape as technical perfection and the communication of aesthetics at one and the same time (ill. 2.4.9).

The glass roof, stuck with silicon, rests on a mounting system of nodes above the framework construction and consists of same-format, flat, rectangular composite safety glass panels (ill. 2.4.10).

Thanks to Peter Rice, this new type of construction was developed by subjecting material to the limits of what was technically possible and would have been unimaginable without the intensive multidisciplinary collaboration between engineers and architects and the innovative steel/glass manufacturer Tuchschmid (Frauenfeld, Switzerland), which manufactured and tested prototypes and also conducted important development work in their implementation, winning the 1993 Steel Construction Prize in the process (ill. 2.4.11).

This type of construction is not an invention, rather a discovery by Rice; it was first used in a building structure in 1993 as part of the collaboration with Arup for the roof over the sculpture hall in the Louvre (architect: Michael Macary; ill. 2.4.12).[67] The spoked wheel principle and, in particular, its use for big wheels[68] had been around for much longer. In 1989, in other words at much the same time as the roof was put on the postal vehicle shed in Chur, Jörg Schlaich developed a analogous roof construction to cover the courtyard at the Museum of Hamburg History (see chapter 1, case study 11).

92   Building as an Art or the Art of Building?

2.4.10

2.4.11

2.4.7: Overall shape, night view

2.4.8: Carcass and construction work

2.4.9: 'Flying' nodes

2.4.10: Detailed view of the glazing

2.4.11: Shaped piece in the workshop of Tuchschmid

2.4.12: Glass roof over the sculpture hall in the Louvre, Paris, 1993

2.4.12

Case Study 28

Waterloo International Terminal

London, England, 1993
Architects:
Nicholas Grimshaw & Partners
Engineers:
Anthony Hunt Associates

Nicholas Grimshaw is one of the pioneers of English light tech architecture. Like Foster, his encounter with Buckminster Fuller left its mark on him. For him, the history of building, with structures such as the Iron Bridge in Coalbrookdale, Crystal Palace and the Palm House in Kew Gardens, is ever present, and he regards pioneers such as Paxton and Prouvé as role models. The London Architectural Association and other architects' federations, such as Archigram and Arup, are also of importance for him. These backgrounds quickened his interest in construction and engineering, material technology and industrial design. Waterloo International Terminal represented a continuation of such experimental projects as the printing buildings of the *Financial Times* in London (1988), and the *Western Morning News* in Plymouth (1992), or the British pavilion at *Expo '92* in Sevilla.[69]

The brief was to symbolise the direct train link between London and Paris through the Eurotunnel in competition with international air traffic by means of an attractive terminus station. Plans envisaged 15 million passengers annually, which called for an extremely high level of efficiency, and in a confined space, which represented particularly difficult conditions (ill. 2.4.13).

The Eurostar train station has recently moved to central London after it's integration into the newly restored St Pancras station.

Most London stations are at a raised level, on a plinth. Waterloo International Terminal also provided an opportunity to spread the functional areas over three levels. The old station features shed roofs that run transverse to the tracks, whereas the new roof follows the rails in the traditional way. Special joints are created between old and new: The new Waterloo International Terminal acts as an adapter in an urban context (ill. 2.4.14).

The trains travelling into the bend create enormous thrust, to which the filigree glass shed roof must respond. The curved structure of the roof references the pioneering stations of the Victorian age, such as Euston Station in London and Lime Street Station in Liverpool. The requisite flexibility, the asymmetric, spatially impressive curvature and the fascination with new technological possibilities led Grimshaw to a synthesis: he designed three-hinged trusses, as if it were as bone structure; and a supple skin of glass scales (ill. 2.4.15).[70]

Construction The load-bearing system is a combination of three-hinged arches and spatial lattice structure: pressure pipes, tension rods, transverse and diagonal beams. The pressure pipes consist of individual pieces with alternating profiles and adapt to the span, which in the course of the 400-metre-long shed increases from 32 to 48 metres (ills. 2.4.16 and 2.4.17).

The latticed structure segments on the short roof side consist of compression arches, which are fed almost vertically into the plinth hinge, whereas the tensile elements are configured as an outward-facing, upper lattice structure (with transverse and diagonally braced dual flanges); the glazing is located beneath the lattice structure. It is precisely the other way round in the flatter arched section of the roof: the dual pressure pipes act as an upper flange, the slanting tension rod is the lower flange; it is likewise connected to a spatial lattice structure with the compressed arch by means of transverse and diagonal beams; the roofing here is above the load-bearing structure. The base hinge is a specially shaped cast piece that accommodates the

2.4.13

Building as an Art or the Art of Building?

2.4.14

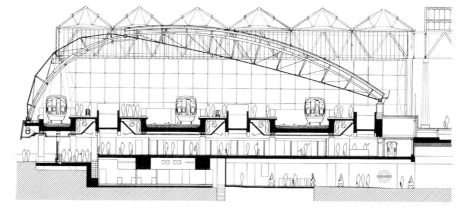

2.4.15

2.4.16

2.4.17

various angles of compressed pipes and tension rods on it (see ill. 2.1.11).

Since Victor Contamin used the three-hinged arch for the Palais des Machines at the 1889 Paris *World Exhibition*[71] there were scarcely any other similar applications for a railway shed. The readdressing of this theme in the highly symbolic Waterloo International Terminal bears witness to a mindset that is both conscious of history and forward-looking. What are entirely new are the movable roof structure and the hinged glass panels, which have to be protected from breakage, as the whole platform moves up to 80 mm lengthways and 6 mm across as trains arrive and depart. So as to cushion this, a secondary construction made of extruded, perforated aluminum profiles assumes the linking function between the glass panels and the stainless cast-steel hinges; only the hinges are connected to the load-bearing structure. Despite the different curvature of the roof this flexible construction allows for a few series of standardised glass elements (ill. 2.4.18).

Designed in a workshop The swivel joints are complex, crucial elements that were developed in a long

2.4.13: Aerial view

2.4.14: The interface between old and new: a collage of structures and materials

2.4.15: Cross-section

2.4.16: Mock-up of a segment in the workshop

2.4.17: Shed construction using the three-hinged arch system

process of experimentation – the result of an industrial design train of thought and working culture in the Grimshaw studio. So as to determine the accuracy and mobility of these nodes and the functional suitability of their shape, prototypes were manufactured with cast-steel works from a foundry. Only after several experiments could they be produced on an industrial scale – an example of design in an industrial context becoming a new field of work. Knowledge of materials, technology and production conditions widen the design scope of both the architect and the multidisciplinary team (ills. 2.4.19 and 2.4.20).

The computer-generated shapes of the roof and handmade models, the mock-up of a segment of the roof,

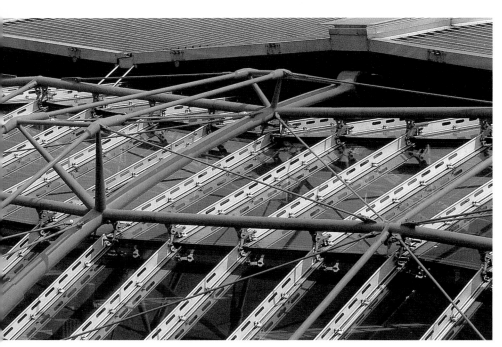

2.4.18

along with 1:1 models of individual details (joints) served to check the structural and technical feasibility as well as the visualisation. Grimshaw himself commented on this: "As such, the entrepreneurs had an opportunity to familiarise themselves with the details and we could develop the concepts for the skin."[72]

Images and appearance   Thanks to the joints being key pieces, a visual effect of mobility and lightness, and in particular of transparency and spatiality, can be created, as was orchestrated in Turner's Palm House in Kew Gardens, a source of inspiration which Grimshaw repeatedly mentions in his lectures and interviews. With regard to the shaping of the roof he likewise refers to the history of English building, in particular Paxton's Great Stove in Chatsworth and his combination of a ridge and furrow roof and a curvilinear primary construction (see chapter 1, case study 3). The ridge in this case, however, consists of a segment-shaped, glass element that is just as curved as the valley gutter (ill. 2.4.21).

The high glass wall at the point of transition from the old to the new shed represents an invention, as it was one of the first that had to withstand wind pressure on both sides. To this end the design and construction team developed a specially transparent structural glazing solution as an advancement on the X-shaped glass holders in Peter Rice and RFR's pavilion in Parc André Citroën (see chapter 1, case study 10). Interdisciplinary design[73] was decisive here, as Grimshaw stated: "A building like our station can come about only through intense collaboration. With regard to the glazing and the roof, which is made of stainless steel, engineering and architecture interact extremely closely."[74] (ill. 2.4.22)

The 'bone analogy' for the structure and spatial design of Waterloo International Terminal comes from Grimshaw's approach of observing and analysing the shaping powers in natural phenomena and 'transposing' them into spatial and building structures. It is not 'bionics' as the basis of imitation, but rather, for inspiration as well, the empirical, British "instinctive feel" for seeing and transferring with this 'inner eye' that finds expression is this masterly way of thinking and acting. Grimshaw commented on this as follows: "Buildings have the ability to be flexible and to adjust to changing conditions. They can be translucent or transparent, their skin can change; they can respond to the activities and the life in them. (. . .) We must get used to seeing buildings as living, vital units. We use them, and as a result transform them, too. (. . .) Regardless of how long a building is meant to stand it has to be a carefully considered, flexible organism and not a rigid, dead monument."[75]

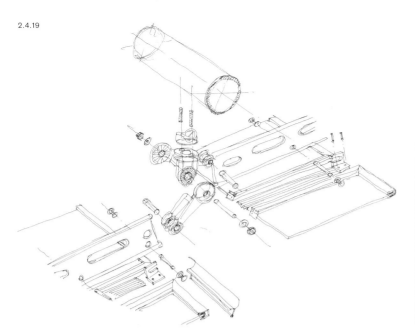

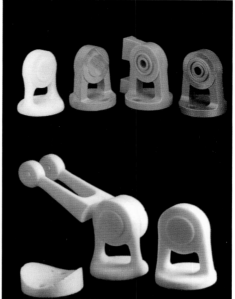

2.4.21

2.4.18: Construction functions and materiality are visualised: a view of the roof; the 'soft' interim aluminum construction with the joints cushions the movement of the primary construction against the glass panels.

2.4.19: Sketches by Nicholas Grimshaw and David Kirkland, prototypes

2.4.20: Industrial design: wax models of cast parts for the swivel joints

2.4.21: View of the roof from the west

2.4.22: Nodes in the glass wall between the old and new station; this marked the first use of wind bracing on both sides with braced struts, which secure the x-shaped brackets for the glass panels affixed using silicon.

2.4.22

Lehrter Central Station

Berlin, 2004
Architects: von Gerkan,
Marg und Partner (gmp)
Engineers: Jörg Schlaich,
Schlaich Bergermann
und Partner

What today is still wasteland and an area undergoing development in a city that is growing together again will soon be a highly concentrated centre with the new Lehrter Central station as a gigantic hub, ICE station, and the heart of the area between the districts of Moabit and Berlin Mitte. Two railroad axes intersect here. Unfortunately, part of the new railway shed was axed, and now suffers from having been disproportionately shortened.

The competition drawing and vision of the architectural studio von Gerkan, Marg und Partner (gmp) promised a terminal of incomparable dimensions with two interacting ICE lines in a megalomanic space, which itself should be a city in a place where there has never been anything of the kind. The core of the original shed is 66 metres wide, spans seven platforms and would have been 400 metres long, but was reduced somewhat in length (ill. 2.4.23).

2.4.23

The drawing from above reveals the volumetric plan and the typology of the lattice structure (ill. 2.4.24). Above a platform on the banks of the River Havel two parallel service buildings rise up at an angle to the tracks,

which the latter penetrate, as if entering a tunnel, after, or before crossing the Havel by bridge; the bridge across the Havel is likewise a joint piece of work between gmp and Schlaich Bergermann und Partner.

The flatly curved arched structure is reinforced underneath at the apex and above at the borders of the bearing; compression members maintain the distance between the primary pressure element and the secondary tensile construction; the upper and lower bracing cables follow the structurally calculated moment diagram. This combination allows the profile dimensions of the supporting arch to be reduced, the apex to be flattened and a steepening peripheral geometry, which complies with the functional requirements of platform accessibility and the overhead clearance of the trains passing through (ills. 2.4.25 and 2.4.26).

This supporting framework follows at intervals of 12 metres. The glazing consists of square panels, which are braced on the diagonal by means of tensile cables – a glass construction that gmp and Jörg Schlaich had tried out for the glass roof over the courtyard of the Museum of Hamburg History (ill. 2.4.27; see chapter 1, case study 11). Here, too, the geometry is irregular; the span of the entire roof ranges from 40 to 66 metres in a typology similar to that at Waterloo International Terminal in London. The longitudinal direction has also been contorted here as well.

Jörg Schlaich conceived a whole range of forward-looking shed constructions for stations, such as the new Spandau station in Berlin (1998), and the extension to the main station in Helsinki (a competition design with gmp). The 'structural expressiveness' in his spatial lattice structures follows a mindset that is geared to lightweight construction: through the efficient use of the flow of force in structuring the load-bearing frame and a material's characteristics the amount of material can be reduced. Instead of welding it 'to death' engineers should allow constructions to 'relate' their task and function. In this way, laymen can also understand the construction, for it explains its mode of operation itself, not least of all through its details.[76] The 'structural expressiveness' is furthermore an expression of Schlaich's biographical background, the Olympic Stadium in Munich being his first major 'journeyman's piece'.

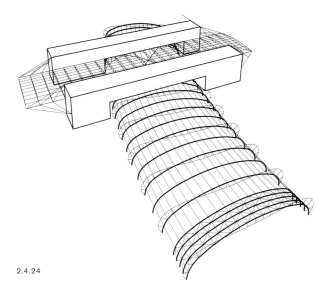

2.4.24

2.4.25

2.4.26

2.4.27

2.4.23: Competition model

2.4.24: View of the volumetry and lattice structure plan

2.4.25, 2.4.26: Arched structure and upper bracing construction (detail)

2.4.27: Museum of Hamburg History, Hamburg: diagonal bracing of the glass construction

New Stations
for Deutsche Bahn
– Visions

Deutsche Bahn (DB), which is facing stiff competition from medium-haul aircraft, is planning new stations along its ICE network that are conceived as 'future terminals', and in its marketing is giving preference to visionary designs by innovative architects and engineers. Some stations link the railroad with an airport, as for example in Frankfurt/Main. The stations are intended to feature urban qualities, as was the case in 19th-century pioneering stations. Is this a reconstruction of what formerly was? They take up again the fascinating steel-and-glass constructions, such as Richard Turner's Lime Street Station in Liverpool. Facilities such as hotels, restaurants, lounges, shops, etc. were always an integral part of city stations. So what is new, what is the next move?

If one considers the competition entry submitted by Bothe Richter Teherani (BRT Architekten Hamburg) for the ICE airport terminal in Frankfurt/Main, what is primarily striking is the 'bionic' inspiration of the sheath – similar to a Manta –, which embraces a communication space that follows the infinite railroad strip – heralding a new culture of networked spatial experience, while at the

same time representing a response to human factors such as emotion and communication (ill. 2.4.28). BRT: "Because what would innovative architecture be without the people who use it?"[77]

The planned sheath, which in the form envisaged resembled the fuselage of an aircraft, could not, unfortunately, be realised, but was adapted to the rapidly changing conditions in the rail and air travel market and mutated into a – still fascinating – glass shed on the upper deck, a 'glass tank', but with no claim to being a new construction typology. The glass framework is to be found in the load-bearing system and is on the lines of the glass hall designed by gmp and Ian Ritchie for Neue Messe Leipzig (1994–95), with the decisive difference, however, that BRT did not design a barrel, but rather a flattened ellipsoid, shaped by means of an arched sheaf with varying degrees of curvature along a flat 'creating piece' in a longitudinal direction (ill. 2.4.29).

BRT's design for the through station in Dortmund follows a similar approach: here, too, it is a shell, a mussel-like figure that encloses a multi-functional urban space. It sits, as if movable, on the iron rails and is not looking for any direct link with the city (ills. 2.4.30 and 2.4.31).

It is to be hoped that the new underground extension to the station Stuttgart 21 will be built. The design is the work of Ingenhoven, Overdiek und Partner, and Frei Otto acted as consultant. It is an attempt to enshroud the new world of communications, which operates in virtual space, with the ephemerally-oriented construction typology of membrane technology and to stand in the face of the monumental train stations by Paul Bonatz and Friedrich Eugen Scholer from 1911–28. The implementation planning of "Stuttgart 21" was activated in 2007 (ill. 2.4.32).

In the form of the TGV terminals, the French railroad is also pursuing visionary concepts (Lille, Lyons), and it would seem that throughout the world the railroad is being rediscovered, with a new 'branding' being defined by means of fascinating constructions: in addition to 'grande vitesse' in a comfortable fauteuil with every media form available, the station is becoming a new identifying urban place – a symbol of forthcoming terminal architecture (ill. 2.4.33).

2.4.28

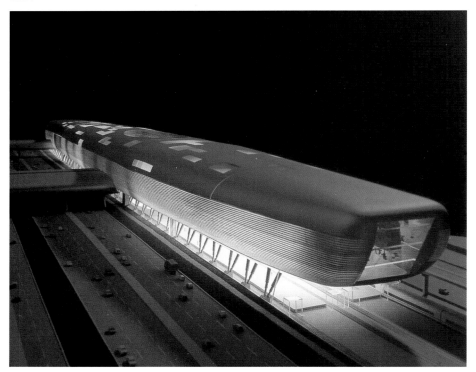

2.4.28: Bothe Richter Teherani: ICE airport terminal, Frankfurt/Main; model photo for the competition entry

2.4.29: ICE airport terminal, Frankfurt/Main: interior of the glass hall on the upper platform

2.4.30, 2.4.31: Bothe Richter Teherani: Dortmund station; photomontages

2.4.32: Ingenhoven, Overdiek und Partner with Frei Otto: design for the new station in Stuttgart; membrane formed canopy with tear shaped 'it eyes' complement the existing monumental train

2.4.33: Vision of Arhem Central station, Netherlands; architects: UN Studio/Ben van Berkel; engineers: Arup Associates, London

2.4.31

2.4.30

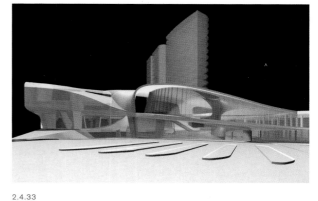

2.4.33

2.4.32

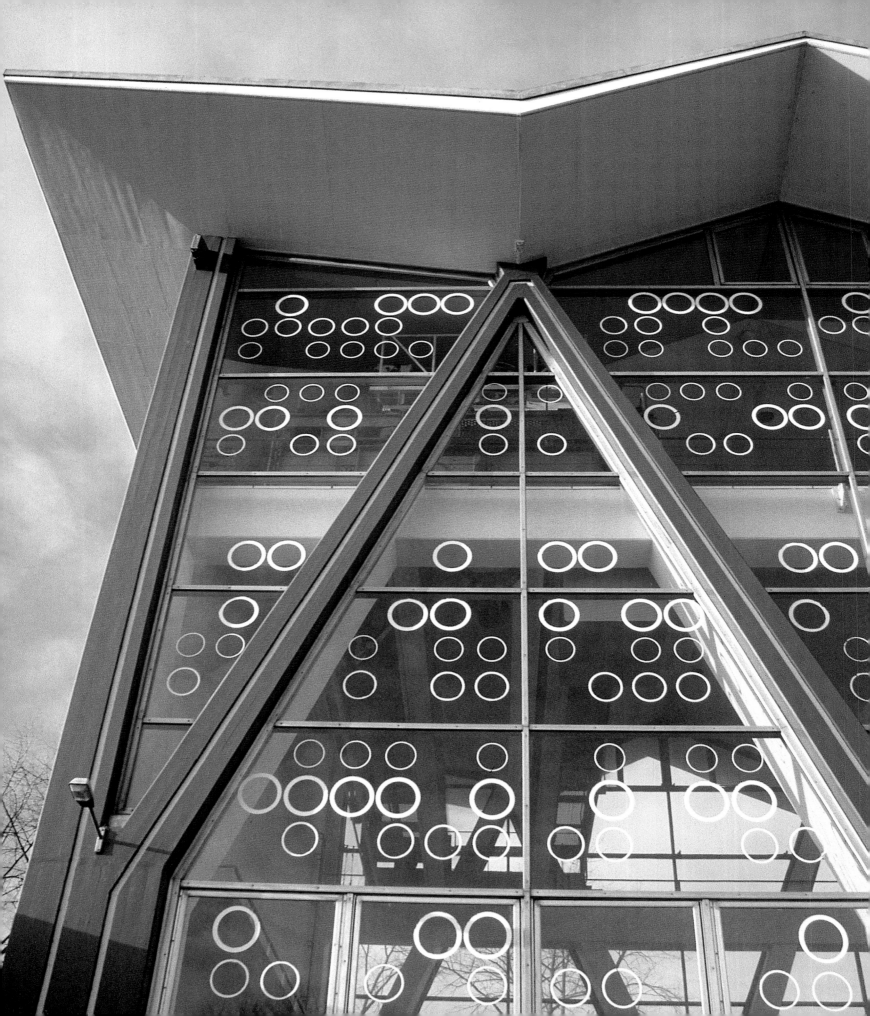

3 How Concrete Became Lighter – 100 Years of Concrete Pioneers

The history of concrete as a building material does not begin only at the end of the 'Age of Iron' around 1900 – in fact, with François Hennebique's patent of 1892 concrete moved into the field of vision of architects and engineering construction. Until this point this material had mostly been used for functions where it was not visible, such as bridge abutments or foundations, or as stabilising filler material. Since the Pantheon in Rome the use of concrete had been restricted to those areas where a material with compressive strength was required, which meant that the design repertoire consisted of arches, barrel vaults and spheres.[1] Chemistry as an 'industrial science' and the École Centrale des Arts et Manufactures in Paris, where this subject had been taught since 1830, played key roles in the research and utilisation of knowledge about concrete and in preparing it for use as a formative building material.

Pioneering period – concrete as a design means The discoveries of François Hennebique (ill. 3.1), Robert Maillart and Eugène Freyssinet, who were the most important developers of concrete's new design importance, were preceded by numerous amateur experiments as well as by scientific investigations. These included the patent for the wire-reinforced flowerpot by the gardener Joseph Monier (1867), who constructed a bridge spanning 16 metres as early as 1875 (ill. 3.2).[2] In 1854 Joseph Louis Lambot presented a boat made of concrete at the *World Fair* in Paris. Monier and Lambot thus introduced a new and modern world of forms made of concrete, comparable, for example, with John Claudius Loudon's experiments in the area of building with glass.[3]

Scientific experiments François Coignet (1814–88), a pioneer of the early days of reinforced concrete, had a pioneering influence with regard to the industrialisation of building in concrete. In England in 1855 he registered a patent for iron rods connected at right angles to be used as reinforcement in concrete beams, and a number of years later he published a scientific treatise with the title *Béton aggloméré à l'art de construire* (Paris 1861). Parallel to this the American Thaddeus Hyatt (1816–1901) made an important contribution to using iron and concrete together in building through his experiments with the correct positioning of the reinforcement iron in the tension zone and in the bearing area of beams (around 1850).[4] Thus he anticipated Hennebique and founded a new technological school of thought that Ernest Leslie Ransome (1844–1917) was later to develop industrially, and from which Albert Kahn also profited in building his automobile factories (ill. 3.3; cf. case study 71).

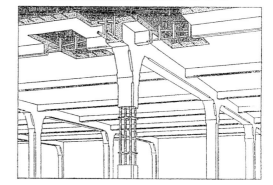

CONSTRUCTIONS EN BÉTON ARMÉ 3.1
Inaltérables et à l'épreuve du feu
Système HENNEBIQUE, Breveté S. G. D. G.

3.1: Logo Système Hennebique, 1892

3.2: A further concrete bridge that employs the Monier System was built in 1890 near Wildegg in Switzerland.

3.3: Albert Kahn's first automobile factory in concrete: Ford Motor Company, Highland Park, Michigan, USA, 1909/10; building skeleton

3.0: Hans Hofmann designed an attractive folded plate structure with a precisely detailed system of splayed columns for Birsfelden Rhine Power Station near Basle; engineers: A. Aegerter and O. Bosshardt

Edmond Coignet (1856–1915) studied at the École Centrale des Arts et Manufactures in Paris (graduating in 1879) and subsequently developed the work of his father François in terms of its industrial application, and perfected the sintering process (*béton aggloméré*). As both scientist and businessman he was also one of the inventors of the concrete column and of earthquake-proof concrete construction, which he carried out in numerous countries. The national concrete award, *Le Prix François Coignet*, goes back to the Coignet family.[5]

Experiment and method Thus two discovery processes that essentially ran parallel to each other characterise the early use of concrete as a design means: the empirical experimentation of the American Hyatt and the French gardener Monier, and the systematic, scientific and industrial research of the chemicals and building entrepreneur François Coignet and his son Edmond in France. The remarkable thing here is that, like with the construction of glasshouses and iron halls, it became clear that the two different schools of thought – the 'shop culture' with its more physics-based experiments, and the 'school culture' in the research area of industrial chemistry – shaped the pioneering era of concrete as a modern building material.

3.4

Concrete – the building material of the 20th century In that it addressed and documented the state of concrete technology since the pioneering days, the 1900 *World Fair* in Paris marks an opening. The great forward thrust of architecture in concrete developed, above all, after 1900 through the mass production of consumer goods for a society that had become more mobile (factories, industrial complexes), and after 1920 through the enormous post-war need for large housing estates, sanatoriums, schools, etc. The modernism of the period between the wars additionally adopted a programme that was based either on committed entrepreneurs or on a strengthened, socio-politically inspired working class: new worlds of work as dignified, bright and healthy workplaces and workshops, factories and studios. In addition to the native countries of the pioneers – France, England and America – in the Netherlands, Germany, Italy and Switzerland there came into being new schools of thought in the area of architecture in concrete which exerted their effect far into the era of post-war modernism (ill. 3.4).

3.5

Post-war modern age A further thrust occurred after 1945 through the reconstruction of destroyed cities and infrastructures as well as due to the economic and industrial boom: the post-war modernism of the 1950s and the 1960s was able to exploit the design means offered by innovations in the area of material technology and considerably lighter structures in concrete. For example, the design of transparent spaces, lightweight construction façades, and 'hovering' roofs, such as those by Egon Eiermann and Sep Ruf, were made possible by slender concrete frame construction: reinforced concrete relieves the façade of the load (ill. 3.5). This is also the era of a new kind of shell constructions, such as those by Eduardo Torroja, Eladio Dieste and Felix Candela, and by Heinz Isler and Heinz Hossdorf – the outcome of experimental form-finding processes.

Système Hennebique: the design strength of reinforced concrete Hennebique's patent of the 'ribbed or T-beam slab' from 1892, which presented the expressiveness of the structural junction between column and beam in the form of a haunch that became a new trademark, suited an era in which a strongly expressive will to create form, 'structural honesty' and the 'Neue Sachlichkeit' of modernism were important tendencies. It meant liberation from the linear structure of the steel frame, a move towards the structured surface, towards the cantilever, freedom from a specific direction, and the removal of weight from the façade. Tony Garnier used the Système Hennebique for his project for *Une Cité Industrielle* (1900/01), and the brothers Auguste and Gustave Perret for their first town palace in Paris shortly after 1900. Modern, naturally-lit factories were inconceivable without the Hennebique licence.

Robert Maillart: the invention of the mushroom column   Through the use of mushroom columns the Swiss bridge-builder Robert Maillart, who also started his career with Hennebique licences, made it possible to avoid disruptive ribs and beams in the soffit: by fictively rotating Hennebique's haunch around its own axis he achieved a regular, circular and – depending on the reinforcement – extensive field of tension around the column axis which rendered downbeams superfluous ('flat slab' construction; 1909). His mushroom ceiling slabs represented a pioneering invention that expanded the possibilities of design in terms of architecture, space and construction. The new 'flatness' of such structures also matched the clarity and simplicity in the visual depiction of the flow of structural forces found in his bridges (ill. 3.6).

3.6

Eugène Freyssinet: concepts for free spatial forms   Eugène Freyssinet ventured a step further by developing a completely new concrete technology that allowed free spatial forms, and through his work on pre-tensioning reinforced concrete. Through research and experiments on the behaviour of concrete in the curing and consolidation processes Freyssinet observed potential methods of forming the material and in this way created the preconditions for a decisive expansion of the design forms used in concrete constructions (cf. ill. 3.0)

Concrete and tectonically formed space   The energy crisis sparked by the October war in 1973 led to a shift of paradigms in the aims and goals of using reinforced concrete: in Central European countries, in particular, there developed a tendency to use massive building methods. This was not the case in England and France, where a parallel development started in the area of lightweight and glass construction, largely a consequence of exploring the use of concrete skeletal frames in building (ill. 3.7).

3.7

Since the 1990s and the critical questioning of postmodernism we can discern also in the area of building in concrete – as in the areas of glass, steel and lightweight construction – a "new constructivism", which allows us recognise an interest in sensitivity to materials, visualised structure and construction, and static or dynamic modes of operation. A variety of possibilities of expression and perception has been produced by new findings in the field of material technology static cognitions, tectonic and structural design, as shown, for example, in the de Menil Collection Museum from Renzo Piano and his football stadium near Bari, the current pre-stressed constructions by Swiss engineers Jürg Conzett and Joseph Schwartz. Thus the area of design for architects, engineers and material technologists has been considerably expanded.

About 100 years have passed since the first buildings based on Hennebique's patent. Numerous engineers, creative architects and businesses shaped the great 'concrete building school' of the 20th century: from Mies van der Rohe and the 'bony' T-beam slabs in his drawings for an office block dating from 1923 to Eero Saarinen and his John F. Kennedy International Airport in New York (1956–62) – a basis for further research in the direction of a light and sustainable concrete construction technology.

3.4: Owen Williams: pharmaceuticals factory, Beeston, England, 1930–32

3:5: Egon Eiermann: Kaufhaus Merkur, Reutlingen, 1952/53

3.6: Robert Maillart: Salginatobel Bridge near Schiers, Canton Grisons, Switzerland, 1929/30

3.7: Norman Foster: Carré d'Art, Nîmes, 1984–93, in context and reference field to the antique temple

3.1 Concrete: The Building Material of the 20th Century

The reason concrete emerged relatively late (around 1900) as a modern building material has to do with the scientific and technical theory and the schools of thought and school cultures that developed it. That concrete technology so rapidly shifted the use of iron and steel as structural materials and design means into second place was due to the brilliant 'project of modernism' and its urgent building tasks: naturally-lit factories, sanatoriums oriented towards the sun, light-flooded schools, large, humane housing developments (in Berlin, Frankfurt, Amsterdam, Rotterdam and elsewhere) profited from the industrial standards of concrete technology and, additionally, influenced a way of thinking based on building systems and standardised building elements (see chapter 5).

Building material for a new urban vision

Ildefonso Cerdà's urban project for Barcelona *Eixample* (1859) founded the modern theory and practice of urbanisation (1867) and was a precursor of the 'new city' of the 20th century, which was continued by Ebenezer Howard's garden city concept (1898). Shortly afterwards the third new kind of urban concept followed: Tony Garnier's → Cité Industrielle, which anticipated the 1933 CIAM concept of functionally distinct zones.[6] Garnier used the Système Hennebique – for the first time since it had been patented – as a uniform, systematic, new building technique, employing the expressive form of its structural effect and efficiency for his vision of the city.

Concrete: ideological raw material of the avant-garde

In the early period of modern architecture *le béton armé* was the benchmark of an epochal trend: Hennebique published a widely-read journal under this title, which, thanks to the ambiguity of the name, could also be understood as a kind of call to arms. The Perret brothers and Le Corbusier also used the slogan as a 'logo' for their notepaper.

The avant-garde saw concrete as the means of overcoming the old, style-based schools and of shaping the new – reinforced concrete was thus coded as the building material of the architecture of the future. According to J. J. P. Oud, architect and member of the De-Stijl group and an important theorist on new ways of seeing in the design of space and form: "Reinforced concrete makes possible the homogeneous combination of supporting and supported parts, as well as allowing horizontal extensions of significant dimensions and a pure definition of areas and mass. Additionally, however, in contrast to the old system of piers and loads in which, from above and below, one can only build inwards (that is, backwards), it allows us also to build from below to above and outwards (namely, forwards). The latter offers us the possibility of a new architectural plasticity, which, when combined with the design opportunities offered by iron and glass – on a structural basis – can lead to the development of an architecture with a visually immaterial, almost hovering appearance."[7] The new building material thus represented a design tool that formed a style; reinforced concrete became a programme (ill. 3.1.1).

The architects who founded CIAM in La Sarraz in Switzerland in 1927[8] worked on specific projects that covered wide areas and demanded social and political acceptance – a sign of the end of the pioneering spirit and the start of normative aspirations. The founding manifesto states that reinforced concrete allows standardisation and, as a modern means of expression, favours the 'liberated plan': "*les murs portants n'existent plus*."[9] Alongside the skeletal concrete structure all that remains are lightweight partition walls in the interior and façades hung in front of the structure. The use of the new building materials, means of construction and production

3.1.1

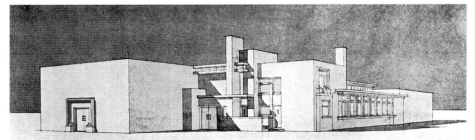

How Concrete Became Lighter

was to become the universal programme of modernism (ill. 3.1.2).

In Italy, parallel to 'futurismo', the architectural avant-garde was forming itself, as the 'Movimento Italiano per l'Architetttura Razionale' (M.I.A.R.) and its advance troops, the Gruppo 7 from Como (see section 2.3, case study 23).[10] Here, reinforced concrete did not play an idealised role as a medium of stylistic meaning that gave 'Neue Sachlichkeit' a material form, as was the case in Holland, but a material role as a medium of function for ideological programmes in the political context of fascism's need to present itself – the architecture debate was shaped by an ideological instrumentalisation of concrete as a material (ill. 3.1.3).

In the fourth document of the Gruppo 7 issued in 1926/27 'stressed concrete' is regarded as the basis for the 'spirito nuovo': "But everyone, or almost everyone, in Italy disputes that stressed concrete can advance to monumental values. Nothing could be further from the truth than this: If there is any material that can achieve a monumental classicism then it is *precisely* stressed concrete and it develops this from *Rationalism*."[11] This dualism – 'spirito nuovo' and monumentality – opened up the way for the protagonists of the Architettura Razionale to coordinate all architectural tendencies under the hegemony of fascist building programmes (ill. 3.1.4).[12]

As early as 1925 the magazine → *ABC* produced a double issue on the theme of concrete which expressed an astonishing degree of modern self-awareness: the issue is no longer the battle for a new style but finding practical instructions that can offer an answer to the simple question: "How do we build in a modern way?"

'Béton armé': expressive design tool of the architecture of the future

The pioneers of modernism used reinforced concrete not merely as a structural and technical means of giving form, but also connected with it a philosophical and theoretical way of thinking and seeing, and thus defined a new style in opposition to the old, academically influenced one. With the possibilities offered by the cantilever, rib slabs (Hennebique) or mushroom columns (Maillart), it became possible to 'liberate' the façade from its structural function and to replace it with a glass skin

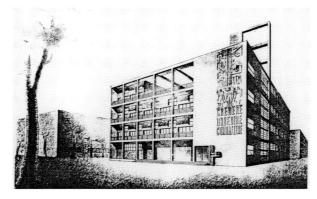

3.1.3

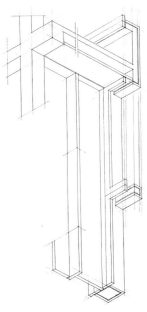

3.1.4

hung in front of the building – which could also be continued around the corner. This innovation in the areas of construction and material technology became the programme of Modernism and was the technical response to the new theory of space and the spatial perception of 'transparency' suggested in Frank Lloyd Wright's Prairie Houses.[13] Reinforced concrete could be used to implement these theories – béton armé became the code of Modernism (ill 3.1.5).

Le Corbusier's → Domino house type is an expression of a synthesis of liberated space with a structure given built form through concrete technology. Here, however, the depiction of the vision is at odds with the construction used to implement it: Six years after Maillart's invention of the mushroom column the possibility offered by columns that carried concrete slabs without the use of downbeams ('flat slab construction') – and therefore with no dominant direction – had not yet been grasped by Le Corbusier, a phenomenon we also encounter in Gropius's Bauhaus in Dessau.

3.1.5

The Ideal Industrial City – Cité Industrielle

Project, 1900/01
Architect: Tony Garnier

Tony Garnier (1869–1948), the son of the famous architect of the Opera House in Paris, Charles Garnier, studied, like his father, at the École des Beaux-Arts, first of all in Lyons (1886) and from 1889 in Paris, under Julien Guadet among others.[14] In 1899 he won the much-coveted 'Prix de Rome', which allowed him to spend two years in Rome, living in the Villa Medici. It was during this period that he produced his design for a virtual city in the Rhône valley, to the south of his native city, Lyons. He called it Cité Industrielle – drawn in an unornamented 'manière Beaux-Arts', organised as a proto-functionalist organism and built in a rational and plain fashion using the Système Hennebique (ill. 3.1.6).[15]

The degree of complexity and concreteness with which ideas are implemented in Garnier's design is extraordinary, if one compares the precision of the statements it contains with, say, the diagrams of the ideas that Ebenezer Howard developed around the same time for his Garden City (1898).[16] About the method of construction Garnier wrote in an accompanying text: "The materials used are aggregate concrete for the foundations and walls, and reinforced cement for the floor and ceiling slabs and roofs. All important buildings are built almost entirely of reinforced cement."[17]

Whereas Garnier still suggested the use of the pisé method for constructing the walls,[18] the floor and ceiling slabs made of reinforced concrete with continuous reinforcement followed the Hennebique method. Garnier drew the precisely dimensioned reinforcement plans himself (ill. 3.1.7).

Various drawings from this enormous oeuvre refer to the Hennebique system, which is characterised by junctions between the verticals of the columns and the horizontal ceiling beams that are strengthened through the use of haunches. This is clearly legible in the building complex containing the meeting halls at the centre of the city, in the clock-tower, the interior of the baths, the hydrotherapy centre, as well as in the heliotherapy treatment centres.

In addition to presenting what were at the time the most modern symbols of the achievements of building technology, the Système Hennebique, the public meeting halls at the centre of the Cité industrielle have a frieze running along the entire external wall above the columnar hall with long quotations from Émile Zola's extremely critical novel *Travail* (ill. 3.1.8). As a member of a Lyons society of friends of Zola, Tony Garnier will hardly have missed the advance extracts from this novel that were printed in 1900 in the newspaper *L'Aurore* and the ideas it contained on the reorganisation of capital and labour, using the example of the ideal city La Crêcherie, probably served as a source of inspiration in developing his new ideal industrial city.[19]

For the widely cantilevered and self-supporting canopy roof to the railway station (ill. 3.1.9) Garnier did not use Hennebique's new construction principles but anticipated future developments by using a ceiling slab carried on mushroom-head columns, and space-defining walls without structural elements – an anticipation of Robert Maillart's invention in 1909, and an important theme of Modernism in the 1920s and 1930s.

Exposing the raw concrete construction in the appearance of the exterior and – to an extent – the interior of the building makes clear that here Garnier is presenting an entirely new, original vision of architecture and urban planning. Perhaps with the fascinating monumental simplicity exuded by the remnants of classical Rome in front of his eyes,[20] he relativised the traditional, style-based school and, using elementary design means and a monolithic approach to materials, conceived a modern framework for his humanist, positivist ideas on the city – very much in the same direction as Saint Simon's[21] school of thought (ill. 3.1.10) – the Cité Industrielle, a synthesis?

Tony Garnier worked in Lyons as an architect and, from 1912, as a teacher of architecture, long before his project for the Cité Industrielle was published in 1917. Thanks to his good connections to the socialist mayor of the time, Édouard Herriot, he was able to carry out fragments of this urban project in his native city Lyons: Grange-Blanche hospital, the stadium and the abattoir, as well as a number of villas.[22]

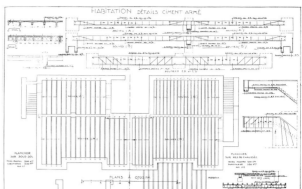

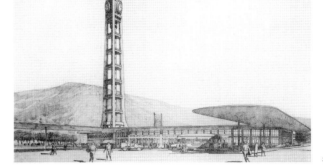

3.1.9

3.1.8

3.1.6: Overall view of the industrial district

3.1.7: Reinforcement and detail plans, drawn by Tony Garnier

3.1.8: Hennebique trademark as the medium that carries quotations from Émile Zola's critical novel *Travail* (1901) on the frieze of the central meeting hall

3.1.9: Railway station canopy and clock tower

3.1.10: Applied arts school designed for the Cité Industrielle: synthesis of 'academicism' and the new school of thought of concrete technology

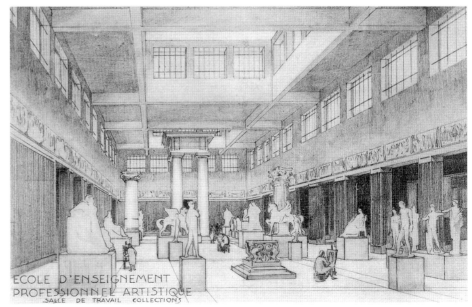

3.1.10

The Magazine *ABC*

1924-28
Published by:
Emil Roth, Hans Schmidt,
Mart Stam, El Lissitzky

In the first issue of the magazine *ABC* (1924) the Russian constructivist El Lissitzky wrote about the principles of modern design: "The modern designer examines the tasks he is set in terms of the functions that they have to fulfil. For each function he selects the appropriate element (...) Where two or more elements are brought together, a kind of tension is created. The manner in which the forces of tension are made to balance determines the construction. In addition to the compressive forces of load and pier, in modernism tension forces emerge as a new kind of expression. In this way the open rib is created. Modernism separates the parts in tension from the adjoining, enclosing elements. It does not wish to cover up, mask, or decorate. It represents the healthiness of nudity. The elements for the material – according to resistance: concrete (compression), iron (tension), etc."[23]

The double issue of *ABC* (no. 3/4) from 1925 already referred to was dedicated to concrete. The introductory text to this avant-garde magazine was devoted to technical demands and new discoveries in the field of concrete shuttering technology for *in situ* concrete. The contribution is illustrated with the example of a largely industrialised building method using movable shuttering that was employed for Eugène Freyssinet's airship hangar built in Orly in 1923. This was followed by a piece about the new materials, with a header that read: "Modern materials are the product of our industry. They are made by chemists from raw materials and produced by machine."[24] Mart Stam showed two examples of his elegant reworking of visionary drawings by Mies van der Rohe, one of which was for the latter's concrete office building of 1923 (ill. 3.1.11).

In addition, building systems are explained (for example, Le Corbusier's Maison Domino), and the advantages offered by prefabricated building elements are loudly praised. Requirements (such as those for prefabricated concrete window frames) are defined in considerable detail, and, although such frames are praised in an advertisement placed by a concrete products factory (ill. 3.1.12), they appear not to have been completely satisfactory, as new solutions were called for. "We need: a frame with a minimum weight and minimal strength, in standard sizes for windows and doors, made in a single

piece (...) with all the necessary rebates for making the joint with the façade render, incorporating the brick or blockwork and fixing the external winter-time window, the blocks for hanging the folding shutters, the sleeves for screwing the sub-frame of the inner window, and all of these poured in concrete."[25] This was de facto an anticipation of the technical perfection of the prefab culture of building that was to develop 30 years later (see chapter 5).

Finally, the magazine introduces new concrete processes: gas, steel and torcrete concrete. The design qualities and effects, in terms of architecture, construction and building physics, are described, as are the technologies of production and processing, and examples of use are shown. The inventors are also mentioned. This concrete issue of *ABC* forced the protagonists of building, in particular the building firms, to take action, to invent rapidly and to implement at almost the same time. This is no longer the age of the pioneers but of the doers. The issues are building, the method of manufacture, material and technology. The idealised style is born, to be followed shortly by the time of patents, standards and implementation on a broad scale. Time is of the essence. The urgent problems of the time encourage construction. The programme of Modernism must be implemented right across the board: in model and large housing estates (ill. 3.1.13), schools and kindergardens, factories for the production of mass goods, sanatoriums (ill. 3.1.14), hospitals as well as leisure facilities, baths and public event halls.

Le Corbusier presented his Pavillon de l'Esprit Nouveau at the 1925 *Exposition des Arts Décoratifs* in Paris. The Schroeder House in Utrecht by Gerrit Thomas Rietveld was built in 1924. A large experimental building site for the construction of mass housing in Berlin was started by Stadtbaumeister Martin Wagner in the form of the Hufeisensiedlung (1925-31) and by the founding of the GEHAG housing association in 1924, and preparations for the New Frankfurt were made by Ernst May (1925-33). The guidelines of the *ABC* avant-garde lay in the field of tension between proto-typical building production for Neues Bauen and the wide-ranging aspirations of the new style.

How Concrete Became Lighter

3.1.11

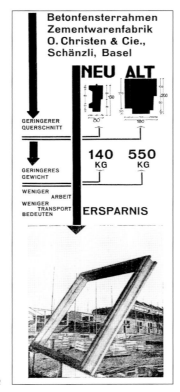

3.1.12

3.1.11: Office building in concrete by Ludwig Mies van der Rohe (1923); reworked by Mart Stam: in contrast to Mies's design the cantilevered concrete beams taper (see also ill. 3.2.4).

3.1.12: Advertisement for prefabricated concrete window frames in *ABC,* no. 3/4, 1925

3.1.13: J. J. P. Oud: workers' housing estate Kiefhoek, Rotterdam, 1925–29

3.1.14: Johannes Duiker, Bernard Bijvoet and Jan Gerko Wiebenga (engineer): Sanatorium Zonnestraal, Hilversum, 1926–28

3.1.13

3.1.14

Case Study 33

The Domino Model

Project, 1915
Architect: Le Cobusier

ESTHÉTIQUE DE L'INGÉNIEUR

MAISONS en SÉRIE

PAR

LE CORBUSIER-SAUGNIER

In the journal *L'Esprit Nouveau*[26] Le Corbusier published 1921 a concept under the title "Houses in Series" (ill. 3.1.15) in which he asserted: "The first effects of industrial development in the 'building industry' are shown in the following early phase: natural building materials are replaced by artificial materials, building materials with heterogeneous and dubious composition are replaced by homogeneous, artificially produced materials tested in laboratories and made of unchanging basic materials. Unchanging material must replace natural, limitlessly changeable material. In addition, the laws of economics assert their presence: steel sections and, since a short time ago, reinforced concrete are an expression of the art of calculation, which precisely and completely evaluates the material, whereas in earlier days old timber beams might have had problematic hidden knots, and giving them their rectangular shape meant a considerable loss of material."[27]

In this study Le Corbusier refers to his patent for the Maison Domino of 1915, a construction system intended to be serially produced in reinforced concrete, and to its industrial potential. The two drawings of the Domino house type reproduced in *Œuvre complète* (ills. 3.1.16 and 3.1.17) show contradictory images: on the one hand, there is a perspective of a two-storey construction with 6 columns, 3 unstructured slabs and a concrete staircase connected with the slabs and with 2 of the columns; on the other hand, there is a two-dimensional construction plan combined with a reflected ceiling plan: this plan shows 8 columns, and 3 longitudinal main beams cantilevered at both ends and one cantilevered at a single end, 2 cross beams of the same dimensions running between the longitudinal beams and connected with the columns, as well as three longitudinal secondary beams to take the *hourdis* elements – here, cantilevers at the ends are not possible. How the problem of the corner in front of the stairs was to be solved remains unclear.[28]

Whereas the plan of the structural system as well as the section through the ceiling slab clearly show a structure with a direction – like the traditional pattern of a timber beam ceiling – and thus implies a direction in the layout of the spaces, the perspective irritates in that it presents a homogeneous slab construction without ribs or mushroom heads. The façade that can apparently be continued freely around the corner, or even has a free

corner, is misleading about the real nature of the building structure. Nor are the structural elements required to brace the load-bearing frame shown. The rigid junctions that are essential could be achieved only by fixed storey-height frames – an erroneous concept?[29]

During 1908/09, for a period of 14 months, Le Corbusier worked half-days in the Paris studio of Auguste and Gustave Perret – the concrete pioneers of the early days – in the building on Rue Franklin that entered the annals of building technology history as the prototype of the Système Hennebique (see following case study 34). Since the Paris *World Fair* of 1900 Hennebique's studio had designed not only rib slabs but also ribbed structures without a dominant direction and even concrete slabs without ribs or downstand beams (cf. ill. 3.2.3). Le Corbusier failed to recognise the design potential of the Système Hennebique or that of the mushroom column and flat slab developed by Maillart in 1909. The space of the Maison Domino is modern, but the structure and construction remain traditional.

Even today, in its renovated state, the basic structure of Le Corbusier's Villa Schwob (Turque) in La Chaux-de-Fonds in Switzerland (1916/17) still illustrates the Domino house type on the lower floor as well as a concrete structure based on the rib slab system and junctions with a dominant direction from the more robust Mörsch system (ill. 3.1.18) – despite Le Corbusier's personal contact to Hennebique through Amédée Ozenfant[30] and despite the declaration: "Ch.-E. Jeanneret – architecte béton armé" used as his letterhead in the correspondence Le Corbusier conducted with his client Anatole Schwob (ill. 3.1.19)![31] Did Le Corbusier flirt with the "state-of-the-art"?

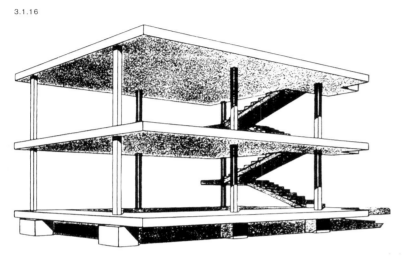

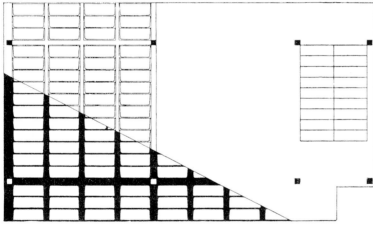

3.1.17

Ch.-E. Jeanneret - architecte
BÉTON ARMÉ

LA CHAUX-DE-FONDS, RUE NUMA DROZ 54, le ...ia   Paris 6 10 mars   TÉL. 959
1917

BUREAU DE PARIS:
13, RUE DE BELZUNCE

3.1.19

3.1.15: Le Corbusier: title page of *Maisons en Serie*, 1921

3.1.16, 3.1.17: Domino house type: two images, different construction typologies. In *Œuvre complète* the ceiling slab construction is erroneously described as a concrete slab.

3.1.18: Le Corbusier: Villa Schwob in La Chaux-de-Fonds, basement ceiling slab with the Mörsch system

3.1.19: Le Corbusier's letterhead

3.2 Système Hennebique: The Strength of Reinforced Concrete in Design

3.2.1: Title page of *Le Béton Armé*

3.2.2: Maurice Braillard: mountain station of Salève cable railway with restaurant and hotel, perspective from 1931

3.2.3: Palais des Lettres, Sciences et Arts, Paris *World Exhibition*, 1900; architect: Sortais; contractor: Cordier

3.2.1

3.2.2

Inventions, patents and the system

François Hennebique (1842–1921), who belonged to the first generation of concrete pioneers, completed an apprenticeship as a stonemason and at the age of 25 set up his own business. The development of the Système Hennebique took about 12 years, until in 1892/93 the decisive patents opened up the way to the development of a worldwide business empire,[32] and simple use in construction and the first prototypes in monolithic concrete building became possible.[33]

The business was so successful that in 1905 the Système Hennebique already had about a fifth of the world market in the area of concrete construction; 380 people were employed in 50 construction offices and every day throughout the world over 10,000 building workers worked on Hennebique building sites.[34] At the same time, Hennebique's advertising and 'activist' magazine *Le Béton Armé* (1894–1914) took on the competition from steel construction systems (ill. 3.2.1).[35]

On the occasion of the 1900 *World Exhibition* in Paris the new school of thought of reinforced concrete presented itself as superior and seemed to signal the end of the 'Age of Iron'. A completely new building material was now available: in the context of the developing mass production of goods, monolithic concrete construction combined the advantages of structural robustness, large spans, simple corner connections and cantilevers. By means of dramatic photographs in *Le Béton Armé* Hennebique propagandised the safety of this material with regard to fire and earthquakes.

The École Centrale in Paris and the Système Hennebique

At the École Centrale des Arts et Manufactures (ECAM) a basic knowledge of chemistry was taught to allow an understanding of the qualities of iron and concrete and their combined use. 'Chimie industielle', the applied theory of building materials, formed the basis for uniform standards in the training of architects and engineers and, at an early stage, opened up for them the way towards the material and building technology of reinforced concrete.[36] Graduates of the ECAM such as Maurice Dumas (graduation 1892) in the studios of François Hennebique took part in the development of reinforced concrete

technology and in the patents; ECAM engineers F. Perret and M. Martinez were journalists with *Le Béton Armé*.[37]

Hennebique's promotion

Hennebique produced good reasons for the use of concrete: safety in the case of earthquakes, fire resistance, and structural reliability – also in the case of movable loads. Whereas concrete itself as a material does not demand any specific forms or sculptural shaping, the typology of iron reinforcement does: Hennebique's invention of continuous reinforcement in the transition from the vertical column to the horizontal beam illustrated concrete's monolithic character and its rigidity, which Hennebique praised as unequalled. Precisely at the point where the bending moment is greatest – or the system is weakest – the Hennebique system's most visible symbol could be employed: the haunch, an expressive element, rigid in terms of material but light in its visual effect, was made by Hennebique into a typical 'branding' and company 'logo'. It was also to develop into a trademark of the constructive and expressive tendencies of Modernism (ill. 3.2.2, cf. also ill. 3.1).

Congresses, visits to building sites combined with technical demonstrations, as well as the involvement of building protagonists and prominent politicians promoted a 'Hennebique lobby'. Instructions for licensees and quality control of all projects connected with the patent[38] helped to spread the system and to prevent damage and catastrophes.

Breakthrough at the 1900 *World Exhibition* in Paris

In addition to rib slabs Hennebique also constructed free shapes and cantilevers, as shown by the concrete pavilion at the 1900 *World Exhibition* in Paris – a demonstration of the lightness of concrete (ill. 3.2.3). The Dutch concrete school built upon this, for example, the architect Johannes Duiker and the engineer Jan Gerko Wiebenga.

A programme for Modernism

The first representative application of the Système Hennebique and a milestone at the beginning of Modernism was the → apartment house on rue Franklin in Paris by the Perret Brothers, who exploited the functional, sculptural, pictorial and expressive strength of this new build-

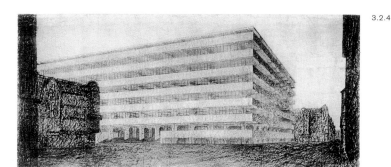

3.2.4: Ludwig Mies van der Rohe: office building made of concrete, Berlin, 1923; T-beam slab with cantilevers at two sides which do not taper, as they do with Duiker or in the reworking by Mart Stam, but still allow a version of the structurally unloaded 'liberated' corner (cf. ill. 3.1.11)

3.2.5: Casa il Girasole, Marcellise, 1929–35, mobile Hennebique construction

3.2.6: Albert Kahn: Ford Motor Company, Highland Park, Michigan, USA, 1909/10

3.2.7: Josef Fuchs, Oldrich Tyl: internal hall of the former Trade Fair Palace in Prague, 1924–28; today it serves as the National Gallery of Modern Art and Architecture.

ing material for their design concepts. The theoretical adaptation of concrete building techniques by the avant-garde, which has already been referred to, was expanded by Mies van der Rohe through his typological differentiation between 'bones' and 'skin', a theme that, while it had emerged in Chicago back around 1880, now opened up new opportunities (ill. 3.2.4).

The Système Hennebique also spread rapidly in Switzerland, as is shown by the example of one of the world's first daylight factories, the → Bally Shoe Factory in Dottikon in Canton Aargau. Numerous buildings followed before this system became a standard.[39]

The Casa il Girasole at Marcellise near Verona is the only building documented that uses the Hennebique construction type to prove its skeletal stability when used in a mobile structure showing the house following the path of the sun (ill. 3.2.5).[40]

The thrust provided by the automobile factories

After 1900, with the introduction of the assembly line, mass production began to exert its influence on industrial architecture. The modern production of motorcars by Henry Ford was the pacemaker in industrial mass production.[41] Detroit was the centre of this development; the first concrete skeleton frame structures for Packard (Detroit 1905) and Ford (1909/10), developed by architect Albert Kahn and his brother Julius, led to a patent which can be ranked with the discoveries of Hennebique and Ransome and did not require haunches (ill. 3.2.6; cf. case study 71).[42]

The 'transatlantic spark' reached northern Italy first. Giovanni Agnelli, the founder of the Fabbrica Italiana Automobili Torino (FIAT), visited Henry Ford on several occasions and regarded Albert Kahn's Ford Motor Company near Detroit as his model.[43] From 1916 to 1920 Agnelli had the → Lingotto works built outside the gates of the old town of Turin – at that time this was largest assembly-line factory, based on the Ford principles, in the old world.

The challenges of building large halls

For large studios, exhibition halls and churches,[44] as well as for market halls and representational buildings, architects, engineers and draughtsmen used rib slabs and rib constructions in reinforced concrete as a structural material. One example that demonstrates the Hennebique standards in virtuoso fashion is the former Trade Fair Palace in Prague, designed by the architects Josef Fuchs and Oldrich Tyl (ill. 3.2.7).

The Dutch culture of building in concrete

The avant-garde De Stijl movement manifested itself in the programme of a new style, a new spirit, and a new consciousness with regard to the architecture of the future. The movement of the 'Nieuwe Zakelijkheid' joined forces with De Stijl in 1926. In this framework the architects Johannes Duiker and Bernard Bijvoet together with the engineer Jan Gerko Wiebenga influenced a Dutch 'school of building in concrete' that referred to Hennebique. A number of → model buildings of Dutch modernism illustrate the principle of the rib slab as a prefabricated system – an industrial interpretation of the Hennebique system. After a period of research and experiment between 1923 and 1926 Duiker, Bijvoet and Wiebenga obtained their own patent

The German school of building in concrete

The culture of building in concrete in Germany was influenced by such theorists as Emil Mörsch, by experimental research work and, above all, by the Nuremberg company of Dyckerhoff & Widmann, which, like Hennebique's studio, had a broad background of experience and employed engineers such as Franz Dischinger and Ulrich Finsterwalder as pioneers of building in concrete. In the standardisation phase of concrete building technology (wholesale market halls, 'Jahrhunderthalle') Robert Vorhoelzer,[45] among others, expanded the range of forms and construction and as a teacher at the Technische Hochschule in Munich established a kind of modern 'school of post office buildings' with a number of model buildings for the Deutsche Post. Representational buildings of Bauhaus architecture such as the → Bauhaus Dessau itself (Walter Gropius and Adolf Meyer; 1925/26), or Hannes Meyer's Bundeschule of the ADGB in Bernau near Berlin (1928–30)[46] seem to refer to Hennebique.

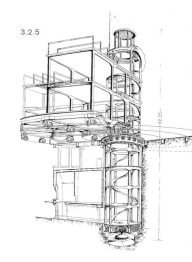

3.2.5

3.2.6

3.2.7

Apartment House

25bis rue Franklin
Paris, France, 1903
Architects: Auguste and
Gustave Perret
Building contractor:
Latron et Vincent

Two influences are detectable in the work of August Perret (1874–1954): the style-oriented and theory-influenced way of thinking of the École des Beaux-Arts that referred to Viollet-le-Duc, and the technical and industrial school of thought which explored new possibilities in building construction. As a consequence of their activities in the Paris Commune of 1870 Perret's parents had been forced to go into exile in Belgium. Auguste returned to Paris in 1881, where he attended the 'École', moved in avant-garde circles and, after completing his training, worked in the studio of Julien Guadet, under whom Tony Garnier also studied (cf. case study 31), until joining his father's building company. Together with his brother Gustave (1876–1952) he took over the management of the company in 1905. Under the name 'Perret Frères' it became one of the leading concrete building companies and was also an architects practice.[47]

In 1932 Pierre Vago described the apartment house at 25bis rue Franklin (opposite the Eiffel Tower, looking

3.2.8

across the Seine; ill. 3.2.8) as a pioneering building: "La première realisation de l'architecture du Béton armé: L'immeuble de Rapport de la rue Franklin à Paris."[48] In the chronicle of the history of reinforced concrete in the journal *Techniques et Architecture* it said in 1903: "A. et G. Perret, Architectes, introduisent le béton armé dans L'Architecture avec l'immeuble de la rue Franklin, à Paris."[49]

The Perret brothers began their work with this grand apartment building: the building at the same time demonstrates the expressive potential of 'béton armé' for the different kinds of building commissions that were to confront emerging modernism, also in the area of representational buildings – reinforced concrete became a stylistically formative construction material (ill. 3.2.9).

The Beaux-Arts influence as well as the modernity of the technical possibilities are perceptible in three dimensions of the concept: (1) the concrete skeletal frame defines the layout of the floor plans in terms of space and construction; (2) within the context of a classical 'triparta' with a pronounced plinth, a central part made up of typical standard storeys and a two-storey rooftop element in which the Perret ateliers were located until the beginning of the 1930s (Le Corbusier worked there), the Perret brothers allowed themselves a decidedly avant-garde solution on the ground-floor; the studios were moved there in 1933 (ill. 3.2.10); (3) while the façade facing towards the city is a decorative landscape composed of flat surfaces developed in a meandering sculptural manner, the 'bony' courtyard façade displays a bare structural skeleton with modern glass block elements (ill. 3.2.11)

The concrete structure was developed in conjunction with the building company of Latron et Vincent, a licence holder of the Système Hennebique. The columns measure 25 x 35 cm in cross-section, the span is 4 metres, and it proved possible to reduce the thickness of the floor slabs to a concrete core of only 8 cm![50] A version of the floor plans dating from 1 May 1903 shows the functional and spatial effects of the skeletal frame concept, but they were concealed in the design of the interior (ills. 3.2.12 and 3.2.13):

The area of tension between Beaux-Arts representation on the reception level and in the appearance of the interior, and the presence of engineering achievements and concrete building technology on the standard storeys remains visible in the overall image – the skeleton frame system organises the spatial plan and elevation. The expressiveness and the main characteristics of the structural, constructional and functional 'skeleton' that creates the overall appearance have a rationality comparable with the First Leiter Building of William Le Baron Jenney (1879) or the Reliance Building of Daniel Burnham in Chicago (1890–94);[51] however, Perret's crust of ornament contrasts with the plainness and practicality of the Chicago School.

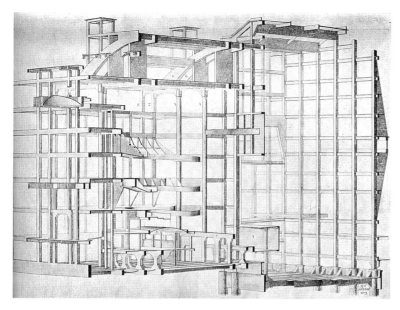

3.2.10

3.2.12

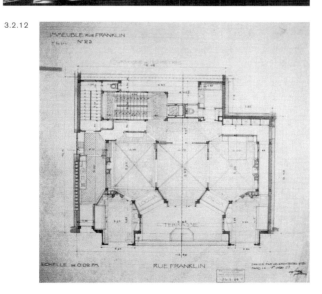

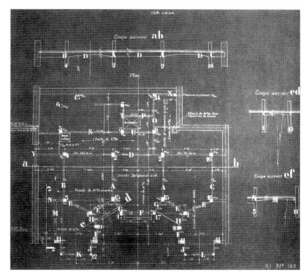

3.2.13

Bally Shoe Factory

At the same time as Albert Kahn built Henry Ford's first assembly line factory in Highland Park in Michigan, a concrete structural system was used for the new Bally shoe factory building in the Swiss village of Dottikon. Whereas Albert Kahn and his brother developed their own patent for a rib slab without haunches, the building contractor Locher & Cie. relied on their Hennebique licence. The Bally factory is probably the first large daylight factory spectacularly constructed according to the Système Hennebique. A year earlier the building contractor Porcheddu, a Hennebique licence-holder, had erected a small building for the Borsalino hat factory in Alessandria in Piemont (architect: Brezzi, engineer: Savoiardo; 1908). In 1911 this was followed by a shoe factory erected by a branch of the Hennebique company in Boston, Massachusetts.[52] And seven years after the erection of the Bally factory the engineer Giacomo Mattè Trucco, commissioned by Giovanni Agnelli to design the Lingotto Works in Turin, the largest motorcar factory in the old world, produced a symbol with considerable impact (here again Porcheddu was the licence-holder and building contractor). It was mere chance that the Bally factory was not based on Maillart's mushroom column and flat slab, given that Maillart also worked with Locher & Cie., and that this invention was already known at the time.

The Bally company erected another large shoe factory outside their headquarters in Schönenwerd to utilise a further catchment area of potential labour. The location Dottikon in Freiamt in Canton Aargau was within easy reach of a number of surrounding villages. The main means of transport used by the 1,500 male and female workers was the bicycle, but company bus services were also operated (ill. 3.2.14).[53]

The 8-storey main wing (with 5 regular storeys above ground level), which is about 85 metres long and only 16 metres wide, was used for the manufacture of different types of shoes. The short, lower transverse wing contained offices and the dispatch department (ill. 3.2.15).

In terms of construction and space the layout was designed for a production system based on Henry Ford's assembly-line principle and Frederick Taylor's system of 'scientific management' in which work was organised according to piecework and time units (ill. 3.2.16).[54]

The Hennebique system was eminently suitable for this rigid organisational model thanks to its large spans and structural robustness, combined with flexibility for the line production units. The relatively thin concrete ceiling slabs allowed the bays between the main beams to be used for ventilation ducts. Depending on the time of year these introduced cold or preheated air into the manufacturing storeys. In winter a central coal-powered steam heating system was used (ill. 3.2.17).

The concrete skeleton system was clad externally at parapet level with exposed clinker brickwork. The window openings filled the entire bay between the columns and offered excellent daylight conditions. Salmon-red awnings provided shade from the sun. Today the original double windows have been renovated to improve their energy efficiency; unfortunately the original solar protection was removed (ill. 3.2.18).

Initially, an entire ensemble was planned consisting of three long wings and two cross wings which would have formed a courtyard – a similar situation to that in the FIAT motorcar factory. In addition to the machine building (today a museum for old-timers) there was a coal store with a connection to the railway network (today it lies on the international Alpine transverse railway line). The Bally factory remained in operation until 1974.[55]

Numerous daylight factories followed this prototype. Here mention will be made only of the huge, 312-m-long, 52-m-wide and 25-m-high building organised around 10 courtyards which once housed the Deutsche Waffen- und Munitionsfabrik in Karlsruhe (Brauerstrasse) and which was built in 1915/16. It was slightly damaged in World War II and today is an industrial monument and the seat of the Zentrum für Kunst und Medientechnologie (ZKM).[56]

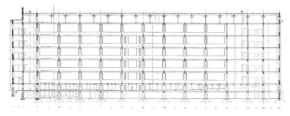

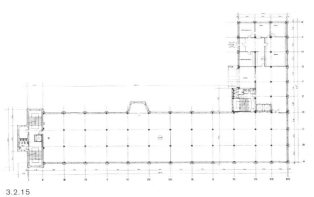

3.2.15

3.2.14: The end of the working day, historical photograph

3.2.15: Longitudinal section and plan of ground floor, original plans from 1909

3.2.16: Unaltered organisation of the workplaces in the Bally factory from its founding until into the 1970s

3.2.17: Concrete skeleton frame with ducts supplying hot or fresh air

3.2.18: The appearance of the façade today

Fiat Automobile Factory Lingotto

Turin, Italy, 1916–20
Engineer: Giacomo Mattè Trucco
Building contractor:
Società Porcheddu

The 'Societa per la construzione e il commercio delle automobili – Torino', which was founded by Giovanni Agnelli and 7 other pioneers on 1 July 1899 and was located in workshops at Via Dante 35, was later renamed 'Fabbrica Italiana Automobili Torino' (FIAT) and was the first automobile factory in the old world intended to be organised according to American principles. Agnelli met Henry Ford in Detroit in 1910 and visited the Ford works in Highland Park that had been erected by Albert Kahn in 1909. Ford's assembly-line principle interested him[57] as did Frederick Taylor's[58] principle of 'scientific manage-

3.2.19

ment' and Kahn's[59] system of building in concrete. With this concept of a thoroughly rationally organised motor-car factory Agnelli returned to Italy and commissioned the engineer Giacomo Mattè Trucco and the large Italian construction company Porcheddu to build the new FIAT works at Lingotto (ill. 3.2.19).

Agnelli had in common with Ford a feeling of certainty about his success. In the production year 1908/09 Ford produced 10,607 cars and a year later – before Agnelli's visit – he was already selling 18,664 from the assembly line. The first town cars cost 850 dollars each, 10 years later only 355 dollars. Ford shaped his era and the pioneering generation of the emerging mass production of goods through the image of a civilisation and culture defined by modern capitalism: "If someone speaks about the growing power of the machine and industry, we can easily conjure up a picture of a cold, metallic world, in which the trees, flowers, birds, meadows have

been driven away by large factories, a world that consist of iron and human machines. I do not share this vision. I believe instead that if we cannot better understand machines and their uses, if we do not learn to better grasp the mechanical aspect of life, we will not be able to find the time to delight in the trees, the birds and the meadows."[60]

Encoding time and space was the driving force of the development and success: the work was brought to the worker, the distance formerly walked to obtain raw materials was eliminated, the optimum time required to complete every step in the work process was calculated and stipulated (ill. 3.2.20). For lack of space and thanks to an unusual idea the designers of Lingotto factory placed the motorcar-testing track on the roof, at the end of the production process – the reverse of the system used in the Ford factory at Highland Park (ill. 3.2.21).

The Lingotto works consists of two long wings (each 507 x 24 m) that are connected by two transverse wings to form three courtyards and that consist of 5 production levels. Two ramps form end elements that terminate the complex. These dimensions demanded a rational construction system. The building company Porcheddu, which held a licence for the Hennebique patent, chose this latter system as it was robust, efficient and expressive. It allowed virtuoso interpretations such as the spectacular ramps, which entered the annals of history as 'cathedrals of concrete' (ills. 3.2.22 and 3.2.23).

The Lingotto works were erected during an experimental phase in concrete technology: Hennebique's constructions were standard, Maillart's mushroom columns had been invented, and Freyssinet's pre-tensioning techniques were being prepared. This building marked the transition from a rigid Hennebique system to the new possibilities of freer forms and structures developed by Freyssinet.

The avant-garde zeitgeist was expressed in the dynamism of the rooftop and the expressive ramps. The major project consisting of the revitalisation, transformation and renovation of the Lingotto works by Renzo Piano (completed in 1993)[61] strengthened the connection between urbanity, spatial quality and the structural rationality of the concrete system (ill. 3.2.24).

3.2.20

3.2.21

3.2.19: General view of the complex (1922)

3.2.20: Assembly-line production in an assembly hall of Lingotto factory, 1924

3.2.21: Spectacular racing and testing track on the roof. This inspired both futurist artists who saw their visions realised here, as well as Le Corbusier, who personally took a test drive in 1925 and 1934 (in a 'Balilla') and described the building as a model of modern urban planning and a new architectural and organisational concept.

3.2.22: Precise geometry of the Hennebique system in the complex structure of the ramp

3.2.23: Construction of the south ramp: adding a dynamic component to the Hennebique system and an upward spiral development in the third dimension. Hennebique's skeletal system was augmented here by the use of diagonal and meridial ribs, braces and ties.

3.2.24: The spatial quality of the skeletal building, new handling of light, the poetry of material of the Hennebique concrete system: transformation of the motorcar factory into a multifunctional urban building by Renzo Piano Building Workshop

3.2.22

3.2.23

3.2.24

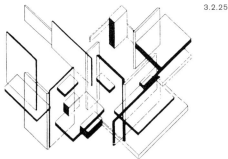

Case Study 37
Key Buildings of Dutch Modernism

3.2.25: The basic elements of architectural expression (1919): compositions of slabs and panels for interconnected, 'transparent' space

3.2.26 Social housing: Spangen estate, Rotterdam, 1918–20; planning: J. J. P. Oud; architects M. Brinkman and L. de Jonge (cf. also ill. 5.5)

3.2.27: Johannes Duiker with Bernard Bijvoet: Montessori open-air school, Amsterdam, 1927/28

3.2.28: Concrete building system with T-beam element, patented by Johannes Duiker, Bernard Bijvoet and Jan Gerko Wiebenga (engineer), 1923–26

3.2.29: Zonnestraal sanatarium, Hilversum: heightening the expressiveness of the Système Hennebique, a suggestion published by Mart Stam in the magazine ABC (no. 3/4, 1925) in his drawn reworking of Ludwig Mies van der Rohe's office building from 1923 (see ill. 3.1.11)

3.2.30: Montessori open-air school, Amsterdam, 1927/28: 'free' corner resulting from the cantilevered slab with tapering 'Hennebique beams'

As a result of the strong influence of the De Stijl movement (from 1917 onwards) on the debate about the principles of architecture after the turn of the century a decidedly experimental architecture developed in the Netherlands. While the new understanding of space – open, 'flowing', transparent space – was inspired by Frank Lloyd Wright,[62] the Système Hennebique formed the reference point in terms of construction and structure. The panel/slab compositions of the theoretical projects by Theo van Doesburg and Cornelis van Eesteren could not be carried out in reinforced concrete as the technology of pre-tensioning was not yet available (ill. 3.2.25).

After World War I the great challenges across Europe were, first, to rebuild destroyed areas, and, secondly, to erect new, large housing estates as quickly and economically as possible, and in addition to build new schools, kindergartens, sanatoriums and clinics, hotels and recuperation homes, daylight factories and modern offices, leisure and sports facilities. These challenges were taken up by pragmatists and theoreticians alike. As early as 1918 Johannes J. P. Oud, the newly-appointed head architect of the Rotterdam urban and housing department, examined the construction of mass housing. The idea was that the reflections and demands of De Stijl should be incorporated and translated into the practical construction of housing. Modern building technology, it was believed, should be used to solve socio-political questions, in particular the question of housing (ill. 3.2.26).

Numerous housing estates and urban development projects characterise the period after 1920. Dutch members of the avant-garde, such as J. J. P. Oud and Gerrit Thomas Rietveld, were represented at the Werkbund exhibitions in Stuttgart (1927) and Vienna (1932). The decisive key buildings of the 1920s and 1930s, however, were built by J. Duiker, Johannes Andreas Brinkman and L. C. van der Vlugt, among others. They defined their approach as 'Nieuwe Zakelijkheid' – 'Neue Sachlichkeit' as a Dutch variation of modern architecture in the interwar period. Whereas early buildings by Duiker still refer to the spatial sculptures of Frank Lloyd Wright and Oud (for example, the first design for the technical school in Scheveningen, 1921), from around 1925 he developed an independent modern direction. The Zonnestraal sanatorium in Hilversum (1926–28; see also ill. 3.1.14), the multi-storey Nirwana housing development in Den Haag (1927) and the Montessori open-air school in Amsterdam (1927/28; ill. 3.2.27), which were all built around the same time, show the new 'objective' style.

Duiker and Bernard Bijvoet, together with engineer Jan Gerko Wiebenga, wanted to use their own standardised concrete construction system (1923–26), which was derived from the Hennebique patent, in a way that would shape a new style. Their system was also based on the rib slab principle, not as a continuous, monolithic method of building but rather in the form of prefabricated, standardised building elements. Two T-shaped columns were connected by a beam and a strip of slab and responded to vertical connections such as staircases, service ducts, etc. by means of standardised cut-outs in the slab – an early concept of prefabrication which in practice turned out to be constricting (ill. 3.2.28).

For Duiker, the design for the Zonnestraal sanatorium in Hilversum was the most important area of experiment.[63] He returned to the Hennebique system, but developed it further in the direction of structural efficiency and aesthetic elegance. Exploiting the possibility of cantilevering the concrete slab that rests on the beam and tapering the beams as they move away from the columns are striking features and represent a sculptural design variation that Duiker also used in his open-air school in Amsterdam (ills. 3.2.29 and 3.2.30).

With further key buildings such as the Winter department store in Amsterdam (1934) or the Hotel-Theatre Gooiland in Hilversum (1934–36) Duiker succeeded, within the context of the 'International Style', in giving the Dutch contribution to the architecture of Modernism an independent character.

3.2.26

3.2.27

3.2.28

3.2.29

3.2.30

Case Study 38
Bauhaus Dessau

Dessau, 1925/26
Architects: Walter Gropius
and Adolf Meyer
Assistants: Carl Fieger,
Ernst Neufert (project supervisor),
among others

3.2.31

The *Suggestions on the Founding of an Educational Institute as an Artistic Consultation Centre for Industry, Commerce and Handcraft* which Walter Gropius published in 1916, as well as the *Programme of the State Bauhaus in Weimar* (1919)[64] developed during the period until the Bauhaus moved 1926 to Dessau into a widely recognised new kind of teaching model with workshops and work groups – an 'amalgamation' of the Anglo-Saxon tradition of the 'shop culture' with the reforming pedagogic theories of the period, which in German-speaking Europe was marked by both industrial and socio-political upheavals (Weimar Republic).[65] The Bauhaus remained a school based on the master principle, but with an industrial orientation. The opportunity to erect a suitable school complex in Dessau offered Gropius a unique chance and led to an architectural concept that depicted the functional requirements and utilised the building materials of 'Neue Sachlichkeit'.

The asymmetrical composition is made up of three tracts: the technical institute of education, the workshop building (ill. 3.2.31) and the residential/studio building for the students. The administration offices are located in a connecting bridge: the dining hall, kitchen and an assembly hall that can be used from two sides form the link between the residential section and the workshops. The entire complex is a spatial and structural continuum and thus breaks with traditional representational appearances. Gropius wrote: "One has to walk around this building to grasp its corporeality and the functions of its members."[66]

As shown by the cross-section (ill. 3.2.32), the construction of the those parts that bridge large areas appears to follow the Hennebique system, in particular (in addition to the bridge with the masters' offices) the workshop wing: a continuous beam connected with the columns by flatly inclined expressive haunches (ill. 3.2.33).

The irritation provoked by Le Corbusier's Domino model appears here in reality as a paradoxical construction type: whereas the extremely robust, load-bearing structure develops in just one direction and has only a slight cantilever at the side, the glass skin is continued around the corner without any direction or hierarchy (ill. 3.2.34). It is, however, one of the most spectacular and extensive curtain walls of its time; it has extremely slender glazing bars and uses a series of centre-hung flaps for ventilation.

Ludwig Mies van der Rohe's vision of an office building from 1923 (cf. ill. 3.2.4) seems to have impressed Gropius just as little as did Mart Stam's refinement of the theme of 'bones and skin', a more elegant solution with a structurally adapted tapering of the beams, which was published in *ABC* (no. 3/4; cf. ill. 3.1.11) in 1925; the Bauhaus Dessau was planned in July/August of the same year (ill. 3.2.35).

The rib slab construction of the upper storeys of the laboratory and workshop buildings (according to Gropius, only a "reinforced concrete carcass")[67] is carried by mushroom columns and flat slab in the 'basement'. Unfortunately, even in the first Bauhaus magazine from 1926 there is no reference to the engineers, building contractors or firms that were responsible for the technical and constructional quality of the Bauhaus buildings. All that is known is that companies from Dessau were engaged for the construction work.[68]

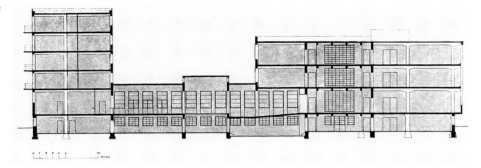

3.2.34

3.2.31: Workshop wing, seen from the bridge

3.2.32: Cross-section through residential building, intermediate wing and workshop wing

3.2.33: Workshop wing (left), structural shell of the building without the glass skin

3.2.34: Corner detail of the glass skin, seen from the outside

3.2.35: Irritation caused by the meeting of 'bones' and 'skin' at the corner

3.2.35

3.3 The Invention of the 'Mushroom Column'

3.3.2

The swiss structural engineer Robert Maillart (1872–1940) from Bern studied at the Eidgenössisches Polytechnikum in Zurich (today known as the Swiss Federal Institute of Technology; Eidgenössische Technische Hochschule, ETH) under Karl Wilhelm Ritter, the successor of Karl Culmann, and completed his diploma there in 1894. After working for the Tiefbauamt (civil engineering office) of the City of Zurich (the Stauffacher Bridge over the River Sihl) and for the construction company Frote & Westermann (Inn Bridge in Zuoz, Grisons), in 1902, together with Max von Müller and Adolf Zarn he set up the construction company Maillart & Cie. In 1904 he won the competition for the Rhine Bridge at Tavanasa (Grison), which is regarded as his real first work. After initially orienting himself on the Hennebique system, in 1908/09 Maillart invented the mushroom column, which opened up new design possibilities

3.3.1

and made concrete construction appear even lighter.[69] In 1911 he was appointed lecturer in 'reinforced concrete building' at the ETH.

In 1905 Maillart designed the Pfenninger clothing factory in Wädenswil on Lake Zurich and in 1907, together with the architects Pfleghard and Haefeli, the Königin Alexandra Sanatorium in Davos. Both these buildings were conceived using the Hennebique system. Other projects followed for which Maillart was both engineer and building contractor, including the warehouse for the Prowodnik company in Riga, which was over 300 metres long (1914), manufacturing halls for the Spanish companies Mata y Pons in Sallent (1920) and Benet in

Barcelona (1920), and the Magazzini Generali in Chiasso (1924). Load-bearing structure broken up into ribs and slender frames allowed lavish amounts of glazing and also led to high-quality spatial structures – Maillart's daylight factories are among the key buildings of modern engineering design (ill. 3.3.1).

Although rib beam constructions formed part of Maillart's successful repertoire, he went a decisive step further around 1908/09 and developed the 'flat slab system' without supporting beams (ill. 3.3.2).[70] This type of structure opened up a wide design area to architects and engineers alike. The mushroom column offers a more elegant capital than Hennebique's rib slabs do: in a sense the haunch is revolved around its own axis and, by means of continuous reinforcement, directs the load of a broader, circular area of the ceiling slab from the horizontal into the vertical.[71] The ceiling has no downstand beams and is a flat surface; the space is therefore no longer structured by primary and secondary beams but is free and without any specific direction. Where the mushroom column stands in an edge bay the ceiling can cantilever outwards and liberate the façade from any load-bearing function – a new spatial quality that was exploited in many of Modernism's industrial buildings, such as the Hoffmann-La Roche building in Basle (1936/37) by Otto Rudolf Salvisberg (ill. 3.3.3). It is remarkable that Maillart, an engineer, put a new design tool into the hands of prominent architects such as Frank Lloyd Wright, Brinkman and van der Vlugt, Owen Williams and others. In recognition of this fact he was made an honorary member of the Royal Institute of British Architects (RIBA) in 1937, at the same time as Eugène Freyssinet – they were the first two engineers to be honoured in this way.

Two building types emerge: the robust and also sharp-edged mushroom column as well as a more slender type with rounded cross-sections. The former was used prominently in the → Van Nelle Factory in Rotterdam by Brinkman and van der Vlugt (1926–29) as well as in Owen Williams's pharmaceuticals factory in Beeston, England (1930–32). Whereas Owen Williams used a slender edge to the slab and thus reveals the structure of the columns and slabs (ills. 3.3.4 and 3.4), Brinkman and van der Vlugt exploited the possibility of the vertical curtain wall. The slender type of column refers to Maillart's dis-

3.3.3

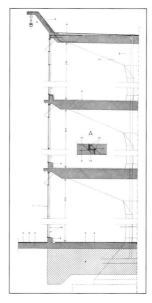

3.3.4

3.3.5

3.3.6

3.3.7

3.3.1: Robert Maillart: weaving hall for the company Mata y Pons, Sallent, 1920

3.3.2: Set-up of a test by Maillart with 9 bays and 4 mushroom colums

3.3.3: Otto Rudolf Salvisberg: company building for the Hoffmann-La Roche chemicals factory, Basle, 1936/37

3.3.4: Owen Williams, pharmaceuticals factory, Beeston, 1930–32; section showing the construction

3.3.5: Robert Maillart: cold storage house and warehouse for Gerhard & Hey, St Petersburg, 1912

3.36: Robert Maillart: Magazzini Generali, Chiasso, 1924: an extremely slender Vierendeel construction made of concrete with compression rods, a polygonal bottom chord and, at the sides, splayed columns as counterweights; a unique imitation of the lightness of the Polonceau truss carried to extremes

3.3.7: Robert Maillart, Hans Leuzinger: cement hall, Swiss National Exhibition, Zurich, 1939

covery. It is shown in the elegant example of the cold storage house and warehouse in St Petersburg from 1912 (ill. 3.3.5) and moves along the boundaries of 'dematerialisation', like Frank Lloyd Wright's → Johnson Wax Administration Building in Racine, Wisconsin (1936–39).

In 1924 Maillart constructed for the Magazzini Generali in Chiasso (ill. 3.3.6) an original, expressive spatial structure that seems to hover.[72] The pavilion for the cement industry – an early example that 'pushes the envelope' in the area of concrete shell technology (ill. 3.3.7) – represents a high point in the further exploration of borderline areas in material technology. It was built on the occasion of the 1939 *Swiss National Exhibition* by Maillart together with the architect Hans Leuzinger from Glarn.

Although Maillart was primarily a bridge-building engineer and as such left behind him an extensive and impressive œuvre – for example, the Salginatobel Bridge at Schiers in Canton Grisons (cf. ill. 3.6), which in 1991 was declared an International Historic Civil Engineering Landmark by the American Society of Civil Engineers (ASCE)[73] – and helped to shape the development of increasingly lighter bridges, with his numerous industrial and infrastructure buildings he also represents a modern engineer with high architectural aspirations.[74]

Van Nelle Tobacco, Tea and Coffee Factory

Rotterdam, Netherlands, 1926–29
Architects: Johannes Andreas
Brinkman, Leendert Cornelius
van der Vlugt, Mart Stam
Engineer: Jan Gerko Wiebenga

The Van Nelle tobacco, tea and coffee factory in Rotterdam (ill. 3.3.8) from 1926–29 is an interpretation of Maillart's mushroom column construction. The architects were Johannes Andras Brinkman (1902–49), Leendert Cornelius van der Vlugt (1894–1936) and, in the design phase, Mart Stam (1899–1986). The engineer was Jan Gerko Wiebenga, who was involved in all the projects and buildings by Johannes Duiker. As one of the leading and most original engineers of the *Neue Sachlichkeit*, Wiebenga has received far too little recognition in the history of building in concrete and of Dutch Modernism.

The Van Nelle factory is an early example of a daylight factory for the consumer goods industry, which completely exploits the possibilities offered by the concrete skeleton system in terms of space, structure and technology of materials. References to the themes of the De Stijl movement are unmistakable – both with regard to the new spatial quality and the transparency of the spaces, as manifested theoretically by Theo van Doesburg and practically, for example, in the Schroeder House in Utrecht, by Gerrit Thomas Rietveld, as well as with regard to the important role played by reinforced concrete as a style-shaping design tool of the architecture of the future as envisaged at an early stage by J. J. P. Oud. Consequently, the 'façade' changed from a load-bearing wall that terminates the space to a building envelope and a 'climatic skin' (ill. 3.3.9).

The Van Nelle factory is a consistent implementation of Mies van der Rohe's concept of 'bones and skin'. In the production wing the structurally effective area in the densely reinforced area of the ceiling around the mushroom capital of the column allowed the columns to be set back behind the line of the façade, which meant the complete 'liberation' of the external wall from any load-bearing function. The 'curtain wall' of glass and aluminium sheeting provides only the necessary protection against the climate (ills. 3.3.10 and 3.3.11). The play between load-bearing and separating or protective layers opened up a completely new design area that provided a joint construction space for architects and engineers.

Vent windows strengthen the dynamics and the spatial quality of the glass façade. This version of the continuous curtain wall façade is differently and, in terms of building technology, more consistently designed than the

factory building erected a number of years later in Beeston by Owen Williams (cf. ills. 3.4 and 3.3.4). Owen Williams continued the ends of the concrete floor slabs to the outside so that the concrete skeletal frame is robustly depicted externally – unlike in the Van Nelle factory.

The entire Van Nelle factory complex consists of several wings. The 8-storey building for tobacco production is about 240 m long and is connected by 4 ramps to the warehouses lying along a canal. The administration building is a front element that lies on the curve of the approach to the complex, reacts to the angled site boundary and gives the ensemble a very definite dynamism. Various expansion wings originally planned were never built.

It seems that the compositional principles to be applied to the connections between the production and warehouse buildings provided material for discussions. The dynamic approach of Brinkman and van der Vlugt contrasted with the rationalist, orthogonal preferences of Mart Stam, which the latter documented in a drawing (ill. 3.3.12). The debate was conducted at a late stage, clearly when the factory was already being built, as today a cantilevered bracket is still visible at the level of the top floor, a remnant of Mart Stam's concept that was dropped in favour of the concept with the inclined ramps – the materialisation of a discussion that was not concluded (ill. 3.3.13).

For the architects and engineers involved the Van Nelle factory represented a field of experiment. Different special cases allowed the team to depart from rationalist rules and to manifest a kind of 'Dutch virtuosity' in the framework of the architecture of Modernism, something that Johannes Duiker also succeeded in doing. The administration building, which is adapted to the entrance curve, reacts with an unusual arrangement of columns to the irregular site boundaries and at the transition to the main wing is given an outward-turned glass layer. The interior is a loosely structured landscape of work with glazed spatial cells and lightweight partition walls, which anticipates the open plan office.

3.3.8

3.3.8: Van Nelle factory Rotterdam, 1926–29

3.3.9: The overlaying of different spatial references, simultaneous perception of space, transparency of space skeleton construction and thanks to curtain wall technology

3.3.10: Primary structure with the octagonal mushroom columns

3.3.11: Building envelope with continuous glass and aluminium skin, and a visible internal structure

3.3.12: Mart Stam: design with horizontal ramps

3.3.13: Built depiction of a debate that was not concluded: horizontal or inclined ramps?

3.3.10

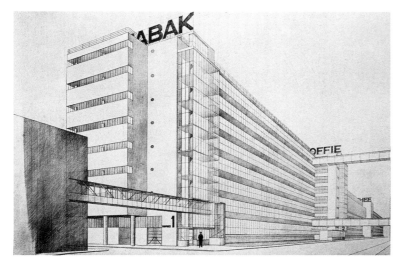

3.3.11

3.3.13

3.3.12

Johnson Wax Administration Building

Racine, Wisconsin, USA, 1936–39
Architect: Frank Lloyd Wright
Engineers: Mendel Glickman,
William Wesley Peters

After the important period of the Chicago School and following the *Columbian Fair* of 1893 in Chicago, American architecture was strongly influenced by the Beaux-Arts style, which had established itself since the mid-19th century on the east coast with New York as its centre.[75] From the beginning of the 20th century to the period after 1945 it experienced a marked revival, if one thinks, for example, of the extensive œuvre of Paul Philippe Cret, the teacher of Louis I. Kahn in Philadelphia.[76] The sons of the pioneers of the Chicago School, John A. Holabird and John Wellborn Root Jr., shaped the architecture of the period between the wars with a traditionally formal style[77] until Mies van der Rohe, and later the architects' office of Skidmore, Owings and Merril (SOM), developed a modern alternative. In terms of concrete construction the system primarily available was the one developed by Ernest Leslie Ransome, which was characterised by a classically inspired treatment of the profiles and junctions. This made the mushroom column construction used by Frank Lloyd Wright seem all the more revolutionary – a symbol of modernity and a depiction of construction in the design of space.

Maillart's invention of the mushroom column, following on the Hennebique system, opened an entire new dimension of design possibilities for architecture. Whereas Hennebique visually depicted the different effects of compression (concrete) and tension (steel reinforcement) in his system and revealed an expressive design potential, Maillart 'liberated' the ceiling slab from the elements that structured it to create an uninterrupted, transparent spatial landscape without any dominant direction. The tectonic debate started by Hennebique at an early stage, which influenced all schools of building in concrete in Holland, Germany, Switzerland, etc., was expanded by Maillart's flat slabs, which added a decisive spatial dimension.

Frank Lloyd Wright, together with the engineers Mendel Glickman and William Wesley Peters, employed the principle of the flat slab for the Johnson Wax Administration Building in Racine Wisconson (ill. 3.3.14). As a consequence he achieved more spacious and flexible work and circulation areas uninterrupted by columns, as well as – between the mushroom columns – sufficient areas for rooflights to introduce a comfortable amount of daylight (ill. 3.3.15).[78]

The 'capitals' of the mushroom columns essentially carry themselves; they are made as independent, flat, spreading mushroom caps, with each quadrant connected with the next cap by bridging elements, and they terminate the space at the top. The interstitial spaces between them are glazed with vacuum glass tubes, similar to the glazing of the building's façades, and in particular to the glazing of the laboratory tower built between 1943 and 1950 (ill. 3.3.16). To protect them from the elements a second robust glazing system had to be fitted externally (ill. 3.3.17).

In contrast to Maillart's constructions the columns – which taper downwards – are hollow and are made of spun concrete; their structural qualities had to be tested initially to acquire the relevance experience (ills. 3.3.18 and 3.3.19).

As early as 1931/32, shortly after the completion of the Van Nelle factory in Rotterdam by Brinkman and van der Vlugt, Wright had used the (more elegant) mushroom column system for Georg Putnam's publishing building for the *Capital Journal* newspaper in Salem, Oregon, USA.[79] And in 1955–58 there followed a considerably larger project for the Lenkurt Electric Company in San Carlos, California, which has a mushroom column structure that theoretically could be extended indefinitely – the model of a landscape of work that could be expanded and adapted as required.[80] In terms of its modernity the Johnson Wax Administration Building lies between the best examples of the Chicago School, such as the buildings of Holabird & Roche, and the first buildings by Mies van der Rohe or by Skidmore, Owings & Merrill, such as the Manufacturer's Trust Company in New York from 1954 (see chapter 4, case study 60, ill. 4.4.21).

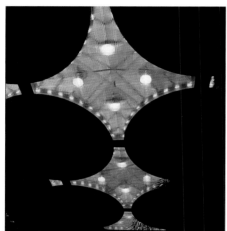

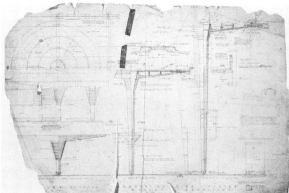

3.3.18

3.3.19

The Invention of the 'Mushroom Column'

3.4 The Further Development of a Modern Culture of Building in Concrete: Concepts for Free Spatial Forms

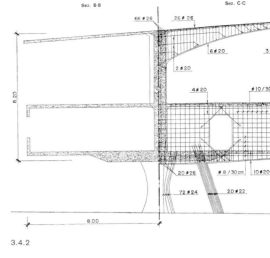

3.4.2

Shortly after Maillart's invention of the mushroom column and flat slab, the theoretical and practical works of Eugène Freyssinet (1879–1962), in which he tested and developed the possibilities of forming and pre-stressing concrete, opened up further design areas for architecture. After his studies at the École Polytechnique in Paris and the École Nationale des Ponts et Chaussées Freyssinet initially worked from 1905 as a bridge-building engineer in the road construction department of Moulins. In 1907, when building a bridge in Praireal-sur-Berbre, he discovered previously unknown deformation characteristics in setting concrete. After various experiments with pre-stressing, in 1911 he succeeded in developing a process that would set concrete more rapidly.[81] From 1914 Freyssinet was head of the construction company Limousin & Cie. From 1928 he worked as a consultant engineer and devoted himself more intensively to research work. He also maintained an experimental factory in Bezons.

With a patent dated 2 October 1928 (Paris) Freyssinet founded the theory and practice of modern pre-stressed concrete technology using high-quality steel and concrete cement. This material technology was also going through a development stage at the time. Freyssinet opened up the way for this development as well as for an entire school of thought and a concrete construction movement that influenced the 20th century and has continued to develop down to the present day (ill. 3.4.1).

Thanks to pre-stressing technology, which keeps reinforced concrete under constant even pressure, every kind of deformation could now be combatted. This made considerably larger spans and more precise forms possible. Thus the structural frame made of apparently monolithic concrete still visible in the Système Hennebique and consciously used as its trademark was moved into the invisible area – the reinforced concrete structure now became a homogeneous flat or linear figure in the form of shells or folded plates that were at the same time space-shaping architectural elements. Concrete became lighter and worked as a space-enclosing envelope or shell; less material was needed (ill. 3.4.2). Thanks to Freyssinet the architecture of Modernism could avail of new possibilities in the field of building technology and made use of reinforced concrete technology in order to realise its world of ideas.

3.4.1

The hangars in Orly (1923)

The two airship hangars by Freyssinet in Orly near Paris are presented here as a mature example (ill. 3.4.3). With a span of 80 m and a height of 56 m these halls were the largest reinforced concrete constructions of their time. The individual arched beams, vaulted in cross-section, were 7.5 m wide, at the bearing points 5.4 m wide and at the crown the vaulted beam was 3 m high. The walls of the beams were only a few centimetres thick (at the side areas 9 cm). The glazed perforation of the arched beams produced an astonishingly bright space. The hangars were destroyed during World War II.

Freyssinet's research did not focus exclusively on the borderline area of the greatest possible spans – but also extended to formwork and assembly technology. The scaffolding, "which ran on tracks that could be raised and lowered by hydraulic lock spacers, solved this problem in a manner appropriate to the purpose."[82] (ill. 3.4.4)

CNIT exhibition hall, Paris, La Défense (1955–58)

The roof over this space, built over a triangular-shaped plan without internal columns, which has sides measuring 225 m and is 48 m high, was originally conceived in the form of three interlocking cylindrical shells. It was ultimately made as a box-section, double concrete shell, in which each shell is 65 mm thick, and with a tolerance of 3 mm. A secondary curvature with a construction height of 2.4 m stabilised the load-bearing system.[83] The architects Robert Camelot, Jean de Mailly and Bernard Zehrfuss worked initially with the engineers Pier Luigi Nervi and Eugène Freyssinet; later a project team under Nicolas Esquillan with the construction company Coignet took over the construction (ill. 3.4.5). The construction of the gigantic 'curtain wall' façade was by Jean Prouvé (see also ill. 4.3.29). Today (2007–08) this hall is being renovated by the Parisian architectural firm Cuno Brullmann (brullmann crochon architects) to reveal its original character and improve on the structure.

Folds, vaults, pre-stressing

Taking Freyssinet's work as a starting point the Italian school of concrete pioneers developed an independent culture of building in concrete. In contrast to the freer, 'organic' vaulted techniques in Spain or in South America, the Italian way of thinking was based on the 'razionalismo' of the inter-war period: on the interpretation of the shaped beam and orthogonal contours. Whereas both during the fascist era and afterwards → Pier Luigi Nervi researched and explored the new boundaries of concrete technology, the virtuoso contributions of Ricardo Morandi[84] and → Angelo Mangiarotti, for example, characterise post-war architecture in Italy.

The concrete shell experiments in the Zeiss planetarium in Jena and the company responsible, Dyckerhoff & Widmann, shaped the German school of building in concrete. The young engineer → Franz Dischinger, who joined this firm in 1922, developed shell technology further and arrived at new forms with cylindrical and double-curved light structures – a design area for architects and engineers that still exists today. The structural tension forces at the edges were dealt with by means of robust frames and beams. More elegant solutions are to be found in the Spanish tradition of building in concrete, for example, in the work of → Eduardo Torroja and → Eladio Dieste, which relates to Catalan vaulting techniques, also in the work of Félix Candela and later with the Swiss engineers → Heinz Isler, Heinz Hossdorf,[85] as well as in Alexandre Sarrasin's retaining wall projects.

Alexandre Sarrasin

Alexandre Sarrasin (1895–1976), a Swiss engineer and contemporary of Maillart and Dischinger, in 1925/26 constructed a retaining wall for an equalising reservoir near Les Marécottes, which was the most innovative retaining wall of its time (ill. 3.4.6).[86] A series of semicircular cylindrical shells at an angle of 57° resist the pressure of a body of water 6 m deep. The shells are strengthened by the use of trapezium-shaped cross walls that deal with tension forces at the edges of the shells; 2 or 3 arches or crossbeams span between the cross-walls. They are 4.6 m apart and 25 cm thick. The concrete shells are only 12 cm thick, which caused amazement among Sarrasin's contemporaries. The cross-walls pro-

vide the necessary edge strengthening to take the bending moments of the cylindrical shells – in a certain sense the reverse of a Dischinger construction.[87]

In the further development of shell technology it was discovered that edge tension, even in the case of larger spans, can be more easily dealt with in flatter shells than in cylindrical shells with their typical wave-shaped bending problems, which Louis I. Kahn together with the engineer August Komendant examined over the space of a year when building the Kimbell Art Museum in Fort Worth, Texas (1966–72) until both the structural and formal demands could be harmoniously resolved.[88]

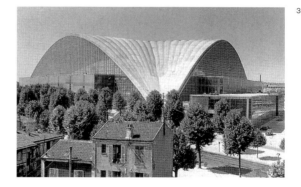

3.4.5

3.4.6

3.4.1: Commercial building on Ottoplatz, Chur; architects: Jüngling & Hagmann, engineers: Jürg Conzett/Conzett, Bronzini, Gartmann. The position and geometry of the rhombical structure of the pre-stressing cables determines the pattern of the openings (see also ill. 3.5.23).

3.4.2: Expanded architectural design possibilities thanks to pre-stressing technology: Palazzo della Regione, Trento, 1963; architect: Adalberto Libera, engineer: Sergio Musmeci; reinforcement plan in the cross-section of the annex building[130]

3.4.3: Eugène Freyssinet: hangars in Orly, 1923. During the construction phase: principle of the cambered cross-section of the arched beams

3.4.4: Mobile scaffolding for the hangars in Orly, 1923: the scaffolding was intended to make it easier to remove, lower and slide the formwork and re-fix it at the next arch, thus avoiding waste of material and time.

3.4.5: Exhibition hall, Centre Nationale des Industries et Techniques, Paris, 1955–58

3.4.6: Alexandre Sarrasin, retaining wall to the equalising reservoir Les Marécottes, Switzerland, 1925/26

Pier Luigi Nervi – Engineer Architect

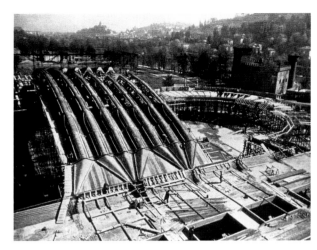

3.4.7

Pier Luigi Nervi (1891–1979) completed his civil engineering degree at the engineering faculty of the University of Bologna in 1913. Immediately following this he began to work as the director of the technical department of the Società per Costruzioni Cementzie di Bologna, a well-known company in Italy. After World War I, in which he served as an officer in the engineer corps, he continued working in the company but in the Florence branch, where he was project head until 1923. Subsequently, and throughout the fascist era, he ran his own office until 1978. Between 1946 and 1962 Nervi taught construction technology and material technology at the architecture faculty of the University of Rome.

Nervi's particular achievements at the beginning of his engineering career lay in the study of prefabricated concrete elements and new developments in the area of material technology, and in his invention of the 'ferro-cemento' process. However, this process is matched by an efficient prefabrication in which wire-reinforced, thin-walled, fine-grain concrete prefabricated elements are laid on a scaffold and used as a 'permanent formwork'. The reinforcement is laid in the joints and then the concrete is poured. This means that concrete is used 'above and below', that is to say, twice[89] (ill. 3.4.8).

As it involved the combination of prefabricated elements and *in situ* concrete the 'ferro-cemento' technique meant that Nervi did not conduct a fundamental study of prefabrication – perhaps he did not wish to do this in order not to destroy the ornamental quality that he saw in the construction of his structures. Stefan Polonyi suggests that "Nervi was, it seems, hindered from properly understanding pre-cast construction by his concept of forms, and also by his invention of ferro-cemento elements."[90] Ferro-cement shells were reinforced with a number of layers of wire mesh ranging in diameter from 0.5 to 1.5 mm and placed 1 mm apart. They were very elastic and flexible but also extremely resistant and eminently suitable for the creation of ornamental forms.[91]

Nervi's first large work was the Giovanni Berta Stadium in Florence (1930–32). This was followed by the cylindrical structures and prefabricated airport sheds for hangars in Orvieto (1935/36), Orbetello and Torre del Lago (1939–41). During the Abyssinian Wars (1935/36) and the Italo-German military alliance between Mussolini and Hitler they were used by the Italian air force.[92] In 1945 Nervi published his main theoretical work, *Scienza o arte del costruire?*, in which, much like Torroja, he argued in favour of a synthesis of construction, structure and artistic expression, and for the unity of the architectural and structure-generating design process.

Nervi's best-known works, such as the Expo Pavilion in Turin (1947–49, ills. 3.4.7, 3.4.9 and 3.4.10), the Palazetto dello Sport in Rome (with Annibale Vitellozzi, 1956/57), the buildings for the 17th Olympic Games in Rome in 1960 – including the Flaminio Stadium and the large Palazzo dello Sport (with Marcello Piacentini) – pursued architectural and constructional considerations on how to roof large halls with an economic use of material. However, it was not the span that interested Nervi but the structure of the elements that defined space: ". . . that every part of a structure . . . harbours an enormous potential of formal possibilities and that the essence of structural design lies in recording and making visible these requirements of an objective nature."[93]

Among the most important of Nervi's architecturally oriented works are the UNESCO headquarters in Paris (with Marcel Breuer and Bernard Zehrfuss, 1953–58).[94] The roof of the conference building in the courtyard of the complex, which looks like a 'folded plate', is essentially a paradoxical construction: the combination of the folded plate with a central, continuous, slightly curved slab in the compression zones leads to a 'box-section' kind of structure (ill. 3.4.11).

Polonyi writes: "The folded plate alone would have sufficed; it would have been perhaps formally less exciting but more difficult to calculate."[95]

Nervi was not just an engineer; his design approach was that of an architect. He was interested in space and its defining elements, in the material and its structural and technological possibilities. He was "engineer doctus, but architect natus".[96]

3.4.8

3.4.9

Vorfabrizierte Elemente

Nachträglich aufgebrachter Beton

3.4.11

3.4.7: Pier Luigi Nervi: Expo Hall, Turin, 1947–49, building shell

3.4.8: 'Ferro-cemento' structure: combination of pre-cast elements and *in situ* concrete

3.4.9: Expo Hall, Turin: cross-section and detail section: maximum possible dissolution of the material

3.4.10: Expo Hall, Turin: sculptural definition of space by the handling of light and construction of the structure

3.4.11: UNESCO Building, Paris, 1953–58: the structural and architectural appearance of

3.4.10

Angelo Mangiarotti –
The Design Impact
of Concrete
Structural Systems

3.4.12: Chiesea Mater Miseri-cordiae in Baranzate, near Milan, 1957; architects: Angelo Man-giarotti, Bruno Morassutti; struc-tural engineer: Aldo Favini

3.4.13: Housing development at 24 via Quadronno, Milan, 1959: richly varied expression of an industrialised building method

3.4.14: Elmag company, Lis-sone, 1964: depiction of the bearing situation at the column head and the use of the geome-try of the structure to determine the 'glass line' of the flanking window slits; structural engi-neer: Alessandro Sbriscia Fioretti

3.4.15: Warehouse near Padua: interplay of the primary and sec-ondary systems, seen at a cor-ner; the system displays the fact that it can be extended: open-ness for a future change of use

3.4.16: Riccardo Morandi: coal loading station, Civitavecchia, 1952

After obtaining his degree in architecture from Milan Polytechnic in 1948 Angelo Mangiarotti (who was born in Milan in 1921) moved to America to work there (1953–55). He met Frank Lloyd Wright, Walter Gropius, Mies van der Rohe and Konrad Wachsmann. Following his return from the USA Mangiarotti set up an architects practice in 1955 together with Bruno Morassutti, with whom he worked until 1960.[97] Wachsmann in particular appears to have exerted a great influence on Mangiarotti: the standardisation of building production and assembly technology and its aesthetic depiction formed the theme of a new school of thought established by Wachsmann, which sought to renew the connection between architec-ture and industrial production. With his reference to a history of development that started with the Crystal Palace in London in 1850/51 and reached a provisional high point with his General Panel System (1947–49), developed together with Walter Gropius (see chapter 5, case study 76), Wachsmann greatly influenced the post-war generation of architects. He documented his views in his famous book *Wendepunkt im Bauen* and enabled many students and colleagues to take part in his pioneer-ing research work at summer schools and experimental seminars in the USA and in Europe. The other important influence on Mangiarotti was Milan's post-war environ-ment of 'doporazionalismo' around the BBPR group (Banfi, Belgiojoso, Peressutti and Rogers, known for the Torre Velasca residential tower in Milan, 1956–58).

In one of his first works, the Chiesa Mater Misericor-diae in Baranzate near Milan (1957), Mangiarotti showed a developed way of thinking in terms of construction that led to a direct architectural expressive strength (ill. 3.4.12).

In the context of a self-defined 'practical research programme', in his first housing projects on the basis of building systems he had developed himself and which exploited the latest achievements of building technology and the possibilities of industrial production, Mangiarotti attempted to create a new world of images in architec-tural design. For the housing development at 24 via Quadronno in Milan (1959), together with Morassutti he combined a concrete skeletal frame with a metal frame construction in the façade zone and inserted timber windows (ill. 3.4.13). The metal structure of the building

envelope can form freely meandering loggias as it does not have to assume a load-bearing function – an example of the 'liberated plan' and of the 'liberated façade' pos-sible thanks to the combination of standardised building systems.

A number of pioneering industrial complexes, ware-houses, and factories such as for Elmag in Lissone (1964) or Lema in Alzate Brianza (1969) formed the basis for a new kind of systematic thinking in the area of concrete technology (ills. 3.4.14 and 3.4.15). Out of the technical ability to make load-bearing structures previously un-known, Mangiarotti generated an ambitious design strength from standardised building parts and their inter-action within an overall system of primary and secondary elements that is more than just the visual depiction of load-bearing functions and structural characteristics (see chapter 5, case study 78). To this extent Mangia-rotti's striving for an 'architectural' method of expression resembles Nervi's, but with Mangiarotti the 'art of building' is depicted more directly – without detours – and points the way to a new 'industrial aesthetic.'

In differently oriented experimental projects Mangia-rotti also dealt with the design and industrial possibilities of steel, metal, and plastic constructions.

Mangiarotti's design system is based on linear, rod-like elements. Their industrial aesthetic is expressed in the way the cross-section is shaped and in the rhythmical interplay, which produces a spatial handling of light.

In contrast to this Riccardo Morandi developed space-shaping, free concrete structures, which develop in a virtuoso manner the possibility of new plane load-bearing structures established by Freyssinet (ill. 3.4.16). Morandi also is among those engineers whose work has been accorded too little appreciation in the history of the culture of building.[98]

3.4.13

3.4.15

3.4.16

The Further Development of a Modern Culture of Building in Concrete

Franz Dischinger and Concrete Shell Technology

3.4.17: Zeiss Planetarium, Jena, 1922: lattice dome with a diameter of 16 m; photograph taken during construction, showing the skyworkers

3.4.18: Lattice of a planetarium dome, sprayed with concrete in sections: spray gun process

3.4.19: Domed hall for the Schott company near Jena, 1923/24

3.4.20: Loading test with 50 people standing on a prototype double-curved plane load-bearing structure with an extremely thin shell, summer 1931; reinforced with 3-mm wire mesh, shell thickness in the bay 1.5 cm, at the edges 2.5 cm!

3.4.21: Louis I. Kahn, August Komendant: Kimbell Art Museum, Fort Worth, Texas, USA, 1966–72; distribution of the compression and tension forces (after A. Muttoni)

3.4.22: Ulrich Finsterwalder: market hall in Cologne, 1940

Franz Dischinger (1887–1953) studied at the Technische Hochschule in Karlsruhe (road and bridge building department) from 1907 to 1911 and taught concrete statics and concrete technology at the Technische Hochschule Berlin from 1933 to 1951. The invention of building statics and theoretical mechanics, with the help of which 100 years previously – before one could speak of concrete technology at all – knowledge was generated about plane load-bearing structures, vaults, domes and double curved shells, is the achievement of the French school of mathematicians and engineers, in particular those from the École Nationale des Ponts et Chauseés (Cauchy, Clapeyron, Lamé, Navier and others).[99] The development of theory which had also taken place in Germany since 'graphic statics' by Karl Culmann and August Föppl contrasted with building practice. At the time there was a lack of innovative construction companies that were prepared to take risks and were willing or able to undertake the erection of prototypes.

The first permanent modern concrete shell was developed in 1922 for the Zeiss Planetarium in Jena. The function, a stereometric projection of the visible cosmos onto the internal surface of a hemisphere, demanded an extremely precise form and surface. Achieving both of these was far from easy (ill. 3.4.17).[100]

A first attempt by the Nuremberg firm of Dyckerhoff and Widmann (D&W) – for whom Dischinger had worked since 1922 – using an iron lattice structure refined with wire mesh and plastered by hand failed, as the form was not sufficiently stable and the surface of the interior too rough. In the second attempt, sprayed concrete was used, which was a new process at the time (gun concrete process, ill. 3.4.18) and which requires a spherical timber formwork. This was made as a single segment and moved from position to position until the entire shell had been cast in concrete (diameter 16 m). Thanks to the finely ground cement which was new for concrete technology at the time, the setting period could be reduced considerably and the surface perfected. At the suggestion of the engineer Mergler from D&W the initiator of the project, Walther Bauersfeld, a Zeiss physicist in the area of optics and precision mechanics, and the Zeiss company itself submitted patents for the thin-walled, curved shells as well as for the junctions –

a physicist and a company that produces optical appliances as the inventors of a resoundingly successful new concrete technology!

After the construction of the Zeiss planetarium the challenges for Dischinger lay in the realisation of larger spans and flatter shells. The next experimental shell for the Schott company, a sister company of Zeiss, was to span 40 m with a radius of curvature of 35 m and a thickness of only 6 cm (ill. 3.4.19). Here, too, the formwork scaffolding was made of segments and in this case it could travel around the centre axis of the dome. In this experiment wave-shaped edge deformation of the reinforcement net occurred – a borderline area of material performance. Exact calculation methods did not exist at the time. To correct this problem struts were used and the problem disappeared after the concrete had set.

In other attempts the inner edge of the shell was strengthened by a steel ring.[101] Whereas over its entire surface the flat shell was subject to compression forces only, the ring at the bearing point took up the tension forces. Later, Dischinger examined spanning vaults over rectangular and square spaces. Here, shells curved in two directions were required, which were augmented by beam panels at the sides. Together with the double-curved shell these formed a kind of spatial rib slab that was placed on four corner columns (ill. 3.4.20).

In the course of these examinations Dischinger returned to cylindrically curved roof surfaces with rigid longitudinal and transverse panels. These in turn became the starting point for more modern buildings, such as the Kimbell Art Museum in Fort Worth, Texas (1966–72) by Louis I. Kahn and engineer August Komendant, which has already been referred to: here, pre-stressing the structure allowed the bracing panels to be dispensed with (ill. 3.4.21).

The engineer Ulrich Finsterwalder (1897–1988) played an important role in the further examination of the edge zone problem in shell structures. After studying at the Technische Hochschule in Munich (1920–23) he joined the firm of Dyckerhoff & Widmann at the time when the concrete shell for the Schott company was being designed. He subsequently dealt mostly with construction problems in barrel-vaulted roofs (ill. 3.4.22).

How Concrete Became Lighter

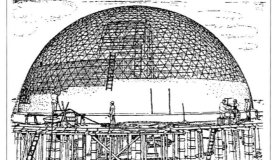

3.4.18

3.4.17

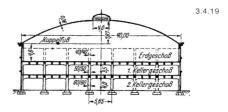

3.4.19

3.4.20

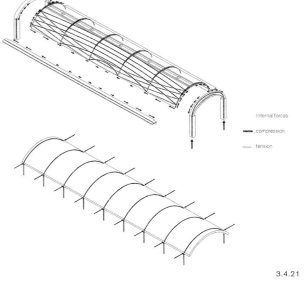

internal forces

compression

tension

3.4.21

3.4.22

Case Study 44

Eduardo Torroja –
The Logic of Form

Eduardo Torroja (1899–1961) developed the work of Freyssinet and Dischinger further and produced new fundamental theoretical and didactic considerations on shell construction. He studied at the engineering school for road, drain and harbour construction which had been founded in Madrid in 1799 by Augustin de Bétancourt on the model of the Paris École Nationale des Ponts et Chaussées. After graduating in 1923 and until the outbreak of the Spanish Civil War in 1935 he designed and carried out numerous buildings with new kinds of structures and form with extremely thin concrete shells (5 to 9 cm), including the market hall in Algeciras (1933), the roof over the stands in the Hippodrome in Zarzuela (1935; ill. 3.4.23), and a hall for ball games in Madrid (1935).

After the civil war Torroja involved himself in the reconstruction of the country as head of the department for bridge building in the Infrastructure Ministry. He taught at the engineering school for road construction and built up a research institute there with a materials testing laboratory at the Institute for Construction and Concrete, which achieved worldwide recognition and today bears his name. The value of his achievements lies in the development of a new aesthetic way of thinking in engineering construction. In his standard work, *The Logic of Form*[102] which appeared in German in 1961 he devoted the chapter "Vaults and Domes" to explaining the structural principles that influence construction, structure and architectural form – a theory of form based on statics as a synthesis of architecture and engineering design (ill. 3.4.24).[103]

To avoid the problem of edge tension forces in curved concrete shells Torroja invented a variety of shells curved in several directions and overlaid figures; in this way he overcame the 'bony' quality of Dischinger's approach with an elegance that is influenced by the Iberian art of building (ill. 3.4.25). He wrote: "The best rule that one can offer to achieve a truly aesthetic structure is that the designer should combine a well-considered and precise artistic sensibility with fruitful creative fantasy, together with the technology required to understand the purpose and the mechanism of function that provides stability."[104]

Frank Lloyd Wright described Torroja as the engineer who best expressed the organic character of concrete construction – the structural forces.[105] For his part, Torroja shows in his publication Wright's little-known project for a bridge in San Francisco (ill. 3.4.26).

In his theoretical studies, as well as with his completed buildings, Torroja points towards a development that was to achieve significance in the architecture of the post-war period, represented, for example, by Félix Candela and the Swiss engineers Heinz Isler and Heinz Hossdorf. Torroja himself wrote: "And so one can successfully build many very different forms (…) which are, in fact, only an announcement and a call for the revolution that will take place in the area of architecture. Sculptural form is in a development phase that is proceeding rapidly and appears as an unknown occurrence in the history of building."[106] (ill. 3.4.27)

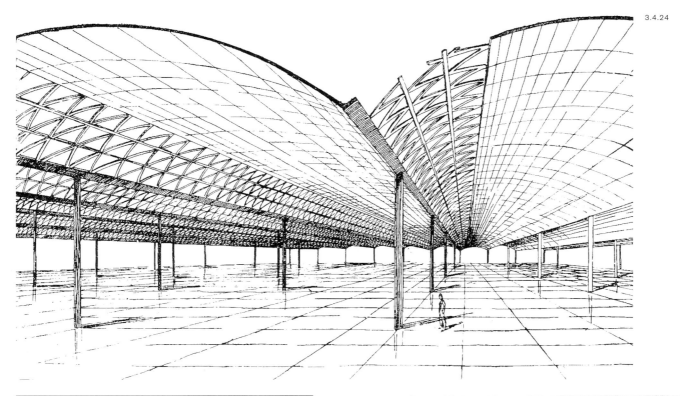

3.4.24

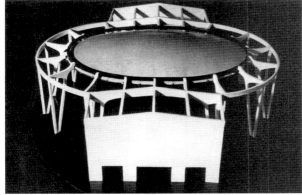

3.4.25

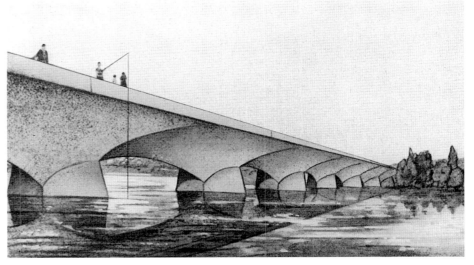

3.4.26

3.4.27

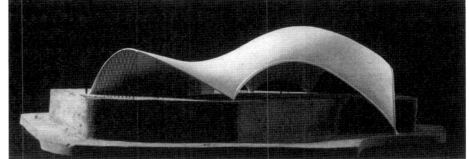

The Further Development of a Modern Culture of Building in Concrete

Eladio Dieste – Thin-shell Brickwork Structures Using Concrete Technology

Eladio Dieste (1917–2000) was born in Uruguay. He obtained his degree in engineering from the University of Montevideo in 1943. His family came from northern Spain. At an early stage he worked with the Argentinian architect Antoni Bonet Castellana, who had also emigrated from Spain and who developed the technology of reinforced brickwork with him. In 1955, together with Eugenio Montañez, Dieste set up his own firm in Montevideo (until 1995). This company carried out numerous buildings in Uruguay, Argentina and Brazil, and later also in Spain, using the thin shells made of reinforced brickwork developed by Dieste. A first exhibition of Dieste's work in Europe was held in Seville in 1996 and was shown at the Technische Universität in Munich in 2001.[107]

Borrowing from Catalonian vaulting techniques Eladio Dieste used his new reinforced brickwork structures to define new boundaries in the relationship between the span and the crown height, and the thickness of the construction (ill. 3.4.28).[108]

Dieste combined the handcraft of vaulting – which had once been standard in Arabian building culture and was revived and made known once again, for example, by the work of Hassan Fathy in the Egyptian village complexes New Gourna (1948) and New Bariz (1967, ill. 3.4.29)[109] – with modern concrete technology and pre-stressed construction methods.

This building technology is characterised by the same economy found in the traditional building methods, which achieved remarkable results using little material. In many epochs, for example, in the era of Gothic cathedrals, restrictions in the availability of material led to inventive aesthetic and constructional solutions. The construction of a space that is reduced to what is absolutely necessary was and remains a depiction of the 'logic of form'. For Dieste the harmonisation of the human building with universally valid ideals of beauty is the worthy goal of the architect.[110] The structure developed with the minimum of material resources suffices to shape the space – the elements that delineate the space are identical with the load-bearing envelope. Dieste's structures are made stable by the way they are shaped. This, in turn, follows the most modern methods of structural calculation. The pliable quality of the vaults and shells, above all those with double curves, was achieved by a fine mesh of brickwork which reacts to the 'textile' structure of the reinforcement and integrates it in the joints, better than the more massive and seemingly monolithic concrete.

Because he combined old techniques with the most modern developments in the area of statics (method of finite elements, field theory), the production of one of Dieste's barrel-vaulted shells demands double precision in both planning and execution. The thin bricks placed on a wooden formwork must be kept an exact distance apart from each other so that the reinforcement steel or pre-stressing cables can be placed in the joints. When the concrete skin has been poured over them they then form a composite construction. The bricks, placed in position by hand and separated by battens, follow the lines of tension. They replace the usual concrete layer in the tension zone of the vault. As they are hollow the construction is considerably lighter – where concrete is used in this layer it does not have to match the performance required in the zone above (ills. 3.4.30 and 3.4.31).

Double-curved shells, too, were made using this 'paradoxical' construction technique that requires handcraft and industrial precision. The serial arrangement of wave-shaped elements allows good day lighting (ill. 3.4.32).

3.4.28

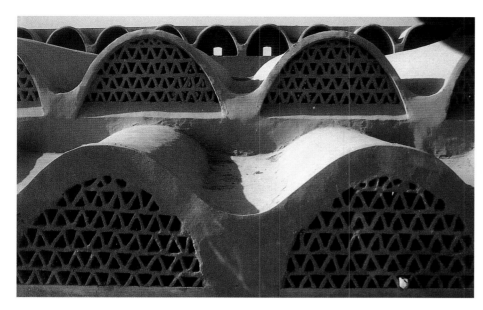

3.4.31

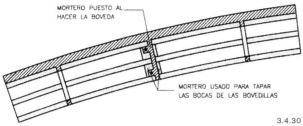

MORTERO PUESTO AL HACER LA BOVEDA

MORTERO USADO PARA TAPAR LAS BOCAS DE LAS BOVEDILLAS

3.4.30

3.4.30

3.4.28: Eladio Dieste: bus station in Salto, Uruguay, 1973/74

3.4.29: Hassan Fathy: revival of ancient cultural techniques. Soukh of New Bariz, Egypt, 1967

3.4.30: Drawing by Dieste of a section through the vault: the notches made in the bricks to take the reinforcement allow extremely thin horizontal joints – thanks to brick and traditional techniques concrete becomes lighter.

3.4.31: Dieste's vaulting techniques require precise manual work.

3.4.32: Eladio Dieste: Julio Herrera & Obes warehouse, Montevideo, 1977–79; double-curved arched shells, span: 50 m, shell thickness: 12 cm, of which 10 cm is brick; edge beams of reinforced concrete

3.4.32

Heinz Isler –
Spatial Form and
Shell Technology

Heinz Isler, who was born in Zollikon near Zurich in 1926, completed his degree in civil engineering at the Eidgenössische Technische Hochschule Zurich (ETH) in 1950 with the design of thin shell structures. He worked for three years as an assistant in the chair for building statics and massive building construction at the ETH under Pierre Lardy, where he examined operable structural models and aesthetic questions of the relationship between load-bearing performance and the shaping of form. A model workshop set up by Hans Hauri, another assistant and later professor for building statics in the architecture department as well as president of the ETH school council, followed the school of experiment, design and modelling of structural systems founded by Eduardo Torroja and gave an entire generation of engineers a new view of their role in the culture of building.[111] As early as 1954 Heinz Isler set up in Burgdorf (near Berne) a 'building laboratory' as a 'design workshop'. From there he developed a worldwide network through exchange with other inventive engineers as well with universities of technology. In 1959 the International Association for Shell and Spatial Structures (IASS) was set up in Madrid. The pioneers, Eduardo Torroja, Nicolas Esquillan, Ove Arup and also Heinz Isler, gave lectures in the context of this body – a milestone and the start of long phase of experimentation.

Before Heinz Isler's experiments, shell construction was confined to classic and mathematically simple forms such as cylindrical, spherical or hyperbolic-parabolic lightweight structures, with exceptions such as in the area of Oriental dome and vault construction or examples that resulted from the properties of an even less well-known material technology (for example, the palm house in Bicton Gardens, see chapter 1, case study 1). In 'vernacular architecture' there were also examples of free forms curved in a number of directions, for example, the Bedouin tent. Since the work of Frei Otto these kinds of figures and self-organising, natural, organic and biological phenomena stimulate present-day designers in particular to emerge from their own specialised field and to explore new areas. Through the study of cushion shapes Heinz Isler arrived at the construction of 'hump-backed' shells built over square and rectangular floor plans that allow zenithal openings to be made (ills. 3.4.33 and 3.4.34).

Looking by chance at a soaked piece of hanging fabric, around 1955 Isler arrived at the idea of revolving the membrane in a frozen state, in which it depicted only tension forces, through 180°, which gave him the automatically produced ideal form of a shell that is subject only to compression forces – an experiment that Antoni Gaudí had made earlier for neo-Gothic stone vaults (ills. 3.4.35 and 3.4.36).[112]

For the shape of the structure and form the decisive aspect is to determine the outline conditions, such as the number of bearing points, the stability of the material, the load, the material, etc. From these givens the structure and form organise themselves, as it were – a methodical approach used again today in the computer-assisted generation of structure and form (for example, design by algorithm; see case study 81).

Isler, too, worked from an early stage with the electronic compilation of fields of tension, shifted loads, variable bearing points and their depiction in operable diagrams, which were used to produce the shell constructions (and also the formwork matrices) (ill. 3.4.37).

Even after 40 years of uninterrupted research and building work the classic shell supported on three points, which Isler used, for example, at Deitingen-Süd motorway service area and filling station between Bern and Zurich (1968), remains the most beautiful spatial form – an artefact of the culture of building (ill. 3.4.38).[113]

In terms of material technology these old shell constructions are in perfect condition, for within a short time, as the concrete began to dry out it grew increasingly stronger, making the shells denser and more weather-resistant with their increasing age. Heinz Isler reckons that they have a further lifespan of 50 years!

3.4.35

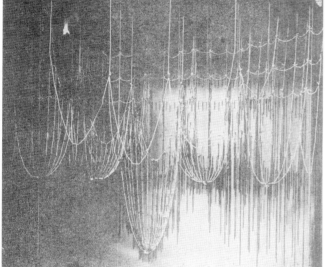

3.4.36

3.4.37

3.4.38

3.5 Concrete and Architectonically Shaped Space

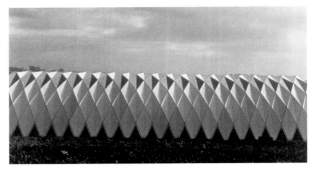

3.5.2

New experiments

After World War II, Ove Arup was one of those who pursued the research goal of building lighter concrete structures. The Sydney Opera (1957–73) is an interesting example of creative collaboration between architect and engineer in a process that extended over many years. For the particular location in Sydney Harbour architect Jørn Utzon suggested a composition of concrete shells that was intended to suggest associations with sails. After numerous attempts using computer-assisted models the two Arup engineers involved in the project, Jack Zunz and Peter Rice, recognised that the desired form could be achieved only by using a ribbed structure and could not be built as a shell construction. However, the form of the composition of shells was put together using segments that appear to have been cut out of the surface of a single sphere. The engineers created this form using a truss-like concrete rib structure with a ceramic brick covering that assists the homogeneous membrane-like effect of the basic architectural figure. However, the engineers were called in only at a late stage, which complicated and extended the length of the entire project process and made it more expensive (ill. 3.5.1).[114]

The 'Portuguese pavilion at the *Oceans World Exhibition* in Lisbon in 1998 gives the impression of an apparently 'paradoxical' load-bearing structure. Here, too, the architect, Álvaro Siza, from Porto in northern Portugal, worked with engineers from Arup, including Cecil Balmond and Fred Illidio. The apparently hovering concrete roof of the pavilion is not a 'tension band' but a 'baldachin' that lies on steel cables.

Ferrocement: a rediscovery

It is certainly no accident that Renzo Piano, who was born in Genoa in 1937 and is a fellow countryman of Pier Luigi Nervi's, took up the latter's research work and experiments with 'ferro-cemento'. Nervi had shaped the culture of building in Italy to a considerable extent, not only through his buildings but also through the example of his personality as a researcher and his will as a designer to derive from the load-bearing structure more than just a statical function. Renzo Piano comes from a family of building contractors who encouraged not only his enthusiasm for building but also his interest in experimenting with new materials and technologies. The building site was the playground of his childhood years. These circumstances and the influence of his teachers at the Polytechnic in Milan, Ernesto N. Rogers and Giancarlo De Carlo, honed his understanding of theory and practice, history and the future, architecture and city, space and construction.

In the post-war era the Italian tradition of massive and robust concrete constructions based for the most part on walls was modified by Richard Buckminster Fuller, Konrad Wachsmann and Jean Prouvé. For Renzo Piano, too, lightweight building technology meant a new world of the future. After completing his studies he carried out his first experiments in building (ill. 3.5.2):[115] "I was searching for the absolute space – without a corset of form, for structures devoid of heaviness, that is, for an elegance without architecture. The theme of lightness was a game in the real sense of the word: a search that was very much based upon instinct. I had the feeling that I belonged to a great circus of constructors. Fragile, indeed 'impossible' structures were for me like the exercises of a high-wire artist, which were developed without the safety net of what had already been seen, already created."[116]

These studies of lightweight building led Renzo Piano to other materials and technologies and to ferrocement – back to the future, as it were. In 1981 Piano entered a phase in which he examined the possibilities of designing, shaping and producing concrete in a lighter way. The 'de Menil Collection Museum in Houston, Texas (1982–86), and San Nicola football stadium near Bari (1987–90) are attempts at freeing concrete of its weighti-

3.5.1

ness and at introducing the spatial effect of light and the handling of light. In the former project Piano was aided by the engineer Peter Rice, in the latter by the engineering office of Vitone Brothers from Bari. In the period that followed he examined the Système Hennebique during his transformation of the Lingotto FIAT automobile factory in Turin and conducted his first experiments with terracotta, which was rediscovered as façade cladding material, for the Cité Internationale project in Lyons (1991–95).

Pre-stressing technology and new spatial figures

Architectural design employing the new technology of pre-stressed concrete opened up new paths for architects and engineers. After it had been recognised early on that it made sense to pre-stress reinforcing steel so as to prevent the formation of cracks (first US patent 1886), it was the French pioneer Freyssinet who, thanks to systematic studies and experiments, first succeeded in the 1920s in actually employing the pre-stressing technique in the construction of bridges and buildings. In the intervening period high-quality steel became available and the theory of building statics advanced. After 1945 this technology spread widely in the USA and in Europe and since that time it has formed an integral part of the repertoire of engineering structural design, no longer only in the area of bridge building (ill. 3.5.3).

While the early concrete panel compositions of the Dutch De Stijl movement (1915–19) did not advance beyond drawings and models, they did illustrate new design possibilities of thinking about architectural space as a completely new kind of life and event space. As concrete pre-stressing technology was not yet available (Freyssinet's first patent was taken out in 1928) it is hardly surprising that the only consistently built manifesto of this epoch is, in fact, an attempt to simulate the effect of a figure of panels and slabs using traditional masonry techniques: the Schroeder House in Utrecht by Gerrit Thomas Rietveld is, in a certain sense, the anticipation of a concrete technology that was yet to come – a 'creative mistaken concept' (ill. 3.5.4).

The design possibilities of creating references between inside and outside, of transparency and penetration in the interior, simultaneous perception, etc.,

through compositions of slabs and panels could not be adequately translated by engineers in terms of technology or materials. However, it had become clear to the protagonists of the avant-garde of the 1920s that the new modern design of space could be achieved only through the use of the material concrete. This realisation itself pointed towards the future. Today, architects and engineers reinterpret this technology discovered 80 years ago, and exploit its potential to advance towards new boundaries, as the works of Swiss engineers ʹJürg Conzett and ʹ Joseph Schwartz illustrate.

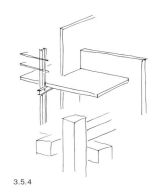

3.5.4

Bridge-building with architectural aspirations

As in the area of iron construction in the 19th century, it is noticeable that in the field of concrete construction, too, important impulses of technological thought flowed from the design area of bridge-building into architecture and continue to do so: Polonceau trusses, three-hinged arches, Gerber beams, lattice structures, Vierendeel trusses, etc., have become architectural design elements. Their application, remodelling and use in solving architectural and spatial problems open up new design areas for cooperation between architects and engineers. In this respect bridges with lofty architectural aspirations are models (ill. 3.5.5).

3.5.5

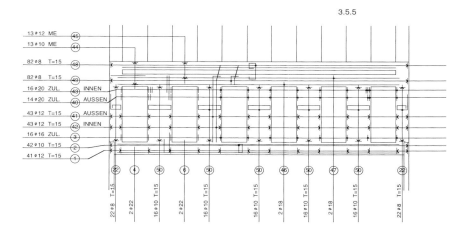

Portuguese Pavilion

World Exposition on the
theme of the oceans
Lisbon, Portugal, 1998
Architect: Álvaro Siza
Engineers: Arup, London/
Cecil Balmond, Fred Illidio
and others

3.5.6: The Portuguese pavilion
during the exhibition

3.5.7: Álvaro Siza's first sketch

3.5.8: Longitudinal section
through the entire complex

3.5.9: The open edge areas
reveal the interplay of the
pre-stressed steel cables and
the flexible concrete slab

3.5.10: Construction process
in 9 steps

The *World Exposition* in Lisbon in 1998, which, under the aegis of the UN, was dedicated to the theme of the protection and use of the oceans, attempted to take new paths as regards the exhibition grounds also. The site made available, which was about 3 km² in area and situated on the banks of the Tagus River on the northern periphery of the city, was an extremely contaminated area: abandoned oil refineries, rusting machinery, cars, ships, war material and containers, as well as rubbish and toxic waste defined the character of the place. The exhibition was thus a means of solving the contamination problem and at the same time an opportunity to create an expansion and relief area for the capital – the Expo as the motor of a new urbanisation. At the same time it was intended that this Expo should be a model for future

3.5.6

World Expositions: national pavilions used for purposes of self-representation were no longer called for, instead there were to be presentations on the theme within the setting of built structures that were recyclable – with the exception of the Portuguese pavilion, which was to remain as the cultural centre of a new urban district created a short time later.

This pavilion, designed by Álvaro Siza, was to be given an enormous covered forecourt, an open gathering place with a roof to provide shade (ill. 3.5.6). A sketch by Siza shows it as an independent spatial element with a baldachin (ill. 3.5.7).

The massive front buildings placed on either side of the baldachin, which are independent of the actual pavilion itself, anchor the roof – or the steel cables – in the unstable ground of this alluvial land area on the banks of the Tagus River. They define a space that is 65 m long, 50 m wide and only 10 m high. The sag of the roof is 3 m, the concrete layer is 20 cm thick (ill. 3.5.8).

The baldachin is a concrete slab hung slackly on a parallel series of pre-stressed carrying cables. It does not extend quite as far as the anchoring points so that the cables are left visible at the edge areas, which offers advantages both as regards the different expansion coefficients of the materials steel and concrete (which are not bonded together here), and also as regards the natural lighting of the entrance areas to the pavilion (ill. 3.5.9; see also book dust jacket).

In contrast to a tension band bridge the roof does not require bracing beams. In the case of fluctuations in temperature or gusts of wind only the amount of sag changes, which leads to slight feathering movement. As the concrete slab 'swims' and is set back from the edges, there are no fixed-end moments. The concrete ceiling was placed on a formwork which was adapted to the catenary line taken by the sheathed cables. After the concrete had hardened the cables were post-tensioned, the slab lifted slightly from the formwork, and the friction forces between the expanding cables and the walls of the sheaths, which put the concrete under tension, could develop. The 20-cm-thick concrete slab was strongly reinforced above and below the sheaths so that hair cracks could be kept to a maximum width of only 0.15 mm. The concrete slab is therefore not a load-bearing structure but only a protective roof: "The appearance of the slab resting on the cables precisely matches the actual structural situation; this is therefore one of the rare non-paradoxical constructions."[117] (ill. 3.5.10)

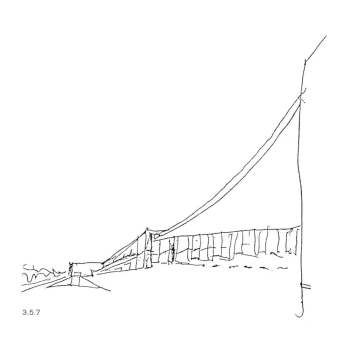

3.5.7

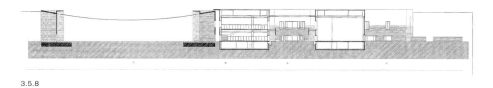

3.5.8

3.5.9

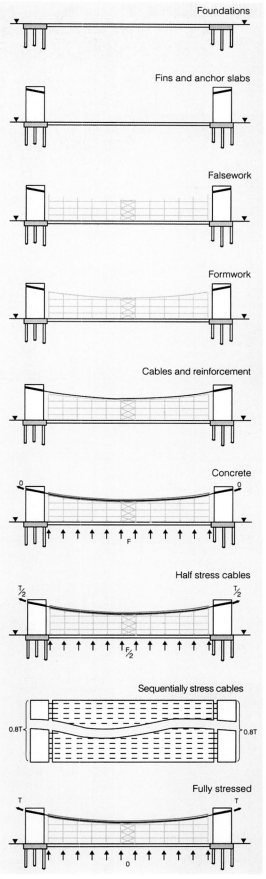

Foundations

Fins and anchor slabs

Falsework

Formwork

Cables and reinforcement

Concrete

Half stress cables

Sequentially stress cables

Fully stressed

3.5.10

Menil Collection Museum

Houston, Texas, USA, 1982–86
Architects:
Renzo Piano Building Workshop
Engineer: Peter Rice

Renzo Piano, who came from a family of building contractors, developed an interest in building at an early stage in life. His studies at the Polytechnic in Milan furthered his understanding of the historical, urban and contextual dimensions of architecture. The architectural developments at the end of the 1950s and beginning of the 1960s relieved buildings of their weightiness, permanence and individually determined functions; with spaces that could be used flexibly, temporary structures and new kinds of building materials and technologies an entire generation captured the design area of the future. The *World Expositions* in Montreal in 1967 and Osaka in 1970, where Renzo Piano was present with the Pavilion of Italian Industry, were milestones in this development. Winning first prize in the competition for the Centre Georges Pompidou in Paris (Renzo Piano with Richard Rogers and Peter Rice; president of the jury: Jean Prouvé), and, above all, the realisation of this cultural centre (1971–78) offered proof that the direction taken was not just a dream and a utopia but could become reality.

In designing the museum for the art collection of Dominique de Menil, Renzo Piano worked from the start with the engineer Peter Rice, who had previously worked for Arup and had set up the RFR consultancy firm after the completion of the Centre Pompidou: since that time Piano has had an office in Paris as well as in Genoa. A special building was required for Dominique de Menil's collection of 10,000 objects of primitive and modern art: "She had a dream of an experimental museum that would be both a recreational centre and a small village. Light was her great love and so we were instructed to work with natural light."[118] (ill. 3.5.11)

The combination of 'village museum' for temporary exhibitions with conservation workshops that can be seen into, recreation zones, cafeteria and shop, etc., and a 'treasure house' on the first floor containing the permanent collection led to a structuralist floor plan with an 'enfilade' of spaces, different spatial qualities, courtyards, and views through the building: a complex that, in principle, could be extended in all three dimensions (ill. 3.5.12).

The structure and the materials followed various systems of reference, which are, however, all influenced by the common theme of lightness. The 'balloon frame' or 'ready-made house', a standardised, transportable product of the prairie style that is popular throughout the American Midwest (cf. section 5.1), provided reference images for the design of the externally closed elements of the complex (ill. 3.5.13).

The second reference figure was 'leaves', which form a shady roof running around the outside of the entire museum, and also spread above the exhibition spaces and the courtyards in the form of thin sections made of ferrocement that direct light, cast shade and shape space (ills. 3.5.14 and 3.5.15).

The lamella section made of thin ferrocement forms the heart of the complex and also of Piano and Rice's joint design process. The shell consists of a special marbled, porcelain-like concrete layer, reinforced with wire, sprayed, sanded by hand and polished – a combination of industrially produced, standardised components and high-quality handcraft.[119] This element that channels light also has to filter out ultraviolet rays and, at the same time, to present the brilliance and the differentiated tones of the art objects in the best possible light. The profile of the modulated lamellas was created using a complex mathematical simulation model with the help of which the extreme outdoor light of 80,000 lux in Texas during the spring could be broken down to 1,000 lux in the interior of the building. Artificial light and ventilation also had to be integrated. In addition to computer simulations, models were also built, and a test module was developed, which, when tested in the desert near Dallas, survived a tornado. The lamellas are hung from a steel space frame that is covered with a layer of glass (ill. 3.5.16; see also ill. 5.4.3).

Important experience gained in this museum project could be applied later in the work on the museum building for the Fondation Beyeler in Riehen near Basle (1992–97), as well as in the Paul Klee Museum near Berne (2003–05).

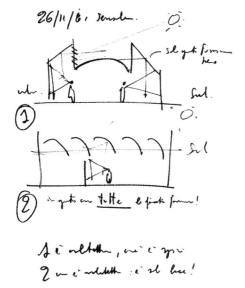

3.5.11

3.5.12

3.5.13

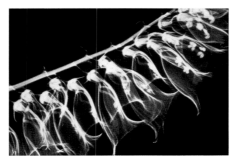

3.5.14

3.5.15

3.5.16

Case Study 49

Hochschule für Technik und Wirtschaft

Chur, Switzerland, 1990–93
Architects:
Jüngling & Hagmann
Engineers:
Jürg Conzett/Conzett,
Bronzini, Gartmann

Commercial Building on Ottoplatz

Chur, 1995–99

3.5.17: Hochschule für Technik und Wirtschaft: polyvalent hall as a foyer, exhibition space and audi max

3.5.18: Full-height point-bearing panels: structure is here a traversable, space-forming system

3.5.19: The conceptual model: stable configuration of free load-bearing walls in the form of a two-storey system of panels. This helps to design concrete buildings in a lighter way and to dissolve the original monolithic function of concrete: two floor plans and an elevation

3.5.20: The first purely industrial skeletal building in the world: British Navy boat store in Sheerness, 1858–60; engineer: Godfrey Greene

3.5.21: Commercial building on Ottoplatz, Chur, 1995–99: overall view, here the structural system is external.

3.5.22: Constellation of the internal walls: photo of the building shell

3.5.23: Diagram of the construction of the façade with the tension bays entered – the rhomboid truss is the conceptual and construction model.

3.5.24: The construction model of the rhomboid frame or truss as demonstrated by the example of the Menier chocolate factory in Noisiel-sur-Marne, 1871/72; engineer and metal structure contractor: Armand Moisant; architect: Jules Saulnier

The technology of pre-stressing brought previously unimaginable spatial compositions into the realm of the possible. In Switzerland in particular a new tectonic culture developed from the 1990s onwards. The Swiss concrete building tradition and the work of the pioneer Robert Maillart, who had a lasting influence on engineering design in this country and throughout the world, encouraged a renewal of concrete building technology. In his current panel and slab constructions Jürg Conzett, who graduated from the ETH Zurich, worked there as an assistant to Christian Menn and subsequently worked as an engineer for Peter Zumthor, among others, refers back to Maillart ". . . whose three-pin box-girder bridges and stiffened 'stabbogen' (arches built on top of bar shaped elements) bridges build upon this principle".[120]

The Hochschule für Technik und Wirtschaft in Chur by Jüngling & Hagmann Architekten and Jürg Conzett is the first larger public building that was constructed according to the principles of point-bearing panels and slabs – so to speak, a 'safe experiment'. Spatial complexity on an extremely tight site led to the concept of linking the various parts to each other by means of spatial interpenetration and transparency, and of designing their functional relationships in a richly eventful way. The central polyvalent hall is an 'urban piazza' that offers a contrast to the anonymity of the surrounding industrial district (ills. 3.5.17 and 3.5.18).

The structural rule that a construction is stable if can be supported on at least three panels, which, if extended, should not intersect at a single point is interpreted as follows by Conzett in relation to free, supporting wall panels: ". . . a construction is stable when in plan it has at least three lines of panel systems, which, in each case, are connected with each other by two bearing points. These three lines can have parts of their length in common but they must not have one point common to all. (. . .) In multi-storey systems the connecting lines can be broken up into individual wall panels on various storeys. The constraint that these panels must touch each other at some point or other remains."[121] (ill. 3.5.19)

Thus 140 years after the first purely skeletal frame building, the Boat House in Sheerness in southeast England (1858–60, ill. 3.5.20), an alternative is presented

to the skeletal system, which provides in non-industrial building a 'plan libre' and a 'façade libre' like Le Corbusier's *Domino* model from 1915.

In the commercial building on Ottoplatz in Chur by the same team the principle of the solid building 'dissolved' into panels and slabs was intended to lead to spatial qualities defined by primary building components rather than by the connection with secondary elements (ill. 3.5.21).

The engineers met the demand for a large ground-floor area free of columns – at the planning phase the requirements of the future users were still unknown – by seeing this as a 'bridge-building problem' for which they used a box-like combination of pre-stressed concrete panels and slabs. This required that the position of all concrete elements in the structural system be immovable. The quality of the space results from the logic of the structure and vice versa. Close collaboration between the architect and engineer during all phases of the project was essential. Both the façade and the corridor wall elements are narrow and are moved apart from each other by a distance about equal to their own width (ill. 3.5.22).

The exterior walls above the column free ground-floor area consists of staggered, slender concrete panels that are connected in the middle of their diagonal lines by pre-stressed cables and serve as a type of virtual open-web girder: The positions of the openings (windows) is achieved through these inter-crossing cables (ill 3.5.23).

The history of building offers various predecessors that employed the same conceptual model in order to react to complex spatial constellations. According to Jürg Conzett, reference buildings include the Dorchester Hotel in London by Owen Williams (1928), as well as the Palazzo della Regione in Trento (1963; cf. ill. 3.4.2) and the Hotel 'Schatzalp' in Davos. The Menier chocolate factory in Noisiel-sur-Marne near Paris is the direct depiction of a rhombic structure and a 'collage' of joint design by engineer and architect (ill. 3.5.24; cf. chapter 4, case study 52).[122]

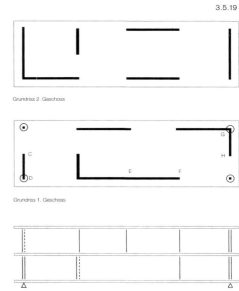

Grundriss 2. Geschoss

Grundriss 1. Geschoss

Ansicht

3.5.20

3.5.21

3.5.22

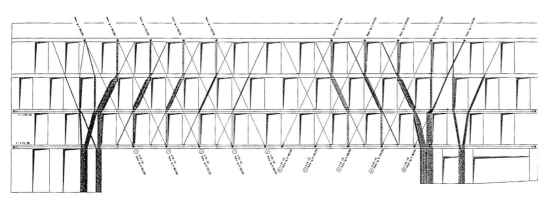

3.5.23

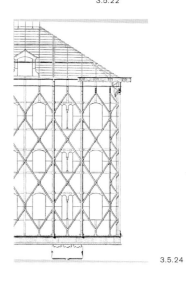

3.5.24

Concrete and Architectonically Shaped Space

Transitions – From Tectonics to Morphology

Tourism Resort Andermatt, Switzerland, 2007 – Architects: Ulrich Pfammatter + Christian Fierz (ArchStudio Zurich), Cuno Brullmann (brullmann crochon architectes Paris and Vienna)

Specialists: Joseph Schwartz (Dr. Schwartz Consulting; structural engineering), Heinz Beiner (Planpartner; urban and traffic planning), Fabienne Kienast (kienastland; landscape architecture), Kurt Hildebrand (Todt Gmür & Partner; climate engineering). Project study and competition.

3.5.25: The abstract figures of the morphological concept make a different effect by day and by night.

3.5.26: Views from and into the communicative centre of the sport and leisure centre

3.5.27: Triangular concrete slabs form the structural elements
of the construction and are supported by branching concrete piers that taper downwards. Daylight cubes allow good natural lighting as well as offering focused views of the surrounding mountains. The intention was to make the large triangular elements, some of which are pre-tensioned, *in situ*, using as aggregate gravel that is found in the Urseren Valley, and to place them in position using a heavy, mobile caterpillar crane. Reinforcing bars were used at the joints and concrete was poured into the relevant areas to create a completely monolithic roof construction, which in its finished state has no joints and is therefore easy to maintain.

3.5.28: Floor plan of the main level and cross-section through the swimming pool and spa

3.5.29: SANAA – Kazuyo Sejima + Ryue Nishizawa; structural engineering: SSC – Sasaki Structural Consultats; environmental engineering: Transsolar ClimateEngineering: Learning Centre at École Polytechnique Fédérale de Lausanne EPFL

3.5.30: Renzo Piano Building Workshop, Arup Engineering: Zentrum Paul Klee near Berne – spatialisation of the existing nature and its continuation by means of vegetation in the setting of a usable, man-made environment

3.5.31: Behnisch Architekten + Transsolar Climate Engineering: offices for the Commune di Ravenna/Italy, Laboratory and Administration Building for the ARPA, project 2004 – 08

The project study for an extensive new sport and leisure centre with spa in the Andermatt tourist resort of Egyptian investor Samih Sawiris represented a challenge on several fronts. As the means of arriving at a solution our interdisciplinary and international project team chose a transformation strategy. The site, which had been used for a longer period by the Swiss army and contained large exercise, manoeuvre and parking areas, was not simply to vanish but should retain traces, as the survival of the mountain village of Andermatt had, to quite some extent, depended for decades on this military presence. The Alpine setting with its natural and cultivated areas was a second context that provided a further source of reference. What was required was a new vision of a modern, future-oriented and environmentally compatible model way of building in the Alps.

For the project team these two sources of reference, along with the dramatic topographical location and the extensive flood area of the Furkareuss river in the valley floor, represented the start of an architectural synthesis of tectonic shaping and meaningful form as a basic concept for design and construction that would exert a spectacular effect by day and by night (ill. 3.5.25).

The 'geomorphological operation' involved in transforming existing territorial and tectonic structures in the natural and cultivated landscape of the Urseren Valley in the heart of the Swiss Alps into a spatial and functional building structure consists both of a historic anchoring in the 'genius loci' as well as contextual new interpretations and the creation of a new, future-oriented area of reference and identification (ill. 3.5.26).

The structural and design unity between function, spatial quality and the materials used in the construction is expressed in a roofscape broken up into triangular areas made of the only material that makes sense for this project, namely, *in situ* concrete slabs. Daylight cubes and cones are cut out of these slabs, which are insulated internally and clad with acoustic elements made of native wood, wherever this material is appropriate (ill. 3.5.27):

Externally, it was planned to cover the concrete triangles with a carpet of vegetation. This geometric natural landscape is planted in such a way that each triangle has a different colouring and in addition expresses the change of seasons. Like in the newer botanical gardens in Barcelona, tall, light panels of Corten steel were to be used to separate the areas, thus serving to accentuate the geometry. The roofscape leads seamlessly to the edge areas, where it connects with the adjoining terrain (ill. 2.5.28).

References to reflections and projects by Cuno Brullmann,[123] Daniel Liebeskind,[124] the group MVRDV,[125] the Japanese team SANAA,[126] to the Zentrum Paul Klee by Renzo Piano Building Workshop near Berne[127] or to the ARPA administration building project in Ravenna, Italy, by Behnisch Architekten + Transsolar Climate Engineering[128] are unmistakable (ills. 3.5.29, 3.5.30 and 3.5.31).

The transformation of existing tectonic structures – in the Andermatt project, the artificial plate tectonics of the former military complex – in shaping form indicates the possibilities of new design scenarios that could create 'ties' in problematic, sensitive and extreme contexts or in transitional zones between the constructed and natural environments, and thus create identities and remarkable places that activate all the senses. Here, the material concrete attains a far-reaching design function as a medium of meaning.[129]

3.5.25

3.5.25

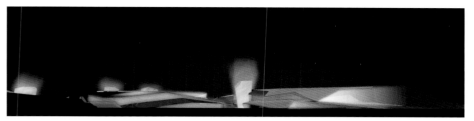

3.5.25

3.5.26

3.5.27

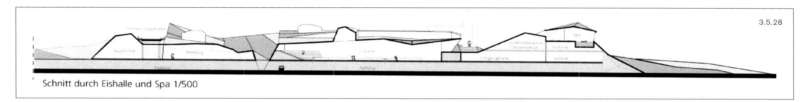

Schnitt durch Eishalle und Spa 1/500

3.5.28

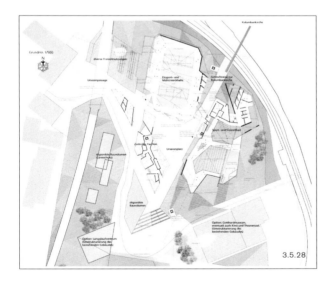

3.5.30

3.5.28

3.5.29

3.5.31

4 The 'Liberated Façade' – From Wall to Partition to Skin

The development of the culture of building is characterised by the tendency to dissolve mass. This is as old as civilisation and is one of the first cultural expressions of building. The model of a Caribbean primitive hut, which in 1851 so impressed Gottfried Semper at the Crystal Palace exhibition in London that he showed it and commented upon it in the second volume of his opus magnum *Der Stil*,[1] proves this fact (ill. 4.1). One hundred years after Semper's discovery Ludwig Mies van der Rohe took up the analogous theme of skeleton and lightweight building using industrial means (ill. 4.2).

Alberti's 'skeleton' Leon Battista Alberti (1404–72) was the first theorist and architect who in his main work, *Ten Books on the Art of Building*,[2] not only dealt with the dissolution of the wall as a conceptual, design and construction task in building but also carried this out as a concrete 'lesson' in his Palazzo Ruccellai in Florence.[3] The structuring of the walls as a load-bearing 'skeleton' that follows the internal layout of rooms, as well as an intermediate layer of leftover pieces of stone, described as 'supplements', between the inner and outer 'incrustations' anticipates new terms such as 'building structure' and 'economy of construction'. Within the wall layer 'stone piers' served 'to carry the layer of beams'.[4] Whereas Vitruvius,[5] Alberti's model, treated the layers of masonry in a similar but two-dimensional way, Alberti developed a building structure that works together in a three-dimensional manner (ill. 4.3).

Alberti thus introduced the transition from the homogeneous wall to the structured and layered wall in terms of both theory and practice, whereas in Gothic buildings this development occurred as a result of 'necessity'.[6] The differentiation between load-bearing and non-load-bearing elements as well as the way the wall is built up in layers anticipates the industrial era and modernism, as manifested by, for example, Mies van der Rohe's 'skin and bone' approach.

Durand's virtual grid – a methodical design instrument 350 years later Jean-Nicolas-Louis Durand at the École Polytechnique in Paris gave the non-material constructional grid based on Alberti's 'skeleton' a theoretical and methodical basis.[7] With his differentiation between valuable, hard, robust materials[8] and less valuable ones for the 'supplements' Alberti had already introduced the economic argument. Durand's rationalism, which was rooted in the Enlightenment, laid down rules of construction as the basis for architectural design and composition. In Durand's school of thought a 'virtual grid' replaces the physical stone-based dimensions used for the old classical orders – the end of 'Vitruvianism' had arrived and ushered in a 'Copernican Revolution' in the methodology of drafting (ill. 4.4).[9]

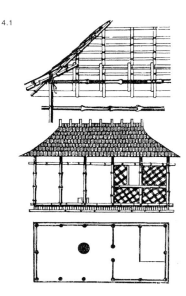

4.1

4.2

4.1: Caribbean primitive hut, after Gottfried Semper: "…the earth raised on piles that serves as a terrace, the roof carried by columns and mats hung to terminate the space or to form a wall".

4.2: Ludwig Mies van der Rohe: Farnsworth House, Plano, Illinois, 1945–50; Mies van der Rohe in front of the structural shell

4.0: Cotton Exchange Building, an example of standardised curtain walls of iron and glass in Liverpool after the buildings of Peter Ellis

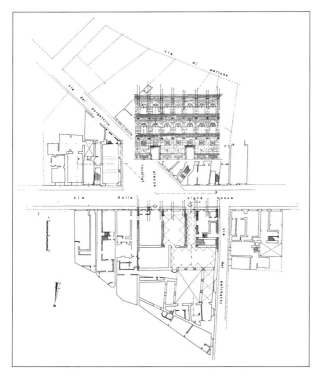

4.3

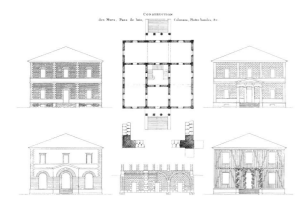

4.4

4.5

Cotton mills At the same time as the French Revolution (1789–94) and the founding of the École Polytechnique in Paris (1794/95) industrial pioneers in the English Midlands built the first modern textile factories with load-bearing iron frames, enclosed by masonry. Following the construction of the first factory of this kind in Derby in 1792/93 this typology developed further in the space of about two decades. Larger wall openings to improve the quality of daylight led to the formation of wall piers with non-load-bearing bays between them and thus transformed the walls into a structural wall – here we encounter Alberti's visionary approach once again.[10] When the iron frame was completed by the use of cast-iron columns on the inner side of the façade the next step was inevitable: the iron skeleton frame 'captured' the wall. This theme was subsequently pursued in the docklands and office buildings in Liverpool until finally the curtain wall was arrived at.

Iron skeleton and 'curtain wall' The introduction of the Bessemer process, which led to the transition from cast iron to the more efficient milled steel, expanded the design possibilities of skeleton construction: parallel developments in England, France and North America after 1850 demonstrate the transition to the new standard of building construction which is expressed in the tendency to separate load-bearing structure and wall into two different design areas for architect and engineer, to make front-hung building envelopes as well as new, industrially influenced façade images. The British Navy Boat Store built by Godfrey Greene from 1858–60 in Sheerness on the Medway estuary is the first pure skeleton structure building with a consistent curtain wall (ill. 4.5; see also ills. 3.5.20 and 4.1.6).

The experience acquired in industrial architecture then flowed into the repertoire of office architecture. The first examples of the application of the building methods used in English textile factories to impressive office buildings are found in the backyards of the old town in Liverpool. A parallel development took place in France, for example, in the construction of the façade of the mill in the Menier chocolate factory in Noisiel-sur-Marne near Paris (1870/71).

From the New York Iron Works to the 'Chicago frame' From 1890, American building history followed developments in Europe with the new construction technology of the 'Chicago frame' – a structural system with a steel frame. Following the appalling fire in Chicago in 1871 William Le Baron Jenney, who was trained at the École Centrale des Arts et Manufactures in Paris and was familiar with English building methods, played a key role in the reconstruction of the city and as the founder of the Chicago School of Architecture.[11] The modern curtain wall was thus continued in the 'Loop' in Chicago, where a second centre (in addition to Liverpool) of future-oriented developments in building and materials technology grew up that was additionally inspired by the iron manufactory (New York Iron Works) of James Bogardus and Daniel Badger, who produced cast-iron façades that they sold by catalogue (ill. 4.6).

It was not only the iron façade, as in New York, but the building structure as a whole with a steel frame structure and terracotta façade cladding that became the programme of the Chicago School. Frank Lloyd Wright, who was critical of this 'commercial architecture' that was less architecturally oriented and more focused on building technology, worked at the turn of the century as an industrial designer for the Luxfer Prism Company and initiated a more architecturally ambitious kind of curtain wall design.

The 'Liberated Façade'

The 'façade libre' – a project of modernism   Despite his assertions in his *Five Points for a New Architecture*[12] the liberation of the wall from the function of carrying the building – the 'façade libre' – is not one of Le Corbusier's inventions. However, through addressing the 'mur rideau' in a new social context, and influencing the background of new developments in the theory of architecture, Le Corbusier did contribute to making the industrial potential of the 'liberated façade' available to the programme of modernism. The anchoring of modernism in the industrial age was, however, already clear, even before its theory was defined and spread by the Werkbundsiedlung in Stuttgart in 1927 and by the founding of the CIAM in 1928. This fact is demonstrated by, for example, buildings for German industry (Steiff Works, Giengen a. d. Brenz; Fagus Works, Alfeld a. d. Leine; Zollverein Collliery, Essen-Katernberg and many others) and by Dutch modernism (Van-Nelle factory, Rotterdam) – all of which are early milestones of the modern programme.

As a further pole in the field of tension between the avant-garde, modernism and post-war modernism, Mies van der Rohe expanded the art of building with industrial means and challenged the new architecture to undertake a consistent search for modern space and style. The curtain wall – the 'skin' – became the depiction of the load-bearing structure – the 'bone'.

The lightness of post-war modernism   The 'uncompleted project' of the architecture of inter-war modernism, in pioneering individual buildings, as well as in the areas of exemplary large and model housing estates was implemented on a broader scale only after World War II. Germany, which had been devastated by bombing, offered an important area for the renewal and the demonstrative revival of living postulates of the architecture of the 1920s and 1930s. The buildings of Egon Eiermann and Sep Ruf and their joint design for the German Pavilion at the 1958 *Expo* in Brussels, the work of J. H. van den Broeks and Jacob B. Bakemas in Holland, Arne Jacobsen in Denmark, Skidmore, Owings & Merrill in the USA as well the architects of post-war modernism in Switzerland, Italy and Austria shaped a new architectural approach and a feeling of belonging to a new era among the generation of young Europeans that emerged after 1945.

After 1973 – the future of the 'intelligent' building envelope   The light, transparent and optimistic architecture of the 1950s and 1960s was abruptly stopped by the oil crisis in 1973. Energy efficient buildings were now called for. Since then the façade has taken on an increasing number of functions with regard to conditioning the internal climate and regulating the building's use of energy. The building is increasingly regarded as an organism that is included in the dynamics of the environment. Glass technology plays a decisive role here. Since that time the building envelope has been subjected to an uninterrupted process of research and development and interdisciplinary teams have worked on visions of the future.

The new curtain wall   The attempts to oppose building construction and technologies that use resources economically, are energy-saving and sustainable by means of the massive, closed quality of post-modern buildings led to the 'triumphant success of glass', which has continued up to the present day. In the future the 'liberated façade' will have to prove itself not only as a 'sustainable skin' (see section 6.4) but also as a 'communication skin' (ill. 4.7).

4.3: Leon Battista Alberti: Palazzo Ruccellai, Florence, 1446–51. New understanding of the building structure as a system made up of the organisation of spaces, a structural 'carcass', the layers of the wall and the image of the façade (colour markings by the author)

4.4: In his textbook *Précis des leçons d'architecture* Durand illustrated the equality of 'construction economy' and 'formation of style' by means of four floor-plan and façade images as variations on the same building structure.

4.5: The world's first iron skeleton building with a curtain wall: the Boat Store of the British Navy in Sheerness, England, 1858–60; engineer Godfrey Greene

4.6: James Bogardus and Daniel Badger in New York anticipated the work of the pioneers in Chicago. The founders of the New York Iron Works experimented as early as 1850 with 'free' iron-and-glass façades; the illustration shows 'The First Cast Iron House Erected, Invented by James Bogardus', New York, 1848.

4.7: The new curtain wall communicates not only a sense of the building's function and significance, epochal model images and technical progress but also the fact that the building is part of the dynamics of the environment: Schneider + Schumacher, Westhafen-Tower, Frankfurt am Main, 2003.

4.6

4.7

4.1 Iron Skeleton Structure and Curtain Wall

The architecture of the Industrial Revolution in England

The modern curtain wall (a wall made of iron and glass that is hung in front of the building) in the office buildings in Liverpool would be inconceivable without the early skeleton building system developed during the initial years of the textile industry in the Midlands. This started a development that has exerted its effect down to the present day. The pioneers of iron skeleton frame construction are St Anne's Church in Liverpool (1770–72), the Iron Bridge in Coalbrookdale (1775–79) and the first modern textile factory, the Calico Mill in Derby by William Strutt (1792/93) – so to speak, 'landmarks' of the future in the core area of the Industrial Revolution. In this pioneering period iron entrepreneurs such as the Darby dynasty and modern factory builders worked together.[13]

The building structure of the Calico Mill consisted of an iron skeleton system surrounded by external walls – a typological basic type that was developed further and,

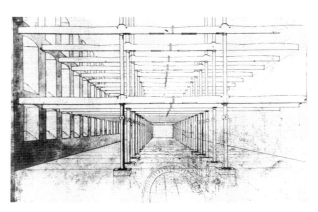

4.1.1

after about 20 years, led to a standardised construction and to the perfection of the junction between column and beam.[14] The rationality of floor plan and building structure and the growing size of the openings in the wall – from 'hole in the wall' to the structuring of the external wall into wall pier and open bays – as shown only 10 years later by the Boulton and Watts Twist Mill (1799–1802) in Salford (ill. 4.1.1), illustrate the logical steps leading up to the complete iron skeleton system building.

The standard construction of the textile factories in the English Midlands

Inverted, slightly upward curved T-beams rest on cast-iron columns, with a vaulted brick ceiling spanned between them – similar to the Catalonian vaults – on top of which a concrete floor is poured; in the cross direction tension rods between the beams stabilise the wrought-iron junctions. This standard construction was the outcome of an inventive development: initially, the drive rods for the machines were led off-centre past the junctions, which endangered the building's stability. The multi-storey, mostly triple-aisled buildings contained hundreds of machines (Jenneys, Arkwrights and others) and were thus subject to dynamic forces that were little understood at the time. Hence the axially positioned split junction of the shaft drives meant a breakthrough – an invention of Charles Bage in the Flax Spinning Mill building in Shrewsbury 1796/97 (ill. 4.1.2).

Transformation of the wall

20 years after William Strutt's pioneering building in Derby the Stanley Mill in Stonehouse in southern England (1812/13) is probably the first example of a pier construction with infill parapets and iron-framed windows (ill. 4.1.3). In the Midlands this breakthrough did not occur in the textile factories, but in the later office buildings in Liverpool. As early as 1800 the architect Samuel Wyatt – who was far ahead of his time – patented a complete iron structure with columns on the inside face of the enclosing wall (ill. 4.1.4).[15] He thus pointed towards the complete dissolution of the wall in the direction of a consistent skeleton building system, even though he did not yet perceive the consequences of his invention – the transforming step towards the curtain wall.

The invention of the curtain wall

In the era of industrial development Liverpool played an important role as the trans-shipment centre of the textile region in the English Midlands; it was also the port for Manchester, to which it had been connected by rail since 1830. Liverpool's importance grew with the productive strength of the cotton industry, the boom in trade with North America and the connection of the industrial regions in Wales, the Midlands and Scotland with London

4.1.3

4.1.4

4.1.5

4.1.6

through the new railway, which rapidly replaced the slow, and sluggish canal network.[16] Liverpool later boomed as an emigration port; the Adelphi Hotel today still bears witness to this era.

It was in Liverpool that a special building type, the early modern commercial office block, developed. As merchants, tradespeople, shipping company owners, banks, insurance companies, etc. moved their headquarters into the port area and the docklands the centre grew increasingly dense. Small and narrow lanes, tight, dark backyards formed the appearance of the city.[17] Thanks to the pioneering invention in the 1860s of the curtain wall and the bay window, it proved possible to improve conditions at the workplace as well as hygiene standards in the city.

Through the bay window, in which the total area of glass was increased by the use of projecting and recessed elements, thus improving daylight comfort in the office spaces, the builders of Liverpool revolutionised traditional window typology (ill. 4.1.5). The stepped glass surfaces also reflected sunlight and top light externally and made the lanes and internal yards considerable brighter. Given the poor existing standards of hygiene in the city and workplaces, the development that led to the curtain wall of iron and glass took place very rapidly in Liverpool. The highpoint was around 1865 in the → office buildings by Peter Ellis. They were the immediate models for the building technology used in the reconstruction of Chicago after the fire in 1871, and the basis for the 'façade libre' as well as a signpost that pointed the way towards Modernism.

Shortly before Peter Ellis's designs of complete skeleton structures and consistent curtain wall façades, Godfrey Greene, a member of the Royal Engineers, designed a boat store for the ships of the English Navy in the Royal Dockyards in Sheerness on the Medway Estuary (1858–60). The triple-aisled structural bay extends across an area of three times 14 m and consists of an iron skeleton structure that is externally visible. The building envelope made of corrugated iron (used here for the first time for such a purpose) lies between the façade columns (ill. 4.1.6).[18]

The French school of iron

If one excludes a few individual pioneering buildings, iron construction in France lagged behind that in England. The Halle au Blé in Paris, the first true iron-and-glass construction with a new kind of lattice truss structure that replaced the old timber-and-glass dome, was not built until 1809–13.[19] After Napoleon's fall in 1815 industrial development was blocked by the Restoration regime until the July revolution of 1830 provided a liberating spark – also in the area of building technology – that was initially visible in the area of railway construction and that also meant the new start of the Industrial Revolution in France.

At the same time, 'Polytechniciens' and disciples of Claude Henri Saint-Simon founded a new school, the École Centrale des Arts et Manufactures in Paris, where architects and engineers together received a scientifictechnhical and industrial training and, as a result, shaped the industrial image of the 19th century with railway stations, exhibition pavilions and modern production workshops. Graduates of the École des Beaux Arts also faced the challenges presented by the new industrial building technology, as is illustrated by the Halles Centrales by Victor Baltard and Félix Callet (1853–66, demolished 1971),[20] in which the first 'façade respirante' was built that could be conditioned with the use of adjustable louvres (ill. 4.1.7).

The first pioneering industrial complex for which a new kind of curtain wall was developed was the → chocolate factory of the philanthropist Émile Menier in Noisiel-sur-Marne near Paris (1871/72). Against this background further 'murs rideaux' were created, above all in fin-de-siècle Paris: metal-and-glass façades of department stores, bay windows in city palaces, etc.[21]

4.1.7

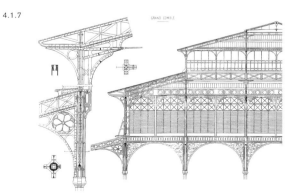

Office Buildings

Liverpool, England, 1864–66
Architect: Peter Ellis

4.1.8

The architect Peter Ellis (1835–84) is the inventor of the first modern metal-and-glass curtain wall that displays architectural aspirations. He transferred the building typology of the skeleton method used in the cotton mills to prestigious office building (ill. 4.1.8). Little is known about Ellis: he was a London architect who opened an office in Liverpool and, according to available sources, carrried out only two office buildings in this city: the Oriel Chambers Building (1864) and the building at 16 Cook Street (1866).[22]

For the Oriel Chambers Building, Ellis was on the receiving end of biting criticism in the construction journal *The Builder*: "The plainest brick warehouse in the town is infinitely superior, as a building, to that large agglomeration of protruding plate glass bubbles in Water Street, known as Oriel Chambers . . . and we sincerely hope that this building will prove unique in its way and the first and last in such a style."[23] The criticism was both correct and incorrect: Ellis's buildings were indeed unique – but they were not the last of their kind. They contained a programme that was industrial, architectural and spatial, and addressed issues of hygiene and health at the workplace and pointed towards the future of both Chicago and also the modernism inspired by Europe – heralds of a new style and a new tectonic culture in architecture (ill. 4.1.9).

Liverpool provided an area of experiment for industrially oriented building methods.[24] The load-bearing structure of cast iron invented for the cotton mills was also used in warehouses in the docks. Even before Peter Ellis, unknown builders in Liverpool attempted to dematerialise the façades of the office buildings and to increase the size of the glass elements to create a complete glass skin (ills. 4.0 and 4.1.10).

A transitional building in this development stands in central Liverpool at the corner of Fazakerley Street and Old Hall Street. Whereas the façades onto the backyard – iron window frames in bays between solid piers, that is, a dissolved external wall – show the standard common around 1860, the street façades could be seen as direct predecessors of Ellis's office buildings (ill. 4.1.11).

Oriel Chambers Building (1864)   In contrast to the neo-Gothic façade to the street, the façade in the narrow backyard reveals the new industrial technology: it is a glass-and-metal façade that projects and steps back like a cascade. In the interior we find a skeleton system borrowed from the cotton mills, consisting of iron columns and beams, a standard vaulted brick ceiling filled with concrete spans between the load-bearing beams. Tension rods in the transverse direction were no longer necessary here, as the iron frame of the façade took over the function of cross bracing (ill. 4.1.12).

The cross-section through the façade (ill. 4.1.13) shows that on the courtyard side the external shell steps back at each floor as the building rises upwards, which means that, starting from the top storey, the inclined top light in the window is somewhat wider on each successive level. This, in turn, led to better daylight conditions and also increased the effect of reflected light in the cramped yard. The importance of this building in terms of construction history was first recognised after damage caused by bombs in World War II (May 1941) to large parts of the building exposed the load-bearing structure made of cast iron.[25]

16 Cook Street (1866)   The second office building by Peter Ellis is on Cook Street, where it fills a gap in a prestigious street (ill. 4.1.14).

As in Oriel Chambers, the courtyard façade represents the industrial character of the new building style, but it goes an important step further. Although the bay window was invented in Liverpool before Peter Ellis, with the aim of improving the amount of daylight and the quality of the workplace by increasing the amount of glass (at the sides, above, or both), Ellis was probably the first to continue this 'bulging' window around the corner and thus became the inventor of the 'free corner' – it was only in 1924, sixty years later, that Gerrit Thomas Rietveld was to completely dissolve the corner, which had previously been defined in terms of architecture and material, in his Schroeder House in Utrecht, the Netherlands, by using two frameless vent windows (ills. 4.1.15 and 4.1.16; see also ill. 3.1.5).

Parallel to the work of Peter Ellis, in France the iron and metal company of Armand Moisant, together with architect Jules Saulnier, developed a curtain wall of high architectural quality for the Menier chocolate factory in Noisiel-sur-Marne (1871/72). This was to become a standard in the later industrial buildings of Modernism (see case study 52).

4.1.9

4.1.10

4.1.11

4.1.12

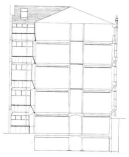

4.1.13

4.1.8: Peter Ellis: Oriel Chambers Building, Liverpool, 1864; the
two street façades of this building on the corner of Water Street and Covent Garden show the newly invented bay window in
an overall neo-Gothic structure: a repetitive arrangement of rounded glazed oriels that depicts the skeleton construction is placed in the framework of a façade cladding made of York stone.

4.1.9: Courtyard façade of the Oriel Chambers Building: the quality and comfort of daylight in the office building is improved, as is the reflection of light in the narrow yard; anticipation of a design and construction strategy that was to be given a commercial application and industrial interpretation only two decades later by the Chicago School of architecture, founded by William Le Baron Jenney.

4.1.10: Curtain wall in a backyard in Liverpool, around 1860

4.1.11: Direct predecessor of Oriel Chambers Building: building on the corner of Fazakerley Street/Old Hall Street, Liverpool; the transition from standard
to new here takes place in the opposite way to Ellis's building: the old (although advanced) façade technology is in the backyard, whereas the new system is used on the street front.

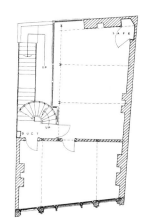

4.1.14

4.1.16

4.1.15

Case Study 52
Menier
Chocolate Factory

Noisiel-sur-Marne
France 1871/72
Engineer and metal construction
company owner: Armand Moisant
Architect: Jules Saulnier

Since 1996, the old Menier chocolate factory has been owned by the Nestlé-France company, whose headquarters are located in the central mill. The entire complex has been renovated, revitalised and extended by the Parisian architects office of Reichen & Roberts, who are specialists in the areas of industrial archaeology and the transformation of run-down industrial sites.[26] In 1864, Émile Menier, together with the architect Jules Saulnier (1817–81), started developing the complex. Saulnier also planned the 'cité ouvrière', which formed part of the complex: a housing estate for the workers of the philanthropist Menier based on the model of the first social housing estates of Émile Muller in Mulhouse, which were characterised by standardised domestic comfort (kitchen, bathroom, heating) and included facilities such as school, library, restaurant, bakery, shops and recreation park.[27]

To meet the requirements of modern fabrication the centrally located mill was to have a functional spatial and load-bearing structure. In 1869, Saulnier decided to use a steel frame for this core element of the complex and to combine this with a metal, front-hung, braced lattice structure and he engaged the services of the engineer and businessman Armand Moisant, a graduate of the École Centrale des Arts et Manufactures (ill. 4.1.17). Saulner artistically used clinker bricks of different colours as infill in this 'mur rideau' to create a more prestigious appearance. Saulnier had not been at a Beaux-Arts masterclass but had attended courses at the École Centrale and at the École Spéciale founded in 1865 by the 'Centralien' Émile Trélat.[28]

The way in which the engineer's metal lattice structure is overlaid with the architectural design creates a synthetic image that combines the two different disciplines of engineer and architect and gives a visible form to the strong presence of the school of thought of the École Centrale (ills. 4.1.18 and 4.1.19).

The crude primary steel structure stands on a concreted platform resting on four massive double piers in a channeled side arm of the river Marne. The structural system is a frame. The lattice not only forms the cladding but also braces the entire structure – forming a shell around highly dynamic machinery (ill. 4.1.20).

The jointed connection between the rigid primary structural elements and the building envelope in front allowed the structure to react elastically to the vibrations and dynamic forces unleashed by the turbines, thus creating a unity between architecture, construction and machinery (ill. 4.1.21).

The technique used to connect the load-bearing façade structure is an early design version of the modern 'curtain wall', as addressed later by, for example, Mies van der Rohe ('skin and bone' concept), defined by Le Corbusier as a building typology theory (together with the overall figure a combination of the 'maison sur pilotis', 'ossature à sec' and 'pan de fer') or elevated to the level of an industrial design task (as a bodywork type) by Jean Prouvé.

Combining the curtain wall construction with a steel frame is Armand Moisant's invention. In 1859, Moisant (1838–1906) completed his studies at the École Centrale des Arts et Manufactures in Paris, earning the title of 'constructeur'– a degree that represented a synthesis of architectural and engineering competences (ill. 4.1.22).[29]

In 1866, Moisant founded a workshop for steel and metal construction, combined with a sheet metal business. Within two decades this business had developed into one of the largest metal construction companies in France.[30] In 1887, it was called Moisant, Laurent, Savey & Cie., after Moisant had involved several of his colleagues from the École Centrale in the development of the business.

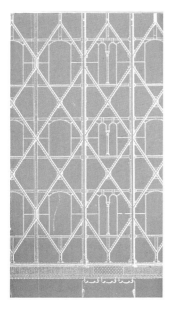

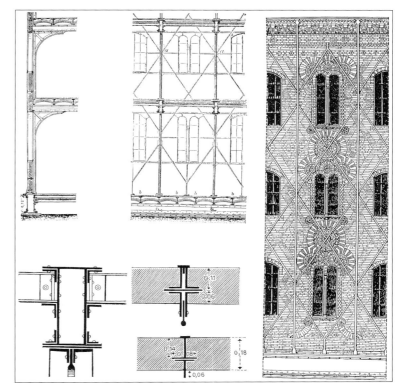

4.1.20

4.1.22

4.1.17: The central mill of the chocolate factory

4.1.18: Construction drawing by Armand Moisant

4.1.19: The overall architectural appearance by Saulnier

4.1.20: A combination of two structural systems to stabilise the machine building: steel frame as a 'bone structure', filigree lattice to stabilise and support the building envelope in front

4.1.21: 'Tableau' of the construction system by Armand Moisant

4.1.22: Corner detail of the central mill: joint work by the engineer-businessman Moisant and architect Saulnier

Iron Skeleton Structure and Curtain Wall

4.2 From the New York Iron Works to the 'Chicago Frame'

The development of building technology in the USA before the Civil War (1860–65) was shaped by 'shop culture': that is to say, inventions and solutions to technical problems were found through workshop knowledge. The success of this work culture was due, in part, to the fact that the 'shops' could stimulate each other to reach increasingly higher levels thanks to the horizontal transfer of knowledge by 'walking workers'. Despite important pioneering schools a true systematic, scientific and technical training in the context of a third-level school system – the 'school culture' – could spread only after the Civil War.[31] The first iron frame constructions inspired by England's industrial potential[32] prepared the ground for the development of an American art of building in iron, which in addition to Philadelphia, the found-

to arguments in favour of a façade cladding of iron – a serious error, as was later revealed. The first important iron constructions on an industrial basis came from two leading New York foundries, those of James Bogardus and Daniel Badger.[33] Thanks to a patent for a building constructed completely of iron, Bogardus was able to erect numerous buildings that, even from a present-day viewpoint, seem modern, for example, the buildings on the corner of Washington Street and Murray Street or at the corner of Centre Street and Duane Street (ills. 4.2.1 and 4.2.2).

In 1854, Bogardus constructed the cast-iron façade for the popular general store Harper's that was an eclectic mix of imported European stylistic elements – Venetian Gothic and Florentine Renaissance – as well as modern

4.2.1

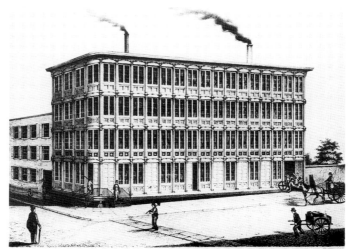

4.2.2

4.2.3

ing city of the USA and the first location of scientific and technical progress, soon spread to numerous other American cities, such as Boston or St Louis, and later to New York and Chicago in particular.

James Bogardus and Daniel Badger

The starting point for the New York Iron Works was a devastating fire on 16/17 December 1835 that destroyed 17 street blocks on the lower East Side: it offered support

materials and new technology: one step backwards, two forwards! Nevertheless, the cast-iron and glass façade placed in front of the conventional load-bearing structure represented an early form of curtain wall.[34]

Daniel Badger, Bogardus's main competitor, also produced systems and components for iron façades and entire buildings. The most prominent among these is probably the Haughwout Store at the corner of Broadway and Broome Street in New York City, which dates from 1857. It was in this building that Elisha Graves Ortis installed his first elevator with an automatic braking system (ill. 4.2.3).[35]

In addition to the iron works of Bogardus and Badger numerous other firms also profited from the emerging boom and, after the great fire in Chicago in 1871, were able to establish themselves there also.[36] The largest iron frame building in New York at the time was the Wanamaker Store at the corner of Broadway and 9th Street (1859–68).[37]

The transformation of Chicago – building technology after the Great Fire of 1871

On the eve of the devastating fire of 8 October 1871 Chicago consisted largely of numerous timber houses built using the balloon frame or 'western system' that had been invented there (cf. chapter 5.1). Only a few buildings, mostly the prestigious ones, consisted of a solid construction. To make matters even worse the streets of Chicago had been paved with wood and the joints filled with tar ('Nicholson's pavement').[38] The fire raged for 48 hours and destroyed the entire core of the city from south to north: the results were 100,000 homeless people and the loss of one third of the real estate value of Chicago.

The fire encouraged the development of a new building technology – the Chicago frame – and, in connection with it, the curtain wall. Fire safety was achieved by cladding the steel frame: in the interior it was enclosed in plaster or brick, and externally encased in shaped terracotta elements (ill. 4.2.4). The building that served as a model and example was the Nixon Building by Otto H. Matz (north-eastern corner of La Salle Street and Monroe Street, demolished in 1889[39]), which had been completed shortly before the fire and survived the blaze.

The reconstruction of the central area of Chicago after the fire gave the city an entirely new physiognomy – a metamorphosis of districts that had originally consisted of numerous timber houses (balloon frame) into an elegant, light, vertical and 'fast' business city – the capital of the 'West'. Just as rapidly as it had grown out of nothing from 1830, the city transformed itself four decades later. Here, building technology played a key role. Massive

building methods and a horizontality based on classical styles retired to the background (ill. 4.2.5).

The new building technology had first to be invented in order to renew, speedily and in the middle of an economic crisis, a city that was growing at an explosive rate. What was new was the use of steel sections readily available on the market[40] to build load-bearing skeleton systems that tapered (and therefore grew lighter) as they rose upwards. A new building type, 'the high-rise', was created, which could be given a fireproof cladding by the use of prefabricated terracotta elements. This technique was first demonstrated and also published in 1891 as a 'skyscraper programme' by → William Le Baron Jenney in the Fair Building,[41] after having anticipated this tendency in his prototypical First Leiter Building in 1879. The Fair Building was a model that pointed the direction for the production of buildings by the Chicago School of Architecture.[42]

In contrast to the Chicago School of the 'Western Architects', skyscraper technology in New York remained at the stage of the 'double structure': the internal steel frame was enclosed by massive walls, which were used by East Coast architects still influenced by the Beaux-Arts style as a medium for stylistic decorative elements.

The constructive typology of the buildings by the → Chicago School consists of a combination of the 'Chicago frame' with the specific form of the curtain wall and is characterised by a thin layer of terracotta cladding cast in moulds, which depicts the load-bearing skeleton, a high proportion of glazing, as well as the typical Chicago window (side tilting/sliding windows) or the 'bay window' imported from Liverpool. The impression made was that of a skin stretched across the steel skeleton frame – a functional and rational preparation for the modernism that was to follow, as in the work of Mies van der Rohe. Frank Lloyd Wright – and later Colin Rowe – offered fundamental criticism of this 'commercial architecture' that had neither spatial nor sculptural aspirations.[43]

4.2.4

4.2.5

Case Study 53
First Leiter Building and Fair Building

Chicago, Illinois, USA,
1879 and 1890/91
Architect:
William Le Baron Jenney

William Le Baron Jenney (1832–97) commenced his studies at the Paris École Centrale des Arts et Manufactures (ECAM) in 1852/53, and graduated there in 1856 (one year after Gustave Eiffel) as a 'constructeur'. Thanks to the influence of this industrially oriented school of thought Jenney was in the position to react to new kinds of problems, such as 'skyscraper technology', which he helped shape after his return to Chicago from Paris.[44] The ECAM had been founded in 1829/30 by former 'polytechniciens' and followers of Saint-Simon. Towards the end of the restoration era there were clear indications of forthcoming change caused by the emerging force of industrialisation and the development of a modern French bourgeoisie. Saint-Simon linked the philosophy of the Enlightenment[45] with the programmatic intentions of the early capitalists. When Louis-Philippe, Duc d'Orleans, who came to power as 'citizen king' in the aftermath of the July Revolution of 1830, was replaced by a second Napoleonic regime in the course of a third French political upheaval in 1848, Paris experienced a planning and building boom under the leadership of Baron Haussmann. The founders of the ECAM, who successfully sold their school to the state in 1857 and in this way secured their pensions, also profited from this development.[46]

In the decade that followed the destruction of central Chicago by fire in 1871 a considerable number of iron businesses, architects and engineers moved to Chicago, among them Jenney. His first modern building (after the eclectic Natural History Museum of 1875) was the First Leiter Building, erected in 1879 on the corner of Wells Street and Monroe Street, in the inner district of Chicago. Here, Jenney invented the 'high-rise' building type, a steel skeleton frame building encased in fire-resistant material, with columns close to the inside face of the external wall and the façade, hung like a shell in front of the structure (ill. 4.2.6).

The floor plan (ill. 4.2.7) shows in detail that Jenney was searching for consistency. The precisely drawn system of columns and the rationally organised plan with just a few 'disturbing' elements, such as lift, staircase and service spaces, contrast with the less pictorial way in which the external wall is shown. In the floor plan it irritatingly looks more like an external wall rather that

what it actually is: a secondary structural system for a curtain wall, a light building envelope or 'skin', which depicts externally the skeleton of the internal load-bearing structure. In this prototype Jenney opened up the bays between the piers to the greatest possible extent.

After further buildings (Home Insurance Building, 1884/85, Second Leiter Building, 1889/91), Jenney in 1891 designed his first consistent high-rise building, the Fair Building, which became a role model for the new building technology. The entire system of this building – with its specific foundation type, standardised steel frame and effective front-hung wall made of prefabricated terracotta elements – forms a kind of 'lesson' of the Chicago School (ill. 4.2.8). The floor slab construction was a new interpretation of the building technology used in the cotton mills 100 years earlier. That the Fair Store became the prototype of the skyscraper was due in part to the 'tableau' of the construction (based on the French tradition), complete with architectural and technical descriptions by Jenney (ill. 4.2.9).

Jenney was an engineer-architect, inventor of building techniques and a propagandist.[47] At a lecture given in 1890 he developed a vision of a modern façade technology using burnt clay in the form of a consistently high-quality, machine-made material, a thin, weatherproof and light layer, made of standardised forms and with a smooth, self-cleansing surface. Twenty years before Henry Ford's principle of the assembly line Jenney also prophesied automated production lines operating on a 365-day and 24-hour basis – terracotta as a mass product that would meet the requirements of the entire city of Chicago. He also predicted similar processes for the production of steel: "And we enter upon a new age – an age of steel and burnt clay."[48] (ill. 4.2 10)

When Ludwig Mies van der Rohe moved to Chicago he took these achievements as his starting point and perfected the typological and tectonic connection of load-bearing skeleton frame and curtain wall, utilising the advances in technology that had been made by the 1950s.

4.2.6

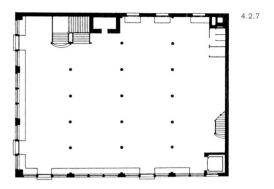

4.2.7

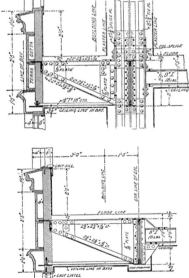

4.2.8

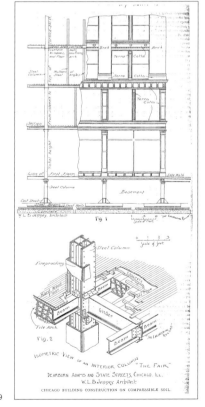

4.2.9

4.2.10

Case Study 54

The Chicago School of Architecture

Holabird & Roche, John W. Root,
Daniel H. Burnham, Louis Sullivan

4.2.11

Jenney's inventions and developments led rapidly to typical standardised building methods and techniques that were employed by the architects and engineers of Chicago. This created a specific image of architecture in Chicago. The character of the 'Loop' in Chicago, which still makes an impact in urban and building terms, was created within the space of a few years following the great fire. The fact that this speedy and efficient rebuilding took place during an economically depressed period may seem amazing, yet it was also based on the availability of inexpensive labour owing to high unemployment levels, as well as on favourable construction loans.

Jenney's practice developed into a 'teaching workshop' for the protagonists of the Chicago School: Jenney's former staff members Louis Sullivan, John W. Root and Daniel H. Burnham worked as innovative interpreters, his assistants William Holabird and Martin Roche as enterprising men of action. While Sullivan, after having gained work practice in Jenney's office, studied at the École des Beaux-Arts in Paris, Holabird and Roche were 'scholars' the Chicago School: in their 'commercial architecture' they developed and brought to maturity the basic ideas of plain, unadorned modernity, technical perfection and functional economy (ill. 4.2.11).

Probably the finest and most original skyscraper from the time of the Chicago School is the Reliance Building, built by Daniel H. Burnham between 1890–94. The concept of the repeated use of bay windows 'imported' from Liverpool (ill. 4.2.12, see also ills. 4.2.5 and 4.2.10) not only created a special spatial quality and gave the figure a sculptural aspect but the larger areas of glass also improved the quality of daylight in the workspaces, reflected light externally and brightened up the surroundings, an effect also noticeable in the backyard of Peter Ellis's Oriel Chambers Building in Liverpool (see case study 51).

Whereas John W. Root trained himself further in the scientific, technical and industrial areas at the Engineering School of New York University, Burnham's experience was based on his apprenticeship period with Jenney and on practice. The fascinating Flat Iron or Fuller Building in New York (1902), which is based on a steel skeletal frame but clad with a layer of real stone, is also by Burnham. The system of the openings in this building illustrates the internal 'skeleton' of construction, a typical characteristic of the Chicago School.

The department store Carson Pirie Scott & Cie. (originally Schlesinger & Mayer) built by Louis Sullivan and Daniel Burnham from 1899–1901 stands at a geometrically slightly irregular junction in the street grid. This offered a chance to solve the problem of the corner by means of a rotunda (ill. 4.2.13). This richly decorated element, visible from a considerable distance, marks the main entrance of the building. As a consequence this building is more complex than the usual commercial buildings in the Loop in Chicago. However, the construction followed the same scheme as the 'Chicago frame' and the building was erected in the shortest imaginable period: two photographs taken within the space of about a week show the rate of 'high-speed assembly' (ills. 4.2.14 and 4.2.15).

When Sullivan was working on the design of the Auditorium Building (1887–89), he employed Frank Lloyd Wright in his office. It may have been the exceptional complex spatial quality of this building and the sculptural nature of the front foyer element that caused Wright to develop into a critic of the standard, spatially uninspired type of 'commercial architecture' and challenged him to produce architectural alternatives, even for the skyscraper. Wright's criticism later led Colin Rowe to produce a new critical evaluation of the architecture of the 'Chicago frame'. In 1956 he wrote in *Architectural Review*: "Due to the open, evenly lit floor and the unlimited number of storeys which it allowed, the steel frame almost imposed itself on Chicago architects as an answer to a practical problem; but the circumstances under which they examined it meant that they were inevitably prevented from exploring its spatial possibilities."[49]

4.2.12

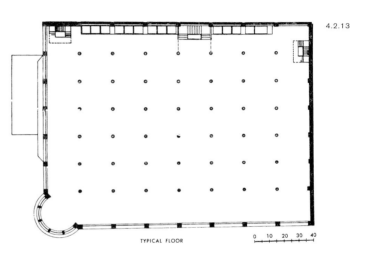

4.2.13

TYPICAL FLOOR

0 10 20 30 40

4.2.14, 4.2.15

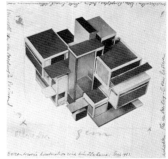

4.3 The 'façade libre' – A Project of Modernism

4.3.1: Johannes Duiker with Bernard Bijvoet and Jan Gerko Wiebenga (engineer): open-air school, Amsterdam, 1927/28; concrete skeleton frame and glass skin

4.3.2: Ludwig Mies van der Rohe: Kaufhaus Adam (department store), Berlin, project, 1928/29; Mies's new curtain wall, a front-hung opaque glass wall as a potential medium for signs and advertising, the horizontal metal bands only represent virtual reference lines, they depict the ends of the internal floor slabs, thin bars articulate the glass bands – an anticipation of the façade technology of the future.

4.3.3: Theo van Doesburg, Cornelis van Eesteren: Maison d'artiste, project for the De Stijl exhibition in Paris in 1923

It took the avant-garde thinking of the Perret brothers and the De Stijl movement, as well as Le Corbusier's propaganda-like radicalism and the technically adept architectural consistency of Mies van der Rohe to apply the achievements of Liverpool and Chicago to the new challenges of the 20th century. Furthermore, the architects and engineers of modernism had to respond to the urgent demands resulting from crises – such as tuberculosis, carried over from the 19th century, or the widespread housing shortage after World War I. The concrete frame building method and the new possibilities of glazing were most useful in meeting such challenges. Replacing the solid wall by the curtain wall façade and membrane-like skin (ill. 4.3.1) meant freedom, lightness, transparency and health – light, air and openness were the formulas of modernism[50] – and a departure from the weightiness and massiveness of styles inspired by classicism.

Visions and industrial reality

From 1894/95 Frank Lloyd Wright was commissioned as an industrial designer by the → Luxfer Prism Company to investigate the theme of lightweight façade technology.[51] His designs and visions were taken up in the buildings of the Chicago School and Wright himself used this glass technology in his designs for high-rise buildings.

Ludwig Mies van der Rohe's vertical concepts for high-rise and office buildings and department stores (1921–23) reflected the context of the metropolis Berlin in their glassy clarity, and thanks to the glass skin allowed the form of the structural skeleton frame to shimmer through – as manifestos for the new, the coming. While the skeleton was used to organise a rational structure of spaces and functions, the principal features are depicted in the 'skin' only in a rough and abstract way; essentially the building envelope follows its own rules. Mies wrote as follows: "The materials are: concrete, iron, glass. Reinforced concrete buildings are essentially skeleton buildings. No dough, no turrets. Where a construction of load-bearing beams is used, then the wall should be non-load-bearing. That is, skin and bone buildings."[52] (ill. 4.3.2).

Dutch modernism

The Kontra-Konstruktion and the projects Maison particulière and Maison d'artiste by Theo van Doesburg and

Cornelis van Eesteren (ill. 4.3.3) show a spatial composition with free references in three dimensions: walls and floors become panels and slabs, the climatic boundary between indoor and outdoor space is not determined, the 'figure' hovers, is not connected to any particular place, has no primary direction, and is independent of the environment – a universal manifesto. The drawing published in the journal *De Stijl* in 1924 is a key depiction of the new way of thinking.[53]

The free design of the façade in the intellectual model of the 'Kontra-Konstruktion' indicates a new dimension of the curtain wall. It is no longer related to the structural skeleton system as in the Chicago School: instead it forms a tectonic figure of the spatial system and follows its own rules about materials. The first building to implement this vision was the Schroeder House by Gerrit Thomas Rietveld (Utrecht, 1924). For the first time in the history of building an absolutely free, immaterial corner was created, when the two side-hung windows of the first-floor living room were opened.

Since the inventions of Hennebique, concrete technology had made cantilevered building elements and free corners possible, which decisively expanded the design area of the glazed curtain wall. The Dutch 'Neue Sachlichkeit' fully exploited this design potential. Johannes Duiker's buildings or the Van Nelle factory in Rotterdam (see chapter 3, case study 39), which are comparable to Owen Williams's pharmaceuticals factory in Beeston, England, show great design virtuosity in the interplay of the concrete skeleton structure and the glass skin. This 'dematerialisation' of the wall became a theme of modernism and established itself as a standard in post-war modernism.

Industrial architecture

A number of → industrial buildings in Germany addressed this new design area that was defined in terms of construction and also mastered the 'liberation of the corner' in both technical and aesthetic terms: the factory of the Steiff-Werke in Giengen an der Brenz (1903), the Fagus-Werke in Alfeld an der Leine by Walter Gropius and Adolf Meyer (1911) or the buildings designed by Fritz Schupp and Martin Kremmer for the Zollverein Colliery in Essen-Katernberg (1928–32) are all symbols

of modernism in the field of industrial building. Albert Kahn, who conceived large production halls for the most important American car manufacturers, used the typology of 'bone' and 'skin' as early as 1910 to visually position factory architecture as the forerunner of an anticipated light, industrial modernity (ill. 4.3.4; see case study 71).

The Maison de Verre in Paris (1928–32) also manifests an industrial lightness. The design was generated by a 'tight building site': a cross block in a narrow courtyard close to the Boulevard St Michel was to be redeveloped, but it was necessary to preserve the top floor of the building. The architects Pierre Chareau, Bernard Bijvoet[54] and Lois Dalbet decided to use the bare underpinning framework as the new structure and employed a glass block wall independent of the structure to define the spatial boundaries – an original interpretation of the 'liberated façade' and of spatial transparency (ill. 4.3.5)

The industrial building envelope of modernism

The possibilities offered by the free design of façades suggested by industrial architecture were implemented by the pioneers → Le Corbusier, Pierre Jeanneret and → Jean Prouvé. They experimented with new materials and technologies; in addition Prouvé examined new achievements in the fields of railway and ship-building technology. Prouvé and Le Corbusier were fascinated by the lightness of flight and the speed of the motorcar and exploited this technical potential for the visionary dimension of a future-oriented architecture.

Gottfried Semper and 'Metallotechnik'

Prouvé's sculpturally shaped, curved, bevelled and deep-drawn metal sheets recall an extraordinary statement by Gottfried Semper in his opus magnum *Der Stil*, which dates from 1863, on the theme of iron construction and 'Metallotechnik'. In this book Semper asks how metal might become part of 'beautiful architecture' and provides the answer to his own question: hollow metal prisms and metal in the form of worked sheets should be used as constructive elements: "But as far as I am aware nobody has still used this method of construction architecturally. I believe that this has to happen if art is to gain its share of the world of iron." For Semper, metal

is "usable for beautiful architecture only in the form of sheets (by this term I mean the form in which, seen in relation to the cross-sectional area, the surface area is extremely significant. I also include cast columns, for example)."[55]

Somewhat later, in his building for the royal and imperial stage-set depot, known as the Semper Depot, which served the court opera house and court theatre in Vienna (ill. 4.3.6),[56] Semper demonstrated what he meant: in two large spaces the ceiling slab is constructed of concave iron sheets, bevelled on all four sides, and riveted to iron beams (inverted T-sections). These sheets were intended as 'permanent shuttering' for the thin cement floor poured on top of them. These 'hump-backed sheets' remain visible and form a wavy, light-reflecting 'sky' and shape the style within the overall context of the building, which internally has an iron skeleton construction much like the English textile factories, while the exterior is designed like a Florentine palazzo.[57]

4.3.4: Albert Kahn, industrial modernity and a brand-related image for Chrysler, Detroit, 1937

4.3.5: Maison de Verre, Paris, 1928–32, glass blocks used as a curtain wall

4.3.6: Gottfried Semper with Karl Hasenauer: ceiling made of curved metal sheets in the stage-set depot (Semper Depot), Vienna, 1874–77, gallery hall on the third floor

4.3.6

Case Study 55

The Luxfer Prism Company
Frank Lloyd Wright's Studies and Projects

Frank Lloyd Wright's collaboration with the Luxfer Prism Company in Chicago began in 1894/95 when the company engaged his services as an industrial designer. The development of Luxfer prism glass after the invention patented by the English engineer James Pennycuick in 1882 led, after the founding of the Luxfer Prism Company, to the production of glass tiles measuring 10 x 10 cm, which were ribbed on one side so that the standardised prism structure of apparently 20 rods redirected light. Like glass blocks, the individual modules could be combined in metal frames to form larger units. They were used as components in non-load-bearing façades and were employed in innumerable buildings, also in Europe, including, for example, Bruno Taut's glass pavilion at the 1914 *Werkbundaustellung* in Cologne, or in the inclined canopy roof to the Kärntner Bar in Vienna by Adolf Loos (1908). The Saint-Gobain glass company in Paris played the leading role in the production of Luxfer prism glass for the European market. In the USA during the first two decades of the 20th century, Luxfer prism technology was used in tens of thousands of office buildings, warehouses, etc.[58]

Through working with Frank Lloyd Wright the Luxfer Prism Company hoped to raise the design level of this industrial product and to create a professional background for the future use of this new building element. The aim was to associate the product's qualities in terms of technical progressiveness, energy-saving and low maintenance with an expression of design modernity – 'industrial design' as a marketing element for the 'century's triumph in lighting'[59] (ill. 4.3.7).

The design patents came from Wright and were initially restricted to impressed patterns on individual modules or ornamental figures across a number of combined panels, until a competition in 1898 made prism glass into a theme for the design of entire buildings and called for examples of 'good modern architecture'. The jury included important promoters of the Chicago School, such as William Le Baron Jenney, Daniel H. Burnham, William Holabird and Frank Lloyd Wright himself, as well as Henry Crew, physics professor at the Northwestern University in Chicago. Two model designs, which probably came from Wright himself, were included among the competition documentation (ill. 4.3.8).

Wright's proposals remained anonymous. He placed the prism glasses in modules measuring 11 x 11 feet and used these units to design the entire façade. The composition with its special ground floor and mezzanine zone conveys a new image of architecture – the technical building element becomes the component that shapes the style of the building. In the January 1938 edition of the magazine *Architectural Forum* Wright published 'Design No. 1' for an office building with prism glass, or as a reference image for later projects such as the St Mark's-in-the-Bouwerie-Towers in New York (1927–31) or the more developed glass technology in the Price Tower in Bartlesville, Oklahoma (1952–56, ill. 4.3.9).

A number of other projects by Wright – for example, the National Life Insurance Company Building in Chicago (1924/25, ill. 4.3.10), the Grouped Towers in Chicago (1930) or the Rogers Lacy Hotel in Dallas Texas (1946/47) – show a variety of ways of translating prism glass technology into architectural compositions.[60]

In the context of the activity of the Chicago School the technology of Luxfer prism glass developed into a highly influential element in the design of plinth zones, and was also, to a certain extent, used in the upper levels of buildings. The deflection of light by prism glass allowed deep spaces to be lit and could make light wells unnecessary – for example, in the building (already referred to) of the Gage Group on Michigan Avenue in Chicago by Holabird & Roche and Louis Sullivan, with a depth of over 50 m where the intention was to improve the daylight situation (see ill. 4.2.11), or in the Carson Pirie Scott & Cie. department store by Louis Sullivan and Daniel H. Burnham, where prism glass as a modern industrial design product is stylistically incorporated in a Beaux-Arts ornament – a collage of stylistic elements from different eras (ill. 4.3.11).

Since the demonstrative presentation in the Siemens Pavilion at the 1992 *Expo* in Seville (architects: Bertram Engel, Christian Hartmann, Gunter R. Standke) the theme of prism glass has again become topical, at least in the world of research.

4.3.7

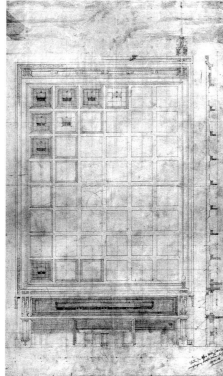

4.3.10

4.3.9

4.3.11

The 'façade libre' – A Project of Modernism

Case Study 56

The Industrial Building Culture in Germany

Steiff-Werke, Fagus-Werke,
Zeche Zollverein

4.3.12: Richard Steiff: Steiff-Werke, Giengen an der Brenz, 1903; the skeleton structure in the end building consists of twin steel sections with visible diagonal struts and a completely glazed façade, which is consistently and independently hung in front of the structure and is continued around the corner: in contrast to Gropius's and Meyer's Bauhaus in Dessau (see case study 38) the corner column has the same profile on both sides – a perfect corner solution by the inventor of the teddy bear.

4.3.13: Interior of the Steiff-Werke: lightness of the primary construction in interplay with a glass envelope conceived independently of it; the ventilation windows and louvres can also be seen.

4.3.14: Steiff-Werke: load-bearing system and glass skin – two structures of construction and space that do not refer to each other shape a vision of architecture unusual for its time.

4.3.15: Walter Gropius and Adolf Meyer: Fagus-Werke, Alfeld an der Leine, 1911; the construction of the façade reveals an irritation: the load-bearing façade piers look like 'isolation joints' in the glass skin.

4.3.16: Fagus-Werke: two steel channels placed back to back form the column; the independent glass skin with its own constructive 'rules' is placed in front of it.

4.3.17: Fritz Schupp, Martin Kremmer: Zeche Zollverein, Essen-Katernberg, 1928–32; section through the standard wall construction

4.3.18: Zeche Zollverein: special solution with a recessed corner column, an image of architecture shaped by industry and the considerations of construction and technique – a landmark for a new aesthetic of industrial culture

Three examples from the period between 1903 and 1933 in Germany illustrate building complexes, which, although very different to each other, all manifest new aspects in the development of building technology. They also illustrate three different schools of thought in architecture: the approach of the boffin and man-of-action, of the kind we have already encountered in the person of Paxton and Monier in earlier chapters, of the artist-architect, and the approach taken by the industrial architect.

Steiff-Werke, Giengen an der Benz, 1903   Richard Steiff, the inventor of the teddy bear (with the 'button in its ear') and graduate of the Kunstgewerbeschule Stuttgart (1898), designed his own factory and commissioned the Eisenwerk München AG (formerly Kiessling – C. Moradelli) to build it. The complex consists of a three-storey end building and a rear area with two long, two-storey production wings (1905 and 1908) bordering a wide courtyard, which were planned by Richard's brother Hugo, a mechanical engineering graduate of Mannheim engineering school (ill. 4.3.12; see also ill. 8, p. 10).

All buildings use an elegant steel skeleton structure made of two separate channels connected by flat steel plates, giving the columns a transparent effect (ill. 4.3.13). The inner glass skin runs between the ceiling and the columns, while the outer skin is fixed continuously in front of the structure; the void between the skins is ventilated – a forerunner of the most modern 'twin skin' technology.[61] The independence of the skin and structure in the flat buildings has a strong visual effect (ill. 4.3.14) – some 25 years before Mies van der Rohe's Barcelona Pavilion!

Fagus-Werke, Alfeld an der Leine, 1911   Carl Benscheidt, who founded the Fagus-Werke (Fagus Works) in 1911, wanted to improve the form of the shoe last and in this way contribute to providing shoes that are good for the foot. The intention to design a modern product was to be combined with a modern, naturally lit factory. Benscheidt commissioned the office of Walter Gropius and Adolf Meyer to design the factory. Gropius and Meyer – not without encountering difficulties with their client – pursued the idea of a consistent skeleton system building made of steel, glass and clinker brickwork. The constructive disposition follows the primacy of form in the order form – construction – function, which Gropius also

referred to in his correspondence with Benscheidt.[62] The cross-shaped brickwork piers in the façade look like isolation joints in the projecting, steel-framed glass layer in which the horizontal bars are larger than the verticals (ill. 4.3.15). Only at the corner of the staircase building are there no piers. The shadow cast on the 'isolation joints' by the projecting 'box' of the window reveals that the masonry piers in fact taper upwards (from 74 to 66 cm; in the visible area between the edges of the window frames from 23 to 13 cm).

However, the most consistent skeleton structure building in the Fagus complex is the boiler house (today the Fagus-Gropius Café) at the extreme north-eastern corner – here, somewhat removed from the rest of the complex, the construction was prioritised and depicts the possibilities of the 'free corner'. In terms of its space-shaping and constructive typology it lies historically between Peter Ellis's office building at 16 Cook Street in Liverpool and the Schroeder House by Gerrit Thomas Rietveld in Utrecht (ill. 4.3.16)

Zeche Zollverein, Essen-Katernberg, 1928–32   'Shaft XII' of the Zeche Zollverein (Zollverein Colliery) was opened in 1932. The buildings were designed by architects Fritz Schupp and Martin Kremmer from Essen and Berlin. The complex is an inventive example of the subtle architectural design of what is a rather crude business. While the load-bearing structure is a steel frame, the purely functionally defined rooms are enclosed by a thin façade skin (ill. 4.3.17).

This envelope consists of a well-proportioned, red-painted frame with an infill layer of brownish-purple clinker bricks and glass panes (some of them wired glass). The façade frames are fixed to the load-bearing structure, that is, unlike in the Steiff-Werke, they refer to the primary system. All parts of the complex use the same design principle: ". . . this architecture is expressly conceived for the gaze of the viewer."[63] (ill. 4.3.18).

These examples also stand for others that indicated new paths and made an individual contribution to the culture of building and the building technology of modernism. The best-known building from this era of modern industrial building history is most probably Peter Behrens's AEG turbine factory in Berlin (1909); the least well known is Godfrey Greene's British Navy Boat Store in Sheerness (1858–60; see ills. 3.5.20, 4.5 and 4.1.6).

4.3.13

4.3.14

4.3.15

4.3.16

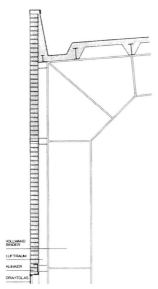

VOLLWAND
BINDER

LUFTRAUM

KLINKER

4.3.17 DRAHTGLAS

4.3.18

'Le mur rideau'
Studies and Projects
by Le Corbusier

1927–39

In connection with the Weißenhofsiedlung of the German Werkbund in Stuttgart, in 1927 Le Corbusier (Charles Édouard Jeanneret, 1887–1965) developed theoretical reflections on the architecture of the future and on a new aesthetic. Alfred Roth (for and with Le Corbusier) published these reflections as the *Five Points on a New Architecture* to accompany the Stuttgart Werkbund exhibition.[64] For the 'free design of the façade' – point 5 – Le Corbusier proposed a concrete slab that projects beyond the posts and moves the façade to the edge of the posts: "It thus loses its load-bearing quality and the windows can be placed wherever required, without a direct relationship to the internal disposition (. . .) therefore the façade has a free design."

Whereas in his subsequent buildings Le Corbusier had problems in applying this idea in a consistent constructional way, for Jean Prouvé the 'mur rideau' was the basis of his thoughts on material technology from the very start. Whereas the former was influenced by Behrens and Gropius, the latter was influenced more by the surroundings of a workshop culture, in which the bodywork for cars was produced.

The building by Le Corbusier and Pierre Jeanneret that apparently comes closest to the concept of the glass or metal curtain wall ('mur rideau', 'pan de verre' or 'pan de fer') is the Immeuble Clarté (or Maison Wanner) built in Geneva from 1928–32 (ills. 4.3.19 and 4.3.20). External, slightly projecting sheet-steel panels are welded to a steel skeleton frame, in which the columns are made of two steel channels facing each other and the ceiling beams are H-sections; the fixed glazing is attached to these steel plates from inside. The fixed connection of the primary structure and the glass skin, without any intermediate space, is an irritation. In fact this is not an independent frontal curtain wall but a wall layer set back between steel columns that project slightly outwards (ill. 4.3.21).

The Pavillon Suisse in the Cité Universitaire in Paris (1932/33), which was built at around the same time, conveys a similarly deceptive picture of a 'mur rideau'. A four-storey metal frame, similar to that of the Clarté, is mounted on a concrete 'table' carried on 'pilotis' (point 1 of the *Five Points*) and serves as the structural system for floor slabs, walls and façades. If one compares this with the completed building, two different pictures emerge: the rear façade, (which represents the side where people arrive), has a solid character, despite the fact that it has isolation joints like a clad façade, whereas the side facing the park is designed as a light metal-and-glass skin (ill. 4.3.22). The technical details of the construction clearly show the transition: the glass skin is positioned in front of the columns lying in the façade plane and is fixed to outward-facing steel angles – it is connected to the primary structure but looks like a front hung 'façade semi libre' (ill 4.3.23).[65]

The apartment building at Porte Molitor in Paris, which was also completed in 1933, illustrates the next step towards a true curtain wall façade with a front façade layer that, in the parapet area, is made of glass windows and glass block modules but still follows the rhythm of the building's structure (ill. 4.3.24).

In 1939, the first year of the war, Le Corbusier and Pierre Jeanneret, who dissolved their office partnership in the same year, undertook an attempt to design prefabricated small houses, the Maisons montées a sec (M. A. S.), using dry construction methods and prefabricated elements (ill. 4.3.25). Here they took a step further towards the 'mur rideau': the façade structure consists of an outward-facing steel channel and a welded, inward-pointing T-section that is rigidly connected with an inner wooden frame construction. Metal plates, curved at the edges, are clamped externally into the channels to form a sealed external skin. The assembly of the construction from outside is a new aspect here, as is the typological independence of structure and envelope – 'pan de fer' similar to car body and coachwork construction. The channel is only the connecting member. In the central mill of the Menier chocolate factory by Armand Moisant and Jules Saulnier (1870/71, see case study 52) we find an essentially similar construction. The M. A. S. project approached Prouvé's way of thinking.

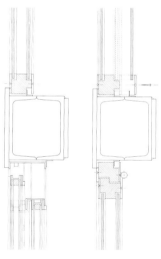

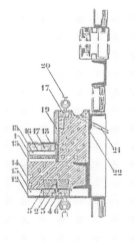

4.3.21

4.3.22

4.3.23

4.3.24

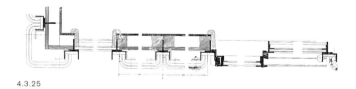

4.3.25

4.3.19: Le Corbusier and Pierre Jeanneret : Immeuble Clarté (Maison Wanner), Geneva, 1928 – 32, the building in its present state

4.3.20: Immeuble Clarté: view of the rear façade, photograph during construction

4.3.21: Immeuble Clarté: fixed glazing, horizontal section

4.3.22: Le Corbusier and Pierre Jeanneret: Pavillon Suisse, Cité Universitaire, Paris, 1932/33; park side

4.3.23: Pavillon Suisse: vertical section through the construction

4.3.24: Le Corbusier and Pierre Jeanneret: apartment building at Porte Molitor, Paris, 1933; part of the front facing the city

4.3.25: Le Corbusier, Pierre Jeanneret: dry construction method (M. A. S.) as a working and intellectual model; horizontal section

Industrial Façade Technology – Studies and Projects by Jean Prouvé

1929–58

4.3.26: Maison du Peuple, Paris-Clichy, 1936–39; metal panel façade by Jean Prouvé before renovation

4.3.27: 'Tableau' of construction details for the standard façade, Maison du Peuple

4.3.28: Garage Marbeuf for Citroen, Paris, 1928/29: early glass façade based on the industrial aesthetic of Jean Prouvé (architects: Albert Laprade and Léon Bazin)

4.3.29: CNIT exhibition hall in Paris-La Defense: around 6,000 m² of curtain wall façade made of glass with multifunctional metal sections, which Prouvé gave an extremely slender cross-section in the front but whose bearing strength is effective at right angles to the façade (see also ill. 3.4.5)

4.3.30: Norman Foster: dome of the Reichstag in Berlin with metal sections designed specifically in terms of bearing strength, light reflection and visualisation of the functions

4.3.31: Jean Prouvé: aluminium anniversary pavilion, Paris, 1954; axonometric showing the spatial, structural, material and technological context[115]

The curtain wall studies by Jean Prouvé (1901–84) have a different background to those by Le Corbusier. As a trained metal worker Prouvé found at an early stage an approach to iron and metal, aluminium and glass and their processing technologies. Professional contacts to architects of modernism such as Robert Mallet-Stevens, Le Corbusier, Pierre Jeanneret, etc. awakened in him an interest in further design possibilities. In his studio and workshop in Maxéville (Nancy, 1947–53) he set up a multidisciplinary workshop with architects, engineers, 'constructeurs' and technicians. Prouvé also invented new kinds of machines to shape metal sheets.[66] His metier meant that he regularly crossed the boundary between the building and the automotive industries – the typology of the chassis and coachwork provided him with a transfer model for building technology. His façade studies from 1929 onwards always point consistently in the direction of the curtain wall.[67]

As early as 1936, after numerous attempts in the area of curtain wall façades, Prouvé invented a new kind of sheet-metal panel for the façade of the Maison du Peuple in Paris-Clichy (ill. 4.3.26), which went a step further than Le Corbusier's M. A. S. constructions. Double-walled metal panels tapered at the edges and spanned against each other by means of clips form standardised modules that are screwed to the sub-construction and, thanks to the clips, can react to temperature changes (ill. 4.3.27).[68]

For Prouvé, 'façade' meant the technical and aesthetic design of the skin or building envelope composed by performed layers. All the services required, such as protection against heat and cold, imperviousness to wind, screening sun and glare, were to be combined in a profiled layer so the elements required could assume a load-bearing function or at least play an auxiliary structural role to relieve the load of the primary bearing structure of the building. Further studies by Prouvé, which continue the work of the pioneers of greenhouse architecture, focus on an attempt to increase the proportion of glass in the surface by developing deeper metal sections (ill. 4.3.28).

The façade for the CNIT exhibition hall in Paris-La Défense, constructed by Prouvé's workshop in 1956, is 206 m long and 50 m high at the crown of the arch (cf. section 3.4). The 'mur rideau' of glass, like the glass front of the Garage Marbeuf, is carried by deep, multi-functional metal sections. The entire entrance area was redesigned in 1991 by Peter Rice/RFR using a structural glazing façade (ill. 4.3.29); unfortunately, the original Prouvé façade was destroyed, and was not restored by RFR.[69] Presently, this building is being completely renewed by brullmann crocon architects in Paris. They are clearing out the inside and redesigning the environment in order to emphasize the original spatial and constructional quality (see also p. 132f.).

It is possible to trace a line of development here that extends from John Claudius Loudon's empirical metal sections to Prouvé's systematic studies and continues to the light-tech references of Norman Foster's aircraft aesthetic in the Reichstag dome (ill. 4.3.30; see case study 89).

The most highly developed 'murs rideaux' and the high points in Prouvé's research are to be found in the apartment building on Square Mozart in Paris (architects: Jean Prouvé, Lionel Mirabaud; 1953) and in the Paris exhibition pavilion *100 Years of Aluminium* of 1954 (built to commemorate the discovery and first uses of bauxite; see chapter 6, case study 85). The building envelope of the apartment house on Square Mozart has movable elements and is a metal-and-glass construction that can react to environmental influences and can be regulated by the residents themselves (see section 6.3 and ill. 6.3.3.). In the aluminium pavilion Prouvé demonstrated all the processes used in the production and shaping of raw aluminium for construction purposes current around 1950: metal shaping, chamfering, rolling, extrusion, deep-drawing, casting, etc. Above all, he showed possible combinations of processes that are still topical in present-day industrial design and that anticipated the sustainable design and construction strategies that employ consciously economical resources (ill. 4.3.31).

From 1957 to 1970 Prouvé worked as a teacher at the Paris Conservatoire Nationale des Arts et Métiers[70] and influenced numerous young designers and 'constructeurs' such as Renzo Piano, who attended his courses at the beginning of the 1960s. According to Piano, it was Prouvé's personality and approach that persuaded him to become an architect rather than a building contractor, and ten years later the fact that Prouvé was president of the jury for the Centre Pompidou competition persuaded Piano and Richard Rogers to enter.[71]

4.3.26

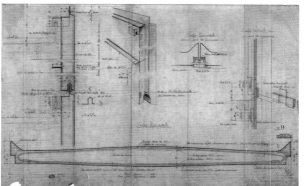

4.3.29

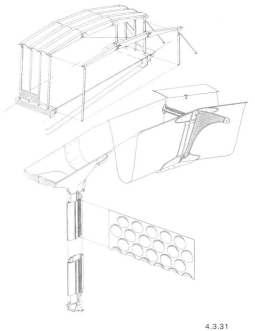

4.3.30

4.3.31

The 'façade libre' – A Project of Modernism

4.4 The Lightness of Post-war Modernism

4.4.1: Adminstration building of the Eternit company in Nieder-urnen (Canton Glarus, Switzerland) by Haefeli, Moser, Steiger architects, 1954/55

4.4.2: Hans Hofmann (architect), A. Aegerter and O. Bosshardt (engineers): Birsfelden Rhine power station, Switzerland, 1953/54

4.4.3: Brussels *Expo* 1958: the German Pavilion by Egon Eiermann and Sep Ruf as the symbol of a new 'liberated space'

4.4.4: Arne Jacobsen: Jespersen office building, Copenhagen, 1952–55

4.4.5: Jespersen office building, cross-section of the 'flying' storey platforms with a true curtain wall

4.4.6: Roland Rohn: Hoffmann-La Roche pharmaceuticals company, Basle, 1947, ramp building

4.4.7: Luigi Figini, Gino Pollini, Annibale Fiocchi: Olivetti factory, Ivrea, Italy, 1955–57

In the 20 years following World War II architecture that referred to the modernism of the interwar period achieved unexpected success. The era of the intellectually oriented avant-garde, of pioneering work and the 'struggle' of the 20s and 30s was followed after 1945 by a widespread phase of development and consolidation that produced major projects of modern architecture such as Le Corbusier's buildings in La Tourette, Marseille and Chandigarh, the main works of Alvar Aalto and Louis I. Kahn, Mies van der Rohe's buildings on the campus of Illinois Institute of Technology and the skyscrapers in Chicago, the emergence of the practice of Skidmore, Owings & Merrill that started with the building of Lever House, Frank Lloyd Wright's Guggenheim Museum in New York, Jørn Utzon's Sydney Opera House, the town hall in Tokyo by Kenzo Tange, the new city of Brasilia by Oscar Niemeyer and Lucio Costa, Kennedy Airport in New York by Eero Saarinen and, for example, James Stirling's Leicester University Engineering Building. In Switzerland, protagonists of the new style developed a modernism that, while internationally oriented, also showed regional influences, as represented by examples such as the administration building of the Eternit company in Niederurnen (Canton Glarus, Switzerland) by Haefeli, Moser, Steiger architects (1954/55; ill 4.4.1)[72] or the Rhine power station at Birsfelden by Hans Hofmann (1953/54; ill. 4.4.2; see also ill. 3.0).

Until around 1960, post-war modernism presented itself as a coherent style of the 1950s and was also taken up by commercial offices. The architects of the period after 1945 undertook pilgrimages to Rotterdam to view the new Lijnbaan shopping and town centre by J. H. van den Broek and Jacob Bakema (1949–53),[73] visited the Berlin *Interbau* (1957) and the 1958 *Expo* in Brussels, where they admired the German Pavilion by Sep Ruf and Egon Eiermann (ill. 4.4.3). This post-war modernism provided a field of reference for both the practice of architecture and the training of architects. A number of schools appointed committed protagonists of modernism or the transitional movement as professors, who then exerted a lasting influence on entire generations of younger students.[74] The seminars held by Konrad Wachsmann should be mentioned in this context, as they had the character of a school of thought and were linked with different school cultures.

Sigfried Giedion's *Space, Time and Architecture* shaped the post-war generation, as did Konrad Wachsmann's *Wendepunkt im Bauen* or, somewhat later, *Transparency* by Colin Rowe and Robert Slutzky.[75] The end of the formal CIAM functionalism still practiced by the 'old guard' came about at the conference in Otterloo in 1959,[76] and was initiated by a new generation that came together in the shape of Team X and the structuralism movement[77] that developed within this framework. These developments also clearly indicated a "turning point in the way of thinking".[78] Claude Levi Strauss's sociological and ethnological studies and Christopher Alexander's *A Pattern Language* of 1977[79] added the broad theoretical background for an examination of the inadequacies of functionalism and rationalism, and for questions about the relationship between the individual, culture and society that extended as far as the habitat problem. The 'democratically inspired' architecture was not confined to Germany (Sep Ruf, Egon Eiermann and, after them, Günter Behnisch) but was combined with an open, transparent spatial quality and lightness of construction that attempted to express itself in freely designed façades that referred to and utilised these qualities.

'Bones' and 'skin': the industrial concept of the 'liberated façade'

Ludwig Mies van der Rohe's glass office, department store, and high-rise buildings for Berlin and Stuttgart that were planned around 1920 not only point to the future of a new kind of building culture, construction technology and world of images, they also reveal this architect's sources of inspiration in the field of tension that extended between De Stijl, the German avant-garde and 'metropolitan architecture'.[80] While the new concrete technology made an efficient skeleton structure possible – forming the bones of the building – the glass skin represented a vision of freedom, openness, lightness and light. During his exile in the Illinois Institute of Technology (IIT) in Chicago (from 1938) Mies was confronted with the rigid market of the American building industry: on the one hand, his concept of glazed office buildings allowed him access to the modern building type of the Chicago skyscraper but on the other, the American situation with its standardised building elements and mass production

4.4.3

edged him towards a new technological way of thinking. While his → faculty buildings at IIT still demonstrates European painstakingness and handcraft, his high-rise buildings on Lake Shore Drive, in the 'Loop' of Chicago, on Park Avenue in New York, in Detroit (Lafayette Park) and elsewhere represent the connection of a European inspired, technically oriented art of building with the 'time is money' attitude of 'Yankee technology' – a synthesis of an illusionist presentation and constructive presence, of building art and the art of building.

The project of modernism and its industrial completion

With their Lever House building in 1952 → Skidmore, Owings & Merrill (SOM) demonstrated that the new international style was possible not only in Chicago and Philadelphia but also in New York. The pure steel-and-glass construction is not simply an unornamented building in the New York high-rise style but in fact its replacement; as a further development of Mies's 'bones and skin' concept it influenced new urban surroundings, anticipated the coming generation of high-rise buildings and was the model for the metropolitan architecture of the future. During this time Frank Lloyd Wright also made a contribution in this field with his space-shaping, sculptural and constructional designs for tall buildings, for example, the Price Tower in Bartlesville, Oklahoma (1952–56; see ill. 4.3.9).

Among the architects particularly involved in generating a style in the 1950s and 1960s through post-war modernism were → Sep Ruf and Egon Eiermann: their buildings contrasted radically with the stone buildings of the German reconstruction project. The post-war work of Arne Jacobsen in Copenhagen – including the SAS high-rise building (1955–60), a kind of gesamt-kunstwerk that refers to Lever House, or the office building for A. Jespersen & Son of 1952–55 (ills. 4.4.4 and 4.4.5) – signified a new orientation based on the principles of modernism, in the case of Jacobsen this took the

form of a further development of his own regionally referenced modernism (for example, the Town Hall in Århus, 1937–42).[81] The office of van den Broek en Bakema presented a 'new town' in the bombed city of Rotterdam: here, rebuilding was understood as the formulation of a forward-looking architectural approach, rather than the reconstruction of the old.

In response to the advances made in concrete technology, with cantilevers, free corners, two-way flat slabs on mushroom-head columns, etc., and inspired by the international network of architects that had developed since the beginnings of modernism as well as by magazines and exhibitions, Swiss architecture and industrial building during the post-war period used the light glass skin as a style-shaping spatial boundary, for example, Roland Rohn in his buildings for the Basle-based pharmaceuticals company of Hoffmann-La Roche (ill. 4.4.6).[82]

In Italy, after the fall of Mussolini it was not possible for a completely new style to develop: post-war modernism was defined somewhere between *continuità* and *dopo-razionalismo*, as essentially it was shaped by the same protagonists. All the same a clear will for renewal is evident, illustrated, for example, by the transparent, light and Dutch-inspired modernism of the Olivetti factory in Ivrea by the team of Figini and Pollini of 1955–57, whose approach in this building is astonishing given their role during the Fascist era (4.4.7).[83]

4.4.5

4.4.6

4.4.7

Ludwig Mies van der Rohe: IIT Campus and Skyscraper Technology in Chicago

4.4.10

4.4.8

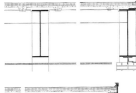

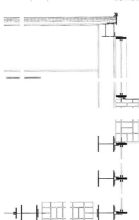

4.4.9

4.4.8: IIT Library: axonometric of the corner

4.4.9: IIT Library: vertical and horizontal sections through the façade; the curtain wall is welded to the outer face of the outer flange by means of two angles, in the long direction the plane of the glass and the frame lies between the columns – hence the curtain wall runs only in one direction.

Mies van der Rohe's early visionary glass building designs clearly show his departure from the English country house style as interpreted by Muthesius and from the neo-Classical manner of the 'Prussian Style'.[84] As the representative of the Deutscher Werkbund (1926–32) he headed the construction of the Weißenhofsiedlung in Stuttgart (1927) and designed the German Pavilion at the *World Fair* in Barcelona (1929).

Mies's vertical designs for office buildings from 1922–25 illustrate a new structural formula, a technically oriented compositional rule. He wrote: "The materials are concrete, steel and glass. Reinforced concrete buildings are essentially skeleton buildings. No dough, no turrets. Where a construction of load-bearing beams is used, then the wall should be non-load bearing. That is, skin and bones buildings."[85] From an early stage this concept shaped Mies's basic architectural approach and allowed him to attain design freedom and to find an approach to new façade technologies.

After going into exile in America in 1938[86] Mies examined the market conditions of 'Yankee technology' – mass production, standardisation and construction processes dictated by the adage that 'time is money' – without ever denying his avant-garde way of thinking. In using easily available standard steel sections in his design work his aim was to raise the general level of the art of building.

Prototype IIT Library   The main beams of Mies's library for Illinois Institute of Technology span about 60 m over three bays in the transverse direction of the building and are welded to slender secondary beams. At the corners this order is changed by means of a flat metal section that covers the outer half of the main beam (which would otherwise be visible) and continues down to the ground. The projecting brick wall hides the lower flange from view, making it seem that the corner seems not to have a primary direction (ills. 4.4.8 and 4.4.9).

Searching for a standard   Both the Chemistry and Metallurgy Building (1945/46) and the Alumni Memorial Hall (1945) at IIT pursue a further combination of 'the presentation of an illusion' with necessities that result from the construction. As the buildings were several storeys high they had to be given a fire-resistant cladding. This meant that the oriented H-section column remained hidden, leading Mies to develop a neutral corner solution

without a primary direction. Although the façade is consistently placed in front of the load-bearing structure, it takes the form of a curtain wall only in the transverse direction (ills. 4.4.10 and 4.4.11).

Crown Hall, reverse figure   This building for the training of architects and designers (1950–56) in which Mies and László Moholy-Nagy headed master classes was conceived as an industrial hall. The body of the hall (which has no internal columns) seems to hang from beneath the external frame system although, in fact, it is carried by secondary beams. The suspended ceiling prevents one from seeing how the construction is organised (ill. 4.4.12).

Skyscraper technology   Lake Shore Drive Apartments in Chicago (1948–51) was the first high-rise building to challenge Mies to develop a new technical and aesthetic approach. As in the Chemistry Buildings on the IIT campus the structure here also consists of H-columns encased in concrete. Regularly positioned steel sections on the façade brace the building envelope (ill. 4.4.13).

To overcome the irregularity in the fenestration and the effect made by the corner of the Lake Shore Drive Apartments, in the neighbouring Esplanade Apartments (1953–57) Mies expanded the space between the glass layer and the load-bearing system (ills. 4.4.14 and 4.4.15).

In the Seagram Building on Park Avenue in New York (1954–58) Mies increased the distance between the primary and secondary construction. The space gained as a result made it possible to convey the illusion of a neutral structure with a skin that continues around the corner (ill. 4.4.16).

This architectural, constructional and technical design of the building envelope became a standard part of Mies's later office buildings, as shown by the residential high-rise buildings in Lafayette Park in Detroit (1960) or by the Federal Center in Chicago (1959–64). In terms of the technical and constructional shaping and the architectural figure created the 'Fed' represents a perfect synthesis in Mies's search for a style-forming corner solution (ill. 4.4.17).[87]

Mies was not only influential as a teacher at IIT in Chicago, his buildings and projects also became models for several generations of architects and engineers, among them the office of SOM.[88]

4.4.12

4.4.11

4.4.13

4.4.15

4.4.16

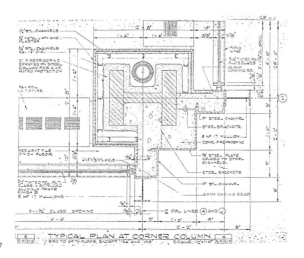

4.4.14

4.4.17

4.4.10: IIT, Chemistry and Metallurgy building, corner detail

4.4.11: IIT, Chemistry and Metallurgy Building: horizontal section; here the curtain wall is welded with steel angles to the inner face of the external flange of the façade I-beams. In contrast to the library the steel beams on the façade change direction around the corner. Mies's detail sketches reveal the search for a pure corner solution – a constant problem. The precise placing of the two outermost façade I-beams along the lines of the physical and virtual axes of the concrete-encased H-column at the corner conceals the asymmetry of the primary system.

4.4.12: IIT, Crown Hall: primary structure during construction

4.4.13: Lake Shore Drive Apartments, Chicago: the order of the secondary structure led to a 'flaw'. The regular positioning of the façade I-beams on the main grid created 'blind areas' at the corner; as a consequence the windows here are narrower than in the other bays.

4.4.14: Horizontal sections comparing Lake Shore Drive and Esplanade Apartments: distance pieces and a corner

cladding that is turned slightly outwards produce a façade and cladding layer that continues uniformly around the corner, which has an impact on the appearance of the building.

4.4.15: Lake Shore Drive (on the right) and Esplanade Apartments (left): different images created by two different constructional solutions of the curtain wall and the corner problem

4.4.16: Seagram Building, New York, 1954–58 (with Philip Johnson)

4.4.17: Federal Center, Chicago; corner detail: horizontal section at parapet level with internal parapet wall and external curtain wall made of aluminium and glass. The 'physical' axis of the corner column (web) and the 'virtual' axis are shown in the plan, the corner I-beams on the façade lie along the extension of these axes. Although they have no structural function here, they mark the regular rhythm of the 'skin'. The way in which the concrete casing is shaped responds to the layers of the façade that are connected to it at the sides – the constructional system is depicted by the sculptural treatment of the corner, analogous to the depiction

An American School of Thought of Post-war Modernism: Skidmore, Owings & Merrill

Louis Skidmore (1897–1962) and Nathaniel A. Owings (1903–84), both of them architects, in 1935 founded an architecture office in Chicago. In 1939 they were joined by engineer John O. Merrill (1896–1975), and since that time the firm has been known as Skidmore, Owings & Merrill (SOM).[89] Thanks to this multidisciplinary configuration SOM (like Albert Kahn some 30 years earlier) were able to take on complex building commissions and to offer ancillary services on the American building and planning market. Through building Lever House in New York in 1952 (ill. 4.4.18) as well as further 'landmarks' of the architecture of the 1950s and 1960s, SOM achieved a worldwide reputation. Committed engineers such as the Indian Fazlur R. Khan and the Chinese T. Y. Lin, as well as a strong group of architects around Gordon Bunshaft, Bruce Graham, Myron Goldsmith and others, also shared the responsibility for these contributions.

An organigram of the architecture firm dating from 1957 additionally shows that further core disciplines in building, such as heating, ventilation, air-conditioning, electrical and plumbing services, as well as landscape architecture and management areas, were integrated in the office structure, so that SOM could offer an overall construction package or, alternatively, provide part services for third parties. In addition, during a period that was marked by the pioneering achievements of the architecture of post-war modernism and by new kinds of high-rise buildings SOM was a 'national organisation' with offices in Chicago, New York, Portland and San Francisco. Each of these independently operating branches took on a specific region of the world where commissions were sought for and dealt with. After Lever House SOM not only developed into one of the largest architecture firms (1958: more than 1,000 staff members), but also into a growing organism (1981: 2,100 employees). 20 years after its founding the firm had 14 partners, 15 associates and 39 shareholders (ill. 4.4.19).[90]

Lever House was designed by SOM partner Gordon Bunshaft together with the architect and designer Nathalie de Blois.[91] The Lever concern, manufacturer of soaps (Lux) and washing powders (Tide) wanted a 'clean building' and an urban symbol of modernism.[92] The choice of blue-green tinted glass strengthens the 'gleaming hygiene' of the building's overall appearance.

A single-storey building carried on *pilotis* surrounds a public courtyard and is a kind of 'ground-scraper' that mediates between the 24-storey vertical slab and its urban surroundings. This was the drafting area of Nathalie de Blois. The employees use the roof garden of the low, flat building for recreational purposes. The high-rise building, carried on 18 concrete-encased steel columns that project through the low building, is a skeleton structure building with flexible floor plans on each level. As it is completely air-conditioned and the glazing has no opening elements, the curtain wall could be made as an extremely smooth metal-and-glass skin (ill. 4.4.20). The peripatetic critic Lewis Mumford described Lever House in *The New Yorker* as "... the first office building in which modern materials, modern construction, and modern functions have been combined with a modern plan."[93]

The masonry held in a steel frame in the lintel and parapet areas is surprising, as only a short time before Mies van der Rohe had dispensed with these elements entirely in his Lake Shore Drive Apartments (1948–51).[94] Generally, however, the Miesian school of thought strongly influenced SOM through the person of Myron Goldsmith, who had studied under Mies at IIT and, like Bruce Graham, developed the starting points provided by Mies's skyscraper designs in the setting of the third generation of the Chicago school and in this way arrived at new types of high-rise buildings.[95]

But Gordon Bunshaft also examined Mies's structural strategies: for example, the design of the tectonic spatial figure of the Manufacturer's Trust Company in New York is a further development of the plastic design of the curtain wall in Mies's Lake Shore Drive Apartments, using expressive means of construction and glass technology (ill. 4.4.21).

Essentially, in Lever House a curtain wall technology was developed that was to be used by the entire following generation of post-war architecture – even SOM never surpassed this achievement, apart perhaps from the visual effect of the 'bones and skin' tectonics, for example, in the Pepsi Cola Company headquarters building in New York, whose chief designer was Nathalie de Blois from SOM (ill. 4.4.22).

4.4.18

4.4.19

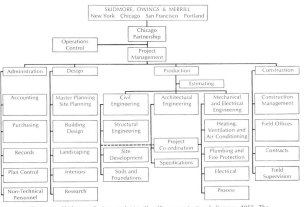

SKIDMORE, OWINGS & MERRILL
New York Chicago San Francisco Portland

Figure 74. Skidmore, Owings and Merrill, office organizational diagram, 1957. The large American architectural office of the twentieth century was typified by a style of organization both complex and rigidly structured.

4.4.18: Lever House, Park Avenue, New York, 1952

4.4.19: Organigram of Skidmore, Owings & Merrill (SOM) 1957: while the vertical line structure encompasses the professional and disciplinary work, in the horizontal levels the disciplines are connected and the project development is coordinated.
As in Albert Kahn's 'industrial office' half a century earlier, the development of the projects took place from station to station under the supervision of a project supervisor from the management area.

4.4.20: Lever House: vertical section through the layers of the building envelope; particularly remarkable are the brickwork parapet and lintel areas, which are clad externally with aluminium panels.

4.4.21: Manufacturer's Trust Company, New York, 1954; design by Gordon Bunshaft: separation of load-bearing structure and building envelope

4.4.22: The standardised tectonic image of the third generation of the Chicago School: Nathalie de Blois and Gordon Bunshaft's design for the Pepsi Cola Company building in New York, 1960; view at night

4.4.20

4.4.21

4.4.22

From 'Liberated Space' to Transparent Skin: Egon Eiermann and Sep Ruf

Like Skidmore, Owings & Merrill, who moved into the global limelight in 1952 with the erection of Lever House in New York, or J. H. van den Broek and Jacob Bakema, whose Lijnbaan shopping centre in Rotterdam (1949–53) developed into a promising 'place of pilgrimage' for post-war architects, with the German Pavilion at the 1958 *Expo* in Brussels Egon Eiermann and Sep Ruf created a symbol of modernism after 1945 (ill. 4.4.23). This pavilion, like the one built by Mies van der Rohe in Barcelona in 1929, was a 'democratic bearer of hope' for a new, liberated world and expressed a feeling of escape from the petrified structures of the century of the dictators.

Egon Eiermann (1904–70) worked as a self-employed architect from 1930. Up until 1945 he built single-family houses and apartment buildings as well as industrial complexes, such as the factory building for Total KG Foerstner & Co. in Apolda (1938/39) or, during the war years 1939–42, the factory of the Märkische Metallbau GmbH in Oranienburg. These buildings were modern, and represented the style of Neue Sachlichkeit and Neues Bauen, which under the National Socialists were permissible for commissions of this kind. The primacy he gave to an 'objective approach' that was defined by clarity of construction, functionality and economy as the characteristics that shaped both form and style allowed Eiermann after the war to regard himself as a continuer of modernism and to work as a pioneer of the architecture of the post-war generation (also as a teacher of architecture at the Technische Hochschule in Karlsruhe).

Thanks to the skeleton structure, which makes the building appear to hover, the façades of Eiermann's buildings could be freed of any load-bearing function and constructed using a lightweight system. The use of large glass fronts, non-load-bearing wall elements and rods at the front that support sun screen systems, railings, etc., became Eiermann's trademark (see ill. 3.5).

For his skeleton buildings Eiermann used both steel and concrete structural systems. Both systems allowed cantilevers and, as a consequence, also permitted curtain walls liberated from carrying the load of the building. While the German pavilion in Brussels had a steel structure, Eiermann, at around the same time, chose concrete

skeleton technology for his buildings for Neckermann Versand KG in Frankfurt am Main (1958–61). Eiermann continued using the themes of layering, dissolution and transparency to visualise and give spatial form to the construction of the building envelope up until his last building, the Olivetti administration and training centre in Frankfurt am Main (1967–72), which was preceded by a number of similar high-rise buildings (ill. 4.4.24).

Through his position in architecture Egon Eiermann prepared the way for a post-war generation whose members, like Günter Behnisch, for example, wanted to see a new socio-political approach – in a democratic spirit – incorporated in architecture. As president of the jury for the competition for the Munich Olympic buildings in 1967, which was won by Behnisch, Eiermann paved the way for such an approach.

Sep Ruf (1908–82) In the historic Munich of Friedrich von Gärtner or Leo von Klenze, Sep Ruf placed congenial counterpoints using a light-footed post-war architecture. The characteristics of his architecture included apparently hovering building structures with slender columns, wide, full-height glass fronts, 'canopies', spiral staircases with a light and lively quality and elegant materials in the interior. In the housing development at the corner of Türkenstrasse and Theresienstrasse (1952/53), the development of the Maxburg (with Theo Pabst; 1953–55), the Erhlicher store in the inner city (1961–63) or the new wing for the Bavarian State Library (1959–66, renovated in 2000) he reacted in the spirit of post-war modernism to the stone rebuilt city that was an artificial reconstruction in terms of both material and construction (ill. 4.4.25).

With his building for the Royal Filmpalast on Goetheplatz in Munich (1956/57) Ruf demonstrated this modernity in a highly visible way: steel rods spanning between the projecting roof and a cantilevered escape gallery function both as a 'useless' definition of the volume as well as a 'useful' support for the surrounding gallery to be used as an emergency exit. In 1997/98 this building was renovated by the addition of a protective glass skin, which could be fixed using these rods. This new envelope also now serves as an advertising medium (ill. 4.4.26; see also ill. 4.5.2).

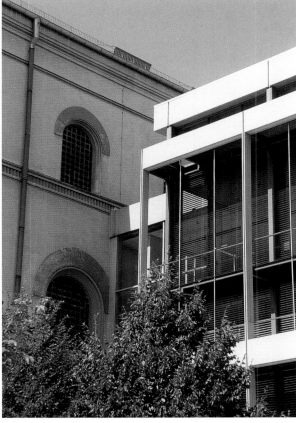

4.4.25

The Lightness of Post-war Modernism

4.5 After 1973 – The Future of the Intelligent Building Envelope

4.5.1

The energy crisis that resulted from the Middle East War in October 1973 exerted an influence on the architecture, construction and material technology of façades that remains unmistakeable to this day: it was soon recognised that there was a need to develop building envelopes composed of several layers that could contribute to reducing energy consumption. This was a challenge not only for the traditional strategies but also for those that pointed towards the future.

The breakthrough of the 'new constructivism'
Norman Foster (together with Peter Rice) was one of the pioneers of the new glass architecture that reacted to the energy crisis not by means of solid façades, hole-in-the-wall windows and a post-modern repertoire of forms, but, in contrast, by employing strategies based on material technology, initiated 'the victory campaign of glass' that continues to the present day. → Peter Rice and his engineering consultancy firm RFR as well as Ove Arup & Partners influenced a broad movement of glass building engineers. Rice is the founder of the school of thought of 'structural glazing' (cf. chapter 1, case study 10). The catalyst was provided by projects for a new kind of glass envelope for the Willis-Faber office building in Ipswich (1975), in which glass fins were used as wind-bracing, as well as by the Renault spare parts warehouse in Swindon in south-west England, where large glass panes were fixed with adhesive (1983; ill. 4.5.1; see also case study 84).[96]

From this point onwards not only glass technology (float glass production, as well as new coatings and methods of treating glass), but also new ways of fixing glass, and the changed role of the structure (now separated into primary and secondary elements) shaped the new means of expression of an architecture based on construction, as is also shown by the details (ill. 4.5.2).

This 'new constructivism' is depicted visually through the use of light cladding materials such as corrugated aluminium sheeting, webbed panels, or shaped terracotta elements, which serve as a 'second skin' that is back-ventilated and provides protection from the effects of the sun and the weather as well as offering a further design area for creating overlays of images in the way the façade is perceived and exerts its effect. In this context

the experiments of → Renzo Piano in the area of material technology deserve special mention.

Flexible building envelopes
Façade elements that react automatically or by means of manual operation to the dynamics of the environment, climate and weather conditions have always formed a part of the culture of building. Old techniques such as sailcloth canopies, reed mats, louvres, meshes, etc., are still used today in places and are being rediscovered. Modern examples of this include the building envelope of the apartment building on Square Mozart in Paris by Jean Prouvé and Lionel Mirabaud (1953; see section 6.3 and ill. 6.3.3), or the adjustable wooden louvres in the apartment building in the Quartier Barceloneta in Barcelona by José Antonio Coderch (1952–55, restored 1992; ill. 4.5.3)[97] – forerunners of projects such as the Bibliothèque Nationale de France by Dominique Perrault (1989–95; ill. 4.5.4).[98]

The high-tech ventilated building envelope of the Bibliothèque de France is augmented by internal elements made of steel angles clad with wood that can be adjusted by the staff to individually modify the internal climate. Both the low-tech examples from post-war modernism as well as the later high-tech solutions show the various ways in which the users of a building can constantly alter the expressive image of the building's façade.

While the effects of the 1973 oil crisis on architecture were, indeed, serious they also introduced new possibilities in the areas of building typology, building structure, construction, choice of materials, material technology, economic use of energy, etc. New worlds of images and a new culture of building emerged from this situation. In → German-speaking Europe a movement started by English architects and engineers – including climate and energy engineers – took a different direction to the post-modern one (Auer + Weber, Schneider + Schumacher, Ingenhoven, Overdiek und Partner, Petzinka Pink

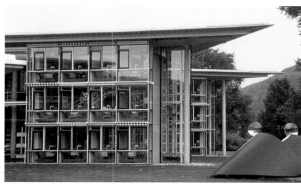

4.5.2   4.5.3   4.5.4   4.5.5

Architekten, Bothe Richter Teherani, Behnisch Architects, Transsolar, Gerhard Hausladen, Klaus Daniels and many others in Germany, Switzerland, Austria and Finland, to name but a few). Interdisciplinary collaboration, the primacy of construction and its visualisation determined the goals set in designing the building envelope. The use of sustainable strategies even led to 'sustainable branding': the belief that buildings ought to demonstrate how they perform in terms of reacting to environmental influences and should also show that they are the product of a multidisciplinary process of thinking and designing (cf. section 6.3).

Worlds of images of the future

Against the background of the discussion on post-war architectural modernism in Germany Günter Behnisch and his design team in Stuttgart developed a democratically inspired concept of 'liberated space', thus giving birth to a new school of thought in German glass architecture. The Central Library of the Catholic University of Eichstätt in Bavaria can be regarded as a high point of this approach (ill. 4.5.5).[99]

Behnisch's buildings pointed the way for an entire generation of younger offices and, in the debate on the architecture of the future, stood for the 'liberating' position of light, transparent and 'optimistic' constructions and structures. Following the arbitrariness of post-modernism, sensitivity towards the aspects of light, materials and colour once again took a direction in the culture of building that led to new worlds of images now being continued by 'communicative building envelopes'.

'Next skin'

The façades of the near future will be presented to an even greater extent in the context of 'communication design' – a depiction of the meaning that the architectural object wishes to communicate, as two examples from → Zurich West show, as well as reactions to long

established ways of perception in visual language expressed by provocative, unfamiliar building envelopes as in → the buildings of Herzog & de Meuron in St Gallen in Switzerland or in London and also the new Olympics buildings in Beijing (see ill. 5.4.5). Toyo Ito's media centre in Sendai (Tokyo, 1995–2002) illustrates the identity and interaction of communication and architectural design (ill. 4.5.6).

With their references to elements from the area of product and packaging design, building envelopes expose themselves to the test of time, deliberately taking into account shorter lifespans, and experiment with new kinds of materials from other areas of industry. Translucent materials in the areas of glass, plastics and metal are the focus of great attention, as they allow designers to achieve new spatial qualities and to utilise the effects of overlaid images.[100]

4.5.6

The Technology of Structural Glazing – Peter Rice and RFR

4.5.7: Glass pavilions, Museum of Science, Technology and Industry, La Villette, Paris, 1981–86; architect: Adrien Fainsilber, engineers RFR (Peter Rice, Martin Francis, Ian Ritchie); the cable tensioning changes direction at the corner.

4.5.8: Glass pavilions, La Villette, sketches by Peter Rice: distribution of the structural-dynamic forces within a module when a glass pane breaks

4.5.9: Within the overall system the components that take tension forces are differentiated from those subject to compression.

4.5.10: Tactile nature of the space-forming structure: Peter Rice (second from the left) with Renzo Piano (right) at a workshop on the Menil Collection Museum

4.5.11: Kaufmännisches Bildungszentrum, Zug, Switzerland, 1999–2001; architects: Bucher, Hotz, Burkart und Wiederkehr Krummenacher; engineers: Wismer + Partner; façade constructed by Ruch Griesemer

4.5.12: Technische Hochschule Rapperswil, Canton St Gallen, Switzerland; architects: Burgdorf + Burren; the sculptural, space-shaping quality of the façade results from the bracing glass fins, enhanced by the use of bronze sheeting.

The new façade technology that emerged after 1973 introduced a development that has continued to the present and that follows the vision of a 'sustainable skin'. Pioneering projects in this area include Norman Foster's Sainsbury Centre for the Visual Arts in Norwich (1974–78) and the Willis Faber office building in Ipswich (1975), Richard Roger's Lloyd's Building in London (1978–86) and Adrien Fainsilber's glass buildings for La Villette Museum for Science, Technology and Industry in Paris (1981–86), where Peter Rice and the RFR team for the first time developed a consistent form of structural glazing that was to be perfected by Patrick Berger and RFR[101] in the greenhouses in Parc André Citroën in Paris (1988–92).

After the construction of the Centre Pompidou in Paris (in which Peter Rice played an important role) had been completed and the role of a construction-oriented and transparent architecture in the city's architectural future had been indicated, Peter Rice, together with Martin Francis and Ian Ritchie, founded the consultancy firm RFR in Paris in 1982. In the Willis Faber office building in Ipswich Martin Francis had developed an all-glass façade (with glass 'fins' as bracing), which was hung from the edge of the roof and glued with silicone; Ian Ritchie had worked with Rice at Ove Arup & Partners in London and with Francis in Ipswich.[102] Thus the first pioneering buildings that use structural glazing, and the studies that preceded this development came from the Arup school of thought.[103]

The concept for the glass pavilion for the museum in La Villette offered the first opportunity to use the new principle of structural glazing on a large scale and thus to set in motion a process that was to open up new design areas (ill. 4.5.7).

The dimension of the complete glazing (4 x 4 modules, each of them a square with sides measuring 8.10 m) demanded new experiments with deformation and breakage scenarios, which influenced all the components, right down to the point fixing. Rice's goal was not merely technical perfection but, in addition, the visual depiction of the individual and overall performance of the structural glazing system in the context of industrial design (ills. 4.5.8 and 4.5.9)

Rice started from the old dream of the glasshouse pioneers – which the Bailey brothers had pursued at the beginning of the 19th century in their palm house in Bicton Gardens (see chapter 1, case study 1) – to create a light and bright space with a thin glass skin structured only by a fine meshed metal lattice. And yet this goal alone was not enough for the engineering personality Peter Rice, who positioned the engineer in the field of tension between the challenges of natural forces (such as gravity, wind, water, snow and earthquakes) and the task of translating these through the design process into structures that are rational in terms of both construction and material: "This is the positive role for the engineers' genius and skill: to use their understanding of materials and structure to make real the presence of the materials in use in the building so that people warm to them, want to touch them, feel a sense of the material itself and of the people who made and designed it."[104] According to Rice, 'constructive intelligence' refers not only to the 'art of building' but equally to the engineer's approach as a cultural mediator (ill. 4.5.10).[105]

Structural glazing gained wide acceptance within the space of only a few years. Anxiety about safety could be dispelled and evidence produced that, in connection with an expanded building envelope (double skin façade) and thanks to back-ventilation and wind-protected solar screening, structural glazing could make a significant contribution to energy-efficient building techniques (see section 6.3). Today, throughout the world, structural glazing forms part of the standard repertoire of architects, engineers and those responsible for construction design in metal, glass, window and façade companies (ill. 4.5.11).

The visual depiction of the constructive and technical functions of the individual components and of the industrial design of the limited number of connecting elements is not a 'pièce de résistance' by designer architects but is intended to provide a key to the overall architectural concept: the detail shaping of the figure expressly refers to this concept. The glass 'fins' not only have a technical function as wind bracing but, for example, through the visible and apparently green edges of the glass they can contribute to the plastic imagery and elegance of an all-glass façade, as shown by the new buildings of Rapperswil Technische Hochschule (Canton St Gallen, Switzerland), designed by architects Burgdorf + Burren (ill. 4.5.12).

4.5.7

4.5.8

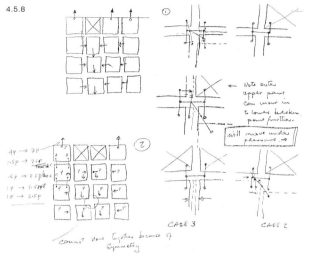

4.5.9

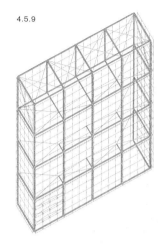

4.5.10

4.5.11

4.5.12

Experiments in the Field of Material Technology – the Buildings of Renzo Piano Building Workshop

In addition to the material technology experiments with plastics that mark the beginning of his building activity, Renzo Piano also investigated unusual building materials and new combinations of materials, a theme that represented an extensive area of research and design and therefore influenced and advanced his current project work. Reference has already been made to the area of concrete technology and *ferro cemento* (see chapter 3, case study 41). Piano has always pursued the goal of understanding materials and their technological development, processing and use as a contribution to lightweight building methods and sustainability. For Renzo Piano the combination of elements with different functions and performances in the layers of the façade is a dimension of the design process and an expression of the architectural concept.

The new building for the Institute for Research into Light Metals in Novara in Italy (1985) offered Renzo Piano an opportunity to develop a new kind of façade technology. The commission from the Società Aluminia did not initially involve a new building but the development of a system of multi-purpose façades. The goals of this study were standardisation, prefabrication and series for the market. The need to build a test façade ultimately developed into a building project for a modular building: a reinforced concrete structural system combined with a 'clip-on', front-hung façade (ill. 4.5.13). This curtain wall consists of a slender, unstable aluminium frame that is fixed to the concrete elements by means of a subconstruction, as well as infill elements of glass and aluminium louvres. It is only when they work together that the façade system becomes stable, that is to say, the glass takes on an auxiliary structural function (ill. 4.5.14).[106]

Renzo Piano developed his next line in material technology with the rediscovery of terracotta. Although this material had proved its worth back in 1890 in the context of the office buildings and skyscrapers of the Chicago School (see case study 53) it had been 'forgotten' again by modernism or replaced by ceramic panels. The changed environmental situation that resulted from the energy crisis in 1973 made it necessary to search for light, natural and durable cladding materials, in particular so as to design back-ventilated façades. Terracotta shells are weather-resistant, self-cleansing, can be shaped as required, can have a warm effect thanks to their natural colouring and provide a fine-grained surface structure. They can be mass-produced or manufactured as bespoke moulded pieces.

Renzo Piano first used terracotta façades in the housing development on the Rue de Meaux in Paris (1987–91). The narrowness of the courtyard dictated a solution with a multi-layered façade that, together with densely planted birch trees, was intended to provide protection against inquisitive glances and prevent the residents from feeling that they were 'on display'. The outer layer consists of a frame made of glass-fibre reinforced concrete as well as various infill elements: terracotta modules in slender metal frames, sun protection louvres, window elements (ill. 4.5.15).[107]

The mesh of the envelope is a composition that is based on the internal function of the apartments and the need for external protection and was optimised in a number of tests. The requirements for protection and transparency shaped the design of the 'mur rideau'.

Further buildings with terracotta 'skins' followed: the extension to the Centre Georges Pompidou in Paris by the addition of a music school (IRCAM, 1988–90), the Cité Internationale in Lyons (1991–95) and the buildings on Potsdamer Platz in Berlin, including the Debis tower (1996–2000). Here, terracotta was used mostly for sun protection, but seen in the overall context of the entire façade it gives a light, transparent, reddish textile structure that extends uniformly across this complex ensemble and, although it refers to the Berlin brick tradition, replaces it with a 'Mediterranean' charm (ill. 4.5.16).

Experiments in material technology influence and determine Renzo Piano's work and his search for new architectural possibilities. In addition to social and functional conditions, intelligent reactions to the dynamics of the environment define the guidelines of his designs and constructions. In addition to local and cultural references, influences such as fluctuations in temperature, sun, wind and noise are therefore important design factors. Equally relevant is the aesthetic visualisation of the solutions to problems (ills. 4.5.17 and 4.5.18; see also case studies 86 and 100).

4.5.13

4.5.14

4.5.16

4.5.15

4.5.17

4.5.18

Concepts for New Glass Façades

RWE central administration building
Essen 1991–97
Architects: Ingenhoven,
Overdiek und Partner
Façade design and construction:
Josef Gartner

Westhafen Tower
Frankfurt am Main, competition: 1996
Built: 2003/04
Architects: Schneider + Schumacher
Façade design: Institut
für Fassentechnik Karlotto Schott
Façade construction: Josef Gartner

GSW main administration building
Berlin, 1995–99
Architects: Sauerbruch Hutton
Structural design and technical
building services: Arup Berlin,
engineering partnership Höpner

4.5.19: Section of the façade of the cylindrical, 31-storey RWE building: air is supplied and extracted from the rooms by means of a double separated system, on the one hand, by adjustable chambers for air extraction or entry into the valves through barely visible air slits in the façade, on the other, through air change on the diagonal
(Konzept und Beratung HL-Technik; see also ill. 6.3.21).

4.5.20: Norman Foster: Haus der Wirtschaftsförderung, Duisburg, 1988–93

4.5.21: Schneider + Schumacher: Westhafen Tower, Frankfurt am Main, 2003/04; atria several storeys high that lie along the building envelope wind upwards through the 100-m-tall, cylindrical building (diameter 38 m; the 28 office levels provide around 1,200 workplaces; Konzept und Beratung HL-Technik).

4.5.22, 4.5.23: GSW central administration building, Berlin. The east and west façades have a different appearance, reflecting their different functions.

4.5.24: Baumschlager & Eberle: ecological secondary school in Mäder, Vorarlberg, 1999: two façade layers using timber and glass allow differentiated reactions to environmental influences, thus creating changing visual effects.

The concepts for new glass façades and energy-efficient building envelopes that were developed in response to the 'oil shock' of October 1973 came to German-speaking Europe from England. After the demonstrative input of English façade technology by Norman Foster in the Haus der Wirtschaftsförderung in Duisburg (1988–93) this movement began to spread in Germany also and many younger architects practices devoted their attention to the challenging task of developing and researching the complex relationships between fundamental questions of architecture and the new requirements of energy efficiency. Grey areas in the field of building physics and new standards, which did not always come from interdisciplinary teams, the interpretative basis for granting permits in individual cases etc. did not, however, restrict the inventive spirit and enthusiasm for research. A 'genealogy' of façade technology emerged both in terms of the energy concept (see also section 6.4 and case study 99) and in the technology for the production of new kinds of imagery.

One of the pioneering buildings of the 'ecological' direction was the central administration building of the Rheinisch-Westfälische Energie AG (RWE) by Ingenhoven, Overdiek und Partner (1991–97). The design and construction team recognised at an extraordinarily early stage the necessity to modularise the building envelope into window or façade units that can be controlled in terms of energy and that take up entire structural bays and storeys (ill. 4.5.19).

By means of this concept the façade technology developed for the RWE offered an alternative to the approach in which a second glass skin (twin skin) is stretched across the entire façade and used for free back-ventilation, which, for example, in Foster's Haus der Wirtschaftsförderung in Duisburg had led to overheating problems in the upper regions.[108]

By this time the danger of flashover fire in double wall façades that extend across several storeys had been recognised by the fire safety authorities, making clear the need for vertical and horizontal fire compartments (ill. 4.5.20).

The concept of the modularisation of the façade construction is nowadays standard and forms part of the repertoire used to deal technically with large glazed façades. In the case of the Westhafen Tower in Frankfurt am Main by Schneider + Schumacher individual sections of the cylindrical building volume are combined in narrow 'atria' several floors high and can consequently be individually controlled in terms of energy. The voids along the façades between the circular external skin and the rectangular geometry of the internal spaces were revolved through 90° and wind their way upwards like the 'hanging gardens' of the Commerzbank in Frankfurt or the 'spatial spirals' in the SwissRe Tower in London (both by Norman Foster). Each of the 'atria' can be naturally ventilated by window vents (ill. 4.5.21).[109]

The central administration building of the Gemeinnützige Siedlungs- und Wohnungsbaugesellschaft (GSW) in Berlin (1995–99) reveals a design strategy that leads further. The architects Sauerbruch Hutton (structural design: Arup; façade consultant: Emmer Pfenninger Partner AG; building services consultant: Arup) reversed the trend towards uniformly designed façades and developed two different types for the east and the west façades. As these sides are exposed to the environment in specific ways and therefore must perform differently, they were also designed in different ways. The east façade has a louvre structure for intake air; this air is directed through the rooms and on the west side of the building is led upwards (by means of thermals) along an exhaust façade with coloured sunscreen louvres, aided by a 'wind catcher' on the roof that creates negative pressure (ills. 4.5.22 and 4.5.23; see also ills. 6.2.14 and 6.4.14–16).[110]

This approach, too, has influenced later projects such as the ecological secondary school in Mäder in Vorarlberg (Austria) by architects Baumschlager & Eberle (1999), who here also designed two different types of building envelope. Additionally, the vertical solar protection glass louvres can be moved so that, depending on the angle and position of the sun, different spatial effects and overlays of images are created (ill. 4.5.24).

The 'Liberated Façade'

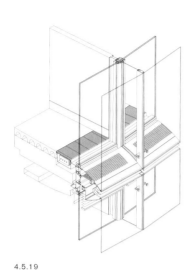

4.5.19

4.5.20

4.5.21

4.5.22

4.5.23

4.5.24

Transformation Strategies

Bluewin Tower
Zurich-West, Switzerland
Architect: Rolf Läuppi
Engineers: Walt + Galmarini
Façade design and construction:
Felix Construction

Headquarters of the Helvetia Patria Insurances
Zurich-Altstetten, Switzerland
Architects: Romero & Schaefle
Engineers: Lüchinger & Meyer

For a considerable time now the sustainable strategy required since the oil crisis of 1973 has no longer been restricted to producing alternative energy or saving energy. In addition to affecting the planning process (urban, spatial and housing planning), this strategy has been extended to design and construction, and research and development in the area of material technology. Based on an awareness that existing building fabric must also be adapted to meet new energy standards ('minergie', 'passive house' and others) a number of architecture and engineering offices have developed specific competence in dealing with the restoration, renovation and conversion of existing buildings and building complexes. In each case the transformation strategies reveal new ways in which existing 'sustainability qualities' such as well-preserved, tried-and-tested load-bearing structures can be supported or made usable for new energy concepts. Two recent examples from Zurich can be used to illustrate this development.

The high-rise building that has become known as the Bluewin Tower and which, owing to its exposed position on Escher-Wyss-Platz in Zurich-West, is visible from a considerable distance (something rare in Switzerland), was 'fitted' over an existing, slab-like office block from the 1960s, which was once the Escher-Wyss administration high-rise building (ill. 4.5.25). The architect modified the load-bearing structure with its external concrete piers in several respects: it was painted and then protected from the elements by adding a second glass skin: the space between the piers has been transformed into a continuous vertical exhaust air façade, which is interrupted only by metal gratings that can be walked across (today the current fire regulations would require them to be fire-resistant); the original façade – the inner skin – has been replaced and is no longer exposed to the external climate and therefore has only a function as a 'Klimagrenze'. In addition, the properties of the load-bearing structure allowed a striking addition to be made on top of the building using a structural system that appears lighter but with the same double glass skin – the 'skin' remains the same, the 'bones' change (ill. 4.5.26).

The new headquarters of the Helvetia Patria Insurances near Zurich-Altstetten railway station were also in need of renovation. The structural fabric of the old building, which dates from 1970, was used for the transformation and given a new building envelope, while an additional floor was added on top (ills. 4.5.27 and 4.5.28). Whereas the new north façade has full-height and full-width glass elements, the other façades have band-like parapets clad with aluminium panels to reduce the amount of glazing. The subdivision of the façades is independent of the system of piers behind. The large areas of fixed glazing are augmented by narrow ventilation vents that are located in spatial isolation joints, into which the rods of the sunscreen awnings retract. In the corner area the main façade is given primacy. It closes its structure with an 'isolation joint at the corner'.

The sun protection awnings that open outwards on drop arms (first use of this system) transform the building from a 'steamship' into a 'sailing ship', as it were: not only is it perceived entirely differently, it also alters its surroundings. The salmon-pink fabric awnings are a favourite of architects Romero & Schaefle and characterise a number of buildings by this practice. They recall old school buildings of post-war modernism (ill. 4.5.29).

4.5.25

4.5.26

4.5.27

4.5.28

4.5.29

4.5.25, 4.5.26: Bluewin Tower: transformation of an existing office building into a glazed high-rise building: the old and new buildings compared

4.5.27, 4.5.28: Headquarters of Helvetia Patria Insurances: transformation of the 1970s building into an office building for the working world of the future: the old and new buildings compared

4.5.29: Headquarters of Helvetia Patria Insurances: salmon-pink awnings strengthen the fascinating presence of the building on the busy forecourt of Zurich-Altstetten railway station.

The 'Communicative'
Building Envelope

In terms of material technology current tendencies in architecture since the turn of century show unusual transfers and elements, borrowed, for example, from product design and the packaging industry. Through this reference to an everyday culture they seem somewhat alien and yet familiar. This is the starting point for projects that will have to prove themselves in the future, ranging from the buildings of Herzog & de Meuron, the National Swimming Centre for the 2008 Olympic Games in Beijing (PTW Architects Sydney and Arup; ill. 4.5.30; see also ill. 5.4.5), 'blob' figures such as the Kunsthaus Graz (architects: Spacelab/Peter Cook, Colin Fournier, 2004) or Selfridges department store in Manchester to the projects of the Rotterdam architects office NOX and UN-Studio with their complex building envelope structures.[111]

The 'movable skin' of Jean Prouvé's apartment building on Square Mozart in Paris was also new and unfamiliar in the 1950s. From the view point of an engineer and 'constructeur', who, as a trained metal worker, had experience in the construction of carriages, lift cabins and bodywork technology, and was familiar with the relevant materials, technologies and workshop organisation, Prouvé had no scruples in seeing a building envelope as a 'bodywork problem' and 'translating' this into the architectural object (see also ills. 6.3.3 and 6.3.6). In this sense he anticipated the model of the 'skin' that reacts to the environment, which became really topical only after the energy crisis in 1973. Today, the technology of fabric skins is being discussed and researched – 'learning from breathable textile skins'?

In their extension buildings for Helvetia Patria Insurances in St Gallen in Switzerland Herzog & de Meuron chose a strategy that reflects the environment in an unusual manner and achieves simultaneously an extraordinary effect on the surroundings. This new kind of office landscape is functionally restricted by a rather tight site, but by the use of modular glass elements which are inclined at 4 different angles it is spatially expanded in a polyvalent way.[112] They exert an effect both inside and outside the building depending of the angle (ills. 4.5.31 and 4.5.32).

The interplay between transparency and reflection breaks up the surroundings into individual images that are shifted in relation to each other, which moves them away from familiar everyday impressions and requires a consciously new kind of perception. At night the impression is reversed, in a certain sense: the building seems like an illuminated 'showcase'. It is always in dialogue with the surroundings, in particular with the seasonal changes of colour in the surrounding park landscape designed by Günther Vogt.[113]

In contrast to the prominent and exposed position of the Helvetia Patria building on the 'university hill' in St Gallen, the location of Herzog & de Meuron's Laban Dance Centre in Greenwich in London is unspectacular, industrial: a peripheral wasteland. It was precisely this setting that inspired the architects to engage in an unusual urban and architectural 'operation'. In this territory the building extends like an amoeba in all possible directions and is enclosed in a translucent shell of profiled, coloured polycarbonate panels that augment the internal glass skin. The shades of colour and the openings positioned with no distinguishable rhythm demonstrate the contradiction between the laid-down function of the internal organisation (with its conventional schedule of accommodation) and the placing of the dance school as a foreign body in an inhospitable but stimulating location (ills. 4.5.33 and 4.5.34).

The new, multi-functional Herti sports hall in Zug in Switzerland by Bétrix & Consolascio (engineers: Lüchinger & Meyer) offers a more noble kind of packaging. The translucent quality of Profilit glass is used not to light the interior spaces; instead, differently coloured areas are placed behind it, giving it a radiant presence that – like in the Laban Dance Centre – confronts the industrial environment with a spectacular building (ill. 4.5.35).[114]

4.5.31

4.5.32

4.5.30: National Swimming Centre for the 2008 Olympic Games in Beijing (architects: PTW, Sydney; engineers: Arup; partner: China State Construction Engineering Corporation, CSCEC): the 'bionically' inspired cellular structure is the outcome of the computer-generated development of form and structure.

4.5.31, 4.5.32: Herzog & de Meuron: Helvetia Patria Insurances, St Gallen (competition: 1989; construction 2000–02; façade design: Emmer Pfenninger Partner; façade construction: Tobler Metallbau; landscape designer: Günther Vogt): the same building envelope creates two different effects.

4.5.33, 4.5.34: Herzog & de Meuron: Laban Dance Centre, London, 1997–2000; an unpredictable organism in an isolated industrial wasteland focuses on surprising and changing its surroundings.

4.5.35: Herti sports hall in Zug, Switzerland (architects: Bétrix & Consolascio; engineers: Lüchinger & Meyer): a jewel in an inhospitable industrial wasteland

4.5.33

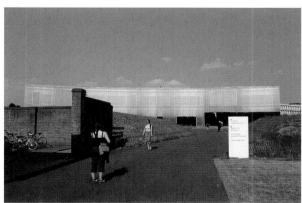

4.5.34

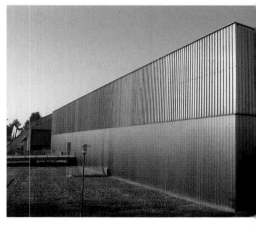

4.5.35

5 Process Thinking Conquers Construction – Industrialisation from the Balloon Frame to the Skyscraper

If one follows 'prefabrication' back to its roots, one realises that in 'vernacular architecture' and 'anonymous construction' this cultural technique was, and indeed still is, an engine room of civilisation (ill. 5.1).

In the development of building, the invention of new cultural techniques, tools and thought models continues to play a decisive role in improving standards with regard to daily life and environmental conditions and the way societies, cultural communities, even nations are organised.

It was not by chance that industrialisation initially took root in England. As a result of the 1666 Revolution the ruling nobility was confronted early on with a civilian world that fuelled industrial development and also forced representatives of the hereditary nobility to become involved. In this reciprocal process the theoretical deliberations of John Locke (1632–1704) were an influential force for almost 200 years.[1] Locke believed that even bricklayers and gardeners had innovative capabilities[2] and in reverse called for the sons of noblemen to engage in workshop activities and acquire practical knowledge and skills. The training was, however, to be in addition, and undergone privately and in their spare time.[3]

Thrusts behind industrial development   With regard to building technology, with the planning and construction of the Iron Bridge in Coalbrookdale (1775–79) in the Midlands in England, a group of iron era pioneers created an initial symbol of the forthcoming revolutionary industrial process (ill. 5.2).

It was, however, neither the material – cast and wrought-iron – (the Darby dynasty, established by the foundry entrepreneur Abraham Darby I, had been operating since 1708) nor the shape which was reminiscent of a pressure-loaded arched stone Romania bridge that was novel, just as little as the building technique, which, by means of dovetails, wedges and cogging adopted a familiar style of wood construction, but rather the transfer of previous industrial techniques and experience into a spectacular bridge: this was the achievement of a multidisciplinary team of an architect-engineer and of entrepreneurs.[4] What was also novel was the speed with, and manner in which, the bridge was built: the five 40-metre-wide arches were prefabricated in Darby's workshop and hoisted into position from a raft (date of commencement: 1 July 1779), with final construction using the lightweight construction method (completion: 23 October of the same year!). The Iron Bridge was something like the first sensational branding of industrial construction culture – and remains so today.[5]

5.1

5.1: Portable house in African culture

5.2: Iron Bridge, Coalbrookdale, England, 1775–79, architect and engineer: Thomas Farnolls Pritchard. The bridge was the first building to herald the forthcoming industrial age.

5.2

5.0: Empire State Building, visiting inspector, 1930/31

5.3

5.4

5.5

Emanating from England, the 'transatlantic spark' wielded its influence far beyond the centres of New England on the eastern US seaboard, journeying to the shops in the new towns in the Midwest. In Chicago, which in the space of just a few years from 1830 grew from being a fort for French missionaries into the centre of the west, a new building technique was discovered: the 'balloon frame', or 'western frame'. It was the construction instrument the settlers used to conquer the west (ill. 5.3).

Balloon frame and skyscraper: the first signs of successful industrial building technique Together with other industrial products manufactured in a similar way (guns and pistols by Colt, agricultural machines by McCormick, etc.)[6] the 'horizontal' conquest of the territory by means of mass production of standardised houses with ready-made timber framing represented an anticipatory thought pattern for the 'vertical' conquest of space. It was the same Chicago in which, on 8 October 1871, a devastating fire destroyed tens of thousands of wooden balloon frame houses, leading as a result to the invention of the forward-looking method of construction with fire-proof high-rises. This enabled the rapid reconstruction of Chicago, despite economic crisis.

Mass production and the industrial program of Modernism The automobile industry was a driving force in the mass production of consumer goods. Detroit, from where the Bessemer process for the manufacture of top-grade iron (steel) took root in America, played a forward-looking role in industrial development. Henry Ford invented the assembly line with a view to producing more cars more quickly, more perfectly and more cheaply (ill. 5.4). While his system of production acted as an impetus for industrialisation in general, it was further accelerated by Frederick Taylor's time and piece-rate model of scientific management, with both dimensions synthetically implemented in car factories designed by the architect Albert Kahn and his own 'industrial office' (see ill. 4.3.4).

Ford and Taylor also had an influence on developments in Europe. Parallel production plants were established, such as the Bally shoe factory in Dottikon, Switzerland, the FIAT Lingotto car factory in Turin, the Van-Nelle factory in Rotterdam, the Fagus works in Alfeld (see case studies 35, 36, 39 and 56).

After World War I, European Modernism developed a forward-looking residential accommodation programme of industrial dimensions, which, after the American timber framing of 1830, represented a second revolution in the mass production of accommodation. Urban visions such as Tony Garnuer's Cité Industrielle pointed the way forward for the industrial solution of problems (see case study 31). The acute shortage of accommodation necessitated swift, efficient planning and construction. Particularly affected city administrative authorities appointed avant-garde architects as city master builders: J. J. P. Oud in Rotterdam, Cornelis van Eesteren in Amsterdam, Martin Wagner in Berlin, Ernst May in Frankfurt am Main, among others (ill. 5.5).

The New Frankfurt was one focal point of this new industrial accommodation construction; the Werkbund housing scheme at Weißenhof hill in Stuttgart was an experiment in new materials and building techniques. The Nazis and World War II put an end to these experiments. Parallel to this, there emerged, primarily in the USA, the movement for prototypes and models of 'case study houses' on an individual basis, a movement that is still much in evidence today.

50 years on from these first developments between the two world wars this horizontal advanced into vertical industrialisation of the second-generation sky-

Process Thinking Conquers Construction

scraper technology mode, of which the 12-month construction time for the 85-storey-high Empire State Building in New York is a high-speed example.

Construction system way of thinking between 'sputnik shock' and 'oil shock' When, on 4 October 1957, the 83.6-kg Russian satellite 'Sputnik I' became the first artificial celestial body to circle the Earth in 95 minutes (the first American satellite, 'Explorer I', followed on 1 February 1958), it was interpreted as the East's technical and scientific superiority and attributed to deficiencies in the West's education and research system (ill. 5.6).

School reform projects, which post-1957 responded to the 'sputnik shock' with a boom in education and led to the mass-production of all levels of classroom, from kindergartens to university campuses, the reconstruction and accommodation construction project of post-war Modernism, new methods in the production and distribution of mass-produced consumer goods and, finally, a third generation of high-rise buildings – all these represented the framework conditions that challenged numerous architects, engineers, constructors and ultimately the building industry to come up with new inventions and fostered unlimited faith in technology.

In this context, the Structuralist school of thought focused on an integrative, interdisciplinary model that included sociologists and ethnologists to counter the functionalist, economic primacy of the 'Wirtschaftswunder' with a humanistic project.

The 1973 energy crisis triggered by the second Middle East war spelled the demise of the 'bony' prefab systems, as the insulation now required necessitated multi-layered outside walls. By way of contrast the 'bodywork model' enjoyed a revival, particularly in England – a new school of thought with regard to system building and lightweight construction responded to the 'oil shock' and delivered a new counter and architectural stance to solid-state building inspired by postmodernism.

From mass to tailor-made production Following several futile attempts on the part of Peter Rice and his team of engineers at Arup, even with the aid of one of the computers that were still a rarity between 1958 and 1961, to employ the free wing shapes in Jørn Utzon's competition sketch for the Sydney Opera House in practical construction purposes, they eventually settled on the simplest of shapes: the sphere.[7] Since then the construction industry has witnessed the 'triumphant success of CAAD'. The decisive breakthrough occurred when it became possible to combine design and production tools (computer-aided manufacturing) and when it became apparent that this technique used in machine, vehicle, aircraft and shipbuilding could be adopted for planning, production and even assembly processes.

Nowadays, with the help of mathematical models, complex volumes, shapes, structures and, ultimately, construction systems, like irregular surface structures, can be generated in general architectural, engineering and structural conditions. Mass production has not been abolished but in the future will extend the tailor-made production of construction systems and components, design freedom and the penetration of as yet unimagined areas of spatial, construction and material concepts (ill. 5.7).

5.6

5.7

5.3: Chicago just before the Great Fire of October 1871: the look of the city 40 years after its founding, a sea of 'balloon-frame' wooden houses

5.4: Henry Ford with his son Edsel on the occasion of the rolling out of the 15 millionth Model T in 1927

5.5: Spangen estate, Rotterdam, 1919–22; architects: M. Brinkman and L. de Jonge

5.6: Model of the 'Sputnik 1' satellite launched on 4 October 1957

5.7: Swiss Re tower, London, 2004: a synthesis of standardised, computer-generated and technically produced components

5.1 Balloon Frame and Skyscraper: The First Symbols of Successful Industrial Building

5.1.2   5.1.3

Being able to construct tall buildings to a high industrial level required not only novel ideas and challenging economic, building law and fire-prevention conditions – and later an Elisha Graves Otis or a Léon Edoux, the inventors of the elevator – but also architecture and engineering pioneers with a forward-looking planning and technical mindset. And this mindset was not new in America. When the new 'balloon-frame' building technique was invented around 1830, in Chicago's founding era, no one could have envisaged St. Mary's Church being a proto-

5.1.1

type for hundreds of thousands of buildings in the great plains, or that entire cities, such as Oklahoma City, would emerge in the shortest of time thanks to this 'ready-made house' type of construction, and that the balloon-frame buildings would provide an everyday motif for painters such as Winslow Homer (1836–1910) and Edward Hopper (1882–1967), or that this method of construction would remain up-to-date until today (ill. 5.1.1).

Balloon frame – the beginning of industrial building history

The success of the original version of the → balloon frame, or western frame, is linked to Chicago's rapid growth and the history of the settlement – the horizontal conquest – of the Midwest. The balloon frame was invented around 1830 by George W. Snow; it was first used two years later, in 1832, in the construction of St. Mary's Church by Augustine D. Taylor (ill. 5.1.2).[8]

5.1.1: Balloon-frame type of construction for 'growing houses'

5.1.2: Augustine D. Taylor: St. Mary's Church, Chicago, 1832

5.1.3: Low-cost housing, Ohio, USA, 1998 (Abacus Architects)

5.1.4: McCormick's first factory in Chicago, 1847

5.1.5: Department store for 'Uncle Sam's way of life' in Chicago

5.1.6: Chicago frame visible during the assembly of Ludwig Mies van der Rohe's Lake Shore Drive apartments (1948–51)

Without this wooden-frame type of construction the building and rapid development of Chicago – which in 1830 was still a French missionary fort (Fort Dearborn), in just four decades until the Great Fire of 1871, when the city had 334,000 inhabitants – would never have been possible. Subsequently, with cities springing up all over the country, this type of construction spread throughout America. It has survived until today and in a modified version geared to European conditions is used as a type of wooden-frame construction in the 'Old World' (ill. 5.1.3).

Chicago's expansion period witnessed the American Civil War (1861–65), which also produced a change in the way construction developed. Whereas previously a shop culture had dominated and production was client and need-oriented, a market structure initiated by the victorious northern states now held sway over construction in the larger field of operation. Production on a large scale and to supply an open market called not only for industrial methods of production, new-style warehouses, and silos, etc., but also for market tools (a nationwide railroad, markets, stores and marketing) and market dominance as well as knowledge acquired through a school culture.[9]

The McCormick story – the source of an industrial mindset in construction

In 1841, → Cyrus H. McCormick founded a factory for agricultural machines in Virginia. For almost 40 years it operated as a steadily growing blacksmith's shop. As was the case with most companies the Civil War led McCormick to switch from a handicraft to an industrial method of production: from production for specific customers to production for an (anonymous) market. With the McCormick factory moving to Chicago in 1847 this step was a matter of course (ill. 5.1.4).

The rapid developments in McCormick's production of lawnmowers, threshers, harvesters and tying machines led to the invention of the 'interchangeable parts' principle, the possibility of their being used in different types

of machine, their being perfected, etc. – in anticipation of the type of bodywork construction practised by, for example, Jean Prouvé 100 years later and the modular system for Norman Foster's Sainsbury Centre for Visual Arts in Norwich (1974–78, see ill. 5.4.2).

After 1865, alongside a domestic market the likes of which had never been seen before, an immense global market dominated by the USA emerged. Distribution, sales, advertising, product development and marketing swiftly led to conglomerates (the first monopolies such as Singer, Woolworth, until the invention of trusts around 1890, for example, US Steel and Standard Oil), a booming banking and insurance sector (Morgan, Home Life Insurances), etc., as well as to a response to the unbridled development of what was to go down in history as the 'period of corruption' of Ulysses S. Grant, a general in the Civil War, who, under his government (1869–77), reconstructed the state under the leadership of the North (ill. 5.1.5).

The first New York banks crashed as early as 1873 and by the mid-1870s America had an unemployment rate of 10 per cent, which led to enormous political unrest and the emergence of the trade union movement.[10] During this period the Great Chicago Fire of 1871 also raged. Astonishingly, Chicago's recovery occurred at a time of major economic crises. However, it was precisely these conditions – cheap loans and labour – that resulted in a new type of construction, the skyscraper: the very image of technical efficiency, of high-speed assembly and – that architectural downfall – the 'time is money' principle (see section 4.2).

'Chicago frame' – vertical conquest of space

Whereas the 'transformation' of the wooden frame type of construction into the steel → 'Chicago frame' was an invention of the 'western architects' and engineers in Chicago, the east coast architects in New York and Philadelphia merely used it as a 'skeleton' which, in Beaux-Arts manner, was to be walled in and decorated. The light terracotta sheath on Chicago skyscrapers, on the other hand, displays the skeleton, visualising the modern type of construction and playing a role in creating a functional style, which, after William Le Baron Jenney's Fair Store (1890–91), influenced the avant-garde

5.1.5   5.1.6

and Modernism, for example, Ludwig Mies van der Rohe, underwent a broad-based revival in post-war Modernism – in particular through Skidmore, Owings & Merrill – and which, since the 1973 energy crisis, has served as a new generator for 'sustainable skins' (ill. 5.1.6).

Frank Lloyd Wright and the balloon frame type of construction

Other 'ready-made' concepts for industrial lightweight construction based on the wooden frame principle are to be found in the work of inventive architects of American construction history. → Frank Lloyd Wright used the framing system, among other things, for his 'Prairie-style' houses, for example, in the case of the Ward W. Willits House in Highland Park, Illinois (1902–03) – according to Hitchcock: "...the first masterpiece among the Prairie houses".[11]

Wooden-Frame Construction: Balloon Frame and Western Frame in the USA

5.1.7

The 'western frame', or platform frame', is a frame with standardised two-by-four-inch planks nailed down on both sides, with posts and bars for bracing. Normed windows and doors are inserted in the partition gaps. In this way it is structurally both a plate and a slab, is simple to assemble on the ground and can be erected vertically by just two people. The floor plate follows the same structure but features additional slating cross bars for bracing. As opposed to 'western frames' and 'platform frames', which represent a complete frame on each storey, with the 'balloon frame' the corner posts cover two storeys. As there was a lack of skilled labour people built the houses themselves. For this purpose there were manuals with precise instructions for each stage of the process and for how to deal with problems – even down to combatting termites (ills. 5.1.7. and 5.1.8).

The industrial manufacture of the component parts depended on the stage of development of tools and machines. Around 1830 the circular saw was widespread; in 1840 the gang saw was available (24–42 teeth), and after 1850 the steam engine multiplied saw production, while the modern band saw was introduced in 1870. The consumption of wood corresponded to this development: 100 per cent increase from 1830–40; 350 per cent from 1840–50, and in each of the following decades an increase of approx. 50 per cent. Between 1830 and 1890 the price of a pound of nails dropped from 6 cents to 2 cents.[12]

In widespread catalogues (such as those Sears, Roebuck & Co.) the balloon frame was available in all manner of styles: the Victorian 'dream house' could just as easily be ordered as a glitzy suburban residence or a prestigious townhouse for New York (ill. 5.1.9). Catherine Beecher's 1869 *American Woman's Home* (both the title of her book and a vision with regard to concrete projects that she drew and published in it; see section 6.4, ill. 6.4.2) followed this industrial construction technique too but also included forward-looking technical features.

The standardised components could be assembled in only one way, the correct way, following the principle of coherence in shape = coherence in force.

The 'ready-made' philosophy is the result of technological development from American 'mechanic shops'. It also had an influence on other branches of industry as did the 'Chicago frame' building technique.

Oklahoma City – balloon-frame city The 'establishment' of Oklahoma City on a single day, 22 April 1889, can be regarded as a late highlight in the 'high-speed' founding of cities using the balloon frame type of construction. The allocation of land by the US government to private railroad companies expanding westwards did not occur free of charge. By reselling individual districts that had been demarcated since 1785 in Land Ordinances and Land Acts and that were suitable for settlement along planned railroads, the companies financed their own progress. Brokers and intermediaries arranged the sale of individual strips of land to settlers, for the most part in towns and stations along the eastern seaboard, where immigrants were waiting to find their fortune.

When information about the founding and approval of a new town in the west became more concrete, large numbers of settlers descended on the 'promised' place by railroad: "At noon on April 22, 1889, when the federal government first opened up the area to white settlement, there was nothing on the site of Oklahoma City but a railroad station and a few wooden buildings. By nightfall a tent town of about 10,000 persons had sprung up."[13] (ill. 5.1.10)

After four weeks of organisation and building work the new balloon-frame town was standing. The first shape Oklahoma City took was primarily one of single-room houses (ill. 5.1.11).

After just one year the new town had acquired an overall appearance and the most important public buildings had been erected: town Hall, court of law and prison, church, assembly hall and school, etc.

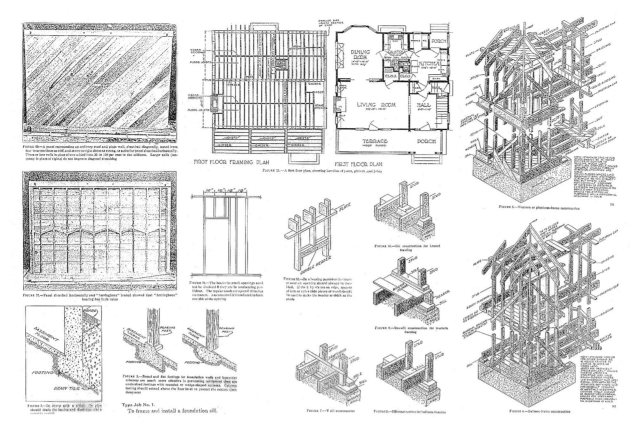

5.1.7: First balloon-frame 'single-room houses' in the new town of Oklahoma, 1889

5.1.8: Breakdown of the timber framing: author's assembly from a manual[81]

5.1.9: Balloon frame as a prestigious town house ('Renaissance Palazzo')

5.1.10: 'Oklahoma City as planned in 1889' – poster as a vision: at the same time, the *World Exhibition* with the Eiffel Tower opened its doors in Paris (6 May 1889).

5.1.11: Oklahoma City after four weeks: the first 'Prairie houses' for 10,000 settlers

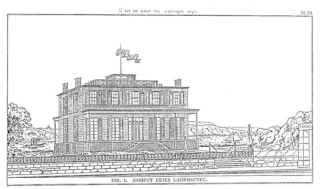

FIG. 1. ANSICHT EINES LANDHAUSES.

5.1.10

5.1.11

The McCormick Factory: 'interchangeable parts' as the Forerunner of Industrial Building

In 1841, the year it was founded, the McCormick factory produced a mere two reaping machines, which were known as 'Cyrus reapers'; by 1842 it had risen to seven, to 29 in 1843, 50 in 1844 and in 1845, and 190 in 1846.[14] From the outset the firm's founder, Cyrus H. McCormick, attempted to establish a broad-based sales area around Virginia, USA. In line with the 'shop culture' capacity production had to be on a decentralised basis. The marketing concept was nothing if not original: McCormick went from farm to farm demonstrating his latest devices and asked the farmers for suggestions for improvements – 'demonstration on the road'. He also granted licences to additional shops in other regions. The purchase of one of his machines also included technical support and repairs – a service principle that was introduced only later in the automobile industry (initially at Ford and Citroën).

Very soon the decentralised production exceeded capacity and Cyrus McCormick decided to move to Chicago and set up a central factory there (1847). An order for immediate delivery of 100 reaping machines had directly prompted this step. In 1848 the factory in Chicago produced 500 reaping machines, in 1849 it was producing 1,500, and so on (ill. 5.1.12).[15]

The special feature of a repair and technical service led to the principle of interchangeable parts, because this very characteristic of being able to put together the very same parts in different machines, for example, combines, as well as their ongoing advancement (along the lines of a new model every year) required component parts that were coordinated. The uniformity of the models (industrial design) and their parts (performance, technical perfection and coherence of shape), as well as quality assurance, went hand in hand with this. McCormick combined advertising and instruction: the images in catalogues and advertisements in newspapers and magazines also contained technical explanations and illustrations of how the products worked, and also drew attention to how the machines were continually being updated along the lines of "never-ending experimental work in progress and of the presence of competition".

On the back of this marketing strategy McCormick was able to expand rapidly; whereas in 1847 the factory measured 12 x 30 metres, had two storeys and 10-hp machines for producing the reaping machines, by 1849 it had already been extended to 60 metres in length; the factory boasted 30-hp steam engines and had a payroll of 120. As early as 1851 McCormick's Chicago Reaper Factory was the largest producer of agricultural machinery in the world (ill. 5.1.13; see also ill. 5.1.4).

The decisive turning point, however, was brought about in 1880 by Lewis Wilkinson, who was employed as managing director of the family-owned company. Having trained as a mechanic in New England he brought to the firm experience in industrial production gained at the Colt Firearms Company in Connecticut and Wilson Sewing Machines Company, in other words, expertise in key modern industries. The model-based production principle was the final step towards standardisation, to the interchangeable parts system, and mass production (ills. 5.1.14 and 5.1.15).

In the reconstruction period under President Ulysses S. Grant following the Civil War, political unrest increased (the army was sent in to deal with the nation-wide railroad strike) and in 1877 led to a change in direction followed by a period of over-production (until 1882). This triggered a railroad building boom and massive waves of immigrants from Europe, primarily northern Europe, who brought not only manpower, but also political ideas and movements (such as anarchists from Germany), which ideologised what was already a chaotic urbanisation process. Chicago in particular, with its abattoirs, industrial factories and the most important stock exchange in the Midwest developed into a centre of political strife.[16]

In the mid-1880s, uprisings and strikes were organised on McCormick's factory grounds, and on Haymarket in Chicago German anarchists were involved in a devastating (and legendary) plot. The events in Chicago played a pivotal role in the emergence of the Labor Day movement, with its principle demand for the eight-hour working day: from 1886 this became the 1 May holiday, which is observed throughout the world (ill. 5.1.16).

5.1.12

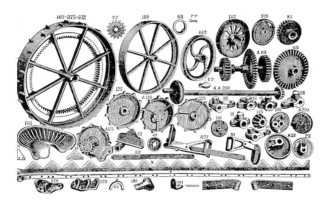

American reaping machine by McCormick. I.L.N. July 1851.

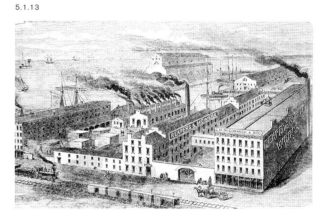

5.1.13

5.1.12: The latest McCormick reaping machine on display at the first *World Exhibition* at Crystal Palace, London, 1851; illustration in the *World Exhibition* catalogue

5.1.13: Factory extension, Chicago, 1868 (first workshop dating from 1847: see ill. 5.1.4)

5.1.14: Breakdown of the interchangeable parts, around 1885

5.1.15: The new McCormick factory, Chicago, 1885

5.1.16: Reaper machine assembly at McCormick's: combination
of manual and industrial production, around 1885

5.1.14

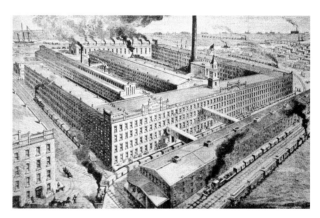

5.1.15

5.1.16

Case Study 69

The Chicago Frame and the Invention of the Skyscraper

The skyscraper owes its genesis not only to the balloon frame form of construction, which had been in use since 1830, but also to the New York Iron Works (see section 4.2) as well as to inventive pioneers and models of thought (such as McCormick's) and economic crises (cheap labour and loans). In terms of construction, New York's response to the requirement of fireproof structures was different to the approach adopted in Chicago (ill. 5.1.17).

The Great Chicago Fire of 1871 – consequences for construction development   Within 48 hours, the fire that broke out on the night of 8 October 1871 in south Chicago had left over 100,000 inhabitants homeless and destroyed about a third of the value of real estate in the booming city. In temperatures of 3,000° Celsius iron structures and façades also melted and even fuelled the fire: a deadly lesson with regard to fireproofing (ill. 5.1.18).

William Le Baron Jenney and the Chicago School of Architecture   Iron companies as well as architects and engineers moved to Chicago, where there was much to be done following the 1871 fire. Thanks to his training at the École Centrale des Arts et Manufactures in Paris, Jenney was familiar with modern skeleton constructions, English iron-and-glass construction methods, as well as technical developments in France (see case studies 6 and 53).[17] His invention of the skyscraper represents a synthesis of this background and the prevailing conditions with regard to 'Yankee technology': a lack of skilled workers, highly industrialised market production of standardised component parts and high-speed construction processes. Jenney's first modern piece of work was the 1879 First Leiter Building (see ills. 4.2.6 and 4.2.7). Though modest in terms of size, it nonetheless featured all the elements that formed the basis for high-rise buildings (ill. 5.1.19).

Jenney's Home Insurance Building (1884–85) already boasted 11 storeys. The Fair Store (1890–91; see ill. 4.2.9) became a lesson in skyscraper design and technology and, in practice and theory, has influenced to this day what was then the emerging high-rise typology as a form of industrial building system.[18] Jenney is the actual founder of the Chicago School of Architecture.

William Holabird, Martin Roche, Corydon Tyler Purdy: Standardisation of the Chicago frame   Further developments in Chicago were dominated by several outstanding teams of architects and engineers, including Burnham & Root (Reliance Building, 1890–94) and Holabird & Roche (former employees of Jenney). The engineer Corydon Tyler Purdy operated behind the scenes in both companies and was a major influence in the development of skyscraper technology to industrial building standards. He graduated from the University of Wisconsin in Madison in 1885 and was later involved in the construction of the Monadnock Building (South Addition, 1893) by Burnham & Root and the Old Colony Building by Holabird & Roche (ill. 5.1.20).[19]

Daniel H. Burnham: Reliance Building   The 'fastest' building was Burnham & Root's Reliance building at 32 North State Street (1890–94; see ills. 4.2.5 and 4.2.10). The structure, with cross pillars, slender parapet strips, bay window strips, and the slender design of the edifice, which towers up on the smallest of sites, makes it one of the most innovative and most attractive of the Chicago School's 1890s skyscrapers.[20] To give an idea of the speed of construction, two photographs from the building phase that have been preserved are reproduced here (ills. 5.1.21 and 5.1.22).

Thanks to the bay windows, the cut of the construction and the interiors reveal design qualities (ill. 5.1.23) – Burnham faced a similar challenge with the Fuller (Flat Iron) Building (1902) in New York.

New York style   As in Chicago, the parallel development of skyscraper technology in New York began with the 'history of fire' in the city (major fires: 1857, 1859, 1866, 1868) and the first high-rise to be built as a result – the Equitable Life Assurance Company Building (1868–70). A fireproof outside wall of natural stone – not a curtain wall like in Chicago – was erected in front of the inner steel skeleton. Thanks to elevators, which had been developed in the meantime, George B. Post's Havemeyer Building, constructed in 1891–92 (at the same time as Jenney's Fair Store in Chicago), set a record height for New York (ill. 5.1.24). In 1893, Post was one of the co-designers of the *World's Columbian Fair* in Chicago. He trained at Richard M. Hunt's Beaux-Arts studio in New York.

5.1.18

5.1.19

5.1.20

5.1.21

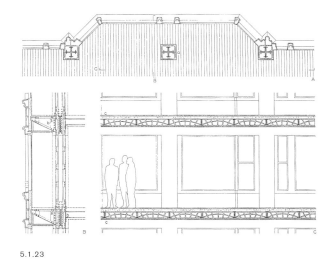

5.1.22

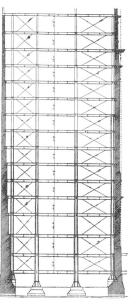

5.1.23

5.1.24

Frank Lloyd Wright – Balloon-frame Construction Technique and Tectonic Design

For Frank Lloyd Wright the industrial production of building elements and the simplification of the assembly process in wooden frame construction spelled a challenge with regard to the raising of architectural quality; after all, before his very eyes the Loop in Chicago personified the simplification of architecture through the commercial and speculative implementation of industrial conditions and markets. Although his Oak Park Studio was sufficiently far south of the centre, in Sullivan's studio he was nonetheless confronted with this environment on a daily basis. Though in the case of Wright, too, the 'framing' principle determined a sort of basic rhythm, an adherence to regularity legible in the footprint and façade, he nonetheless integrated the wooden frame as a dimension that created or influenced the style.[21]

For Frank Lloyd Wright the ready-made timber framing and the balloon frame methods of construction were sources from which to develop his own wooden frame construction method in two different versions: the light timber system, and the American Model C3 version. The light timber system was an advance on, and primarily an architectural and spatial interpretation of, wooden houses available on the market for individual villas that Wright built between 1898 and 1909, at the time his Oak Park Studio existed. The constructions were based on

a 3-foot grid, were modular and machine-made, like the balloon frame, which was still popular after some 70 years (ills. 5.1.25 and 5.1.26).[22]

Wright used wood as a building material not only for practical reasons but also because, given the numerous machining possibilities, it could be shaped in any number of ways for architectural purposes. Whether wood, concrete or glass, Wright always used natural materials to create a style, be it in the 'forest period', for his 'Prairie houses', or for the Usonian House project (ill. 5.1.27).

In a second phase of wooden frame designs, Wright developed the American Model C3 system of house construction for the builder Arthur L. Richards from Milwaukee. This was, likewise, a modified balloon-frame type of construction and was patented (ill. 5.1.28).

A completed example of this type of house is the one built in 1919–20 for Thomas P. Hardy on a slope near the Johnson Wax Administration Building in Racine, Wisconsin (ill. 5.1.29).

For Wright, wood as a construction material also had textile properties, which he used to develop Semperesque tectonics, which were employed to create a plastic effect: through joints, scales and layers. As he wrote: "Wood can never be wrought by the machine as it was lovingly wrought by hand into a violin, for instance, except as a lifeless imitation. But the beautiful properties of wood may be released by the machine to the hand of the architect. His imagination must use it in true ways – worthy of its beauty. His *plastic* effects will refresh the life of wood, as well as the human spirit that lost it – as inspiration – long since"[23] (ill. 5.1.30).

Wright embraced the era of early industrial mass production and technological inventions and, when he left Sullivan's studio in 1893 and before he founded Oak Park Studio, spearheaded experiments with the new materials and forms of technology that were becoming available; "Having to respond to technological and cultural transformations, which he himself did nothing to engender, Frank Lloyd Wright was caught in just such a vortex of dynamic change."[24]

5.1.25

Process Thinking Conquers Construction

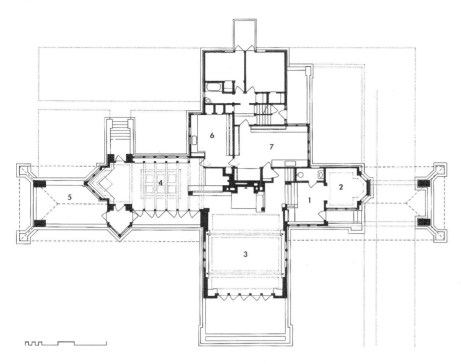

5.1.25: Ward W. Willits House, Highland Park, Illinois, 1902–03: façade rhythm as an illustration of the modularised wooden frame construction system

5.1.26: Ward W. Willits House: footprint typology with module construction 3-foot grid

5.1.27: Summer house for George Gerts, Whitehall, Michigan, USA, 1902: construction plan for this Usonian type of building

5.1.28: American system-built houses for the Richards Company, 1915–17: patent drawing

5.1.29: House for Thomas P. Hardy, Racine, Wisconsin, 1919–20: the 'ready-cut' method influenced the shape from the volume to the smallest detail.

5.1.30: House for Herbert F. Johnson (Wingspread House), Racine, Wisconsin, 1937–39: horizontal strengthening of the projecting 'streamline' figure by means of scaled wooden panelling

5.1.27

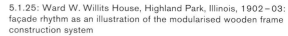

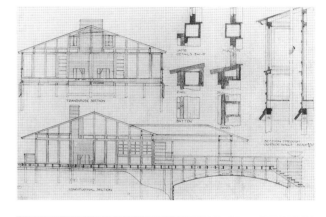

5.1.28

5.1.29

5.1.30

5.2 Mass Production and the Industrial Programme of Modern Architecture

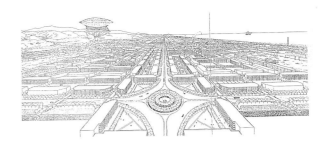

5.2.2

After 1900 the American automobile industry and its promoters set an industrial development in motion that furthered the mass production of consumer goods on a scale never witnessed before. The instruments for organising the distribution and sales market were already in existence: precisely the 'timber framing' method of house construction had performed much preliminary work. Among the automobile pioneers it was Henry Ford who, through series production and the assembly line system, was the first to develop automated manufacturing, which he had in fact adopted from other areas of consumer goods, for example, from the meat processing operations in the Chicago stockyards (since 1866; ill. 5.2.1).[25] Ford complemented this production set-up, which required linear, reticulate space, with a time management system and division of labour, clearly delineated tasks, and piece work. The empirical, theoretical and practical basis for this stemmed from Frederick Taylor's scientific management concept.

→ Albert Kahn, who in Detroit ran a multi-discipline 'industrial office' and was the leading architect of automobile factories, combined the assembly line and scientific management systems in his building for the Ford Motor Company in Highland Park, Michigan (1909–10), a state-of-the-art factory with natural daylight and of high architectural quality. In Europe, modern industrial plants (the FIAT Lingotto car factory in Turin, the Bally shoe factory in Dottikon, Switzerland, the Van-Nelle factory in Rotterdam, the Fagus works in Alfeld, to name

but a few), all followed these standards, representing an important branch of the construction programme of modern architecture.

Whereas the 'vertical' industrialisation of Chicago's high-rise technology relied exclusively on steel, 'horizontal' production employed patented concrete building systems already in existence (the Ransome system in America, Hennebique in Europe; see section 3.2). Like steel, they were suited to automobile and consumer goods production in that they enabled wide spans, support-free production lines and flexibility with regard to space and function, even over several storeys. Concrete had the advantage of its structural robustness and resilience and the fact that it was fire and earthquake-proof, whereas the advantage of steel was that it could be dismantled if buildings were extended or production lines changed.

The residential construction programme of modern architecture

Modern architecture took hold in three areas of industrial production: mass residential accommodation, pilot developments and 'case study houses'. Following 'timber framing' in America from 1830, this ambitious programme represented the second industrial revolution with regard to accommodation.

Based on drawing board projects such as the 1859 city project Eixample conceived by the engineer Ildefonso Cerdà for the expansion of Barcelona (ill. 5.2.2) and Tony Garnier's Cité Industrielle (1900–01; see case study 31), in the 1920s numerous architects came up with utopian visions for cities that could only be built with industrial means (Le Corbusier's Plan Voisin, 1925, among others).

With regard to practical building construction, however, a trend was emerging. "Europe is observing American production," was how Sigfried Giedion described the early tendency among the European avant-garde and modernity to 'go West'.[26] Not only does the relocation of Rudolph Schindler, Albert Frey and William Lescaze to the USA bear witness to this, but also publications by, for example, Richard Neutra[27] and Le Corbusier. *A Concrete Atlantis* by Reyner Banham presents a lively description of the mood at the time.[28]

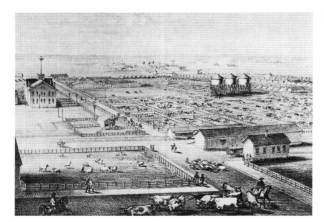

5.2.1

5.2.3

5.2.4

5.2.1: Stockyards, Chicago: role model and forerunner of 'horizontal industrialisation'

5.2.2: Ildefonso Cerdà: Eixample project (a vision for the expansion of Barcelona), 1859. It was, however, still too early for the realisation of this urban planning project by means of industrialised construction; the abattoirs in Chicago were opened at the same time.[83]

5.2.3, 5.2.4: Industrialisation and creative design were the objectives behind the construction programme of the major Berlin housing developments: two types of building in Bruno Taut's forest housing development in Zehlendorf (Onkel Toms Hütte) in comparison

5.2.5: Baba Werkbund housing development in Prague: a Mart Stam building (1928)

5.2.6: Carson Pirie Scott & Cie. department store, Chicago, 1899–1901; architects: Louis Sullivan, Daniel H. Burnham; a forerunner of Neue Sachlichkeit

Far-sighted municipal administrations that were committed to the question of accommodation appointed architects whose roots were to be found in the avant-garde, Neue Sachlichkeit and Neues Bauen, to be 'city master builders' or to city building authorities: J. J. P. Oud in Rotterdam, Cornelis van Eesteren in Amsterdam, Martin Wagner in Berlin, Ernst May in Frankfurt am Main, and others.

The field of industrial prefabrication in construction was new. The large number of identical parts, the reduction in component parts to just a few series, and the standardisation of windows, doors and installations – a prerequisite for cutting costs – required the type of construction, footprint and opening typology to be standardised. In this respect → Neues Frankfurt went furthest. In Berlin, Martin Wagner, together with a group of prominent architects,[29] attempted to combine industrial production with design criteria, which in Frankfurt was not paramount. The idea of a coherent urban shape also influenced future development principles, for example, major projects such as Britz, Onkel Toms Hütte, Siemensstadt and Weisse Stadt (ills. 5.2.3 and 5.2.4).

Neither in Berlin nor in Rotterdam was the industrial method of building as advanced as in Frankfurt. The quality of urbanity, construction type, and spatial quality, on the other hand, were higher there. In particular the residential quarters of Spangen and Kiefhoek (built with J. J. P. Oud in charge of construction) revealed architectural qualities that are still valid today. The 1981–90 concept for the rejuvenation of Spangen exploited this potential and made the small town attractive again for the next generation (ills. 3.2.26 and 5.5).[30]

Whereas major developments were built using ready-mixed concrete – the prefab process was tested only in industrial construction – those architects involved with the Werkbund developments, in particular → Weißenhof in Stuttgart, 1927, experimented with new materials and types of construction. In this case they attempted to combine new material technology and building techniques with new types of living and a new lifestyle (in particular Le Corbusier's two residential buildings), and thus to dominate the new style. The Baba development in Prague (1928; ill. 5.2.5), like the Werkbundsiedlung in Vienna (1932), primarily reflected the Neues Bauen and Neue Sachlichkeit style; innovation in terms of construction and experiments were rare. The architects of the Neubühl Werkbundsiedlung in Zurich (1931–32), on the other hand, featured coordination in size, standardisation and new building techniques which had already proved their worth.[31]

Modern architecture's third field of experimentation in the search for new forms of building were the → 'case study houses'. Numerous architects addressed this challenging subject matter, and indeed still do so today, far removed from planning, urban politics, social and economic compulsion, and largely independent of rigid market mechanisms. Visionary projects that were not, in fact, built were just as important in this specific line of development as prototypes and model houses that were completed. Anonymous architecture also played, and still plays, its part in the history of prefabrication.[32]

The vertical industrial programme:
the second generation of skyscrapers

The work of William Le Baron Jenney's assistants William Holabird and Martin Roche, and in particular Louis Sullivan's department store Carson Pirie Scott & Cie. in Chicago (1899–1901; heightened and extended in 1960–61 by Holabird & Root) represent the transition from the pioneering era of the first skyscrapers to the high-rise building of modern architecture. While the speed of construction (see ills. 4.2.14 and 4.2.15) illustrates the highly developed nature of state-of-the-art high-rise technology, the urban constellation and the design of the façade reveal stylistic elements that point in the direction of Neue Sachlichkeit (ill. 5.2.6).

The → Empire State Building in New York was built within a single year (1930–31), in the period following the Wall Street crash! The planning, delivery, transport and storage logistics, as well as the assembly process for the 85-storey, steel structure, which had a construction site railway on each storey, bear witness to the high level of Yankee technology with regard to the industrial erection of high-rises as well as to the 'time is money' mindset in the construction industry. It was only post-1945 that this technology was able to take root in Europe.

5.2.5

5.2.6

Albert Kahn
and the
'Industrial Office'

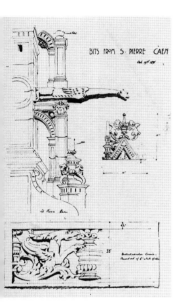

BITS FROM S. PIERRE CAEN

5.2.7

In 1880, Albert Kahn's (1869–1942) family of ten moved from Rhaunen near Mainz, in Germany, to Detroit. In Old Europe, the widespread belief in an America of freedom and unlimited opportunities also proved to be fateful for Albert's father, Joseph. He had to go in search of occasional work and the children had to earn money, too. Albert also took on various jobs, including work in the Michigan Central Railway depot. During his childhood, economic housekeeping and thriftiness were a matter of course, which helps to explain why he withdrew a mere 40 dollars a week, even in the 'Golden Twenties', at a time when his architectural office had weekly construction costs of one million dollars.[33]

As a 14-year-old Albert Kahn was able to familiarise himself with the skills of the draftsman in an architect's studio in Detroit (without pay) as well as practise drawing by hand at a sculptor's. From 1884 onwards he took over drawing work at Mason & Rice, an architecture firm. In 1890 he received a 500-dollar scholarship from *American Architect and Building News*, which enabled him to take an educational trip to Europe. As Kahn put it himself, the four months spent in Italy with Henry Bacon as his guide were "my real education in architecture"[34] (ill. 5.2.7).

In 1891, having returned from Europe, Kahn was appointed chief designer of the studio. In 1893 he received an offer from Louis Sullivan to take Frank Lloyd Wright's position, which was becoming vacant, though he declined. In 1896, together with two colleagues from Mason & Rice, he founded Nettleton, Kahn and Trowbridge (until 1900). As such, he embarked on his career in an independent practice; he had acquired his education through his trip to Europe and his literature studies.

For Kahn, Detroit had the advantage of binding him neither to Chicago's 'western architects' scene, nor to the Beaux-Arts current on the eastern seaboard. He admired both and kept an open mind with regard to forthcoming assignments. Detroit helped in the architect's rapid success: as a centre of the steel industry (in 1864 it became the first place in America to have a Bessemer furnace), a major Great Lakes port, a railroad hub (with the Pullman factory as of 1871) and, as such, a city that attracted engineers, technicians and skilled workers, it was well prepared for the emerging automobile industry.

Kahn's first forward-looking assignment was the construction of a small machine-tool workshop for Joseph Boyer. In 1902, the latter introduced him to Henry B. Joy, whose father, James, was an influential Detroit railroad magnate. When, in 1903, Joy became general manager of the Packard Motor Car Company, he appointed Kahn to be company architect for all building work that needed to be done as well as for all non-industrial buildings (ill. 5.2.8).

In 1902, Julius Kahn, Albert's brother and the office's chief engineer, founded the Trussed Concrete Steel Company, which designed an efficient, robust reinforcement system for wide spans (approx. 20 metres), heavy loads from travelling cranes, and large glass walls and roofs. It was first used in 1906 in the scarcely known automobile factory G. N. Pierce in Buffalo, New York (ill. 5.2.9).

In 1908 Kahn signed his first contract with Henry Ford: the new car factory erected in 1909–10 in Highland Park, Detroit, was used to produce the Model T. Giovanni Agnelli's FIAT Lingotto works in Turin (see case study 36 on Ford's first production plants (see ills. 3.3 and 3.2.6) was based directly on it. To be able to handle the growing number of assignments from a modern point of view, Kahn adopted Ford's goal and organisation model for his own company: annual doubling of production rates, highly standardised mass production, continual material flow, work sequence from station to station, performance and time monitoring, etc. It became an industrial office itself. When Kahn began designing for Ford he had 40 people working for him; in 1918 this figure had grown to 80, and in the 'Golden Twenties' to 400. Of these, 180–200 were architects, engineers and technical drawers, 80–90 in-house technology engineers and draftsmen, 40–50 heads of construction, 40 secretaries, almost 20 bookkeepers et al. – an early model of multidisciplinary office organisation along the 'under-one-roof' principle with a complete range of services (ill. 5.2.10).

In the 1920s the company was working on 20–30 projects daily, with a lead time of 6–10 working days. In almost 40 years of construction activity by Alfred Kahn Inc. – not just for the automobile industry – its total turnover was worth 800 million dollars![35] (ill. 5.2.11; see also ill. 4.3.4).

Process Thinking Conquers Construction

5.2.9

ORGANIZATION

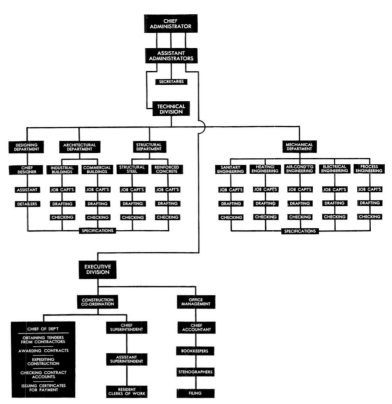

5.2.7: Albert Kahn, sketch, made on his European trip 1890, of St. Pierre in Caen, not far from the Eiffel Tower

5.2.8: Albert Kahn: Packard Motor Car Company, factory no.10, Detroit, 1905: the break-through of a modern style of concrete construction

5.2.9: Albert and Julius Kahn, (with Lockwood, Greene, & Cie., Boston): G. N. Pierce Company, New Automobile Plant, Buffalo, New York, 1906; one of the first factories to be lit by natural daylight

5.2.10: Organigram of Albert Kahn's 'industrial office'

5.2.11: Press shop, Ford Motor Company, River Rouge plant, Dearborn, Michigan: standard-ised construction and industrial design for factories lit by natural daylight and future working environments

5.2.11

Major and Model Developments

Neues Frankfurt

Head: Ernst May

Frankfurt am Main, 1925–33

Werkbundsiedlung, Weißenhof

Head: Ludwig Mies van der Rohe

Stuttgart, 1927

5.2.12: Hellerhof major housing development, part of the Neues Frankfurt programme

5.2.13: Manufacturing hall for the industrial production of large-format component parts

5.2.14: Praunheim housing development, Frankfurt am Main; Frankfurt assembly procedure

5.2.15: Manufacture of ceiling beams in wooden and iron moulds with grid-like iron inlays or hollow iron cores

5.2.16: "The assembly procedure enforces objectivity and clarity in the design" (Ernst May): The Neues Frankfurt type of building – the first trial group in the Praunheim housing development

The shortage of accommodation caused by World War I caused the authorities in several cities to develop refurbishment programmes for their outdated and unhealthy city centres, as well as an effective new building programme with state-of-the-art accommodation in order to cope with a growth in the population and influx of new city dwellers. The extensive rejuvenation and modernisation programmes in Rotterdam, Amsterdam, Berlin and Frankfurt am Main initiated industrialisation on a large scale. The founding of CIAM (Congrès Internationaux d'Architecture Moderne) in 1928 in La Sarraz, Switzerland, came late, and shortly after construction of the Werkbundsiedlung at Weißenhof, in Stuttgart, but served the theoretical clarification of the accommodation question by means of subsequent congresses.

Neues Frankfurt: from brick walls to assembly Frankfurt-style   The Neues Frankfurt residential building programme included the construction of several major developments with 10,000 residential units, which, as of 1925, were to be manufactured and constructed within a decade (ill. 5.2.12). A group centred around the architect Ernst May founded not only a factory to produce the component parts, but also a school, the Frankfurter Kunstschule, which, in a similar and yet again different way from Bauhaus, faced concrete tasks and was committed to an industrial programme. Though far less well known than Bauhaus, it was in fact far more effective.[36] The Frankfurt school of building also wielded forward-looking influence on CIAM: the 'subsistence-level apartment' had already been the focal theme of the 2nd CIAM Congress in 1929 in Frankfurt.[37] New types of buildings, residential and spatial models were developed and presented, for example, the 'Frankfurt' kitchen.

The residential building programme was at the same time a development concept for the new city. As Ernst May wrote: "The concentric, homogeneous growth of big cities has endangered the health conditions of their inhabitants. Cities must be decentralised, with self-contained urban complexes embedded in open land."[38] As the driving force of the new Frankfurt and international school of thought Ernst May founded the magazine *Das Neue Frankfurt*, thereby setting in motion a broad-based discussion while at the same time continuously documenting building activity.

The Frankfurt residential building programme was intended to advance a rational form of construction and the extensive mechanisation of apartment production (including series of component parts: door frames, plywood doors, standardised windows, boilers and kitchens, etc.). In the autumn of 1926 the first factory for the manufacture of large-format component parts opened in an empty machine hall at the Frankfurt trade fair grounds: the first step towards the rationalised fabrication of an edifice (ill. 5.2.13).

Prefabricated concrete slabs formed the core of apartments in the programme. The standard slab measured 3 x 1.1 metres, was 20 centimetres thick, and consisted of a mixture of materials containing assorted-grain Rhineland pumice 'Bimskies', which boasted excellent heat insulation qualities (corresponding to those of a 46-centimetre-thick solid brick wall). The same material served as mortar for sealing joints. These were aligned using 4-cm-high lumps of concrete.[39] The concrete mass was initially poured into moulds and pounded by foot ". . . in order to use a large number of unemployed for the production of the slabs".[40] An initial trial block

5.2.12

with 10 apartments in the Praunheim housing scheme confirmed that the preliminary work had indeed been correct. Work immediately began on another 200 buildings in order to be able to make definite comparisions with regard to cost-effectiveness (ill. 5.2.14).

Machine production of a slab now took 3–5 minutes, setting it on the building site with grouting half an hour; the average building time for a residential unit was reduced from 5–6 months to 1–2, including fittings! Using hollow beams, the floors and ceilings were made of reinforced concrete, which, pushed against each other, produced unfinished floors that were coated in gypsum screed and covered with linoleum (ill. 5.2.15).

The Frankfurt production and assembly procedure was based on a modular system that accommodated any component parts that could be standardised. The rational design in terms of footprint and elevation produced a type of building that illustrated the Neue Sachlichkeit and Neues Bauen idea of the 'apartment for the subsistence level'. Ernst May had this to say: "Just as the design of the prefabricated concrete buildings is not initially drawn and then modeled, but is first of all built up the other way round, using small bits of wood like a child's toy and then put to paper, so the finished edifice reveals an unconditional clarity and harmony between the footprint and elevation."[41] (ill. 5.2.16)

Neues Frankfurt addressed the design of products for everyday use in the new housing schemes. To this end various Frankfurter Kunstschule classes and workshops, which were closely associated with the Neues Frankfurt residential building programme, developed designs and fit-for-purpose prototypes, among them the following departments: Construction (head: Adolf Meyer, who worked with Gropius at the same time; Franz Schuster; engineer: H. Craemer); Apartment Construction and Interiors (head: Franz Schuster); Textiles (head: Richard Lisker; Anne Wever, Marianne Uhlenhuth); as well as the Metal workshop (head: Christian Dell), which developed luminaires for industrial manufacture (ill. 5.2.17).

All those teaching the construction classes were primarily employed by the Building Surveyor's Office: Ferdinand Kramer, Martin Elsaesser, Adolf Meyer and Fritz Wichert, who built up the Kunstschule and, until his dismissal by the Nazis in 1933, served as its director.

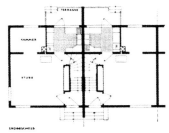

Bild 18: Grundriſſe vom Plattentyp

The courses and practical work at the Frankfurter Kunstschule were less experimental than those at Bauhaus and were specifically geared to the major projects in the city of Frankfurt. In addition, there were classes for painting (among others, Max Beckmann), graphics, sculpting, commercial art and typography (among others, Willi Baumeister), fashion, jewellery and other subjects.[42]

Werkbund housing scheme at Weißenhof, Stuttgart The Werkbund housing scheme on Weißenhof hill in Stuttgart was headed by Ludwig Mies van der Rohe. Here, too, several selected architects of the modern era were able to construct experimental buildings, and others were not (for example, Adolf Loos). As a 'trial colony' the Weißenhof development was intended to try out different types of residence, construction methods and new materials technology, and construction systems, which were suitable for common and low-rent residential buildings (ill. 5.2.18).

According to the extensive documentation and comments compiled by Heinz and Bodo Rasch on the building techniques applied at the Werkbund housing scheme, in addition to individual building materials (such as pumice hollow blocks, linoleum flooring) and parts ('rapid' reinforced concrete supporting ceilings, 'Pelikan' reinforced concrete panel ceilings, tubular cell ceilings, 'Tekton' lightweight planks, 'Torfisotherm' insulation panels, 'Luxfer' prism glass, etc.), procedures ('Torkret' concrete injection procedure) and entire construction systems (reinforced concrete framework masonry, concrete rib and filler tile slabs, iron skeleton system) as well as technical fitting techniques (central heating for small houses, steel radiators, fireclay bathtubs, etc.) were used, while inventions such as Japanese-style, transformable dividing walls of lightweight construction (the Rasch brothers) and 'thermal walls' in buildings by Hans Scharoun, Max Taut, Adolf Rading and many others were all tried out (ills. 5.2.19 to 5.2.22).[43]

280 new products by various companies were used at Weißenhof: "The vast number of tests at the experiment area at the Weißenhof exhibition were summarised and presented for criticism by the still hesitant visitor. Much is still being completed, not yet ready. On the whole, however, the impression gained was that new technology is beginning to flourish and that sooner or later the old will have to succumb to it. This is the point of departure. This is where new architecture is emerging. Not in the debates about a sense of shape and style."[44] (ill. 5.2.23)

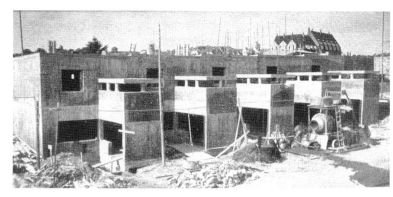

5.2.22

5.2.21

5.2.17: Popular work lights from Christian Dell's workshop, who as well as teaching at the Frankfurter Kunstschule was previously master of the metal workshop at Bauhaus in Weimar

5.2.18: Werkbund experimental housing development on Weißenhof hill, Stuttgart, 1927

5.2.19: Weißenhof housing development, Stuttgart: terraced house by Mart Stam, with pumice hollow block masonry and 'rapid' supporting ceilings

5.2.20: Terraced house by J. J. P. Oud – a monolith made of insulating concrete: "The way Oud's houses were built is magical. In a short space of time the moulds were set up, concrete poured in, the moulds removed again, and the houses were ready. (…) With this type of house there was nothing left for the mason to do."[84]

5.2.21: The carcass of the house Ludwig Mies van der Rohe used for material testing

5.2.22: The same terraced house for renting by Mies van der Rohe: iron framework, masonry, insulated with 'Torfisotherm' panels and plastered

5.2.23: Vision of the industrial, automated erection of a residential block

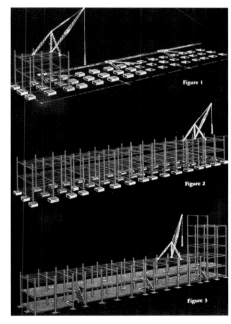

5.2.23

Case Study Houses

Richard Neutra,
Charles Eames and
Eero Saarinen,
Richard Buckminster Fuller,
Le Corbusier

5.2.24

There have always been case study houses. Even the transportable African hut (see ill. 5.1), the Caribbean 'primitive hut' Semper admired so much (see ill. 4.1) and the tree houses in New Guinea[45] are 'case study houses': the results of a long development with regard to cultural techniques that enabled individuals, groups and societies to respond intelligently to environmental conditions and gradually improve their own circumstances. The essence of these forms of architecture is their exemplary nature, their characteristic feature lightness: they are light materials and constructions, simple to assemble and dismantle, easy to transport. In its rediscovery of these primeval forms of housing modern architecture pursued a goal of extending the field of design and experimentation with regard to architecture in the hope of new access to modern style creation. The heterogeneity of the results in terms of design is revealed in the various examples – from the Eames House to Shigeru Ban's emergency accommodation for earthquake victims, from Le Corbusier's Pavillon de l'Esprit Nouveau to the digital technology trial pavilion developed by Toyo Ito and Cecil Balmond (Arup) for the Serpentine Gallery London 2002, from Albert Frey's case study houses (ill. 5.2.24) to Richard Horden's Micro Compact Home project for student accommodation in Munich, from Richard Buckminster Fuller's Wichita House to Itsuko Hasegawa's type of house.[46]

All the inventors aimed to wield influence on future developments. Several 'case study house' projects in modernity reveal a trend to industrial mass production and saw themselves as 'models' or prototypes for series construction. Even single-family dwellings and other one-offs, such as Richard Neutra's 1935 prefabricated school building made of rounded sheet metal, were trials; Neutra's building represented one stage on the path from his vision of the Diatom modular houses developed in 1928 (ill. 5.2.25) to completed major projects such as the Channel Heights development for 600 workers near Los Angeles in 1942.

The American case study houses took advantage of the range of industrial products available and as such were part of the market-related 'ready-made' building technique that had been advancing since the settlement of the west, as illustrated in studies by Rudolph Schindler,[47] Albert Frey,[48] and the case study house no. 9 (Entenza House) by Charles Eames and Eero Saarinen in Pacific Palisades (ill. 5.2.26). Frank O. Gehry's first house, his own, represents the continuation of this school of thought.

Richard Buckminster Fuller's 1927 Dymaxion House project is an industrially manufactured, hexagonal, five-room apartment, suspended, like Neutra's house, from a mast, around which mobile installations can be moved (ill. 5.2.27). A dual-shell roof skin and a draft channeling device provide natural ventilation. According to Fuller, an aircraft factory would be in a position to produce 50,000–60,000 of this type of residential unit annually. A few slightly more advanced types were actually completed as Wichita House around 1945 in Kansas.[49]

With his Pavillon de l'Esprit Nouveau, erected for the *Exposition Internationale des Arts Décoratifs et Industriels Modernes* in Paris in 1925, Le Corbusier intended propagating a building model and a form of living that was produced totally on an industrial basis and featured standardised component parts ("un logement-type de réalisation exclusivement industrielle avec l'emploi systématique d'éléments standards") as well as its application in urban planning dimensions ("l'étude de ces principes de standardisation dans leur généralisation urbaine et interurbaine").[50] In Le Corbusier's development as an architect the pavilion comes in between the Domino type of house (1915; see case study 33) and the prefabricated 'maisons montées à sec' (M. A. S., 1939; see case study 57): all these were attempts to achieve lightness and speed of construction, inspired by automobile, ship and aircraft production and other lightweight construction methods, which Le Corbuiser published in the magazine *L'Esprit Nouveau* (ill. 5.2.28).

5.2.24: Albert Frey: weekend house in Northport, New York, 1934; sail cladding with an aluminium coating; reconstructed by students at a college on Long Island

5.2.25: Richard Neutra: 'Prefabricated one plus two expandable dwellings of Diatom construction', 1928. The modular houses accommodate growing or dwindling family or neighbourly circumstances; the structure consists of floor and ceiling panels suspended from a mast and stabilised by aluminium façade panels; the suspension principle enables it to fit in with various topographies.

5.2.26: Charles Eames, Eero Saarinen; case study house no. 9, Pacific Palisades, California, USA, 1945–49: the carcass

5.2.27: Richard Buckminster Fuller: diagram for the Minimum Dymaxion House study, 1927

5.2.28: Le Corbuiser: Pavillon de l'Esprit Nouveau, Paris, 1925; this type of footprint reveals the skeleton construction, which regulates the rational footprint and organises the space – not yet a 'plan libre'.

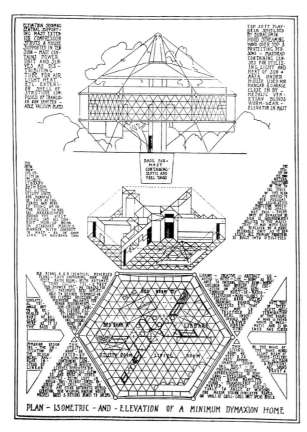

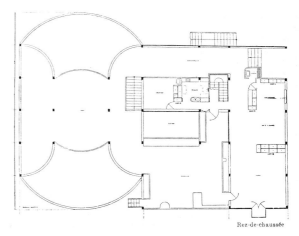

Rez-de-chaussée

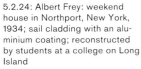

Mass Production and the Industrial Programme of Modern Architecture

Empire State Building

New York, USA, 1930–31
Architects:
Shreve, Lamb & Harmon

The 'vertical' industrial organisation of a construction process is expressed not only in the space and time management on the building site itself, but also in the organisation of the flow of materials, from the industrial production of component parts (such as steel girders), and transport and storage logistics, to the assembly process, where industrial techniques encounter craftsmanship. The Empire State Building is proof of an organisational achievement completed in narrow confines and in the shortest of time – and in the context of the 1929 Wall Street Crash![51]

In place of the renowned Waldorf-Astoria Hotel, whose owner was no longer able to cope with the rising prices on Fifth Avenue, Bethlehem Engineering Corporation, which bought the site in 1928, intended erecting an office complex (ill. 5.2.29).

What was then the world's tallest building (and remained so until the construction of the World Trade Center in 1972) was planned and built between 1928 and 1931, around the time of the 1929 Wall Street Crash! At the time, however, there was cheap labour available, and the final investment costs actually turned out to be US$ 8 million below the projected US$ 50 million. The revised plans and more ambitious aims of the group of architects Shreve, Lamb & Harmon called for an 85-storey building which, at the tip of the aerial, was to be 381 metres high and have a rentable surface area of 230,000 square metres. 64 elevators and 8 emergency staircases had to be accommodated, which, together with the access area, accounted for almost 30 per cent of the surface area of the ground floor, and for almost 50 per cent on the 7th to the 19th storeys (ill. 5.2.30).

Construction and assembly of the basement of the steel framework edifice began on 7 April 1930 and was completed on the 85th storey on 3 September, fewer than five months later! Slightly later than the carcass, from the bottom upward the façades and fittings were completed, such that building could be officially opened on 1 May 1931 after just one year and 45 days, as not only the tallest, but also the 'fastest' building in the world (ill. 5.2.31)! The detailed programme for construction planning, ordering, provision, transport and assembly of

the steel framework illustrate the 'time is money' strategy: the time span for the material flow was between two and four months. There was very little time between delivery and assembly: at this particular spot in Manhattan there was no space for storing things longer than four to five days (ill. 5.2.32).

According to the material, space and schedule diagram, the erection of the steel framework appears to be the logical continuation of the process of continual industrial mass production of standardised component parts which are then put together in a specific way.

The logistics behind the construction process were not all that astonishing. In a logbook found in 1996, page 14 reveals that on 14 August 1930, shortly before the steel framework was completed, there were 3,439 workers at the building site, the majority of them during the entire construction period. On that particular day Starrett Brothers & Eken, the main contractor, who had 104 foremen and supervisors on site, had to coordinate 1,928 workers of its own from dozens of different trades, as well as 27 subcontractors. The general contractor's organisation chart reveals a combination of direct monitoring (e.g. costs, structural engineers), as well as indirect monitoring (e.g. time, in-house technicians). Like Albert Kahn's 'industrial office' it illustrates the rationalised implementation of linear, multidisciplinary organisation (ill. 5.2.33).

The industrial orientation of the construction method was supported by a railroad on each storey (ill. 5.2.34) and complemented by large numbers of craftsmen going about their trade, with regard both to the steelwork and the fittings – a combination of industrial and manual precision and discipline. On top of this there was meticulous inspection of each and every step in the proceedings.

There were also new types of problem that had to be solved: the setting up of an on-site hospital, the difficult monitoring of every single worker (four times a day) with regard to working time and output, the laborious payment of wages on presentation of ID under police supervision: on average, every Friday some 250,000 dollars were paid out in cash on the building site!

5.2.29: The Empire State Building in the urban environment of New York

5.2.30: Tableau with selected footprints

5.2.31: Image sequence: the first support was erected on 7 April 1930 and the 85th storey completed on 3 September of the same year.

5.2.32: The skeleton programme: construction planning, delivery, storage and assembly of the steel framework in the 'time is money' diagram

5.2.33: Project-specific organigram for the construction of the Empire State Building

5.2.34: An example of the industrial railroad from the 1st floor.

5.2.29

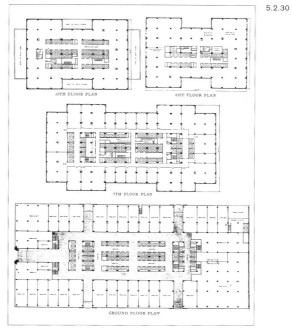

5.2.30

5.2.31

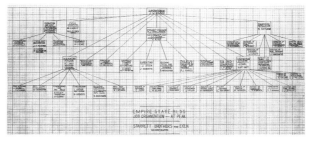

5.2.32

5.2.33

5.2.34

5.3 Construction System Mindset Between the 'Sputnik Shock' and the 'Oil Shock' – Precursors and Consequences

5.3.1: Jean Prouvé: model of barracks that can be dismantled for the French Air Force, 1938; image of assembly

5.3.2: Centre Le Corbusier, Zurich, 1964–65, built by Heidi Weber, supported by professors at ETH Zurich (et al. Alfred Roth, Berhard Hoesli, Heinz Ronner); Le Corbusier's standardised construction type 'Le Brevet 226 x 226 x 226' marked the point of departure.

5.3.3: The CLASP (Consortium of Local Authorities Special Programme) lightweight construction system and an image of the prefab model

5.3.4: Peikert school construction system, Zug, Switzerland

5.3.5: Ludwig Mies van der Rohe: Lake Shore Drive Apartments, Chicago, 1948–51; Mies used the 'Chicago frame' as a skeleton to create an industrially-based pictorial language of modern detailed architecture with European inspiration.

5.3.6: James Stirling: hall of residence at St. Andrews University, Scotland, 1964–68; axonometry of the assembly process

→ Jean Prouvé's experiments and his development of lightweight, prefabricated, temporary structures that could be dismantled (1939–45) were in response to the war situation and the refugees, wounded, homeless, etc. They stand for architectural and construction prototypes in the line of development from Richard Buckminster Fuller's Minimum Dymaxion House (1927), Richard Neutra's Diatom project (1928), as well as the 'case study house' movement. As early as 1938 Prouvé developed a rational construction principle for small houses for the French Air Force that could be dismantled (patented in 1939), of which 800 were produced during World War II (ill. 5.3.1). They were followed in 1944–45 by another 800 for the homeless and people whose accommodation had been destroyed through air raids. Every day, four workers assembled a unit and slept in it before building the next one the following day.

In 1949, based on preliminary studies, he developed the perfected, architecturally sophisticated Maison Standard building type. Rationalised production took place in Prouvé's own workshops in Maxéville near Nancy, where between 1947 and 1953 he oversaw multi-disciplinary operations. The design of the Tropique type of house followed in 1950–51 – a precursor to the 'sustainable habitat' concept (see ill. 6.3.6 and case study 96).

Le Corbusier's modular system 'Le Brevet 226 x 226 x 226', which had already been preceded in the 1920s by deliberations about mass-produced houses and industrialisation,[52] formed the basis for the Centre Le Corbusier in Zurich built in 1964–65 (ill. 5.3.2).

Mass production for the construction of residential accommodation, schools and industrial architecture

Post-1945, a third generation of mass residential accommodation production appeared to be emerging. The → General Panel System designed by Walter Gropius and Konrad Wachsmann was an early attempt to achieve mass production for the construction of residential accommodation using genuine industrial manufacturing methods: by means of production lines all the component parts and their connecting elements were to be prefabricated and, in some cases, assembled.

Post-war architecture saw the development of construction systems using steel and metal, as well as concrete. CLASP, SCOLA and USM were lightweight construction systems with steel frameworks and non-supporting metal components (building sheaths, dividing walls). The CLASP school building system developed by the Consortium of Local Authorities Special Programme as a direct consequence of the 'sputnik shock' in 1957, and which was presented Europe-wide at the 1960 Milan *Triennale* and given broad support by the Labour government in the UK after 1964, was based on the industrial production of system components (ill. 5.3.3).[53]

For the Swiss architect Fritz Haller, who in 1948–49 followed the major developments of the post-war Dutch reconstruction and rejuvenation project, coping with the future problem of the mass production of residential accommodation and the enormous amount of space required by the boom in education would be possible only by means of industrialisation. The relationship to post-war Dutch Modernity and Mies van der Rohe, as well to Skidmore, Owings & Merrill, is evident even in Haller's very first school buildings in Switzerland. He designed → USM 'Maxi', his first steel construction system, together with the steel company Ulrich Schärer Münsingen (USM). Between 1966 and 1971 Haller was a visiting professor at Konrad Wachsmann's building research institute at the University of Southern California in Los Angeles (see ill. 1.3).

Among the pioneers of concrete prefab systems Angelo Mangiarotti in particular stands out; taking up the school of thought established by Pier Luigi Nervi he was interested not only in the structural and material dimension but also in the expressive visualisation of specific struc-

5.3.1

Process Thinking Conquers Construction

tural functions and new designs for frameworks. The → 'U70 Isocell' and 'Briona 72' construction systems prompted Mangiarotti to address framework typology, rationalised and industrialised manufacturing processes, transport logistics, assembly methods and aesthetics.

Among the numerous concrete construction systems, such as the Habraken system in Holland, and the Peikert school construction system (in Zug, Switzerland, ill. 5.3.4), the → Marburg university construction system was the dominant system at that time. It represents the systematic search for extreme consistency in the creation – in terms of structure, technology, infrastructure and design – of a spatially unlimited campus, which was to guarantee maximum flexibility as well as the possibility of future changes. 'Marburg' also stands for the exploitation of mass production in construction at a high point in prefabrication between the 'sputnik' shock (1957) and the 'oil shock' (1973), and for the last stage in construction before the aid of computers began to eliminate the need for mass production.

Skyscraper technology

The development of a third generation of skyscrapers (after the pioneering era and modern architecture) is linked with the work of Ludwig Mies van der Rohe in Chicago after 1938. The American construction industry suited Mies's concept of 'skin and bones' architecture while at the same time demanding an inventive way of dealing with just a few standardised component parts. Mies succeeded in stamping the European tradition of detailed technical and aesthetic precision on the genre of the commercialised US skyscraper and to counter 'Yankee technology' with sensitivity to materials and accuracy.

Whereas the 'skeleton' was the simple continuation of the 'Chicago frame' with improved steel but profiles that were still assembled, the building sheath signified an interesting design space for Mies (see case study 59). It was a paradoxical synthesis: on the one hand, "the simplicity, the technical accuracy and the assurance of shape", which Sigfried Giedion defined as characteristics of American production and a consequence of the lack of skilled workers;[54] and on the other hand, the reduction, constructive presence and illusionist effect in the work of Mies, which stemmed from a European-influenced

background with high-quality craftsmanship (ill. 5.3.5; see also case study 60).

Mies wielded a dominant and decisive influence on post-war modernity architects, in particular on Skidmore, Owings & Merrill, on his students at the Illinois Institute of Technology in Chicago (IIT), and even on his mentor, John Holabird of Holabird & Root.[55]

The Structuralist movement and its Humanist project

A younger generation of architects, which even before the last CIAM congress in Otterloo in Holland in 1959 had joined forces as 'Team X', as well as the Dutch group 'Forum' accused Functionalism of a lack of social interest and dismantled its legend: the International style. It was not until 1981 that Arnulf Lüchinger coined the term → 'Structuralism' for this movement. Its protagonists, such as James Stirling, Herman Hertzberger, Alison & Peter Smithson, Kenzo Tange, Kisho Kurokawa and Louis I. Kahn, translated the basic structural elements of a construction assignment (activities, functions, spatial units and their relationships) into a technical structure and developed construction systems for it that illustrated this relationship (ill. 5.3.6).

From the first steps towards structural industrialisation with Crystal Palace in London in 1851, involving standardisation (type catalogues), production rationalisation (work organisation), the mechanisation of production (tools) and provision of productive power, (procurement of labour, energy sources, and investment and operating capital), there emerged a school of thought that is still valid today.

5.3.5

5.3.6

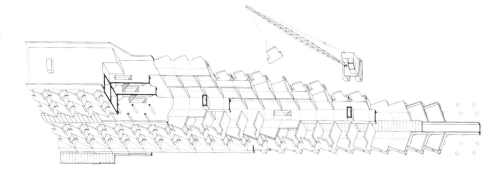

Jean Prouvé: From the 'baraque démontable' to the '2CV de l'habitat'

Immediately after the outbreak of World War II in 1939, one of Jean Prouvé's first assignments to go beyond his projects that until then had included holiday camps and pavilions that could be put up quickly and club buildings was on the back of an enquiry from General Dumontier, prior to the war director of the École Polytechnique, to manufacture barracks for 12 soldiers that could be assembled, dismantled and moved within hours. As 90 of his 120 employees had been called up, Prouvé was left with minimum development possibilities in his workshop in Nancy. He was, however, able to fall back on previous work, in particular a project he had completed just before the war for Onville holiday village, and his 1938 studies for the Ministry of Aviation for lightweight construction buildings that could be dismantled, which he patented,[56]

5.3.7

as well as the development project begun in 1938 for prefabricated metal buildings for the architects Eugène Beaudouin and Marcel Lods (until 1944).[57]

In September 1939, General Dumontier ordered 20 barracks in three different sizes to be delivered monthly to the 5th Army. Having made a prototype and conducted additional development work, Prouvé presented the first trial building in Alsace. Its functionality and assembly time of just three hours won over the general, who immediately placed an order for 275 units to be delivered within a month (ills. 5.3.7 and 5.3.8)! Prouvé also had this invention patented.[58]

Together with Le Corbusier and Pierre Jeanneret he then developed the 'Écoles volantes' for refugees

(1939–40; ill. 5.3.9). This type of structure consisted of a central framework with splayed supports made of bent sheet metal and wooden panels for the sheath. Le Corbusier considered the space and method of construction forward-looking ("digne de l'esprit nouveau").

These studies now formed the basis of a major temporary accommodation project, which Prouvé and Pierre Jeanneret fleshed out, for the war wounded for the Société Centrale des Alliages Légers (SCAL) in 1939–40 in Issoire. For the first time the concept was able to be realised using central supports, which Prouvé, as mentioned, had devised in 1938 for the Ministry of Aviation (see ill. 5.3.10). The 'supporting framework' with splayed supports and projecting supporting arms on both sides is an unstable system that assumes its structural function only after it has been put together with the equally unstable walls: it was a forward-looking principle of material-saving, lightweight construction in anticipation of 'sustainable building design' (see chap. 6, case studies 85 and 86). In Issoire, a small housing development featuring all manner of variations on the SCAL type of building was erected using this prefab system (ill. 5.3.10).[59]

In 1944–45 there followed numerous pavilions, emergency accommodation (including 800 houses for the homeless), prefab and lightweight construction systems, even for Prouvé's studios in Maxéville near Nancy (1946–48), in 1947–48 a prefabricated barracks development for construction workers in Ottmarsheim, in 1949–50 an industrial building system for school pavilions for the Ministry of Education, and also during that same period the patented, matured 'Maison Standard 8 x 12' project (architect: Henri Prouvé) with an exterior load-bearing frame. In 1950, this type of building was exhibited at the Salon des Arts Ménagers in Paris and was completed in several instances, including 14 units on a trial site in Meudon. The 'Maison Standard' was so popular that it went down in construction history as the '2CV de l'habitat' (ill. 5.3.11).[60]

'Tropique' (1950–51; see ill. 6.3.6), which was preceded by numerous prototypes and trial buildings, was one variation on this development, as was 'Alba' (1952–53), an aluminium building with no supports, just a supporting sanitation core as well as non-supporting façade panels, all on a concrete plinth.

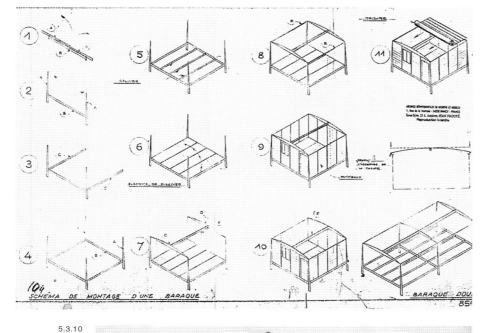

5.3.10

5.3.11

5.3.7: Jean Pouvé: Army barracks that can be dismantled, 1939; assembly of the prototype

5.3.8: Army barracks, 1939: diagram for assembly and dismantling

5.3.9: Jean Prouvé with Le Corbusier and Pierre Jeanneret: 'flying classrooms' for refugees, 1939–40

5.3.10: Jean Prouvé with Pierre Jeanneret: SCAL prefab, temporary accommodation for the war-wounded, Issoire, 1939–40; construction type

5.3.11: Jean Prouvé: 'Maison Standard', Tourcoing, 1950–52; reconstruction

The General Panel System

Architects: Konrad Wachsmann,
Walter Gropius

Konrad Wachsmann (1901–80) was a pioneer of wooden construction, Walter Gropius (1883–1969) a pioneer of the Bauhaus school of thought. The thriving industrialised building methods of the New World influenced both Wachsmann and Gropius, and were an inspiration and a challenge at one and the same time. Both architects were interested in the panel construction method in wood, which in America had been popular and in widespread use under the name 'balloon frame' and 'western frame' since 1830 (see case study 67), and, using the principle of assembly line production developed by Henry Ford, attempted to process them using prefabricated elements and to reinterpret them architecturally.

Based on the 'balloon frame' Konrad Wachsmann presented this system as early as 1930 in his book *Holzhausbau, Technik und Gestaltung*[61] and illustrated the technical description with examples from Germany, including one of his own projects (ill. 5.3.12).

"The panel construction method enables the best possible mechanical construction of houses. The building elements in panel houses are ready-made wall panels, door panels, roof, ceiling and floor panels, which can be perfectly standardised. Given the systematic configuration of room sizes and sequences it is possible to produce the individual panels in large numbers. Depending on requirements, the number of panels needed is taken from the storage area and used to construct the particular house required."[62]

This designation of the wood panel method of construction holds the key to the American ready-made timber framing and marked the starting point for the general panel system that Wachsmann and Gropius developed. Advantageous general conditions (a high level of industrialised approach and construction as well as market organisation), as well as disadvantages (no trained construction workers) led the European architects to new deliberations about how to develop construction systems that could be put together only in a single, correct manner. The decisive 'pièce de résistance' was the joining and linking technique, the node: Wachsmann and Gropius's universal metal hook fastener represented a ground-breaking invention (ill. 5.3.13).

The system Construction system mindset begins with benchmark and dimension, stereometry and spatial organisation. With the general panel system the cube represented the starting point for methodical approach in the form of a basic unit and module. The cube has the potential of individual parts and the wide variety of spatial, structural and technical relationships with each other; it is the 'thinking room' for dimensions of time and space, motion sequences and operative procedures (ill. 5.3.14).

Based on a contract Konrad Wachsmann landed from the state-subsidised General Panel Corporation in New York aimed at channelling armament money into construction, in 1941 Wachsmann and Gropius, together with a team of experts, began development work on a dividing wall system.[63] Industrial production enforced simplicity and universality, and the use of as few building parts as possible and just one joining technique. This was intended to result in unlimited combinations (ills. 5.3.15 and 5.3.16).

At the time, wood was the only material available and was easy to process. For manufacturing purposes machines had to be invented that combined the various automatic work stages in a 'transfer line': profiling the planks of wood, slits in two directions, insertion of the locking hook in the slits, adhesive bonding as a frame with the pre-cut 3 x 1-metre base plate, dual side glueing of plywood, weatherproof resin treatment, change from the horizontal assembly to the vertical storage and transport position – as of 240 metres the general panel was ready for transport and assembly (ill. 5.3.17).

Production of the general panel system commenced in 1947 in Los Angeles. It could be ordered in any combination, be transported to prepared building sites within a radius of 500 kilometres, and in eight hours be erected by five unskilled workers: "a complete house, with windows, doors, wardrobes, bathroom, kitchen, electric light, hot and cold water and a heating system (. . .) in which all that was missing was the final coating of paint".[64] A total of 150–200 general panel units were sold and erected. As early as 1948 financial difficulties began to threaten their production and development; liquidation of the company was unavoidable and occurred in late 1952.[65]

5.3.12: Konrad Wachsmann: BVG office building, Berlin

5.3.13: Universal metal hook lock for the general panel system

5.3.14: Spatial diagram, developed from a cube, of the operative relationship between component parts of a building structure

5.3.15: A 3D modular construction system with panels and connecting rods

5.3.16: Image of assembly of the general panel system on the building site: "No dirt, no waste, no material loss, no measuring instruments, as all the parts align themselves, no tools apart from a hammer, no skilled workers."

5.3.17: View of the machine and assembly shed: parallel transfer lines

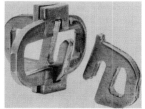

5.3.13

5.3.14

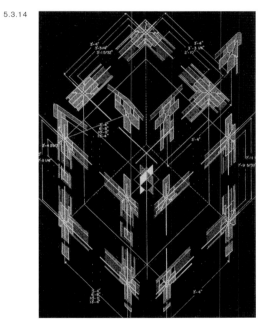

5.3.16

5.3.15

5.3.17

The USM Construction System

Switzerland, as of 1960
Architect: Fritz Haller
Metal construction company:
Ulrich Schärer Söhne (Sons)
Münsingen (Berne)

This construction system philosophy influenced an entire generation of post-war architects, in particular a group that referenced Mies van der Rohe and Skidmore, Owings & Merrill and under the label 'Solothurn school' conceived numerous school and institute buildings as well as factories and warehouses on the southern foot of the Jura mountains between Baden and Geneva, and also had a profound influence on building in Switzerland: Alfons Barth, Franz Füeg, Max Schlup, Hans Zaugg; Fritz Haller played a long-term leading role.[66]

After completing his apprenticeship, Fritz Haller (b. 1924) worked in various architecture studios and in 1948–49 for van Tijen and Maaskant in Rotterdam, who in Modernity had become well known for their Bergpolder (1933–34) and Plaslaan (1937–38) high-rises as well as several buildings in the port of Rotterdam (ill. 5.3.18).

Until 1960, Fritz Haller designed several school buildings that lean heavily on constructions by Mies van der Rohe and Egon Eiermann. That year, together with the metal construction company Ulrich Schärer Münsingen, he conceived the USM construction system, to which the company gave its name. For the company itself, the first application followed with the USM 'Maxi' construction system (1st building phase up until 1964, the 4th until 1987). Between 1962 and 1964, together with his father, Bruno Haller, Fritz Haller built one of his first school complexes, Baden Canton School, the forerunner of the 'USM-Systems Haller', in anticipation of the standardisation, characterisation and modularisation to come (ill. 5.3.19).

The 'Mini' system was developed as of 1962; the 'Midi' from 1972 onwards, with it first being used for the Swiss Railways training centre in Löwenberg, near Murten (Canton Berne, 1976–82). Thanks to the volume of the lattice girders the construction system enables the effortless integration of the technical fittings required since 1973 (ill. 5.3.20).

As of 1982, the integration of heating, ventilation, air-conditioning, electricity, water, sprinkler and alarm systems, etc. led to more deep-rooted deliberations, which Haller, as professor at Karlsruhe University (TH), addressed as a research project. Together with Therese Beyeler and the Karlsruhe research team he developed, as a computer-generated process, an integrative HVACR system to optimise operations within the potential provided by the USM system and to adapt to the different requirements every building had (ill. 5.3.21).

The additional Armilla service system follows the same working model that served as the basis for the development of the USM system from the outset, namely the demands of a particular era, and of society undergoing change in the 1960s, for absolute flexibility (types of usage) and variability with regard to space (change of function) that is minimally hampered by supporting elements and can be subdivided with light construction walls positioned and adjusted at will, and just as easily surrounded by a light-tech climate sheath by means of sealed, transparent or translucent panels.

The USM was, and still is, not a purely technical system: Fritz Haller succeeded in making the dream of industrial aesthetic appeal in system construction using standardised parts come true. The school and laboratory buildings for the University of Applied Sciences in Brugg-Windisch (Canton Aargau; 1964–66) also reveal a streamline figure. Not least of all the machine and turbine technology department at the school (which is close to the BBC/ABB mechanical engineering industry in Baden) inspired the industrial design of the façade finish, which is the work of Hans Diehl (ills. 5.3.22 and 5.3.23).

Today, only a few buildings are ever built by USM; the furniture construction system of the same name, however, which was developed by the same team between 1962 and 1970, still enjoys uninterrupted success.[67]

5.3.18

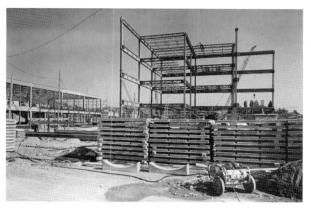

5.3.19

5.3.20

5.3.22

5.3.23

5.3.21

5.3.18: Van Tijen and Maaskant: port building, Rotterdam

5.3.19: Fritz and Bruno Haller: Canton School, Baden, 1962–64, assembly of the load-bearing system; direct forerunner of the USM building system

5.3.20: Fritz Haller: SBB training centre in Löwenberg near Murten; high-installation ceiling integrated in the USM construction system

5.3.21: 'Armilla' integral HVACR system

5.3.22, 5.3.23: University of Applied Sciences (north-west Switzerland), Brugg-Windisch, 1964–66; corner detail: carcass and image of finished product in comparison

Case Study 78

Concrete Construction Systems

The Marburg university construction system
Germany, 1962–65
Architects: Kurt Schneider, Helmut Spieker,
Günter Niedner, Winfried Scholl,
Gottfried Gondzio, Günter Herold,
Structural and construction
consultation: Rudolf Müller

U70 Isocell and Briona 72
construction systems
Italy, 1969–72
Architect: Angelo Mangiarotti

5.3.24: Typical Marburg construction system corner: 3D growth potential

5.3.25: Axonometry of the carcass system

5.3.26: Joint impact of the primary (carcass) and secondary (fittings) grid

5.3.27: Industrialised building site with manufacturing area, sliding protective roof, and storage space for completed parts; at rear of picture: beginning of assembly

5.3.28: Angelo Mangiarotti: U70 Isocell construction system developed for production sheds and warehouses; pictured: shed in Alzate Brianza near Como, 1969; structural and formal design in node area

5.3.29, 5.3.30: Model and building site assembly of the Briona 72 construction system

A wide range of reinforced concrete and steel construction systems dominated post-war architecture. Among other things 'Sputnik 1', the Russian satellite put into orbit on 4 October 1957, triggered in the West a wave of increased effort in the field of science, technology and education aimed at countering the supposed lead the East had in these areas. First school reforms followed the 'sputnik shock', including, in particular, wider access to further education based on a less selective reform process, resulting in massive investment in a boom in the construction of a new type of school building, even new-style campuses.

The construction system developed for Philipps University in Marburg was in response to the changed political situation. It illustrates a method of thought and construction that responded with an efficient, well-founded concept to the prevailing conditions. The functional neutrality of the construction system met the demands for flexibility, variability and adaptability in the use of space, for opportunities for growth, conversion and transformation of the entire structure and its individual modules (ill. 5.3.24).

This type of construction was based on the principle of the 'strip grid', of the joining together of spatial modules in any direction and number. Furthermore, the joints are used to remain flexible also with regard to the alignment of technical building fittings and to avoid openings for cables being made by hand (ill. 5.3.25).

The framework typology responds to the different locations of the supports, to concave and convex corners, and to extensions to the system. It is coordinated with the secondary interior building system (ill. 5.3.26).

Production of the component parts was conducted at a sort of 'factory building site': the supports, girders and panels were prefabricated in a manufacturing area, in the open air and, if necessary, beneath a sliding protecting roof, before being stored beside it. (ill. 5.3.27).

In Italy the architect Angelo Mangiarotti developed a construction system for each of his building assignments (see case study 42). Two of the systems he conceived, however, are more general in character and also reveal a different type of thought model: the U70 Isocell and Briona 72 construction systems. With its 'hammer-like supporting capitals' the former is a direct continuation of previously developed systems (see ills. 3.4.14 and 3.4.15). From the H-shaped support cross-section a dual-section support head with a trapeze-shaped superimposed geometry is formed for the 'trough-shaped' longitudinal girders. At a height of 75 centimetres they allow for various spans: the 'trough' profile reduces the thickness of the material to 3 cm! The tapered shape of the support head reveals the force-fit and form-fit figure at the point of transition from the vertical to the horizontal (ill. 5.3.28).[68]

The Briona 72 construction system emerged from collaboration between Mangiarotti and the Sacie company in 1972. In this case the design centred not on the dovetailing of the point of transition between support and girder but on a more classically oriented additive principle. The supporting capital is shaped in such a way (positive) that with their complementary shape (negative) the adjoining side girders can be used as fitting pieces: a transition from supporting and load-bearing that is flush with the edge by means of the prefab method (ills. 5.3.29 and 5.3.30).[69]

Continuing Pier Luigi Nervi's work, Angelo Mangiarotti invented a specifically architectural, design set of aesthetics in industrial construction systems that unfortunately was scarcely imitated, and which is for the most part missing in many textbooks and manuals as well as in literature about building culture and building history in general.[70] By way of contrast the Marburg university construction system stands out for its utilitarian rationality, efficiency, technical perfection and aesthetic pragmatism.

5.3.24

5.3.25

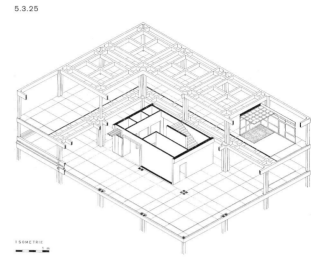

5.3.26

5.3.27

5.3.28

5.3.29

5.3.30

Structuralism

James Stirling
Herman Hertzberger

Among the most influential architects of the Structuralist movement James Stirling (1926–92) and Herman Hertzberger (b. 1932) in particular addressed prefabrication, system construction and construction systems. However, Kenzo Tange, Kisho Kurokawa and Louis I. Kahn also played their part in the broad range of structuralist forms of expression: in the case of Tange this was visible in his press and broadcasting centre in Kofu (1964–67), of Kahn in the buildings for the University of Pennsylvania in Philadelphia (Richards Medical Research Center, 1957–64) and for Olivetti in Harrisburg (1966–69).

James Stirling Nine years after graduating, Stirling's first major project (with James Gowan), the engineering department buildings at Leicester University (1959–63), reveals a fully developed concept for the spatial, volumetric, constructive and formal relationship between various sections as part of a structural principle (ill. 5.3.31).

Stirling's first drawings for the Sheffield University project (1953) show structuralist thought patterns in the constructive, technical image of the different spatial types. The rhythmic division of the façade, which is a 1:1 reproduction of the inner rooms, is the basis of a systematic transformation into a prefab construction system (ill. 5.3.32).

In his projects for a students' hall of residence at St. Andrews University (1964–68), the Runcorn New Town housing scheme (1967–76), a residential accommodation programme in Lima, Peru (1969–76), and the Olivetti training centre in Haslemere (1969–72) Stirling addressed industrialised manufacturing and assembly technology. Whereas the latter represents a 'bodywork' made of reinforced fibreglass polyester, to reproduce industrial standardisation parallel to a design product, the previous edifices were made of ready-made concrete parts developed on the basis of an industrial prefab system (ill. 5.3.33; see also ill. 5.3.6).

Herman Hertzberger Early on, the Dutch group Team X confronted their younger fellow architects with the basic questions of structuralism. From this emerged the magazine *Forum*, which Herman Hertzberger also joined. From the outset he developed a form of vocabulary, grammar and syntax in the translation of functional and spatial relationships in material, construction and image. System thought in construction very much helped the Structuralist approach, according to which construction, material and technology served as the reflection of a spatial and building programme based on the element, structure and system of functionally definable human activities, and their relationship with each other, that could be structured, put in hierarchy and interpreted spatially. The span of this thought model ranged from urban planning to technical detail.

Hertzberger's second major project, the Lin Mij factory extension in Sloterdijk, Amsterdam (1962–64), reveals what was to become standard in his work: the development of an operable construction system with modularised elements made of different materials that follows the variety and complexity of spatial qualities and references, and that strengthens their contents and statements by means of the presence of and sensitivity to materials (ills. 5.3.34 and 5.3.35).

In addition to the famous school buildings (including the Montessori school in Delft, 1960–66 and the De Evenaar primary school in Amsterdam, 1983–86), the office building for the Centraal Beheer insurance company in Apeldoorn (1967–72) provided a reason for Hertzberger to develop an industrialised manufacturing and assembly method that exploited the structural principles of the spatial and constructional structure (ill. 5.3.36).

Like Mangiarotti, Hertzberger also developed a support typology to respond to spatially complex structures systematically and in a way that is innate to the system – a theme that had already appeared in Konrad Wachsmann's research studies.[71] The combination of constant and variable relationships between elements in the system creates a design discipline in between detailed architectural design and urban planning concepts.

Kisho Kurokawa Kurokawa's 1972 Nakagin Capsule Tower is the metabolistic 'translation' of European-inspired Structuralism and a 'translation' of *Expo '67* Montreal Visions. 140 integral, comfortable residential modules, each measuring around 10 square metres, create a vertical structure that is a vision and constructed image of the permanent process of change in society (ill. 5.3.37).

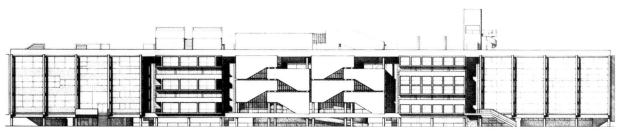

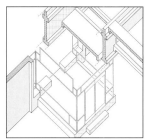

5.3.35

5.3.31: James Stirling, James Gowan: Department of Engineering at Leicester University, England (1959–63)

5.3.32: James Stirling: Sheffield University, project, 1953; the façade is structured in the rhythm AAAABAABACACACABAABAAAA, whereby
A = 2 x B and B = 2 x C.

5.3.33: James Stirling: students' hall of residence at St. Andrews University, 1964–68; assembly of the ready-made concrete parts

5.3.34: Herman Hertzberger: Lin Mij factory extension, Sloterdijk, Amsterdam, 1962–64; typical interlacing of spatial quality and constructive penetration with a material image

5.3.35: Isometric portrayal of the context of spatial relationships and constructive design

5.3.36: Herman Hertzberger: office building for the Centraal Beheer insurance company, Apeldoorn, 1967–72; assembly phases of the prefabricated concrete construction

5.3.37: Kisho Kurokawa: Nakagin Capsule Tower, Tokyo, 1969–72; the constructed vision of permanently changing life forms and constructed indi-vidualism

5.3.34

5.3.36

5.3.37

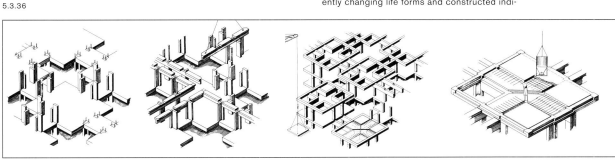

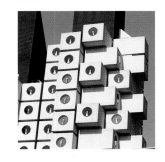

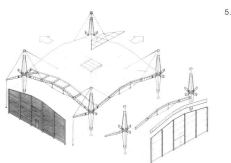

5.4 From Mass-made to Customised Production

Richard Buckminster Fuller's intellectual outlook in terms of 'geodesic domes', Jean Prouvé's lightweight construction technique and in particular Norman Foster and Anthony Hunt's bodywork construction systems for the Renault distribution centre in Swindon (see case study 84) and the Sainsbury Centre for Visual Arts at the University of East Anglia in Norwich, England, as well as new standardised construction systems such as Richard Horden's European house system[72] 'saved' the lightweight method of construction beyond the October 1973 crisis and at the same time formed a new basis for computer-aided and computer-generated operable construction techniques in the building industry (ills. 5.4.1 and 5.4.2).

The team centred around Norman Foster and Ove Arup & Partners transferred the interchangeable parts hypothesis inspired by 'Yankee technology' to architecture. Whereas the load-bearing system assumes multi-functional tasks but in its material substance remains a constant in the overall system, the sheath is made up of different elements that serve variable purposes: a solid wall, transparent and translucent openings, ventilation lamellas, sun protection – a 'bodywork' with replaceable component parts. Their standardisation allowed for adjustments to accommodate changes in operations or usage, as well as replacement when worn out or damaged, etc. The load-bearing frame and sheath had different life spans. The components catalogue still does not feature a pre-defined design for the entire system, as is the case with automobiles. Overall it represents the implementation of the idea of 'instant architecture' developed by Archigram as early as the 1960s.

CAAD as a tool

The general panel system reveals that standardisation, modularisation and system thought are fundamental principles in the industrial production of construction parts. The experience the Arup team gained through the building of Sydney Opera House illustrates that in the beginning these were an indispensable basis for computer-aided design and construction. In the pioneering era of computer-aided architectural design (CAAD) programs were used as a tool and means of portrayal as well as to monitor and check the precision of complex structures and shapes. For Renzo Piano's → Bercy 2 shopping

centre CAAD was used to calculate an operable structure. CAAD is also a joint instrument for communication between architects, engineers and constructors (ill. 5.4.3).

Building simulation programs serve as a design aid when it comes to gaining knowledge about air flows in dual-skin façades and atriums, about the behaviour of fire in complex spatial contexts, and about multilayered building sheaths (ill. 5.4.4).

CAAD as a design instrument

Once again it was the English school of thought which, in addition to other research teams, such as teams in Italy,[73] undertook concrete steps in the direction of design – a 'pièce de résistance' on the part of architects. Using computer-generated structures and designs, architects and studios such as Future Systems, Frank O. Gehry, Zaha Hadid, UN Studio, and NOX, as well as Arup engineers, including Cecil Balmond, penetrated, and indeed still are penetrating, new realms of space and image previously accessible only in the mind but which today can be realised (ill. 5.4.5).

In order to be able to complete complex structures operable models are necessary that reinterpret the fundamental rules of construction, explore new boundaries and redefine constants. The implementation process – choice of material, industrial manufacture, assembly technology – requires the linking of CAAD and CAM (computer-aided manufacturing) tools. Neither is new; what is new is the transfer of numerically controlled manufacturing processes from mechanical engineering, automobile, aircraft and shipbuilding technology to construction and making it available for CAAD. The fact that computer-aided design and computer-controlled production merely offer a form of electronic representation is forward-looking; in other words, the entire multidisciplinary team involved in a planning and construction process – architects, engineers, constructors, and technicians, foremen, as well as developers, operators, and service providers (facility management) – works with just one instrument for communication and a uniform language and nomenclature, which also alters thought and cognitive processes, the consequences of which (opportunities as well as potential restrictions) have yet to be researched.

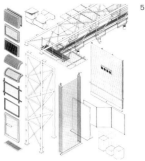

5.4.2

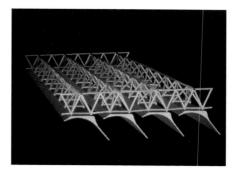

5.4.3

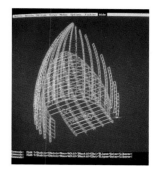

5.4.4

Major projects such as Norman Foster's roof over the → atrium at the British Museum in London and the irregular figure of the Greater London Authority require mathematical models as a basis initially for structural calculations, which, given the circumstances, permit only a limited selection of structures and shapes. Many projects are subject to concrete framework conditions: the characteristics of the site, of the structural support lines, load-bearing framework mounting points, etc. By way of contrast there have always been fields of experimentation such as Expo pavilions, and Olympic buildings, whose specifications are becoming ever more restrictive (ill. 5.4.6).

The *Architecture Biennale* in Beijing in 2004 and the catalogue *Fast Forward. Hot Spot. Brain Cells*[74] featuring all the exhibits of (Western) computer-based design technology reveal not only implementation strategies for construction but also inspiring "dream buildings" (Neil Leach). As a result of this Western presence, the Chinese architecture scene, represented, for example, by Xu Wei-Guo, who is also co-editor of the exhibition catalogue, has hopes of new perspectives and ways of thinking, in order to tackle fundamental problems in society in a different way: "and so enabling Chinese architects to establish a new basis for their theory and practice. In essence, this means a brand new beginning."[75]

Hybrid constructions

In the concrete realisation of irregular, freer structures and shapes several media can be used to control the planning process: 'the first sketch', with the advantage of an initial lack of precision at the time of fundamental decision-making, CAAD for generating operable building shapes, load-bearing structures and for 'translation' into plans, the model for sensitive checking and portraying in front of experts and laymen alike, the industrial prototype as test object and manual labour on the object itself.

Two case studies serve to provide illustration of this: the industrial manufacture and assembly concept for the → Daimler B4 and B6 office buildings on Potsdamer Platz in Berlin by Richard Rogers and Lüchinger & Meyer engineers (Zurich, Switzerland), as well as Norman Foster's → Swiss Re Tower in London.

Craftsmanship will not lose its significance: it is capable of providing 'tailor-made' special fabrications that are in evidence in almost all buildings. Computer-generated blobs and bubbles result in complex details, whose number and variety cannot be industrialised at will, as, for example, the 'watercube' for the 2008 Olympic Games in Beijing (architects: PTW, Sydney; engineers: Arup; see ills. 4.5.30 and 5.4.5) illustrates. Craftsmanship is also required for prototype products: components, mock-ups, test models. This is where constructors and technicians play a role in the design and construction process as 'anonymous designers': modelling as a part of the 'design process'. Peter Rice was of the opinion that manual work, such as the clearly visible blow of a hammer on a cast

5.4.5

part – for example, the 'Gerberette' at the Centre Georges Pompidou in Paris (see case study 83) – visualises the human input dimension and is able to convey in particular the enormous dimensions of the engineering work with regard to the tactile aspect (a desire to touch it). Architects such as Nicholas Grimshaw and Renzo Piano, who see the workshop as "an extension of the design studio", are striving for new expertise with regard to materials and production – they use the place of production to increase their knowledge, to experiment, as a source of inspiration and to open up the design scope in the overall project development and construction process.

5.4.6

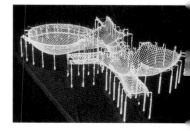

Bercy 2 Shopping Centre

Charenton le Pont
near Paris, 1987–90
Architects:
Renzo Piano Building Workshop
Engineer: Peter Rice

Non-orthogonal shapes are a constant theme in Renzo Piano's work. Even with his early buildings (a workshop for wood treatment, Genoa, 1965; sulphur production plant, Pomezia, 1966; pavilion for the 14th Milan *Triennale*, 1967, among other things), Piano's aim was to "combine lightness, flexibility and effortless construction" with each other in structures (see also ill. 3.5.2).[76] The concept for the IBM travelling pavilion (1983–86; see case study 86) as well as the underground stations in Genoa (1983–91), both elliptic arch structures, represent the highpoint of his attempts with plastics, membranes and composite materials. The studio devised a concept for an ellipsoid shape for the conference room in the FIAT Lingotto transformation project in Turin (1983–93) and the dream figure of the sphere on the IMAX cinema on Potsdamer Platz in Berlin (1992–2000) and 'La Bolla' in the old harbour in Genoa. Ever since the irregular sheath around Kansai International Airport near Osaka (1988–94), developed together with Peter Rice, Renzo Piano Building Workshop and its consultants have also been involved 'en connaisance de cause' in the devising of free spatial shapes and structures.

The Bercy 2 shopping centre falls within the timeframe of these projects and forms part of the search for new solutions to complex problems and increased expertise (ill. 5.4.7). It is situated right next to a motorway interchange, its shape determined by a feeder road: the continuous line of the 'infinite strip' that is the motorway is reflected in the building's streamlined volume; the shopping centre is not only a functional part of the spacious traffic system but also fits in with regard to shape (ill. 5.4.8).

The challenge lay not in the layout of the interior, which boasts a conventional design and is in line with conventional standards, but in the building's concept and construction of its supple sheath (ill. 5.4.9).

Calculating the dual curvature framework was a particularly challenging task. Model studies and simulation models were used for the purpose ((ill. 5.4.10). Modelling the entire building would have been an expensive, arduous procedure, but as Renzo Piano reports, "Peter Rice gave me an idea: why not use ready-made parts? The challenge was not without its charm, as it presupposed a close link between the geometry of the entire building, the design of the individual parts, and the manufacturing procedures. Perhaps I recognised in it an analogy to my early works."[77]

The supple shape of the wooden framework was to be covered with a material that best visualised and designated it. Determined by the rules of geometry, the intersecting lines of the primary system formed the basis of a mathematical model for optimising the shape of the roof panel pieces, which resulted in the selection of a modular metal cladding (ill. 5.4.11).

The roof, which measures almost two square kilometres, features a dual shell with a climate buffer zone in between. The metal skin is made of thin, smooth, sheet stainless steel and reflects the sun's rays, which facilitates the cooling of the interior. Whereas the structural skeleton resembles a Zeppelin (ill. 5.4.12), the modularised, industrially-manufactured 'bodywork' references automobile production, as well as the motion, speed and momentum of the location.

The construction and materiality lend weight to the architectural concept, emphasising it as a landmark and 'branding' for the shopping centre, which is catching on account of its coherence in all design aspects and as such is firmly rooted in the memory of all those that drive past it.

5.4.8

5.4.9

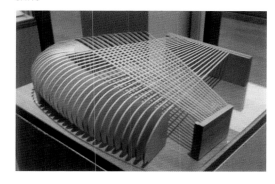

5.4.10

5.4.11

5.4.12

5.4.7: The shopping centre viewed from the side

5.4.8: Aerial view: the shopping centre in relation to the motorway system

5.4.9: The different layers of the building's sheath

5.4.10: Model study of the dual curvature framework

5.4.11: Skylights in the modulated roof skin

5.4.12: The Zeppelin as a reference image

From Mass-made to Customised Production

Spheres, Blobs and Digital Tectonics

Chris Williams, Cecil Balmond

Jørn Utzon's Sydney Opera House was the first prestigious building that was constructed with the help of a computer. At the time there were just three major IBM computers: one belonged to the Pentagon, Ove Arup used the second, and IBM itself the third. Despite the seemingly unlimited possibilities a tendency has persisted even until today: the simplification of basic stereometric shapes through circles, barrels and cylinders, cones and spheres. The Pantheon and the Maxentius Basilica in ancient Rome, the granary in Paris (1807–11), William Le Barron Jenney's Crystal Dome at the *Columbian Fair* in Chicago (1893), Richard Buckminster Fuller's 'geodesic domes', and not least of all the US pavilion at *Expo '67* in Montreal all bear witness to this; one up-to-date example would be Nicholas Grimshaw's Eden Project (see case study 13). Whereas the regular, geometric 'standard shape' affirms itself, computer programs enable irregular structures and figures with multi-curvature surfaces. The techniques go by the name of 'design by algorithm', 'digital tectonics', etc.

CAAD and CAM – design and construction in the virtual workshop One future trend that was emerging, namely research into new shapes and structures as the image of coming spatial realms, marks the continuation of a line of development that at the latest began to adopt systematic features with Antoni Gaudí's experiments. *Exploring Form. Space, Geometry, Structure and Construction* was the name of an exhibition to mark the international Gaudí year in Barcelona in 2002.[78] Continuing the approach of the Catalan architect (b. 1882), the authors made an attempt to experiment virtually, to replicate Gaudí's shapes and structures using computer models and advance them further.[79] The fact that the conoids used in Catalonian vaults represent the most promising chapter in the presentation revised by the Barcelona school of architecture is hardly surprising; it is, after all, still influencing architects and engineers today (see case study 45). One of his least known buildings, Gaudí's temporary school next to the Sagrada Familia in Barcelona (ill. 5.4.13), required ingenious craftsmanship – whereas the planning and production of the roof over the atrium at the British Museum in London almost 90 years later (ill.5.4.14; see also case study 12) involved a high-performance computer program. This enabled the creation of thousands of differently shaped beams, nodes and panels whose best possible structural forming limit was calculated using an algorithmic program. In this way in the multidisciplinary team of architects, engineers, constructors and entrepreneurs were able to acquire new expertise in their quest to produce as yet undreamt of spatial figures.

According to the mathematician Chris Williams (together with Buro Happold), the computer's mathematical high performance and the capabilities of human intelligence work well together. Algorithmic design involves the laying down of rules. These define constants and variables. Superimposing different sets of rules produces complex figures. For the structure and shape of the Japanese pavilion at *Expo 2000* in Hanover (Shigeru Ban, Buro Happold; see case study 88) and the roof over the atrium at the British Museum (Norman Foster, Buro Happold) Chris Williams used a mathematical model that also involved structural and material framework conditions. In the case of the British Museum the geometry and single-axis position of the rotunda, as well as the corner areas of the side support lines formed the framework conditions and at the same time posed extremely difficult mathematical problems (ill. 5.4.15).

New dialogues In the early 1970s Chris Williams was a member of Ted Happold's team at Ove Arup & Partners in London and was involved in generating the structure and shape of the multi-purpose hall at the German Horticultural Show in Mannheim (see case study 11 and ills. 1.4.6, 5.4.6 and 6.2.9). Later on, Happold set up business on his own and was the structural engineer responsible for the roof over the atrium at the British Museum. The Ove Arup school of thought was also the background of Cecil Balmond, who in 2002, together with Toyo Ito, conceived the Serpentine Gallery Pavilion in London. For this project the team aimed to do away, by way of experiment, with vertical supports and reduce to the limits the material (positive) elements of a spatial box – "a capsule of drifting space" (Cecil Balmond). A 'drifting' alignment left traces of empty spaces: "Like ice floats, the solid is at risk."[80] (ills. 5.4.16 and 5.4.17)

Process Thinking Conquers Construction

5.4.14

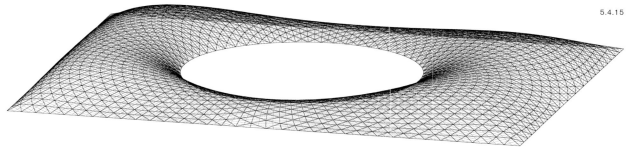

5.4.15

5.4.13: Antoni Gaudí: temporary school next to the Sagrada Familia, Barcelona, 1909; super-imposition of facing, continuous vaulting

5.4.14: Atrium roof, British Museum, London, 1998–2001; architects: Foster and Partners; engineers: Buro Happold, Chris Williams; problem areas at the point of transition from the curved roof to the orthogonal support lines at the edge of the courtyard

5.4.15: Chris Williams, Buro Happold: computer-generated model of the atrium roof at the British Museum; the various colours represent pressure and tension.

5.4.16: Toyo Ito, Cecil Balmond: Serpentine Gallery Pavilion, London, 2002

5.4.17: Digitally designed and produced structure assembled manually

5.4.16

5.4.17

Combination of Industrial and Manual Techniques

B4 and B6 office buildings, DaimlerChrysler
Potsdamer Platz, Berlin, 1992–99
Architects: Richard Rogers Partnership
Engineers: Lüchinger & Meyer, Zurich
Outer façade: Karl Steiner, Zurich
Glass roof and atrium façade:
Tuchschmid, Frauenfeld

SwissRe Tower
London, 1999–2004
Architect: Norman Foster
Engineers: Arup, London
Façade construction:
Schmidlin, Aesch (Switzerland);
Ruch Griesemer, Altdorf (Switzerland)

5.4.18: Richard Rogers: separated perimeter block development for the B4 and B6 office buildings on Potsdamer Platz, Berlin

5.4.19: Detailed view of the main façade

5.4.20: Precise manual assembly of the industrially produced components to form standardised modules in the workshop in Oerlikon, Zurich

5.4.21: SwissRe Tower, London: the final stages in the assembly of the façade with 'skyworkers'

5.4.22: Combination of manual and computerised mass production. The special profiles made by Ruch Griesemer in Altdorf, Switzerland, span the atrium in those places where they do not join up to the ceiling.

5.4.23: Robots in construction: not only the computerised manufacture of elements and modules in factories but also automated assembly on building sites is
a topic architects and engineers will need to address in the future; assembly structures that advance from bottom to top as 'mobile workshops' are changing the face of building: 'irritating perfection'?

B4 and B6 office buildings, Potsdamer Platz, Berlin   The 1992 overall building plan for Potsdamer Platz, which was the result of the competition won by Renzo Piano together with Hilmer & Sattler, readopted the old Berlin pattern of courtyards and perimeter block development. It also enabled them to be broken down and separated, which Richard Rogers also exploited in the planning of the B4 and B6 office buildings (ill. 5.4.18). The Berlin climate and the new climate and energy standard requirements were fundamental circumstances that spoke in favour of the concept of an atrium and an energy-efficient building sheath.

A building system that minimised the amount of energy required resulted in differentiation in terms of volume, structure and materials. The glass-roofed atrium forms the heart of the complex. The racking of the west fronts and the additional reduction of the building mass enables the atriums to be lit from the sides as well; furthermore, a distinct entrance area emerges on account of the free space that is created as a result.

The façade modules adopt various functions that were determined following extensive climatic investigations into various façade areas using computer simulations (glass types, protection from the sun, etc.). The modules measure 2.7 x 3.6 metres and are divided up into different 'functional areas' (ill. 5.4.19).

The reduction in the width of the centre post of the modulated windows to 10 cm demanded by the architect was implemented by the company that built the façade, Karl Steiner, in Oerlikon, Zurich (as in the case of Jean Prouvé's 'curtain wall' design the profile is reinforced inwards; see case study 89). The final size of 106 x 163 mm is the result of multi-disciplinary collaboration between the architects, engineers, companies, designers, constructors and the workshop. The names of the constructors in the workshop and the technicians in the construction company are unknown, but they are important developers, inventors, and not mere implementers. Assembly of

the standardised components to form a module occurred manually in the workshop and the same company transported them directly to the building site 'just in time', as there was a lack of storage space (ill. 5.4.20).

SwissRe Tower, London   The computer-generated conversion of the shape into an operable structure was less complicated than the next step: the constructive typology and the materials to be used. This included determining the individual components and modules, which are only ever the same within a horizontal ring, and also the assembly technique for the primary load-bearing structure, the secondary façade framework and the glass panels (ill. 5.4.21).

The spiral-shaped atriums, which continually wind their way upwards, required special treatment of their cross girders (bars), as in each case the connection to the ceiling was missing in these places. Whereas all the other parts with their different dimensions and lug angles could be industrially made to measure using numerically controlled machines – similar to Foster's roof over the atrium at the British Museum – the 'flying bars' are the product of the superb craftsmanship of the KMU company Ruch Griesemer in Altdorf, in Canton Uri, Switzerland. The special profiles were manufactured here using high-precision, manually operated machines (ill. 5.4.22).

On account of their complex figure, computer-generated shapes and structures in particular require different production methods when being constructed. Numerous recent case studies reveal construction and assembly methods that are still far removed from the visions of, for example, the 'general panel system' and automobile assembly line production. Since the early 1990s, however, primarily in Japan and in the meantime also in China and South Korea, there have been approaches and examples that herald the next logical step: computerised assembly using robot technology. Buildings such as these will lead to different appearances and forms of expression (ill. 5.4.23).[81][82]

5.4.18

5.4.19

5.4.20

5.4.21

5.4.22

5.4.23

6 "Sustainable Building Design" – A Future Project

The history and prospects of sustainable building techniques   Environment-related building and constructions and complexes built with sustainability in mind did not come into being with the UN Conference on the Environment and Development in 1992 in Rio de Janeiro.[1] Ideas for the economic use of natural resources in the broadest sense can be found in the 'ancients', in Vetruvius and Alberti, who gave just as much thought to topography, the climate, wind direction, marshes, quarries, etc. – the area to be taken into consideration and the character of a town that was being established – as they did to the configuration of sensitive rooms (such as the kitchen, pantry, animal husbandry, etc.) with regard to, say, land, soil characteristics, ground water, the environment, path of the sun, or main weather direction.[2]

The master builders of medieval cathedrals were left with no choice but to use materials sparingly as antique know-how and the relevant technical instruments had largely been destroyed and had made 'economy in construction' imperative. In the *Dictionnaire raisonné* of 1854–68 Eugène Viollet-le-Duc (1814–79) interpreted it as follows: "This school of artists that has taken on this particular role based its art on the law of equilibrium that had not been known until then, on geometry, on the observation of natural phenomena, on the laws of crystallisation, in other words on everything that does not deviate one iota from what is logical. In an attempt to replace tradition with principles the school went about studying the natural flora in minute detail in order to make its subtleties its own, to learn from flora and even fauna to apply a thoroughly logical procedure that was to enable them to create an organism from stone that had the same characteristics as organism in nature."[3] (ill. 6.1)

The industrial revolution also produced astonishing inventions relating to construction and material technology, enabling, for example, load-bearing frameworks to be more effective using less material. Without the spirit of enlightenment that was liberating itself from lingering medieval shackles and without the drive to research, which turned the philosophers of the 'siècle des lumières' into players with a long-term influence, the industrial achievements would have remained technical and could have been dismissed as the fall of an 'unbound Prometheus'.[4] The main 'philosophes' in France, such as Voltaire, d'Alembert, Diderot and Condorcet, combined the idea of scientific and technical progress with an improvement in the standard of living of the population in general, independent of origin, status and religion. Condorcet demanded more gentle treatment of the environment and resources so as to maintain them for future

6.1

6.1: Antoni Gaudí: works with the nature of material and the logic of structure[58]

6.2: Bridges as symbols and 'materialisation' of the trend towards improved mobility, communication, social exchange and life in general: the former stonemason Thomas Telford not only designed even flatter arched stone bridges, he also attempted to transfer the stone technique to iron constructions appropriate for the material, and thus to achieve greater efficiency with less material (see also ills. 6.1.6 and 6.1.7).

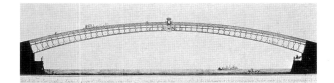

6.2

6.0: Jean-Marie Tjibaou Cultural Centre, Nouméa, New Caledonia, 1993–98; architects: Renzo Piano Building Workshop; engineers: Arup

6.3

6.3: A trend towards the decomposition of mass – pioneers in the 19th, breakthrough in the 20th century; Richard Buckminster Fuller's flying Ford dome, 30-metre span, aluminium bars with a plastic sheath

6.4: Tate Modern, London (architects: Herzog & de Meuron): extension of the lease of life of industrial witnesses as sustainable strategy

6.5: Sigfried Giedion: *Befreites Wohnen*, 1929: improved living standards and spatial comfort as a programmatic topic of modern architecture

6.6: Christian Menn: Sunniberg Bridge near Klosters, Graubunden, Switzerland: an example of a new perspective of architecture

6.7: Lloyd's Building, London (architect: Richard Rogers, engineers: Ove Arup & Partners): representative building and an early manifesto shortly after the 1973 energy crisis; a technoid building that references Archigram, with (almost) no heating, with natural ventilation that displays everything it has to offer

6.4

generations. In this pre-revolution era these philosophers, scientists and mathematicians also worked on concrete technical projects to improve living standards and make working conditions easier. Their famous encyclopaedia revealed the way forward and was a major illustration of the advances in culture that we would nowadays refer to as sustainability. In particular the development of bridge-building since the Industrial Revolution represents a material symbol of this trend (ill. 6.2).[5]

Once the importance of the node and, later, the joint in the overall supporting system became apparent, engineers and construction engineers worked on extending boundaries, on the development of an improved degree of efficiency and improved material: buildings generally became lighter. Jean Prouvé, Richard Buckminster Fuller, Konrad Wachsmann et al. discovered just how light construction systems can be when two unstable systems are combined with each other: their structures were far lighter than the usual state of the art (ill. 6.3).

The term sustainability Since the term tends to have fundamental overtones and, as such, is of no great help to us, we ought at this point to consider how concepts such as the 'spirit of sustainability' and a 'culture of sustainability' can be interpreted differently. In the 1995 Reith Lectures, Richard Rogers defined application of the term in the range between spatial and urban planning to individual objects and construction. His arguments have lost none of their relevance today and can be illustrated using current examples.[6]

On another level, Ove Arup, in his key speech of 1970, had already depicted the perspectives of ethical responsibility in the thought and work process that takes place in the field of tension between man, the environment, and technology. Given that it pointed a project for the future in the right direction as long as 38 years ago, the full text of the speech is included in the appendix.

The focus here should be on construction response strategies that reflect a sustainability mindset and make a contribution to a future sustainability building culture. Developments with regard to materials and technologies provided and, indeed, from today's point of view, still do provide basic principles and opportunities for actually implementing sustainable strategies for buildings. What is decisive here is an integral way of thinking, and not individual criteria such as recyclability. If we consider, for example, Gustav Eiffel and Maurice Koechlin's 1889 "tour de 300 mètres" in Paris and John A. Roebling's Brooklyn Bridge in New York, have they not already long since proved their sustainability? Is Tate Modern, which Herzog & de Meuron transformed, sustainable? Despite the enormous amounts of material and technology involved in the revitalisation of the former Bankside Power Station, built by Sir Giles Gilbert Scott on the banks of the Thames between 1933 and 1953 and shut down in 1986, to become a luxury museum, the mighty structure, which was not actually in service that long, but which had taken huge numbers of man-hours to build, could be given a new function; the existing building fabric was used and its lease of life extended by different usage and renewal measures (ill. 6.4).

The structural and technical inventions, experiments and visions addressed here illustrate behavioural patterns, types and strategies on the part of pioneers, schools of thought, project groups and interdisciplinary teams, which, for some 150 years (since the Crystal Palace in London in 1851[7]), have been attempting to clarify the relationship between mankind and the environment in terms of mutual and forward-looking compatibility. In this, working with natural, renewable raw materials has been and, indeed, still is the focal point, partly in contradiction of its self-conception and claim to continually improve the standard of living and comfort (ill. 6.5).

6.5

The efficiency and effectiveness of systems, structures and elements Decisive impulses in 'structural efficiency' in modern architecture after 1850 came from engineering, in particular from bridge-building. The division into compression and tension zones, dividing these into elements and the creation of triangles, the invention of nodes and joints, the differentiation between load-bearing frame and sheath, down to the combination of unstable structures, influenced the art of building, and initially differentiated between architects and engineers before ultimately bringing the two disciplines together again (ill. 6.6).

Material and technology, resources and processes The Industrial Revolution forced architects and engineers to address material and technology-related problems and provided them with scientific access to the fundamentals. The inventors among them used the new findings to redefine building and restructure buildings. Durand's invention of the 'structural (virtual) grid' around 1800 represented a 'Copernican revolution' in the tendency to dissolve mass. It also opened up the methodical field of experimentation and thought transfer that drew on engineering, and accelerated the emergence of new types of building such as greenhouses, railway sheds, covered markets, Expo pavilions, etc.[8] At this time, the discovery, still valid today, was made that a material's characteristics are not pre-determined but are likewise the result of a creative process of invention and development.

6.6

'Light tech' and 'low energy' – a turning point in thought Up until the oil crisis of October 1973 the pioneers of lightweight construction and inventors in the field of energy efficiency went different ways. Exceptions such as, Jean Prouvé's 1950–51 *Maison Tropique*, marked the starting point for a new interest in combining lightweight construction and low-energy consumption. The result has been new types of building, new appearances and a new 'branding'.[9] Analogous to Konrad Wachsmann's *Wendepunkt im Bauen*, which he saw as the 1851 Crystal Palace, there was quite clearly a turning point in thought after 1973 – the first representative buildings followed immediately (ill. 6.7).

6.7

'Sustainable building design' – 10 points for a culture of sustainability This book concludes with a list of discussion points that are intended to help ensure sustainable building in order to satisfy the brief of architectural culture. This should mean more than scientific and technical pragmatism – it involves far more a stance with historical and political dimensions.

6.1 Efficiency and Effectiveness of Systems, Structures and Elements

6.1.1: The Pantheon in Rome, 118–125; master builder: Apollodorus of Damascus; the typology of the cross-section reveals the thinning dome profile and the increasingly light consistency of the purely compression-loaded construction with non-reinforced concrete from the base to the summit with a 9-m-wide opening.

6.1.2: Museum of Hamburg History, Hamburg (architects: von Gerkan, Marg und Partner, engineers: Schlaich Bergermann und Partner); 'flying node' (see also ill. 1.3.23 and other examples in case study 27)

6.1.3: 'Tensegrity' structure at the University of Oregon

6.1.4: Jean Prouvé: 'curtain wall' as a multifunctional performed element; development study for a residential building in Saint-Jean-de-Maurienne (1953–54)

6.1.5: Genuine image of membrane construction technology: Lord's Cricket Ground, London, 1985–87; architects: Michael Hopkins & Partners

In addition to increased performance through more efficient load-bearing systems and building structures, which result in an advance to new visible, external boundaries, the penetration of an inner 'micro world' of molecules and nanotechnology pursues a strategy of increasing the effectiveness of traditional building materials and new materials. The development from degradable iron ore to iron capable of being cast and forged, and to high-grade steel, from bauxite to aluminium that can be processed and recycled, from mouth-blown glass panes to infinite strips of float glass that is as long as the life cycle of the furnace that makes it, from 'cementum romanum' to 6-cm-thin concrete shells – this sort of development is set to continue and extend to new materials, e. g. textile materials that will make buildings lighter still.

System mindset and framework typology: increased performance, less material

Many of the projects and case studies depicted or mentioned in the previous chapters reveal a common characteristic: 'less for more'. The aim to achieve greater performance through less material has dominated the entire history of engineering, which has left its mark, indeed still does, on architecture – starting with the Pantheon in Rome, whose structure represented the limits of what could be built with pure compression, non-reinforced concrete (ill. 6.1.1).

Following various experiments and patents with ridge and furrow structures and curvilinear shapes in greenhouse construction post-1800 (see section 1.1), after 1830 the knowledge of how to replace the traditional method of construction and function with regard to support and pressure was used in the construction of railway sheds and covered markets (see section 2.1). The decisive breakthrough, using a systematically thought-through and graphically operable load-bearing structure occurred in 1837 with Camille Polonceau's invention of the lower-span girder divided into triangles using pure compression and tie members: the 'Polonceau truss'. The discovery that the construction principle of the spoked wheel, which had been in use for some time, could be transferred to building structures was the next logical step and occurred more than 150 years later. This also enabled irregular shapes to be given equilibrium (ill. 6.1.2).

With his experimental research into nodes, which he immediately undid in 'tensegrity' structures, Richard Buckminster Fuller pursued a different line. Logically, however, 'tensegrity' was restricted to sculptural use; only later did it become suitable for use in spaces with different climatic conditions through reinforcement. However, this approach did lead to the classic paradigm of load and force, which had been declared unalterable, being changed into an integral model (ill. 6.1.3).

The transfer of construction types used in bridge-building to architectural concepts accelerated the trend to lighter building structures, to a reduction in the amount of material used and an increase in performance. The → Centre Georges Pompidou in Paris is a demonstrative 'lesson' in the application and reinterpretation of the German bridge-builder Heinrich Gerber's principle and invention: the 'Gerber girder' was transformed into a 'Gerberette'. Arup engineers used a similar principle for Norman Foster's design for the → Renault distribution centre in the English town of Swindon (1983): considerably shorter spans enabled a plastic-coated membrane construction suspended from pylons.

Improved effectiveness through combined construction performances

What had already been in evidence in the Bailey brothers' palm house in Bicton Gardens around 1825 (see case

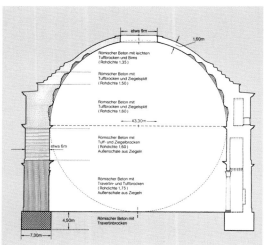

6.1.1

6.1.3

study 1) emerged 130 years later as the central theme of Jean Prouvé's → aluminium pavilion (1954): the combination of different construction performances in a coherent part, in particular the construction of a light, single-layer building sheath, that offers both support and protection. In the 20th century this search for an integrated sheath led to a forward-looking research and development project that was influenced by a new school of thought in lightweight construction (ill. 6.1.4).

It formed the exact counterpart to the Mies van der Rohe-style 'skin and bone' concept, which by means of a skeleton construction approach stripped buildings of their weight and solid state too. And both trends stood in contrast to solid state construction, which rigidly followed classic-style schools, indeed still does, finding a more contemporary form of expression in Post-modernity: the 'less for more' mindset was countered by Venturi's 'less is bore'. Solid-state structures could perhaps compensate for the comparably greater strain on building resources through lower energy consumption.

Renzo Piano and Peter Rice's → IBM exhibition pavilion (1983–86) represents an example of extreme reduction in environmentally occasioned, climatically required, spatial, functional, structural and material requirements to a 'hybrid' combination sheath, without neglecting architectural design. The pavilion, built in the 'new Constructivism' style bears just as much likeness to constructed space as the Pantheon in Rome – boasting here, as there, an elementary shape: barrel vaults and a dome, only the sheath of the touring IBM pavilion is the result of an ingenious composition of light materials that

produce different effects and not the ingenious structuring of a homogeneous, heavy building material.

In order to turn membranes and plastic foils into sheaths that are acceptable in terms of climatic conditions, several layers and possibly surface coating and superficial treatments are absolutely indispensable. Whereas membrane technology works with fixed shapes, with patterns that follow manufacturers' techniques and brace the entire structure, foils need to be shaped through air-borne condition. Membrane materials with an added insulation layer and additional physical functions (insulation diffusion, acoustics) leave the original path, which the simple, convincing tent roof laid out. The curved peripheral lines resulting from immanent stress are intended to unfold in the free space; as soon as a vertical sheath is added, which mostly occurs using adjustable 'foil cushions', the typical shape and structure system becomes falsified and is destroyed (ill. 6.1.5).

It is easier to conceive building sheaths, including roofs, with foils. This technique has long since formed part of the tradition of panels, which, thanks to the frame, can accommodate all manner of fields. Two methods are used to influence the climatic conditions: the use of multi-layered foil cushions filled with compressed air or the possibility of extracting air by means of vacuum-isolating panels. Working and building with → air, or its opposite, a vacuum, is a new approach and stands in the line of development that began with the invention of the hot-air balloon. It is still used today in the construction of Zeppelins. One particular branch results in the construction of mostly dubious, air-inflated halls in sports, shopping and leisure facilities, and (looking backwards) unsightly pneumatic 'blobs', such as at *Expo '70* in Osaka. This technique can, however, reveal a perspective if designed with panels.

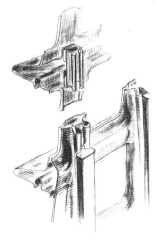

6.1.4

6.1.5

The Invention
of the Joint

Structural inventions by bridge-builders have provided, and continue to provide, important impulses in the trend to reduce mass in construction. In bridge–building, the introduction of joints and soft, pliable links was an invention that came from the earliest engineering work in the Industrial Revolution in England: as early as 1795(!), in his experimental bridge near Longdon-on-Tern, Thomas Telford placed a strip of rubber between the bevelled sheet steel of the bridge girder and its counterpart in the seating. He did this to test a new technique of pliable joints and, without envisaging it, paved the way for the invention of the articulated link (ills. 6.1.6 and 6.1.7).

The joint was the key to the second revolution in bridge-building: the breakthrough to lightness. Like the first, the transfer of the stone arch technique to the cast- and wrought-iron structure of the Iron Bridge in Coalbrookdale (1775–79; see ills. 1, 2 and 5.2), the pliable structure introduced by the German engineer Johann Wilhelm Schwedler in 1865 and which the 'ingénieur centralien' Armand Moisant used for the 115-metre-span machine hall at the 1889 *World Exhibition* in Paris, represented a transition from engineering to architecture (see case study 22). The spectacular framework of the Palais des Machines next to the Eiffel Tower doubtless provoked a new image of space and contributed to a change of paradigm in the question of style; gravity appeared to have been overcome: "Visually, the arch adopted an unusual hovering position."[10]

The Centre Culturel Georges Pompidou   The bridge over the River Main near Haßfurt (1866–67), which was designed by Heinrich Gerber, inspired Peter Rice, who played a pivotal role in the discussion about structure with Richard Rogers and Renzo Piano in the Arup team 'Structure 3' (with, among others, Ted Happold), to a transfer in the load-bearing system for the Centre Georges Pompidou (Paris, 1971–78; see section 2.4). The urban development, as well as functional and spatial framework conditions of maximum flexibility with regard to use (50-metre, support-free platforms) and maximum free space next to the building, as illustrated by one of Renzo Piano's sketches, led to a 'reversal' of the Gerber principle: the intermediate section, suspended from two joints, was not to be the shortest, but rather the longest (ills. 6.1.8 and 6.1.9).

The 'Gerberette' forms the key piece of the entire structure, not just in structural terms but also with regard to allowing lay observers to see and sense 'major component parts'. Peter Rice wrote that: "We can make people – people who would normally be alienated by things – feel comfortable. It proved to me that the thing that really matters is to introduce elements and materials in a way that reflects their real nature."[11] The gigantic cast piece was not only cast at Krupp, but was also finished off by hand to improve the material and load-bearing qualities. The still visible hammer blows reveal the way the girder was made as well as its function: it is a visualisation of the interplay between industrial and manual technique (ill. 6.1.10).

The different treatment of the 'Gerberette' profile provides another dimension to the history of the invention of lightweight construction: at each interface the transverse section does just as much as is absolutely necessary. The changes in it along the projecting section meet the different statical requirements between the inner seating and the outer stay joint – yet another example of 'constructive' economy (ill. 6.1.11). The 'constructive economy' working model was introduced by Jean-Nicolas-Louis Durand at the École Polytechnique in Paris around 1800 and made available as the method of construction for the assignments the coming industrial era entailed (see case study 2).

6.1.6

6.1.7

6.1.8

6.1.9

6.1.10

6.1.11

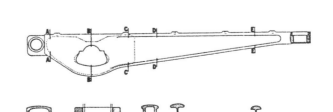

6.1.6, 6.1.7: Thomas Telford, the 'first great engineer' of the Industrial Revolution in England; the bridge near Longdon-on-Tern, built in 1795, a trial bridge prior to construction of the Pontcysyllte aqueduct near Llangollen in 1805; rubber strips provided (and 200 years later still do) a soft link and were a precursor to the invention of the joint in bridge-building.

6.1.8, 6.1.9: Comparison of Heinrich Gerber's bridge over the River Main near Haßfurt with the concept of Peter Rice's invention the 'Gerberette'

6.1.10: Workshop at Krupp: industrial manufacture and subsequent manual finishing of the 'Gerberette'; traces of manufacture and finishing by manpower

6.1.11: Changes to the cross-section of the 'Gerberette': a response to different statical functions along the projection and an illustration of 'constructive economy'

The Renault Distribution Centre

Swindon, England, 1983
Architect: Norman Foster
Engineers: Over Arup &
Partners/Anthony Hunt

The working environment in the new Renault building was intended to correspond to the design quality of the automobile marque. This included work areas that could be used for different purposes with a non-obstructing 'bone structure', a 'bodywork' façade as design field and a modular type of construction enabling swift assembly and a low-cost strategy. Norman Foster wrote that: "This quest for excellence was to be sought within demanding limits of time and cost in ways which would also accommodate the dynamic of change during the building's life."[12] (ill. 6.1.12).

The complex was built on greenfield land on an irregular site measuring 6.5 hectares. The modular division of the available space enabled maximum exploitation of the field. And it was based on the construction and market-related design strategy. It was possible to combine the spacious roof, which as a result of the way it was structured avoided the bulkiness of industrial buildings, with a type of façade, which, because it does not support anything, was able to respond to the outside in different ways: open in the foyer and social areas, closed in the warehouses, and equipped with large gates in the delivery area (ill. 6.1.13).

Each space module, which in terms of construction is defined by four pylons, measures 24 x 24 metres and is 7.5 to 9.5 metres high; the pylons reach a height of 16 metres. The individual, almost 580-square-metre modules can be divided up or used as a single, continuous unit in any direction. The height of the building allows for the construction of work galleries (ill. 6.1.14).

The construction and the component parts catalogue, as illustrated in the assembly diagram (ill. 5.4.1), reveal the composition of the lightweight structure. Polygonal, perforated steel girders are hung on joints between the pylons with lower bracing in the middle field; the bracing cable is continued to the head of the posts. The pylons in the peripheral and corner fields have to be braced on the outside and firmly anchored in the ground (ills. 6.1.15 and 6.1.16).

The roof of a module consists of a single pre-stressed, plastic-coated membrane, which is stretched over a 75-mm-thick insulating layer of mineral wool; this rests on a trapezoid metal plate, connected to secondary supporting elements. The peripheral fields and the areas around the pylons on the inside are made of glass. The skylight elements in the peaks of the modules also serve ventilation and smoke dispersion purposes.

The curtain wall, which is divided up into standardised components, is also based on a components catalogue, enabling it to respond to the different requirements of the facilities on the inside. It is set back one layer from the front edge of the primary construction. Because it encounters slight instances of deformation in the field of the suspended roof, an intermediate layer or buffer zone made of hard rubber was inserted between the façade and the roof (see ills. 5.4.1 and 6.1.15), like in car-making, when different moving parts encounter each other. The façade, which was made entirely of glass, involved the first use of the 'Planar' system developed by Pilkington on a major scale: the patented anchorage allows vertical movement across roof deformations of up to 75 mm, and up to 30 mm as a consequence of horizontal wind pressure (ill. 6.1.17; see also ill. 1.3.15, first diagram left relates to Swindon).

Like Waterloo International Terminal in London, in whose construction Anthony Hunt was also involved in the role of engineer (see case study 28), here, there is not only a differentiated structure for different functional and statical performances, but, through the controlled movement of building components, the additional potential of structural systems, from building materials and technology, is exploited, with a view to creating an easier method of construction and simpler assembly procedures. This "structural logic" is visualised, indeed orchestrated, by means of a new appearance.

6.1.12

6.1.13

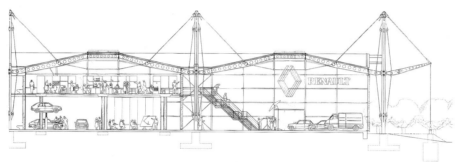

6.1.14

6.1.12: Overview of the entire plant

6.1.13: Glass foyer

6.1.14: Cross-section of two modules

6.1.15: Detailed view of the suspended roof

6.1.16: Anchorage point of the pylons in the ground: industrial design in the entire plant, down to the very last detail

6.1.17: 'Planar' glazing by Pilkington: a 'bodywork' design; section of the building sheath

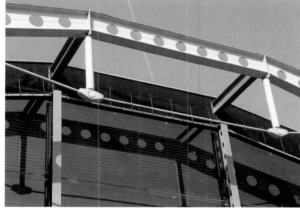

6.1.15

6.1.16

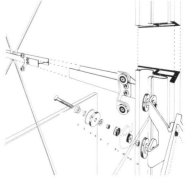

6.1.17

Aluminium
Jubilee Pavilion

Paris, France, 1954
Architect and engineer:
Jean Prouvé

An exhibition held in 1954 in Paris honoured the 100th anniversary of the very first industrial transformation by Henri Sainte-Claire Deville in 1854 of bauxite into aluminium suitable for construction purposes. Jean Prouvé landed a contract from the French aluminium industry to use the method of construction and the structure of the exhibition hall to demonstrate the aluminium's state-of-the-art processing technique and to "illustrate" its usage – the idea was to construct a demonstration pavilion. It was located on the banks of the River Seine between Pont des Invalides and Pont de l'Alma and revealed a totally new look. Prouvé primarily demonstrated the possibility of combining the functions of various building parts, thereby presenting an example of material reduction and the probing of new limits with regard to structural logic (ill. 6.1.18).

In the roof area the 4-mm-thick aluminium rainwater drains are shaped in such a way that they play a role in the crosswise bracing (dummy girder ribs); spacers keep them 'in shape' and, together with the pavilion's lengthwise cover panels (1.6 mm), and complemented by cable stays per group of three, have a stabilising effect. The jamb consists of two complementary extruded sections, which, at their point of overlap, form a continuous vertical groove for mounting the façade panels. The base of the prop is a hinged cast part and the façade pieces are of deep-drawn, flat, corrugated sheet aluminium (0.8 mm). In total, 114 load-bearing modules, each with a 15-metre span, were erected (ill. 6.1.19; see also ill. 4.3.31).

For processing procedures such as reshaping and bevelling, among other things, Prouvé designed special machines in his workshops in Maxéville. With regard to structural calculations, further works ensued in collaboration with the Aluminium Français research centre and engineering department as well as with Armand Copienne (structural engineering and execution planning). As far as structure was concerned the entire building, for which Prouvé also served as the architect, was divided into standardised components and designed as assembly modules (ill. 6.1.20).

As a result of its specific profile, the jamb – as a multifunctional part – can assume a wide variety of functions. The load-bearing effect is heightened by the hollow shape, the elliptical cross-section and the grooves at the end of the longitudinal section, as well as by the additional crosswise raises. These also serve the clip assembly of the various façade elements (aluminium panels, glass panes, doors). By means of screws and springs the inner groove can also be used for the mounting of spatial installations (ill. 6.1.21).

A series of preliminary studies and sketches made accessible by Peter Sulzer illustrates Prouvé's search for new possibilities with regard to combined performed elements and material reduction – an increase in the effectiveness of aluminium through new structuring, shaping and technological processes (ill. 6.1.22).

Jean Prouvé's construction-oriented research and development work ran parallel to Richard Buckminster Fuller's empirical experiments. Both defined a new 'extension of boundaries': Prouvé inwards, within the micro-world of material technology and the structuring and design of construction parts with the aim of achieving more efficient systems; Fuller, by means of 'geodesic domes', outward, in the field of ever-bigger spans and macro-worlds of new spatial settings. As inventors, both represent a school of thought whose aim is to construct fascinating spaces while at the same time reducing expenditure for material resources suitable for construction purposes. They are pioneers with whom the likes of Renzo Piano, Norman Foster, Richard Horden, Richard Rogers and Nicholas Grimshaw, to name just a few, associate.

6.1.18

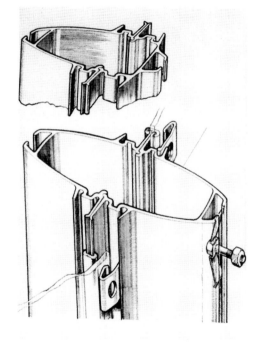

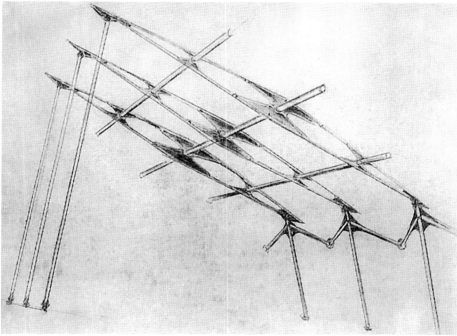

6.1.18: Current photograph of the reconstructed aluminium pavilion in Paris

6.1.19: A view from below of a prototype load-bearing module

6.1.20: Transition pieces from the gutter to the vertical jamb laid out

6.1.21: Jean Prouvé: publication drawing of column profiles

6.1.22: Jean Prouvé's preliminary study for the aluminium pavilion

IBM Travelling
Exhibition Pavilion

1983–86
Architects: Renzo Piano
Building Workshop
Engineer: Peter Rice

The pavilion was used to present future developments and visions in IBM information and communications technology at various locations in European cities. Consequently, its design and construction had to respond to differing local conditions and themselves be an image of a future vision. The vault-shaped space, and likewise the polycarbonate pyramids, represent classic geometric figures, which reference local features anywhere, whereas the structure is a new take on a, for the most part, 'dematerialised' load-bearing system, all of whose component parts demonstrate the highest level of efficiency (ill. 6.1.23).

The exhibition pavilion is 48 metres long, 12 metres wide, and at its tip 6 metres high. It stands on a platform that is raised from the ground and has a hollow floor for technical installations. The exhibition space is encased in 34 automatically stable, arched modules that are put together from both sides (ill. 6.1.24).

The individual component parts of the differentiated structure were designed in an inter-disciplinary process in which material technology specialists took part alongside architects and engineers: "For the IBM exhibition we decided to use a hitherto unknown cocktail: laminated wood for the small cross beams, cast-aluminium parts for the joints, and polycarbonate (a particularly light, transparent material) for the pyramid-shaped roof elements."[13] (ill. 6.1.25).

In the overall structural design the materials assume various functions that correspond to their characteristics. Wood, which in this case is not used as an assembly material, i.e. as a board, but rather in its original linear, grained texture, can absorb compression as well as tensile forces, and as such is used as a lower and upper flange; laminating it prolongs its life.

Aluminium tends to be a soft building material which, as Prouvé demonstrated with his 1954 aluminium pavilion, can be treated and used in a wide variety of ways. Various attempts to link the wooden planks using methods appropriate to the material involved resulted in a 'logical shape-structure': in a linear, finger-like dovetail that corresponds to the direction of the wood's grain and gives the aluminium an 'extended area of contact' (ill. 6.1.26).

The polycarbonate pyramids consisted of four surfaces glued together. The idea behind the design aimed at total transparency – a 'feeling of non-materiality', communication between inside and outside. As opposed to what is usually the case with glass, polycarbonate's transparency is two-directional; its materiality also seems ephemeral, of unlimited duration, which corresponds to both its changing location and the structure's ability to be transported and re-assembled, as well as its unforeseeable length of usage. The polycarbonate panels are robust and demountable. They were connected using extra-hard solidifying glue on the edges, which provides additional structural stability: "Polycarbonate as a material is light and robust but it is also not very strong: its load-carrying capacity and its stiffness are low. (...) Making the polycarbonate perform a structural role meant that all the joints had to perform properly and predictably."[14] (ill. 6.1.27)

The increase in load-bearing performance and degree of efficacy in connections of different materials in 'hybrid' structural systems is the result of an interdisciplinary design and construction process. The resultant urge to reach new limits in terms of 'dematerialised' constructions and spaces created new forms of expressions and images that trigger new spatial and material-related emotions.

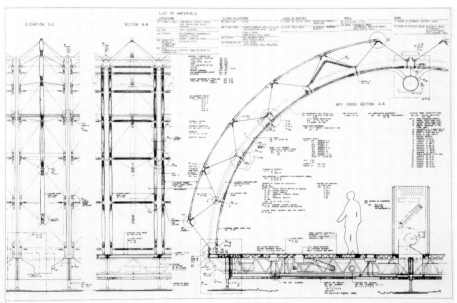

6.1.25

6.1.23: The IBM pavilion was assembled in various locations: in a park in Milan, on the banks of the Seine in Paris and, shown here, in front of Castel Sant'Angelo in Rome.

6.1.24: Assembly of the half-arches

6.1.25: The stability of the arched pieces and the fact that they can be assembled are the result of joining three unstable components: wooden planks as compression and tension linear elements, aluminium nodes entwined with these, and polycarbonate panels glued to form pyramids; chart depicting construction, structure and shape

6.1.26: Finger-like dovetailing of aluminium and wooden plank length-wise, as well as plate-like linking of the aluminium end sections cross-wise: 1:1 experiments using wooden model, and final consistent thrust and shape design in the detailed node

6.1.27: 1:1 test arch: visualisation of the interplay between the com-ponents and the efficacy of their functions in an entire module arch

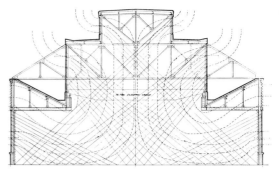

Case Study 87
Air as Construction Material

6.1.28: Albert Kahn: Packard Motor Car Company, forge shop, Detroit, 1911; relationship between building profile, ventilation and daylight comfort

6.1.29: The hangar originally intended for the design and construction of cargo airships in Brand (architects: SIAT GmbH; engineers: Arup; 2000), which is currently used as 'event space'; framework and membrane technology for the conversion into the 'Tropical Islands' leisure centre: form TL, Radolfzell, Germany

6.1.30: Pneumatic cushion forming the roof over the atrium at the Festo Technology Centre in Esslingen, Germany; architect: Ulrich Jaschek, Stuttgart; framework planning, roof and glass: form TL Ingenieurplanung Leichtbau, Radolfzell

6.1.31: Pneumatic shading principle through compressed-air-controlled shifting of the middle ETFE foil

6.1.32: Cross-section of one of the three atriums that connect the plant's 'finger docks'

6.1.33: 'Stingray' by prospective concepts ag: air-inflated membranes provide the framework.

6.1.34: 'tensairity^R' supporting structure (air beam) for a car park roof in Montreux, Switzerland, 2005; architects: Rodolphe and André Luscher (Airlight Ltd.), engineer: Mauro Pedretti

Air, a renewable, natural raw material, was only recently discovered as a component part for construction purposes. Ever since Frank Lloyd Wright's Larkin Building (Buffalo, New York, 1902–06) the artificial treatment of air for climatic conditioning has been influencing (and continues to influence) spatial design (spacious open-plan offices), volume, and building structure (installed, structurally effective elements), even down to spatial installation and furnishings. Until the 1973 energy crisis, climate conditioning provided a challenge for new design and construction concepts, as evidenced, for example, by Frei Otto's Arctic City, the most extreme example of a project that used membranes supported by compressed air (see case study 8). Parallel to this, architects and engineers were working with the principle of natural through ventilation, which had a conceptual impact first and foremost on the cross-sections and profiles of buildings (ill. 6.1.28).

After the 1973 'oil shock' the use of air-based climate control systems was extended to include dual-skin glass façades (an advancement on thermopane glazing), which were considered to be part of the energy supply of the building as a whole. This typological change in paradigm with regard to the sheath of a building, as well as the increased use of technical methods of natural through ventilation and controlled room aeration, altered the physiognomy and 'branding' of new buildings and plants.

Air-inflated structures The hot-air balloon was an early discovery of the structural effect of conditioned (heated or cooled) air: limp material becomes stiff and can perform supporting functions. The air'ship' and Zeppelin represented an advancement on the air balloon and by means of a light inner frame were given the reinforcement necessary to carry large sizes. This approach was reverted to in the design of the 'later type' Zeppelins, from 'Cargolifter' airships to assembly hangars (ill. 6.1.29).

Air-inflated roofs such as that for the Eden Project in Cornwall, the Masoala-Halle at Zurich Zoo and the Orang-utan House at Hagenbeck Zoo in Hamburg (see case study 13 and ills. 1.0 and 1.3.8) are special cases serving to balance extreme climatic conditions. The first 'normal case' of an air-inflated roof over an atrium was completed for and with Festo in Esslingen, a company which

itself designs and manufactures pneumatic products (ill. 6.1.30).

This new-style atrium roofing is made of triple-layer ETFE foils (ethylene tetrafluorethylene), which, using controllable compressed air, is inflated to form cushions, whose external and middle layers are also printed in the from of a 'chessboard' and can be pressed together in such a way that a desired shading effect of 47–93 per cent can be achieved (ill. 6.1.31).

By means of a curved framework made of tie rods and compression members on which connecting platforms rest, the atrium roof is brought into 'dynamic balance' with the front façade, with tangible vertical and horizontal movement (ill. 6.1.32).

The Swiss company prospective concepts ag was made famous by designing and testing the 'Stingray', an inflatable manned aircraft, which, like a manta, boasts an expansive two-dimensional structure and shape (ill. 6.1.33).

Together with prospective concepts ag, extensive design work on the part of Airlight Ltd. resulted in the new load-bearing structure 'tensairity^R', which can also be used for building purposes. In comparison with traditional load-bearing structures the actual weight of an air-inflated girder with the same load-bearing qualities can be reduced several times over (ill. 6.1.34).[15]

In 2006, for the first time, the façades of an office building in Lausanne, Switzerland, were to be clad in 4-layer ETFE-foils (architects: Brauen and Wälchli, Lausanne).

Building with vacuum It is not the load-bearing capacity of vacuum construction parts, but primarily their insulating qualities at the smallest cross-section that make this field of research and experimentation of continuing interest. Here, consideration has to be given to aspects of transfer that use natural phenomena or vehicle and aircraft-building techniques as a source of inspiration: among other things, problems related to load-bearing capacity, (chambers, combs or such like), types of connection and soft protective shields are as yet unsolved (see case study 95).

6.1.31

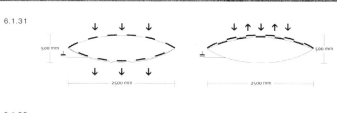

500 mm

2500 mm

500 mm

2500 mm

6.1.32

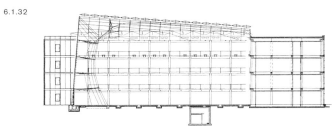

6.1.33

6.1.34

6.2 Material and Technology, Resources and Processes

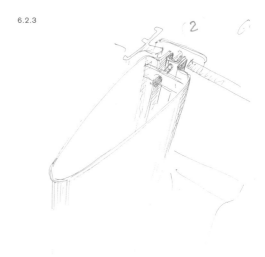

The history of the development of sustainable design and construction strategies follows two main paths. In addition to load-bearing structures, construction materials, and technology that serve the construction of architectural space, it is references to the environment, energy and the climate that inspire master builders, architects and engineers to go down new roads, and develop and invent lighter structures and more efficient energy systems – topics that are as old as the 'métier' or the profession itself. On the one hand, the 'dematerialisation' of building structures presents, on the other, a challenge to give new consideration to the indoor environment, to energy efficiency and the structure of building sheaths. Does a reduction in energy requirements and consumption result in solid-state construction? Or to new types of construction, to even lighter methods of building? The seemingly paradox task of combining lightness and energy efficiency requires thought transfer, a willingness to experiment, a research urge and inventiveness (ill. 6.2.1).

6.2.1

6.2.2

The trend to dissolving mass

From the Pantheon in Rome, gothic cathedrals, Alberti's structural 'skeleton', to Durand, Semper and Mies van der Rohe, and on to Fuller and Foster, Rice, Piano and Shigeru Ban, there is evidence of a major 'structural evolution' towards ever lighter constructions and striking spatial design. All the previous chapters have traced this history and its perspectives. The → Japanese pavilion by Shigeru Ban and Buro Happold (with Frei Otto) at *Expo 2000* in Hanover was an unusual construction made of laminated paper and roles of cardboard to create a fascinating space: it represented a concept for a 'robust lightweight construction', which, on account of its functional reusability and material recyclability, boasted a sustainable quality. The 'paper tube structure' represented a forward-looking construction principle, which for Shigeru Ban was uncharted territory.

Load-bearing structures are becoming lighter, structures more slender, construction materials, which anyway had been improved, are becoming even more effective, and construction systems and connecting nodes more efficient: previous limits have been broken and pushed back further – an extension of limits through

material and technology inventions. This development is ongoing and is receiving a new, sustainable dimension as a result of the increasing demand for the sparing use of non-renewable resources and for construction materials to be reusable (ill. 6.2.2).

Richard Buckminster Fuller, Frei Otto, Heinz Isler, Eladio Dieste, Jörg Schlaich, Thomas Herzog and many others were, indeed still are, pioneers of a new school of thought with regard to sustainable building that has only recently become known as such, but that has been researched and practised almost as a matter of course for some time now.

Experiment and transfer thought

It is in the work of Jean Prouvé that we find the most far-reaching and most extensive studies and experiments on material and technology. As a trained craftsman he had a different perspective and direct access to the manual as well as the industrial dimension of construction. He was familiar with materials and technology, as he was with the design opportunities they opened up. Contact to leading architects of Modernity such as Mallet-Stevens, Le Corbusier, Pierre Jeanneret and others inspired him to set up links and develop projects that were able to translate architectural programs into industrial 'languages' (ill. 6.2.3).

With spatial-depth → profile systems Prouvé was ahead of his time and was an influence on Norman Foster. Even in the early 1960s he was working with separate profiles and multi-layered connection opportunities for sandwich panels and dual-layer glass packets.[16] New processing machines, designed in part by Prouvé in his studio, as well as improved material qualities enabled the manufacture of previously unknown structures and shapes, which led to new forms of expression and effects.

The invention of material characteristics

The transition from Roman circular arches to flatter

"Sustainable Building Design" – A Future Project

6.2.1: Hot-air balloon with integrated architectural space; "Exposphere" project by the architects Gerster & Haelfinger, Basle, Switzerland

6.2.2: Nicholas Grimshaw: Eden Project, St. Austell, Cornwall, 2001; extension of material limits

6.2.3: Profiling as a constant design theme in the history of construction: a sketch by Jean Prouvé, made during his courses at the Conservatoire des Arts et Métiers in Paris

6.2.4: Ethyltetrafluorethylene foils (ETFE) were also used as a multi-layered cushion for Herzog & de Meuron's Allianz Arena in Munich;

thanks to the partial UV permeability, which is also advantageous to tropical houses such as the Eden Project in St. Austell, Cornwall (see case study 13), and the Masoala-Halle in Zurich, the harmful UV-C is absorbed.[59] Shown here: the Masoala-Halle at the Zurich Zoo, 2003

6.2.5: Mike Davis: concept for a polyvalent building sheath, 1981[60]

6.2.6, 6.2.7: 9 Metre-high, hanging glass panels used for stabilisation and reinforcement against wind at the Sainsbury Centre for Visual Arts in Norwich (architect: Norman Foster; engineers: Anthony Hunt Associates) (see also ill. 5.4.2)

stone-arch bridges, the Bessemer process for the manufacture of steel from iron, concrete pre-stressing techniques, glass load-bearing systems, the emergence of plastics and air-inflated load-bearing systems in building – these developments never followed immediate material characteristics or a 'material's logic': in this case, 'state of the art' was not the goal behind all the thought, research and work, but rather its point of departure. Taking new paths was based on observation, experiments and vision.[17] The new technologies mentioned led, and still lead, to new inventions with regard to material characteristics! And this development is continuing, in fact, it is increasing in speed; one only has to think of the new achievements in the field of nanotechnology and plastics (ill. 6.2.4).

As a result of new challenges with regard to building assignments, of different mindset systems, of requirements such as time-saving and cost-cutting (time is money), of new tools and instruments, and of the spirit of invention on the part of pioneers and schools of thought, materials are, in their substance (materiality) and treatment (technology) seen differently and in a new light and given highly diverse fields of application – material characteristics are an open field for technological inventions and innovative thought.

What does material-appropriate construction mean?

Combining various construction materials can lead to a change in their characteristics and, in fact, new creations. Physical, chemical, electrolytic, as well as mechanical, compounds of various construction materials or of materials in various conditions widen the field of design with regard to material-appropriate construction. Compound systems and compound materials increase performance: reinforced concrete, fibreglass-reinforced plastics, laminated glass and structural glazing are examples of this (ill. 6.2.5).

Making compounds of various materials for the purposes of energy efficiency also broadens the design and construction scope.

Whereas combining different materials results in a 'functional cocktail' as far as the construction module is concerned, and to lighter, energy-saving parts, the joining technique acquires a key role in the system as a whole: it is here, and not in the 'centre field' of the module, that the potentially weak points and scope for invention on the part of architects, engineers, constructors, technicians and material experts of industrial design and innovative companies are to be found.

The transformation of existing materials by means of new technology

Available materials can be changed in terms of their function, e.g., glass that serves as division and protection into glass with a structural function: glass panels for bracing façades, cross pillars with several dovetailed glass layers, etc. (ills. 6.2.6 and 6.2.7).

Thanks to profiling technology (rolling, casting, pressing), shaping (bending, cambering, deep-drawing), and so on, steel and aluminium panels, for example, can be transformed into highly efficient load-bearing structures. Thanks to new technological processes there are transformations, metamorphoses and new products in particular in the field of → plastics, new materials and composites. As a result of altered shapes, construction materials such as these assume new structural functions in the overall system, serving as image-bearers of industrial and machine-made structures.

By means of layering, laminating, pre-stressing and partial pre-stressing, materials can adopt different physical and chemical conditions, and be 'tailor-made' to perform specific functions. The thermal pre-stressing of → glass, for example, alters the traditional characteristics of glass planes in building. As with the pre-stressing of concrete, this process remains concealed from a cursory glance but not, however, from our perception in terms of material and technology, which inevitably attributes the extraordinary efficiency of such a part to 'background' measures: Technology is only indirectly present.

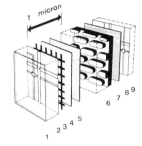

6.2.4

6.2.5

6.2.6

6.2.7

Shigeru Ban: The 'Paper Tube Structure' Technique

Japanese pavilion,
Expo 2000, Hanover
Architect: Shigeru Ban
Engineer: Ted Happold
Consultant: Frei Otto

Shigeru Ban used the main theme of ecology and sustainability at *Expo 2000* in Hanover in several ways to conduct inter-disciplinary development work on a new construction method and structure using previously recycled construction materials: "In accordance with the main theme of *Expo 2000* – environmental conservation – I have designed a temporary pavilion that uses recycled materials to a great extent. The building should also produce minimum waste when dismantled and be highly reusable or recyclable."[18] (ill. 6.2.8)

Shigeru Ban sought to collaborate with Frei Otto on account of the latter's many years' experience in lightweight construction. And the challenge he faced was the condition that the pavilion could be totally dismantled and the objective of building an outstanding structure: "It must be a masterpiece of the art of building." He also saw himself as an interpreter between architecture and engineering (ill. 6.2.9).[19]

Given the large number of visitors to *Expo*, the need to create spacious structures favoured the choice of paper or cardboard as a construction material: almost infinite rolls of card with no joints are easy to produce from recycled paper. To avoid permanence, steel frames filled with stones and sand were used for the foundations. In the discussions between Shigeru Ban, Frei Otto and Ted Happold the 'curvilinear' structure and shape discovered in the pioneering era of glass and greenhouses held sway, as it improved stability in all directions. The space was around 80 metres long, almost 30 metres wide and almost 18 metres high (ill. 6.2.10).

An inventive spirit was required in particular for joining together the rolls of card. The 3D stereometry of the nodes resulted in a flexible, soft connection that could be dismantled and reassembled, like those Frei Otto had designed as early as 1971 for the multi-purpose hall in Mannheim (ill. 6.2.11).

In order to be able to mount additional struts and stabilise the entire structure, as demanded by the German authorities, Ted Happold proposed metallic connections. The roof took the form of a translucent, waterproof membrane foil (ill. 6.2.12).

Other temporary structures designed by Shigeru Ban along the same principle served to research and test new structures, wider spans, and new shapes with regard to the assembling of rolls of card to form fascinating, special spaces, such as the cover over the sculpture garden at the Museum of Modern Art in New York (ill. 6.2.13).

In Japan, the Building Ministry recognised the new 'paper tube structure' technique as a form of construction – not least of all given the temporary housing that needed to be produced swiftly and cheaply in the case of natural disaster. After the 1995 earthquake at Hanshin near Kobe, the office of the United Nations High Commissioner for Refugees (UNHCR) commissioned Shigeru Ban to come up with an alternative solution to the UN tents that had been in use until then (see case study 96). On the basis of the experiments with rolls of paper, he designed and built, in an honorary capacity and together with a group of Japanese students, a 'community centre' and an emergency accommodation quarter as a contribution to the field of socio-cultural sustainability. He wrote about it as follows: "Even in disaster areas, as an architect I want to create beautiful buildings. I want to move people and improve people's lives. If I did not feel this way, it would be impossible to create meaningful architecture and to make a contribution to society at the same time."[20]

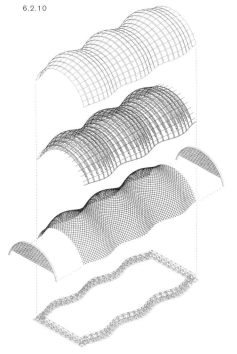

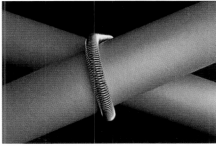

6.2.8: A model of the Japanese pavilion at *Expo 2000* in Hanover

6.2.9: Frei Otto: multi-purpose hall, Federal Horticultural Show, Mannheim, 1971

6.2.10: Curvilinear structure and shape: explosion axonometry of the different layers

6.2.11: Experimentation with connecting techniques: visualisation of temporary, recyclable technique from the entire structure to the connection in detail

6.2.12: Visualisation of the temporary structure by means of a recyclable membrane foil

6.2.13: Roof over the Abby Aldrich Rockefeller sculpture garden at the Museum of Modern Art, New York, 2000

Material and Technology, Resources and Processes

Case Study 89
Profiling: a Constant Theme of Industrial Design

Jean Prouvé, Nicholas Grimshaw, Norman Foster

6.2.14: Aerodynamically structured and shaped wind wing designed to increase the speed of upward thrust and flow of waste air between the glass layers on the GSW high-rise in Berlin by Sauerbruch Hutton Architects, Berlin

6.2.15: Wood-processing machine for the 'Paxton gutter' at Crystal Palace in London (1851)

6.2.16: Nicholas Grimshaw: British Airways building at Heathrow Airport, London; profiling as an architectural theme from the building geometry, technical multi-functionality to detail shaping in detail

6.2.17, 6.2.18: Buildings by Jean Prouvé and Norman Foster in comparison: Citroën garage in Lyons, 1930–31 – streamline profiling that was ahead of the Citroën design; the 'aircraft wing' at the Reichstag building in Berlin

6.2.19: Hendrik Petrus Berlage: Municipal Museum, The Hague, 1927–35; elegant solution to the division of load-bearing function and 'curtain wall'; the load-bearing profile is screwed to the 'curtain wall' in selected places.

6.2.20: Ingrid Burgdorf, Barbara Burren architects: new buildings at Rapperswil University of Applied Sciences, St. Gallen Canton, Switzerland; glass panels mounted on the outside for bracing purposes

The profiling of building components and systems, indeed entire buildings, represented a constant theme in the development of building techniques. For some time now aerodynamic structures and shapes have no longer been restricted to mobile vehicles; buildings and sections of buildings also follow aerodynamic circumstances, such as Richard Buckminster Fuller's Wichita House, Richard Horden's Wing Tower in Glasgow, and Norman Foster's Greater London Authority. Sun protection lamellas and windscreens also reveal aerodynamic shapes, which directly influence climatic conditions (ill. 6.2.14).

Even in the pioneering era of the industrial age the profiling of the balusters for glass and greenhouses provided a design, construction and technical challenge. Profiles that were as thin and slender as possible and allowed the maximum amount of light to enter had to perform their structural function by means of longer webs, in other words, they were given spatial depth. This train of thought, which emerged for the first time in 1817–18 in the work of John Claudius Loudon and which is still in evidence today in the Bailey brothers' Palm House in Bicton Gardens (see case study 1), runs right through the history of the development of construction-influenced architecture. The first ground-breaking patent for a fully developed, multifunctional profile that combined load-bearing functions with glazing and drainage technical features was the 1850 'Paxton gutter', (see ill. 1.1.25 and case study 20). This almost 40-kilometre (24-mile) gutter for Crystal Palace in London was manufactured using a wood-processing machine designed specially for the purpose (ill. 6.2.15).

The discovery of the industrial aesthetics of the multifunctional capabilities of façade profiles is attributed to Jean Prouvé. He utilised the web's requisite profile depth to anchor, among other things, double glazing, to balance different degrees of thickness in the construction, and to visualise the actual function (see case study 58).

This profile geometry can also feature on the outside and be strengthened and optimised, e.g., through perforation, or fitted with additional functional profiles that can serve, for example, as guide rails for sun and weather protection equipment. On Nicholas Grimshaw's British Airways building at Heathrow Airport this multifunctionality was taken a step further: projecting consoles serving as supports for a number of sun protection lamellas extend the concave glass façade, whose shape, together with the position of the lamellas, was optimised such that radar interference by flights could be avoided at computer workstations (ill. 6.2.16).

Current industrial design is inspired by the 'streamline' world of the 1950s, as well as by natural structures and shapes such as fish bellies and blades of grass, or, in terms of shape, references the typology of aircraft wings and helicopter rotor blades. In doing so it transfers the rather covert world of engineering and mechanical engineering, technical construction and unfamiliar natural phenomena to the visual and emotional brand language of everyday culture.

Jean Prouvé and Norman Foster's endeavours in terms of design point in precisely this direction. If one considers the design of cars at the time – the DS was not launched until the 1960s – the profiling of Prouvé's early façade for the Citroën garage in Lyons (1930–31) was way ahead of the streamlined Citroën design! Foster's transfer of an aircraft wing model to the side ramp in the cupola atop the Reichstag building in Berlin triggers in visitors a sensation of flying – were the ramp to move vertically one would experience the confusing sensation of being on a bridge . . . (ills. 6.2.17 and 6.2.18).

The division or selective connection between the load-bearing profile and joint supporting 'curtain wall' in Hendrik Petrus Berlage's 1927–35 Municipal Museum in The Hague (ill. 6.2.19) represents a variation on profile reinforcement. Nowadays, glass panels are a popular substitute for steel and aluminium profiles. On the new buildings at Rapperswil University of Applied Sciences (St. Gallen Canton, Switzerland) they are mounted on the outside (ill. 6.2.20; see also ill. 4.5.12).

6.2.14

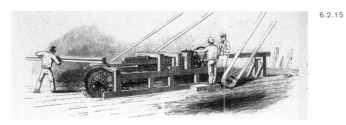

6.2.17

6.2.18

6.2.19

6.2.20

Material and Technology, Resources and Processes

Plastics, New Materials, Composities

The development of new
material characteristics

In building there is a sheer unlimited number of plastics in use, and the trend is rising. Building construction and technique provide an attractive research field for new materials and technology. Since time immemorial, ephemeral, temporary pavilions for international exhibitions, sports events, building trade fairs, visitor centres for large infrastructure projects, etc., have been used as a field of experimentation for penetrating previously uncharted territories in terms of material technology. In the 1960s, plastics were discovered as unusual materials for industrialisation projects and transferred from automobile and wagon construction and product design to building (ill. 6.2.21).

After the 1973 energy crisis, man-made insulation materials were increasingly used in building sheaths. At the same time, engineers such as Peter Rice at Arup 'transferred' the silicon adhesive technique from its area of application for car windscreens to the new pictorial language of 'structural glazing' (ill. 6.2.22).

The fact that plastics provide a solution to the characteristics required in building today is decisive in their use in construction: structural aspects (stability, elasticity, malleability), fire prevention, safety (tear resistance, indestructibility), durability, usability (re-use in the same or even a different shape or structure), and the ability to be dismantled. There are no limits to ideas, research is progressing full steam ahead, and recycling tests are producing interesting results. The number of relevant publications is increasing, as is the number of landmark buildings and projects that are going down new paths (ill. 6.2.23).

Plastic-coated fabrics (textile or man-made) have long been used for tent roofs and membrane constructions. Their discovery is attributable to a pioneering generation of engineers working on the borderline between nature and technology: Frei Otto, Walter Bird, Klaus-Michael Koch, Horst Berger, David Geiger, et al. Even today, structuring and design are achieved using 'hybrid technology': the combination of industrial and weaving techniques and the use of computer-generated patterns (ill. 6.2.24).[21]

Nowadays, foils and coated fabrics are being used increasingly whenever a sheath that needs to perform multifunctional and dynamic functions is to be built, for example, transparent interior and exterior views, or the ability to respond to varying, occasionally extreme, climatic fluctuations. One of Norman Foster's early works, the compressed-air-inflated office pavilion for Computer Technology Ltd. in Hertfordshire (1968) was made from a nylon-reinforced PVC foil of less than one cubic metre in volume for a working area of 800 square metres and was assembled using a mobile crane in under 55 minutes.[22] Ethyltetrafluorethylene foils (ETFE) are being increasingly used for greenhouses (Eden Project, Cornwall), pavilions in zoos (the Masoala-Halle in Zurich, the Orang-utan House in Hamburg), or sports venues (the Allianz Arena in Munich). Multi-layer 'cushions' inserted in load-bearing structures enable volumes to be altered using compressed air in response to fluctuating climatic requirements (see case study 13).

The roof over the atrium at the Festo Research and Development Centre in Esslingen produced an original solution using ETFE foils: printed foils resembling a chessboard and positioned next to each other in the middle and on the outside are pressed against each other using compressed air in such a way that controllable shading of 50 to almost 100 per cent can be created (see case study 87).

Fibre-reinforced plastics in 'duroplastic' condition are being tested with a view to making load-bearing structures lighter. Initial attempts using profiles and connections borrowed from steelwork (rivets, screws) led to structures, shapes and connections that are designed in a manner appropriate to the material (e.g., gluing). Here, too, however, what is appropriate for a material emerges not from the material or by itself, but has to be discovered or invented. Methodical thought transfer, 'translation work', and visions are always necessary, and mistakes inevitable.[23]

6.2.21

6.2.21: Plastic building in the pioneering era of material transfer from other areas of application to building: Monsanto House, made of glass-fibre-reinforced plastics, USA, 1957 (architect: R. Hamilton); Futuro House, made of a polyurethane, high-resistance foam core and polycarbonate coating, Finland, 1971 (architect: Matti Suuronen; engineer: Yrjö Ronkka)[61]

6.2.22: Conference Centre 'Grünenhof', Paradeplatz, Zurich, 1987–91 (architect: Theo Hotz): glass façade stuck with silicon[62]

6.2.23: Old material rediscovered: Scobalit webs with or without aerogel filling as a building sheath; *Swissbau*, Basle, 2000

6.2.24: Membrane roof at Munich Airport

Traditional glass-blowing companies encountered their first industrial challenge prior to the construction of Crystal Palace in London for the first *World Exhibition* in 1851. For the Great Stove on the grounds of Chatsworth House (1836–40), Joseph Paxton, at the time still the Duke of Devonshire's head gardener, demanded glass panels that had been extended from three to four feet to combine the curvilinear ridge and furrow strips. This entailed hard work and required strong glass-blowers. The enormous quantities of glass needed for Crystal Palace revealed the limits of this technique: for the production of around 100,000 m² of glass for the façade and roof the commissioned company, Chance, had to devote a third of its annual production for this one building, and within the space of five months! (ill. 6.2.25; see also case study 3 and case study 20)

The lowering of the 'window tax' in England in 1845 paved the way for industrial mass production using new processes and glass technology: from continuous rolling and via the pulling procedure to the invention of float-glass technology by Pilkington between 1950 and 1960.

As a result of the architectural requirement for the further 'dematerialisation' of building sheaths for glass and greenhouses that followed the 1973 energy crisis, engineers such as Peter Rice from Ove Arup & Partners discovered and invented the 'structural glazing' assembly technique. And through this technique and the practice of punctual affixing there emerged a new, previously unknown problematic area, that of 'glass structural engineering,' when experiments with it began being conducted with in various places. The precise description of the questions in conjunction with the construction of the 'serres chaudes' for La Villette Museum of Science, Technology and Industry in Paris, as well as with the transition to a higher level for the greenhouses in Parc André Citroën by Peter Rice (see case study 10), reveals the uncharted territory that glass technology represented, and which from that point on was to be a design project that pointed way into the future (ill. 6.2.26).[24]

With regard to new opportunities in terms of architectural space, further scientific and technical research based on 'structural glazing' inevitably led to the topic of load-bearing glass. For atrium roofs, high-rise façades and other exposed types of glazing, various layers of glass had to be glued together with foils to form composite safety glass in order to make it unbreakable. This represented another metamorphosis for glass, whose qualities were no longer self-evident. Technology that assigns glass primary load-bearing functions is even more concealed to our sight and senses: thermal pre-stressing and partial pre-stressing alter the characteristics of glass and extend its area of application. After concrete and wood, this particular form of technology has now embraced glass (ill. 6.2.27; see also case study 14).[25]

Thanks to this spectrum of glass technology, 'tailor-made' characteristics are now possible. Glass is not used just as a pane that can be walked on or as overhead roofing – composite glass tubes are increasingly being used as structural components. Reinforced with interior cable stays, they also perform a load-bearing function as compression members in all-glass façades. In the wake of experiments that were presented at *glasstec '96,* composite glass tubes were used for the first time on a large scale for the atrium façade on Richard Rogers's Tower Place office complex (2000–02). Via a tensile structure it transports wind loads to the primary load-bearing structure. In the case of wind pressure the glass influences the balance of forces in the entire system, whereas in the case of suction it is the pre-stressed stainless steel stay on the inside (ills. 6.2.28–6.2.30).

This also opens up a whole new field of design for the future. Glass constructions can turn atriums into 'power stations' and buffer zones that can considerably reduce energy consumption levels. As a result of this transformation in characteristics the visually perceivable 'logic of the structure' becomes a source of confusion – the presence of technology is indirect, whereas that of the engineer is more direct than normal.

6.2.25

6.2.27

6.2.26

Rohrendenbauteil mit
Kugelgelenk-
anschluss zur Krafteinleitung   Basisplatte aus Stahl

Durchgehendes   Spannseil   1 bis 3 Paare
Tragrohr   hydraulisch   Schutzschalen
                        vorgespannt   pro Rohrlänge   6.2.28

6.2.25: Blown glass: the end of traditional glass-blowing companies on the threshold of a new industrial challenge

6.2.26: Structural glazing: the transition from window typology to glass skin; 'serres chaudes' in the Parc André Citroën in Paris (architect: Patrick Berger; engineers: Peter Rice/RFR)

6.2.27: Pedestrian bridge across Corporation Street in Manchester, 2001; architects: Hodder Associates; engineers: Arup

6.2.28: Diagram of a composite glass tube

6.2.29, 6.2.30: Richard Rogers (architect), Dr. Lüchinger & Meyer, Zurich (engineers); Tower Place office building, London, 2005: insertion of a composite glass tube in the tensile structure of the atrium façade

6.2.29

6.2.30

6.3 'Light Tech' and 'Low Energy' – A Watershed in The Way of Thinking

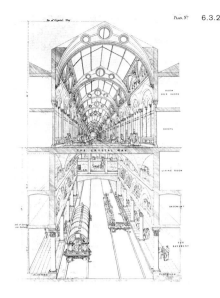

One of the very first fantastic lightweight structure projects featuring climate control was Joseph Paxton's 1855 Crystal Way, a vision that fed off tried and tested greenhouse construction techniques and the experience in industrial iron construction that Paxton was able to gather during the building of Crystal Palace in London in 1850–51. To a certain extent, Crystal Way was an 'extended' Crystal Palace surrounding central London; 16 kilometres long, 22 metres wide and 33 metres high it was to link all the city's peripheral stations. It was intended to be a multifunctional blend of a permanent, multi-storey 'splendid station' consisting of hotels, offices and flats and comprising a ring-shaped city of the future (ills. 6.3.1 and 6.3.2).[26]

120 years later Richard Buckminster Fuller and Norman Foster designed another lightweight 'superstructure' with artificial climate control: the Climatroffice (1971), an exciting development for the future featuring offices and other spaces and related to Frei Otto's 1971 Arctic City project, but, even two years before the 1973 'oil shock', already very much last year's 'high-rise' model (see case study 8). Ten years later the same team devised another ground-breaking concept that this time, however, was efficient in terms of energy and was integrated in the environmental momentum and natural conditions: the 'autonomous dwelling' of 1982 was able to respond to changing demands on its own (see section 1.3 and case study 9). As a working model it represented a point of departure that paved the way forward in terms of research approach. Dual-skin building sheaths with buffer zones as well as functional layers that were integrated in the sheaths and were able to respond to changes through motion are now par for the course.

Types of building for the future

The fact that structural elements, components, layers, indeed entire systems that are part and parcel of the environmental momentum take the form of lightweight constructions lies in the very nature of things. Manoeuvrability and malleability were initially achieved through doing away with outside walls, layering walls and the new way of viewing façades as a sheath (ill. 6.3.3).

Breaking down the sheath into several layers was a result of the wide range of demands made of it: trans-

parency and protection from the sun, a view outside and glare protection, density and ventilation, insulation and light permeability, etc. (see chap. 4). From Mike Davis's micro polyvalent 'wall' a development stage was required for the 'twin skin' featuring two layers of glass and a ventilated space in between, and yet another development stage until the space in the buffer zone could actually be used as a walk-in area (ill. 6.3.4).

Out of the usable 'climatic buffer zone' a new type of building could emerge: a new type of multi-storey 'arcade'. Its naturally conditioned climate serves to exchange inside and outside air, even in extreme climatic conditions, and is suitable for special types of use: as a place for recreation, encounters, communication, as a winter garden, parking space for low-energy vehicles, as an exhibition, information event and party venue – extended urban space for use at the interface between the private, neighbourly and public spheres, as this project by Richard Horden demonstrates (ill. 6.3.5).

The → 'new atrium', which, as opposed to 19th-century atriums, a product of the iron and glass era, was to become a type of building for the future, represented the next step: independent of changes in the seasons and the weather, under its roof it served as both a summer and winter garden, making available at all times outside urban space that was becoming increasingly more important.

The → city mall in urban context as an up-and-coming type of building went one step further: in this case, an exclusive functional relationship with an existing or new building is not previewed. A 'city mall' can be a covered market, an 'event space', an independent space with a climate all of its own that contributes to the appeal of inner cities, which, on account of peripheral shopping malls located at motorway junctions, are threatening to become wasteland. The 1846–47 Jardin d'Hiver on the

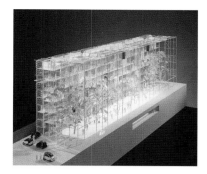

Champs Élysées can be seen as an original example of this phenomenon (see section 1.1, ills. 1.2 and 1.1.4 and Paxton's Crystal Way).

It remains to be seen whether this extended urban space will appeal more through 'horizontal' new types of building, or the vertical trend, to a public which, given a global networking that is becoming more virtual, is increasingly pushing for 'physical communication'. The concept of the → 'green skyscraper' demonstrates this possibility, albeit for a select public made up of the thousands of residents, users, visitors and workers who are anyway to be found in the skyscraper.

The challenge of an extreme environment

Buildings exposed to extreme environmental conditions have always been a source of new findings about light-weight construction methods and energy-reducing strategies. The process of learning from natural structures and shapes, from organisms and phenomena that configure and regulate themselves influences the trend-setting research sector of a school of thought that has made 'bionics' its theme. Here, too, though, as long as 50 years ago pioneers such as Jean Prouvé were charting unknown territory, as, for example, his Maison Tropique project reveals (ill. 6.3.6).

Among these new approaches the concept of 'transparent heat insulation' played a pioneering role: the most diverse materials, like glass, plastic structures (such as tubes, combs), foils, concrete and loam are suitably layered together in such a way that the heat absorbed is stored and discharged into the room with a delay: similar to the natural function of a polar bear's skin the result is a balanced ambient temperature (ill. 6.3.7).

Problems with filling that collapsed or became deformed led to further experiments with web panels and aerogel or nanogel filling. This combination of materials lowers the thermal conductivity value of the building sheath, without its losing translucency. In doing so, the air, as a renewable raw material, also always plays a key role. In the case of vacuum-insulated panels (VIP) even this no longer applies. Using VIPs in projects such as the experimental → Newspirit and peak_lab pavilions serves as an attempt to make structures lighter, and to make do with natural sources of energy such as air, big differences

in temperature, sun, water, snow and ice, and create new settings for 'life-style' and 'work-style' concepts, as well as 'work spaces' and 'event spaces' as part of a sustainable building design programme. Here, there is also a need for temporary buildings as research projects, be they high in the mountains, in places of environmental dangers and risks or in desert regions – architecture of climate change as a coming programme.

The habitat question

An increasing amount of autarkic living space is also

6.3.6

being created in areas that are confronted with disasters triggered by natural or wartime occurrences. This → habitat consists of both living space and infrastructure: community centres provide supplies of food and drinking water, classrooms and cultural venues, washing facilities and hygiene centres, medical help and social care, etc. For social areas such as these, building techniques must be developed just as swiftly, efficiently and on a sustainable basis as for residential accommodation. Specific cultural techniques play a key role in this future area of research and development: every culture has its own building techniques, from which even highly industrialised and highly technical societies can learn – the intercultural synthesis is the only sustainable aspect here.

6.3.7

Case Study 92
The 'New Atrium'

Sauerbruch Hutton Architects,
Berlin
Bothe Richter Teherani, Hamburg
Cuno Brullmann, Paris and Vienna

The 'new atrium' references the Egyptian, Greek and Roman originals, their special function in the city and the specific quarter they are in, their microclimate and their purpose in terms of communication. Modern 19th-century atriums represented a continuation of glass and greenhouses following their first change in function, of which the Jardin d'Hiver (1846–47) in Paris marked the introduction. Nowadays it is no longer industrial but communicative societies that need new spatial forms: no longer in order for them to be networked virtually, but to physically 'assemble'. The architects Kevin Roche and John Dinkeloo's Ford Foundation building in New York (1964–68), which features an atrium and overhanging office tracts, was a prototype for the 'new atrium', but, boasting as it did an artificial climate was "in tune with the times". At the same time, with their Hyatt Regency Hotel in Atlanta (1967), the design of whose atrium represented a continuation of the glass-roofed interior courtyards of pioneering-era hotels, Portman and Edward, for example, were pursuing the same idea. Whereas the Ford Foundation anticipated the concept of new work areas that were extended to included urban space, Portman's design represented a trendsetting type of hotel that reached its zenith with, for example, the Hotel Kempinksi at Munich Airport with its technically perfect sheathing of a spectacular public space (ill. 6.3.8).

In cases of refurbishing as well, the addition of an atrium to buildings also entails advantages, not only as far the extension of usable space is concerned but also inasmuch as it provides an opportunity to subject courtyard façades that are weak in terms of structure and energy and, in particular, those worthy of preservation, to gentle rejuvenation. The roof over the courtyard at the 'Hamburg Museum' is an illustration of this 'avoidance strategy': this enabled the materiality of the clinker façade, the original window frames, and ultimately the valuable appearance to be preserved and protected from the environment (see case study 11; ills. 1.3.23–24 and 6.1.2).

The 'new atrium' is a theme in the private sector construction of office buildings, hotels and shopping malls, as well as the public sector, represented, for example, by the new building for the Federal Environment Agency in Dessau by Sauerbruch Hutton Architects (ill. 6.3.9).

The architects Bothe Richter Teherani featured this type of 'new atrium' in their 'Double-XX' office high-rise, as well as the 'Berliner Bogen' office building in Hamburg. In the former the core structure of the dual, x-shaped footprint is directly surrounded by the first sheath, which follows the double x, while the prismatic volume of the entire building is defined by a second glass sheath. The sheaths follow different contours, such that atriums are created in the spaces in between (ill. 6.3.10). Together with the additional, horizontal areas, which are not used for office space but which serve as communication zones, they form a complex spatial figure that alternates between 'full' and 'hollow', 'positive' and 'negative' volumetric and spatial qualities (ill. 6.3.11).

In the 'Berliner Bogen' office building the atriums are built in segments and are wholly independent. Here, they also serve as a climate balance, though also entail a high level of sun protection measures to prevent overheating in the summer (ill. 6.3.12). Norman Foster's 'finger-shaped' Microelectronic Centre in Duisburg, Germany (1990–96) represented a forerunner).[27]

A solution to the question of whether and to what extent atriums can serve as 'power stations' that support the low energy standards concept is reserved for future research projects.[28] An atrium that served as an experiment in this direction was completed by Behnisch, Behnisch & Partner and Transsolar Climate Engineering (both offices in Stuttgart, Germany) in the 'Alterra' research building in Wageningen, in Holland (ill. 6.3.13).

Alongside energy-related criteria, other 'sustainable' aspects also speak for the atrium as a form of construction: the increased quality of urban lifestyles, the fact that inner city areas become concentrated and multifunctional, the concentration of circulation and traffic and the interlinking of work, residential and leisure facilities, which Richard Rogers made the subject of his Reith Lectures as early as 1995. In this greater sphere, new projects feature such as the Fünf Höfe in Munich by Herzog & de Meuron or projects by Cuno Brullmann, which reveal the atrium as a commercial and cultural type of construction for the future (ill. 6.3.14).

"Sustainable Building Design" – A Future Project

6.3.8

6.3.9

6.3.10

6.3.11

6.3.12

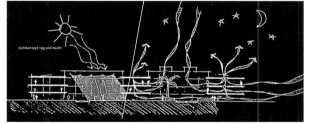

6.3.13

6.3.14

6.3.8: Hotel Kempinski, Munich Airport, 1993; architects: Murphy/Jahn, Chicago; engineers: Schlaich Bergermann und Partner, Stuttgart

6.3.9: Sauerbruch Hutton Architects: Federal Environment Agency, Dessau, 2005; the atrium as a communicative work landscape (photo of model)

6.3.10: Bothe Richter Teherani: 'Double-XX' office high-rise, Hamburg, 1997–99; a meandering and a surrounding glass sheath define spaces and hollows, work landscapes and communication worlds.

6.3.11: A view of the social areas in 'Double-XX'

6.3.12: Bothe Richter Teherani: Berliner Bogen office building, Hamburg, 1998–2001; a series of atriums serving as climatic buffer zones dominates the spatial structure and dovetails the office landscape with the environment.

6.3.13: An environmentally-friendly, energy-efficient and spatially fascinating atrium of the new generation: the Alterra research building in Wageningen, Holland (competition 1993, built 1996–98; architects: Behnisch, Behnisch & Partner), night and daytime cooling concept by Transsolar Climate Engineering, Stuttgart, Germany

6.3.14: Cuno Brullmann, Jean Luc Crochon & Associates, Paris: Centre d'information sur la France contemporaine in Mexico City; future atrium landscape

The City Mall

Itsuko Hasegawa,
Richard Horden

The city mall as an up-and-coming type of construction means the transformation of former covered markets and the 19th-century 'Jardin d'Hiver' (see section 1.1) into a building structure and spatial form that will be part of future sustainable urban development programmes. Concrete projects are already emerging. As is evident from Emile Zola's novel *The Fat and the Thin*, the Halles Centrales in Paris were not merely a multifaceted shopping centre but a place for various social classes to meet and intermingle (ill. 6.3.15).[29]

In terms of energy efficiency and sustainability there must in Europe be a reappraisal of, and change in, thought away from fully air-conditioned city malls like the ones in the urban context of New York and other up-and-coming regions in Asia (ill. 6.3.16).

6.3.15

Two trends are emerging: the new-style orangery, which avails itself of tried and tested greenhouse construction techniques, and the environmentally independent city mall. Old greenhouses are no longer used just for making botanical observations but are being converted and equipped for multi-purpose use, for example, shops, cafeteria, exhibitions and to accommodate cultural events (e.g., the Sundial House on the grounds of Schloss Schönbrunn in Vienna; see case study 5). New greenhouses are being used more extensively for cultural and leisure activities (Kew Gardens in London; Parc André Citroën in Paris; the Eden Project in St. Austell, Cornwall) or built in connection with zoos, such as the Masoala-Halle in Zurich. Itsuko Hasegawa's Museum of Fruit in Yamanashi, Japan, unites these trends and combines them with educational and research projects (ill. 6.3.17; see also ills. 1.4.28 and 1.4.29).[30]

City malls represent a concept for the sustainable rejuvenation of inner cities, which, given the competition from shopping malls located on the edge of cities, in concentrated conurbations and beside motorway intersections, face the prospect of becoming deserted. Increased attraction, functional as well as social concentration, the linking of a wide range of urban uses, the provision of an urban structure as a 'stage' for cultural, entertainment, and political activities – these are the purposes a city mall can fulfil (ills. 6.3.18 and 6.3.19).

This strategy programme for the sustainable development of quarters and cities must be supported through a spatial, building, and construction structure for such 'event spaces' which makes efficient use of resources. If multi-purpose halls are used as permanent spatial installations in urban contexts, HVACR facilities can be provided through the network of utility providers. Natural ventilation, the active and passive use of solar energy, greenery and water elements should contribute all the more to a reduction in energy requirements. Temporary and mobile spaces represent a greater challenge. Here, additional foil cushions can serve as tanks for water supplies and storage, and movable sun-protection lamellas as a mount for photovoltaic panels, and lush interior greenery for conditioning the interior climate – new hothouses?

A project conducted by the author of this book together with students at Bauschule Chur[31] addressed this topic for cities in the Mittelland region of Switzerland (for example, the city of Frauenfeld). It is an open research field; combining it with the 'autarkic' use of space and climate engineering technology, even under extreme conditions, would seem purposeful. There are already glass pavilions and event spaces in abundance, but they are not as yet sustainable.[32]

6.3.18

6.3.19

6.3.15: The covered markets in Paris 'Les Halles Centrales' by Victor Baltard and Félix Callet (project 1853; execution 1854 – 57; torn down 1971)

6.3.16: Public glass hall in New York: a permanent venue for leisure-time activities, lunchtime concerts, picnics and interaction featuring artificial climate control to prevent fast and extreme fluctuations in climate

6.3.17: Itsuko Hasegawa, Arup engineers: The Museum of Fruit, Yamanashi, Japan, 1992 – 95; the mix of exhibition hall, tropical greenhouse, fruit garden, glasshouse workshop, water garden and communication centre makes this a spacious leisure and education facility (portrayal for promotion purposes).

6.3.18, 6.3.19: Richard Horden (architect), Ove Arup & Partners, (engineers): project to revamp the South Bank in London (1992); the four glass cubes, measuring 50 metres in height and width, house the National Theatre, the Hayward Gallery, as well as two exhibition rooms for new technology and art.[63]

Case Study 94
The Green Skyscraper

Ingenhoven, Overdiek und Partner
Dominique Perrault,
Norman Foster, Kenneth Yeang,
Richard Horden

The Commerzbank high-rise in Frankfurt am Main (1994–97) represents if not the first, certainly a prominent example of the concept of the 'green skyscraper' (ill. 6.3.20). It marks a totally new type of construction, which in the vertical strives to achieve similar effects to those of the horizontal workplaces built during the 1990s with atriums, winter gardens, and dual-skin façades. The ecologically orientated high-rise concepts range from ingenious 'twin-skin' technology (e.g. the RWE headquarters in Essen) to the stacked natural landscape of MVRDV's Dutch pavilion at *Expo 2000* in Hanover.

The approach in terms of energy and façade technology employed by Ingenhoven, Overdiek und Partner for the headquarters of Rheinisch-Westfälische Energie AG (RWE) in Essen (1991–97; see case study 64)[33] produce a climate that is generated or supported by natural means, and which is able to respond to different scenarios with regard to the environment and requirements (global or individual). The cylindrical shape of the structure avoided the tedious problem of corners and enabled a standardised façade throughout (ill. 6.3.21).[34]

This trend towards a low-energy strategy stands in contrast to the high-tech solution for the Bibliothèque Nationale de France. The architect Dominique Perrault's concept is based on four angled, glass cubes – in the shape of opened-up books – which house the book store and workplaces, and which are aligned around an interior courtyard planted with tall spruce trees. The natural elements 'implanted' throughout the complex compensate for a 'breathing' high-tech façade, which, being a compact 'twin skin', needs to be ventilated with compressed air (ill. 6.3.22; see also ill. 4.5.4).[35]

Sauerbruch Hutton Architect's elegant GSW high-rise headquarters on Kochstrasse in the Kreuzberg district of Berlin is a demonstration of the advancement of the 'green skyscraper' genre: each of the building's façades is different in structure and design depending on its required function – a tailor-made 'twin skin'(see case studies 64 and 98).

Norman Foster's Frankfurt skyscraper for Commerzbank represents a new form of construction, which, being 'big and green', is set to dominate 21st-century high-rise architecture.[36] The 'hanging gardens' spiral over the height of four storeys, assuming as they do the function

of passive solar-energy-producing winter gardens. Thanks to the integrated energy and climate concept, which was new for tall buildings and produced a halving of heating requirements, natural ventilation thanks to dual façades, an atrium and winter gardens and active solar support of the interior lighting – the high-rise appears to be a prototype of the 'green skyscraper'. The double-loaded offices have spatial depth and an additional middle zone, providing a high concentration of workspaces, the comfort of whose natural light is enhanced by the central atrium, the tall winter gardens, as well as façade elements that channel natural light into the building (ills. 6.3.23 and 6.3.24).

The architect Kenneth Young has been the source of original, forward-looking proposals for the 'big and green' type of construction. One of his research and building projects involves working with wind. In the hot and humid climate of Malaysia the type of ventilation usual in Europe, which circulates outside air on the inside and expels the used air through the façades, was not sufficient to create an appropriate degree of climatic comfort: Hamzah & Yeang's 'Menara UMNO' high-rise, for example, which is conceived as a wing tower, uses the energy that is constantly generated and reinforced through the structure and shape of the building to completely regenerate and freshen the air inside, helping to reduce energy requirements by half (ill. 6.3.25).

Richard Horden followed a similar approach with his 100-metre-high, revolving 'Wing Tower' in Glasgow (engineer: Peter Heppel), whose structure is conceived such that the constant wind force provides up-thrust for the building. Thanks to its aerodynamic design, which British Aerospace checked in simulations, the tower rotates depending on the wind's direction, thereby improving its structural qualities and the economic aspects of the building construction: the tower appears to be lighter than it is, like a vertical aircraft wing with spoilers (ill. 6.3.26).[37]

6.3.20

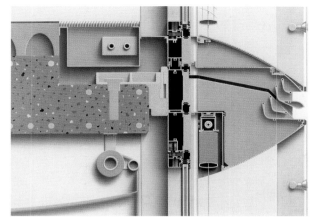

6.3.21

6.3.22

6.3.23

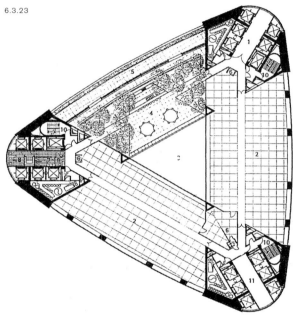

6.3.24

6.3.25

6.3.26

Case Study 95
The Newspirit and Peak_Lab Research Projects

Architects: Ulrich Pfammatter, Richard Horden, Christian Fierz, Burkhard Franke, Mathias Frey, Lydia Haack, Walter Klasz, Brigitta Kunsch, Armando Meletta

Engineer: Joseph Schwartz
HVACR: Urs Rieder, Kurt Hildebrand, Gerhard Zweifel et al.[38]

6.3.27

The Newspirit and peak_lab projects conducted by the author of this book together with Richard Horden and the assistance of Christian Fierz, Walter Klasz and a broad-based inter-disciplinary team were experiments aimed at designing lightweight constructions for exposure to extreme conditions and building a new type of spatiality. Between 1998 and 2003, students at the Hochschule für Technik und Architektur (university of applied sciences in technology and architecture) in Lucerne and, from 2002 on, the Technical University in Munich (with Richard Horden) took part in the research projects. For peak_lab the international interdisciplinary team from Lucerne and Munich received the 'Award 2004' from the ETH in Zurich.[39]

To begin with, Newspirit appeared to be a seemingly straightforward assignment: to design a visitors' centre at the airfield at La Chaux-de-Fonds, the town in the Jura region famous for its clocks. The problem was nothing if not straightforward: there was neither electricity nor running water, and the climate in the Jura is raw. The pavilion would be required to stage receptions, exhibitions, presentations and media conferences, but would also have to boast high climatic standards, as well as an attractive interior and a branding (ill. 6.3.27).

On the back of interdisciplinary student workshops, in which building engineers and HVACR specialists as well as material technology experts participated, two outstanding approaches were ultimately devised that served further research and professional work. Parallel to this in workshops in Lucerne and Munich, Richard Horden, Andreas Vogler and the teaching team at the Technical University in Munich became involved in the proceedings, influencing the structure and design of the lightweight construction and thereby contributing to the blending of different backgrounds and areas of expertise (ills. 6.3.28 and 6.3.29).

The peak_lab project on the Klein Matterhorn at an altitude of 4,000 metres above Zermatt represented, on the one hand, a continuation of Newspirit, but, on the other, was subject to far more extreme conditions. The Alpine research station was intended to provide workspace for three researchers and be suitable for stays of at least three weeks. The location had neither electricity nor running water, merely sun, glacier ice, thin air

and strong winds. The terrain is difficult, with the helicopter service of Air Zermatt on hand for emergencies and disposal purposes (ills. 6.3.30 and 6.3.31).

This scenario was initially dealt with in a broad-based preliminary competition study involving 60 students, before being addressed in greater detail in three teams.[40] One group looked into the 'horizontal version,' featuring a skiing and research centre, a second into the vision of a mobile station, while the third, an international, interdisciplinary group, into the most difficult model of a vertical tube (ills. 6.3.32, 6.3.33 and 6.3.34).

The core problems were related to the load-bearing structure, anchorage in the vertical mountain rocks, assembly by helicopter, the wall sheds, the technical features, and the interior design to the extent that lifestyle = work style. The project's objective was, and indeed still is, the probing of new boundaries, in particular with regard to lightweight construction, for example, by reducing the number of points and joints where the structure is anchored in the vertical cliff to just three, as in mountain climbing. The jointed link between the supporting scaffolding and the assembly ledges had to be designed with greater assembly tolerance than normal in order to enable the hovering helicopter to insert the joint in the existing hollow during assembly; as soon as it was in place 'sky worker' mountain climbers had to connect the joints to the main scaffolding using stays (framework engineer: Joseph Schwartz). A 1:1 steel mock-up of the 'pièce de resistance', the joint, was modelled by the metal construction company Vitus Fux in Visp (ills. 6.3.35 and 6.3.36).

In the case of peak_lab, the wall originally envisaged for Newspirit, featuring translucent galley panels

6.3.31

6.3.27: Initial design by HTA Lucerne students for the visitors' centre for the airfield at La-Chaux-de-Fonds, a major centre of Swiss clock production

6.3.28, 6.3.29: Newspirit: two studies for the project: a rhombic, diagonal construction aimed at efficient material use and design and at branding for the visitors' pavilion, and a model for the exhibition at *Swissbau* 2002 in Basle; in an altered version the pavilion was to be prepared for construction for the Federal Institute for Snow and Avalanche Research on the Weissfluhjoch above Davos (not realised).

6.3.30, 6.3.31: peak_lab: preliminary studies by students at the Hochschule für Technik und Architektur in Lucerne and the Technical University in Munich

6.3.30

'Light Tech' and 'Low Energy'

(Scobalit) filled with aerogel, as well as vacuum-insulated panels (VIP), had to be consistently made using VIPs in order for the lightweight construction to be able to withstand storms of up to 250 km/h and temperatures of −30°Celsius (with differences in temperature of up to 50°C) that occur at this altitude. In order to avoid the worse thermal conductivity readings on the edges of the VIPs they are dual-layered and positioned against each other (each one 30 to 45 mm). Between or within the VIP layers there is a load-bearing structure made of vertical, ring-shaped profiles (steel or fibreglass-reinforced plas-

6.3.32

tic). The inner lining of 3-mm-thick plastic can be part of the interior furnishings and installation at one and the same time. The outer protective shield of 3- to 5-mm-thick aluminium is rear-ventilated and features additional sealing and protective foils in order to counteract global radiation, which at this altitude is greater by a factor of 1.5.

In total, the thickness of the wall can be reduced to 150 mm with a thermal conductivity reading (calculated by means of simulation) of 0.07 w/m²K! (ill. 6.3.37).

Whereas for the Newspirit preliminary study the supporting framework was made with folded, U-shaped sheet metal (invented and developed by the Swiss company Müller-Kaltbach), so as to accommodate the requisite storage mass in the form of paraffin panels as well as LEDs in the profile's hollow, in the case of peak_lab the HVACR engineers forewent storage mass, preferring instead to bank on a natural passive and active solar heating system. To this end, with the exception of the

rear, the entire outer sheath is covered with photovoltaic cells, guaranteeing electrical supplies (the location has a high number of sunshine hours throughout the year). The rear ventilation beneath the photovoltaic/aluminium layer enables the air to be preheated by means of a low-energy ventilation system, lowering heating energy requirements. The air intake occurs by means of two clearly distinguishable extra-high chambers (spoilers), whose geometry prevents snow and dust collecting, which would endanger the system. The dimensions of this relaxation space were checked by means of simulation and it was enhanced with a volume current regulator and filters (ill. 6.3.38).

So what do Newspirit and peak_lab have to do with sustainability? They are research projects that emerged from students' work and that can be advanced as working models. They serve to set new limits with regard to material-saving lightweight construction and technology and energy-efficient climate control. The findings that experiments such as these produce always lead to new, more in-depth questions and problems: can the sheath be made even softer, suppler, into a breathable skin, with air, or through a vacuum, which needs honeycomb or mesh-shaped load-bearing structures? How can plastics be recycled? How can recycled aluminium, which requires less energy to be reprocessed, be identified in the material cycle in order for it to be used on a sustainable basis as secondary aluminium?

Since the construction industry consumes and wastes a great deal of energy and material worldwide, while at the same time producing vast amounts of waste, there is a need to invent and develop counter models. If we succeed in minimising the resources needed for construction purposes, be they renewable, recycled or reusable, using a methodical 'vehicle' or model of a project under extreme conditions, an autonomous camp, or living space that is autarkical in terms of energy, then considerations such as these can be transferred to other climatic, cultural and social contexts, for example, with regard to desert, mountainous, Alpine, and Antarctic regions, disaster areas and the problem zone of the question of habitat.

6.3.34

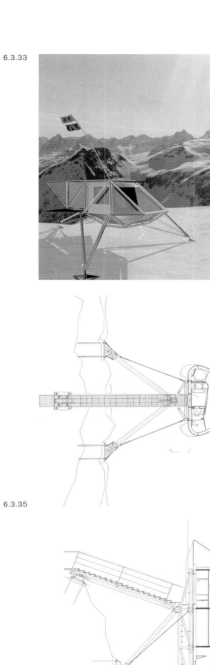

6.3.33

6.3.35

6.3.36

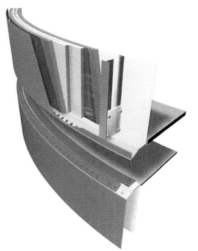

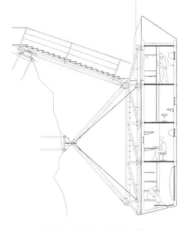

6.3.32, 6.3.33, 6.3.34: Three
different project approaches in
the advanced phase of peak_lab

6.3.35, 6.3.36: peak_lab: footprint of the ground floor with
the anchoring in three places
in the cliff

6.3.37: peak_lab: 1:1 model
of the 150-mm wall

6.3.38: peak_lab: view from
above with the entrance galley
and spoilers

6.3.37

6.3.38

Regarding the Question of Habitat

Balkrishna V. Doshi,
Hassan Fathy,
Shigeru Ban

In the wake of decolonialisation from 1960 on, Third World societies also succeeded in liberating themselves from architecture that had merely been imported and opened their doors to architectural concepts that referenced the industrial world in a different way. Not the major monumental projects of the likes of Le Corbusier and Louis I. Kahn in India and Lucio Costa and Oscar Niemeyer's new city Brasilia, but the 'other pupils' of modern architecture, such as the Indian Balkrishna Vithaldas Doshi (for many years dean of the architectural school in Ahmadabad) and the Egyptian Hassan Fathy, set about blending traditional cultural techniques with modern thought (ill. 6.3.39).

In numerous special editions of international trade journals and competitions in connection with UN habitat conferences, Western, tri-continental and multicultural teams addressed traditional cultures and attempted to tackle the question of habitat on a sustained basis.[41] Whereas it was the Structuralist school of thought centred round the Dutch magazine Forum that probed this field of research to the greatest extent, it was Hassan Fathy who revealed a consistent path involving modernised tradition as cultural synthesis with the construction of two new villages, New Gourna and New Bariz, in Upper Egypt (see ill. 3.4.29).

For some time the 'continuity of Modernity' in construction played a role in developing countries becoming emerging or transformation countries. As under Boumediène in Algeria, pure 'autarky' and a recourse to traditional values could lead to withdrawnness, or alternatively to the challenge of learning about different cultures, as the INDEL courses at the ETH in Zurich and elsewhere were able to teach. Stefano Bianca's train of thought, method of work, and research on Islamic architecture and also the work of the Aga Khan Foundation, for example, reveal such forward-looking approaches.[42]

In the 1980s, in conjunction with the second wave of decolonialisation, in particular on the back of Portugal's withdrawal from Africa and the fall of the Boumediène regime in Algeria, entirely new problems had to be solved, this time in and around major European cities, including Lisbon, Paris, Marseille and Lyons. Squatters brought the question of habitat directly to the First World, which was now experiencing similar conditions to Rio, Bombay and the British Crown Colony Hong Kong. The methodical approach of Herbert E. Kramel, who together with students at the ETH in Zurich devised examples of development strategies, among others for the Sudanese city of Khartoum, offered, and still offers, a feasible route to a 'sustainable community'. The projects had names such as 'Amal – a concept for shelter and urban integration in Khartoum, Sudan', or 'Mawa, unauthorised and squatter settlements in Khartoum', and can be considered as helping others to help themselves while also 'learning from Arab habitat'.[43]

Since the new millennium this work has been being increasingly channelled into disaster and conflict areas. Following the devastating earthquake in Kobe in 1995 the Japanese architect Shigeru Ban developed the Paper Loghouse, a form of standard house made of materials found lying around: "The foundations are plastic beer-bottle cases packed with sandbags, the walls and framework are paper tubes, and tent material is used for the ceiling and roof."[44] (ills. 6.3.40 to 6.3.43).

The representational variation of this 'paper tube' technique is presented in case study 88.

Ban's 'emergency shelter' concept enables swift, efficient and sustainable use. During and after the civil war in Rwanda in 1994, which left over two million people homeless, the UN humanitarian organisation UNHCR provided aluminium frames and sheets of plastic, with the result that the refugees sold the aluminium and in its place felled trees and used the wood from them: "Contributing to already critical deforestation, it was obvious that alternative materials had to be found. A low-cost alternative, paper tubes, was introduced. The proposal was adopted and the development of prototype shelters began." These prototypes were durable, waterproof and termite-proof. Paper rolls can be produced using on-site machines, thus saving transportation costs. In 1998, 50 such emergency houses were built and tested in Rwanda.[45]

6.3.39

6.3.40

6.3.41

6.3.42

6.3.43

6.3.39: Balkrishna V. Doshi: industrial settlement, Baroda, India, 1971

6.3.40, 6.3.41: Shigeru Ban: Paper Loghouse, project in India; temporary emergency accommodation, view from outside and of the interior

6.3.42, 6.3.43: Shigeru Ban: Paper Loghouse, project in Turkey; construction and assembly of emergency accommodation

6.4   10 Points Regarding
a Culture of Sustainability

'Learning from nature'

Bionics, the combination of biology and technology is a relatively new science. It also points the way forward for construction, leading as it does to observations of how nature itself uses resources sparingly to organise its structure and form and produce efficient performance.[46]

(1) Self-organisation and self-control by natural structures, forms and phenomena form the background for observations with regard to 'translations' to building structures, spatial shapes and appearances. The proof that the imitation, interpretation and transformation of naturally generated material is a purposeful strategy in terms of design and construction lies in the fact that nature saves material yet is highly efficient, that it is self-regulating and can respond in an intelligent way to hanging environmental conditions and can attain higher quality levels. These facts were decisive for a series of esearch studies and projects, some of which resulted in finished structures, others not, by the interdisciplinary team of the → Renzo Piano Building Workshop and Peter Rice.

(2) For several years the cross-border, interdisciplinary science of bionics had been emerging as a field of inspiration for the construction world. Lightweight construction in particular is benefiting from findings in this area, and is attempting to imitate biological structures, forms and processes, or replicate or transform them: jellyfish, which are able to withstand enormous water pressure, corals, which respond to currents, pebble algae, which create material-efficient structures, birds, which in terms of aerodynamics behave like feather-weights, the metamorphosis of caterpillars into butterflies, the structural construction of elephants' skulls, to name but a few (ill. 6.4.1).

Iconography and the branding
of 'sustainable' strategies

In the future, buildings will respond even more sensitively to the environment. They will be conceived in such a way that they are integrated in environmental dynamics, and that their use occasions new approaches to cultural techniques with regard to the question of the environment and energy. This will lead to new types of buildings, new forms of construction, to visionary forms of expression, to visualisation and to the branding of sustainable achievements in terms of construction and material performances.

(3) In many places sustainable urban systems are being tested and gradually introduced. Whereas concepts such as solar cities, eco-cities and energy labels, etc. strive for pragmatic, technical solutions, approaches that exhaust the multi-layered nature of possible measures are far more promising. In this respect the Reith Lectures that Richard Rogers gave on the BBC in March 1995 provide an all-embracing vision of sustainable developments in architecture in the widest sense, even when they are reread today.[47] As aspects of a modern urban structure that is no longer overused in terms of industry, energy and traffic, in Rogers's opinion, close neighbourhood concepts, compact urban life, efficient energy consumption, and a reduction in traffic by means of the overlaying of functions are the criteria that should be pursued with regard to sustainable urban development.[48]

(4) In terms of energy-related and technical fittings, buildings will in the future be conceived and designed on a more sustainable basis – there is no getting round energy efficiency. Courtyard houses in Antiquity, the design of markets, the configuration of city grounds, and ultimately Catherine Beecher's 1869 *American Woman's Home,* which functioned on the basic of an 'integrated' in-house technical system, were the precursors of recent low-energy strategies (see ill. 6.4.2).[49] Even today, in Arabic and Islamic regions, for example, it is still possible to observe traditionall climate-related types of construction and technology based on examples from Antiquity (ill. 6.4.3).[50] Two examples in Berlin illustrate this new school of thought referring to old techniques: Sauerbruch Hutton Architect's → GSW headquarters and Norman Foster's new design for the Reichstag building.

(5) Nowadays, thanks to sustainable city development scenarios, the 'liberated space' of post-war architecture is enjoying an expansion of typology: new urban spaces such as atriums, arcades, multi-purpose halls, cultural pavilions – event spaces, which serve social concentration and density, overlaying in terms of function and infrastructure, and neighbourhood as well as urban communication, and which transform types of building from the 19th century and earlier into forms of future buildings. They are operated and managed using natural resources:

6.4.1

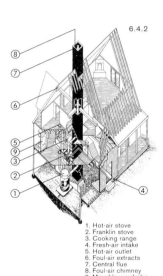

6.4.2

1. Hot-air stove
2. Franklin stove
3. Cooking range
4. Fresh-air intake
5. Hot-air outlet
6. Foul-air extracts
7. Central flue
8. Foul-air chimney
9. Movable wardrobe

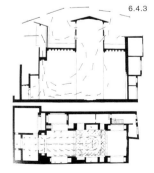

6.4.3

6.4.1: An elephant's skull: together with air chambers enclosed between thin bone lamellas an upper and lower membrane form a sort of sandwich construction.

6.4.2: Catherine Beecher's American Woman's Home, 1869: cut-away showing the complete house as an environmental system, working with only renewable energy sources

6.4.3: Naturally ventilated residential complex in Cairo with a multi-storey interior courtyard, climatic zoning according to summer and winter use, and wind traps

6.4.4: Riverparc Development, Pittsburgh, PA, USA; Behnisch architects and Transsolar Climate Engineering, Stuttgart, Germany; integral and interdisciplinary urban planning project for sustainable development in the New World, 2007–15

6.4.5: Norman Foster: sketch of the Commerzbank high-rise in Frankfurt am Main; atriums and 'hanging gardens' – according to the basic concept, the spatial areas for natural ventilation and energy saving

6.4.6: Micro-Compact Home, a project by the student union in Munich for temporary student accommodation in an urban context; architects: Richard Horden, Technical University, Munich; Lydia Haack + John Höpfner architects, Munich; Horden Cherry Lee Architects, London; engineers: Brengelmann engineers, Munich

6.4.7: Caribbean primeval hut, immortalised by Gottfried Semper in his work *Der Stil in den technischen und tektonischen Künsten* (style in the technical and haptic arts), vol. 2, 1863

6.4.4

natural ventilation, solar-generated electricity, the use of rain water, etc. They can even be operated as 'summer and winter gardens' that are autarkic in terms of energy: cool in summer, with a pleasant ambient temperature in winter (ill. 6.4.4).

(6) Ever since the building of Norman Foster's 260-metre-high Commerzbank building in Frankfurt am Main (1994–97, ill. 6.4.5), the concept of the 'green skyscraper' as a future form of construction has been a topic of discussion. Corresponding to the size, spacious measures throughout serve to make it possible to generate active and passive solar energy, to benefit from wind power that specifically affects skyscrapers and the air currents this produces, while at the same time positioning the vertical work landscape as an integral part of urban living space.

(7) The concept of → sustainable skin is inspired by natural phenomena (polar bear skin). The multi-layered structure of transparent heat insulation is derived directly from his. Textile skins such as the thickly woven cloth for Bedouin tents or multi-layer, high-tech fabrics assume additional functions, including insulation from the wind and rain, humidity exchange – does this involve learning from breathable membranes and fabrics as a future strategy for 'next' building sheaths? Experiments with temporary buildings and those that are autarkic with regard to energy represent a highly promising field of research.

A turning point in approach

Strategies that have a sustainable effect on the environment and resources, on effective and efficient construction and material technology, as well as on societal and cultural trends can be influenced only by interdisciplinary schools of thought – a 'sustainable avant-garde' should be invented.

(8) For the case studies and working models presented in this book, 'state of the art' was not, and is still not, the objective, but rather the point of departure for work and research. Cultural techniques and new dialogues are the driving force and the drivers of change behind the development of architecture. For this reason the intercultural exchange of knowledge and skills can lead to more advanced, improved achievements, as the example of the New Caledonian 'primeval hut' reveals, which for the planned → cultural centre in Nouméa

prompted the Renzo Piano Building Workshop to 'transpose' the structural, material and formal response of local building culture to extreme conditions into the meta-language of architecture.

(9) Without interdisciplinary working hypotheses and models the development of sustainable strategies is unimaginable. The trend revealed here towards lightness and the dissolution of mass represents a progression from schools of thought that link various disciplines, points of view, approaches and stances. The comprehensive interdisciplinary model set in motion by Ove Arup has produced not only outstanding achievements, but also an ongoing process-orientated search for new solutions, the penetration of new boundaries and the invention of new things.

(10) Autarkic and temporary building provides the greatest challenge in the future. Natural disasters in Asia, the Alps or Latin America show that no area is safe from

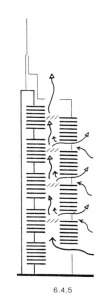

6.4.5

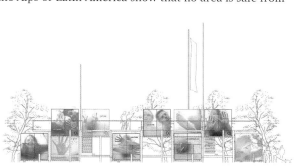

6.4.6

6.4.7

them – or from disasters caused by humans and societies, which occur everywhere. What is our task in this world? We can think, learn and conduct research anywhere. For this reason projects such as 'Minergie'-, 'Passive House'-standardised projects and research in German-speaking cultures or also Student Habitat by Richard Horden, his colleagues and students at the Technical University in Munich can fuel development work in order to transfer know-how (ill. 6.4.6),[51] likewise, vice versa, the Caribbean primeval hut, described by Gottfried Semper in his opus magnum (*Der Stil*, 1863), which even today can still have an influence on architecture in terms of space, structure and style (ill. 6.4.7).

Learning from Nature

Renzo Piano Building Workshop
and Peter Rice

Numerous joint projects between Renzo Piano and Peter Rice reference natural, organic and biological structures, forms and phenomena. They inspire similar related considerations as to how – using as little material as possible, with reduced resources and with great efficiency in terms of structures, load-bearing components and node typologies – great building performances can be achieved. Three projects serve to illustrate this.

Kansai International Airport on a man-made island off Osaka was the last joint project between Renzo Piano and Peter Rice, who did not live to see the opening ceremony. Constructing the terminal, with a planned length of 1.7 km, to a level of technical perfection, and to complete it within four years to the precise deadline was a masterpiece of interdisciplinary and international cooperation (competition 1998, construction period 1990–94). Peter Buchanan, Renzo Piano's biographer, refers to the Kansai terminal as an organic machine: "This represented the pinnacle of the Building Workshop's claim to integrate nature in technology – an ambition that harks back at least to Viollet-le Duc. Given its anatomic logic, the exact compliance of form with function and its formal insularity, the terminal (...) has the look of a gigantic organism."[52]

Whereas the terminal's overall shape resembles a glider, the skeleton of the core area, which consists of 20 identical, 80-metre-long, quadruply curved spatial frameworks, is an allusion to the structure of a dinosaur's skeleton (ills. 6.4.8 and 6.4.9).

For two years (1978–80) after the completion of the Centre Georges Pompidou in Paris, Renzo Piano and Peter Rice ran a joint operation, Piano & Rice Associates. This period produced several experimental works and projects that are totally interdisciplinary in nature, such as the FIAT VSS trial car, the results of which to a large extent were used for the FIAT TIPO, which was produced from 1988. What was new about this car's design was the separation of the structural steel frame from the plastic panels of the bodywork, which were glued onto the frame from outside, making them easier to design and, furthermore, replaceable, enabling them to be customised to changing models and customer wishes. The supporting steel pipe frame became more stable, enjoyed greater protection and was multifunctional. It is based on the natural structure of pebble algae, whose 'structural design' is sourced from a self-organising growth process (ills. 6.4.10 and 6.4.11).

As opposed to the first IBM pavilion (see case study 86), the IBM Lady Bird travelling pavilion, which was never realised (only a 1:1 mock-up was built), was conceived as movable, and could be opened up and then folded back together again. Cast-aluminium parts connected the laminated wooden profiles, making them flexible, which was inspired by insect and bat limbs (ills. 6.4.12 and 6.4.13).

Nature challenges us to think. Renzo Piano views it as a source of inspiration, not as something to imitate: "My use of natural materials and shapes has frequently given rise to misunderstandings, to the opinion that I emulate nature in my work. I do no such thing. The fact is, though, that nature does a good job and through close observation you can always learn a lot from it. Pure imitation, however, would be naïve, not to say ridiculous. At best one can speak of common elements that emerge from the application of physical and mechanical rules. The covering for a building can be reminiscent of a mussel, because a mussel is a fantastic construction, the result of millions of years of evolution; but beware: it is not a metaphor, there is no hidden meaning. A church is a church, and a mussel is a mussel. Where there is no denying a certain degree of similarity I would, if anything, talk of reference rather than imitation: one recognises something – as sometimes happens when we listen to music – but one is not sure what. Which brings us back to the relationship between structure, space and emotion, which is the focal point of my work."[53]

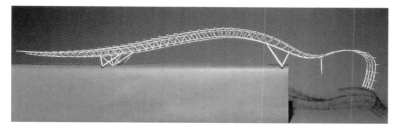

6.4.8

6.4.9

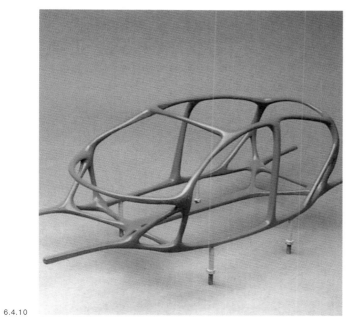

6.4.10

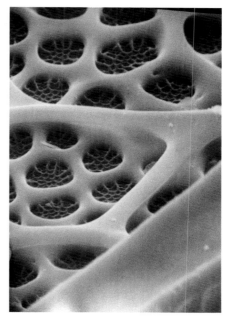

6.4.11

6.4.12

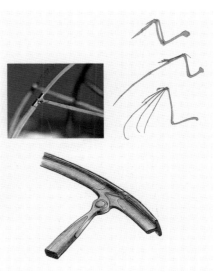

6.4.13

6.4.8, 6.4.9: Kansai International Airport. Osaka, Japan: skeleton of the terminal compared with that of a dinosaur

6.4.10, 6.4.11: Model of the steel frame for the FIAT-VSS trial
car, and the natural structure of pebble algae

6.4.12, 6.4.13: Structure of the IBM Lady Bird travelling pavilion and jointed skeleton compared with the flexibility of insect or bat limbs

Low-energy Strategies

GSW Headquarters
Berlin, 1995–99
Architects: Sauerbruch Hutton
Framework planning
and low-energy concept:
Ove Arup & Partners

**Redesign of the
Reichstag building**
Berlin, 1993 (competition)
1995–99
Architect: Norman Foster

Structural engineers: Leonhardt,
Andrä und Partner; Ove Arup
& Partners; Schlaich
Bergermann und Partner
HVACR and environmental
technology:
Amstein+Walthert, among others

The image of the headquarters of the Berlin-based Gemeinnützige Siedlungs- und Wohnungsbaugesellschaft (GSW), which was designed by Sauerbruch Hutton Architects, is an architectural reproduction of the HVACR concept. From the outset the architects collaborated with specialist planners to achieve a low-energy standard that was reduced by 50 per cent in comparison with normal office buildings and high-rises. Whereas in the case of the GSW building this strategy was pursued using architectural means, in the redesign of the Reichstag building in Berlin it was a geothermal solution that won out.

The GSW building complex in Berlin consists of several edifices, including a 22-storey high-rise dating from the 1950s, which serves the new high-rise slab placed in front as a 'backbone' and service tower. The slightly curved, slender slab boasts a spatial depth of a mere 10 metres and is 65 metres in length. This shape allows for an efficient natural ventilation concept (ill. 6.4.14).[54]

The east and west façades are an expression of the different functions with regard to energy and HVACR: whereas the east façade has to allow in outside air that tends to be cooler and as such must feature relevant openings and ventilation, the west façade, which faces the sun in the west, where it tends to be warmer, is conceived as an exhaust-air buffer area and has an upthrust enhancing air vane on the roof (ills. 6.4.15 and 6.4.16; see also case study 64 and ill. 6.2.14).

The fresh air flows in through lamellas on the east façade and throughout the offices, where, individually controlled, it is channelled into the dual-layer glass skin in the west. In order to prevent overheating, in the east as well, which would impact negatively on the overall climate, this sheath was also designed as a twin skin, though more slender. Sun protection lamellas on the west front enable users to set the ambient temperature to a desired comfortable level; in winter, the warmer air flows from the west to the east façade (ill. 6.4.17).

Following the fire in 1933 and its destruction in World War II, the Reichstag building in Berlin, which dates from the Wilhelmine era (1884–94), was subsequently reconstructed and refurbished in 1995. Here, too, indeed at the same time as the GSW building complex, there was a call for an energy-efficient concept in terms of construction and technical features. The old air ducts were used for fresh-air supplies. Ventilation continues through the 'pressure floor' beneath the plenary chamber and ends in the spoiler in the apex of the new glass cupola (ill. 6.4.18).

The fresh air is heated in winter and cooled in summer by two separate sets of underground stores at a depth of 60 and 300 metres. According to the plans, tri-generation by means of a block-type thermal power station was to account for 80 per cent of total energy requirements. The glass cupola fulfils several functions: it serves as a viewing platform for visitors and affords a view down to the plenary chamber, for which it also provides shade by means of a screen that follows the course of the sun; and the exhaust funnel accelerates the ventilation of the entire complex thanks to its thermodynamically designed cross-section (ills. 6.4.19 and 6.4.20).

Both projects, the GSW high-rise and the new Reichstag building, are demonstrations of new paths towards sustainable strategies that form part of an urban rejuvenation project. In the case of the Reichstag building, planners, architects and engineers used the existing or reconstructed building fabric and the natural environment, earth, air and sun, to make it an effective component in the environmental dynamics. For the very first time the GSW high-rise represents a forceful, highly visual expression of how energy and HVACR-related measures can result in different structures, shapes and appearances, and also that it is possible to devise a high-rise concept that in the long term stands out from the normal 'boredom' of many skyscrapers.

6.4.14: Architectural reproduction of the HVACR concept: GSW Headquarters on Kochstrasse in Berlin by Sauerbruch Hutton Architects

6.4.15, 6.4.16: GSW Headquarters, Berlin: the different appearances of the east and west façades correspond to the ventilation or passive solar energy concept.

6.4.17: GSW Headquarters: diagrams of different cases of cross-ventilation

6.4.18: Reichstag, Berlin: ventilation scheme

6.4.19, 6.4.20: Exhaust-air spoiler, sunscreen and three-dimensional transparency in the visitors' centre beneath the Reichstag cupola

6.4.14

6.4.15

6.4.16

6.4.17

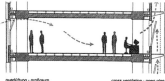

querlüftung - großraum · cross ventilation - open plan

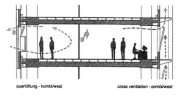

querlüftung - kombi/ost · cross ventilation - combi/east

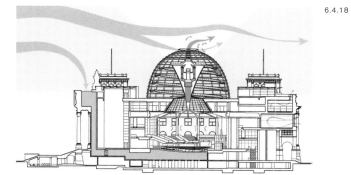

6.4.18

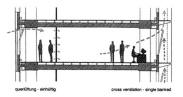

querlüftung - kombi/west · cross ventilation - combi/west

querlüftung - einhüftig · cross ventilation - single banked

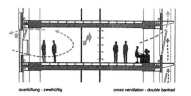

querlüftung - zweihüftig · cross ventilation - double banked

6.4.19

6.4.20

The Sustainable Skin Concept

Skin is not an independent membrane, but rather part of an overall organism. The same is true of a building. It assumes a number of vitally important functions, in particular climate exchange, moisture regulation, protection, sensitivity and much, much more. Various natural 'skins' have always been, and are once again, a source of inspiration to imitate them technically, to attempt replication or the direct transformation of them in an attempt to enclose living spaces.

The structure of a shark's scales (ill. 6.4.21) creates references to 'breathing' façades, such as the layering of the 'curtain wall' on the residential building on Square Mozart (Jean Prouvé; see ill. 6.3.3), the 'compressed air façade' on the Bibliothèque Nationale de France (Dominique Perrault; see ill. 6.3.22), and the

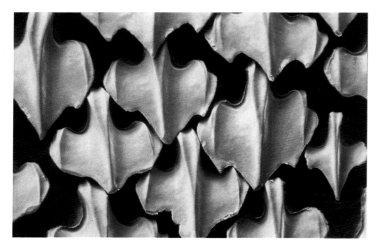

6.4.21

compressed-air-inflated ETFE foil sheaths (see case study 13).

Lotus leaves serve as a role model in the development of self-cleaning window panes using nanotechnology. The previously mentioned structure of an elephant's skull entices imitation in the form of vacuum-insulated panels (VIP), which to date were not used for free shapes but only at level or slightly curved slabs or sheets. Classified as 'transparent heat insulation', by means of a series of layers that in terms of structure, material and technique is quite straightforward, it has already been possible to imitate the skin of a polar bear (ill. 6.4.22).

Industrial sectors, which for some time now have been making advances in terms of R&D in the bionics-related field of industrial design, provide a forward-looking context for learning for building technology and construction. Whereas the automobile, aircraft and lightweight construction sectors are experimenting with new materials, technology and composites, and are using replaceable sandwich panels, for example, with fibre composite materials, which can be used in building, the textile and plastics industries are going down new paths with multi-layered and integrated fabrics, which can perform polyvalent, multifunctional tasks. It is precisely these which respond only in an overall exchange system between mankind and the environment – in other words, a dynamic exchange between the building as an entire system that is subjected to numerous variables, and environmental conditions, which are likewise constantly changing (ill. 6.4.23).

The mathematical and computer-generated know-how for determining the structure and shape of pre-stressed sails can be used directly in the conception of aerodynamic building parts such as spoilers, sun screens that are exposed to wind, skyscrapers, bridges and wing towers.

Building sheaths on free-shape spaces and constructions can be realised in two different ways: with rigid structures or soft membranes. Whereas, for example, the acrylic glass skin on the new Kunsthaus in Graz (2004, architects: Peter Cook, Colin Fournier, among others [55]) required an enormous amount of filigree substructure and anchoring technology, Norman Foster's glass roof over the atrium at the British Museum in London required a long period of mathematical calculations, but no substructure. By way of contrast, free membrane and foil constructions can be balanced through a combination of unstable load-bearing structures that are divided strictly according to compressive and tensile force (ill. 6.4.24).

Shigeru Ban's Japanese pavilion at *Expo 2000* in Hanover (see case study 88) is an example of economic construction in which structures such as weave and tissue, which themselves represent techniques derived from natural phenomena, can be reinterpreted and transformed (ill. 6.4.25).

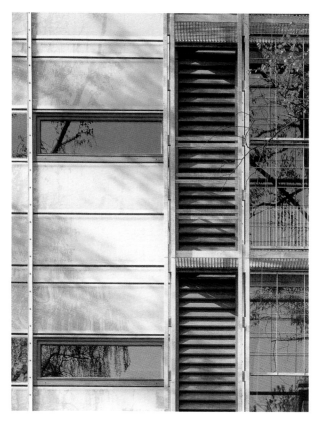

6.4.22

6.4.21: Shark scales

6.4.22: Structural interpretation of the function of a polar bear's skin: office and pioneering building with 'transparent heat insulation'; Thomas Herzog, Munich 1993

6.4.23: Network materials: rigid, textile, semi-finished products used for the most part as the middle layer in composites, pliable crosswise

6.4.24: Tropical landscape in the Eden Project, St. Austell, Cornwall (see case study 13): MERO spatial framework with additional wide span; ETFE foil cushions inserted in hexagonal steel frame and equipped with aluminium clipping system

6.4.25: Shigeru Ban: Japanese Pavilion, *Expo 2000*, Hanover; paper-roll weave, derived from the principle of fabrics and mats used in several cultures to portray an imitation of natural structures

6.4.24

6.4.25

Case Study 100
Jean-Marie Tjibaou
Cultural Centre

Nouméa, New Caledonia
1991 (competition), 1993–98
Architects: Renzo Piano
Building Workshop
Engineers: Arup

Nouméa, the capital of New Caledonia, was to be home to a cultural centre, donated by the former French colonial power, for the Kanak population, which was spread over several Pacific Islands. In its finished form it forges a link between tradition and Modernity, between the past and the future of the Kanak people, a "proper little village", as Renzo Piano describes his project, "with promenades, parks and public areas in a constant relationship with the sea. The use of wind and the search for modern forms of expression in the tradition of the built environment" represent "a pivotal anthropological contribution" for Piano.[56] He was, however, not concerned with the creation of a prestigious museum, but rather with the preservation and reproduction of a 'cultural memory'.

In order to define and organise themselves in the raw climate, the South Sea islanders developed their own construction structures and shapes, as well as behavioural patterns and techniques. Even in his competition entry Renzo Piano was at pains to work in a strange, well-nigh contrasting culture and empathise with the natives' way of thought. The Kanaks' constructions emerge directly from weatherproofed materials found in nature, to which they are exposed; what are important are not their durability and robustness, but rather typology and construction principles, in particular the traditional huts and walls. One can learn from this (ills. 6.4.2 and 6.4.27).

Together with Ove Arup & Partners and others, Renzo Piano and his colleagues transformed the characteristic building typology features they had come across in terms of structure, shape and material techniques into new prototypes they constructed using new materials in order to expose them first of all as trial objects to the forces of nature (ill. 6.4.28).

A fundamental element that influenced structure and shape was the power of the wind, which was not only to be withstood, but also utilised: "Don't fight forces, use them", Richard Buckminster Fuller, who, like Renzo Piano, also engaged in experimentation, once remarked. Simulation programs and wind tunnel experiments led, analogous and delayed in time, to similarly differentiated spatial structure and wall construction, though using present-day materials and technology, as the South Sea

island inhabitants had empirically achieved over the course of their long cultural development (ill. 6.4.29).

The new 'huts', there are 10 in total, of which the highest is 28 metres high, make up a multifunctional complex, but are structured in line with a uniform principle. In response to the particular climatic conditions the design featured a twin skin made of laminated wood mesh: the outer layer is structured such that the monsoon blowing in from the sea can be used for passive ventilation. In a light breeze, movable lamellas open up to accelerate natural ventilation; should the strength of the wind increase, these close gradually from bottom to top (ill. 6.4.30).

This dynamic modelling is the result of simulations, trial models and tests, as well as interdisciplinary collaboration. On the subject, Renzo Piano wrote: "This system of air circulation also gives the huts a 'voice'. Together they create the sound peculiar to Kanak villages and their woods – or for seafarers, that of a harbour on a windy day."[57] (ill. 6.4.31; see also ill. 6.).

The cultural centre in Nouméa is an example of mutual learning between cultures. Shapes transformed into structures and reinterpreted cultural techniques reveal a forward-looking thought, research and work model for sustainable architectural achievements and stances: the resonance of unfamiliar environmental dynamics, the learning of spatial, structural and material economy, and respect for different types of culture and social set-up.

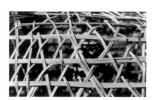

6.4.27

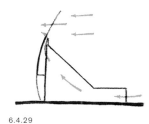

6.4.28

6.4.26: New Caledonian huts: structure and shape are a response to environmental conditions.

6.4.27: Four types of traditional wall constructions that can respond in different ways to wind: increments in wind-resistance to through-ventilation

6.4.28: Prototype of a new structure 'transformed' from ancient culture

6.4.29: Diagrams of different cases of wind load; example of cyclone effect

6.4.30: Structure and shape for the use of different wind strengths for natural ventilation; 1:1 mock-up

6.4.31: Analogy with regard to shape to the vegetation and the natives' huts and transformation to the modern world of architecture generated from intercultural exchange

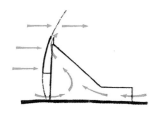

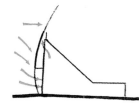

6.4.29

6.4.30

6.4.31

The Key Speech

Sir Ove Arup

"We could become a small-scale experiment in how to live and work happily together." (Ove Arup: "Aims and Means: Part I", *Newsletter, 37,* Nov. 1969)

On 9 July 1970 Ove Arup spoke to a meeting at Winchester of his partners from the practices around the world bearing the Arup name. His talk was in response to the collective desire to continue working together, despite the changes that would take place as the founding partners progressively retired and gave up ownership, handing over control to the successors they would choose for these practices.

The pre-natal name of 'key speech' for this talk has endured, in recognition of the fact that in it Ove both states the aims of our firm and analyses in his very distinctive way the principles through which they may be achieved. From time to time we have asked ourselves whether what he said in 1970 remains valid for us, despite the fact that inevitably some specifics about the firm's organisation and individuals' roles therein to which he refers in passing have changed over the years. On each occasion we have found that it does, and thereby reaffirmed our commitment to these principles.

The Key Speech is required reading for each person who joins Arup or who wants to be reminded of what we are all about, and for those who want to learn about us.

In its pre-natal stage, this talk has been honoured with the name of 'key speech'. It is doubtful whether it can live up to this name. What is it supposed to be the key to? The future of the firm? The philosophy? The aims? At the moment, sitting in my garden and waiting for inspiration, I would be more inclined to call it: 'Musings of an old gentleman in a garden' – and leave it at that.

I have written before a piece called 'Aims and Means' for a conference of Senior and Executive Partners in London on 7 July 1969. It did not manage to deal much with means, however, and it is of course difficult to generalise about means, for they must vary with circumstances. The first part of this paper was published in *Newsletter 37*, November 1969. This you may have read – but I will shortly summarise the aims of the firm as I see them.

There are two ways of looking at the work you do to earn a living:
One is the way propounded by the late Henry Ford: Work is a necessary evil, but modern technology will reduce it to a minimum. Your life is your leisure lived in your 'free' time.

The other is:

To make your work interesting and rewarding. You enjoy both your work and your leisure.

We opt uncompromisingly for the second way.

There are also two ways of looking at the pursuit of happiness:
One is to go straight for the things you fancy without restraints, that is, without considering anybody else besides yourself.

The other is:

to recognise that no man is an island, that our lives are inextricably mixed up with those of our fellow human beings, and that there can be no real happiness in isolation. Which leads to an attitude which would accord to others the rights claimed for oneself, which would accept certain moral or humanitarian restraints.

We, again, opt for the second way.

These two general principles are not in dispute. I will elaborate them a little further: The first means that our work should be interesting and rewarding. Only a job done well, as well as we can do it – and as well as it can be done – is that. We must therefore strive for quality in what we do, and never be satisfied with the second-rate. There are many kinds of quality. In our work as structural engineers we had – and have – to satisfy the criteria for a sound, lasting and economical structure. We add to that the claim that it should be pleasing aesthetically, for without that quality it doesn't really give satisfaction to us or to others. And then we come up against the fact that a structure is generally a part of a larger unit, and we are frustrated because to strive for quality in only a part is almost useless if the whole is undistinguished, unless the structure is large enough to make an impact on its own. We are led to seek overall quality, fitness for purpose, as well as satisfying or significant forms and economy of construction. To this must be added harmony with the surroundings and the overall plan. We are then led to the ideal of 'Total Architecture', in collaboration with other like-minded firms or, still better, on our own. This means expanding our field of activity into adjoining fields – architecture, planning, ground engineering, environmental engineering, computer programming, etc. and the planning and organisation of the work on site.

It is not the wish to expand, but the quest for quality which has brought us to this position, for we have realised that only intimate integration of the various parts or the various disciplines will produce the desired result.

The term 'Total Architecture' implies that all relevant design decisions have been considered together and have been integrated into a whole by a well-organised team empowered to fix priorities. This is an ideal which can never – or only very rarely – be fully realised in practice, but which is well worth striving for, for artistic wholeness or excellence depends on it, and for our own sake we need the stimulation produced by excellence.

The humanitarian attitude   The other general principle, the humanitarian attitude, leads to the creation of an organisation which is human and friendly in spite of being large and efficient. Where every member is treated not only as a link in a chain of command, not only as a wheel in a bureaucratic machine, but as a human being whose happiness is the concern of all, who is treated not only as a means but as an end.

Of course, it is always sound business to keep your collaborators happy – just as any farmer must keep his cattle in good health. But there is – or should be – more in it than that. (We know what happens to cattle.) If we want our work to be interesting and rewarding, then we must try to make it so for all our people and that is obviously much more difficult, not to say impossible. It is again an ideal, unattainable in full, but worth striving for. It leads to the wish to make everybody aware of, and interested in, our aims and to make the environment and working conditions as pleasant as possible within the available means.

This attitude also dictates that we should act honourably in our dealings with our own and other people. We should justify the trust of our clients by giving their interest first priority in the work we do for them. Internally, we should eschew nepotism or discrimination on the basis of nationality, religion, race, colour or sex – basing such discrimination as there must be on ability and character.

Humanitarianism also implies a social conscience, a wish to do socially useful work, and to join hands with others fighting for the same values. Our pursuit of quality should in itself be useful. If we in isolated cases can show how our environment can be improved, this is likely to have a much greater effect than mere propaganda.

There is a third aim besides the search for quality of work and the right human relationships, namely prosperity for all our members. Most people would say that this is our main aim, this is why we are in business. But it would be wrong to look at it as our main aim. We should rather look at it as an essential prerequisite for even the partial fulfilment of any of our aims. For it is an aim which, if overemphasised, easily gets out of hand and becomes very dangerous for our harmony, unity and very existence.

It costs money to produce quality, especially when we expand into fields where we have no contractual obligations and can expect no pay for our efforts. We may even antagonise people by poaching on their domain or by upsetting and criticising traditional procedures.

It also costs money to 'coddle' the staff with generosity and welfare, or to lose lucrative commissions by refusing to bribe a minister in a developing country, or to take our duty too seriously if nobody is looking.

Money spent on these 'aims' may be wisely spent in the long term, and may cause the leaders of the firm a certain satisfaction – but if so spent it is not available for immediate distribution among the members, whether partners or staff. So aim No. 3 conflicts to that extent with aims 1 and 2. Moreover, if money is made the main aim – if we are more greedy than is reasonable – it will accentuate the natural conflict about how the profit should be distributed between our members – the partners and staff or the different grades of staff.

The trouble with money is that it is a dividing force, not a uniting force, as is the quest for quality or a humanitarian outlook. If we let it divide us, we are sunk as an organisation – at least as a force for good.

So much for our aims. As aims, they are not in dispute. What is debatable is how vigorously each shall be pursued – which is the most important; how to balance long-term against short-term aims. Let us first see what these aims imply.

Obviously, to do work of quality, we must have people of quality. We must be experts at what we undertake to do. Again, there are many kinds of quality, and there are many kinds of job to do, so we must have many kinds of people, each of which can do their own job well. And they must be able to work well together. This presupposes that they agree with our aims, and that they are not only technically capable but acceptable to us from a human point of view, so that they fit into our kind of organisation; and that they are effectively organised, so that the responsibility of each is clearly defined and accepted. In short, we must be efficient – individually, in all our subdivisions, and as a world organisation.

I have tried to summarise the foregoing in a number of points. Like all classification, it is arbitrary and rough –

but may nevertheless be useful as a help to understanding and discussion, if its imperfections and its incompleteness are borne in mind.

The main aims of the firm are:
Group A
  1 Quality of work
  2 Total architecture
  3 Humane organisation
  4 Straight and honourable dealings
  5 Social usefulness
  6 Reasonable prosperity of members.

If these aims could be realised to a considerable degree, they should result in:
Group B
  7 Satisfied members
  8 Satisfied clients
  9 Good reputation and influence.

But this will need:

Group C
  10 A membership of quality
  11 Efficient organisation
  12 Solvency
  13 Unity and enthusiasm.

Of course, there is not really any strict demarcation between aims *(Group A)* and means *(Group C)* and the results *(Group B)* flowing from the whole or partial fulfilment of the aims in A. And it is not absolutely certain that these results are obtained. For instance, A3 and 4 (a humane organisation and straight dealings) can as well be considered as a means, and in fact all the points are to some extent both aims and means, because they reinforce each other. And there will be members who are dissatisfied no matter how good the firm is, and the same may apply to clients, who may not appreciate quality at all. But on the whole, what I said is true. We should keep the six aims in A in view all the time, and concentrate on the means to bring them about.

But before I do this I will try to explain why I am going on about aims, ideals and moral principles and all that, and don't get down to brass tacks. I do this simply because I think these aims are very important. I can't see the point in having such a large firm with offices all over the world unless there is something which binds us together. If we were just ordinary consulting engineers carrying on business just as business to make a comfortable living, I can't see why each office couldn't carry on, on its own. The idea of somebody in London 'owning' all these businesses and hiring people to bring in the dough doesn't seem very inspiring. Unless we have a

'mission' – although I don't like the word – but something 'higher' to strive for – and I don't particularly like that expression either – but unless we feel that we have a special contribution to make which our very size and diversity and our whole outlook can help to achieve, I for one am not interested. I suppose that you feel the same, and therefore my words to you may seem superfluous; but it is not enough that you feel it, everybody in the firm should as far as possible be made to feel it, and to believe that we, the leaders of the firm, really believe in it and mean to work for it and not just use it as a flag to put out on Sundays. And they won't believe that unless we do.

On the other hand, who am I to tell you and the firm what you should think and feel in the future when I am gone – or before that, for that matter? It wouldn't be any good my trying to lay down the law, and I haven't the slightest inclination to do so. That is my difficulty. I dislike hard principles, ideologies and the like. They can do more harm than good, they can lead to wholesale murder, as we have seen. And yet we cannot live life entirely without principles. But they have in some way to be flexible, to be adaptable to changing circumstances. 'Thou shalt not lie', 'Thou shalt not kill', are all very well, generally, but do not apply if, for instance, you are tortured by fanatical Nazis or Communists to reveal the whereabouts of their innocent victims. Then it is your duty to mislead. What these commandments should define is an attitude. To be truthful always, wherever it does no harm to other ideals more important in the context, to respect the sanctity of human life and not to destroy life wantonly. But where to draw the line in border cases depends on who you are, what life has taught you, how strong you are.

In the following 13 points, which I must have jotted down some time ago – I found them in an old file – I am grappling with this question, perhaps not very successfully. I give them to you now:

Principles
  1 Some people have moral principles.
  2 The essence of moral principles is that they should be 'lived'.
  3 But only saints and fanatics do follow moral principles always.
  4 Which is fortunate.
  5 Are then moral principles no good?
  6 It appears we can't do without them.
  7 It also appears we can't live up to them.
  8 So what?
  9 A practical solution is what I call the *star system*.
  10 The star – or ideal – indicates the course. Obstacles in the way are *circumnavigated but one gets back on the course* after the deviation.

11 The system is adopted by the Catholic Church. Sins can be forgiven if repented – it doesn't affect the definition of good or evil.

12 That this system can degenerate into permanent deviation is obvious.

13 One needs a sense of proportion.

Incidentally, they should not be taken as an encouragement to join the Catholic Church!

I found also another tag:
'The way out is not the way round but the way through.'
That's rather more uncompromising, more heroic.
It springs from a different temperament. It's equally useful in the right place. But the man that bangs his head against a wall may learn a thing or two from the reed that bends in the wind.

The trouble with the last maxim is that it says something about the way, but not about the goal. The way must be adapted to the circumstances – the goal is much more dependent on what sort of person you are. I admit that the last maxim also says a good deal about the man who propounds it, a man of courage, of action, perhaps not given too much to reflection, perhaps not a very wise man. The wise man will consider whether this way is possible, whether it leads to the desired result. Unless, of course, his goal is to go through, not to arrive anywhere, like the man in the sports car. But this only shows that it is the goal which is important, whatever it is.

The *star system* is an attempt to soften the rigidity of moral principles. But it doesn't really solve this dilemma. It is a little more flexible than moral precepts as to the way, but surely the 'stars' must be fixed – for if they can be changed *ad lib* the whole thing wobbles. And that in a way is what it does – I can't do anything about that. I should have loved to present you with a strictly logical build-up, deducing the aims for the firm from unassailable first principles. Or perhaps this is an exaggeration – for I know very well that this can't be done. All I can do is to try to make the members of the firm like the aims I have mentioned. I would like to persuade them that they are good and reasonable and not too impossible aims, possessing an inner cohesion, reinforcing each other by being not only aims but means to each other's fulfilment.

'Stars' like goodness, beauty, justice have been powerful forces in the history of mankind – but they so often are obscured by a mental fog – or perhaps I should say the opposite – they are created by a mental fog, and when the fog lifts, they are seen to have been illusions. They are man-made. I do not rate them less for that reason – but they are too remote, too indefinable, to be of much practical use as guidelines. They sustain or are born of the longings of mankind, and belong to the ideal world of Plato – which is fixed for ever. Rigid ideologies feed on them. Not so practical politics.

Our aims on the other hand are not nearly so remote. We will never succeed in fulfilling them *in toto*, but they can be fulfilled more or less, and the more the better. And they are not grasped arbitrarily out of the sky or wilfully imposed, they are natural and obvious and will, I am sure, be recognised as desirable by all of you: so much so, in fact, that the thing to be explained is not why they are desirable, but why I should waste any words on them. I do, as I pointed out at the beginning of this argument, because our aims are the only thing which holds us together, and because it is not enough to approve them, we must work for them – and the leaders must be prepared to make sacrifices for them. Temporary diversions there must be, we have to make do with the second best if the best is not within reach, we have to accept expediencies and from a strict point of view all our activities can be considered as expediencies, for in theory they could all be better still – but the important thing is that we always get back on the course, that we never lose sight of the aims. Hence the name *star system* derived from comparison with old-fashioned navigation. But I propose to abandon this expression, partly because its meaning in the film industry may confuse, especially as it is very opposed to our point of view, which is in favour of teamwork rather than stardom: and also because it suggests stargazing, which I find uncomfortably near the bone because I might with some justification be accused of it. So I am afraid we have to fall back on 'philosophy'. Having dabbled in this subject in my youth I have been averse to seeing the term degraded by talk about the philosophy of piledriving or hairdressing, but it is, of course, useless to fight against the tide. The word has come to stay – and in 'the philosophy of the firm', it is not used quite so badly. So that's what I have been giving you a dose of.

I will now discuss what we have to do in order to live up to our philosophy. And I will do it under the four headings 10 to 13 in my list of aims and means:

10 Quality staff
11 Efficiency
12 Solvency
13 Unity and enthusiasm.

But it will, of course, be necessary to mix them up to some extent.

Quality of staff   How do we ensure that our staff is of the right quality, or the best possible quality?

Key question. The whole success of our venture depends on our staff. But what can we do about it? We have the staff we have – we must make do with them, of course (and I think we have a larger proportion of really good people than any other firm of our kind). And when we take on new people – the choice is limited. Again we have to take the best we can get. We cannot pay them a much higher salary than our average scale, because that would upset our solvency and sink the boat. Naturally our method of selection is important, and what we can do to educate our staff and give them opportunities to develop is important, but I can't go into details here. All I can say is that staff-getting and staff-'treating' must not degenerate into a bureaucratic routine matter, but must be on a personal level. When we come across a really good man, grab him, even if we have no immediate use for him, and then see to it that he stays with us.

The last is the really important point, which in the long run will be decisive. Why should a really good man, a man – or woman – who can get a job anywhere or who could possibly start out on his own, why should he or she choose to stay with us? If there is a convincing and positive answer to that, then we are on the right way.

Presumably a good man comes to us in the first instance because he likes the work we do, and shares or is converted to our philosophy. If he doesn't, he is not much good to us anyhow. He is not mainly attracted by the salary we can offer, although that is, of course, an important point – but by the opportunity to do interesting and rewarding work, where he can use his creative ability, be fully extended, can grow and be given responsibility. If he finds after a while that he is frustrated by red tape or by having someone breathing down his neck, someone for whom he has scant respect, if he has little influence on decisions which affect his work and which he may not agree with, then he will pack up and go. And so he should. It is up to us, therefore, to create an organisation which will allow gifted individuals to unfold. This is not easy, because there appears to be a fundamental contradiction between organisation and freedom. Strong-willed individuals may not take easily to directions from above. But our work is teamwork, and teamwork – except possibly in very small teams – needs to be organised, otherwise we have chaos. And the greater the unit, the more it needs to be organised. Most strong men, if they are also wise, will accept that. Somebody must have authority to take decisions, the responsibility of each member must be clearly defined, understood and accepted by all. The authority should also be spread downwards as far as possible, and the whole pattern should be flexible and open to revision.

We know all this, and we have such an organisation: we have both macro, micro and infra-structure. It has been developed, been improved, and it could undoubtedly be improved still further. We are, of course, trying to do that all the time. The organisation will naturally be related to some sort of hierarchy, which should as far as possible be based on function, and there must be some way of fixing remuneration, for to share the available profit equally between all from senior partner to office boy would not be reasonable, nor would it work. And all this is very tricky, as you know, because, as soon as money and status come into the picture, greed and envy and intrigue are not far behind. One difficulty is particularly knotty, the question of ownership, which is connected with 'partnership'. There is dissatisfaction amongst some of those who in fact carry out the functions of a partner – dealing with clients, taking decisions binding on the firm, etc. – because they cannot legally call themselves partners but are 'executive' partners – or have some other title. I have discussed this problem in my paper "Aims and Means". If some viable way could be found to make 100 partners, I wouldn't mind, but I can't think of any.

In the Ove Arup Partnership we have all but eliminated ownership – the senior partners only act as owners during their tenure of office – because someone has to, according to the laws of the country. And I wish that system could be extended to all our partnerships. It no doubt irks some people that the money invested in the firm may one day (with some contriving) fall into the turban of people who have done nothing to earn it – but what can we do? The money is needed for the stability of the firm, it makes it possible for us to earn our living and to work for a good cause, so why worry? It may be possible to devise a different and better arrangement than the one we have now, more 'democratic', more fair: it may be possible to build in some defences against the leaders' misbehaving and developing boss complexes and pomposity – and forgetting that they are just as much servants in a good cause as everybody else – only more so. This is partly a legal question depending on the laws of the country. But I have neither the ability nor the time to deal with all that here. What I want to stress is the obvious fact that no matter how wonderful an organisation we can devise, its success depends on the people working in it – and for it. And *if* all our members really and sincerely believed in the aims which I have enumerated, if they felt some enthusiasm for them, the battle would be nearly won. For they imply a humanitarian attitude, respect and consideration for persons, fair dealings, and the rest, which all tend to smooth human relationships. And anyone having the same attitude who comes into an atmosphere like that is at least more likely to feel at home in it. And if the right kind of people feel at home with us, they will bring in other people of their kind, and this again will attract a good type of client and this will make our work more interesting and rewarding and we will turn out better work, our reputation and influence will grow, and the enthusiasm of our members will grow – it is this enthusiasm which must start the process in the first place.

And they all lived happily ever after?   Yes, it sounds like a fairy tale, and perhaps it is. But there is something in it. It is a kind of vicious circle – except that it isn't vicious, but benevolent, a lucky circle. And I believe that we have made a beginning in getting into this lucky circle. I believe that our fantastic growth has something to do with our philosophy. And I believe our philosophy is forward-looking, that it is what is needed today, is in tune with the new spirit stirring in our time. But, of course, there are many other and dangerous spirits about and too much growth may awaken them. Too much growth may also mean too little fruit.

My advice would be:
  'Stadig over de klipper',
or if you prefer:
  'Take it easy!'
  'More haste less speed!'
  'Hâtez-vous lentement!'
  'Eile mit weile!'
  'Hastvaerk er lastvaerk!'

It's the fruit that matters. I have a lingering doubt about trying to gain a foothold in various exotic places. Might we not say instead: Thank God that we have not been invited to do a job in Timbuctoo – think of all the trouble we are avoiding. It's different with the work we do in Saudi Arabia, Tehran and Kuwait.[1] There we are invited in at the top, working with good architects, doing exciting work. We are not hammering at the door from outside. But as a rule, grab-and-run jobs are not so useful for our purpose. I think the Overseas Department agrees with this in principle, if not in practice.

It's also different with civil engineering work, provided we have control – complete control – over the design and are not 'sharing' the job or having a quantity surveyor or 'agent', etc., imposed on it preventing us from doing the job our way. The general rule should be: if we can do a job we will be proud of afterwards, well and good – but we will do it our way. In the long run this attitude pays, as it has already done in the case of Arup Associates. And incidentally, the control of such jobs should be where our expertise resides.

To export Arup Associates' jobs is much more difficult, for whilst we may be able to build a bridge or radio tower in a foreign locality, good architecture presupposes a much more intimate knowledge of the country. Long-distance architecture generally fails. But that does not mean that the ideal of Total Architecture is irrelevant to our purely engineering partnerships or divisions. In fact, they have been founded on the idea of integrating structure with architecture and construction, and in Scotland, for instance, they are trying to give architects a service which will unite these domains.[2]

Coming back to my main theme, I realise that when I have been talking about quality, about interesting and rewarding work, about Total Architecture, and attracting people of calibre, you may accuse me of leaving reality behind. 'As you said yourself', you may say, 'our work is teamwork. And most of this work is pretty dull. It is designing endless reinforced concrete floors, taking down tedious letters about the missing bolts, changing some details for the nth time, attending site meetings dealing with trivialities, taking messages, making tea – what is exciting about that? You are discriminating in favour of an elite, it's undemocratic. What about the people who have to do the dull work?'

Equality of opportunity   You have certainly a point there. Of course, I am discriminating in favour of quality, and I would do anything to enable our bright people to use their talents. You cannot equate excellence with mediocrity, you cannot pretend they are the same. We would be sunk if we did that. We need to produce works of quality, and we need those who can produce them. One perfect job is more important for the morale of the firm, for our reputation for producing enthusiasm, than 10 ordinary jobs, and enthusiasm is like the fire that keeps the steam-engine going. Likewise one outstanding man is worth 10 men who are only half good. This is a fact of life we cannot change. It is no good pretending that all are equal – they aren't. There should be equality before the law, and as far as possible equality of opportunity, of course. But the fact that you are good at something is something you should be grateful for, not something to be conceited about. It doesn't mean that you are better as a human being. And there are probably many other things you are hopeless at.

No man should be despised or feel ashamed because of the work he does, as long as he does it as well as he can. What we should aim at, naturally, is to put each man on to the work he can do. And, fortunately, there is nearly always something he can do well. We will have square pegs in round holes, we shall have frustrated people, unfortunately – those who are not frustrated one way or another are in the minority. But fortunately, people vary, as jobs vary, and few would want to do the job another calls interesting if they are no good at it.

If we can reach a stage where each man or woman is respected for the job they do, and is doing his or her best because the atmosphere is right, because they are proud of what we are and do and share in the general enthusiasm, then we are home. And each job is important. Secretaries, for instance. They could have a tremendously civilising influence on our staff. They could teach them to write English, for instance, a most important and necessary job. But secretaries who can do that are, of course, at a premium. We must try to find them. It is even more important than that they are good-looking – and nobody could accuse me of being indifferent to that.

Our messengers and cleaners – how important it is that they are reliable and likeable, human, with a sense of humour. A cheerful remark can brighten the day. All our people are part of us, part of our 'image', create the atmosphere we live in.

But it doesn't alter the fact that the services of a messenger are less valuable to the firm than those of a gifted designer or an imaginative mechanical engineer, a fact that even the messenger will understand.

But there are, of course, people we cannot employ usefully. Masses of them, in fact. Those we should not take on, obviously, except on a strictly temporary basis. But sometimes they are found inside the firm. They may have been good once, but are on the way down. I am a case in point myself. But their loyal service, their place in the hierarchy, makes it difficult to de-grade them. To deal with them requires much tact, and is embarrassing. But they should not be allowed to pretend to do jobs they are no good at. They must not prevent the good ones from functioning. It's a problem all firms have, it's one of the cases where humanity and efficiency clash. To resolve it tactfully may be expensive, not to resolve it is fatal.

So far I haven't said much about solvency. Stuart Irons[3] can tell you something about that. I compare it to stability in engineering structures – without it the whole thing collapses but if you have much more money than you need the usefulness of it declines until it becomes distracting and dangerous. That danger need not worry us for the time being. At the moment the need for solvency is restricting, and is the most frequent cause of having to compromise. That we may have to do – but let's not do it unnecessarily, and let's get back on course.

And Unity and Enthusiasm, the last item, is, in a way, what my talk has been about. It is a question of giving the firm an identity. What do we mean, when we speak about the firm, about 'we' or 'us'? Is it the whole collection of people in dozens of offices in different places? Are 'we' all of them or some of them, and which?

I think it is unavoidable that 'we' should mean different things in different contexts. Sometimes what is said is only relevant to the upper layers of management, sometimes it is meant to include everybody. What we must aim at is to make 'we' include as many as possible as often as possible. To increase the number of those who have a contribution to make, however small, who agree wholeheartedly with our aims and want to throw in their lot with us. We might think about them as members of our community; the others, who come and go, might be called staff. Of course, there can never be any clear line of demarcation – it is not a question of signing a form or bestowing a title – it is a matter of how each feels and what we feel about them. For it is a two-way business.

But what binds our membership together must be loyalty to our aims. And only as long as the leaders of the firm are loyal to these can they expect and demand loyalty from the members. This speech is too long already, and I have not even touched on what you perhaps expected to be the main subject of my talk, the relationship between the Ove Arup Partnership and the Overseas Partnerships. But from the foregoing my point of view should be clear.

The fact that we have these outposts all over the world is, of course, an enormous source of strength to us and to you, it helps to establish our reputation and power for good, and opens up opportunities for all our members. This is, however, only because the leaders in these places are our own people, bound to us by common aims and friendships. But as the old leaders retire and growth takes place mainly locally, the ties that bind us together may weaken. We should prevent this by forging more ties, forming new friendships, and always being true to our principles. Improve communications – the universal injunction nowadays. Absence does not make the heart grow fonder, unfortunately. There will always be a need for a strong coordinating body – which is at the moment formed by the senior partners – which has the power to interfere if our principles are seriously betrayed. For should that happen, it would be better to cut off the offending limb, less the poison should spread. Our name must not be allowed to cover practices which conflict with our philosophy. But at the moment there is no danger of that, and we can take comfort from what has been achieved. Perhaps that should have been the gist of my talk? But you are seeing it for yourself. I could also have dwelt on how far we still have to go; it would perhaps have accorded more with my stargazing habits. But my time is up – my speech should have been condensed to one third – but it is too late now. I hope at any rate that I haven't deserved the warning which the Duke of Albany addressed to Goneril in *King Lear*:

How far your eyes may pierce I cannot tell. Striving to better, oft we mar what's well.

Arup's core values maintain the vision established by Sir Ove Arup (1895–1988):
- We will ensure that the Arup name is always associated with quality.
- We will act honestly and fairly in dealings with our staff and others.
- We will enhance prosperity for all Arup staff.

Our priorities are:
- our clients and our industry
- our creativity
- our people
- sustainable development.

We shape a better world:
- to enhance prosperity and the quality of life
- to deliver real value
- to have the freedom to be creative and to learn.

Notes

Introduction

1 Rowe, C. and R. Slutzky, B. Hoesli, 1968
2 *Arch+*, no.172, December 2004
3 Concrete also acquires a lightness that results from the material through reinforcement with steel or textile fibres as well as through other new processes.

4 Pfammatter, U., 2000
5 Landes, D. S., 1968
6 Mostafari, M. (ed.), 2006; Luebkeman, Ch., 2006
7 Horden, R., 2004

8 ArchStudioLab: www.archstudio.ch
9 www.fskb.ch/Architekturgalerie

1 From Greenhouse to 'High-tech Hothouse'

1 John Locke (1632–1704) committed his ideas on education to paper some years after the Glorious Revolution in England (1666) in *Some Thoughts Concerning Education*, Locke, J., 1693.
2 The biographies of, for example, Thomas Telford (stone mason) or Joseph Paxton (gardener) illustrate this unrestricted possibility of making a career that was not dependent upon one's social origins.
3 Extensive description of the glasshouse as a building type in: Kohlmaier, G. and B. von Sartory, 1988.
4 In the area of structural systems these were, in terms of construction, building and material technology, the product of the art of engineering as demonstrated in the construction of railway stations; a synthesis of bridge-building technology and the method of constructing halls and sheds (see chapters).
5 Architect of the Cité des Sciences et de l'Industrie La Villette in Paris: Adrien Fainsilber; engineers: RFR (Peter Rice, Martin Francis, Ian Ritchie); built 1981–86.
6 *Remarks on the Construction of Hothouses* (1817), *Sketches of Curvilinear Hothouses* (1818); Loudon set up specialist journals including *The Gardener's Magazine* and, as the first architecture journal, *The Architecture Magazine*; comprehensively in: G. Kohlmaier and B. von Sartory, 1988, pp 227–43.
7 The first modern scientific and technical school of thought in France developed at the École Polytechnique, which was founded in 1794 immediately after the French Revolution. Its first generation of students included such well-known and inventive masters of building as Leo von Klenze, Guillaume-Henry Dufour and many others: Pfammatter, U., 1997, chapter 1.
8 Förster, L. (ed.), *Allgemeine Bauzeitung*, Vienna 1837, no. 48, pp. 395–400, and no. 49, pp. 403–08.
9 Chadwick, G. F., 1961, p. 93; after Sigfried Giedion, who on this point refers to L. A. Boileau, Paxton used this opportunity to visit the Jardin des Plantes, where he looked at Fleury's greenhouses, which served as a model for his greenhouses in Chatsworth: Giedion, S., 1928, p. 40.
10 First of all Hippolyte Meynadier de Flamalens, who in 1846 could not convince the Société Immoblière, which had commissioned him, to erect a building at such dimensions, and then Charles-Théodore Charpentier.
11 Playing water guarantees regulated air humidity, the powerful heating system a constant room temperature of 12 degrees Celsius. The building services achieved a 'state-of-the-art' completely new for that time.
12 In the boutiques, exotic birds, perfumes, soaps, etc. were offered for sale.
13 *Zeitschrift für praktische Baukunst*, 1849, quoted from Kohlmaier, G. and B. von Sartory, 1988, pp. 470 and 466.
14 Paxton mentioned it in a letter to his wife dated 16 Oct. 1848, it was also described in the *Gardener's Chronicle* of 1848; Cole, H., 1884, vol.1, pp.116–205; Chadwick, G. F., 1961, p.139; Hix, J., 1974, p.117; Giedion. S., 1976, p.174; Kohlmaier, G. and B. von Sartory, 1988, p. 466.

15 The original design appears to be from Decimus Burton, who also worked for Paxton in Chatsworth.
16 The Italian garden at the centre of the large park is by André Le Nôtre, the landscape designer of Versailles. Kohlmaier, G. and B. von Sartory, 1988, p. 314 ff.
17 It was only in 1845 that these duties were reduced by around 70 per cent, thus permitting larger complexes such as Kew Gardens and the Crystal Palace to be built. Elliott, C. D., 1992, p.128.
18 In 1985 the glass panes were replaced by Pilkington float glass, of the same format but flat and no longer with thicker edges by the sides in cross-section so that the original ventilation of the interior and the draining of condensation to the outside no longer functions.
19 The proto-industrial type with wrought-iron glazing bars and glass panes of various dimensions, as well as the heat storage wall at the rear strongly suggest the first pioneering period between 1820 and 1830. The construction date of 1843 given by Kohlmaier and von Sartory, who rely on Hix, would be only three years before Kew Gardens and the Jardin d'Hiver in Paris – building-technology structures of enormous dimensions and industrially manufactured – which is simply too short a time for such a development. Also, the glass pavilions by Rohault de Fleury in Paris (1833) and Great Stove in Chatsworth by Joseph Paxton (1836–40) represent a comparatively more advanced level of industrial precision. Kohlmaier, G. and B. von Sartory, 1988, p. 315 f., and Hix, J., 1974, p. 27.
20 After visiting England in 1834, Rohault de Fleury himself wrote in 1837 a two-part report for the Vienna *Allgemeine Bauzeitung* (ed. Ludwig Förster), no. 48, pp. 395–400 and no. 49, pp. 403–08, Vienna, 1837, where the early curvilinear hothouses of the Bicton Gardens type are described and illustrated.
21 Rice, P., 1995, p.14
22 He was later prominent in the area of monumental and representational buildings in Haussmann's Paris, for example, in the construction of the Grand Hôtel on the Place de l'Opéra, together with Armand, Hittorff and Pellechet, which had 700 beds and a skeletal, iron load-bearing frame; it was opened in 1862.
23 In more detail in Pfammatter, U., 1997, chapter 1
24 Unfortunately they stood for only a short time and were replaced by similar but more robust structures which have survived to the present.
25 Monge was the inventor of 'géometrie descriptive' from the pre-revolutionary era of French Enlightenment philosophy and taught this subject at the École Polytechnique, the first new scientific and technical school after the French Revolution: Pfammatter, U., 1997, pp. 40–42
26 'Feuille quadrillée: standard sheet of squared drawing paper, 45 x 29.2 cm, with a printed red or orange grid of 4-cm squares, intended to be used for 1:100 scale drawings; cf. on Durand in particular Szambien, W., 1984
27 Pfammatter, U., 1997, pp. 83–87
28 First drawn for his degree work at the École Centrale in

Paris: the 'Polonceau truss' was conceived for 15- to 40-m spans, but was used in railways stations in Paris for spans of up to 60 m without intermediate columns! Pfammatter, U., 1997, pp.150–53
29 The elevated longitudinal beams (also superfluous) meant that the top section of the roof could be placed higher, allowing a strip of high-level glazing on either side. Columns that were cross-shaped in section were new at the time; they surface later in an industrial setting, for example, in the Reliance Building in Chicago (1890–94) or in Mies's Barcelona Pavilion and his National Gallery in Berlin; cf. chapter 5 case study 69
30 Vienna 1837; no. 48, pp. 395–400 and no. 49, pp. 403–08
31 Chadwick, G. F., 1961, chapters 1–4
32 A documented plan is signed by Decimus Burton, who 10 years later produced a design for the Palm House in Kew Gardens which served as a basis for Turner's project; Chadwick, G. F., 1961, p. 86
33 In the studios of Georges Bontemps near Paris larger-format glass panes could be blown thanks to the cylinder glass process. On account of the glass tax the use of this process in England was senseless until 1845; Elliott, C. D., 1992, p.131 f.
34 Exhaustively in Hix, J., 1974, p.117 ff.; see also: McCracken, Eileen, 1971
35 This term coined by Colin Rowe and Robert Slutzky followed analyses of the floor plans and sections of F. L. Wright's Prairie Houses and of buildings by Corbusier and others that relate to Cubism; Rowe, C., R. Slutzky and Hoesli, B. (eds.), 1989.
36 Hix, J., 1974, p.122
37 The Palm House in Kew Gardens was one of the first glass pavilions to be erected after the abolition of the glass tax (1845).
38 Kohlmaier, G. and B. von Sartory, 1988, p. 498
39 At the same exhibition Peter Behrens built a winter garden in the Austrian Pavilion in an arts and crafts manner; Marrey, B., 1997, p.175
40 Architects: Jacques Adnet and René Coulon
41 A product newly launched by Saint-Gobain under the name 'Verisolith'
42 Marrey, B., 1997, p.78
43 Taut's further glass buildings: glass dome in the light well of Mittag department store in Magdeburg (1913/14), glass lantern in the entrance pavilion to apartment house no. 34 a Tiergartenstrasse in Berlin (1912); on the subject of 'Frühlicht' and 'Gläserne Kette': *Bruno Taut*, exhib. cat., 1980
44 De Long, D. G., 1998, pp.152, 158
45 Engineer: Walter Bauersfeld, in collaboration with the company Dyckerhoff & Widmann; Kind, F., in *Betonatlas*, 2002, p. 23
46 Buckminster Fuller, *Inventions* (1983), quoted from Pawley, M., 1990, p. 115
47 The project was designed at the same time as the Climatroffice by Fuller with Norman Foster, and the Multihalle

at the Bundesgartenschau in Mannheim by Frei Otto, Ted Happold from Ove Arup and the architects K. Mutschler and J. Langner.

48 Architects: Davis, Brody, Chermayeff, Geismar, de Harak; engineers: David Geiger and Horst Berger

49 Heinle, E. and J. Schlaich, 1996, p.192

50 Turak, T., 1986: on the 1893 exhibition in Chicago in particular see chapter 12, p.303ff.

51 All these architects were prominent representatives of the Beaux-Arts system that had been exported to the USA; Bancroft, H. H., 1893, p. 65; Pfammatter, U., 1997, pp. 265–93

52 Jenney, W., in Inland Architect, vol. XVII, no. 5, Chicago, June 1891; see also Pfammatter, U., 1997, p.175

53 Alongside the Crystal Palace from 1851 that measured 616 x 144 m; this building stood until 1936.

54 Bancroft, H. H., 1894, extensive description of the Horticultural Building: pp. 427–50 and 464 f.

55 Turak, T., 1986, p. 315 ff.

56 Kohlmaier, G. and B. von Sartory, 1988, p. 329

57 Lemoine, B., 1986, p.155 ff.; Graefe, R., 1989, pp. 99–116

58 Josef Albers, Marcel Breuer, Walter Gropius among others; in addition, John Dewey, John Cage and Robert Rauschenberg and many more studied and taught here.

59 Elucidations by Jörg Schlaich, in Heinle, E. and J. Schlaich, 1996, pp. 155, 173 and 180

60 The experiments made with concrete constructions from 1900 onwards are examined in chapter 4.

61 Up until the beginning of the 1980s a further 300,000 geodesic domes were built. Heinle, E. and J. Schlaich, 1996, p.157

62 Comprehensive report by Fuller, in Krause, J. and Lichtenstein, C., 1999, pp. 238–45

63 Hix, J., 1974, p.193 ff.; Frei Otto, 1995, p.120 f.

64 Heinle, E. and J. Schlaich, 1996, p.155; Nerdinger, W. (ed), 2005

65 Horden, R., 1995, pp. 94–101

66 This project followed the study at a seminar at Karlsruhe University in 1980 which in turn referred to a student workshop run by Haller at MIT in 1976, where an attempt was made to produce the space capsule out of raw material from the moon; Haller, F. 1988, Doc. 3.6.0–3.6.6 as well as Wichmann, H. (ed.), 1989, p. 280 ff.

67 He belonged to the 'Structure 3' team at Ove Arup, which was headed by Ted Happold and worked together with Frei Otto, who introduced Rogers to the team: Rice, P. 1994, p. 25

68 From 1969 onwards Frei Otto also ran his own design and development in Warmbronn Atelier, near Stuttgart.

69 Frei Otto and Bodo Rasch, 1995, p. 45

70 Holgate, A., 1997, pp. 64–79; Schlaich, I. and R. Bergermann, 2003; Nerdinger, W. (ed), 2005.

71 The American 'sustainable development' movement started to become effective in the mid-1980s, when a group of East Coast architects moved the solar architecture phase out of the hands of 'grass roots' and 'shelter and society' tinkerers and led a transition to more binding concepts with European references: Giessen, D. (ed) 2002

72 Jodidio, P., 1997, pp.116–21

73 Together with Richard Horden

74 Norman Foster, 1988, pp.154–57; on the SwissRe Tower see chapter 5, case study 82

75 Rice, P., 1994

76 Within the firm of Ove Arup & Partners, with T. Barker.

77 Dini, M., 1983, pp.74–79; Renzo Piano Building Workshop, in a+u, 3/1989, pp.104–15; Brookes, A. J., 1991, pp. 60–63; Renzo Piano Building Workshop, in process architecture, 100/1992, pp.132–39; Rice, P., 1994, p.107 ff.; Piano, R., 1997, pp. 82–85

78 Work on the technology and construction was also carried out with Ove Arup & Partners and, in this case also, with T. Barker: Renzo Piano Building Workshop, in a+u, 3/1989, p.117

79 After the Centre Pompidou, Rice set up the engineering consultancy firm RFR in Paris together with Martin Francis, who had designed the curtain wall in the Willis Faber office building in Ipswich for Foster, and with Ian Ritchie, who worked with both Martin Francis in Ipswich and with Peter Rice at Ove Arup. The most important constructions in the area of glass architecture in Paris in the 1980s and 1990s originate from this team. The RFR team was finally expanded by the inclusion of the engineer Henry Bardsley (who worked with Peter Rice at Ove Arup and with Renzo Piano), and the architect Hugh Dutton, a graduate of the Architectural Association in London.

80 Brookes, A. J., 1991, pp. 88–91; Rice, P., 1994, p.110 ff.; Rice, P., 1995

81 Rice P., 1995, p. 29

82 Peter Rice, quoted in ARCH+, no.102, Jan. 1990, p. 44 f.

83 Rice, P., 1995, pp.124–26

84 Architects: Richard Brosi, Robert Obrist

85 Pfammatter, U. (ed.), 1995, pp.103–07

86 Heinz Isler, Frei Otto and others worked as consultants.

87 Holgate, A., 1997, pp.104–09; Bögle, A., P.C. Schmal and I. Flagge (eds.), 2003, p. 120–121.

88 Holgate, A., 1997, p.110 ff.

89 Architect: Michel Macary (built 1993): Marrey, B. and J. Ferrier, 1997, p.183

90 J. Schlaich, in Heinle, E and J. Schlaich, 1996, p.156

91 Horden Cherry Lee Architects, London

92 Since 1996; Horden, R., 1999; Horden, R., 2005

93 Blaser, W. (ed.), 1995, p. 94 ff.; Horden, R., 1996

94 Blaser, W. (ed.), 1995, p.71 ff.

95 Behling. S. and St. (eds.), 1999; cf. also the contribution from U. Knaack, in: Fassade, 3/2002, pp. 5–9

96 Schittich, C. 1998, pp. 282–85

97 Frei Otto, 1995, p.149 ff.

98 Chris Williams, Cecil Balmond among others; Balmond, C., 2002; Williams, C., 2004

99 Mike Cook and Steve Brown from Happold's office, as well as Chris Williams, mathematician at Bath University; Foster, N., 2001, p. 46

100 Giedion, S., 1928, p. 55, in depth in chapter 2

101 Foster, N., et al., 2001; Anderson, R., 2000

102 Eden: The inside story. The Eden Project, Bodelva, St Austell, Cornwall, 2002 (DVD)

103 Pearman, H., in Davey, P. and H. Pearman, 2000, p.7; NGP = Nicholas Grimshaw & Partners.

104 Quotation and essential details in ARUP Journal, no.1, 2002, pp. 3–12 (authors: Chris Barrettt, Andy Bascombe, Mark Bostock, Hugh Collis, Geoff Farnham, Alistair Guthrie)

105 For example, in England at Arup London in collaboration with the glass industry; in Switzerland, in addition to university institutes, above all at planning firms (among others Daniel Meyer from the engineering office of Meyer & Lüchinger, Zurich), in firms in the metal/glass branch that had their own testing departments (among others Schmidlin AG, Aesch, Baselland) and at glass manufacturers such as Glas-Trösch, who played a leading role in research and development

106 Extensive description by W. Sobek, in Fassade, 3/1999, pp. 59; see also idem in Schittich, C. et al. (eds.), 1998, p.106 f. as well as S. Behling, in Behling, S. and St. (eds.), 1999, pp.110–13

107 Compagno, A., in Fassade, 3/1998, pp. 5–11, as well as Behling, S. and St. (eds.), 1999, pp.114–17.

108 Broad description of glass research and practical examples in Compagno, A., 2002 (5th edition); Behling, S. and St. (eds.), 1999; Achilles, A. et al. (eds.), 2003; on material technology see Stattmann, N., 2000

109 Schittich, C., (ed.), 1998, pp. 282–85

110 Sobek, W., 2004, p.108 ff.

111 Schéou, A. (ed.), 1997, pp. 36–45; Falter, H., in Achilles, A. et al. (eds.), 2003, p.73 f.; Hugentobler, P., 2004

112 Shigeru Ban, 1999

113 French partner architects: Jean de Gastines and Philip Gumuchdjian; official competition publication: Communauté d'Agglomération de Metz Métropole, CAMM (ed.), 2004; Shigeru Ban's project: pp. 39–56

2 Building as an Art or the Art of Building?

1 Heinrich Heine, 1843, quoted from Treue, W. and K.-H. Manegold, 1966 p. 85 f.

2 For the history and significance of ECAM, see Pfammatter, U., 1997 p. 103 ff.

3 Engineering graduate from the polytechnic school in Karlsruhe, first professor of civil engineering at the Swiss Federal Institute of Technology in Zurich, founded in 1855; Pfammatter, U., 1997, p. 239 ff.

4 After its sale to the state in 1857, ECAM, which, since it was founded in 1829/30, had not differentiated in this way, also primarily trained engineers. Two years previously, the Zürcher Polytechnikum had been founded with, for the first time in the history of polytechnic schools, different departments.

5 Even Brunel in his guise as president of the building commission, of which Mathew Digby Wyatt was also a member, saw a link to Crystal Palace; see below

6 Frank Newby, in Picon A. (ed.), 1997, p. 353

7 Pfamatter, U., 1997, chaps. 1 and 2

8 Architect: Pierre-Louis Renaud, engineer: Louis Sévène; 1865–69

9 Architect: Jacob Ignaz Hittorff; engineer Edouard Couche; 1861–65

10 Architect: François-Alexandre Duquesney; engineer: Pierre-Alexandre Cabanel de Sermet; 1847–52

11 Architect: Sir Gilbert Scott, engineers: William Henry Barlow and Rowland Mason Ordish; 1863–73; Ordish had worked since 1850 for Fox & Henderson (see Crystal Palace below)

12 Named after the reign of Queen Victoria (1837–1901), in the first few years of which Euston Station was built

13 Maurer, B., 1998, p. 295 (in Culmann's "technical journey description" of England)

14 Maurer, B., 1998, p. 298

15 Lemoine, B., 1986, p. 304; Pfammatter, U., 1997, p. 203

16 Auguste Renoir, qv. from Sagner-Düchting, K., 1994, p. 94 f.

17 Pfammatter, U., 1997, p.73–76

18 Parissien, S., 1997, p.100 ff.

19 Pfammatter, U. 1997, pp. 293–301

20 Thanks to the disbanding of the state-owned railway construction company in 1849, Cramer-Klett was able to secure most of the follow-up contracts, such as buildings and bridges and steam machines. Early on, the entrepreneur and pioneer substituted production on demand for supply production. In order to raise the capital he founded banks, such as the Darmstädter Bank (1853). Numerous subsidiaries followed, and by 1868 the company had achieved the status of a veritable industrial and financial operation. In 1880 Cramer-Klett founded the reinsurance company Münchener Rückversicherungsgesellschaft and later MAN (Maschinenfabrik Augsburg-Nürnberg AG). In 1867–68 in Switzerland, Klett built the railway shed in the main station in Zurich, for which it also compiled the working plans (the architecture of the entire complex was inspired by Semper) and in 1913 MAN constructed and assembled the railway shed at Badischer Bahnhof II in Basle (architect Karl Moser); Stutz, 1983, pp.176 f., 238 and 240.

For a history of the company see Die Geschichte der MAN, 1895; Bitterauf, O., Die Begründung und Entwicklung der MAN, 1924; 100 Jahre Geschichte der MAN, 1940.

21 It linked the industrial region of the Midland with London, which was to be decisive for the construction of Crystal Palace.

22 He studied under Friedrich von Gärtner at the Academy in Munich (1822).

23 August von Voit built the Winter Garden for Maximillian II in the southern part of the Residence in Munich (1854; with Franz Jakob Kreuter), the Large Palm Building in the Old Botanical Garden (1860–65) as well as the Winter Garden for Ludwig II in the northern part of the Residence (1867–69); Kohlmaier, G. and B. von Sartory, 1988, pp. 454–60.

24 There is an illustration of this French-inspired construction by Leo von Klenze, a pupil of Durand, who influenced the École Polytechnique school of thought, in: Pfammatter U., 1997, p.75 f.

25 Built directly before and during the planning of the Glass Palace (1852–54)

26 Biographical notes in: Hütsch, V., 1985, pp.76–77; Picon A., (ed.), 1977, pp. 210 and 238 f.

27 Two investors in railways, (the Duke of Buccleuch, the co-owner of the Furness Railway, and the Earl of Ellsmere), three architects (Charles Barry, R. Cockerell and T. L. Ronaldson), as well as three engineers (I. K. Brunel, W. Cubitt and R. Stephenson); the most famous representatives in the higher-ranking Exhibition Committee in-

cluded Henry Cole and Matthew Digby Wyatt, in the Finance Committee, Lord Granville and W. E. Gladstone, and in a special commission, Lyon Plyfair; Gibbs-Smith, C. H., 1950, p. 36

28 Project authors: Isambard Kingdom Brunel, Matthew Digby Wyatt, Owen Jones

29 Size: 160,000 square feet

30 The felling of 600,000 square feet of forest that would have been necessary, the danger of fire and the construction time in winter spoke against the use of wood as a construction material; nor could the requisite uninterrupted supply of wood by barge, and with it the opening date, have been guaranteed. A solid construction was ruled out on account of it being impossible to produce six million bricks in six months and dry, fire and lay them in winter; there was no alternative but to construct the edifice using iron and glass based on buildings in London and New York; the Exhibition of the Industry of all Nations in New York was also held in 1853–54; Hütsch, V., 1985, p. 14

31 Qv. Hütsch, V., 1985, p. 19

32 The 3,300 supports and 2,159 girders in Crystal Palace consisted of 3,800 tons of cast and 700 tons of wrought iron; 100,000 square metres of glass as well as some 40 kilometres of wooden 'Paxton gutters' were laid; in addition, 20,000 cubic metres of wood were required for the 'Paxton gutters', the floors and galleries, which is why, though purported to be fireproof, Crystal Palace actually burnt down 85 years later, in 1936. In Munich, around 1,700 tons of cast iron and almost 20,000 square meters of glass (37,000 glass panels) were used; here, too, some 10,000 m³ of wood was used; however, when the building was later converted into a greenhouse the elongated iron profile bars had to be clad in wood. The Glass Palace in Munich also fell victim to fire, in this case arson, in 1931, five years before Crystal Palace.

33 Three weeks before the building was handed over, an additional, unintended second gallery was erected (a wooden construction; construction time: 7½ days). As a result, the usable space increased in size by 30,000 to 210,000 square feet (17,900 square metres).

34 Furthermore, in London almost half the time, approx. 12 days (from 12 to 24 June), was wasted trying to win over all the specialist and political decision-makers to the first version of the project; this involved consulting the Society of Arts, the engineers Stephenson, Barlow and Brunel, the Building Commission and its individual members, and, ultimately, Prince Albert. Paxton quickly engaged the services of William Henry Barlow to check the calculations for the size of the load-bearing elements: on 15 June 1850, four days after his first sketch!

35 The contract was officially awarded on 26 June 1850.

36 In transforming Paxton's concept into precise work drawings Fox was assisted by the young engineer Rowland Mason Ordish (1824–86). He had been working at Fox & Henderson since 1850 and (as a 26-year-old) in principle took over the company's draughtsman's duties.

37 Durant, St., 1994; Lemoine, B., 1986, p. 228 ff.; on school culture: Pfammatter, U., 1997

38 Giedion, S., 1928, p. 55

39 Angus Low, qv, in: Durant, St., 1994, p. 56 f.

40 Peters, T. F., 1996

41 Whereas Five-Lilles & Cie., with on average 250 workers, daily erected four pre-fabricated parts of the framework with three sets of scaffolding, which needed two days to be transported, Cail & Cie., with 215 workers on the building site every day, divided the framework into six components that were manufactured on site and needed five sets of scaffolding cranes for it, but which needed only 1½ hours to be erected and taken down again; both companies reached the middle after six months; Durant, St., 1994, p. 23 f.

42 On Suchov's different visions for a major hall for the *All Russian Exhibition* in Nizhny Novgorod 1896: Graefe, R., 1989, p. 184 ff.

43 Antonio Sant'Elia: born 1888 in Como, died 1916 in battle in World War I; biography in Caramel, L., 1987, pp. 298–301. On the occasion of the first exhibition of Lombard architecture, the Messaggio by Antonio Sant'Elia impressed Marinetti (the founder of the futurist movement) so that it appeared in the exhibition catalogue on 1 August 1914 as *Manifesto dell' archtiectura futurista* in the futurist newspaper *La Voce;* Banham, R., 1964, chap. 10; likewise German translation, though less eloquent in Schmidt-Bergmann, H. (ed.), 1993, p. 230–35; English translation in Caramel, L., 1987, p. 302 f.; on the placing of *futurismo* in an architectural history and political context: Pfammatter, U., 1996, chap. 3 and Pfammatter, U., 2005

44 Quoted from Banham, R., 1964, p. 104 f.

45 The regime's guiding principles were based on the 'antichità' (represented by the traditionalists of the 'Scuola di Roma') and 'Modernità' (represented in the Milan Novecento group and the supporters of the Architettura Razionale and the Gruppo 7 from Como) as well as on 'nuovo futurismo'; Pfammatter, U., 1996, chap. 3

46 Berger, H., 1996, p. 29 f; Heinle, E., Schlaich, J., 1996, p. 193

47 Gruppo Toscano was an association, founded in 1932, of the young, recently graduated architects Nello Baroni, Italo Gamberini, Sarre Guarnieri, Leonardo Lusanna and Pier Niccolò Berardi with the Florentine professor and renowned architect Giovanni Michelucci. Under the overall control of the railway company a studio was set up headed by the engineer Gino Checcucci; the construction work was awarded to the Rome construction company Decio Costanzi; see Savi, V., in Berti, P., 1993, pp. 43–45

48 Pfammatter, U., 1996, pp. 95–97, 99 f., 103 f., also the sources in Patetta, L., 1972, p. 363 ff.

49 The test assignment was the competiton for the Palazzo del Littorio in Rome in 1934: Pfammatter, U., 2005

50 Home to the famous Biblioteca Laurenziana

51 'Autarchia debate', in Pfammatter, U., 1996, chap. 3

52 Pfammatter, U., 1996, p. 99 f., see also the sources for this in Patetta, L., 1972, p. 315 ff.

53 The construction portrayals used here stem from a four-week workshop organised by the École d'Architecture et Urbanisme de Genève, which led to an exhibition of this 'De-Composition Project' and the previously mentioned catalogue or monograph *La Nuova Stazione di Firenze*; responsible for the students' work: Prof. Jean Claude Ludi, École d'Architecture et Urbanisme de Genève; published in Berti, P. (ed.), 1993, annex

54 Quoted from Krausse, J. and C., Liechtenstein, 1999, p. 394

55 Description in Behling, S. and St., (eds.), 1999, p. 114 f.

56 Paronesso, A., Passera, R., 2003, pp. 6–12

57 Paronesso, A., Passera, R., 2003

58 Berger, H., 1996, p. 15

59 Heinle, E., Schlaich, J., 1996, p. 192; Berger, H., 1996, p. 15; Koch, K.-M., 2004, pp. 44 and 115

60 Peter Rice, quoted in Rice, 1996, p. 25

61 Competition success against 687 competitors; jury president: Jean Prouvé ›architects: Richard Rogers, Renzo Piano, Cuno Brullmann for mobile elements; engineers 'Structure 3' at Ove Arup & Partners with Peter Rice, Ted Happold, Lenart Grut et al.; Competition 1971, commissioning 1978

62 Mattie, E., 1998, p. 235 ff.

63 Together with Martin Francis, an engineer and the inventor of the glass façade for the Willis-Faber office building in Ipswich, and Ian Ritchie, who worked with Francis in Ipswich and Rice at Arup; under Rice's supervision RFR developed almost all the new structural glazing constructions in Paris until his death in 1992, such as, the glass pavilions at the museum in La Villette and the greenhouses in Parc André Citroën (see chap. 1, case study 10).

64 'Key speech' by Ove Arup in the annex of this book

65 By way of example: New Bangkok International Airport; architects: Murphy/Jahn; engineer: Werner Sobek

66 Charles de Gaulle airport, Paris (architects: Paul Andreu, Jean-Marie Dutillheul; engineers: RFR); Berlin Brandenburg International airport, (architects: von Gerkan, Marg und Partner); long-distance station at Frankfurt airport (architects: Bothe Richter Teherani; engineer: Binnewies)

67 Marrey, B. and J. Ferrier, 1997, p. 183

68 The first big wheel was an invention by the English engineer G. W. G. Ferris, who made it for the *World's Columbian Fair* in 1893 in Chicago; the diameter was 76 metres: Picon, A. (ed.), 1997, p. 539

69 Extensive portrayal in Powell, K., 1993

70 The asymmetry is the result of the irregular curvature of the tracks due to the fifth track, which veers westward on account of its location and requires a steeper arch in the framework.

71 Span 115 metres, height 45 metres; see case study 22.

72 Grimshaw, quoted from Powell, K. (ed.), 1993, p. 241

73 Together with the construction company YRM Anthony Hunt Associates; Powell, K. (ed.), 1993, annex p. 252

74 Grimshaw, quoted from Powell, K. (ed.), 1993, p. 245 f.

75 Grimshaw, quoted from Powell, K. (ed.), 1993, p. 243; read Grimshaw's lecture ("Structure, Space and Skin"), which he gave in the Design Museum in London on 15 October 1992, in its entirety; printed in ibid., pp. 236–43

76 Jörg Schlaich on the occasion of a lecture at the "New Dialogues Between Architects and Engineers" symposium at the Hochschule für Wirtschaft und Technik (HTW) in Chur, Switzerland, construction and design department, 5 November 2004

77 Accompanying text to *BRT-Fächer*, Hamburg, 2003

3 How Concrete Became Lighter – 100 Years of Concrete Pioneers

1 On the history of the pre-industrial use of concrete and on the development of cement as a binder: Straub, H., 1992, pp. 267–69

2 Picon, A., 1997, p. 311

3 At the transition from the purely functional greenhouse to the architecturally ambitious glasshouse, cf. chapter 1

4 Straub, H., 1992, p. 270

5 Coignet also supported his former school in his function as vice-president of the school council; Guillet, L., 1929, p. 310 f. and 264; Pfammatter, U., 1997, pp. 187–93

6 Drawn 1900/01 for the Rome prize that he won at the École des Beaux Arts in Paris

7 Lecture for the group 'Opbouw' in February 1921 in Rotterdam, in Oud, J. J. P: *Über die zukünftige Baukunst und ihre architektonischen Möglichkeiten*, in ibid., 1926, p. 23 f.

8 Congrès Internationaux d'Architecture Moderne: Steinmann, M. (ed.), 1979

9 Quoted from Steinmann, M. (ed.), 1979, p. 12 ff.

10 Pfammatter, U., 1996, section 3

11 Gruppo 7, Nota 4: *Una nuova epoca arcaica*, in the journal *La Rassegna Italiana*, May 1927, quoted and translated into German in Pfammatter, U., 1996, p. 184 f.

12 Pfammatter, U., 1996, section 4, and Pfammatter, U., 2005

13 Rowe, C. and R. Slutzky (with B. Hoesli), 1989

14 Frampton, K., 1987, chapter 10

15 Further sources in Frampton, K., 1987, p. 335

16 The urban project *Cité Industrielle* was first published in 1917, in 164 plates. It is not known how many were shown at the first presentation in 1904.

17 Jullian, R. (ed.), 1989, p. 18

18 This traditional technique was particularly widespread in North Africa, but also in the area of southern France around Lyons, where Garnier was born and worked; François Coignet, father of Edmond, initially also used the Pisé technique in his work in Saint-Denis near Paris: Picon, A. (ed.), 1997, p. 129

19 Garnier felt close sympathies with the socialist workers movement of his native city Lyons; references by René Jullian, in ibid. (ed.), 1989, p. 10, as well as Frampton, K., 1987, pp. 100–04

20 During his stay in Rome Tony Garnier also took part in the reconstruction work on the ruins of the ancient city of Tusculum. In 1904 he submitted his modern urban project, as well as an elevation of a reconstruction of Tusculum, to the Académie des Beaux-Arts.

21 Claude Henri Saint-Simon (1760–1825); principle work: *Catéchisme des industriels* (1823/24); his reflections formed the philosophical and political connection in the founding of the École Centrale des Arts et Manufactures in Paris (1829/30).

22 Julius Posener in the foreword, in Jullian, R. (ed.), 1989, p. 8

23 El Lissitzky, in: *ABC*, no. 1. 1924, p. 3 f.; the editorial department of *ABC* was made up of Emil Roth, Hans Schmidt and Mart Stam. The headquarters were in Thalwil near Zurich.

24 *ABC*, no. 3/4, 1925, p. 1

25 *ABC*, no. 3/4, 1925, p. 5 (edge column)
26 Von Moos, St. (ed.), 1987, no. 13, December 1921, pp. 1525–42
27 Published also in Le Corbusier's *Vers une architecture*, Paris 1923 (first German edition: *Kommende Baukunst*, edited by Hans Hildebrand, Stuttgart 1926; re-issued in: *Bauwelt Fundamente*, vol. 2 (U. Conrads and others, eds.), Braunschweig/Wiesbaden 1964, reprinted 2000
28 Boesiger. W. and H. Girsberger (eds.), 1967, p. 24
29 Contributions by Wolf Hanak and Rolf Schaal in *Le Corbusier im Brennpunkt. Vorträge an der Abteilung für Architektur ETHZ*, Zurich 1988, pp. 104–09 and pp. 124–31
30 Jenger, J. (ed.), 2002, p. 142 and p. 151f.
31 Garino, Cl., 1995
32 8 January 1886: first patent in Brussels with the proposal to take up the tension forces in a ceiling slab by means of iron reinforcement; 8 August 1892: second patent for France under the title "Combinaison particulière du métal et du ciment en vue de la création de poutraisons très légères et de haute résistance" (Brevet No. 223546; same patent as for Belgium from 8 February 1892); Delhumeau, G., in Picon, A. (ed.), 1997, pp. 223–25
33 Moulin du Dru, Raffinerei de Sucre Bernard Frères in Lille; Hackelsberger, Ch., 1988, p. 75ff.; Delhumeau, G., 1999, pp. 81–97
34 Delhumeaus, G., in Picon, A. (ed.), 1997, p. 223
35 Numerous branches in France as well as innumerable licenced companies spread the concrete technology throughout the world. The company 'Bétons armés Hennebique' remained in existence until 1967 and from its headquarters at no. 1 rue Danton in Paris worked on about 150,000 projects, the majority of which were carried out by licenced firms, whose detail plans were checked in Paris.
36 In contrast to the École Polytechnique, where mathematics, which had assumed dominance during the Enlightenment, shaped scientific and technical thought and action, at the ECAM theoretical and applied chemistry permeated all disciplines and specialised areas; the École Polytechnique (EP) was founded in Paris directly after the revolution (1794/95), the dominant science was 'Géometrie Descriptive' which was introduced by Gaspard Monge. The first architecture textbook to treat applied chemistry in depth was written by Charles-Louis Mary, a former 'Polytechnicien' and the first teacher of architecture at the ECAM; Pfammatter, U., 1997, p. 40ff. (EP) and p. 103ff. (ECAM)
37 Dumas produced the construction drawings and the calculations for the first reinforced concrete bridge near Châtellerault. Léon Guillet, a school biographer at the ECAM, mentions a series of further 'architect-engineers', who graduated from this school in the special area of concrete between 1895 and 1897 – that is, during the pioneering period of reinforced concrete technology – and who formed a first generation of 'Ingénieurs de ciment armé': Flament, Papa, Richaux and Serra (graduated 1895), Béra, Latron and Quost (1896), Genouville and Guéritte (1897); Guillet, L., 1929, p. 311
38 All project plans were examined, checked and stamped at a central office in Paris.
39 Swiss National Library, Bern, architect: Oeschger (1931; renovated and restored 2001); construction of the stands in the Hallestadion (indoor stadium) in Zurich, architect: Karl Engender; engineer: Robert A. Naef and Ernst Rathgeb (1938/39; cf. here Pfammatter, U., in Carrard, Ph. and M. Hanak (eds.), 2005, pp. 49–58) and many others
40 Architect: Ettore Fagiuoli: engineer: Angelo Invernizzi, who also built the big carport building in Venice, Italy (Isle of Tronchetto)
41 The abattoirs of Cincinnati and later the stockyards of Chicago were pioneering complexes for the 'continuous flow of material'. According to Sigfried Giedion, the invention of the 'assembly line' goes back to the grain mills with a continuous flow of material by Oliver Evans in Delaware 1783: Giedion, S., 1982, p. 105
42 His brother was director of the Trussed Concrete Steel Company; the patent: "Kahn System of Reinforced Concrete"; Hildebrand, G., 1974, p. 29ff.
43 Banham, R., 1990, chapter 3
44 For example, the Perret brothers: Ateliers Esders, Paris, 1919/20, Musée des Travaux publics, Paris, 1936–38, Notre-Dame Le Raincy, Seine-Saint-Denis, 1922/23
45 1884–1954; *Oberpostbaurat* (chief post office building official) in Bavaria (1920–30), teacher at the Technische Hochschule (TH) Munich until expelled in 1933, after 1945 rector of the TH Munich; best-known building: post office at Goetheplatz, Munich, 1931–33
46 ADGB: Allgemeiner Deutscher Gewerkschaftsbund; Droste, M., 1999, pp. 188–217
47 Complete biography of the company 'Perret Frères' in Cohen; J.-L., 2002, chapter 3
48 Pierre Vago, journalist, in *L'Architecture d'Aujourd'hui*, no. VII, October 1932, p. 19
49 At that time the president of the editorial committee of the journal *Techniques et Architecture* was August Perret himself!
50 Capacity to take the standard load of 200 kg/m^2 is guaranteed; technical description by P. Poitevin in Rassegna, 1986, p. 32ff.
51 Abram, J., in Rassegna, 1986, p. 14, as well as chapter 4, case studies 53 and 54 in the present book
52 Delhumeau, G. et. al. (eds.), 1993, p. 156, fig. 146 (Borsalino), and p. 160f., figs. 150 and 151
53 Precise description in *Schweizerische Bauzeitung*, no. 25, 22 June 1912, pp. 333–38
54 Documentation and virtual tour at: www.fskb.ch/Architekturgalerie (author with M. Homberger and T. Suter)
55 It was acquired in 2000 by Hanspeter Setz, the former owner of the transport company Setz, since then rented out and maintained.
56 Werner, J., and the city of Karlsruhe (eds.), 1997, 2 vols.
57 Ford, H., 1923
58 Hebeisen, W., 1999
59 Banham, R., 1990, pp. 149–59
60 Ford, H., 1923, p. 1; on the other side of 'Fordism' see, for example, Sinclair, U., 1936
61 Competition 1983, construction period 1985–93; Renzo Piano Building Workshop, 1992, pp. 140–47; Piano, R., 1997, pp. 90–97
62 Fanelli, G., 1985, p. 26f.
63 Exhaustive history and building history, also on the ancillary lightweight construction buildings in Idsinga, T., 1986
64 Hüter, K.-H., 1976
65 Pfammatter, U., 2002, p. 54
66 Gropius, W., quoted in Wingler, H. M. (ed.), 1997, p. 19
67 Wingler, H. M., 1975, p. 383
68 Gropius, W. (ed.), 1926; Kutschke, C., in *Rassegna* 15, 1983, p. 75; Jaeggi, A., 1994
69 Marti. P. (ed.), 1996: numerous warehouses and manufacturing halls were carried out in the mushroom column system by Maillart & Cie.: the Giesshübel warehouse in Zurich (1910), the filter building in Rorschach (1912), the Eidgenössisches Getreidelager in Altdorf (1912), the cold storage house and warehouse of the company Gerhard & Hey in St Petersburg (1912), the Lance cardboard factory (1913/14), the shoe factory in Lyons (1914), later the Von Roll ironworks in Gerlafingen (1932), the Sihlpost in Zurich (1930), and many more.
70 Marti, P., 1997
71 The mushroom column introduced by the American C. A. P. Turner (1906, shortly before Maillart) did not achieve the architectural quality of Maillart's invention; Marti, P. (ed.), 1996, p. 44.
72 Muttoni, A., 2004, pp. 107–14
73 Kessler, A., 1996
74 Billington, D. P., 1997
75 Pfammatter, U., 1997, p. 287ff.
76 Grossman, E. G., 1996
77 Blaser, W., 1992
78 On the significance of this project in Wright's oeuvre in terms of tectonics and material technology: Frampton, K., 1994, pp. 73–75
79 Quinan, J., 1998, p. 83, figs. 13 and 14
80 Quinan, J., 1998, p. 87, figs. 26 and 27
81 In an attempt that then followed to span a 2-m-wide concrete arch over a span of 50 m, thanks to hundreds of pre-stressed steel cables 8 mm in diameter, he succeeded in keeping this arch under permanent pressure of 2,500 t structurally balanced and without deformation. Until into the 1930s Freyssinet achieved genuine records with a concrete setting time (for a compressive strength of 1,000 kg/cm^2) of 28 days, and for 500 kg/cm^2 of only 48 hours! Ordonet, J.A.F. in Picon, A. (ed.), 1997, p. 194 ff.
82 Torroja, E., 1961, p. 221; on the scaffolding technology in timber in Freyssinet's Plougastel bridge: ibid., p. 91
83 Polonyi, S., 1989, p. 74f.; see also the extensive description of shell construction in Joedicke, J. (ed.), 1962; on C.N.I.T.-Halle, see. idem.; pp. 82–87
84 Piccinato, L. (ed.), 1954
85 An extensive self-description of Heinz Hossdorf's 'hybrid statics' has been published: Hossdorf, H., 2003.
86 It served the electrification system of the Swiss Federal Railways in the area of Canton Valais; Brühwiler, E. (ed.), 2002, pp. 117–19
87 In a contribution to the *Schweizerische Bauzeitung* in 1939 Sarassin emphasises the economic aspects of this method of building with inclined cylindrical shells. After this work Sarrasin was invited to take part as an expert in similar construction projects, for example, in France and in the French African colonies; Sarrasin, A., 1939, pp. 231–35
88 Extensively in Muttoni, A., 1999, p. 105ff.
89 Polonyi, S., 1989, p. 70
90 Polonyi, S., 1989, p. 71
91 Between 1942 and 1948 Nervi strongly urged the use of ferro-cement technology for ship-building, a theme later to be taken up again by his fellow-countryman, Renzo Piano.
92 'Steel Agreement', 22. 5. 1939
93 P. L. Nervi, 1963, quoted in: Polonyi, S., 1989, p. 77
94 Further important projects include the participation in the planning phase for the CNIT in Paris (1958) (already referred to in the section about Freyssinet), the Pirelli high-rise building with Gio Ponti in Milan (1955–59), The Palace of Labour at the *International Exhibition* in Turin in 1961, and the headquarters of the International Labour Organisation (ILO) in Geneva with Alberto Camenzind and Eugène Beaudouin (1966–78).The large audience hall in the Vatican, commissioned by Pope Paul VI, can be mentioned here as one of the concluding works (1967–70).
95 Polonyi, S., 1989, p. 76
96 Polonyi, S., 1989, p. 69; Joedicke, J. & E. N. Rogers (eds.), 1957
97 Campioli, A., 1998; Krippner, R., 1998; Bona, E. D., 1980; Mangiarotti, A., 1964/65
98 I am indebted to Jürg Conzett (Dipl. Ing., ETH Zurich, Chur, Switzerland) for the valuable reference to Riccardo Morandi's importance.
99 Picon, A., 1988
100 Prof. Walther Bauersfeld, physicist with Zeiss in the area of optics and precision mechanics, took up the idea of the civil engineer Oscar von Miller, the initiator of the Deutsches Museum in Munich, to develop a planetarium for this museum. Initially a prototype was to be built in Jena. With this aim in mind Bauersfeld turned to the engineer Mergler, who worked for the famous Nuremberg construction company, Dyckerhoff & Widmann.
101 Similar to the rings of iron chains in the Pantheon, the dome of St Peter's in Rome and in the dome of Florence Cathedral
102 Original version: Razon y ser de los tipos estructurales, Madrid, 1957.
103 Chapter 8; pp. 98–114
104 Torroja, E., 1961, p. 243f.
105 Reference from Ordonez and Vera, in Picon, A. (ed.), 1997, p. 506
106 Torroja, E., 1961, p. 114
107 Barthel, R. (ed.), 2001
108 Contribution from J. Tomlow, in Barthel, R. (ed.), 2001. pp. 11–16
109 Fathy, H., 1970; Cousin, J.-P., 1978: Steele, J. (ed.). 1988
110 Dieste's remarks in *Eladio Dieste – Frei Otto*, 1996, pp. 13–20
111 Ramm. E. and E. Schunck, P. Marti (eds.), Zurich 2002; Marti, P., Monsch, O., Schilling, B., 2005
112 Giralt-Miracle, D. (ed.), Barcelona, 2002
113 Virtual tour at: www.fskb.ch/Architekturgalerie (author with M. Homberger and T. Suter)
114 Sauer, C., 2003
115 Spatial structures made of strengthened polyester for a wood-processing workshop in Genoa 1965, a mobile plant for the production of sulphur in Pomezia 1966, a pavilion for the 14th Milan *Triennale* 1967, and the Pavilion of Italian Industry at the 1970 *Expo* in Osaka
116 Piano, R., 1997, p. 22
117 Conzett, J., commentary on the descriptions of constructions by Arup engineers, in *HCB-Betonkalender*, July 2000; cf. also *The Arup Journal*, no. 2, 1999, pp. 16–18; Balmond, C., 2002, pp. 309–43; the author gratefully used personal information supplied by Fred Illidio and Jürg Conzett.
118 Piano, R., 1997, p. 70
119 Nerdinger. W. (ed.), 2002, p. 150f.
120 Conzett, J., 2000, p. 4; Mostafari, M. (ed.), 2006, p. 11
121 Conzett, J., 2000, p. 5f. Naturally, the term 'point' is used in building to mean an adequately strong possibility of connecting materials.

122 Both buildings in Chur can be visited and walked through virtually at: www.fskb.ch/Architekturgalerie (author with M. Homberger and T. Suter).

123 Cf. Pfammatter, U. (ed.), 1995, Projects Centre Nature in Versailles and at Parc de la Villette, Paris 1976, p. 57ff.

124 For example, the leisure and shopping centre in Bern-Brünnen, Switzerland

125 For example, the Netherlands Pavilion at *Expo 2000* in Hanover

126 For instance, the project for the new Learning Centre of the École Polytechnique Fédérale de Lausanne EPFL, Switzerland; cf. EPFL (ed.), 2004, pp. 52–55 as well as EPFL/Revue Tracés (ed.), 2004

127 Cf. Irace, F. et al. (eds.), 2007, pp. 242–47

128 Cf. Behnisch, S. and Schuler, M., 2006, pp. 16–17

129 Cf. discussions between Cecil Balmond and Rem Koolhaas, in C. Balmond (with J. Smith), 2002

130 I am indebted to Jürg Conzett (Dipl. Ing.; ETH Zurich, Chur, Switzerland) for the valuable reference to Sergio Musmeci's importance.

4 The 'Liberated Façade' – From Wall to Partition to Skin

1 Semper, G., 1863, p. 276

2 *De re aedificatoria*, 1443–52

3 Borsi, F., 1986

4 Alberti, quoted from Theurer, M. (ed.), 1991, third book, eleventh chapter, p. 147

5 What Vitruvius had already seen was the build-up of the wall in layers: in contrast to the Greek master builders who produced a "continuous wall with a uniform thickness", the Romans built in a manner that allowed "rapid execution", "two outer layers with a filling between them": Vitruvius; *Ten Books on Architecture*, Second Book, Eighth Chapter: "The Kinds of Masonry"; cit. nach Fensterbusch, C. (ed.), 1981, S. 107

6 Eugène Viollet-le-Duc, in Düttmann, M. (ed.), 1993

7 Pfammatter, U., 2000, pp. 53–67; Szambien, W., 1984

8 With regard to the load-bearing skeleton, as well as the external shell, to withstand the forces of sun, wind, rain, and damp, fire, snow and violence; Alberti, in Theurer, M. (ed.), 1991, third book, eighth chapter, pp. 137–39

9 J.-N.-L. Durand, 1802–05, 1st section, pl. 3. On "the end of Vitruvianism": cf. the two chapters about Durand and Semper in Germann, G., 1980, pp. 229–54; Pfammatter, U., 2000, pp. 53–67

10 Giedion, S., 1976 (1941); Bannister, T., 1950; Skempton, A.W., 1962

11 Turak, T., 1986; Pfammatter, U., 2000, pp. 166–77 and pp. 285–90

12 Made known by Alfred Roth following the erection of Le Corbusier's two villas in the framework of the Werkbundsiedlung on the Weißenhof hill in Stuttgart 1927; Le Corbusier, 1927, pp. 5–7

13 Giedion, S., 1976 (1941), part III; Bannister, T., 1950, pp. 231–46; Skempton, A.W. and Johnson, H. R., 1962, pp. 175–86; Trinder, B., 1974; Condit. C.W., 1982, chapter 6

14 A theme that was to be taken up again later by the 'Chicago School' and in modernism by Richard Buckminster Fuller and Konrad Wachsmann as well as by the schools of thought that they influenced (Ove Arup, Peter Rice)

15 Reference to Wyatt's patent in Bannister, T., 1950, p. 244

16 The 'first British engineer' Thomas Telford planned and built the canal network; Pearce, R.M., 1978, Penfold, A., 1981

17 In Liverpool, where there is little sun in winter and where smoke and soot darkened the skies, solid building methods and 'hole-in-the-wall' windows made conditions in the workplace only worse. The conditions in the working class districts in Manchester, descriebed by Friedrich Engels, were even worse still – the excesses of Manchester Liberalism as shown in the questions of housing and hygiene in the workplace.

18 Skempton, A. W., 1959–60; Ronner, H. (ed.), 1982, pp. 50–58; Picon. A., (ed.), 1997, p. 455f.

19 Architect: François-Joseph Bélanger, engineer and enterpreneur: François Brunet

20 Lemoine, B., 1980

21 Marrey, B., 1989

22 From a few references by the architectural historian Henry-Russell Hitchcock we learn that Peter Ellis was not only an architect but also a civil engineer. H.-R. Hitchcock, after Woodward, G., 1956, p. 268: Hitchcock, H.-R., 1994. p. 329ff.

23 The builder, 20 January 1866, quoted from Woodward, G., 1956, p. 268f.

24 The different development of iron façades around and after 1850 in New York (New York Iron Works by James Bogardus and Daniel Badger) will be examined further below.

25 In 1958, the Liverpool School of Architecture (Professors R. Clarke and W. H. G. Housen) commendably remea-sured this building, made precise drawings of it and published them in the journal Architectural History, Journal of the Society of Architectural Historians, vol. 1, 1958, pp. 84–94 (supplement: *Records of Buildings*); the University of Liverpool holds the copyright of these drawings.

26 Reichen & Robert, 2003, p. 22ff.; Pélissier, A., 1994

27 Garner, J. S., 1992. pp. 43–73; on the 'Centralien' Émile Muller: Pfammatter, U., 2000, pp. 155–57

28 Émile Trélat, like Muller and Moisant, studied at the École Centrale des Arts et Manufactures in Paris; the founding of the École Spéciale, which still exists today, was supported initially by Viollet-le-Duc and Henri Labrouste: Pfammatter, U., 2000, p. 154f.

29 Armand Moisant received his degree at the École Centrale three years after William Le Baron Jenney, the founder of the 'Chicago School of Architecture', four years after Gustave Eiffel and one year before Victor Contamin, the builder of Palais des Machines at the Paris *World Exhibition* of 1889; on A. Moisant: Pfammatter, U., 2000. pp. 177–82

30 Between 1868 and 1889 the production of the company rose from 2,000 to 10,000t of steel structures annually; short portrait of the firm in Lemoine B., 1986, p. 303

31 Pfammatter, U., 2000, pp. 265–92, and sources mentioned therein

32 Christ Church by Benjamin Latrobe from 1808 in Washington, D. C., or the Chestnut Street Theatre (1820–22) and the United States Naval Asylum (1826–30), both built by William Strickland in Philadelphia, referred to an English tradition: Latrobe worked for the English architect C. R. Cockerell and for J. Smeaton, one of the leading engineers of the English industrial era; Strickland was a student of Latrobe's – the early American school of thought in the area of iron construction technology, which was inspired by England, developed in this manner.

33 James Bogardus was initially a clockmaker, inventive mechanic and builder in iron. He owed his knowledge of cast-iron techniques to Daniel Badger as well as to a long visit to Europe (1836–40): in 1848 he set up a foundry in New York and produced columns, beams and entire façades made of iron on an industrial basis.

34 In 1856 Bogardus published a textbook on this subject, as well as the project catalogue *Cast Iron Buildings: Their Construction and Advantages*.

35 Condit. C. W., 1982, p. 84f. and fig. 25

36 For example, the Trenton Iron Works, founded by Peter Cooper and Abram Hewitt, pioneers in the development of rolled-iron technology for tall buildings; they also built for Harper's and erected the Cooper Union: this was from the very start a multidisciplinary educational institute and was given a large auditorium, in which political demonstrations – later also by German anarchists such as Emma Goldman – were held. Later, the famous architecture, engineering and art school The Cooper Union for the Advancement of Science and Art was to develop out of it: Pfammatter, U., 2002, p. 52–60

37 Wanamaker, one of the pioneers of the American general store, commissioned architect John Kellum and the Cornell Iron Works of New York to erect this huge predecessor of the modern-day supermarket. It had a sales area of around 36,000 m² and after 100 years, was destroyed by fire in 1956.

38 Additionally, during a particularly dry autumn the fire brigade was called out on an almost daily basis and the firemen were exhausted, including the 'fire watcher', who stood in a stone tower that has been preserved as a landmark, and who at the decisive moment at 9 in the evening failed in his duty. A strong south wind whipped up a fire that was started by a cow knocking over with her hind leg a petroleum lamp in the stable of Pat O'Leary's house on De Koven Street in southern Chicago. The wind was so strong that the fire spread across the Chicago River and ultimately destroyed a large part of the city. The history of this fire forms the subject of a permanent exhibition in the museum of the Historical Society in Chicago.

39 Randall. F. A., 1949

40 They had been available for some time, in particular through the introduction around 1864 of the Bessemer process to the North American continent via Detroit. First production of 'Bessemer steel' in England in 1856 by Henry Bessemer (1813–98), through blowing air into molten pig iron in the Bessemer converter.

41 On 14 November 1891 in *The Engineering Record*, Chicago

42 In the same year Jenney set up an office partnership with William B. Mundie (1863–1939).

43 In his article "Chicago Frame": Rowe, C., 1956

44 On Jenney's biography: Turak, T., 1986

45 Influential 'philosophes' who also influenced Diderot's famed *Encyclopedia* included Voltaire, d'Alembert, and Condorcet: Pfammatter, U., 2000, pp. 22–24, 103–05.

46 Pfammatter, U., 2000, pp. 120–23

47 He appeared at numerous events, also internationally, for instance, at the international architecture congresses in Brussels in 1887, at the *World's Columbian Exposition* in 1893 and in Paris in 1900.

48 Reprinted and reworked version of the lecture by William Le Baron Jenney to the Chicago Architectural Sketch Club on 6 October 1890, published in *The Inland Architect and News Record*, vol. XVI, no.7, Dec. 1890, pp. 75–77 (archive and library of the University of Illinois)

49 Rowe, C., 1956

50 Giedion, S., 1929

51 Bruno Taut designed the Glaspavillon at the 1914 German Werkbund exhibition in Cologne, also for this company (see also section 1.2).

52 L., Mies van der Rohe, quoted from Frampton, K., 1993, p.178, from the text accompanying the publication on Mies's designs for high-rise buildings in the journal *G*, no.1, July 1923 (reprint Munich 1986)

53 Reference has already been made to the importance of this new way of thinking in the history of the concrete pioneers in chapter 3, and also to the fact that the concrete pre-stressing technique, which was invented by Freyssinet at around this same time, could not yet be used; the projects remained a vision: De Stijl, vol. VI., no. 6–7, p. 93

54 Bijvoet worked together with Duiker on numerous designs in Holland up to 1929, and was subsequently in Paris, after the collaboration with Duiker in the 1929 competition for a beach hotel in Salesel an der Elbe (today Dol Zàlezly) broke down completely; Molema, J., 1989, p.120

55 Semper, G., *Der Stil in den technischen und tektonischen Künsten* (1863); final chapter on 'Metallotechnik' quoted from Wingler, H. M. (ed) 1966, pp. 22–24; Pfammatter, U., 2000 in chapter on the Zurich Polytechnic, p. 225f.

56 Pruscha, C., 1997

57 Pfammatter, U., in: tec21, no. 45, 2003, pp. 6–10

58 Extensive background information on the history of the Luxfer Prism Company in Neumann, D., 1996; the explanation given here follow this contribution.

59 Title of an article in *The Inland Architect and News Record*, no. 34, 1900, p. 39f. quoted in Neumann, D., 1996, p. 26

60 Riley. T. (ed.), 1994

61 Section through construction with part of façade in Staib, G. (ed.), 1998, p. 24, fig. 1.1.32, as well as Herzog, T. et al. (eds.), 2004. p. 241; on the history of the building and the company, see Cieslik, J. and M. (eds.), 1997

62 Weber. H., 1961, pp. 42–47; Wilhelm, K. in *Rassegna* no. 15, 1983, p. 15ff.; Jaeggi, A., 1994.

63 De la Chevallerie, H., 1997, p. 28

64 *Zwei Wohnhäuser von Le Corbusier und Pierre Jeanneret* by Alfred Roth, Stuttgart 1927; reprint Stuttgart, 1977; the *Five Points* are on pp. 5–7.

65 Christian Sumi, who in research work carried out at the

ETH Zürich examined Le Corbusier's way of thinking about construction (using the examples of the Immeuble Clarté in Geneva compared to the Pavillon Suisse, the Maison Loucheur and the technological way of thinking of Jean Prouvé), describes the detail design of the Maison Loucheur as 'bricolage', working with building materials readily available on the market without any inventions in terms of material technology or detail design; much the same can be said about the details of the Pavillon Suisse; Sumi, C., 1989, p. 57.

66 Biographical notes in Sulzer, P, (ed.), 1991, pp. 47–51

67 Sulzer, P., 1991; Sulzer, P., 1995, 2000, 2005 and 2007 (Œuvre complète) and 2002 (highlights); Eveno, C. and Grillet, T., 1990; Lavalou, A. (ed.), 2001

68 Sulzer, P., 2000, pp.186–209

69 Rice, P, and Dutton, H., 1995, p.122 f.

70 Archieri, J.-F. (ed.), 1990

71 Piano, R. in Domus no. 807, September, 1998, p. 52 f.

72 Diethelm, A., in Schweizer Ingenieur und Architekt, SIA, no. 3, 1999, pp. 22–26

73 Joedicke. J. (ed.), 1963, pp.174–79

74 Examples: Aldo van Eyck worked at the TU Delft from 1960, Jacob B. Bakema from 1963, the University of Karls-ruhe (TH) engaged Egon Eiermann (1947–70), the Conservatoire des Arts et Métiers in Paris appointed Jean Prouvé (1957–70), the universities in Rome and Florence appointed Adalberto Libera (1952–55 and 1962/63) as well as Luigi Nervi (in Rome from 1948), Sigfried Giedion, Alfred Roth (from 1955), Rino Tami (1957–61), as well as Werner Moser influenced the training at the ETH Zurich in advance of the famous 'basic design courses' of Bernhard Hoesli and Heinz Ronner (from 1954): Pfammatter, U., 1998, p. 9

75 Giedion, S., 1965; Wachsmann, K., 1959; Rowe, C., and Slutzky, R., 1964

76 Newman, O. (ed.), 1961; Risselada, M. and van den Heuvel, D. (eds.), 2005

77 Lüchinger, A. (ed.), 1981

78 Pfammatter, U., 1998, pp. 9-12

79 Alexander, C., 1977; dissertation of C. Alexander, see idem 1964

80 Tegethoff. W., 2001

81 Thau, C. and Vindum, K. (eds.), 2002

82 Numerous other architects influenced post-war modernism; this area is currently being examined; for part of it see Zschokke, W. and Hanak, M. (eds.), 2001

83 Pfammatter, U., 1996, especially chapters 4 and 5, as well as idem 2005

84 The reasons for his change to an avant-garde approach to architecture after the Riehl House (Potsdam-Neubabels-berg, 1906/07), the competition entry for the Bismarck Memorial (1910) and the designs for the Perls House in

Berlin-Zehlendorf (built 1911/12) or the Kröller-Müller House in Wassenaar (Netherlands, 1912/13, never built) remain unclear. Was it the rejection of his Kröller-Müller project for the Exhibition for Unknown Architects, organised by Gropius in 1991, where the latter disqualified Mies's proposals with the remark: "We cannot exhibit it, we are looking for something completely different" quoted from Mertins, D., 2001, p.107. Mies moved in the field of tension between the traditional handcraft of the training as a stonemason that he had received in his father's business in Aachen, and the modern, industrially oriented work in the office of Peter Behrens in Berlin (1908–10, at the same time as Gropius and shortly before Le Corbusier).

85 Quoted from Frampton, K., 1993, p.178, from Johnson, Philip C., Mies van der Rohe, New York 1947, p.183, or from the journal G, no. 1, July 1923 (reprinted Munich 1986)

86 Five years after the seizure of power by Hitler and the National Socialist German Workers Party he moved to the USA, taking on a teaching job at Armour (later Illinois) Institute of Technology in Chicago (IIT), as well as the redesign of the institute campus (1938–58).

87 In collaboration with Schmidt, Garden & Erikson, C. F. Murphy Associates and A. Epstein & Sons, Inc; on the planning and Mies's high-rise buildings in Lafayette Park, Detroit: Waldheim, C., (ed.), 2004

88 Interestingly, these include one of his mentors, John A. Holabird – the son of William Holabird, who once worked with William Le Baron Jenney in the pioneering era of the Chicago School – who as a member of the appointment committee at IIT was partly responsible for selecting Mies as head of the architecture school. After completing his studies at West Point engineering school (1907) John Holabird attended the École des Beaux-Arts in Paris, where he met John W. Root, who graduated from Cornell University in 1909; John W. Root was the son of John Root, co-owner of the equally well-known firm of Burnham & Root in Chicago. After their studies John Holabird and John W. Root returned to America and worked in the firm of Holabird & Roche, and again after World War I, and in 1928 set up the successor firm Holabird & Root in Chicago. Their designs and projects followed the influence of the Beaux-Arts and a monumental art deco style, as with Paul Philippe Cret – until the emergence of Mies van der Rohe's new kind of work after 1938, when Mies came to influence the architectural approach of the younger generation of architects; Blaser, W., 1992

89 While Owings ran the Chicago office, Skidmore moved to New York to open up a branch office there; Krinsky, C. H., 1988, p. 6

90 Kostof, S., 1977, pp. 325–30; Picon, A., (ed.), 1997, pp. 457, 213 and 251 f.

91 Bunshaft monograph: Krinsky, C. H., 1988; on Lever House see pp.18–26; on the designer Nathalie de Bloisat at SOM, see SOM-journal no. 4, D-Ostfildern, 2006, p.133 ff.

92 The soap and soda factory was founded in 1888/89 with the Sunlight brand in Port Sunlight City on the far side of the River Mersey in Liverpool; architect: William Owen; following the erection of the factory the construction of the 'corporate city' continued until 1913; Williams, E., 1988

93 Lewis Mumford in The New Yorker, 9 August 1952, pp. 48–54; quoted from Krinsky, C. H., 1988, p.18; on Lewis Mumford's Sidewalk Critic see Wojtowicz, R. (ed.), 1998

94 Blaser, W., 1999, vertical section, p. 47

95 Bruce Graham designed the John Hancock Center (1969) and the Sears Tower (1974), among other buildings, together with the engineer Fazlur R. Khan.

96 4.0 x 1.8 m; glass point fixings on a grid measuring 1.8 x 1.33 m. Structural glazing projects compared in Brookes, A. J. and Grech, C., 1991, p. 90 f.

97 Coderch, G. and Fochs, C. (eds.), 1995

98 Perrault, D., 1994

99 Behnisch & Partner (ed.), 1987, pp. 209–23; Katholische Universität Eichstätt (ed.), 1987; Behnisch, Behnisch & Partner (ed.), 2003

100 Kaltenbach, F. (ed.), 2004

101 Peter Rice, Martin Francis, Ian Ritchie

102 Rice P., 1995, p. 9

103 See 'The Key Speech' by Ove Arup in the appendix to this book

104 Rice P., 1994, p.76 f.

105 Rice P., in Arch+, no.102, January 1990, pp. 42–45

106 Piano, R., 1997, p. 99

107 Piano, R., 1997, pp.138–45

108 Compagno, A., 1999, p.120 ff.

109 Schneider + Schumacher (eds.), 1997, pp.132–51; Architektur-Galerie am Weißenhof, Stuttgart (ed.), 2004, p. 30 ff.

110 Sauerbruch & Hutton (eds.), 1996, p. 21 ff.; Sauerbruch & Hutton (eds.), 2000

111 Leach, N. and Wei-Guo, Xu (eds.), 2004

112 Details of construction in Fassade, no. 4, 2002, p. 40 f.

113 Mack, G., 2002

114 Virtual tour: www.fskb.ch/Architekturgalerie (author with M. Homberger and T. Suter)

115 Reconstruction drawing by Pascal Ninivaggi, Prouvé seminar at Stuttgart University, 1989/90

116 Details of the construction in Baumeister, no. 11, 1998, pp. 32–35

5 Process Thinking Conquers Construction

1 Hager, F.-P., 1986; Pfammatter, U., 1995 (diss.), pp. 422–446

2 Which was to prove to be true: Thomas Telford, the "first English engineer", a great builder of roads, bridges and canals, was a trained bricklayer; Joseph Paxton, the inspir-ator behind and organiser of Crystal Palace in London in 1851, was also a railroad engineer and greenhouse designer, and trained as a gardener.

3 Locke, J., 1970 and 1981

4 Thomas Farnolls Pritchard as architect and engineer, and the entrepreneurs Abraham Darby III and his brother Samuel, as well as John Wilkinson (Willey Ironworks)

5 Trinder, B., 1974

6 Hounshell, D. A., 1984; Giedion, S., 1948

7 Rice, P., 1994, p. 60 ff.

8 Mayer, H. M. and Wade, R. C., 1969; Giedion, S., 1941; Condit, C. W., 1982; Cavanagh, T., 1997

9 Pfammatter, U., 2000, p. 265 ff.

10 Brecher, J., 1975; Wehler, H.-U., 1987; Adams, W. P., 2000

11 Hitchcock, H.-R., 1942, comment on fig.73 in the appendix

12 Heinz Ronner archive

13 Encyclopedia Americana, New York, 1976

14 The following is according to Hounshell, D. A., 1985, pp.153–87

15 Production statistics from 1841 to 1885: Hounshell, D. A., 1984, table 4.1

16 By way of example: Upton Sinclair, The Jungle, and Jack

London, The Iron Heel; whereas Sinclair stuck to facts, London creates a visionary perspective from this bleak chapter of American history.

17 Pfammatter, U., 2000, pp.166–77

18 Jenney published his basic thoughts on the matter as well as a sort of 'tableau' of the French construction school of thought in the magazine The Engineering Record, New York, 14 Nov. 1891, pp. 388–90 (see ill.4.2.9).

19 In 1894 he relocated his office to New York, where he was responsible, for example, for Daniel H. Burnham's Flat Iron (Fuller) Building (1902) and the Waldorf Astoria Hotel (replaced in 1930–31 by the Empire State Building). Peters, Tom F. in Picon, A. (ed.), 1997, p. 33 and Condit, C. W., 1964, pp. 119 and 123

20 In 1995–96 the building was roughly restored, Inland Architect, July/August 1996, p. 11

21 On Frank Lloyd Wright's relationship with industry, Frampton, K., 1993 and 1994

22 Frampton K., 1993, pp.106–16

23 Wright, Frank Lloyd, In the Cause of Architecture IV: The Meaning of Materials – Wood, 1928, quoted in Pfeiffer, B. B. (ed.), 1992, p. 283

24 Frampton K., in T. Riley (ed.), 1994, p. 58

25 According to Sigfried Giedion, the assembly belt was invented by Oliver Evans, who, in 1783, used an Archimedes screw to drive the entire belt and bucket chain assembly system in his grain mill: Giedion, S., 1948

26 Giedion, S., 1941

27 Neutra, R., 1930

28 Banham, R., 1986

29 Including Bruno Taut, Hugo Häring, Otto R. Salvisberg, Hans Scharoun, Walter Gropius, Otto Bartning and others: Huse, N., (ed.), 1984

30 For documentation and evaluaton, Silke Hopf, degree thesis, ETH Zurich, Department of Architecture, Zurich, 1986

31 Marbach, U., and A. Rüegg, (eds.), 1990; on Baba-Werk-bund Housing Estate Prague: Templ, St. (ed.), 1999; on Wiener Werkbundsiedlung; Krischanitz, A. and Kapfinger, O. (eds.), 1985

32 Herbert, G., 1978

33 Hildebrand, G., 1974. p. 5–24

34 Albert Kahn, quoted from Hildebrand, G., 1974, p. 14

35 The Architectural Forum, no. 2, August 1938 (special edition on Albert Kahn); see Ueli Zbinden, in Zbinden, U., Wassmer, M. and Fischer, F. (eds.), 2006, pp. 6–11

36 Bothe, R., 1977

37 Steinmann, M., (ed.), 1979, pp. 35–71

38 Ernst May, in Das Neue Frankfurt, no. 5, 1925–27

39 This method of assembly was patented.

40 Ernst May in Das Neue Frankfurt, no. 2, 1926–27, p. 37

41 Ernst May in Das Neue Frankfurt, no. 2, 1926–27, p. 38

42 Bothe, R., 1977, pp.148–65

43 Rasch, H., and B., 1927

44 Rasch, H., and B., 1927, p.169
45 *Detail* no.12, 2004 (edition devoted to Micro Architecture), pp.1417–21
46 Literature on this topic (a selection): Smith, E.A.T., (ed.), 1989; Steiner D., (ed.), 1997; Stiller, A., 1998; Steurer, A., 1999; Buisson, E. and Billard, T., 2004; *Detail* no.12, 2004; on Jean Prouvé's model types: see further below
47 Kovatsch, M., (ed.), 1985
48 In 1934, Albert Frey, a Swiss architect working in the USA, devised concepts for the American Ministry of Agriculture to make farmers' houses self-sufficient; Rosa, I. (ed.), 1995, p.58 f.
49 Diagram of the 1927 Dymaxion house type in *L'architecture d'aujourd'hui*, no. 6, May/June 1946 (special Richard J. Neutra edition), p.78
50 Le Corbusier, quoted from Rüegg, A., 1987, p.135 ff.
51 Willis, C. (ed.), 1998
52 "Les maisons voisins", published in *L'Esprit Nouveau*, no. 2, Nov. 1920, pp. 211–15; "Maisons en série", in *L'Esprit Nouveau*, no.13, Dec. 1921, pp.1525–42; "Industrialisation du bâtiment", in *L'Esprit Nouveau*, no. 20, Jan./Feb. 1924; Nerdinger, W., in v. Moos, S. (ed.), 1987, pp.168–73, as well as appendix p. 284
53 Russel, B., 1981

54 Giedion, S., 1941
55 John Holabird had helped Mies to get his position at IIT; Blaser, W., (ed.), 1992, p.112
56 Brevet no. 849.762: "Construction à ossature métallique démontable", in Sulzer, P., 2000, pp. 230–36 (Prouvé inventory no.786); a compilation of important patents entitled *Prouvé inventore: 32 breviti*, in *Domus*, no. 807, Sept. 1998, pp. 52–59
57 Sulzer, P., 2000, p. 238 f. (Prouvé inventory no.790)
58 Patent no. 865.235: "Baraque démontable", Sulzer, P., 2000, p. 261, (Prouvé inventory no. 851)
59 Sulzer, P., 2000, pp. 264–71, (Prouvé inventory no. 854)
60 Sulzer, P., 2005, p.118, (Prouvé inventory no.1089); V. Wegesack, A. (ed.), 2005, p.176 ff.; Ludwig, M., 1998
61 Wasmuth Verlag, Berlin, reprint 1995, pp. 26–29 and pp.109–28
62 Konrad Wachsmann, idem., 1930, p. 26
63 Wachsmann and Gropius's directly preliminary project was The Packaged House, their first joint concept: Herbert, G., 1984.
64 Wachsmann, K., 1959, p.154
65 Herbert, G., 1984, pp. 304–07
66 *Werk, Bauen + Wohnen*, no.7/8, 1981, special edition *Die Solothurner Schule*, 1981; Wälchli, R. (ed.), 2005
67 Wichmann, H. (ed.), 1989

68 Bona, E. D. (ed.), 1980, pp. 40–43
69 Bona, E. D. (ed.), 1980, p. 44
70 Krippner, R., 1998 and 1999; Ackermann, K. (ed.), 1985; Bona, E. D. (ed.), 1980; Mangiarotti A., 1964–65
71 Herzog, T., idem (ed.), 1988, pp. 5–15
72 Development and realisation as of 1988: *Detail*, no. 5, 1998, pp.761–66
73 Saggio, A., (ed.), 1999
74 Leach N. and Xu Wei-Guo (eds.), 2004
75 Xu Wei-Guo in Leach, N. and Xu Wei-Guo (eds.), 2004, p.13
76 Piano, R., 1997, p. 22
77 Piano, R., 1997, p.136
78 Giralt-Miracle, D., 2002; Crippa, M.A., 2003
79 Burry, M. in Leach, N., Turnbull, D. and Williams, C. (eds.), 2004, pp. 22–33
80 Balmond, C. in Leach, N., Turnbull, D. and Williams, C. (eds.), 2004, p.131; see also Balmond, C., 2002 and Toyo Ito, 2005
81 National Committee on Wood Utilization et al. (ed.), 1953
82 Condit, C. W., 1982, caption to fig. 39
83 Busquets i Grau, J., (ed.), 1992, p. 87
84 Rasch, H. and B., 1927, p. 63

6 "Sustainable Building Design" – A Future Project

1 United Nations Conference on the Environment and Development, UNCED, Rio de Janeiro, 1992
2 Alberti L.B., in Theuer, M. (ed.), Darmstadt, 1991; in particular, *Viertes Buch: Über Anlagen allgemeiner Art*, p.173 ff.
3 Viollet-Le-Duc, E., in Düttmann, M. (ed.), 1993, p. 34 f.; see also Colins, G. R., (ed.), 1983
4 Landes. D. S., 1968; Hobsbawm, E. J., 1969
5 Pfammatter, U., 1995 (diss.)
6 Rogers, R., 1995; Kisho Kurokawa represents a fundamentally different concept of sustainability in his "Symbiosis Manifesto": Kurokawa, K., 2005
7 Crystal Palace, 1850–51, the pavilion for the first *World Exhibition* can be regarded as a landmark in the new mindset of sustainable building: renewable resources such as greenery, natural ventilation and fountains were used to condition the air in the 85,000-square-metre exhibition hall.
8 Pfammatter, U., 2000, pp. 53–67
9 Pfammatter, U., in *archithese*, no. 4, 2004, pp. 20–27
10 Giedion, S., 1928, p. 55; Giedion refers to Vierendeel's criticism: " Les sommiers du Palais des Machines présentent encore un autre défaut, ils sont trop évidés.", in idem, p. 55, note 3
11 Rice, P., 1994, p. 46
12 Foster, Norman, 1998, p.170
13 Piano, R., 1997, p. 82
14 Rice, P., 1997, p.107
15 The author is indebted to Andreas Reinhard and Rolf Luchsinger of prospective concepts ag for information, views and discussions (see www.airlight.biz).
16 Example: Patent no.1.163.238 from 1958; Sulzer, P., 1991, pp. 40–43
17 Ferguson, E. S., 1992
18 Shigeru Ban, 1999, p.7
19 Frei Otto, quoted in Shigeru Ban, 1999, p. 32
20 Shigeru Ban, 2001 (in the introduction)
21 Koch, K.-M. (ed.), 2004
22 Norman Foster, 1988, pp. 50–52
23 In this context see, among other things, Swiss R & D studies: Prof. Otto Künzle at ETH Zurich (www.hbt.arch.ethz.ch); Prof. Thomas Keller, EPFL Lausanne (www.cclab.ch); Borch, I. et al. (eds.), 2004; Genzel, E. and Voigt, P., 2005; Hirsinger, Q. and Ternaux, E. (ed.), 2006; Hirsinger, Q., Ternaux, E. and Kula, D., 2007.

24 Rice, P. and Dutton, H., 1995
25 Behling, S., and St., (eds.) 1999; Wurm, J., 2007
26 Geist, J. Fr., 1979, p. 216
27 Jodidio, P., 1997, pp.102–07; on BRT: Weiss, K.-D. (ed.), Basle u. a. 2005, pp. 328–47 ('Double-XX'), pp. 360–85 on 'Berliner Bogen'
28 This was based on the manual *Atrien der Zukunft* (atriums of the future), initiated and co-written by the author of this book; see *Autorenkollektiv*, 2005; Elsaid, P., 2000; further experts in climate engineering: Klaus Daniels, Gerhard Hausladen (TU München), Matthias Schuler (Transsolar), among many others.
29 Zola, É., 1957 (1873); Marrey, B., 1989
30 Schéou, A. (ed.), 1997
31 Hochschule für Technik und Wirtschaft Chur, HTW, Dept. of Construction and Design
32 See various projects in *Glas*, no. 6, 2004, Leinfelden-Echterdingen 2004
33 Framework engineers: Buro Happold; HVACR fittings and light planning: HL-Technik, Klaus Daniels; façade consulting and technology: Josef Gartner & Co.
34 Feireiss, K., (ed.), 2002, pp. 214–41; Nagel, A. and Frankenheim, K., 1995, pp. 59–62
35 Dominique Perrault, exhibition catalogue, 1994, pp. 49–64; Perrault, D., 1996, pp. 56–59
36 Gissen, D. (ed.), 2002
37 Blaser, W., 1995, pp.70–81
38 Participating students in the final peak_lab project: Yann Friedl, Felix Häusler, Christian Heck, Christine Neumann, Florian Uhl (Technical University Munich); Vitus Erni, Stefan Gassmann, Daniel Schatzmann, Christian Schmidiger, David Schneeberger (HTA Lucerne, architecture); Christoph Baumann, Iwan Plüss (HTA Lucerne, heating, ventilation, climate control)
39 Pfammatter, U., in *Schweizer Ingenieur und Architekt SI + A* (Swiss engineer and architect), no. 42, 20 Oct. 2000, pp. 4–7; Pfammatter, U., in *Intelligente Architektur*, no. 9/10, 2003, pp. 48–51; Horden, R. and Pfammatter, U. (eds.), Technical University Munich, 2003; Klasz, W., in *Detail*, no.12, 2004, pp.1459–1462; Klasz, W., in Design Report, no.1, 2005, pp.16–25
40 Project development: October 2002 to July 2003
41 *Architecture d'aujourd'hui*, no.140, October/November 1968 (Tiers-Monde); *The Architectural Review*, no. 898, December 1971 (*India Today*); *Bauen + Wohnen*, no.7/8,

July/August, 1976 (*Bauen südlich des 35. Breitengrades*); *Bauen + Wohnen*, no.10, October 1977 (*Dritte Welt- Kontinuität der Moderne unter einheimischen Architekten*) and many more
42 Bianca, S., 2000; Jodidio, P., 2007
43 Project, research work and publication series by the Habitat Group, ETH Zurich School of Architecture, Prof. Herbert E. Kramel, 1995–2000
44 Shigeru Ban, 1999, p. 58
45 Shigeru Ban, 2001; project 'mobile_emergency_platform' by the author of this book
46 Nachtigall, W. and Blüchel, K. G., 2000
47 Rogers, R., 1995
48 A realised concept for rainwater use as part of a major project and urban quarter: planning and building section, Daimler-Benz on Potsdamer Platz in Berlin: *Deutsche Bauzeitung* (DBZ), no. 2, 1999; as a current example of an urban sustainable concept: 'Riverpare Development', Pittsburgh, PA, USA, Behnisch architects and Transsolar Climate Engineering Stuttgart, project 2007–15, Behnisch, St. and Schuler, M., 2006.
49 Torre, S. (ed.), 1977, p. 45; Banham, R., 1969, p. 98 f.
50 Bianca, S., 2000
51 Topic: Microarchitecture, in *Detail*, no.12, 2004
52 Buchanan, P. (ed.), 1994, p. 2
53 Piano R., 1997, p. 254 f.; see also Irace, F. et al. (ed.), 2007; Conforti, C. and Dal Co, F., 2007.
54 Sauerbruch Hutton Architects, 2000: *Intelligente Architektur*, no. 21, 1999, pp. 29–41; *Baumeister*, no. 2, 2000, pp.19–31
55 Burgard, R. (ed.), 2004, pp.111–19
56 Piano R. 1997, p.174; see also Zabalbeascoa, A. and Marcos, J.R. (eds.), 1988; Buchanan, P. (ed.), 2000, pp. 86–116
57 Piano, R., 1997, p.178
58 See Collins, G. R., (ed.), 1983
59 Zettlitzer, W., in Burgard, R. (ed.), 2004, p.125
60 Davis, M., 1981
61 Wick J., *Kunststoffe in der Architektur, 1950–1980*, 2000
62 Adam, H., et al. (eds.), 2003
63 Blaser, W. (ed.), 1995, p.112 f.

The Key Speech

1 In 1970, Arup worked on numerous projects in the Middle East.
2 In 1970, Arup's office in Scotland had just begun to offer a multidisciplinary engineering service for construction projects.
3 The financial director at the time

Bibliography

ABC – *Beiträge zum Bauen 1924–1928*, no. 6, 1925.

Achilles, A. et al. (ed.), *Glasklar. Produkte und Technologien zum Einsatz von Glas in der Architektur*, Munich 2003.

Ackermann, K. (ed.), *Industriebau*, Stuttgart 1985 (exh.cat., Universität Stuttgart 1984).

Adam, H. u. U. Jehle-Schulte Strathaus, Ph. Ursprung (eds.), *Theo Hotz Architecture 1949–2002*, Baden, Switzerland 2003.

Adams, W. P., *Die USA vor 1900* (vol. 1) and *Die USA im 20. Jahrhundert* (vol. 2), Munich 2000.

Akademie der Künste Berlin (ed.), *Bruno Taut 1880–1938*, Berlin 1980 (exh. cat., Akademie der Künste Berlin).

Albert Kahn, *Industrial Buildings*, in: *The Architectural Forum*, no. 2, Aug. 1938.

Alexander, Ch., *Notes on the Synthesis of Form*, London 1964 (Dissertation Harvard University Press, Cambridge, Mass.).

Alexander, Ch., *A Pattern Language. Towns, Buildings, Construction*, New York 1977.

Allgemeine Bauzeitung (ed. L. Förster), Vienna 1837, no. 48 (pp. 395–400) and no. 49 (pp. 403–408).

Anderson, R., *The Great Court and The British Museum*, London 2000.

Anderson, St., *Eladio Dieste: Principled Builder and Master in Structural Art, in: Architecture and Urbanism* (a + u), no. 395, Aug. 2003, pp. 63–137.

Angelo Mangiarotti 1955–1964, Tokyo 1964/65.

Archieri, J.-F. (ed.), *Prouvé. Cours du CNAM 1957–1970. Essai de reconstitution du cours à partir des archives Jean Prouvé*, Liège 1990.

Architektur-Galerie am Weißenhof (ed.), *Schneider + Schumacher*, Stuttgart 2004.

Arch+, no. 172, Dec. 2004: *Material*.

Aregger, H., and O. Glaus, *Hochhaus und Stadtplanung*, Zurich 1967.

Arup, Ove, *The Key Speech*, 9 July 1970, in: Dunster, D., *Arup on Engineering*, Berlin 1996, pp. 262–273.

ARUP-Journal, no. 1, 2002, London 2002.

ARUP-Journal, no. 2, 1999, London 1999.

Autorenkollektiv, *Atrien der Zukunft*, Basle 2005.

Balmond, C. (with J. Smith), *Informal*, Munich 2002.

Bancroft, H. H., *The Book of the Fair. An Historical and Descriptive Presentation of the World's Science, Art, and Industry, as Viewed through the Columbian Exposition at Chicago in 1893*, vol. 1, New York 1894.

Banham, R., *Theory and Design in the First Machine Age*, London 1960.

Banham, R., *The Architecture of the Well-tempered Environment*, London 1969.

Banham, R., *A Concrete Atlantis*, Cambridge, Mass., 1986).

Bannister, T., *The First Iron-Framed Buildings*, in: *The Architectural Review*, no. 640, Apr. 1950, pp. 281–346.

Barbieri, U., *J. J. P. Oud*, Zurich, Munich 1989 (1st edn. Bologna 1986).

Barthel, R. (ed.), *Eladio Dieste. Form und Konstruktion*, Munich 2001 (Technische Universität Munich, Lehrstuhl für Hochbaustatik und Tragwerksplanung).

Bauhaus-Archiv Museum für Gestaltung Berlin (ed.), *Der vorbildliche Architekt. Mies van der Rohes Architekturunterricht 1930–1958 am Bauhaus und in Chicago*, Berlin 1986.

Behling, S., and. St. (eds.), *Glas. Konstruktion und Technologie in der Architektur*, Munich 1999.

Behnisch, Behnisch & Partner, *Bauten und Entwürfe – Buildings and Designs*, Basle u. a. 2003.

Behnisch, St., and M. Schuler (eds.), *Ecology.Design.Synergy, Behnisch Architekten + Transsolar ClimateEngineering*, Berlin, Stuttgart 2006 (exh. cat.).

Behnisch & Partner (ed.), *Architekten Behnisch & Partner. Arbeiten aus den Jahren 1952–1987*, Stuttgart 1987.

Benevolo, L., *Die Geschichte der Stadt*, Frankfurt a. M./New York 1990 (1st German edn. 1983; ital. 1st edn. Rome, Bari 1975).

Berger, H., *Light Structures – Structures of Light. The Art and Engineering of Tensile Architecture*, Basle 1996.

Berti, P., and V. Savi (eds.), *La Nuova Stazione di Firenze*, Florence 1993 (exh. cat., together with Ferrovie dello Stato, Stazione di Firenze and École d'Architecture et Urbanisme de Genève).

Bianca, St., *Urban Form in the Arab World. Past and Present*, Zurich 2000 (Institut ORL, ETH Zurich).

Billington, D. P., *Robert Maillart. Builder, Designer, and Artist*, Cambridge University Press 1997.

Blaser, W. (ed.), *Chicago Architecture. Holabird & Root 1880–1992*, Basle 1992.

Blaser, W. (ed.), *Renzo Piano: Centre Karnak. Kulturzentrum der Karnak*, Basle 2001.

Blaser, W. with R. Horden (eds.), *Light tech – towards a light architecture; Ausblick auf eine leichte Architektur*, Basle 1995.

Blaser, W., *Mies van der Rohe*, Basle 1997.

Blaser, W., *Lake Shore Drive Apartments. Wohnhochhaus*, Basle 1999.

Bock, Th., *Robotnik im Bauwesen*, in: *Detail*, no. 6, 1988, pp. 1005–12.

Bögle, A., P. C. Schmal, and I. Flagge (eds.), *leicht weit – light structures. Jörg Schlaich and Rudolf Bergermann*, Munich 2003 (exh. cat., DAM Frankfurt a. M.).

Boesiger, W., and H. Girsberger (eds.), *Le Corbusier 1910–65*, Zurich 1967.

Boesiger, W., and H. Girsberger (eds.), *Le Corbusier, Œuvre Complète 1929–1934*, Zurich 1974.

Boesiger, W., and H. Girsberger (eds.), *Le Corbusier, Œuvre Complète 1938–1946*, Zurich 1977.

Bona, E. D. (ed.), *Angelo Mangiarotti: il processo del costruire*, Milan 1980.

Borch, I. et al. (ed.), *Skins for Buildings. The Architect's Materials Sample Book*, Amsterdam 2004.

Borsi, F., *Leon Battista Alberti. Opera completa*, Milan 1986 (1st edn. 1973).

Bothe, R., *Die Frankfurter Kunstschule 1923–1933*, in: Wingler, H. M. (ed.), *Kunstschulreform 1900–1933*, Berlin 1977, pp. 141–99.

Brecher, J., *Streiks und Arbeiterrevolten. Amerikanische Arbeiterbewegung 1877–1970*, Frankfurt a. M. 1975.

Brookes, A. J., and Ch. Grech, *The Building Envelope*, Guilford, Surrey, England, 1990).

Brühwiler, E., and P. Frey (eds.), *Alexandre Sarrasin. Structures en béton armé, audace et invention*, Lausanne 2002 (exh. cat., Presses polytechniques et universitaires romands).

Buchanan, P. (ed.), *Renzo Piano Building Workshop. Complete Works*, vol. 1, 2, 3, 4, 5, London/New York 1994–2000.

Buisson, E., and Th. Billard (eds.), *The Presence of the Case Study Houses*, Basle 2004.

Burgard, R. (ed.), *Kunststoffe und freie Formen. Ein Werkbuch*, Vienna/New York 2004.

Busquets i Grau, J. (ed.), *Cerdà i el seu Eixample a Barcelona*, Barcelona 1992 (report and exh. cat., Laboratori d'Urbanisme, Universitat Politècnica de Catalunya).

Campi, M. (ed.), *Skyscrapers. An Architectural Type*, Basle 2000 (a study at the ETH Zurich).

Campioli, A., *Mangiarotti e Milano*, in: *Domus*, no. 807, Sept. 1998 (Itinerario 148).

Caramel, L., and A. Longatti, *Antonio Sant'Elia. The Complete Works*, Milan/New York 1987.

Cars, J. des & P. Pinon, *Paris Haussmann*, Paris 1991 (exh. cat., Pavillon de l'Arsenal).

Cavanagh, T., *Balloon Houses: The Original Aspects of Conventional Wood-Frame Construction Re-examined*, in: *Journal of Architectural Education*, vol. 51, no. 1, Sept. 1997, pp. 5–15.

Chadwick, G. F., *The Works of Sir Joseph Paxton 1803–1865*, London 1961.

Cieslik, J.,and M. (eds.), *Die Geschichte der Margarete Steiff GmbH*, Jülich 1997 (1st edn. 1989).

Coderch, G., and C. Fochs (eds.), *Coderch. La Barceloneta*, Barcelona 1995.

Cohen, J.-L., and J. Abram, G. Lambert (eds.), *Encyclopédie Perret*, Paris 2002.

Cole, H., *Fifty Years of Public Work*, London 1884, vol. 1, pp. 116–205.

Collins, G. R. (ed.), *The Designs and Drawings of Antonio Gaudi*, New Jersey 1983.

Communauté d'Agglomération de Metz Métropole (ed.), *Centre Pompidou-Metz*, Paris 2004.

Compagno, A., *Bürogebäude B4 und B6*, in: *Fassade*, no. 4, 1999, pp. 33–39.

Compagno, A., *Intelligente Glasfassaden. Material, Anwendung, Gestaltung*, Basle 2002 (1st edn. 1995).

Condit, C. W., *The Chicago School of Architecture. A History of Commercial and Public Building in the Chicago Area 1875–1925*, Chicago/London 1964 (1st edn. 1952).

Condit, C. W., *American Building. Materials and Techniques from the Beginning of the Colonial Settlements to the Present*, Chicago/London 1982 (1st edn. 1968).

Conforti, C., and F. Dal Co (eds.), *Renzo Piano. gli schizzi*, Milan 2007.

Conrads, U. (ed.), *Programme und Manifeste zur Architektur des 20. Jahrhunderts*, Frankfurt a. M./Vienna 1964 (Bauwelt Fundamente, vol. 1; new edn. 2000).

Conzett, J., *Tragende Scheiben im Hochbau*, in: *Werk, Bauen + Wohnen*, no. 9, 1997.

Conzett, J., *Bemerkungen zu räumlichen Scheibensystemen*, in: *Schweizer Ingenieur und Architekt (SI + A)*, no. 26, Jun. 2000, pp. 4–8.

Conzett, J., *Structure as Space*, London 2005 (Architectural Association AA).

Cousin, J.-P., *Hassan Fathy*, in: *L'Architecture d'aujourd'hui*, no. 195, Feb. 1978, pp. 42–80.

Crippa, M. A., *Antoni Gaudi 1852–1926. Von der Natur zur Baukunst*, Cologne 2003.

Cuadra, M., *Weltflughäfen. Vision und Realität, Kultur und Technik, Geschichte und Gegenwart*, Hamburg 2002 (exh. cat., Deutsches Architekturmuseum Frankfurt a. M.).

Danesi, S., and L. Patetta (eds.), *Il razionalismo e l'architettura in Italia durante il fascismo*, Venice 1976 (exh. cat., La Biennale di Venezia).

Das Neue Frankfurt, Reprint in: Hirdina, H. (ed.), *Neues Bauen, Neues Gestalten. Das Neue Frankfurt/die neue stadt: eine Zeitschrift zwischen 1926 und 1933*, Berlin/Dresden 1984.

Davey, P., *Engineering for a Finite Planet. Sustainable Solutions by Buro Happold*, Basle 2009.

Davey, P., and H. Pearman, *Equilibrium. Nicholas Grimshaw & Partners*, in: *The Architectural Review* (supplement Sep. 2000) London 2000.

Davis, M., *A Wall for all Seasons*, in: *RIBA Journal*, Feb. 1981, pp. 55–57

De la Chevallerie, H., *Gebauter Gedanke. Die Zeche Zollverein Schacht XII in Essen*, Ostfildern 1997 (Universität Witten/Herdecke).

De Long, D. G., *Frank Lloyd Wright. Die lebendige Stadt*, Geneva/Milan 1998 (exh. cat., Vitra Design Museum).

Delhumeau, G. et al. (ed.), *Le béton en représentation. La mémoire photographique de l'entreprise Hennebique 1890–1930*, Paris 1993.

Delhumeau, G., *Hennebique*, in: Picon, A. (ed.), *L'Art de l'Ingénieur. Constructeur, Entrepreneur, Inventeur*, Paris 1997 (exh. cat., Centre Georges Pompidou Paris).

Delhumeau, G., *L'Invention du Béton Armé. Hennebique 1890–1914*, Paris 1999.

design report, no. 1, Jan. 2005: *Extrembedingungen*.

Diethelm, A., *Das FCW-Lagerhaus in Zürich-Altstetten*, in: *Schweizer Ingenieur und Architekt (SI + A)*, no. 3, 22 Jan. 1999, pp. 22–26.

Diethelm, A. (ed.), *Roland Rohn 1905–1971*, Zurich 2003 (Institut gta/ETH Zurich).

Dini, M., *Renzo Piano. Progetti e architetture 1964–1983*, Milan 1983 (2nd edn. 1992).

Droste, M., *Hannes Meyer 1889–1954. Architekt, Urbanist, Lehrer*, Berlin 1989 (exh. cat., Bauhaus-Archiv Berlin).

Dunster, D., *Arup on Engineering*, Berlin 1996.

Dupré, J., *Wolkenkratzer. Die Geschichte der berühmtesten und wichtigsten Wolkenkratzer der Welt*, Cologne/New York 1996.

Durand, J.-N.-L., *Précis des Leçons d'Architecture données à l'École Polytechnique*, vol. 2, Paris 1802–05, 2ème partie (new edn.: *Nouveau Précis*, Paris 1819/1817).

Durant, St., *Palais des Machines*, London 1994.

Düttmann, M. (ed.), *Viollet-le-Duc, É., Definitionen: Sieben Stichworte aus dem Dictionnaire raisonné de l'architecture française du XIe au XVIe siècle*, Basle 1993.

Ecole Polytechnique Fédérale de Lausanne EPFL (ed.), *Building the Future of Learning*, Lausanne, Switzerland 2004 (competition documentation).

Ecole Polytechnique Fédérale de Lausanne EPFL, and *Revue Tracés* (eds.), *learningcenter epfl*, Lausanne, Switzerland 2004 (project documentation SANAA).

Eladio Dieste – Frei Otto. Esperienze di architettura: generazioni a confronto, Mendrisio, Switzerland, 1996 (i Quaderni dell'Accademia di architettura Mendrisioo).

Elliott, C. D., *Technics and Architecture. The Development of Materials and Systems for Buildings*, Cambridge, Mass./London 1992.

Elsaid, P., *Das Atrium. Ursprünge, Bedeutung und Entwicklung*, Zurich 2000 (author's diploma studies, ETH Zurich, Department of Architecture).

Eveno, Cl., and Th. Grillet (eds.), *Jean Prouvé 'constructeur'*, Paris 1990 (exh. cat., Centre Georges Pompidou Paris).

Fabrikneubau in Dottikon der Schuhfabrik C. F. Bally AG in Schönenwerd, in: *Schweizerische Bauzeitung*, no. 25, 22 Jun. 1912, pp. 333–38.

Falter, H., *Geometrie und Verglasung*, in: Achilles, A. et al. (eds.), *Glasklar. Produkte und Technologien zum Einsatz von Glas in der Architektur*, Munich 2003, pp. 68–75.

Fanelli, G., *Stijl-Architektur. Der niederländische Beitrag zur frühen Moderne*, Stuttgart 1985 (1st edn. Rome/Bari 1983).

Fathy, H., *Construire avec le peuple*, Paris 1970 (vol. 2.; 1st edn. Cairo 1969).

Feireiss, K. (ed.), *Ingenhoven Overdiek und Partner. Energies*, Basle 2002.

Fensterbusch, C. (ed.), *Vitruv. Zehn Bücher über Architektur*, Darmstadt 1981 (1st edn. 1964).

Ferguson, E. S., *Engineering and the Mind's Eye*, Cambridge, Mass., 1992.

Fernandez-Galiano, L., *Mies van der Rohe Berlin/Chicago*, in: *AV Monografias*, 92, Nov./Dec. 2001.

Flagge, I. (ed.), *Hassan Fathy, Traumbilder der Architektur*, Frankfurt a. M. 2005 (exh. cat., Deutsches Architekturmuseum Frankfurt a. M.).

Flagge, I. et al. (ed.), *leicht weit – Light Structures. Jörg Schlaich, Rudolf Bergermann*, Munich u. a. 2003 (exh. cat., Deutsches Architekturmuseum Frankfurt a. M.).

Ford, H., *Mein Leben und Werk*, Leipzig 1923

Foster, N., and D. Sudjic, S. de Grey, *Norman Foster and The British Museum*, Munich 2001.

Frampton, K., *Modern Architecture. A Critical History*, London 1987 (1st edn. 1980).

Frampton, K., *Grundlagen der Architektur. Studien zur Kultur des Tektonischen*, Munich/Stuttgart 1993; on Mies van der Rohe: ch. 6, pp. 175–227.

Frampton, K., *Modernization and Mediation: Frank Lloyd Wright and the Impact of Technology*, in: Riley, T. (ed.), *Frank Lloyd Wright. Architect*, New York 1994 (exh. cat., Museum of Modern Art, New York).

Freitag, J. K., *Architectural Engineering, with Special Reference to High Building Construction*, New York 1904.

Freyssinet, E., *Mein Leben für den Betonbau (Selbstportrait)*, in: Haegermann, G. et al., *Vom Caementum zum Spannbeton*, Wiesbaden/Berlin 1964 (section C).

Garino, Cl., *Le Corbusier. De la Villa Turque à l'Esprit Nouveau*, Grandson, Switzerland, 1995.

Garner, J. S., *The Company Town. Architecture and Society in the Early Industrial Age*, New York/Oxford 1992.

Geist, J. Fr., *Passagen. Ein Bautyp des 19. Jahrhunderts*, Munich 1979 (1st edn. 1969).

Genzel, E., and P. Voigt, *Kunststoffbauten: Teil 1 – Die Pioniere*, Weimar 2005 (Bauhaus-Universität Weimar).

Germann, G., *Einführung in die Geschichte der Architekturtheorie*, Darmstadt 1980.

Geurst, J., and J. Molenaar, *Van der Vlugt. Architect 1894–1936*, Delft 1983.

Gibbs-Smith, C. H., *The Great Exhibition of 1851*, London 1950, Reprint 1964 (exh. cat., Victoria & Albert Museum).

Giedion, S., *Bauen in Frankreich. Bauen in Eisen. Bauen in Eisenbeton*, Leipzig/Berlin 1928.

Giedion, S., *Befreites Wohnen. Licht, Luft, Öffnung*, Zurich/Leipzig 1929.

Giedion, S., *Space, Time and Architecture*, Cambridge, Mass., 1941.

Giedion, S., *Mechanization Takes Command*, Oxford University Press 1948.

Giralt-Miracle, D. (ed.), *Gaudi. Exploring Form*, Barcelona 2002 (exh. cat., Barcelona City Council, Institut de Cultura).

Gissen, D. (ed.), *Big & Green. Towards Sustainable Architecture in the 21st Century*, New York 2002.

Glaeser, L. (ed.), *Ludwig Mies van der Rohe. Drawings in the Collection of the Museum of Modern Art*, New York 1969 (exh. cat.).

Godoli, E., *Il Futurismo. Guide all'architettura moderna*, Rome/Bari 1983.

Graefe, R., *Die Bogendächer von Philibert de l'Orme*, in: *Zur Geschichte des Konstruierens*, Stuttgart 1989, S. 99-116.

Graefe, R., *Hängedächer des 19. Jahrhunderts*, in: *Zur Geschichte des Konstruierens*, Stuttgart 1989.

Graefe, R. (ed.), *Zur Geschichte des Konstruierens*, Stuttgart 1989.

Grimshaw, N., *Fusion. Industrial Design*, London 1998.

Gropius, W. (ed.), *bauhaus 1*, Dessau 1926 (Bauhaus newspaper; facsimile reprint, bauhaus-archive Berlin, Nendeln 1977).

Gropius, W., *Internationale Architektur*, Reihe *Neue Bauhausbücher*, Mainz/Berlin 1981 (ed. H. M. Wingler, 1st edn. 1927).

Gropius, W., *bauhaus bauten dessau*, Reihe *Neue Bauhausbücher*, Berlin 1997 (Reprint).

Grossman, E. G., *The Civic Architecture of Paul Cret*, Cambridge University Press 1996.

Grube, O. W. (ed.), *100 Jahre Architektur in Chicago. Kontinuität von Struktur und Form*, Munich 1973 (exh. cat., Staatl. Museum für Angewandte Kunst).

Guillet, L., *Cent ans de la vie de l'École Centrale des Arts et Manufactures 1829–1929*, Paris 1929.

Hackelsberger, Ch., *Beton: Stein der Weisen? Nachdenken über einen Baustoff*, Braunschweig/Wiesbaden 1988 (*Bauwelt Fundamente*, vol. 79).

Hackelsberger, Ch. (ed.), *Gestalten in Beton. Zum Werk von Pier Luigi Nervi*, Cologne 1989.

Haegermann, G. et al., *Vom Caementum zum Spannbeton*, Wiesbaden/Berlin 1964.

Hager, F.-P., and D. Jedan (eds.), *The notion of enlightenment. Conference papers for the 1st meeting of the International Standing Working Group on Education and Enlightenment, ISCHE*, Zurich 1986, pp. 15–30).

Haller, F., *Bauen und Forschen*, Solothurn 1988 (exh. cat.).

Hausladen, G. et al., *ClimaDesign. Lösungen für Gebäude, die mit weniger Technik mehr können*, Munich 2005.

Hayden, D., *Catharine Beecher and the Politics of Housework*, in: Torre, S. (ed.), *Women in American Architecture: A Historic and Contemporary Perspective*, New York 1977.

Hebeisen, W., *F. W. Taylor und der Taylorismus. Über das Wirken und die Lehre Taylors und die Kritik am Taylorismus*, Zurich 1999 (ETH Zurich).

Heine, H., letter from 5 May 1843, in: *Sämtliche Werke*, vol. X., 1874, p. 121 f.

Heinle, E., and J. Schlaich, *Kuppeln aller Zeiten – aller Kulturen*, Stuttgart 1996.

Herbert, G., *Pioneers of Prefabrication. The British Contribution in the Nineteenth Century*, Baltimore/London 1978.

Herbert, G., *The Dream of the Factory-Made House. Walter Gropius and Konrad Wachsmann*, Cambridge, Mass./London 1984.

Herzog, Th. (ed.), *Vom Sinn des Details. Zum Gesamtwerk von Konrad Wachsmann*, Cologne 1988.

Herzog, Th. et al. (ed.), *Façade Construction Manual*, Basle 2004 (Edition Detail Munich).

Heusler, W., and J. Ernst, *Commerzbank Frankfurt*, in: *Fassade*, no. 4, 1996, Dietikon/Zurich 1996, pp. 47–56.

Hildebrand, G., *Designing for Industry. The Architecture of Albert Kahn*, Cambridge, Mass. 1974.

Hirdina, H. (ed.), *Neues Bauen, Neues Gestalten. Das Neue Frankfurt/die neue stadt: eine Zeitschrift zwischen 1926 und 1933*, Berlin/Dresden 1984.

Hirsinger, Q., and E. Ternaux (eds.), *Material World 2. Innovative Materials for Architecture and Design*, Basle 2006.

Hirsinger, Q., E. Ternaux, and D. Kula, *Materiology. Handbuch für Kreative: Materialien und Technologien*, Basle 2007.

Hitchcock, H.-R., *Early Victorian Architecture in Britain*, New Haven 1954.

Hitchcock, H.-R., *Die Architektur des 19. und 20. Jahrhunderts*, Munich 1994 (1st edn. London 1990).

Hitchcock, H.-R. with F. L. Wright (eds.), *In the Nature of Materials. The Buildings of Frank Lloyd Wright 1887–1941*, New York 1942.

Hitchcock, H.-R. et al., *The Rise of an American Architecture*, New York 1970.

Hix, J., *The Glass House*, London 1974.

Hobsbawm, E. J., *Industrie und Empire. Britische Wirtschaftsgeschichte seit 1750*, Frankfurt a. M. 1969.

Hole, J., *An Essay on the History and Management of Literary, Scientific & Mechanics' Institutions*, London 1853 (reprint London 1970).

Holgate, A., *The Art of Structural Engineering. The Work of Jörg Schlaich and his Team*, Stuttgart/London 1997.

Horden, R., *Light Tech. Towards a Light Architecture; Ausblick auf eine leichte Architektur* (ed. with. W. Blaser), Basle 1995.

Horden, R., *Light Architecture. The 1996 John Dinkeloo Memorial Lecture*, The University of Michigan, Ann Arbor, Mich., 1996.

Horden, R., *Architecture and Teaching. Buildings, Projects, Microarchitecture Workshops*, Basle 1999.

Horden, R., *Sixty Projects*, Munich 2004 (ed. Lehrstuhl für Gebäudelehre und Produktentwicklung, Technische Universität Munich).

Hossdorf, H., *Das Erlebnis Ingenieur zu sein*, Basle 2003.

Hounshell, D. A., *From the American System to Mass Production 1800–1932*, Baltimore/London 1984/85 (p. 153–87).

Huberti, G., *Die erneuerte Bauweise*, in: Haegermann, G. et al., *Vom Caementum zum Spannbeton*, Wiesbaden/Berlin 1964 (section B).

Hugentobler, P., *Räumliche Flächen mit ebenen Gläsern*, in: *Fassade*, no. 2, 2004, pp. 11–15.

Huse, N. (ed.), *Vier Berliner Siedlungen der Weimarer Republik. Britz, Onkel Toms Hütte, Siemensstadt, Weiße Stadt*, Berlin 1984 (a project of the IBA 1987).

Hüter, K.-H., *Das Bauhaus in Weimar*, Berlin 1976 (documents in appendix).

Hütsch, V., *Der Münchner Glaspalast 1854–1931. Geschichte und Bedeutung*, Berlin 1985.

Hwang, I. et al. (eds.), *Verb Natures*, Barcelona 2006 (Actar's boogazine, vol. 5).

Idsinga, T., *Zonnestraal*, Amsterdam 1986.

Industrial Chicago, Chicago 1891 (vol 2.).

Institut für leichte Flächentragwerke (ed. Frei Otto), *IL 34: Das Modell*, Stuttgart 1989.

Irace, F. et al. (eds.), *Renzo Piano. le città visibili*, Milan 2007 (exh. cat., Triennale di Milano).

Ito, T., *Sendai Mediatheque*, Barcelona 2003.

Jackson, M., Eden: *The first book*, Bodelva, St. Austell, Cornwall, 2000.
Jaeggi, A. (ed.), *Egon Eiermann (1904–1970). Die Kontinuität der Moderne*, Universität Karlsruhe (TH; Südwestdeutsches Archiv für Architektur und Ingenieurbau), Städtische Galerie Karlsruhe, Bauhaus-Archiv Berlin 2004.
Jaeggi, A., *Adolf Meyer. Der zweite Mann – Ein Architekt im Schatten von Walter Gropius*, Berlin 1994 (exh. cat., Bauhaus-Archiv, Museum für Gestaltung Berlin).
Jaffé, H. L. C., *De Stijl 1917–1931. Der niederländische Beitrag zur modernen Kunst*, Frankfurt a. M./Berlin 1965 (*Bauwelt Fundamente*, vol. 7; engl.1st edn. Amsterdam 1956).
Jaffé, H. L. C. (ed.), *De Stijl: 1917–1931*, New York 1982 (exh. cat., Stedelijk Museum Amsterdam and Rijksmuseum Kröller-Müller Oterloo).
Jenger, J. (ed.), *Le Corbusier. Choix de lettres*, Basle 2002.
Jenney, W. L. B., *An Age of Steel and Clay*, reprint and revision of Jenney's speech before the Chicago Architectural Scetch Club from 28.1.1889, in: *The Inland Architect and News Record*, vol. XVI, no. 7, Dec. 1890, pp. 75–77 (archive and library of the University of Illinois).
Jenney, W. L. B., *Chicago Construction, or Tall Buildings on a Compressible Soil, in: The Engineering Record. Building Record & The Sanitary Engineer*, vol. 24, no. 24, New York, 14. Nov. 1891/London, 28. Nov. 1891, pp. 388–90.
Jenney, W. L. B., *Perspective View of Horticultural Building, World's Columbian Exposition, Chicago*, in: *Inland Architect*, vol. XVII, no. 5, Chicago, Jun. 1891.
Jodidio, Ph., *Sir Norman Foster*, Cologne 1997.
Jodidio, Ph. (ed.), *Under the Eaves of Architecture. The Aga Khan: Builder and Patron*, Munich 2007.
Joedicke, J., *Geschichte der modernen Architektur*, Teufen, Switzerland/Stuttgart 1958.
Joedicke, J., and E. N. Rogers (eds.), *Pier Luigi Nervi. Bauten und Projekte*, Teufen, Switzerland/Stuttgart 1957.
Joedicke, J. (ed.), *Architektur und Städtebau. Das Werk van den Broek und Bakema*, Zurich 1963.
Jones, P., *Ove Arup, Masterbuilder of the Twentieth Century*, New Haven, London 2006 (Yale University Press).
Jullian, R. (ed.), *Tony Garnier: Die ideale Industriestadt – Une Cité industrielle. Eine städtebauliche Studie*, Tübingen 1989 (french 1st edn. Paris 1988).

Kaltenbach, F. (ed.), *Translucent Materials. Glass, Plastic, Metals*, Basle 2004 (Edition Detail).
Katholische Universität Eichstätt (ed.), *Universitätsbibliothek von Behnisch & Partner*, Eichstätt 1987 (anniversary writing).
Kessler, A., *Vom Holzsteg zum Weltmonument. Die Geschichte der Salginatobelbrücke*, Schiers, Switzerland, 1996.
Kind, F., *Beton in der Architektur*, in: *Betonatlas. Entwerfen mit Stahlbeton im Hochbau*, Basle 2002 (2nd ed.).
Klasz, W., *Forschungsstation Peak_Lab*, in: *Detail*, no. 12, 2004, pp. 1459–62.
Knaak, U., *Fachwerke aus Glas*, in: *Fassade*, no. 3, 2002, Dietikon/Zurich 2002.
Koch, K.-M. (ed.), *Bauen mit Membranen. Der innovative Werkstoff in der Architektur*, Munich 2004.
Kohlmaier, G., and B. v. Sartory, *Das Glashaus. Ein Bautypus des 19. Jahrhunderts*, Munich 1988 (1st edn. 1981).
Kostof, S., *The Architect. Chapters in the History of the Profession*, New York/Oxford 1977.
Kovatsch, M. (ed.), *Rudolph M. Schindler. Architekt 1887–1953*, Munich 1985 (exh. cat., Museum Villa Stuck Munich).
Krausse, J., and Cl. Lichtenstein (ed.), *Your Private Sky. R. Buckminster Fuller – Design als Kunst einer Wissenschaft*, Baden, Switzerland, 1999 (exh. cat., Museum für Gestaltung Zurich).
Krinsky, C. H., *Gordon Bunshaft of Skidmore, Owings & Merrill*, Cambridge, Mass./London 1988.
Krippner, R., *Die Sprache des Systematischen – Bausysteme aus Stahlbeton von Angelo Mangiarotti*, in: *Detail*, no. 5, 1998, pp. 776–79.
Krippner, R., Der Systemgedanke in der Architektur. Bausysteme aus Stahlbeton von Angelo Mangiarotti, in: Beton- und Stahlbetonbau, no. 94, 1999, issue 11, pp. 476–82.
Krischanitz, A. and O. Kapfinger (eds.), *Die Wiener Werkbundsiedlung. Dokumentation einer Erneuerung*, Vienna 1985.
Kurokawa, K., Das Kurokawa-Manifest (and other writings ed. by Ezawa Kennosuke), Berlin 2005 (1st edn. Symbiotisches Denken, Tokyo 1987).

Landes, D. S., *Der entfesselte Prometheus. Technologischer Wandel und industrielle Entwicklung in Westeuropa von 1750 bis zur Gegenwart*, Cologne 1983 (dtv wissenschaft; 1st edn. Cambridge University Press 1968).
Langer, F. (ed.), *Lewis W. Hine. The Empire State Building*, Munich 1988.
L'architecture d'aujourd'hui, no. VII, Oct. 1932: *Spécial Perret* (reprint Paris 1991).
Lavalou, A. (ed.), *Jean Prouvé par lui-même*, Paris 2001.
Le Corbusier, and P. Jeanneret (ed.), *Fünf Punkte zu einer neuen Architektur*, in: *Zwei Wohnhäuser von Le Corbusier und Pierre Jeanneret* (ed. with Alfred Roth), Stuttgart 1927 (new edn. Stuttgart 1977).
Leach, N. et al. (ed.), *digital tectonics*, London 2004.
Leach, N., and Xu Wei-Guo (eds.), *Fast forward, Hot spot, Brain cells*, Hong Kong 2004.
Lemoine, B., *Les Halles de Paris*, Paris 1980 (with an facsimilie print of the original essay from Victor Baltard and Félix Callet, including entire plan material).
Lemoine, B., *L'architecture du fer. France: XIX siècle*, Seyssel 1986.
Lemoine, B., and M. Mimram, *Paris d'Ingénieurs*, Paris 1995.
Lepik, A., *Mies und die Photomontage, 1910–38*, in: Riley, T., and B. Bergdoll (ed.), *Mies in Berlin. Ludwig Mies van der Rohe. Die Berliner Jahre 1907–1938*, Munich 2001, pp. 324–29.
Lichtenstein, Cl., *O. R. Salvisberg. Die andere Moderne*, Zurich 1995 (Institut gta/ETH Zurich).
Locke, J., *Einige Gedanken zur Erziehung*, Stuttgart 1970 (1st edn. 1693: *Some Thoughts Concerning Education*).
Locke, J., *Versuch über den menschlichen Verstand*, Hamburg 1981 (4 books; 1st edn., written in 1671, published in 1689: *An Essay Concerning Human Understanding*).
Luebkeman, C., *drivers of change 2006*, Arup London 2006.
Lüchinger, A., *Strukturalismus in Architektur und Städtebau*, Stuttgart 1981.
Lüchinger, A. (ed.), *Herman Hertzberger. Bauten und Projekte 1959–1986*, Den Haag 1987.
Ludwig, M., *Mobile Architektur. Geschichte und Entwicklung transportabler und modularer Bauten*, Stuttgart 1998.
Lyall, S., *Masters of Structures: Engineering Today's Innovative Buildings*, London 2002.

Mack, G., *Reflexion und Transparenz. Zwei Bauten für Helvetia Patria St. Gallen – eine Architektur von Herzog & de Meuron*, St. Gallen 2002.
Mallgrave, H. F., *Gottfried Semper. Ein Architekt des 19. Jahrhunderts*, Zurich 2001 (Institut gta/ETH Zurich).
Mangiarotti, A., *Angelo Mangiarotti 1955–1964*, Tokyo 1964/65.
Marbach, U., and A. Rüegg (ed.), *Werkbundsiedlung Neubühl in Zürich-Wollishofen 1928–32. Ihre Entstehung und Erneuerung*, Zurich 1990 (Institut gta/ETH Zurich).
Marrey, B., *Le Fer à Paris. Architectures*, Paris 1989.
Marrey, B., and J. Ferrier, *Paris sous verre. La ville et ses reflets*, Paris 1997 (exh. cat., Pavillon de l'Arsenal).
Marti, P., and O. Monsch, B. Schilling, *Robert Maillart. Betonvirtuose*, Zurich 1996 (ed. Gesellschaft für Ingenieurbaukunst).
Marti, P. with A. Fürst, *Robert Maillart's Design Approach for Flat Slabs*, in: *Journal of Structural Engineering*, no. 8, Aug. 1997, pp. 1102–10.
Marti, P. et al., *Ingenieur-Betonbau. Hintergrund, Stahlbeton, Betontragwerke*, Zurich 2005 (ed. Gesellschaft für Ingenieurbaukunst, ETH Zurich).
Mary, Ch.-L., *Cours d'Architecture, à l'École Centrale des Arts et Manufactures*, Paris 1852/53 (hand written dictated manuscript and plate section; printed edn.).
Mattie, E., *Weltausstellungen*, Stuttgart/Zurich 1998.
Maurer, B., *Karl Culmann und die graphische Statik*, Berlin 1998 (diss.).
Mayer, H. M., and R. C. Wade, *Chicago. Growth of a Metropolis*, Chicago/London 1969.
McCracken, E., *The Palm House and Botanic Garden Belfast*, Ulster 1971 (on Richard Turner).
Mertins, D., *Architektonik des Werdens: Mies van der Rohe und die Avantgarde*, in: Riley, T., and B. Bergdoll (eds.), *Mies in Berlin. Ludwig Mies van der Rohe. Die Berliner Jahre 1907–1938*, Munich 2001, pp. 107–33.
Molema, J., *J. Duiker*, Rotterdam 1989.
Molenaar, J., *Van Nelle's fabrieken. Bureau Brinkman en Van der Vlugt 1925–31*, Utrecht 1985.
Möll, H., *Der Spannbeton*, in: Haegermann, G. et al., *Vom Caementum zum Spannbeton*, Wiesbaden/Berlin 1964 (section C).
Mostafavi, M. (ed.), *Structure as Space. Engineering and Architecture in the Works of Jürg Conzett and His Partners*, London 2006 (AA Publications).
Mumford, L., *Sticks & Stones. A Study of American Architecture and Civilization*, New York 1955 (1924)
Musmeci, S., *Rapporto tra struttura e architettura nell'ultima esperienza dell'Architetto Libera: il palazzo della Regione a Trento*, in: *L'Industria Italiana del Cemento*, no. 4, Apr. 1976.
Muttoni, A., *An Analyses of the Structure*, in: *Louis I. Kahn. The Construction of the Kimbell Art Museum* (ed. Academia di architettura dell'Università della Svizzera italiana, Mendrisio), Milan 1999, p. 105 ff.
Muttoni, A., *L'art des structures. Une introduction au fonctionnement des structures en architecture*, Lausanne 2004 (École Polytechnique Fédérale de Lausanne).

Nachtigall, W., and K. G. Blüchel, *Das große Buch der Bionik*, Stuttgart/Munich 2000.
Nagel, A., and K. Frankenheim, *Fortschritt im Fassadenbau. Hauptverwaltung RWE AG in Essen*, in: *Fassade*, no. 4, 1995, Dietikon/Zurich 1995, pp. 59–62.
National Commitee on Wood Utilization, United States Department of Commerce, U. S.-Department of Health, Education, and Welfare, Office of Education: *Handbuch balloon framing*, Washington 1953 (reprint).
Nerdinger, W., *Standard und Typ: Le Corbusier und Deutschland 1920–1927*, in: Moos, St. v. (ed.), 1987.
Nerdinger, W. (ed.), *Exemplarisch. Konstruktion und Raum in der Architektur des 20. Jahrhunderts*, Munich 2002 (examples from the collection of the Architekturmuseums of the Technischen Universität Munich).
Nerdinger, W. (ed.), *Architektur der Wunderkinder. Aufbruch und Verdrängung in Bayern 1945–60*, Salzburg 2005 (exh. cat., Technische Universität Munich).
Nerdinger, W. (ed.), *Leicht Bauen, Natürlich Gestalten. Frei Otto – Das Gesamtwerk*, Basle 2005 (exh. cat., Architekturmuseum TU Munich).
Nestler, P., *Neues Bauen in Italien*, Munich 1954.
Neumann, D., *»The Century's Triumph in Lighting." Die Luxfer-Prism-Gesellschaften und ihr Beitrag zur frühen Moderne*, in: *archithese*, no. 6, 1996, pp. 26–33, 56.
Neumann, M., *Grundsätze und Erfahrungen über die Anlegung, Erhaltung und Pflege von Glashäusern aller Art*, Weimar 1852 (reprint Wiesbaden/Berlin 1984).
Neutra, R. J., *Amerika. Die Stilbildung des Neuen Bauens in den Vereinigten Staaten*, Vienna 1930.
Norman Foster 1964–1987, a + u Extra Edition, no. 5, Tokyo 1988.
Norman Foster, GA Document Extra, no. 12, Tokyo 1999.

Olmo, C., *Il Lingotto 1915–1939. L'Architettura, L'Immagine, Il Lavoro*, Turin 1994.
On Tour with Renzo Piano, London 2004.
Ordonez, J. A. F., *Eugene Freyssinet*, in: Picon, A. (ed.), *L'art de l'ingénieur*, Paris 1997 (exh. cat., Centre Georges Pompidou), p. 194 ff.
Ordonez, J. A. F., and J. R. N. Vera, *Eduardo Torroja*, in: Picon, A. (ed.), *L'art de l'ingénieur*, Paris 1997 (exh. cat., Centre Georges Pompidou), p. 506 f.
Otto, F., *B. Rasch, Gestalt finden*, Stuttgart/London 1995.
Oud, J. J. P., *Holländische Architektur*, Munich 1926 (*Bauhausbücher*, no. 10).

Palazzeschi, A., and G. Bruno, *L'opera completa di Boccioni*, Milan 1969.
Pampaloni, G., and M. Verdone, *I Futuristi Italiani. Imagini, Biografie, Notizie*, Florence 1977.
Paravicini, U., and P. Amphoux (ed.), *Maurice Braillard. Ein Schweizer Pionier der modernen Architektur 1897–1965*, Basle 1994 (exh. cat., Fondation Braillard Architectes and Architekturmuseum Basle).
Parissien, St., *Station to Station*, London 1997 (reprint 2001).
Paronesso, A., and R. Passera, *Schwebende Strukturen mit Durchblick. Evolution und Anwendung eines alternativen Leichtbaukonzepts; zur Entwicklung von Tensegrity-Systemen*, in: *tec21*, no. 40, 2003, pp. 6–12.
Patetta, L., *L'Architettura in Italia 1919–1943. Le polemiche*, Milan 1972 (documents and commentary).
Pawley, M., *Buckminster Fuller*, London 1990.
Pearce, R. M., *Thomas Telford. An illustrated life of Thomas Telford, 1757–1834*, Aylesbury, Bucks, UK 1978.
Pélissier, A., Richen & Robert. Transforming Space, Basle u. a. 1994.

Penfold, A., *Thomas Telford. Collossus of Roads, Priorslee Hall*, Telford, Shropshire, UK 1981.

Perdonnet, A., *Traité Élémentaire des Chemins de Fer* (vols. 1 and 2), Paris 1858/1860.

Perrault, D., *Dominique Perrault*, Basle 1994 (exh. cat., arc en rêve centre d'architecture, Bordeaux).

Perrault, D., *Des Natures. Jenseits der Architektur*, Basle 1996 (exh. cat., Edition Architekturgalerie Luzern).

Perret: 25bis rue Franklin, in: *Rassegna*, no. 28, Bologna 1986.

Peters, N., *Jean Prouvé 1901–1984. La dynamique de la création*, Cologne 2006.

Peters, T. F., *Time is Money. Die Entwicklung des modernen Bauwesens*, Stuttgart 1981.

Peters, T. F., *Building the Nineteenth Century*, Cambridge, Mass./London 1996.

Pfammatter, U., *Casa del Fascio – ein Bau der Moderne?*, in: *Bauwelt*, no. 41/42, 7 Nov. 1986, pp. 1560–80.

Pfammatter, U., *Ursprung, Entwicklung und Bedeutung des polytechnischen und industriellen Unterrichtsmodells. Elemente zur modernen Architekten- und Ingenieurausbildung*, Zurich 1995 (diss. ETH no. 11125).

Pfammatter, U. (ed.), *Cuno Brullmann Architecte*, Basle 1995 (with texts by Paul Virilio, Kenneth Powell, Cuno Brullmann, Ulrich Pfammatter and an interview with Marianne Brausch).

Pfammatter, U., *Moderne und Macht. ›Razionalismo‹: Italienische Architekten 1927–1942*, Braunschweig/Wiesbaden 1996 (*Bauwelt Fundamente*, vol. 85; 2nd edn.).

Pfammatter, U., *Die Erfindung des modernen Architekten. Ursprung und Entwicklung seiner wissenschaftlich-industriellen Ausbildung*, Basle 1997.

Pfammatter, U., *Ausbilden nach 1945. Zur Geschichte einer didaktischen Entwicklung im Kontext der modernen Architekturbewegung – eine Skizze*, in: *Schweizer Architekt und Ingenieur (SI + A)*, no. 37, 10. Sep. 1998, pp. 9–12.

Pfammatter, U., *The Making of the Modern Architect and Engineer. The origins and development of a scientific and industrially oriented education*, Basle 2000.

Pfammatter, U., *Ohne Heizung – aber mit Haustechnik. Das Konzept Passivhaus in Leichtbauweise*, in: *Schweizer Architekt und Ingenieur (SI + A)*, no. 42, 20. Oct. 2000, pp. 4–7.

Pfammatter, U., *Die Erfindung des modernen Architekten*, in: *Arch+*, no. 163, Dec. 2002, pp. 52–60.

Pfammatter, U., *2003: Paxton-Jahr, Semper-Jahr*, in: *tec21*, no. 45, 7 Nov. 2003, pp. 6–10.

Pfammatter, U. with R. Horden, *Peak_Lab. Forschungsstation auf dem Klein Matterhorn*, Munich 2003 (ed. Technische Universität Munich, Lehrstuhl für Gebäudelehre und Produktentwicklung).

Pfammatter, U., *Peak_Lab. Interdisziplinäres Projekt zu einer Forschungsstation auf dem Klein Matterhorn, Schweiz*, in: *Intelligente Architektur*, no. 9/10, 2003, pp. 48–51 (rubric outlook).

Pfammatter, U., *Warum immer Neues? Für eine Kultur der Nachhaltigkeit*, in: *archithese*, no. 4, 2004, pp. 20–27.

Pfammatter, U., *Größe und Größenwahn. Wie die italienische Architekten-Elite zwischen Razionalismo und Postmoderne vielen Herren diente und dabei immer unschuldig blieb*, in: *du*, no. 755, Apr. 2005, pp. 29–31.

Pfeiffer, B. B. (ed.), *Frank Lloyd Wright. Collected Writings*, vol. 1: 1894–1930, New York 1992.

Piano, R., *Mein Architektur-Logbuch*, Ostfildern-Ruit 1997 (ital. edn. Paris/Genoa 1997).

Piano, R., *Sustainable Architectures*, Barcelona 1998 (ed. Gustavo Gili).

Piano, R., *Un ricordo di Prouvé/Memories of Prouvé*, in: *Domus*, no. 807, Sep. 1998, pp. 52–66 (with 32 commented patends).

Piccinato, L. (ed.), *Riccardo Morandi. Strutture di calcestruzzo armato e di calcestruzzo precompresso*, Rome 1954 (ital./engl. edn.).

Picon, A., *Architectes et Ingénieurs au Siècle des Lumières*, Marseille 1988.

Picon, A., *L'invention de l'ingénieur moderne. L'École des Ponts et Chaussées 1747–1851*, Paris 1992.

Picon, A. (ed.), *L'Art de l'Ingenieur. Constructeur – Entrepreneur – Inventeur*, Paris 1997 (exh. cat., Centre Georges Pompidou).

Polonyi, St., *Analyse der Tragwerke von Pier Luigi Nervi*, in: Ch. Hackelsberger (ed.), *Gestalten in Beton. Zum Werk von Pier Luigi Nervi*, Cologne 1989, pp. 69–78.

Powell, K., and R. Moore, *Struktur, Raum und Haut. Nicholas*

Grimshaw & Partners, Bauten und Projekte, London/Berlin 1993.

Pruscha, C. (ed.), *Das Semper-Depot*, Munich/New York 1997.

Quinan, J., *Bauten für die gemeinschaftliche Arbeit*, in: De Long, D. G. (ed.), *Frank Lloyd Wright. Die lebendige Stadt*, Geneva/Milan 1998 (exh. cat., Vitra Design Museum Weil am Rhein), p. 70 ff.

Ramazotti, L., *Das Werk von Pier Luigi Nervi*, in: Ch. Hackelsberger (ed.), *Gestalten in Beton. Zum Werk von Pier Luigi Nervi*, Cologne 1989, pp. 53–68.

Ramm, E. et al. (ed.), *Heinz Isler. Schalen*, Zurich 2002 (1st edn. 1986, ETH Zurich); with essays by D. P. Billington, F. Leonhardt, J. Joedicke, E. Ramm, E. Schunck, H. Isler (new ed. P. Marti, Gesellschaft für Ingenieurbaukunst, ETH Zurich).

Randall, F. A., *History of the Development of Building Construction in Chicago*, Chicago 1949.

Rasch, H., and B., *Wie bauen? Bau und Einrichtung der Werkbundsiedlung am Weißenhof in Stuttgart 1927*, Stuttgart 1927.

Reichen & Robert, Bernard Reichen and Philippe Robert, Basle u. a. 2003.

Renzo Piano Building Workshop: 1964–1988, a + u Extra Edition no. 3, 1989.

Renzo Piano Building Workshop. In search of a balance, Process Architecture, no. 100, 1992.

Renzo Piano Building Workshop, *On Tour with Renzo Piano*, London/New York 2004.

Rice, P., *Konstruktive Intelligenz*, in: *Arch+*, no. 102, Jan. 1990, pp. 42–45.

Rice, P., *An Engineer Imagines*, London 1994 (ed. Sylvia Rice).

Rice, P., and H. Dutton, *Transparente Architektur. Glasfassaden mit Structural Glazing*, Basle u. a. 1995 (french 1sr edn.: *Le Verre Structurel*, Paris 1990).

Richard J. Neutra, in: *L'architecture d'aujourd'hui*, no. 6, May/Jun. 1946 (reprint Paris 1992).

Richard Rogers + Architects, Paris 2007 (exh. cat., Centre Pompidou 2007–08).

Richards, J. M., The Functional Tradition in Early Industrial Buildings, London 1958.

Riley, T. (ed.), *Frank Lloyd Wright Architect*, New York 1994 (exh. cat., Museum of Modern Art, New York).

Riley, T., and B. Bergdoll (eds.), *Ludwig Mies van der Rohe. Die Berliner Jahre 1907–1938*, Munich 2001 (exh. cat.).

Robert Maillart. Betonvirtuose, ETH Zurich 1996 (ed. Gesellschaft für Ingenieurbaukunst, ETH Zurich).

Rogers, R., five lectures in the Reith Lectures series titled: *Cities for a Small Planet* in Radio BBC London 1995, in: *Arch+*, no. 127, Jun. 1995, pp. 25–64.

Rogers, R. and A. Power, *Cities for a small country*, London 2000.

Roisecco, G., *L'architettura del ferro. L'Inghilterra (1688–1914); La Francia (1715–1914); Gli Stati Uniti (1776–1914)*, Rome 1972.

Ronner, H., and A. Corboz (eds.), *Industriearchäologie in England. Eine Bestandsaufnahme und Dokumentation einer Seminarwoche 1981*, ETH Zurich 1982 (2nd edn. 1983).

Rosa, J. (ed.), *Albert Frey, Architekt*, Zurich 1995 (1st edn. New York 1990).

Roth, A., *Die Neue Architektur 1930–1940*, Zurich/Munich 1975 (1st edn. Zurich 1939).

Rowe, C., *Chicago Frame. Chicago's Place in the Modern Movement*, in: *The Architectural Review*, no. 718, Nov. 1956, S. 285–289

Rowe, C., and R. Slutzky, *Transparenz*, Basle 1989 (ed. commentary and addendum by B. Hoesli; 1st edn. 1964 in *Perspecta 8*).

Rüegg, A., *Der Pavillon de l'Esprit Nouveau als musée imaginaire*, in: Moos, St. v. (ed.), 1987, pp. 136–151.

Russell, B., *Building Systems, Industrialization, and Architecture*, London 1981.

Saggio, A. (ed.), series *The ITRevolution*, Basle since 1999.

Sagner-Düchting, K. (ed.), *Claude Monet 1840–1926. Ein Fest für die Augen*, Cologne 1994.

Sarrasin, A., *Notes sur les barrages a arches multiples*, in: *Schweizerische Bauzeitung*, 13 May 1939, pp. 231–235.

Sartoris, A., *Introduzione alla Architettura Moderna*, Milan 1949 (1st edn. 1943).

Sauer, Chr., *Sydney Opera House*, Zurich 2003 (author's diploma studies, ETH Zurich, 2002/03).

Sauerbruch Hutton Architects (ed.), *Sauerbruch Hutton. Projekte 1990–1996*, Basle 1996.

Sauerbruch Hutton Architects (ed.), *Sauerbruch Hutton Architekten. GSW Hauptverwaltung Berlin*, Baden, Switzerland, 2000.

Savi, V., *Storie di Santa Maria Novella*, in: Berti, P., and V. Savi (ed.), *La Nuova Stazione di Firenze*, Florence 1993 (exh. cat., together with Ferrovie dello Stato, Stazione di Firenze and École d'Architecture et Urbanisme de Genève).

Schädlich, Chr., *Der Baustoff Eisen als Grundlage für die Herausbildung qualitativ neuer Baukonstruktionen im 19. Jahrhundert*, in: R. Graefe (ed.), *Zur Geschichte des Konstruierens*, Stuttgart 1989, pp. 138–151.

Schéou, A. (ed.), *Itsuko Hasegawa. Recent Buildings and Projects*, Basle 1997 (exh. cat., Institut français d'architecture, Paris).

Schild, E., *Zwischen Glaspalast und Palais des Illusions. Form und Konstruktion im 19. Jahrhundert*, Braunschweig/Wiesbaden 1983 (*Bauwelt Fundamente*, vol. 20; 1st edn. 1967).

Schirmer, W. (ed.), *Egon Eiermann 1904–1970. Bauten und Projekte*, Stuttgart 2004 (1st edn. 1984).

Schittich, Chr. et al. (ed.), *Glasbau Atlas*, Basle 1998.

Schmal, P. C. et al. (ed.), *Kisho Kurokawa. Metabolismus und Symbiosis*, Berlin 2005 (exh. cat., Deutsches Architekturmuseum Frankfurt a. M.).

Schmidt-Bergmann, H., *Futurismus. Geschichte, Ästhetik, Dokumente*, Reinbek b. Hamburg 1993 (vol. 535).

Schneider + Schumacher (ed.), *Schneider + Schumacher, Architekten. 7 Projekte*, Tübingen/Berlin 1997.

Schulz, B., *Der Reichstag. Die Architektur von Norman Foster*, Munich 2000.

Semper, G., *Der Stil in den technischen und tektonischen Künsten* (2 vols.), Munich 1860 (vol. 1) and 1863 (vol. 2); reprinted in Mittenwald 1977.

Sheppard, Ch., *Bahnhöfe. Meisterwerke der Architektur*, Cologne 1996.

Shigeru Ban, Projects in Process to Japanese Pavilion, Expo 2000 Hanover, Tokyo 1999.

Shigeru Ban, London 2001.

Simmen, J., and U. Drepper (eds.), *Der Fahrstuhl. Die Geschichte der vertikalen Eroberung*, Munich 1984.

Singer, C. et al. (eds.), *A History of Technology*; vol. IV., *The Industrial Revolution, 1750–1850*, Oxford 1958 (4th edn. 1975); vol. V., *The Late Nineteenth Century, 1850–1900*, Oxford 1958 (4th edn. 1970).

Siry, J., *Carson Pirie Scott. Louis Sullivan and the Chicago Department Store*, Chicago/London 1988.

Skempton, A. W., *The Boat Store Sheerness (1858–60), and its Place in Structural History*, Excerpt Transactions of the Newcomen Society, vol. XXXII, 1959/60.

Skempton, A. W., and. H. R. Johnson, *The First Iron Frames*, in: *The Architectural Review*, no. 781, Mar. 1962.

Slessor, C., and J. Linden (photos), *Eco-Tech. Umweltverträgliche Architektur und Hochtechnologie*, Ostfildern-Ruit 1997 (1st edn. London 1997).

Smith, E. A. T. (ed.), *Blueprints for Modern Living. History and Legacy of the Case Study Houses*, Cambridge, Mass./London 1989.

Sobek, W. (with M. Kutterer), *Konstruieren mit Glas – Festigkeit und Tragverhalten*, in: Schittich, Chr. et al. (ed.), *Glasbau Atlas*, Basle 1998, p. 88 ff.

Sobek, W., *Show me the Future. Engineering and Design by Werner Sobek*, Ludwigsburg 2004.

Sommer, D. et al., *Ove Arup & Partners – Ingenieure als Wegbereiter der Architektur/Engineering the Built Environment*, Basle 1994.

Staib, G., *Von den Ursprüngen bis zur Klassischen Moderne*, in: Schittich, Chr. et al. (ed.), *Glasbau Atlas*, Basle 1998.

Stattmann, N., *Handbuch Materialtechnologie*, Ludwigsburg 2000 (ed. D. Kretschmann, Rat für Formgebung/German Design Council, Ludwigsburg).

Steele, J. (ed.), *Hassan Fathy*, New York 1988.

Steiner, D. et al. (ed.), *Standardhäuser. Das Fertighaus: Idee, Geschichte, Industrie*, Wien 1997 (exh. cat., Architektur Zentrum Wien).

Steinmann, M. (ed.), *CIAM. Dokumente 1928–1939*, Basle/Stuttgart 1979 (Institut gta/ETH Zurich).

Steurer, A., *Das vergessene Haus in Stahl*, Zurich 1999 (presentation on the occasion of the convention: Bauen mit Stahl 99 given by the Stahlbau Zentrum Switzerland (SZS), Luzern).

Stiller, A., *Standardhaus versus Häuslebau. Normierte Gestaltung von der Stange oder individueller Formenmix*, in: *archithese*, no. 1, 1998, Teufen, Switzerland, 1998, pp. 28–33.

Stirling, J., *James Stirling. Bauten und Projekte 1950–1983*, Stuttgart 1984.

Stirling, J., *James Stirling. Bauten und Projekte 1950–1974*, Stuttgart 1996.

Straub, H., *Die Geschichte der Bauingenieurkunst*, Basle 1992.

Stulz, R., and Chr. Hartmann, *Die Verwandlung des Quartiers Gundeldingen in Basle*, in: *tec21*, no. 3/4, 2005, pp. 5–9.

Stutz, W., *Bahnhöfe in der Schweiz. Von den Anfängen bis zum Ersten Weltkrieg*, Zurich 1983.

Sullivan, L. H., *The Autobiography of an Idea*, New York 1956 (1st edn. 1924).

Sulzer, P., Jean Prouvé. *Meister der Metallumformung*, Cologne 1991.

Sulzer, P., Jean Prouvé. *Œuvre complète/Complete works*; Vol. 1: *1917–1933*, Vol. 2: *1934–1944*, Vol. 3: *1944–1954*, Vol. 4: *1954–1984*, Basle 1995, 2000, 2005, 2007.

Sulzer, P., *Jean Prouvé. Highlights 1917–1944*, Basle 2002.

Sumi, Chr., *Immeuble Clarté Genf 1932. Von Le Corbusier und Pierre Jeanneret*, Zurich 1989 (Institut gta/ETH Zurich).

Syrett, H. C. (ed.), *American Historical Documents*, New York 1960.

Szambien, W., *Jean-Nicolas-Louis Durand. 1760–1834. De l'imitation à la norme*, Paris 1984.

Taylor, B. B., *Pierre Chareau. Designer and Architect*, Cologne 1992.

Templ, St. (ed.), *baba – Die Werkbundsiedlung Prag/The Werkbund Housing Estate Prague*, Basel 1999.

Tegethoff, W., *Wege und Umwege zur Moderne: Mies van der Rohes Frühwerk und der 'Preußische Stil'*, in: Riley, T., and B. Bergdoll (eds.), *Mies in Berlin. Ludwig Mies van der Rohe. Die Berliner Jahre 1907–1938*, Munich 2001, pp. 135–151.

Thau, C., and K. Vindum (eds.), *Arne Jacobsen*, Copenhagen 2002 (1st edn. 1998).

The Architectural Forum, no. 2, Aug. 1938: *Albert Kahn: Industrial Buildings*.

Theuer, M. (ed.), *Leon Battista Alberti. Zehn Bücher über die Baukunst*, Darmstadt 1991 (reprinted 1st edn. Vienna/Leipzig 1912).

Thorne, M (ed.), *Modern Trains and Splendid Stations. Architecture, Design, and Rail Travel for the Twenty-First Century*, London/Chicago 2001.

Torre, S. (ed.), *Women in American Architecture: A Historic and Contemporary Perspective*, New York 1977.

Torroja, E., *Logik der Form*, Munich 1961.

Toyo Ito 2001–2005: beyond modernism, Madrid 2005 (El Croquis).

Treue, W., and K.-H. Manegold, *Quellen zur Geschichte der industriellen Revolution*, Göttingen 1966.

Trigueiros, L. et al. (ed.), *Lisbon Expo 98. Projects*, Lisbon 1996.

Trinder, B., *The Darbys of Coalbrookdale*, Chichester, Sussex, 1974.

Turak, Th., *William Le Baron Jenney. A Pioneer of Modern Architecture*, Ann Arbor, Mich., 1986.

Union Stock Yard Gate, City of Chicago 1976 (ed. Commission on Chicago Historical and Architectural Landmarks).

v. Vegesack, Alexander (ed.), *Jean Prouvé – Die Poetik des technischen Objekts*, Weil a.R. 2005 (exh. cat., Vitra Design Museum).

Van Berkel, B. and C. Bos, *UN Studio – Designmodelle. Architektur – Urbanismus – Infrastruktur*, Sulgen, Switzerland 2006.

Van Doesburg, T., *Grondbegrippen van de nieuwe beeldende kunst*, Nijmegen 1983 (1st text publication 1919, 1st publication with images in German: *Grundbegriffe der neuen gestaltenden Kunst*, Munich 1925).

Viollet-le-Duc, É., in: M. Düttmann (ed.), *Definitionen: Sieben Stichworte aus dem Dictionnaire raisonné de l'architecture française du XIe au XVIe siècle*, Basle 1993.

Von Moos, St. (ed.), *L'Esprit Nouveau. Le Corbusier und die Industrie 1920–1925*, Berlin 1987 (exh. cat., Museum für Gestaltung Zurich, Bauhaus-Archiv Berlin, Musées de la Ville de Strasbourg).

Wachsmann, K., *Holzhausbau. Technik und Gestaltung*, Berlin 1930; reprint: Chr., and M. Grünig, Chr. Sumi (ed.), Basle 1995.

Wachsmann, K., *Wendepunkt im Bauen*, Wiesbaden 1959.

Wälchli, R., *Impulse einer Region. Solothurner Architektur 1940–1980*, Solothurn 2005.

Weber, H., *Walter Gropius und das Faguswerk*, Munich 1961.

Wehler, H.-U., *Der Aufstieg des amerikanischen Imperialismus*, Göttingen 1987 (1st edn. 1974).

Werk, Bauen + Wohnen, no. 9, Sep. 1997: *Ingenieur formt mit*.

Werner, J., Stadt Karlsruhe (ed.), *Jenseits der Brauerstraße. Der Hallenbau A krönt eine neue Stadtlandschaft* (Bd. 1); *Kunstfabrik im Hallenbau A. Zentrum für Kunst und Medientechnologie u. a.* (Bd. 2), Karlsruhe 1997.

Wichmann, H. (ed.), *System-Design: Fritz Haller. Bauten, Möbel, Forschung*, Basle 1989.

Wick, J., *Kunststoffe in der Architektur 1950–1980*, Zurich 2000 (author's diploma studies, ETH Zurich, Departement Architektur).

Williams, Chr. (with N. Leach, D. Turnbull), *Digital Tectonics*, Wiley Academy, 2004.

Williams, E., Port Sunlight. *The First Hundred Years 1888–1988*, Port Sunlight 1988 (ed. Lever Brothers Ltd.).

Willis, C., *Building the Empire State. A rediscovered 1930s notebook charts the construction of the Empire State Building*, New York/London 1998 (ed. The Skyscraper Museum New York).

Wingler, H. M., *Das Bauhaus*, Bramsche 1975.

Wingler, H. M. (ed.), *Gottfried Semper. Wissenschaft, Industrie und Kunst und andere Schriften über Architektur, Kunsthandwerk und Kunstunterricht*, Mainz 1966 (*Neue Bauhausbücher*).

Wingler, H. M. (ed.), *Walter Gropius. Bauhausbauten Dessau*, Berlin 1997 (*Neue Bauhausbücher*; vol. 12 from the older series *Bauhausbücher*, 1930).

Witte, R., *Toyo Ito. Sendai Mediatheque*, Munich 2002.

Wojtowicz, R. (ed.), *Sidewalk Critic. Lewis Mumford's Writings on New York*, New York 1998.

Woods, Mary N., *From Craft to Profession. The Practice of Architecture in Nineteenth-Century America*, Berkeley 1999.

Woodward, G., Oriel *Chambers*, in: *The Architectural Review*, vol. 119, no. 712, May 1956, pp. 268–70.

Wurm, J., *Glas als Tragwerk. Entwurf und Konstruktion selbsttragender Hüllen*, Basle 2007.

www.fskb.ch/Architekturgalerie guter Betonbauten (with virtual walk-in rooms).

Zabalbeascoa, A. and J. R. Marcos (ed.), *Renzo Piano. sustainable architectures – arquitecturas sostenibles*, Corte Madern, CA, USA 1988 (ed. GG Barcelona).

Zbinden, U., M. Wassmer, and F. Fischer (eds.), *Wechselseitig. Zu Architektur und Technik*, Munich 2006 (TU Munich Publishing).

Zevi, B. (ed.), *Giuseppe Terragni*, Bologna 1980.

Zola, E., *Der Bauch von Paris*, Berlin 1957 (1st edn. Le Ventre de Paris, Paris 1873).

Zschokke, W., and M. Hanak (ed.), *Nachkriegsmoderne Schweiz*, Basle 2001 (exh. cat.).

Zukowsky, J., and M. Thorne, *Skyscrapers. The New Millennium*, Munich 2000.

Index

Page numbers in italics refer to illustrations, page numbers in bold to case studies.

Index of Places and Projects

Exhibition and Expo Projects

Picture Credits

1 From Greenhouse to 'High-tech Hothouse'

Akademie der Künste Berlin (ed.), Bruno Taut, 1980: 1.2.4 (p. 43)

Allgemeine Bauzeitung, Vienna 1837, no. 48: 1.1.20

Anderson, R., 2000: 1.4.9 (p. 67), 1.4.10 (p. 85)

L'architecture d'aujourd'hui, Oct. 1932: *Spécial Perret*, reprint 1991: 1.2.2 (p. 57)

Archive author: 1.3.9, 1.3.10

Archive Heinz Ronner: 1.1.23, 1.1.28, 1.2.14, 1.2.15

author: 1.0, 1.3, 1.5, 1.1.3, 1.1.5, 1.1.6, 1.1.7, 1.1.8, 1.1.9, 1.1.10, 1.1.11, 1.1.12, 1.1.13, 1.1.14, 1.1.21, 1.1.26, 1.1.29, 1.1.30, 1.1.31, 1.1.33, 1.1.34, 1.1.35, 1.1.36, 1.2.5, 1.2.19, 1.3.6, 1.3.8, 1.3.14, 1.3.16, 1.3.17, 1.3.18, 1.3.23, 1.4.3, 1.4.4, 1.4.5, 1.4.7, 1.4.12, 1.4.13, 1.4.14, 1.4.21, 1.4.22, 1.4.25, 1.4.27

Bancroft, H. H., 1893: 1.2.7 (p. 25), 1.2.8 (p. 41), 1.2.9 (p. 436)

Behling, P., and St. (eds.), 1999: 1.4.23 (pp. 112–13), 1.4.24 (pp. 116–17)

Bibliothèque Centrale du Muséum National d'Histoire Naturelle, Paris: 1.1.15, 1.1.17, 1.1.18

Blaser, W. (ed.), 1995: 1.4.1 (p. 96), 1.4.2 (p. 101)

Brookes, A. J., 1991: 1.3.15 (pp. 90–91)

Cuno Brullmann: 1.3.4, 1.3.19, 1.3.20

Chadwick, G. F., 1961: 1.1.22 (p. 82), 1.1.24 (p. 89), 1.1.25 (p. 91)

Communauté d'Agglomération de Metz Métropole CAMM (ed.), 2004: 1.6 (p. 49), 1.4.30 (pp. 54–55), 1.4.31 (p. 47)

Davey, P., and H. Pearman, 2000: 1.4.15 (p. 7), 1.4.17 (p. 8, fig. 8), 1.4.20 (p. 9, fig. 10)

Durand, J.-N.-L., 1802–1805, 2. section: 1.1.16 (plate. 21)

Norman Foster, 1988: 1.3.1 (p. 159), 1.3.7 (p. 83)

Foster, N. et al., 2001: 1.4.11 (p. 65)

Frei Otto: 1.3.5 (p. 58)

Frei Otto, and B. Rasch, 1995: 1.4.6 (pp. 140–41, fig. 4)

Fritz Haller: 1.3.2

Heinle, E., and J. Schlaich, 1996; Universität Stuttgart: 1.2.6 (p. 173), 1.2.12 (p. 157), 1.2.18 (p. 162), 1.2.25 (p. 191)

Hitchcock, H.-R., 1954, section XV: 1.1.27 (fig. 32)

Hix, J., 1974: 1.2.21 (p. 195), 1.2.23 (p. 194), 1.2.24 (p. 194)

Horden, R., 1995: 1.2.22 (p. 94)

Jackson, M., 2000: 1.4.16 (p. 38), 1.4.18 (p. 35), 1.4.19 (cover p. 4)

Jenney, W. L. B., in: *Inland Architect*, Jun. 1891: 1.2.1

Jodidio, Ph., 1997: 1.3.3 (p. 106)

Kohlmaier, G., and B. v. Sartory, 1988: 1.1 (p. 241), 1.1.1 (p. 229), 1.1.2 (p. 240), 1.1.32 (sketch p. 497), 1.2.10 (p. 329)

Lemoine, B., 1986: 1.2 (p. 133), 1.1.4 (p. 131)

Lyall, S., 2002: 1.2.20 (p. 64)

Marrey, B., 1997: 1.2.3 (p. 78)

Mary, Ch.-L., 1852/53: 1.2.11 (pl. X and XI)

Neumann, M., 1852: 1.1.19 (pl. VIII)

Pawley, M., 1990: 1.4 (p. 151), 1.2.13 (p. 117), 1.2.16 (p. 136), 1.2.17 (p. 143)

Renzo Piano Building Workshop: 1.3.11, 1.3.12, 1.3.13

Schéou, A. (ed.), 1997: 1.4.28 (p. 42), 1.4.29 (p. 45)

Schittich, Chr. (ed.), 1998: 1.4.26 (p. 284)

Schlaich, J., and A. Holgate, 1997: 1.3.21 (p. 109), 1.3.22 (p. 108, fig. 6.20), 1.3.24 (p. 111)

Williams, Chris: 1.4.8

2 Building as an Art or the Art of Building?

ABC, no. 6, 1925: 2.3.4 (p. 3)

Archive Heinz Ronner: 2.1, 2.1.8, 2.1.16, 2.2.3, 2.2.4, 2.2.6, 2.2.7, 2.2.16, 2.2.17

author: 2.0, 2.1.11, 2.1.13, 2.1.14, 2.1.15, 2.1.18, 2.1.22, 2.1.23, 2.1.24, 2.1.26, 2.1.27, 2.3.7, 2.3.8, 2.3.17, 2.3.19, 2.3.20, 2.4.4, 2.4.9, 2.4.12, 2.4.14, 2.4.17, 2.4.21, 2.4.22, 2.4.25, 2.4.26, 2.4.27, 2.4.29

Barthel, R. (ed.), 2001: 2.3.3 (p. 68)

Behling, P., and St., 1999: 2.3.13 (p. 116)

Berger, H., 1996: 2.6 (p. 29), 2.3.16 (p. 29), 2.3.21 (p. 15), 2.3.22 (p. 15)

Berti, P., 1993: 2.3.9 (p. 81), 2.3.10 (apendix A1, Bl. 2)

Bothe, Richter, Teherani: 2.4.30, 2.4.31

Cuno Brullmann: 2.1.19, 2.1.20

Chadwick, G. F., 1961: 2.2.11 (p. 92)

Cuadra, M., 2002: 2.4.6 (p. 30)

Danesi, S., 1976: 2.3.6 (p. 149)

Detail, no. 4, 1995: 2.4.15 (p. 672), 2.4.18 (p. 677)

Durant, S., 1994: 2.2.18 (p. 28, fig. 53), 2.2.19 (p. 21, fig. 37), 2.2.20 (p. 41, fig. 73), 2.2.21 (p. 57, fig. 4), 2.2.22 (author's image montage: pp. 42–43, figs. 75 and 77)

Norman Foster, 1988: 2.4.3 (p. 283)

Gibbs, C. H., 1950: 2.2.12 (p. 46), 2.2.14 (p. 47)

Giedion, S., 1928: 2.2.1 (p. 44, fig. 37), 2.2.2 (p. 42, fig. 34)

Godoli, E., 1983: 2.3.1 (p. 124, fig. 5)

Grimshaw, N., 1998: 2.4.20 (p. 133)

Heinle, E., and J. Schlaich, 1996; archive Universität Stuttgart: 2.3.5 (p. 192), 2.3.24 (p. 192)

Hitchcock, H.-R., 1954: 2.3 (fig. XVI/36), 2.1.5 (fig. XVI/30), 2.1.6 (fig. XVI/31)

Hix, J., 1974: 2.1.12 (p. 126), 2.2.9 (p. 127), 2.3.23 (p. 192, fig. 311)

Holgate, A., 1997: 2.3.18 (p. 99)

Hütsch, V., 1985: 2.2.8 (p. 54, fig. 74), 2.2.10 (p. 69, figs. 97 and 98), 2.2.13 (p. 28, fig. 29), 2.2.15 (p. 28, fig. 28)

Krausse, J., and Cl. Lichtenstein, 1999: 2.3.11 (p. 393)

Lemoine, B., 1986: 2.5 (pp. 230–231), 2.1.1 (p. 145), 2.1.4 (p. 73), 2.1.17 (p. 73), 2.1.25 (p. 147)

Lemoine, B., and M. Mimram, 1995: 2.4 (p. 21)

Mattie, E., 1998: 2.4.2 (p. 237)

Paronesso, A., and R. Passera, 2003: 2.3.14 (p. 11), 2.3.15 (p. 8)

Pawley, M., 1990: 2.3.12 (p. 150)

Perdonnet, A., 1858: 2.1.3 (p. 371, pl. 6)

Renzo Piano, 1992: 2.4.1 (p. 33, fig. 3)

Renzo Piano Building Workshop: 2.4.5

Picon, A., 1992: 2.2 (p. 358)

Picon, A. (ed.), 1997: 2.1.2 (p. 353), 2.1.7 (p. 175)

Powell, K., 1993: 2.4.13 (p. 26), 2.4.16 (p. 48), 2.4.19 (p. 38)

Rogers, E. N., and J. Joedicke, 1957: 2.2.5 (p. 97)

Roisecco, G., 1972: 2.1.9 (p. 147), 2.1.10 (p. 146)

Sagner-Düchting, K., 1994: 2.1.21 (p. 94)

Jörg Schlaich: 2.4.23, 2.4.24

Thorne, M., 2001: 2.4.28 (p. 86, fig. 3), 2.4.32 (p. 92, fig. 6), 2.4.33 (p. 117, fig. 2)

Torroja, E., 1961: 2.3.2 (p. 159)

Tuchschmid AG Frauenfeld, Switzerland: 2.7, 2.4.7, 2.4.8, 2.4.10, 2.4.11

3 How Concrete Became Lighter

ABC, no. 3/4, 1925: 3.1.11 (p. 4), 3.1.12 (p. 6, edge column)

Archive author: 3.2.5

Archive Heinz Ronner: 3.1.2, 3.2.8, 3.3.1, 3.3.14, 3.3.17, 3.3.18, 3.3.19, 3.4.12, 3.4.13, 3.4.14, 3.4.15

The Arup Journal, no. 2, 1999: 3.5.10 (p. 18)

author: 3.0, 3.7, 3.1.4 (sketch author), 3.1.5, 3.1.18, 3.2.7, 3.2.15, 3.2.17, 3.2.18, 3.2.24, 3.2.26, 3.2.30, 3.2.31, 3.2.34, 3.2.35, 3.3.8, 3.3.9, 3.3.11, 3.3.13, 3.3.15, 3.3.16, 3.4.1, 3.4.33, 3.4.34, 3.4.37, 3.5.3, 3.5.6, 3.5.9, 3.5.17, 3.5.18, 3.5.21, 3.5.22, 3.5.24, 3.5.25, 3.5.26, 3.5.28

Barbieri, U., 1989: 3.1.13 (p. 104)

Barthel, R. (ed.), 2001: 3.4.28 (p. 76), 3.4.30 (sketch Diestes, p. 18, fig. 3), 3.4.31 (p. 31, fig. 24), 3.4.32 (p. 63)

Behnisch, St., 2006: 3.5.31 (p. 17)

Le Béton armé, no. 21, Feb. 1900, year 2.: 3.2.1 (title page; ETH-Bibliothek Zurich: edition shown here 1898/99 in year 1)

Boesiger, W., and H. Girsberger (ed.), 1967: 3.1.16 and 3.1.17 (p. 24)

Brühwiler, E. (ed.), 2002: 3.4.6 (p. 117)

Cemsuisse (ed.), *Architekturpreis Beton 01*, Bern 2001: 3.5.26 (p. 24)

Conzett, J., in: *Werk, Bauen + Wohnen*, no. 9, 1997: 3.5.23 (p. 39)

Conzett, J., 2000: 3.5.19 (p. 7, fig. 7)

Delhumeau, G. et al. (eds.), Paris 1993: 3.1 (p. 46, fig. 39), 3.2.3 (p. 169, fig. 161)

Diethelm, A. (ed.), 2003: 3.3.3 (p. 58)

van Doesburg, Th., 1983: 3.2.25 (fig. 3)

EPFL, *Revue Tracés*, Lausanne 2004: 3.5.29 (p. 24)

Fanelli, G., 1985: 3.1.1 (p. 38, fig. 40), 3.5.4 (p. 165, fig. 13)

Garino, Cl., 1995: 3.1.19 (documentation appendix, after p. 312)

Geurst, J., and J. Molenar (ed.), 1983: 3.3.12 (p. 55)

Giedion, S., 1928: 3.2.10 (p. 72, fig. 71)

Giralt-Miracle, D., 2002: 3.4.35 (p. 99)

Haegermann, G. (ed.), 1964, section B: 3.4.3 (p. 163)

Heinle, E., and J. Schlaich, 1996: 3.4.17 (p. 173)

Hildebrand, G., 1974: 3.3 (p. 46, fig. 12), 3.2.6 (p. 49, fig. 15)

Huberti, G. (ed.), 1964: 3.4.18 (p. 154, fig. 382), 3.4.19 (p. 153, fig. 381), 3.4.20 (p. 156, fig. 389)

Heinz Isler: 3.4.38

Joedicke, J. (ed.), 1957: 3.3.7 (p. 145, fig. 245), 3.4.7 (p. 66, fig. 13), 3.4.10 (p. 62, fig. 5)

Jullian, R. (ed.), 1989: 3.1.6 (p. 31, pl. 13), 3.1.7 (p. 181, pl. 156), 3.1.8 (p. 46, pl. 25), 3.1.9 (p. 74, pl. 74), 3.1.10 (p. 75, pl. 53).

Andreas Kessler: 3.6

Marti, P. (ed.), 1996: 3.3.2 (p. 43), 3.3.5 (p. 49)

Molema, J., 1989: 3.1.14 (p. 78), 3.2.27 (p. 115), 3.2.28 (p. 74), 3.2.29 (p. 61)

Molenaar, J., J. H. M., 1985: 3.3.10 (p. 8, fig. 8)

von Moos, St. (ed.), 1987: 3.1.15 (p. 170)

The Museum of Modern Art, New York, 1969: 3.2.4 (pl. 4)

Musmeci, S., 1976: 3.4.2 (p. 13)

Muttoni, A., 1999: 3.4.21 (p. 110)

Nerdinger, W. (ed.), 2002: 3.5.1 (p. 58, fig. 6)

Olmo, C. (ed.), 1994: 3.2.19 (pl. 15), 3.2.20 (pl. 72), 3.2.21 (pl. 18), 3.2.22 (pl. 7), 3.2.23 (pl. 37)

Paravicini, U., and P. Amphoux (ed.), 1994: 3.2.2 (p. 39)

Perret, *L'architecture d'aujourd'hui*, 1932: 3.2.9 (p. 25)

Perret, *Rassegna*, 1986: 3.2.11 (p. 53), 3.2.12 (p. 21), 3.2.13 (p. 37)
Renzo Piano Building Workshop: 3.5.13, 3.5.14, 3.5.15, 3.5.30
Renzo Piano Building Workshop, *a+u*, no. 3, 1989: 3.5.12 (p.74)
Piano, R., 1997: 3.5.2 (p. 26), 3.5.11 (p.70), 3.5.16 (p.76)
Piccinato, L. (ed.), 1954: 3.4.16 (p. 24)
Picon, A. (ed.), 1997: 3.2 (p. 81), 3.3.6 (p.121), 3.4.4 (p. 343), 3.4.5 (p.126), 3.4.22 (p.185), 3.5.20 (p. 456)
Polonyi, St., in: Hackelsberger, Ch. (ed.), 1989: 3.4.8 (p. 69, fig. I), 3.4.11 (p.75, fig. 26)
Ramazotti, L., in: Hackelsberger, Ch. (ed.), 1989: 3.4.9 (p. 57, fig. 8 and 9)
Ramm, E., and E. Schunck, P. Marti (ed.), Zurich 2002: 3.4.36 (p. 85)
Roisecco, G., 1973: 3.5.25 (p. 293, fig. 228)
Roth, A., 1975: 3.4 (p. 219), 3.3.4 (p. 228)
Schirmer, W. (ed.), 2002: 3.5 (p.104)
Joseph Schwartz: 3.5.27
Steele, J. (ed.), 1988: 3.4.29 (p.16)
Torroja, E., 1961: 3.4.23 (p.167), 3.4.24 (p.106), 3.4.25 (p.112), 3.4.26 (p. 105), 3.4.27 (p.114)
Trigueiros, L., and Cl. Sat, C. Oliveira (eds.), 1996: 3.5.7 (p.134), 3.5.8 (pp. 136–137)
Verein Ortsmuseum Dottikon/Switzerland: 3.2.14, 3.2.16
Wingler, H. M. (ed.), 1997: 3.2.32 (p. 30, fig.15), 3.2.33 (photo Lucia Moholy, p. 23, fig. 8)
www.fskb.ch/Architekturgalerie: 3.5.5
Zevi, B. (ed.), 1980: 3.1.3 (p.71, fig. 4)

4 The 'Liberated Facade'

Architectural History, vol. I, 1958: 4.1.13 (p. 90), 4.1.15 (p. 93)
Archive author: 4.3.1
Archive Heinz Ronner: 4.2, 4.6, 4.1.2, 4.1.3, 4.1.18, 4.1.19, 4.2.1, 4.2.2, 4.3.9, 4.4.10, 4.4.12, 4.4.16, 4.4.17,
Aregger, H., and O. Glaus (eds.), 1967: 4.4.18 (p.79)
author: 4.0, 4.7, 4.1.5, 4.1.8, 4.1.9, 4.1.10, 4.1.11, 4.1.12, 4.1.14, 4.1.16, 4.1.17, 4.1.22, 4.2.4, 4.2.10, 4.2.11, 4.3.12, 4.3.14, 4.3.15, 4.3.16, 4.3.19, 4.3.22, 4.3.24, 4.3.26, 4.3.29, 4.3.30, 4.4.2, 4.4.4, 4.4.13, 4.4.15, 4.4.24, 4.4.25, 4.4.26, 4.5.1, 4.5.2, 4.5.3, 4.5.4, 4.5.5, 4.5.7, 4.5.11, 4.5.12, 4.5.15, 4.5.16, 4.5.21, 4.5.22, 4.5.23, 4.5.25, 4.5.26, 4.5.29, 4.5.31, 4.5.32, 4.5.33, 4.5.34, 4.5.35
Hans-Peter Bärtschi: 4.5, 4.1.6
Bannister, T., 1950: 4.1.4 (p. 244)
Blaser, W., 1997: 4.4.8 (p.79), 4.4.9 (p. 82), 4.4.11 (p. 92)
Boesiger, W., and H. Girsberger (eds.), 1974: 4.3.23 (p. 88)
Boesiger, W., and H. Girsberger (eds.), 1977: 4.3.25 (p. 40)
Borsi, F., 1986: 4.3 (collage author, pp. 54 and 61)
Karin Bucher: 4.3.18, 4.5.24
Campi, M. (ed.), 2000: 4.4.20 (p. 33)
de la Chevallerie, H., 1997: 4.3.17 (p. 25)
Cieslik, J., and M. (ed.), 1997: 4.3.13 (p. 55, fig.138)
Condit, C. W., 1964: 4.2.5 (fig. 67), 4.2.6 (fig. 40)
Condit, C. W., 1982: 4.2.3 (fig. 25)
Diethelm, A., in: *Schweizer Ingenieur und Architekt*, SIA, no. 3, 1999: 4.4.1 (p. 24)
Diethelm, A., 2003: 4.4.6 (p. 54)
van Doesburg, Th., 1983: 4.3.3 (appendix fig. 11)
Durand, J.-N.-L., 1802–05, 1ère partie: 4.4 (pl. 3)
Fassade, no. 1, 2002: 4.5.27 (p. 44, fig. 3)
Feireiss, K. (ed.), 2002: 4.5.19 (p. 225)
Fernandez-Galiano, L. (ed.), 2001: 4.4.14 (montage, p. 41)
Grube, O. W. et al., 1973: 4.2.7 (p.10), 4.2.12 (p.17), 4.2.13 (p. 23)
Lucien Hervé, in: Sumi, Chr., 1989: 4.3.20 (p. 35)
Hildebrand, G., 1974: 4.3.4 (fig.77)
Industrial Chicago, vol. I: 4.2.8 (p. 410)
Intelligente Architektur, no. 9/10, 2003: 4.5.30 (p.10)
Jaeggi, A. (ed.), 2004: 4.4.23 (p.168)
Jenney, W. L. B., 1891: 4.2.9 (p. 388)
Jodidio, Ph. (ed.), 1997: 4.5.20 (p.102)
Kostof, S., 1977: 4.4.19 (p. 329)
Krinsky, C. H., 1988: 4.4.21 (p. 87), 4.4.22 (p.113)
Lemoine, B., 1980: 4.1.7 (pl. XXIV)
Marrey, 1989: 4.3.28 (p.137, fig.154)

Nestler, P., 1954: 4.4.7 (p.155)
Neumann, D., 1996: 4.3.7 (p. 28, fig.7), 4.3.8 (p. 28, fig. 8)
Renzo Piano Building Workshop: 4.5.13, 4.5.17, 4.5.18
Piano, R., 1989: 4.5.14 (p. 249)
Picon, A. (ed.), 1997: 4.1.20 (p. 294)
Pruscha, C. (ed.), 1997: 4.3.6 (p. 92)
Rice, P., 1994: 4.5.10 (p. 92)
Rice, P., and H. Dutton, 1995: 4.5.8 (p. 59), 4.5.9 (p. 32)
Riley, T. (ed.), 1994: 4.3.10 (p. 218, fig. 205)
Riley, T., 2001: 4.3.2 (photo montage, p. 231)
Roisecco, G., 1973: 4.1.21 (p. 293; montage of author from: Schild, E., 1983, p.79 f.)
Schirmer, W. (ed.), 2002: 4.4.3 (p.144)
Semper, G., 1863: 4.1 (p. 276)
Siry, J., 1988: 4.2.14 (fig. II-22), 4.2.15 (fig. II-23), 4.3.11 (p.160, fig. III-24)
Skempton, A. W., and H. R. Johnson, 1962: 4.1.1 (p.184, fig.17)
Sulzer, P., 1991: 4.3.31 (p. 37, fig. 80, (c) SCE Jean Prouvé)
Sulzer, P., 2000: 4.3.27 (p. 28, fig. 30, (c) SCE Jean Prouvé)
Sumi, Chr., 1989: 4.3.21 (sketch, p. 36)
Taylor, B. B., 1992: 4.3.5 (p.109)
Thau, C., and K. Vindum (eds.), 2002: 4.4.5 (p. 411)
Witte, R., 2002: 4.5.6 (p. 8)

5 Process Thinking Conquers Construction

The Architectural Forum, no. 2, Aug. 1938: 5.2.10 (p. 92), 5.2.11 (p.132)
Architectural Review, no. 982, Dec. 1978: 5.4.2 (p. 354)
L'architecture d'aujourd'hui, no. 6, May/June 1946; *Sonder-nummer Richard J. Neutra*; reprint 1992: 5.2.25
Archive author: 5.6, 5.1.1, 5.1.3, 5.2.2, 5.4.12
Archive Heinz Ronner: 5.3, 5.4, 5.1.5, 5.1.6, 5.1.7, 5.1.8, 5.1.9, 5.1.10, 5.1.11, 5.1.12, 5.1.14, 5.1.23, 5.1.25, 5.2.18, 5.2.23, 5.3.2, 5.3.3, 5.3.4, 5.3.22, 5.3.23, 5.3.24, 5.3.26, 5.3.29, 5.3.30
author: 5.2, 5.5, 5.1.29, 5.1.30, 5.2.3, 5.2.4, 5.2.5, 5.2.12, 5.2.19, 5.2.22, 5.2.29, 5.3.5 (from a photo in the foyer of Lake Shore Drive Apartments), 5.3.18, 5.3.20, 5.3.31, 5.4.10, 5.4.14, 5.4.18, 5.4.20, 5.4.21, 5.4.22
Bock, Th., 1998: 5.4.23 (p.1010, fig.17)
Boesiger, W., and H. Girsberger (ed.), 1967: 5.2.28 (p. 28)
Compagno, A., 1999: 5.4.19 (p. 35, fig. 6)
Condit, C. W., 1964: 5.1.17 (fig. 50), 5.1.20 (fig.79)
Condit, C. W., 1982: 5.1.24 (fig. 39)
Das Neue Frankfurt (*dnf*), no. 2, 1926/27: 5.2.13 (p. 34, fig. 8, in: Hirdina, H. (ed.), 1984, p.106), 5.2.14 (*dnf*, no. 2, 1926/27, title image, in: Hirdina, H. (ed.), 1984, p. 85), 5.2.15 (*dnf*, no. 2, 1926/27, p. 37, fig. 13 + 14, in: Hirdina, H. (ed.), 1984, p. 109), 5.2.16 (*dnf*, no. 2, 1926/27, p. 38 f., fig. 17 + 18, in: Hirdina, H. (ed.), 1984, p.197), 5.2.17 (*dnf*, no.7/8, 1929, add., in: Hirdina, H. (ed.), 1984, p.110 f.), 5.2.17 (*dnf*, no.7/8, 1929, add., in: Hirdina, H. (ed.), 1984, p.197)
Foster, N., 1988: 5.4.1 (p.171)
Frampton, K., 1993: 5.1.27 (p.108, fig. 4.12)
Freitag, J. K., 1904: 5.1.21 (p. 69, fig. 33), 5.1.22 (p.71, fig. 34)
Giralt-Miracle, D. (ed.), 2002: 5.4.13 (p.157)
Fritz Haller: 5.3.19, 5.3.21
Hildebrand, G., 1974: 5.2.7 (p. 13, fig. 4), 5.2.8 (p. 30, fig. 6), 5.2.9 (p. 42, fig.11)
Hounshell, D. A., 1984: 5.1.13 (p.169, fig. 4.4), 5.1.15 (p.183, fig. 4.10), 5.1.16 (p.185, fig. 4.14)
Industrial Chicago, 1893: 5.1.19
Kisho Kurokawa Architect & Associates, Tokyo: 5.3.37
Krippner, R., 1999: 5.3.28 (p. 479, fig. 5)
Langer, F. (ed.), 1998: 5.0 (photo Lewis W. Hine p. 82)
Leach, N., and D. Turnbull, Chr. Williams (eds.), 2004: 5.4.6 (p. 44), 5.4.16 (p.128), 5.4.17 (p.133)
Hwang, I. and T. Sakamoto et al. ed., 2006: 5.4.5 (p. 83)
Lüchinger, A., 1981: 5.1 (from: *Forum*, no.7, 1959, p.17)
Lüchinger, A. (ed.), 1987: 5.3.34 (p. 45, fig.16), 5.3.35 (p. 47, fig. 27), 5.3.36 (p.143, fig. 97)
Marburg, exh. cat. ETH Zurich (ed. Heinz Ronner), 1966: 5.3.25 (p. 30), 5.3.27 (p.11)
Mayer, H. M., and R. C. Wade, 1969: 5.1.2 (p. 22, fig. 2), 5.1.4 (p. 31, fig. 2), 5.1.18 (p. 119, fig. 5)

Pawley, M., 1990: 5.2.27 (p. 51)
Renzo Piano Building Workshop: 5.4.3, 5.4.4, 5.4.7, 5.4.8, 5.4.11
Piano, R., 1997: 5.4.9 (p.137)
Rasch, H., and B., 1927: 5.2.20 (p. 62), 5.2.21 (p.122)
Riley, T. (ed.), 1994: 5.1.26 (p.134, fig. 46), 5.1.28 (p. 200, fig.176)
Rosa, J. (ed.), 1995: 5.2.24 (p. 60)
Andreas Ruch (Ruch Griesemer): 5.7
Siry, J., 1988: 5.2.6 (fig.1)
Smith, E. A. T. (ed.), 1989: 5.2.26 (p.105)
Stirling, J. (ed.), 1984: 5.3.33 (p.114)
Stirling, J. (ed.), 1996: 5.3.6 (p. 97), 5.3.32 (p. 29)
Sulzer, P., 2000: 5.3.1 (p. 231, fig.786.a,1, (c) SCE Jean Prouvé), 5.3.7 (p. 260, fig. 850.10; Prouvé-Inventar no. 850, (c) SCE Jean Prouvé), 5.3.8 (p. 260, fig. 850.12; Prouvé-Inventar no.790, (c) SCE Jean Prouvé), 5.3.9 (p. 266, fig. 854.a,1; Prouvé-Inventar no. 853, (c) SCE Jean Prouvé), 5.3.10 (p. 265, fig. 854.10 and 13; Prouvé-Inventar no. 854, (c) SCE Jean Prouvé)
Sulzer, P., 2005: 5.3.11 (p. 30, fig. 9; Foto: Florian Kleine-fenn)
Union Stock Yard Gate: 5.2.1 (1976, pp. 6–7)
Wachsmann, K., 1930: 5.3.12 (p.121), 5.3.13 (p.143, fig. 211), 5.3.14 (p. 59, fig.79), 5.3.15 (p.139, fig. 204), 5.3.16 (p.157, fig. 241), 5.3.17 (p.149, fig. 223)
Chris Williams: 5.4.15
Willis, C. (ed.), 1998: 5.2.30 (p. 23), 5.2.31 (p. 45), 5.2.32 (montage from notebook pp. 41 and 39), 5.2.33 (from notebook p. 9), 5.2.34 (from notebook p. 24)

6 'Sustainable Building Design'

Achilles, A. et al. (ed.), 2003: 6.2.28 (p.154), 6.2.29 (p.156), 6.2.30 (p.157)
Archieri, J.-F. (ed.), 1990: 6.2.3 (p.131)
The Architectural Review, no. 898, Dec. 1971: 6.3.39 (p. 350, fig.19)
Archive author: 6.6, 6.7, 6.1.29, 6.2.1, 6.4.9
Archive Heinz Ronner: 6.2 (from: Telfords Brückenatlas 1793), 6.2.15, 6.2.25, 6.3.6
author: 6.1, 6.4, 6.1.5, 6.1.6, 6.1.7, 6.1.9, 6.1.12, 6.1.13, 6.1.15, 6.1.16, 6.2.2, 6.2.4, 6.2.6, 6.2.7, 6.2.14, 6.2.16, 6.2.18, 6.2.19, 6.2.20, 6.2.22, 6.2.23, 6.2.24, 6.2.26, 6.2.27, 6.3.3, 6.3.10, 6.3.11, 6.3.12, 6.3.15, 6.3.16, 6.3.22, 6.3.29, 6.3.37, 6.4.3, 6.4.14, 6.4.15, 6.4.16, 6.4.19, 6.4.20, 6.4.24
Shigeru Ban Architects: 6.3.40, 6.3.41, 6.3.42, 6.3.43
Shigeru Ban, 1999: 6.2.8 (p. 21), 6.2.9 (p. 30)
Shigeru Ban, 2001 (n.p.): 6.2.10, 6.2.12, 6.2.13, 6.4.25
Banham, R., 1969: 6.4.2 (p. 99)
Behnisch, St., and M. Schuler (eds.), 2006: 6.4.4
Blaser, W. (ed.), 2001: 6.4.29 (p.71)
Cuno Brullmann: 6.3.14
Buchanan, P. (ed.), 1994: 6.1.23 (p.127), 6.1.24 (p.122, fig. 3), 6.1.25 (p.123, fig. 9), 6.1.26 (p.116, fig.1 and 2), 6.1.27 (p.117, fig.12)
Compagno, A., 1995: 6.2.5 (p. 8)
Peter Dransfeld: 6.3.7
Feireiss, K. (ed.), 2002: 6.3.21 (p. 224)
Christian Fierz: 6.3.27
Norman Foster, 1988: 6.1.14 (p.169), 6.1.17 (p.171)
Geist, J. Fr., 1979 (catalogue section): 6.3.1 (fig.119), 6.3.2 (fig.121)
Gerster & Haelfinger architects, Basle, Switzerland: 6.2.1
Giedion, S., 1929: 6.5 (title page *Befreites Wohnen*, Zurich/Leipzig 1929)
Gissen, D. (ed.), 2002: 6.3.25 (p.77)
Glas, no. 3, 2002: 6.1.30 (p.15), 6.1.31 (p. 15), 6.1.32 (p.16)
Herzog, Th. et al. (ed.), 2004: 6.2.21 (p. 211, fig. B 1.7.3 and B 1.7.4), 6.4.22 (p. 26)
Heusler, W., and J. Ernst, 1996: 6.3.23 (p. 48, fig. 3), 6.3.24 (p. 49, fig. 4)
Hildebrand, G., 1974: 6.1.28 (p. 57, fig.18)
Richard Horden: 6.3.5, 6.3.18, 6.3.26, 6.4.6
Horden, R., 2004: 6.3.19 (p. 47), 6.3.28
Richard Horden, and TU Munich: 6.3.30, 6.3.31, 6.3.32, 6.3.33, 6.3.34, 6.3.35, 6.3.36, 6.3.38

Intelligente Architektur, no. 18, Sep. 1999: 6.3.9 (pp. 41–42); no. 19, Nov. 1999: 6.3.13 (p. 48)

Jodidio, P., 1997: 6.3.20 (p. 129), 6.4.5 (p. 128)

Luscher, R., and A. architects, Lausanne, Switzerland: 6.1.34

Nachtigall, W., and K. G. Blüchel, 2001: 6.4.1 (pp. 240–41), 6.4.11 (pp. 274–75), 6.4.21 (p. 51)

Pawley, M., 1990: 6.3 (p. 143), 6.1.3

Renzo Piano Building Workshop: 6.1.10, 6.4.8, 6.4.26, 6.4.27, 6.4.28, 6.4.31

Piano, R., 1988: 6.0 (p. 7), 6.4.30 (p. 9)

Renzo Piano, 1989: 6.4.12 (p. 117), 6.4.13 (p. 118)

prospective concepts ag: 6.1.33

Rice, p., 1994: 6.1.8 (p. 32), 6.1.11 (p. 33)

Sauerbruch Hutton Architekten, 2000: 6.4.17 (p. 195)

Schéou, A. (ed.), 1997: 6.3.17 (p. 36)

Jörg Schlaich: 6.1.2, 6.3.8

Schlaich, J., and E. Heinle, 1996: 6.1.1 (p. 23)

Schneider + Schumacher: 6.3.4

Schulz, B., 2000: 6.4.18 (p. 106)

Semper, G. (1863), 1977: 6.4.7 (p. 276)

Stattmann, N. (ed.), 2003: 6.4.23 (p. 85)

Erika Sulzer-Kleinemeier: 6.1.18

Sulzer, P., 1991: 6.1.4 (p. 33, fig. 73, (c) SCE Jean Prouvé), 6.1.19 (sketch: Pascal Ninivaggi from a Prouvé seminar at the Universität Stuttgart 1989/90; p. 37, fig. 80)

Sulzer, P., 1995: 6.2.17 (p. 146, fig. 181.1,4)

Sulzer, P., 2005: 6.1.20 (p. 342, fig. 1287.5,1), 6.1.21 (p. 340, fig. 1287.3,6, (c) SCE Jean Prouvé), 6.1.22 (p. 338, fig. 1287.2,5, (c) SCE Jean Prouvé)

Front cover: Álvaro Siza and Cecil Balmond, Arup: The Portuguese
Pavilion from the 1998 Lisbon World Exposition: "The Oceans, a
Heritage for the Future"; detail (photo: Ulrich Pfammatter)

Back flap: photo: Hanspeter Setz

Frontispiece: Foster and Partners: Great Court, British Museum,
London; detail of the glass ceiling (photo: Ben Johnson)

The Library of Congress Control Number: 2008921849

British Library Cataloguing-in-Publication Data: a catalogue record for
this book is available from the British Library. The Deutsche Bibliothek
holds a record of this publication in the Deutsche Nationalbibliografie;
detailed bibliographical data can be found under: http://dnb.ddb.de

Prestel Verlag
Königinstrasse 9
80539 Munich
Tel. +49 (0) 89 24 29 08-300
Fax +49 (0) 89 24 29 08-335

Prestel Publishing Ltd.
4 Bloomsbury Place
London WC1A 2QA
Tel. +44 (0) 20 7323-5004
Fax +44 (0) 20 7636-8004

Prestel Publishing
900 Broadway, Suite 603
New York, N.Y. 10003
Tel. +1 (212) 995-2720
Fax +1 (212) 995-2733

www.prestel.com

Translated from the German by Jeremy Gaines, Frankfurt, and James
Roderick O'Donovan, Vienna
Editorial direction by Reegan Finger and Katharina Haderer
Copy-edited by Danko Szabó, Munich
Design concept: Matthias Hauer
Design: Iris von Hoesslin, Munich
Cover design: Cilly Klotz
Typesetting by Max Vornehm GmbH, Munich
Lithography by Reproline Mediateam, Munich
Printed and bound by Finidr, s.r.o., Český Těšín

Printed on acid-free paper

ISBN 978-3-7913-3926-9

Without the generous support of the following institutions, companies
and individuals, the realisation of this English edition would not have
been possible in its present format:

G. und N. Schnitter Fonds zur Förderung der Technikgeschichte an
der ETH Zürich, the Gesellschaft für Ingenieurbaukunst (Prof. Dr. Peter
Marti, ETH Zürich), ARUP London, USM Münsingen, SIKA Zurich,
Glas-Trösch Bützberg, Tuchschmid Frauenfeld, Gasser-Membranbau
Lungern, Ruch-Griesemer Altdorf, Fritz Haller (GmbH Solothurn), Jörg
Schlaich (Schlaich Bergermann und Partner Stuttgart) and Hanspeter
Setz (Oskar Setz AG, Dintikon)

Sydney Opera House, Australia

Michael Lewis, Ove Arup and Jack Zunz on site at the Sydney Opera House in 1966

Pompidou Centre, Paris, France

Øresund Bridge, Denmark - Sweden

The Channel Tunnel Rail Link, UK

© Grant Smith/VIEW

30 St Mary Axe, London, UK

© Ben McMillan

Beijing National Stadium, China

Arup is a global design and engineering firm and a leading creative force in the built environment. It was founded in 1946 by the engineer and philosopher, Sir Ove Arup, who instigated the concept of 'total design', in which teams of professionals from diverse disciplines work together on projects of exceptional quality. This integrated-design approach has been the hallmark of Arup's achievements, visible in the design of the structure of the Sydney Opera House in the 1960s, in the development of the alternative route for the UK's Channel Tunnel Rail Link in the 1990s, and in the current master-planning of the world's first eco-city at Dongtan, Shanghai, China.

www.arup.com

ARUP

The future begins with a visionary system.

USM
Modular Furniture

Sika Solutions
from Basement to Roof

- Concrete and concreting Technology
- Waterproofing below Ground
- Protecting Floors
- Steel Corrosion Protection
- Fire Protection

- Sealing and Bonding the Building Envelope
- Sealing and Bonding in Interior Finishing
- Concrete Repair and Protection
- Structural Strengthening
- Roofing

Tuchschmid

Tuchschmid –
Partner for demanding projects in steel, glass and combined traffic

Over the past few years, Tuchschmid has made a name for itself in the execution of ambitious projects in steel and glass.

Zurich Airport's Airside Center roof structure and the façades of the Paul Klee Centre in Berne are the most recent examples. Construction that places high demands on geometry, engineering, production and erection is our core activity. Thanks to our team of specialists, we are able to meet the needs and demands of clients, architects and engineers with project-specific solutions.

Tuchschmid has been honoured time and again for outstanding achievement in steel and glass. In 2007, our Company was awarded the European Steel Structure Award for the fourth time: this time for the façade at the Paul Klee Centre in Berne.

Services
Steel bridges and walkways
Steel halls and covered areas
Customized steel and glass structures
Steel-glass structures

Tuchschmid AG / Tuchschmid Constructa AG
Langdorfstrasse 26
CH-8501 Frauenfeld
www.tuchschmid.ch
info@tuchschmid.ch

Pictures
1 Paul Klee Center, Berne
2 Airside Center Zurich Airport
3 Culture and Congress Center Lucerne
4 Hurlingham Club, London